Symbol Formation

Symbol Formation

An Organismic-Developmental Approach

to Language and the Expression of Thought

Heinz Werner and Bernard Kaplan

Clark University

John Wiley & Sons, Inc., New York · London · Sydney

SECOND PRINTING, AUGUST, 1964

Library of Congress Catalog Card Number: 63-20643
Printed in the United States of America

preface

Our basic aim in this volume has been to set forth a certain perspective on psychological phenomena and to show how this perspective enables one to order and integrate data on symbolization and language behavior—data obtained by a variety of methods and garnered from domains that are too often treated in isolation from each other.

We recognize and respect the fact that there are multiple approaches to the problems of language and symbolization, each of which probes into these problems with its own presuppositions, its specific concerns, its own techniques and modes of analysis. Naturally, we believe that each approach yields some information on the complex and many-sided problems, and none can reasonably claim to be the only avenue to truth, though some of them seem to us more fruitful than others for elucidating the distinctive characteristics of symbolization and language behavior.

It has not been our intention here to describe or appraise those alternative ways of looking at symbolization. Rather than evaluating the theories and experimental work of others, we have been primarily oriented towards presenting our own view and demonstrating concretely how our approach operates in the analysis of phenomena and in the suggestion of appropriate experiments. On the few occasions when we have dealt with other theories, we have done so chiefly to clarify and distinguish our own position.

Just as our book is not a summary and criticism of extant theories of symbolization and language behavior, so too is it not a compendium of numerous separate facts. As has become increasingly recognized, the "facts" that one obtains are typically dependent upon the general approach followed and the particular methods employed. We have tried to be systematic in the selection of data, considering only findings that had relevance to our approach. Even in this respect, we have been far from exhaustive. To have tried to take account more fully of the immense range of pertinent phenomena and findings would have led either to a considerable sacrifice in the presentation of our own work or would have made this volume prohibitive in size and cost. In brief, then, we hope we have succeeded in articulating our principal conceptions clearly and unambiguously, in indicating how these conceptions can be utilized to bring some degree of order and intelligibility into the variegated manifestations of symbolic activity, and in demonstrating how these notions may lead to certain novel and productive kinds of experimental and empirical inquiry.

We have characterized our approach to symbol formation as "organismic-developmental," thus indicating its two main aspects. It is *organismic* in that it emphasizes the role of ongoing, partly covert processes and states in the shaping and maintaining of the symbolic end-product; in that it stresses the interdependence and reciprocity between the construction of the objects or concepts and the structuring of the symbolic forms; and, finally, in that it views symbolic activity as a process of forging means (forms) for the realization of the individual's ongoing and emergent psychosocial functions. It is *developmental* in that it views the various manifestations of symbolic activity in terms of a principle of orderly, directed change in organization. This "orthogenetic principle" distinguishes developmental change from other kinds of change in terms of increasing differentiation and hierarchic integration; it provides a formal standard in terms of which to assess not only changes with age (some of which are nondevelopmental) but also changes due to psychopathology, variations in adult behavior under different internal or external conditions, etc. We should add that though the orthogenetic principle must be recognized as the "constitutive" principle of development, it is by no means the only principle that underlies genetic and evolutionary changes. We shall throughout this book refer to other important basic developmental notions, such as that of "functional shift" and of the "form-function interrelationship" for the theoretical understanding of the evolution of novel forms for novel functions—to the principle of "spirality" for the understanding of the interweaving of continuity and discontinuity in genetic progression;

to the notion of an unceasing interdependence of regression and progression for the understanding of the language in normal and abnormal behavioral activity.

In applying organismic-developmental conceptions to the area of symbolization, we have focused on four basic components of symbol-situations: the addressor (symbolizer), the addressee or audience, the symbolizer's object or referent, and the symbolizer's means (medium and vehicles) for representing the referent. Our aim has been to show the variation in the relations among these four basic components as being caused by variation of the underlying genetic condition. Thus, we have tried to demonstrate how these relations are transformed in the course of ontogenesis—the progressive transformation conforming, in the main, to the principle of increasing differentiation and hierarchic integration. In other terms, there is an increasing *distance* among the various components and the emergence of novel means of linking or integrating the components. Complementing the study of symbolic progression we have also attempted to show how, under naturally occurring and experimentally induced conditions, a dedifferentiation or decrease in distance occurs, analogous to that which obtains in early ontogenesis.

The volume is divided into five parts: Part I is devoted to a general exposition of the organismic-developmental approach; it is designed to orient the reader to the principal conceptions of this viewpoint and to acquaint him in a preliminary way with the kind of empirical and experimental evidence that renders this perspective plausible and intelligible. Part II is concerned with the formation and general changes in verbal-symbolic behavior in the course of ontogenesis, emphasizing the conformity of these transformations with general developmental principles. Part III attempts to cast light upon processes which we believe underlie the primordial stages of linguistic representation by studying linguistic behavior occurring in adult human beings under special conditions or in special states—experimentally induced orientations as well as schizophrenic and dream states. Part IV focuses on changes in linguistic representation under different conditions of communication, that is, with the addressor providing information for different kinds of audiences; here we deal with the important issue of the genetic differentiation between speech for others and speech for oneself. Finally, Part V deals with symbol formation in nonverbal media of representation (in particular with representation by expressive line patterns, and visual imagery): through such inquiry into nonlinguistic symbolization we sought to bring out into the open the major features of all symbol formation, of which verbal expression, though most important, is only one kind. To show the pertinence of our assumptions we conclude with a chapter on parallels between linear representation and features of various linguistic codes.

Limitations of space have obliged us to forego discussion of other viewpoints. This does not mean that we underestimate the importance of the contributions of such contemporary students of psychology of language as R. Brown, J. Carroll, J. Church, S. Ervin, E. Lenneberg, G. Miller, O. H. Mowrer, C. E. Osgood, J. Piaget, and H. Wallon. Nor have we dealt with the profound contributions of philosophers of symbolization such as M. Black, E. Cassirer, E. Gombrich, S. Langer, G. H. Mead, H. H. Price, W. Urban, and A. N. Whitehead, and of theoretical linguists, such as F. De Saussure, R. Jakobson, and N. Chomsky, all of whom have influenced our thinking.

Again, despite the extreme importance of aphasic phenomena for a truly comprehensive analysis of symbol formation, the tremendous complexity and ramifications of this field of inquiry obliged us to omit consideration of these phenomena. We also had to leave aside any discussion of some of the recent revolutionary findings and hypotheses concerning the neurophysiological bases of language and symbolization (especially those advanced by Penfield and his collaborators), although we believe that these hypotheses are consonant with our organismic-developmental view.

During the past sixteen years, this research has been supported by a number of foundations and institutions, to all of which we are deeply grateful. These include the Social Science Research Council, the Rockefeller Foundation, the Ford Foundation, the Foundations' Fund for Research in Psychiatry, and the National Institute of Mental Health (Grant M-3853). We would also like to acknowledge our indebtedness to our younger colleagues, those who have worked with us on the problems presented in this book (their names are listed on the following page), and those who have helped make the manuscript more readable and comprehensible than it would otherwise have been; of the latter group, we would like to thank especially Sandor Brent, Leonard Cirillo, Joseph Glick, Jane Kaplan, Bernhard Kempler, Jonas Langer, George Rand, and Melvyn Schnall. Finally we would like to thank Barbara Kastenbaum and Emelia Thamel for their patient care in typing the manuscript.

HEINZ WERNER
BERNARD KAPLAN
September, 1963

acknowledgments

The following is a list of the names and present locations of former and current members of the Clark University Graduate Group whose theses and findings have been extensively utilized in various chapters of this work:

BAKER, ROBERT, PH.D., Associate Professor of Psychology, Clark University

BODANSKY, MARGERY, PH.D., Assistant Professor of Psychology, Vassar College

CIRILLO, LEONARD, M.A., Research Fellow, Clark University

DOWLING, ROBERT, PH.D., Assistant Professor, Department of Psychology and Psychiatry, The Catholic University of America

ERLE, RICHARD, M.A., Psychologist, Maimonides Hospital, Brooklyn, New York

GOLDMAN, ALFRED E., PH.D., Senior Research Executive, National Analysts Inc., Pennsylvania

IRITANI, TOSHIO, PH.D., Research Psychologist, Tokyo University

KADEN, STANLEY E., PH.D., Research Psychologist, Worcester State Hospital

KAPLAN, EDITH, M.A., Research Psychologist, Veterans Administration Hospital, Boston

LANGER, JONAS, PH.D., Assistant Professor of Psychology, University of California

MILLER, ARNOLD, PH.D., Assistant Professor of Psychology, Montana State University

SLEPIAN, HOWARD, PH.D., Chief Psychologist, Worcester Youth Guidance Center

SPEIER, SYBIL, PH.D., Assistant Professor of Psychology, Yeshiva University

contents

part *I*
Theory

chapter **1**

The Organismic-Developmental Framework

The organismic-developmental framework, though a unitary one, consists of the coordination and integration of two distinct orientations: one *organismic-holistic;* the other, *developmental.* The general nature of our framework will perhaps be best understood if we treat the organismic-holistic aspect first and then indicate how the developmental orientation intertwines with the organismic one.

The Organismic-Holistic Orientation

Basic to any organismic approach are two closely related general assumptions concerning the nature of behavior. One of these general assumptions is the *holistic* one, which maintains that any local organ or activity is dependent upon the context, field, or whole of which it is a constitutive part: its properties and functional significance are, in large measure, determined by this larger whole or context. The second general assumption is that of *directiveness:* it is assumed that the various organs or activities of an organism function in the realization of ends immanent in the activity of the organism as a whole. These two general assumptions may be briefly elaborated.

The Holistic Assumption

The significance of whole or context in determining the properties and values of parts has been maintained by various philosophers, e.g.,

Whitehead (279), Smuts (232) and theoretical biologists, e.g., Goldstein (82) and von Bertalanffy (16; 17). In psychology, the holistic notion has been most vigorously introduced and advocated by the various schools of Gestalt psychology.[1] The classic paradigm of the role of the whole in the determination of parts is von Ehrenfels' demonstration of the relation between tones and melodies. As von Ehrenfels showed, individual tones differing in acoustic properties may be functionally identical in melodic units transposed to a higher or lower pitch level (principle of invariance), but tones identical in isolation may be functionally different in markedly distinct melodic wholes (principle of variance). Since the time of von Ehrenfels, numerous studies in quite different domains of psychology have shown the general validity of the holistic thesis.[2]

In general, the holistic assumption is opposed to any view that would treat an element (for example, a movement, a momentary experience) as if it possessed a fixed structure and meaning, irrespective of the whole or context of which it is a part. It thus makes one doubt the value of relating, solely on the basis of a material similarity, elements torn from quite different functional contexts.[3] For example, it leads one to question the justification of relating the vocalization of animals or even of pre-speech infants to the actual speech sounds of a child. Again it leads one to question the value of identifying two bodily movements before having considered the possibility of different functions which these externally (materially) similar movements may subserve. The rejection of analysis in terms of absolute material similarity does not, of course, entail an opposition to analysis per se: the thesis is that analysis should take into consideration the context, especially the functional significance, of an action. In brief, then, in terms of the organismic-holistic assumption, every behavioral act, whether outward bodily movement or internalized cognitive operation, gains

---

[1] See Scheerer (212), Guillaume (89) for the history and critical evaluation of Gestalt psychology. See also (137).

[2] The so-called Berlin Gestalt school (Wertheimer-Köhler-Koffka), though holistic, is principally agenetic in contradistinction to the developmentally oriented Leipzig school of Krueger-Sander-Volkelt. It is also noteworthy that the holism of the Berlin group is, with few exceptions, nonorganismic in approach insofar as it studies functions (perception, etc.) unrelated to total organismic activity. Again, in contrast, the Gestalt theory of the Leipzig school, in its stressing of pervasive feelings as the psychophysiological background of all functioning, bears a relatively close relation to more recent organismic theories.

[3] See, in this connection, E. Galanter and G. Miller (72, pp. 279, 285 ff).

its significance and status in terms of its role in the overall functioning of the organism.

With regard to the holistic assumption, one more point should be made explicit; this pertains to the reciprocal relationship between an organism and its environment: we hold with von Uexküll (255; 257) that the analysis of behavior in its fullest scope should not be directed toward an organism in isolation, but an organism embedded in its own vital field or "Umwelt."

The Umwelt, however, should neither be confused with nor reduced to the physical-geographical environment: the fact that one may describe an organism's Umwelt in physical-geographic terms makes it no more a mere geographic-physical environment than would a physical description of an organism or a physical analysis of its movement in space render that organism an exclusively physical entity. The nature of an organism's Umwelt is, of course, dependent on the physical-geographic environment; but it is to a large extent determined by the "ends" of the organism and by its species-specific and individual apparatus for engaging in transactions with its surroundings.

The Directiveness Assumption

There are some indications of a tendency to reintroduce teleogical conceptions in the analysis and description of behavior,[4] though the majority of American psychologists are not inclined to accept such notions.[5] It is our view that, like organismic theory of biology, organismic theory of psychology requires teleological concepts: organismic activity, whether biological or psychological, is by its very nature directed activity. There is, on one hand, the tendency of organisms to *conserve* their integrity, whether biological or psychological: in the face of variable, and often adverse, external or internal conditions, the organism tends to maintain its existence as an integrated entity. There is, on the other hand, the tendency of organisms to *develop* towards a relatively mature state: under the widest range of conditions, organisms undergo transformations from the status of relatively little differentiated entities to relatively differentiated and integrated adult forms.

---

[4] See, for instance, Miller, Pribram and Galanter (168), E. Russell (204; 205).

[5] Such notions often appear covertly in psychological theorizing: the very concept of "behavior" as distinct from "movement" appears to be a teleologically "tainted" notion.

It must be stressed that directiveness should not be understood to imply conscious effort toward an end, so-called "subjective teleology." Directiveness in the sense of "objective teleology" is an observable characteristic of organismic behavior irrespective of any consciousness of ends on the part of the organism (Hofstadter, 106; 107). Purposive or planning behavior, in particular, should not be confused with directiveness in its generic sense, though it is likely that planning behavior, consciously entertained in human beings, is a specialization of that general directiveness immanent in all organic activity.[6]

In the maintenance and attainment of biological and psychological ends, organisms bring into play built-in and acquired organs and operations. Such apparatus constitutes, collectively, the *means* by which organisms exploit their milieus in the realization of their *ends*.

In such realization of ends, organisms may use one rather than another of several available means or may utilize diverse means in a complementary or cooperative way. The *use of one rather than another of several potential means* may arise either through a free voluntary choice or through conditions wherein the normally preferred means for the attainment of an end is blocked. To illustrate the situation of "free choice," one may consider a normal adult who in issuing some command, may use speech *or* gesture. For an example of a situation in which one turns to an alternative means because the normally preferred way is blocked, one may refer to Gelb and Goldstein's case (74), in which the patient, unable to read written material in a normal manner, utilized tracing movements with his head in order to "read" the material. As an illustration of the *complementary use of several means,* one may refer to a normal adult's tendency to combine speech, gesture, facial expression, etc., in order to communicate more effectively.

One must stress the organic relationship between the means and ends of an organism not only by and in itself but also in its relevance for the interaction between the organism and its milieus: on one hand, "means" and "ends" are correlative notions and cannot truly be considered in isolation from each other. On the other hand, an organism "copes" with its milieus by carrying forth its species-specific and individual operations upon that portion of the geographical environment to which its instrumentalities are adequate; it structures the environment into its Umwelt through specific apparatus in the service of its biological and psychological ends. This process of forming one's Umwelt requires some degree of congruity between means and ends: that is, the ends are formed in relation to the available means and the

---

[6] Cf. Whitehead (280), Goldstein (82), E. Russell (205), Agar (2), E. Harris (97).

means undergo formation with respect to the ends to be attained. This interdependence manifests itself with particular clarity in regard to changes in the modes of structuring the environment in the normal course of phylogenesis and human ontogenesis; the reciprocity between means and ends is also quite clearly observable in the deviant ways of "coming to terms with the environment" (Goldstein) in cases of psychopathology.

Implied in this notion of reciprocity between means and ends is the thesis that changes in means affect the character of the ends, and conversely, changes in ends influence the character of the means. The full importance of this notion, as we shall see, becomes manifest when one examines the developmental changes in means-ends relationships, that is, when one observes the effects that newly emerging goals or ends have on the formation and restructurization of biopsychological equipment and the effects which in turn such newly formed equipment has in the determination of biopsychological ends.[7]

The Developmental Orientation

The organismic-holistic orientation, in our framework, is closely interwoven with a developmental orientation: development is a constitutive moment of organismic functioning. We assume that organisms are naturally directed towards a series of transformations—reflecting a tendency to move from a state of relative globality and undifferentiatedness towards states of increasing differentiation and hierarchic integration. It is this tendency, formulated as "the orthogenetic principle," which serves for us to characterize development as distinct from other types of change over time.

With regard to these developmental transformations, one of the important issues concerns the much-discussed question whether these changes are continuous or discontinuous. There are some who argue for a pervasive continuity and insist on deriving the new from the old; there are others who believe in a radical discontinuity, in an irreducible emergence of novel means or ends. Our point is that developmental changes necessarily entail both continuity and discontinuity. On the one side, the orthogenetic principle in *overall terms*, that is, in terms of an increase in differentiation and hierarchic integration, necessarily implies continuity; on the other hand, in terms of

---

[7] We shall sometimes refer in our later discussions to the notion and the genetic principle of "means-ends" relationship by the term "form-function" relationship.

the specific, concrete forms and operations, novel functions and structures "emerge," and in this respect changes are discontinuous. Even in the emergence of novel functions and forms, however, there is, as a rule, an intertwining of continuous and discontinuous changes: though novel features come about by qualitative change, which necessarily implies discontinuity, the *manner* in which such features emerge may be gradual in various respects, e.g., there may be a gradual increase in the frequency of occurrence of the new over the old, or there may be employment of older forms for new functions before the new functions secure the formation of novel, function-specific means, etc. (Mayr, 162; Werner, 273).

A further issue, of equal importance, concerns the "fate" of the genetically earlier modes of functioning when higher functions and forms have emerged. At least with regard to humans it must be maintained that with the attainment of higher levels, lower levels of functioning are not lost. Under normal circumstances, such lower levels of functioning (both in terms of means and of ends) are subordinated to more advanced levels of functioning; they may come to the fore again under special internal or external conditions, for example, in dream states, in pathological states, under intoxication by certain drugs, or under various experimental conditions. They also, and characteristically, may come to the fore when the organism is confronted with especially difficult and novel tasks: in such cases, one often finds a partial return to more primitive modes of functioning before progressing towards full-fledged higher operations; we may refer to this tendency as a manifestation of the *genetic principle of spirality*.[8]

The general principle concerning the survival of lower levels of functioning in the course of development has been perhaps no more succinctly expressed than by Hegel in his *Lectures on Philosophy of History* (99, p. 98): "The life of mind is a totality of levels, which on one hand exist side by side, but which on the other, appear transitorily one after the other. The moments which the mind seems to have left behind actually exist in it at the present time in full depth."

Let us now turn to a brief examination of the ways in which the developmental principles intertwine with the organismic principles of behavior discussed in the previous section.

Taking first the *holistic* assumption, that is, the principle pertaining to the determination of local, part processes by larger contexts or wholes, one finds that with development—both in phylogenesis and

---

[8] Werner (274); cf. Gesell's related "principle of interweaving" (77).

in human ontogenesis—local activities become more and more interrelated and integrated, that is, come more and more under the control of and the determination by the focal, goal-directed activities of the organism. Concurrently, the nature of the organism-environment transactions undergoes marked changes.

At phylogenetically earlier levels, the milieu impinges upon the organism and to a great extent affects its behavior in the form of *physicochemical stimuli*—as energies which evoke direct and relatively stereotyped reactions from the organs or parts affected. At higher levels, the environment defined earlier by physicochemical stimulation and reactivity is converted through both species-specific instrumentalities and individually learned patterns of response into a field or fields of *stimulus-signs* or *signals*, instigating and guiding sensory-motor, goal-directed actions upon things—actions serving predominantly biological ends of maintaining the existence of individual, group, and species. Finally—and most characteristically and elaborately at the human level—the environment is not only reacted to and acted upon but is cognized, or "known," in the form of perceptualized and conceptualized *objects*. Implied in this development, there is an increasing *diversification* of the milieus or Umwelten in which an organism lives—with the lower levels of organism-environment transactions becoming, to an increasing degree, subordinated to and integrated within the higher levels. We have sketched these major developmental transformations of organism-Umwelt relationships in the left-hand column of Table 1-1.

Hand in hand with these developmental transformations in organism-Umwelt relations, and indeed, ingredient in such transformations,

Table 1-1
Diagram of developmental transformations

Organism-Umwelt relationships			Means-ends relationships
I. Tropistic-reflex reactions	*to*	Stimuli	Biophysical and biochemical transmission culminating in stereotyped reaction patterns of parts of, or whole, organism.
II. Goal-directed sensory-motor action	*upon*	Signaled things	Species-specific behaviors and individually learned patterns of response ("habits"); formation of signals (mammals); "natural" tool usage (apes); all predominantly in the service of biological ends.
III. Contemplative knowledge	*about*	Objects	Construction of tools and formation of symbols in the service of knowing about and manipulating the environment.

are genetic changes in the *ends* to which organisms are directed and in the *relationships of means to the realization of ends*. Whereas more primitive organisms—again both phylogenetically and ontogenetically—are directed predominantly toward the satisfaction of biological ends, in higher organisms, ends of a quite different order come into play; in man especially such novel, emergent functions are clearly manifested. Among the novel ends immanent in the nature of the developing human being—and most central in the context of the present discussion—is that of *knowing* about his world. This end plays an intrinsic role in man's transformation of his milieus into objects to be cognized and conceptualized. Indeed this end is so strong in man that even in the absence of certain normally employed instrumentalities of cognition (for example, sight and hearing), man may use alternative, compensatory means for attaining knowledge.

As we have indicated, with the phylogenetically increasing range of ends, and especially with the shifts in dominance towards the novel, "higher" ends, there is a correlative change in the instrumentalities by which the ends are striven for or attained (see Table 1-1, right-hand column). Where the Umwelt is primarily constituted through physical-chemical stimulation and reactivity the instrumentalities are biophysical and biochemical processes culminating in relatively fixed, stereotyped patterns of reaction, with part processes often reacting directly to the impinging stimulations without being subjected to and integrated into any more central organismic end.[9]

At higher levels of functioning, the sovereignty of the stimulus-issuing environment is reduced to some extent, and the "directly stimulus-determined patterns of behavior" (Maier and Schneirla, 161, p. 75), found even among the higher invertebrates, give way to an increasing freedom of "action upon things" in the course of vertebrate evolution. In this shift, there is a transformation, via organismic apparatus, of the physicochemical stimuli into signals for biologically relevant action, a production of signals through organismically initiated action,[10] and occasionally the use of environmental properties as momentary "tools" for the realization of momentary ends.[11]

Finally, at the post-neonatal human level, with the emergence of a

---

[9] Cf. for instance, Viaud (260), Maier and Schneirla (161), Herrick (104).

[10] An example of signal building in mammals would be the urination of male dogs; one of its functions, according to Uexküll, is that of putting up a "flag" as a signal of domination of the territory (256).

[11] See K. Oakley (177), W. Köhler (136), P. Guillaume and I. Meyerson (90).

basic directiveness towards knowing, man's hand and man's brain participate in the construction of tangible tools out of the properties of the environment and the construction of cognitive objects (percepts and concepts) which mediate between man and his physical milieu: it is primarily toward these objects that man's distinctive behavior is oriented.[12] It is in this context, as we shall attempt to show, that the most significant of man's instrumentalities, *the symbol*, is formed.

---

[12] See DeLaguna (54), Kahler (123), Révész (201).

chapter 2

The Organismic Basis of Symbol Formation

The Nature of Symbol Formation and
Its Role in Cognition: Theoretical Considerations

THE KNOWING OF OBJECTS: SYMBOLS VERSUS SIGNS

The developmental transformation from animal to human existence entails a radical change in the nature of the transactions between the organism and its milieus: human beings are not merely, nor mainly, organisms reacting to stimuli or responding to things-of-action. Man forms his Umwelt by relating to his environments in a new manner: he is directed toward knowing. The orientation toward, and the capacity for, knowing are essential and irreducible characteristics of man, characteristics that come clearly into relief when one compares the nature of the adaptiveness of animals and men to their respective environments. In animals—particularly in lower animals—organism and environment are closely attuned to each other; one might say that both are elements in a comparatively closed system, within which stimulation and response are tightly interlocked. With ascendence on the evolutionary scale, the closed system begins to open up: the relative rigidity of adaptive responses, the species-specific conformity to environments, gives way increasingly to choice responses, to modifiability and plasticity of behavior, and to an increasing trend toward learning through individual experience.

The radical transformation in the adaptive process at the human level has its profound effect on human ontogenesis: that comfortable closeness between organism and environment so characteristic of the existence of lower animals, and so quickly attained in the young even of higher animals, is—except for some vital-biological functions—practically absent in the human infant; most of the things in an organism's environment to which infrahuman animals become so quickly adapted remain in the realm of anonymity for the young human being. Only through arduous and painful effort does the human being progressively conquer his environments and render them increasingly familiar.

This human process of becoming familiar with one's milieu is not simply a mirroring of an external, prefabricated "reality," but it involves a formation of the world of objects by the human being in terms of his equipment and biopsychological "goals." The human world, then, cannot claim to reflect an independent "reality per se;" it is rather a coherent, man-specific Umwelt, a representation of "what there is" by means available to the human being.

Thus man, destined to conquer the world through knowing, starts out with confusion, disorientation, and chaos, which he struggles to overcome. This struggle is a never-ceasing process, continuing throughout life: man's objects are always touched with a coefficient of indeterminacy and, as long as he is open to new environments and experiences, they are constantly in the process of transformation, changing in their significance. One may indeed say that man lives constantly in a world of becoming rather than in a world of being.[1] Now it is our contention that in order to build up a truly human universe, that is, a world that is known rather than merely reacted to, man requires a new tool—an instrumentality that is suited for, and enables the realization of, those operations constituting the activity of knowing. This instrumentality is the *symbol*.

Symbols can be formed for, and employed in, the cognitive construction of the human world because they are not merely things on the same level as other existents;[2] they are, rather, entities which subserve a novel and unique function, the function of *representation*. The function of representation is a constitutive mark of a symbol;

---

[1] See Ortega y Gasset (181); Allport (4); Schachtel (211, p. 200 f).

[2] This implies that symbols do not function as *substitutes* of things or signs: only things can substitute for things or signs substitute for signs of things. Thus, Pavlov's bell sound, as a substitute for food stimuli, is a sign or signal, not a symbol.

it distinguishes anything qua symbol from anything qua *sign, signal,* or *thing*. Signs and signals are elicitors (or inhibitors) of action; they lead one to anticipate rather than to represent an event. In our view, therefore, symbols can never be considered a mere species of the genus "sign." [3]

The correlate of our assumption is the thesis that symbols emerge primarily from cognitively oriented rather than pragmatically oriented operations. Thus, against the arguments of some students of linguistic symbolization, we maintain that speech is not genetically derivable from the vocalizations of animals or from vocalizations of infants that subserve biological needs. In maintaining the primary role of cognitive factors in the emergence of true speech, we do not, of course, imply that verbal activity serves no pragmatic function in young children: it would be absurd to deny that early names are exploited in the fulfillment of practical needs. Nevertheless, we insist that in early genesis the pragmatic aspects of naming are subordinate to the cognitive function (see pp. 160 f).

THE CONCEPT OF "SYMBOLIC REPRESENTATION"

Here we essay only a preliminary clarification of what we intend by the thesis that representation is the constitutive characteristic of symbols as opposed to signs. In order to provide this clarification, let us first make, and briefly discuss, a number of terminological distinctions. Generally, in a symbol situation, one distinguishes simply between the symbol and its referent, that is, between the entity which represents and the entity which is represented. An organismic theory finds it necessary to introduce more refined distinctions.

We use the term *referent* in two ways: in some contexts, it is employed solely to designate a perceptual or conceptual "object" to which reference is made, irrespective of the manner in which this object is organized or connotatively structured; in other usages, it is employed to designate the object both as denoted and connoted. Where we wish especially to emphasize the connotational structuring or semantic organization of the referred-to object, we employ the term *significate;*

---

[3] Cf. B. Russell's dictum, "Language is a species of the genus sign" (203, p. 13). This view, which assumes a known world independent of language (symbolization), to which language signs are attached, has been strongly criticized by philosophers such as Cassirer (42) and Urban (259). This latter view—close to our own—is conveyed in Urban's statement, "Knowing in any significant sense of the word is inseparable from language" (259, p. 347).

thus, *referent* and *significate* may sometimes be used synonymously.

Correspondingly, we use the term *symbol* in two senses: in one, it is employed when we wish to emphasize a fusion or indissolubility of form and meaning; in the other, it serves to designate a pattern or configuration in some medium (sounds, lines, body movements, etc.) insofar as this pattern is taken to refer to some content. Where we wish especially to emphasize the structuring of the configuration or pattern in a medium, we employ the notion of *symbolic vehicle;* thus, symbol and symbolic vehicle may sometimes be used interchangeably.

When a symbolic vehicle is taken to "represent" a referent, it is our view that the vehicular structure functions to "depict" or "reveal," through some sort of correspondence or analogy, the connotational structure of the referent. It should, however, be emphasized—a point to be elaborated later on—that correspondence or analogy is not, in our view, "given objectively" in and by itself, but is *established through an intentional act:* the members of a speech community articulate a linguistic form so that it bears a structural correspondence to its significate (referential meaning).

Note that, in our view, symbolizing enters directly into the construction of the "cognitive objects," determining how events are organized and what they mean. Our thesis is thus opposed to the widespread view which treats symbolic vehicles and referents as two fully formed entities that are externally linked to each other through contiguous pairing (and reinforcement). If one accepts this latter view, one implicitly denies to symbolization (including language) any creative role in the cognitive organization of experience and thought: symbolic vehicles then become reduced to a complex system of markers, useful merely for routine indication of referents and for communication about preformed judgments and concepts.

At this point a few comments may be added to clarify somewhat further the terms "representation," "language," and "symbol."

1. The term "representation" is a rather common word used in various areas of discourse. In the area of cognition, the term is sometimes used to designate the relation between an abstract concept and a concrete example: one may thus be said to "represent" the concept *tree* by a percept or image of a particular tree. This "exemplificatory representation" differs clearly from symbolic representation: the concrete object, tree, is a "substantialization" of the connotations of the concept but does not symbolize or depict the concept; it would be preferable to speak here of "reification" instead of "representation" of a concept. In contrast, the word "tree" truly signifies or symbolizes the

concept tree: the dynamic structuring of the word by the speaker (and the hearer) is taken within the linguistic medium to correspond to the significate (connotational structure of the referent). In order for such correspondence [4] between vehicles and significates to be attained, the symbolic vehicles—e.g., the word-forms—have to be constructed systematically; language has become the medium of representation par excellence precisely because its vehicular forms, from the phonemic sound elements to the most complex syntactic structures, are built on systematic principles,[5] making it possible to reveal, within the linguistic domain and by genuinely linguistic devices, the connotational structure of the referent.

2. In regard to the term "symbol" we note again the wide range of meaning this word has in common usage. The distinctive mark of the concept as employed here is its inherent duality: as stated before, a symbol entails a "vehicle" which, through its particular formal and qualitative properties, represents a "referent," that is, an object, a concept, or a thought. "Representation" in the sense used here implies more than simple and direct expression of meaning by a vehicle: it implies some awareness, however vague, that vehicle and referential object are not identical but are, in substance and form, two totally different entities. Thus a name, when handled—as in magic—entirely as the thing which it ordinarily represents, is no more a "symbol" than the object itself. Similarly, a gesture directly and unintentionally expressing an emotion such as joy or disgust is not symbolic; the so-called "symbolism" of gestural and postural patterns may be symbolic for the interpreter, but they are not for the producing individual. Again, the "latent thought" of dream images may render these images symbolic for the interpreting psychotherapists; for the dreamers, the dream images are taken as such and are thus not symbolic.

From true symbols we distinguish, then, those productions whereby the vehicular structures (imagery, visual or verbal patterns, gesture, etc.) directly "present" a meaning rather than "represent" it. One might call these productions *protosymbols*. Though on the surface often indistinguishable

---

[4] The notion of "correspondence" is further discussed in the following section on symbol formation and also in Chapter 4.

[5] In view of the systematic nature of language, the claim of many scholars as to the "arbitrariness" of linguistic forms seems to us to be unwarranted. The widespread characterization of language as "arbitrary" appears to derive from a connectionist theory of learning: since a language has to be "learned," and since there are many languages, all of which refer to apparently the same universe in distinctly different ways (tree = arbre = Baum), the relation between meaning and its linguistic expression "must" be a product of arbitrary, conventional connections. Without going into any argumentation here, we may simply point out that from our constructivist, idealist standpoint, this thesis is untenable: in the last analysis, it goes back to the pre-Kantian attempt to construe system, law, and order out of cognitively blind associative links in which everything can be related to everything else.

from true symbols, protosymbols lack the *intentional* act by which a vehicular form is taken to represent a referent. Nevertheless, protosymbols are extremely important in the genetic processes of symbolization: protosymbols may be transformed into true symbols by progressive differentiation of vehicle and referential meaning; true symbols may regress to protosymbols through dedifferentiation of vehicle and referent.

3. Finally, the term "language" is itself a word to which a rather wide range of meanings is commonly attached. As defined here, the distinguishing mark of language is its function of symbolic representation. From this point of view, it seems quite obvious that von Frisch's (71) "language of the bees" (dancing patterns of a bee, which communicate to other bees the direction and distance of food places) is not language at all but is rather a complex of well-organized behavior patterns which function as biochemically transmissible signals. Even the gesture and vocal communications of anthropoids, however expressive they may appear to an onlooker, must be regarded as nonlinguistic asymbolic signals, lacking any representative function (Köhler, 136).

At the human level, too, it may be noted, many forms of communication are used which do not fulfill our criterion of "language." Take, for instance, the flag signs which in earlier times communicated—by the combinations of three elements (circle, triangle, square)—"sentences" such as: "we have no food," "you are in danger," "we have a leak." True, in contradistinction to animal communication, one deals here with constructed patterns. However, these patterns are purely "arbitrary" combinations based on prior agreement; they are neither built on a systematic principle nor do they mirror, or correspond to, the connotational characteristics of the referent. The "flag language," therefore, is typically no more symbolic than "stop" and "go" traffic lights; it is a complex sign code which indicates but does not represent meanings.

SYMBOL FORMATION AS "DYNAMIC SCHEMATIZING ACTIVITY"

And now we come to the crux of an organismic theory of symbol formation, an attempt to account for how the organism forms its objects, transforms material into symbolic vehicles, and establishes a relationship of representation between vehicle and referent. The central notion in this account is that of *dynamic schematization*. This central notion may be characterized as a *directive, regulative, form-building process*.

Schematization in the Formation of Objects-of-Reference

That objects come to occupy the status of referents in symbolic activity can best be understood in terms of their genetic origin in cognitive (contemplative) behavior. As we have stated earlier, the (pre-symbolic) world of the very young infant is primarily one of things-of-action, articulated in terms of affective-sensory-motor patterns. Soon, however, the directedness towards knowing begins to emerge, and the world undergoes a most significant transformation from things-of-action to objects-of-contemplation. In this process aimed at the knowing of objects, the growing child makes use of some of the specific sensory-motor and affective response patterns by which he had articulated the things-of-action surrounding him; these patterns thus undergo a *shift of function*. They are now utilized for allowing the child to become aware of the characteristics of objects: in other words, they become the means by which he comes to know objects, to reflect on them, to present them to himself. Clearly related to this shift from outward reaction towards inward reflection upon objects is the *internalization* of sensory-motor patterns; in other words, objects are given form, structure, and meaning through inner-dynamic schematizing activity which shapes and intertwines the sensory, postural, affective, and imaginal components of the organismic state.

This view of object perception is consonant with the main tenets of the sensory-tonic theory of perception (265, 277). In rejecting the atomistic notion of the purely sensory (for example, visual, tactual) character of percepts, this theory maintains that percepts come about through an organism's "interpretation" of the sensory stimuli issuing from physical objects, by reference to its own ongoing, dynamic state.

This inner-dynamic activity through which objects of cognition are formed must be considered genetically, that is, as an unfolding or "microgenetic" [6] process: we hold that the formation of referential objects starts from a primordial matrix composed of affective, interoceptive, postural, imaginal elements, etc., that is directed or channelized into a full perceptual articulation by the schematizing activity. Quite naturally, the more familiar an object becomes, the less time this process of articulation requires. Nevertheless, however instantaneous, however automatic the perception of objects may seem, the articulating (form-building) activity leading to a meaningful percept never drops

---

[6] By the use of a variety of techniques, for example, tachistoscopic presentation with exposure time increasing from trial to trial, experimental evidence has been brought forth, demonstrating microgenetic formation of perception, going through an orderly sequence of developmental stages. Cf. Werner (270; 272).

out. In other words, an object as a meaningful entity issues from, and remains linked to, an underlying process of schematization. If this bond breaks, meaning is lost.[7]

Some readers may object to the construct of "dynamic schematization" as being rather vague and may feel more comfortable with terms such as "set" or "anticipatory set." Surely, the notions carried by those terms bear some similarity to our notion and may have the advantage of more common usage. On the other hand, we feel that the notion of set, as usually employed, refers to something static and fixed; we coined the phrase "dynamic schematization" to intimate a dynamic, vectorial, mobile process as well as to hint at the sensuous-postural-imaginal components of this process.

Schematizing in the Formation of the Symbolic Vehicle

From the consideration of the construction of the object-of-reference (the denotable thing as signified), we may now turn to the symbolic vehicle—the means within a medium for representing the referent. In dealing with the formation of a symbolic vehicle, one is faced with the complex and baffling problem of understanding how it is possible that a material pattern, for example, a sound, a pattern of lines, a bodily movement—pragmatically-technically so different in substance and qualities from the object of perception or thought which it can come to symbolize—can ever be exploited for the representation of such an object. One might find no difficulty in understanding how imitating sound-forms represent their content. But the problem of how nonimitating sound-forms are endowed with significance, that is, become symbols, has perplexed all students of language who have recognized that speech serves more than an indicatory function. Indeed, Humboldt (111), that profound philosopher of language, focused upon this problem as the one basic to the understanding of human thought and communication.

It seems to us that a solution to this problem can be approached only by taking into consideration a number of factors that are often overlooked. One of these factors is the (actual or potential) *expressiveness of objects,* that is, the experience of expressive features in

---

[7] The effects of a rupture of the bond between the schmatizing activity and sensory stimulation are most strikingly seen, in normals, under conditions of prolonged fixation, inattention, etc. They are also reflected in psychotic "loss of objects" (Searles, 221, p. 55 f).

things seen and heard; [8] a second is the *transcendence of expressive qualities,* the manifestation of the "same" expressive-dynamic features in objects that are otherwise dissimilar; a third factor is the *intentional act of denotative reference,* the intention to use one item of experience to denote another; finally—and closely tied up with denotative reference—is the *establishment of semantic correspondence,* namely, the construing of the pattern qua vehicle so that its expressive meanings correspond to the connotational structure of the referent.

The nonrepresentational construing of *objects as expressive* is basic, and genetically prior, to the use of expressive properties in representation. Dynamic-vectorial characteristics, physiognomic qualities, rhythms, etc., inhere in the objects and events of our perceptual experience as much as do the geometric-technical properties. Such expressiveness also inheres in the actions of organisms, for example, in their bodily movements, in their vocalizations, and so on. Philosophers of language, such as Humboldt, who have seen the importance of the problem of expressiveness but have examined it solely with respect to speech, have overlooked the possibility that an answer to the question of how sounds are transformed into significant symbols might come, partly, from an understanding of general expressivity rather than from a consideration of vocal patterns alone. (See 103; 111).

The greatest insight here comes from culture-bound or culturally constrained actions, which take on the appearance of "naturalness" and "direct expressivity" within a community. Consider the non-linguistic gestural expressions of such attitudes as doubt, puzzlement, contempt, or haughtiness, which clearly reflect the human tendency towards the shaping of external patterns to convey inner states and meanings. Since such gestures are characteristically culture-bound and yet attain the appearance of "naturalness," one can see in such instances how material patterns (for example, bodily movements) become infused with meaning—infused to the extent that one cannot separate the pattern and its meaning: the gesture is the indissoluble unity of form and content. The "pervasive interpenetration" of sound by meaning which, for Humboldt (111, p. 99), was the most astonishing

---

[8] Many psychologists still insist on a bifurcation between geometric-technical features, as "given" or "out there," and expressive qualities, as derivative and "subjective." This bias is surely one of the factors that lead agenetic sign theorists—who generally take the adult pragmatic-technical world as the mirror of a given "objective" world—to overlook the importance of expressive-dynamic qualities both in perception and symbolization.

feat of human speech is, in principle, not basically different from the pervasive interpenetration of bodily movement by meaning which occurs when attitudes like those just mentioned are expressed gesturally and posturally.[9]

It is characteristic of organismic schematization of events in terms of expressive features that the same dynamic-physiognomic qualities may be perceived in a variety of objects and actions—phenomena which are markedly different from a pragmatic-technical standpoint. It is this *transcendence of expressive qualities,* that is, their amenability to materialization in disparate things and happenings, that makes it possible for one to feel and see equations and similarities that find no place in the physical-technical construction of the world— a construction oriented towards manipulation, control, and prediction. Such transcendence prompts the formation of similes, metaphors, analogies, etc., or at least provides the basis for such formations. It also provides the basis for the manifestation of similar expressive qualities in entities otherwise as unrelated as a sound-pattern and a perceptual or conceptual object.

It should be emphasized here that expressive similarity of two entities does not suffice to establish one of the entities as a symbolic vehicle for the other: expressive similarity obtains between many entities without these entities being conceived in a symbolic relationship. In order for a symbolic relationship to be established, an *intentional act of denotative reference* is required: it is this act which culminates in one entity being "taken" to designate another and which transforms an expressive entity into a *symbolic vehicle.*[10]

Here we come to an important tenet of an organismic theory of symbol formation: the act of denotative reference does not merely, or mainly, operate with *already formed* expressive similarities between entities. Through its productive nature, it brings to the fore latent expressive qualities in both vehicular material and referent that will allow the *establishment of semantic correspondence* between the two entities. It is precisely this productive nature of the denotative act

---

[9] It should be clear from our discussion here that we do not question that "learning" takes place in the process of taking a material movement as a significant gesture. Our concern, however, is with the processes that occur in a person learning that a body movement has a certain meaning or that a sound represents some object. Such "learning" can never be reduced to external conditions of contiguity or to an extrinsic motivational factor, for example, reinforcement.

[10] Through this act of reference, the symmetrical relationship which obtains between entities that are merely similar is transformed into an asymmetrical relationship, in which one entity is taken as signifier and the other as signified.

that renders possible a symbolic relation between any entity and another. Such a possibility could never be realized if one were dealing with *static* entities, namely, the symbolic vehicle as an end product and the referent as a preformed "thing out there." It is only realized because it rests on *twin form-building processes,* one directed towards the establishment of meaningful objects (referents), the other directed towards the articulation of patterns expressive of meaning (vehicles).

Our view of symbol formation as a productive-expressive act is fully consonant with Humboldt's dictum that language—the symbolic form par excellence—comes into being "in the very act of its production" (111, p. 57). It was in connection with this dictum that Humboldt presented his profound distinction between language as *ergon* (objective product or work) and language as *energeia* (energy, activity). "Language," he remarks, "is (in its very essence) not a product but an activity. Its true definition can therefore only be a genetic one; it is the ever-repeated workings of the mind towards making the articulated sound capable of giving expression to thought." Humboldt also emphasized, as we do, the correspondence between the perceptual and conceptual organization carried out by the intellect and the linguistic articulation by the sound-producing mind (111, p. 97). From Humboldt's characterization of language, one can see that he is a forerunner of modern genetic theory of language as dynamic activity. One can also see in his definition the grounds on which one can regard as futile all attempts to treat meaning as a static external connection between stimuli (objects, ideas) and responses (sounds, linguistic forms).

The first of these conjoint form-building processes has already been characterized, as a schema-regulated microgenetic activity leading—through a series of stages—to the articulation of *meaningful objects* (referents as connotatively structured). Similarly, the symbolic vehicle is established through a correlative schematizing process: through this schematizing process the material pattern (body movement, vocalization, etc.) becomes incorporated into an organismic state (comprised of interwoven affective, postural, imaginal, and sensory components) and is shaped into a symbolic vehicle. The pattern as imbued with significance—a word or a sentence—is thus the final manifestation of a comprehensive, microgenetically unfolding structure; it is maintained as a significant form only by virtue of its participation in this structure. Again, analogous to what has been said in regard to object-formation, the more automatized and easily activated are the vehicular forms (for example, word-forms), the more rapidly is the microgenetic process of articulation consummated; it must be stressed once more, however, that no matter how rapidly and automatically the verbal utterance takes place, the forms are still rooted in the expressive act and retain their organismically embedded expressive meaning. Once they lose this tie to the organismic matrix and to the form-building process, they become empty and meaningless.[11]

It must be emphasized again that the relation between the schematizing process and the articulated end-form (the symbolic vehicle) is not a sequential one. The process of schematizing operates throughout, in a regulatory, directive manner, on the inner organismic states as well as on the final (externalized) articulation; it directs all the mental operations involved in the formation of the symbolic vehicle, such as scanning, selecting, discarding, and sequentializing. It is the directed means-ends character of the schematizing activity that binds the vehicular form to its organismic matrix and gives meaning to the vehicular pattern.

Our view concerning form-building, schematizing activity bears some kinship to that presented by Lashley (149) in his revolutionary attempt to provide a neurophysiological account of the temporally unfolding, seriated yet unified character of linguistic expressions. Lashley argues convincingly that prevailing notions of a purely associative linkage between successive elements can account neither for the temporal order of constituents of a serial pattern nor for the presence in one's experience—prior to actual expression—of the configuration as a whole. He is thus led to assume that the neurophysiological basis of the unified seriated expression must be a mechanism independent of the mechanisms underlying the activation of the elements per se. Lashley sees the actualization of serial order as a scanning operation, by which a quasi-spatial trace or neurophysiological network arrangement is translated into temporal articulation.

It is significant that Lashley finds himself at a loss to characterize, even in general terms, the neurophysiological character of the scanning mechanism. We feel that Lashley's difficulty is caused by his reluctance to free himself completely from an adynamic bias: he still tends to conceive of trace-net and scanning mechanism as two distinct entities, one relatively spatial, the other relatively temporal. It seems to us that only if one conceives of the underlying schematization process as *dynamic-vectorial,* directive in nature, and thus not spatiotemporally differentiated, will one be able to dissolve (at least theoretically) the difficulty of "translating" a static spatial entity into a dynamic temporal unfolding.

In brief, then, the *establishment of semantic correspondence* between the vehicular pattern and the referential object—the formation of the symbol—comes about through the operation of schematizing, form-

---

[11] See our discussion of "lapse of meaning."

building activity which shapes the pattern on one hand and the referent on the other. Correspondence is achieved when both pattern and object are rooted in similar or identical organismic states, the formation of these states being directed and regulated by the underlying activity of schematization.[12]

The view presented here may seem, at least superficially, to have some similarity to the well-known "mediation hypothesis" of C. Osgood (182; 183). As we understand it, Osgood's theory holds that words (e.g., "apple") are essentially signs that come to signify their objects by evoking in the organism some fraction of the total response evoked by the stimulus object (e.g., apple); it is thus by virtue of sharing some common response properties that sign (word) and object are related to each other. Thus, both our view and Osgood's hold that there is "similarity" (partial identity) between "reaction" to the referent and "reaction" to the vehicle. But here the agreement of the two viewpoints ends. Osgood's view, rooted in a stimulus-response psychology, is agenetic and does not distinguish fundamentally between mere *reacting* and *knowing*;[13] representational activity is treated as a response essentially no different from other responses. Our view, on the other hand, is genetically oriented and makes a fundamental distinction between *reacting to* and *knowing about;* representation is thus an emergent activity not reducible to the overlap of responses. Finally, for us, but apparently not for Osgood, representational activity goes hand in hand with the *construction* of a world of objects ("knowables").[14]

We may conclude this discussion by trying to communicate to the reader via a concrete—admittedly simplified—hypothetical example what is meant by our notion of the establishment of semantic correspondence. Let us (following Uexküll) assume an individual confronted by a configuration, which he apprehends as possessing a "sitting tone": that is, the configuration instigates in him a postural-affective state which is organized schematically as "something there to move towards and sit down on." It is this schematizing activity and the ingredient organismic state that leads the individual to apprehend the configuration as a "chair" rather than, for example, a "table" (even though the same configuration, considered physically, for example, a

---

[12] The dialectical interaction between vehicle- and referent-formation which takes place in the course of establishing semantic correspondence is further discussed in Chapter 20 under the concepts of *vehicular rotation, conceptual rotation,* and *reciprocal rotation.*

[13] See also Blanshard (20, I, p. 55).

[14] See also Cassirer (42, I, pp. 85–114).

"tree stump," might be articulated—depending of course on organismic states—as either "chair" or "table").

Now we assume that the vocable *chair*, in an English-speaking individual, issues forth from the same schematizing activity: as an essentially dynamic, intonationally molded sound stream—not as a static sonic configuration—the material, phonemically unique sequence, *ch-ai-r*, is articulated into a production whose expressive features parallel those ingredient in the percept "chair." As a mere sound configuration, the utterance *chair* functions as a sign or label (as it actually is for one learning a foreign language). Only when the vocable has become embedded in an organismic matrix, regulated and directed by an activity of schematizing or form-building, does it enter into a semantic correspondence with the object (referent) and does it become transformed from the status of sign to that of symbolic vehicle.

Experimental and Empirical Evidence Consonant with an Organismic Theory of Symbolization

Our aim here is to offer some evidence—all pertaining to symbolization in a linguistic medium—which may serve more directly to support our general view of symbolic activity.

In our attempt to determine the nature of a symbolization, we concluded that the central distinguishing feature of a symbolic vehicle as opposed to a sign lies in its representational function: the vehicle is exploited by the organism to represent or depict a referent. Such representation, we concluded further, comes about through schematizing activity of the organism; it rests on the establishment of an inner-dynamic, rather than external, similarity between the total articulatory processes entering into the formation of cognized objects, on one side, and symbolic vehicles, on the other.

Our aim in this section is to clarify more concretely the main tenets of our theory by presenting some experimental and empirical data which we believe are most consonant with an organismic approach to symbolization.

First, we shall discuss several studies which demonstrate the fact that linguistic forms qua symbolic vehicles may be endowed by individuals with the same dynamic features as the referents they represent. Second, we shall cite findings from experiments on "lapse of meaning" which we take to support the view that vocal forms that are transformed into symbolic vehicles may undergo dissolution, thus reverting to the status of signs. Third, we shall show how the phenomenon of "word-realism" is best interpreted as involving organismic schematizing activity in the establishment of both vehicle and referent. Finally, we shall touch briefly upon an early experiment dealing with the "physiognomization" of linguistic forms—an experiment which points up the organismic roots of verbal symbols.

Experiments on Similarity of Inner Dynamics of Symbolic Vehicles and Referential Objects (Significates)

One argument frequently leveled against a general theory of symbols as representational invokes the fact that linguistic forms, "objectively" considered, typically manifest no trace of similarity to the objects they signify: language, the argument runs, is "arbitrary." Insofar as words are taken as products or impersonal signs, that is insofar as language is abstracted from concrete, active, living individuals, this argument is undoubtedly valid: with the exception perhaps of onomatopoetic word-forms, one can see no *external similarity* between the properties of objects to which reference is made and the properties of the forms used to refer to these objects. However, when one considers the view that perceptual objects as well as symbolic vehicles are established in terms of organismic schematizing activity, one may entertain the possibility that an *inner similarity* between vehicle and referent may occur without this similarity being apparent to an observer who regards solely the external, geometric-technical properties of word-form and object.

One study, designed to demonstrate the infusion into word-forms of dynamic features which enter into the constitution of the referent, was undertaken in the Clark University laboratories by S. Kaden and collaborators (122). Kaden, et al., devised a technique for indirectly measuring dynamic properties inhering in pictured objects and then extended this technique to the determination of such properties in meaningful word-forms.

The technique is based on the assumption that visual dynamics ingredient in a perceived object will be a determinant of the individual's location of that object in space; that is, objects with dynamically upward-directed features will, other things being equal, be seen as relatively higher in space than objects with dynamically downward-directed features.

In their study of the effects of visual dynamics in pictured objects, Kaden, et al., determined first the "neutral apparent eye-line" of each subject, that is, the physical location of an illuminated horizontal rod in the dark which the subject experienced to be at his own eye-level.

The experimenter then presented illuminated pictures of hands, pointing either upward or downward. These pictures were initially placed in a position corresponding to the physically measured ("objective") eye-line of the subjects. Under instructions to *adjust* the pictured hands to their "neutral" eye-line, the subjects placed the upward-pointing hand below the "neutral" eye-line and the downward-pointing hand above the "neutral" eye-line. This placement indicated that at the beginning of the experiment the upward-directed hand was actually *seen above* "neutral" eye-line, and the downward-directed hand was actually *seen below* "neutral" eye-line. The *magnitude* of the shift in apparent location was determined by measuring how much the hands had to be physically moved from objective eye-line in order for them to appear to the subject to be at his eye-level. In Fig. 2-1, the findings are presented diagrammatically.

What happens when the items to be located with respect to one's eye-line are not pictures but word-forms—linguistic vehicles, presumably lacking any visual dynamics, but merely connoting or referring to movements in an upward or downward direction? In this part of the experiment by Kaden, et al., luminescent words were presented to subjects again under darkroom conditions. The words—some referring to upward movement (*climbing, rising*), others connoting downward movement (*falling, plunging*)—were first placed at the objective eye-level of the observer and then shifted up or down, at the request of the observer, until they appeared to him to be at his eye-level (at "neu-

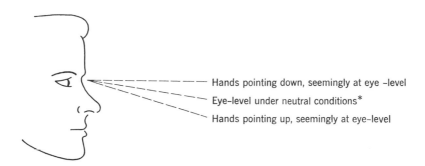

FIGURE 2-1. Apparent eye-levels of pictured hands differing in directional dynamics: Down, −2 mm; up, −42.3 mm. (After Kaden et al.)

* The "neutral" eye-level is, for adults, below the physical eye-line.

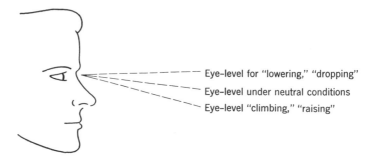

FIGURE 2-2. Apparent eye-levels for word-forms connoting referents differing in directional dynamics: Down, +1.4 mm; up, −11.3 mm. (After Chandler.)

tral" eye-line). The results were strikingly analogous to those found with the pictured hands: in order for the different words to be located at subjects' eye-level, "climbing" had to be placed at a spatial position measurably below "falling" and "plunging."

Recently, in a refinement and extension of this study, K. Chandler conducted an experiment in which the results seem to be clearly in agreement with the general findings of Kaden, et al. Chandler's results [15] are summarized in Fig. 2-2.

Chandler is at present engaged in extending the study to another important aspect of symbol-formation, which bears some relation to experiments on "lapse of meaning," to be discussed later. He induced in his subjects the posthypnotic suggestion that the words to be seen on the screen were those of an unfamiliar language, carrying no connotation for an English speaking person. Preliminary findings seem to indicate that this condition of experimental "word-blindness" induces a striking change in the way in which these, now meaningless, word-forms are located at eye-line, as compared with their location under nonhypnotic conditions. It so happens, at least with the subjects studied so far, that a reversal of location of the word-forms occurs: under normal conditions, upward-connoting words had to be adjusted downward to be perceived at eye-line, but under experimental "word-blindness," the same word-forms were adjusted upward to be perceived at eye-line; an analogous reversal occurred for the downward-connoting words. In order to understand the nature of such reversals, one has to assume, first of all, that the word-forms presented to the subjects have lost

---

[15] Dr. Chandler's study is as yet unpublished.

their status as true words: they are no longer symbols representing a referent but have become configurations, with their own expressive properties and dynamics, based most probably on rhythm, sound properties, etc. In other words, they have become physiognomic syllables whose intrinsic directional properties now determine their placement in space. Some other findings of Chandler's support this interpretation. He was able to demonstrate that two-syllable "nonsense" forms, namely, *budraf* and *medref*, are *located* at different places when each of them is *seen* by subjects at apparent eye-level. Chandler, in attempting to account for these results in terms of the physiognomic properties of the sound patterns, points out that people rate the two words as being different in "weight" or "ponderosity": *budraf* is apprehended as "heavier" than *medref*.

The studies by Kaden, et al. and Chandler provide evidence clearly consonant with two propositions of an organismic theory of symbolization: first, they indicate that dynamic features are no more indirectly inferred from symbolic vehicles than they are from perceptual objects; such dynamic features are the result of behavioral events—organism-environment transactions—which affect the perceptual organization of symbolic vehicles as they do that of objects. Second, they suggest that certain dynamic qualities immanent in objects may also be manifested in verbal forms: they thus point to the fact that dynamic features may transcend a particular material and may occur in externally dissimilar entities. For us, this fact underlies the possibility of the representation of objects by symbols.

Lapse of Meaning, Facilitation of Meaning-Retention,
and the Organismic Basis of Symbol Formation

For most sign theories of symbol formation, the meaning of a symbol is established through an external tie between an object (referent) and a sign-vehicle: when a linguistic form comes to mean something, all that has occurred is that the linguistic sign has been connected to a stimulus-object on the basis of spatiotemporal contiguity (and, perhaps, reinforcement); in this process the sign-vehicle undergoes no change, but merely becomes attached to the referent and serves to indicate or evoke it. In contrast, from an organismic-developmental point of view, the tie between vehicle and referent rests on an *organismic process of schematization:* the sign-vehicle becomes transformed into the overt face of a symbolic vehicle and the referent into a connotatively defined referent (significate); the bond established between the *vehicle* and the *significate*—both structured by a schematizing process—is one of inner similarity.

Among the phenomena consonant with the view that a process of symbol formation and referent-structurization underlies the everyday connection between vehicle and referent is that of "lapse of meaning." "Lapse of meaning," with regard to linguistic forms, refers to the fact that a linguistically meaningful sound-pattern or written pattern, a "word," when uttered or seen in continuous repetition, suddenly begins to sound or look strange, to lose its status as a meaningful word, and in extreme cases to become a mere configuration of sounds or lines.

It is important for the theoretical understanding of this curious phenomenon to realize that in "lapse of meaning" the word-pattern need not, and usually does not, become altogether meaningless: most observers agree that they can experience a "lapse of meaning" even when they still know "abstractly" what the pattern denotes; in other words, a lapse of meaning can occur even though there is still some associative tie between the vehicle and the referent. What really appears to dissolve here is the embeddedness of the vehicle in the total symbol: the loosening of this participation results in the weakening of the inner bond between symbol and significate; as a consequence the linguistic form and the referent lose the close connection they have gained through the schematizing process. Stated more specifically, the continuous repetition of a vocable tends to encapsulate the articulatory activity per se and to loosen the tie of the utterance to the underlying activity of schematization. As we have argued earlier, a vehicle acquires its semantic function—its status as a unity of form and meaning —by virtue of its full participation in this underlying organismic activity; by the same token, when this full participation in the schematizing process and organismic matrix is reduced, the word-form loses its dynamics and reverts to the status of an indicator or sign, or even of a mere configuration.

Some sign-theorists may, of course, argue against our interpretation and maintain that "lapse of meaning" merely involves some disruption or dissociation of the bond linking sign-vehicle and referent; they would deny that there is any alteration in the physiognomy of the word-form, any dissolution of a "constructive" process leading to the structurization of a symbolic form. To confute this argument, one may simply cite the reports about such experienced changes in the configuration constituting the word-form in the course of "lapse of meaning" experiments (see, for example, Severance and Washburn, 226). Nonsymbolic entities such as familiar objects, nonsense syllables, or ornamental patterns do not, under the kinds of conditions promoting "lapse of meaning," lose their characteristic structures or undergo those kinds of changes which take place when word-meaning lapses. It is difficult to see, therefore, why word-forms—were they merely objects—should undergo these changes in configuration. In sum, the facts suggest that "lapse of meaning" is not basically a loss of an external tie between a sign and object but is rather a loss of inner-dynamic organization—a loss of the physiognomy of the word-form because of its loss of participation in the total symbol-forming activity.

In this connection, we may refer to an extremely interesting study on "verbal satiation" (lapse of meaning) by Jakobovits and Lambert (116). This study was specifically based on a distinction made by S. Ervin and C. Osgood (61) between two forms of bilingualism: "compound bilingualism," in which the two languages are functionally interdependent, and "coordinate bilingualism," in which the speaker makes use of two functionally independent language systems. In "compound bilinguals," a common "mediation process" (in Osgood's terms) is presumed to underlie semantically equivalent words (for example, house–maison) in the two languages; in "coordinate bilinguals," such "equivalent" words are thought to lack such common mediation. The underlying hypothesis of the Jakobovits-Lambert study—formulated within Osgood's theoretical framework—was that the effects of "verbal satiation" of a word in one language system on the retention of meaning of the corresponding word in the other language system would differ depending upon whether the individual was a compound bilingual or a coordinate bilingual: in a compound bilingual, lapse of meaning of a word in one language would be expected to spread to the equivalent word in the other language whereas such a spread would not be expected to occur in a coordinate bilingual. The amount of "satiation" or degree of lapse of meaning was measured by the change in the word's "potency" as determined by the "semantic differential" technique. The findings were in complete agreement with the expectations: transference of "satiation" occurred with the compound bilinguals but not with the coordinate bilinguals.[16]

Although this study was carried out within a different theoretical framework than our own, we believe that the findings are completely consonant with our organismic theory of symbolization. It seems to us that the sort of linkage between word-forms of different languages

---

[16] In fact, with the coordinate bilinguals, there was an increase in "potency" of meaning, rather than a decrease, for the "equivalent" words.

that would allow the spread of "lapse of meaning" from one form to the other does not depend upon connections of each of these word forms qua signs to the same class of referents, but is rather dependent upon inner organismic processes—through the participation of the externally different forms in a common symbol-forming activity. Where the forms of both words are structured as overt facets of this common organismic schema, "lapse of meaning" of one—entailing some disruption of the underlying schema—will lead to "lapse of meaning" of the other; where the forms participate in different organismic matrices, "lapse of meaning" will not spread from one form to the other.

Whereas the Jakobovits-Lambert study was concerned with factors conducing to "lapse of meaning," some investigations at Clark University have been particularly concerned with factors that would delay "lapse of meaning" or facilitate the retention of meaning of word-forms. One such study was recently carried out by A. Miller (167), a study designed to demonstrate that the dynamic organization holding a word-form together as a meaningful unit is rooted in schematizing activity in which postural-motor components play a significant part: in this experiment, the "lapse of meaning" phenomenon was used to assess the role of organismic activity.

The following considerations underlie Miller's experiment: it is reasonably well established, on the basis of studies on "sensory deprivation," that the integrated activity of the organism begins to dissolve under repetitive stimulation (homogeneous stimulation); stable relationships, habitually obtaining among experiential entities, become disrupted. Now one may argue that the repetitive exposure to verbal stimuli—a condition serving to promote "lapse of meaning"—induces a disruption in the habitual relation between organismic activity and the linguistic form, eventuating in a dissolution of the dynamic features that constitute the linguistic form as a symbolic vehicle. Given this premise, one would expect that any strengthening of the organismic activity through which a linguistic sign is transformed into a symbolic vehicle would serve to maintain the symbolic nature of the word-form and hence would delay "lapse of meaning": thus, one would expect that a sufficiently intense sensory-motor activity, consonant with a word-meaning, would retard "lapse of meaning" for that word-form. This hypothesis was tested in Miller's study.

Since Miller's experiment constituted a first attempt to probe into a relatively unexplored problem area, rather simple sensory-motor activities were chosen for studying effects on the maintenance of word-meanings. Two action words were used: "push" and "lift." The subjects were requested, under three conditions of concomitant activity, to repeat each word until it lost its meaning. One condition was "concordance" of meaning and action, that is, the subject *pushed a drawer* while repeating the word "push" and *exerted a lifting motion* while repeating "lift." The second condition was "discordance" of meaning and action: the word "push" was accompanied by a *pulling action*, the word "lift" by a *lowering motion*. The final condition was "tangentiality" of action with regard to word-meaning: a *lowering movement* accompanied the word "push," a *pulling motion* the word "lift." The findings of Miller's study were entirely in support of an organismic view of symbolization: motor activity, accompanying the repetition of an action word and consonant with the word-meaning, resulted in greatest delay in "lapse of meaning;" actions related to the word-meaning by opposition or contrast had significantly less effect in retarding "lapse of meaning;" with tangential action, lapse of meaning occurred in the shortest time.[17]

What, from one point of view, may be regarded as an activity delaying or retarding "loss of meaning" may, from a different angle, be taken as an activity facilitating the formation or maintenance of meaning. In this light, an experiment by R. Dowling (56) relates directly to Miller's study. In his investigation, Dowling probed into the role of concordant sensory-motor activity in facilitating word-recognition. His hypothesis was as follows: involvement in motor activity consonant with, or related to, a word-meaning should lead to a relatively lower visual recognition threshold for that word than would involvement in unrelated activity or lack of involvement in a motor activity. Two action words, "pull" and "push," and a neutral word, "part," were exposed tachistoscopically. Each of these words was viewed under three conditions—subject pushing, pulling, or sitting motionless. The results were in full accord with the hypothesis: concordant activity resulted in a lower visual recognition threshold for words than did either discordant activity or nonactivity.

In a subsequent inquiry, Dowling (56) was able to uncover evidence against any thesis that the word-recognition threshold is lowered because of the arousal of word-associations to the sensory-motor activity itself. In examining the "errors" made in a forced-guessing situation, under different conditions of sensory-motor involvement, he did not find that the "erroneous" words uttered by his subjects bore any special relationship to the sensory-

---

[17] With regard to the lesser effect of tangential action rather than opposing action in retarding "lapse of meaning," see Kaplan (130).

motor activity they were carrying out: were the sensory-motor activity to give rise to associations which determined recognition-threshold, one would expect that such activity-related associations would be more prevalent among the "errors."

In sum, then, it seems to us that the findings from the studies by Miller and Dowling—demonstratiing the role of organismic activity in either delaying loss of meaning or facilitating formation of word-meaning—clearly support an organismic view of verbal symbol formation.

Within this context of lapse and facilitation of symbol-meaning we may finally refer to an early experiment by N. Ach (1), which attempted to study processes that appear to be a complete reversal of those involved in lapse of meaning, that is, processes involved in the transformation of signs or labels into true symbolic vehicles. In the study—part of Ach's well-known classification experiment—the task of the subjects (children and adults) was to find the conceptual meaning of four arbitrary verbal patterns. Each pattern was printed on paper and attached to a group of 12 colored cardboard objects: such a group consisted of 4 cubes, red, blue, yellow, and green; 4 similarly colored pyramids; and 4 cylinders. There were, of these groups of cardboard objects, some which differed from another in weight-size. *Gazun* was the label attached to the 12 *heavy* and *big* bodies (cubes, pyramids, cylinders); *Ras* to the 12 *light* and *big* bodies; *taro* to the 12 *heavy* and *small* bodies; and *fal* to the 12 *light* and *small* bodies.

The most important aspect of Ach's study [18] was an examination of the genetic transformations that take place in the word-like patterns as they change from signals or labels to meaningful class names.

Ach, requiring his adult subjects to report on changes in the apprehension of the arbitrary patterns during their performance, found that all the participants, sooner or later, clearly experienced a striking transformation in the character of those patterns: "these patterns, originally indifferent signs that stood only in associative connection with their referential—concrete or ideal—objects, eventually *merged* with their referent, fused with it into full unity" (1, p. 125). Ach concluded that the transformation from mere signs or labels to names entails a merging or fusion of the syllabic pattern and referent so that the particular pattern can be used, irrespective of the presence or absence of concrete referential objects, and can serve in thinking about

---

[18] Subsequent grouping tests based on Ach's method, for example, the Vigotsky test, have regrettably neglected this aspect completely.

these objects, in detecting new characteristics of the groups and of their relation to each other, etc.

We believe that we are warranted in interpreting Ach's somewhat strange notion of "fusion" of pattern and referent to mean that the syllables qua names acquired the function of depicting or representing the concept. In this connection, it is interesting to observe how the choice of the word-patterns (capital and small initials, indicating differences in size; double and single syllables, together with properties of consonants and vowels, indicating differences in weight) obviously served to facilitate the representation of the class characteristics by the patterns. It is through such internal organization of the pattern— not necessarily a conscious organization—that the subjects eventually arrived at the symbolic form, that is, the establishment of a correspondence between verbal pattern (vehicle) and referential concept (significate).

Word-Realism and the Organismic Basis of Object and Symbol Formation

Another phenomenon which seems to us to be refractory to explanation in terms of sign-theory, but which is clearly intelligible in terms of an organismic point of view, is that of *symbol-realism*, of which *word-realism* is a special case. Symbol-realism, especially as exemplified in the magical use of language, is, we believe, of considerable importance and must be comprehended within any adequate theory of symbolic functioning. Ethnologists, psychiatrists, psychologists, and linguists have all commented upon the widespread existence of the tendency to treat entities which are patently symbolic to advanced mentality, as if they were consubstantial with their referents, that is, as if they possessed the properties and the causal efficacy of the objects which they denoted.

It cannot be denied that symbol-realism, the handling of and response to words as if they were concrete objects or actions, pervades primitive cultures, is ontogenetically at the very beginnings of word-usage, occurs with great frequency among psychotics, and so on. The facts are clear. The question is whether these facts can be reconciled with an associationist, contiguity, or redintegrative theory of symbolic activity such as that expounded by Ogden and Richards (178) and most stimulus-response psychologists. (See 169; 170; 183).

Interestingly enough, Ogden and Richards themselves offer considerable evidence for the thesis that vehicle and referent are on many occasions intimately fused and strikingly confused. In the second chapter of their book *The Meaning of Meaning*, they present a large number of illustrations where a symbolic vehicle was either taken as somehow "containing" its meaning or as comprised of the same substance as its referent. The authors, while deploring the fact that symbolic vehicles and their referents are often confused, are obliged at the same time to acknowledge the ubiquity of this "confusion." It is, however, one thing to concede the widespread existence of symbol-realism and quite another thing to account for it on the basis of a contiguity theory. Ogden and Richards do not attempt to account for symbol-realism; they merely resort to a wholesale condemnation of it. It seems to us that it is well-nigh impossible to account for symbol-realism in terms of a contiguity-reinforcement theory of symbolization, that is, in terms of a theory that *reduces symbols* to *signs*. Neither animals nor humans, insofar as they respond to entities qua signs, confuse the sign with what it indicates or foreshadows: no conditioned dog treats a bell or buzzer as if it were of the same substance as the food it signalizes or indicates; no normal man opens his umbrella to protect himself against clouds or thunder as signs of rain.

Taking the symbolic vehicle as the real object is, however, exactly what does happen in magical use of language: the vehicle in such handling takes on the substantial and pragmatic character of the referent which, in nonmagical usage, it merely represents. As we see it, such substantiation of the vehicle and such confusion between vehicle and referent can only occur if the symbolic form is endowed with features (structural-dynamic in nature) which also pervade the object it ordinarily represents. In other words, it is only because the material comprising the vehicle is structurized to possess or embody those features which are apprehended in the object that one can treat both vehicle and referent as identical objects or as objects belonging to the same class.

Magical handling of language has an important bearing on theory of symbolization in another respect. Beyond the fact that such handling reflects the role of organismic schematizing activity in establishing dynamic similarities between vehicle and referent, it also reflects the embeddedness of overt symbolic forms in an organismic matrix: the magical efficacy of words does not rest in the linguistic forms themselves as detached products; rather, it is rooted in the whole organismic process of forming the vehicles—of shaping them, pronouncing them, etc. Magical spells are to a considerable degree articulatory gestures, intonational action patterns: the sorcerer's utterance is breath and spirit infused into words; in the conjurer's mind, and in the minds of those who are affected by the spell, the whole postural-motor activity involved in articulating the linguistic forms endows them with the potency of real objects or actions.

It would be mistaken to believe that magical handling of language has faded out in technologically and scientifically advanced cultures. Invectives as well as words of love derive their efficacy, in great measure, from their substantialized character: one can hit a person with a word as with a weapon; an insult or invective word is produced by the speaker as a vocal-intonational gesture and is, in this respect, not too far removed from the magical spell cast by "primitive" man.[19]

The use of euphemistic terms for tabued words is of particular interest in this connection: euphemisms are constructed because the original (tabued) word-form has become fused with the referent, and its utterance is equivalent to bringing the referent into substantial actuality. Through the introduction of a euphemism, the referent is now "pushed away" and maintained at some distance. If used too frequently, however, the euphemisms may themselves become intertwined with their referents: the distance between vehicle and referent may once again dissolve. Thus frequency of usage, interestingly enough, seems to affect euphemisms in a manner opposite to the effects of frequency of utterance in "lapse of meaning" phenomena: rather than dissolving the tie between vehicle and referent, frequency here leads to an increasing embodiment of the referent in the vehicular form. Eventually the novel euphemistic form also becomes tabued, and a new verbal expression must be created to replace the previously euphemistic form (see Ferenczi, 65).

In summing up the evidence presented in the last two sections, one may observe that, paradoxically, the representational and organismic nature of symbols is most clearly revealed under those extreme conditions where they have begun to lose their character as symbols: that is, under conditions of lapse of meaning where the symbol, because of loss of the represented referent, changes into a mere sign; and under conditions of magical speech, where the symbol because of its fusion with the referent loses its representational function and becomes a substantial thing—an object in itself.

---

[19] See Burke (38), Blackmur (19).

In concluding this section, we may refer briefly to an early study by Werner (269), dealing with the physiognomization of verbal forms.[20] In Werner's inquiry, subjects were given the task of apprehending words—printed on cards—so that these linguistic forms appeared to express or embody their meanings; although the linguistic forms were presented visibly, the expression or embodiment could be experienced auditorially as well.

The first point to note here is that there was no difficulty in eliciting physiognomization of the linguistic forms: the subjects could easily envisage the meanings in tangible features of the vehicle. This fact is directly relevant to our view that symbols are not arbitrary signs but dynamic representational forms; the ease with which subjects could physiognomize the linguistic forms suggests that such an apprehension of words is not a rare or curious phenomenon, permanently discarded by adults; rather, it indicates that physiognomic tendencies operate covertly in normal adults and can be rather quickly realized in perceptual material through experimental instruction. Not one of the large number of subjects who participated in Werner's study was unable to physiognomize the linguistic forms, and with but one or two exceptions all the subjects found the task a quite natural one.

Secondly, many of the reports of the subjects indicated the intimate relationship of physiognomization of word-forms to specific body-postural organizations: this serves to support our view that symbolization entails organismic activity.

To illustrate, we may cite one of the protocols quoted in Chapter 14. In this protocol the subject described his experience in perceiving the (German) word *hart* ("hard") physiognomically. He there reports how, at the sight of the word-form, he immediately experienced something of a "steel-like structuring" of the back of his body, clearly coalescing with the visible word-structure. After a short while, this postural organization dissolved, and with it there was a dissolution of word-meaning. Soon a second stage was reached, consisting in the objectification of the physiognomic-dynamics in the visible form: the dynamic organization, previously fused with body structurization, was now, so to speak, externalized—tangibly present in the word-form confronting the observer.

From this and other experiments cited in Chapter 14, we may draw the conclusion that the presence of organismic activity is a determin-

---

[20] The findings of this study will be presented in greater detail in Chapter 14.

ing factor in symbol-formation; conversely, absence of organismic activity tends to preclude symbol-formation. The just-cited instance concerning the physiognomic apprehension of the word *hart*—an instance paradigmatic of many of the cases we shall discuss subsequently —is clearly consonant with our organismic thesis: with a disruption of a relevant bodily organization, the stability of the linguistic form qua symbol is disrupted, and symbol-formation is impaired; the word-form undergoes a lapse of meaning.

chapter *3*

General Nature of Developmental Changes
in the Symbolic Process

In this chapter, we present an overview of some of the major developmental changes in symbol-situations, that is, changes which—in accord with the "orthogenetic principle" (Chapter 1)—occur in the direction of an increasing differentiation of the components of symbol-situations and of increasing integrative systematization (autonomization) of symbolic forms. In the following, then, we focus predominantly on the aspect of differentiation utilizing the developmental notion of "distancing" or "polarization," and shall only briefly touch in this chapter on the correlative developmental aspects of "autonomization."

The situation in which symbolic activity occurs may basically be viewed in terms of four principal (generic) components: two persons —an *addressor* and an *addressee*—, the object of reference or the *referent,* and the *symbolic vehicle* employed in referential representation. In the course of development,[1] each of these principal components comprising symbol-situations undergoes change, e.g., the *addressor* matures, the *addressees* change from parents to peers to generalized others, the *referents* become increasingly complex and abstract, and the *symbolic vehicles* are of an increasingly conventional and com-

---

[1] Although our thesis pertains to developmental changes in general, our discussion here is chiefly in terms of ontogenesis of verbal symbolization.

40

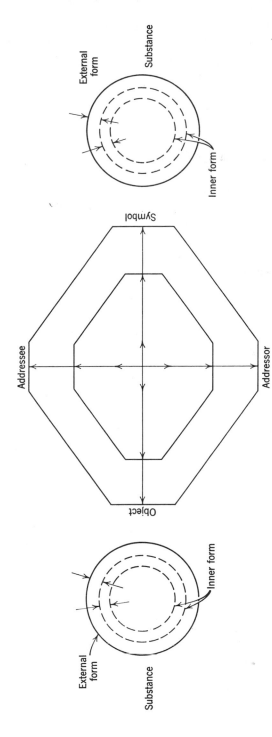

FIGURE 3-1. Diagram of developmental changes (distancing) in relations among components of symbol-situations.

munal nature. Concurrently, the components become related to each other in different ways. Initially, they are more or less fused with each other; they then become progressively differentiated from each other and at the same time linked or integrated with each other in various ways. For a reasonably full account of the development of symbolization, one must consider conjointly both the changes within the components and the changes between components.

For the designation of the process of differentiation in the domains of object formation and symbolization, we shall employ the concept of *distancing* or *polarization*. Here, then, we shall indicate how in the course of development there is a progressive distancing or polarization between person and object of reference, between person and symbolic vehicle, between symbolic vehicle and object, and between the persons in the communication situation, that is, addressor and addressee. Figure 3-1 may serve as a shorthand diagram of the changes involved in the developmental relationships we have termed "distancing."

THE PRIMORDIAL "SHARING" SITUATION

The increasing distancing or polarization of the four components in interpersonal commerce emerges slowly in ontogenesis from early forms of interaction which have the character of "sharing" experiences *with* the Other rather than of "communicating" messages *to* the Other. The primordial sharing situation (see Figure 3-2) may be described as one in which the distancing between the components has hardly begun to form; it is a pre-symbolic situation in which there is little differentiation in the child's experience between himself, the Other (typically the mother), and the referential object.

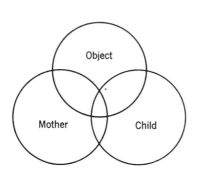

FIGURE 3-2. Diagram of primordial sharing situation.

Initially, inter-individual interaction occurs in purely sensory-motor-affective terms. Sooner or later, however, a novel and typically human relationship emerges, that of "sharing" of experiences, which probably has its clearest early paradigm in the nonreflexive smile of the infant in response to the mother's smile.[2] This sharing attitude in its true sense then becomes manifest when the infant begins to share contemplated objects with the Other.

It is worthy of note that within this primordial sharing situation there arises *reference* in its initial, nonrepresentational form: child and mother are now beginning to contemplate objects together—however slightly these objects are detached from the child's self. Thus, the act of reference emerges not as an individual act, but as a social one: by exchanging things with the Other, by touching things and looking at them with the Other. Eventually, a special gestural device is formed, *pointing* at an object, by which the infant invites the Other to contemplate an object as he does himself.

One of the few demonstrations of the significance of primordial sharing for the establishment of reference, and eventually for communication through symbols, is that given in V. Lowenfeld's ingenious method (156) of introducing an understanding of symbolic communication in blind-deaf individuals: his method consists in sharing with his pupil the creation of sculptures out of clay; in other words, in a teacher-pupil communion, a representative clay object is formed together, examined together, perceived together.

In a primordial sharing situation, that which is shared is the concrete object, perceived by both persons but not explicitly delineated; referring to an object by touching, looking, or pointing entails mainly an invitation to the other person to "look at that thing over there!" with the expectation by the pointing individual that the other person will perceptually articulate this object in a way similar to his own. But sooner or later a higher stage is reached at which sharing in contemplated objects is achieved through *symbols,* particularly through verbal symbols or *names.* The constitutive mark of a symbol, as we have indicated, is its representational function: a symbol represents a referent. Thus, whereas pointing entails only reference, the indication or denotation of a concretely present object, symbolization involves differentiation and integration of two aspects: reference to an object and representation of that object. In reference by pointing, the referent (the object) remains "stuck" in the concrete situation; in reference by symbolization, the characteristic features of the object (its connotations) are lifted out, so to speak, and are realized in another material medium (an auditory, visual, gestural one, etc.). From this early situation, in which symbolic vehicles (names) are

---

[2] Cf. Kaila (124), Spitz (238).

intimately bound to the concrete situation and shared by persons intimately linked to each other, there ensues in the course of ontogenesis an increasing distance between the four components of the symbolizing activity.

DISTANCING BETWEEN PERSON AND OBJECT

The progressive distancing between the person (addressor or addressee) and the object of reference is, of course, a manifestation of the well-known developmental principle of increasing polarization between subject and object, that is, the correlative and progressive establishment of a stable world of objects and a stable self from a matrix in which these two poles of experience exist in relative fusion and undifferentiatedness. The early objects, even on the human level, are probably much like the "things-of-action" characteristic of the infrahuman level, that is, they are things of momentary affective striving and of biologically directed action. Perceptual presentations are assimilated to the ongoing, rapidly changing states and are apprehended in terms of those states. In other words, early objects are defined almost entirely in conative-pragmatic terms, formed and re-formed through the changing affective-sensory-motor patterns of the individual.

In the initial phases of the transition from the apprehension of presented contents as pragmatic things-of-action to their comprehension as cognitive objects, the degree of subject-object differentiation remains relatively slight. There is still considerable fusion with respect to psychological and physical substance, a fusion reflected in that *animistic apprehension* of phenomena in which properties specific to things and properties specific to persons are almost indistinguishable from each other. Gradually, however, a fundamental transformation in the relation of person and object occurs with the shift from ego-bound things-of-action to ego-distant objects-of-contemplation. As we have stated in the previous chapter, implied in this change is the functional shift wherein the externalized sensory-motor pattern by which an object is initially grasped is transformed into an internalized cognitive schema: whereas the sensory-motor schema pertaining to the *external form* of an object is intimately tied to its signal-for-action character, the cognitive schema pertaining to the *inner form* renders the object amenable to representation in another medium; in other words, the object via its connotations (as a "significate") becomes susceptible to representation by a symbolic (signifying) vehicle.

In sum, then, in the relation between person and object, a stage is eventually reached where the fusion of the two moments gives way to the apprehension of the referential object as an ego-independent entity, more or less systematically related to other objects and represented, both in itself and in its relation to these other objects, via a symbolic medium.

DISTANCING BETWEEN PERSON AND SYMBOLIC VEHICLE

Analogous to the increasing polarization between person and object, the person and the symbolic vehicles he employs for representation also become increasingly differentiated from each other. In order to understand this process of distancing between symbolizer and symbol more clearly, one must make a distinction—similar to that made with regard to objects—between the *external, material* nature of a vehicle, that is, the specific character it has in a certain material medium, and the *inner cognitive structure* with which it is endowed through the schematizing activity of the addressor or addressee. In other words, one must distinguish between the *external form* and the *inner form* of the symbolic vehicle.

As to the *external* form of the vehicle, the increasing distance between the person and the symbol is reflected in the shift to a medium which is more or less function-specific with regard to representational reference: with development, the principal medium for representation becomes progressively differentiated from the person's immediate affective-motor-imaginal transactions with the world. Whereas the earlier media of representation are those of bodily movements and images —only slightly differentiated in form from the person's pragmatic activity—the dominant medium for representation becomes that of vocal utterances, which are not central to the individual's direct, pragmatic operation upon things.

Because the medium of vocal utterances is both external (audible) to the symbolizer and relatively detached from actual commerce with things of the environment, this medium permits a considerable degree of functional specificity, conducive to representation per se and hence to the autonomy of the symbol. Phonic forms, at least in their typical use, are specifically tailored to their function as vehicles of representational reference: unlike gesture, the phonic material can be clearly differentiated from pragmatic-conative bodily mobility; unlike imagery, the phonic material lends itself to external, interpersonal shaping, and thus is amenable to formation as speech symbols—more or less objective, person-independent entities, which can be "handed over" from one person to another in social intercourse.

As to the *internal* form of the symbolic vehicle, that is, the connotations or meanings the vehicle expresses, the increase in distance manifests itself in a reduction of "egocentricity" and "idiosyncrasy." Genetically early symbols—even those formed from the conventional patterns of the communal language—express meanings that are highly individualized: such symbolic forms, imbued with private experiences and personal feelings and reactions, are relatively lacking in precise and stable connotations necessary for communication to others. At genetically later stages of symbol formation, the interpersonal vehicle is more or less freed of private and idiosyncratic connotations and serves to represent relatively the same content for the communicants.

Many chapters of this book contain illustrations of symbol formations displaying a relative lack of distance obtaining between the symbolizers and the symbolic vehicles. For example, normal adult subjects, when representing an ostensibly impersonal event by means of expressive line patterns—that is, in a medium of lesser autonomy than that of language—quite frequently infuse in their linear symbols their own attitudes and feelings toward that event. Similarly, primordial speech-forms such as occur in the representational activity of the young child are inordinately interwoven with gross bodily gestures as well as with gestural-intonational elements of the articulatory organs: here too, the medium of representation is really a fusion of bodily states and externalized vehicular forms, in which the speech vehicle typically carries only a portion of the total representation.

DISTANCING BETWEEN SYMBOLIC VEHICLE AND REFERENTIAL OBJECT

In discussing the developmental changes in symbol-referent relationships one may, as before, consider separately the *external or material form* and the *internal or cognitive form* of both components. First, however, a few remarks may be advanced concerning the *substance* of symbols and objects.

It is well attested that at primitive levels of cognitive functioning —in infantile states, in pathological regression, etc.—symbolic vehicles and referential objects are scarcely differentiated from each other in terms of their substantial nature. Where a developed mentality would typically distinguish between vehicle and object, at primitive levels of mentation vehicle and referent are treated as consubstantial.

Thus one finds, at early stages of representation, that a name is treated as if it were of the same nature and causal efficacy as a thing, and action with or upon a name is akin to action with or upon the thing. This, of course, is the phenomenon of "symbol-realism" or "word-realism," briefly discussed in the previous chapter. In the course of development, vehicle and referent become distinct as to their substantial nature. The vehicle becomes "desubstantialized," so to speak, transformed into a device for describing and referring to things and events rather than retained as a thing on the same level, and of the same nature, as that to which it refers.

At advanced levels, then, the vehicle loses its "thing-like" status and acquires the status of a mediator, whose substance might perhaps best be characterized as "transparent": a person, so to speak, apprehends meaning "through" these "transparent" forms. The characteristic of "transparency" probably defies any precise definition; nevertheless, it at least serves to locate symbolic vehicles in a particular domain of reality uniquely their own—a domain at some remove from the domain of objects.

It should be further noted that on the way towards the desubstantialization of the vehicle—the distancing in substance between vehicle and referent—intermediate stages can be observed where vehicles still possess a quasi-thing-like character. In studies on the physiognomization of language (see Chapter 14), for instance, one finds that physiognomically apprehended words are typically "psychophysically neutral" entities; that is, they are relatively undifferentiated with regard to the distinction between psychological and physical properties.

We may now turn to distancing with respect to *external* and *inner form* of vehicle and referent. Let us first consider distancing with regard to *external form*.

It is our contention that, at genetically early levels of representation, the vehicle is produced or taken as a mimetic facsimile of the referent: for example, there are the onomatopoetic vehicles that represent referents by phonemically imitating noises characteristic of the referents. A developmentally more advanced representation is indicated by a relation between vehicles and referents still formed by a bond of external "similarity" where, however, the similarity is carried by *different* modalities: thus, phonic properties may "synaesthetically" represent shapes, sizes, or colors of figures (for example, "zig-zag"). Still more advanced genetically are representations by conventionalized patterns; here the external forms of vehicle and referent have lost most, if not all, of their surface similarity. Thus, there is a progressive distancing—a decrease in tangible "likeness"—between the external forms of vehicle and referent.

Intimately related to the genetic differentiation of the external form of vehicle from the external form of referent, there is an increasing distance between *inner and external* form with regard to the vehicle as well as with regard to the object of reference. At primordial levels, the inner and external form of the vehicle are very close together, that is, the connotative dynamic features of the vehicle are almost completely externalized—visible or audible in the external form. For example, in onomatopoetic expressions the meaning of the vocal form is given in the sound pattern itself. As one moves towards conventional forms, the connotative dynamics so to speak "retreat" from the external, material surface of the natural expression into the covert domain of organismic schemata. The inner and outer forms of the vehicle become clearly differentiated, though, to be sure, they never —except in pathological conditions—completely lose their tie to each other. Seen from this perspective, the physiognomization of language (Chapter 14) involves a return to a mode of representation in which the inner dynamics of words again become externalized in the material forms of the verbal symbols.

With regard to the object-of-reference, the differentiation between inner and external form manifests itself in handling of the object when it is no longer perceived as a concrete, particular entity but as an exemplification of general concepts. At later stages, the referent is apprehended as possessing an inner structure quite removed from the tangible, perceptible features: thus, at the highest level at which the scientific mind operates, the referential object becomes characterized in terms of a network of properties far removed from those open to everyday, unreflective perception. In brief, with development, the meaning or connotative schema of the referent becomes less bound to a concrete external form and eventuates in an invariant inner structure distinct from the ever-varying appearances which an object presents to perception.

As the inner and external forms of both vehicle and referent become increasingly distanced from each other, one would expect that the linkage between vehicle and referent would be carried through the inner forms of both. In other words, as the inner form of the referent becomes more abstract, so too must the inner form or inner dynamic schema constituting the symbolic vehicle. An abstract reference therefore requires a vehicle in which the inner form is not intimately tied to the external form; accordingly, onomatopoetic and physiognomic expressions are not ideally suited to represent abstract references. Indeed, as we shall see later on, the more "primitive" a medium, that is, the more it conduces to the formation of vehicles in which inner forms are manifest in external forms, the more difficult it is to employ this medium for the representation of relatively abstract concepts or abstract conceptual relations; the only way such a task can be meaningfully executed is by concretizing the referent.[3]

DISTANCING BETWEEN ADDRESSOR AND ADDRESSEE

As stated before, symbols emerge in an intimate interpersonal context, whose ontogenetic paradigm we defined as the primordial sharing situation involving child-mother-object. In the course of development, there is an increasing polarization of the persons involved in symbolization—an increase in interpersonal distance. This distancing between the addressor and addressee is a highly significant factor in the transformations which take place in the development of symbolization; it profoundly affects symbol formation in all the aspects just discussed. That is, concomitant with the addressor-addressee polarization there occurs polarization of the referents and of the symbols from the communicants (i.e., increase in objectification, impersonalization), polarization of symbol and referent (i.e., denaturalization), and polarization of inner and external form in symbols and in referents (i.e., increase in abstractness). These polarizations, in toto, bear all-importantly on the *autonomization* of symbols, that is, on the development toward a system of vehicles which enables a person to communicate adequately with an audience psychologically quite distant from the addressor. In other words, the greater the interpersonal distance between individuals involved in a communication situation, the more autonomous must be the symbolic vehicles in order to be understood, that is, the more communal and the less egocentric, idiosyncratic, and contextualized must the vehicles become.

These considerations lead us to one issue of prime interest for study: the different characteristics comprising adequate symbolic formulation under varying degrees of interpersonal distance. What, we may ask, are the characteristics of those symbolic representations that one employs—and takes to be adequate—in symbolizing some content for oneself (under the extreme condition in which addressor and addressee

---

[3] See, in particular, Part V.

are identical) as compared with the characteristics of those symbolic forms that one normally employs in representing that content for others? A related question concerns the degree to which a person who is very close to the symbolizer—an alter ego or a loved one—can garner the general meaning a symbolizer seeks to convey when the symbolic formulation may be rather condensed, elliptical, and ambiguous for others who are remote from the symbolizer.

With the interpersonal situation moving away from conditions in which addressor, addressee, and referential object are more or less closely linked, and with the concomitant formation of language as an instrument of interindividual communication, a further issue arises: it pertains to the relation between language as an "objective" phenomenon and language as a "subjective" event, or, in von Humboldt's terms, of language as "ergon" and language as "energeia" (see Chapter 2). This is indeed an important issue, which will come up in several chapters [4] of this volume: in particular, the question may be asked how, to what degree, and in what way can the objective, impersonal, universal usage of linguistic forms be reconciled with the individuality and subjectivity of the meanings infused into these forms when enlivened by the communicants? One must of course grant that language, in order to be transpersonal, must follow the rules of usage, and hold in relative abeyance or subordination any personal idiosyncrasies in manipulating the instrument of speech. This subordination of individual manipulation to collective usage allows the code to be employed with relative consensuality. But does this necessarily imply—as many theorists have assumed—that such consensuality can only come about where the connotations carried by a vehicle are *identical* for both addressor and addressee? In contradistinction to such assumptions, we do not believe that consensus with respect to the meanings of verbal symbols requires identity of connotations in the different participants: the only requirement is that the connotations evoked in both addressor and addressee occupy a *comparable position* within each individual's *personal* network of meanings.

Humboldt clearly and lucidly anticipated our position in stating: "Men do not understand one another by causing one another to produce exactly the same concept but by touching the same link in each other's sense perceptions and concepts, by striking the same key in each other's individual instrument whereupon corresponding, but not

---

[4] See Chapters 14 and 18.

identical concepts arise in each of them. When the link in the chain, the key of the instrument is touched in this way the whole organism vibrates and the concept that springs from the self stands in harmony with everything surrounding—even at great distance—the individual link" (111, p. 169).

As it is true for all forms of socially organized interrelationships, the execution of communication by speech involves the integration of individual and transpersonal expressiveness: normally conducted speech requires that a balance be maintained between the objective vehicular forms comprising the code and the variable individual meanings expressed in and carried by these forms in interpersonal commerce. This balance, in normal individuals, is rapidly reestablished when it breaks down momentarily. In cases of pathology, however, the balance between the use of the transpersonal code and the expression of personal meanings may be rendered unstable for long periods of time, perhaps even permanently. The instrumentality which is the linguistic code is then handled and used in idiosyncratic and "inadequate" ways in the communication of reference.

A final and truly central issue which has yet to be considered here concerns the *nature of autonomous language* itself. The next chapter will be devoted to this problem.

chapter 4

On the Nature of Language as an Autonomous Medium

In order to round out our theoretical discussion on the genesis of symbol formation as it culminates in full-fledged linguistic representation, we shall attempt in this chapter to give a brief logico-analytic account of the nature of language as an autonomous form. In this presentation, we shall draw considerably upon the views of Karl Bühler, whose *Sprachtheorie* (37), we believe, presents the most advanced contemporary psychological analysis of the general structure of language as an autonomous symbolic system.[1]

One must be cognizant of the character of Bühler's theory and the nature of his subject matter in order to assess his important contribution fairly. For the sake of clarification, it seems best to establish Bühler's position by underlining the differences between his approach and ours. First, Bühler's theory is essentially agenetic—a formal analysis of language as an ideal structure; our view is, of course, essentially developmental. Second, for Bühler the central focus is on language as an *ergon;* for us, as organismic theorists, the central focus is on language as *energeia.* Third—and consequent upon Bühler's agenetic concern with language as ergon—his approach searches for logico-constructive principles of representation; we are particularly oriented towards the psychological processes entering into representation. Despite these differ-

---

[1] It is regrettable that Bühler's book is neither discussed nor even cited in any of the recent works on language by American psychologists.

ences, it seems to us that many of Bühler's formulations are translatable into developmental terms.

Perhaps Bühler's major contribution consists in his *field-theoretical* approach to language.[2] For him, fully developed language is comprised of two substructures. On one hand, there are the elementary signs: lexical units, words. On the other hand, there is a "field," e.g., sentential structures into which the signs are placed. Each sign receives its full meaning and significance, its "field value," in terms of its location in a particular field.

Such sign-field structures, also found outside of language, may be illustrated by a geographical map: here signs for mountains, rivers, or cities, when placed on the map, become determined in their geographical locations, their relations to other signs, etc.; this is possible because of the systematic character of the map as a network of lines, ordered in terms of directional and quantitative spatial values (latitude and longitude). Another example of a sign-field structure is that of musical notation, whereby note-signs are put into a net of five horizontally placed parallel lines. In essence, language for Bühler has a similar dichotomized structure: "lexical elements placed in a field."

On the basis of this characterization of language, one may exclude from the domain of language per se other forms of communication which superficially resemble language. For example, on the basis of Bühler's criterion, flag-signals do not comprise a language because they lack the dichotomized structure of true language: they consist solely of combinations of colors or of geometric forms. In contradistinction to language proper, their communicative value accrues from "arbitrary" agreement. Moreover, such devices belong to the category of *signals* rather than *symbols* because they are substitutes for their referents rather than representations of them.

From Bühler's characterization, therefore, it would follow that where there is no field there cannot be language. Linguistic symbols without a linguistic field would be a contradiction in terms. We are inclined, however, to regard as linguistic in nature the idiomorphic names uttered by the young child, some of the utterances of schizophrenics, etc., even though they occur in the absence of a syntagmatic field. True, these forms have one distinguishing mark which sets them apart from language proper: though they function representatively, that is, they are depictive in character, they lack autonomy; their

---

[2] Anticipations of Bühler's view may be found in the writings of P. Wegener (266); see S. Langer (148, pp. 59 f).

significance derives from their embeddedness in a concrete-perceptual-motor-affective situation rather than from their placement in, and interdependence with, a linguistic field.

In brief, then, full-fledged language entails the correlative linkage of symbolic "signs" to a symbolic field. The symbolic sign—the word —is defined by its fitness for placement into the symbolic field; the field is determined by rules of construction, according to which symbolic signs placed within it acquire determinate meanings. In Bühler's terms, these symbolic signs or words are "synsemantic," insofar as their meaning is determined by the semantic-syntagmatic field, whereas the primitive names—fused with concrete sensory-motor reality— may be designated as "symphysic" or "sympractic."

The distinction between *sympractic* and *synsemantic* symbolic signs is, as will be discussed later (Chapter 10), to a great extent analogous to our distinction between "names" and "words." The developmental progression from "names" to "words" that we shall discuss in Chapter 10 may be conceived as a shift from symbolic signs that are "field-less," that is, linked to the concrete-pragmatic sphere of action, to signs that are located in a linguistic field.

A further distinction made by Bühler is also significant for developmental theory. This distinction pertains to kinds of "fields" rather than to kinds of "signs." On the one hand, there is an earlier or "lower" field—a *field of pointing;* on the other hand, there is a later or "higher" field—a *symbolic field.* The rules of construction pertaining to the field of pointing are concerned with spatial orientation in terms of direction and distance; certain linguistic signs—the demonstratives [3]—are placed into the *field of pointing* and receive their localistic determination through this placement.

In comparison with the *field of pointing,* which is to a considerable degree bound to concrete surroundings, the *symbolic field* reaches a relatively high level of autonomy. By virtue of syntactic principles governing the *symbolic field,* and by certain construction devices (particles, flexion, etc.), there are built up within language symbol structures which permit the depicting of relationships between referents quite unambiguously, that is, rather independently of the presence in concrete perception of the events to which reference is made.

In characterizing language as an autonomous system constituted

---

[3] According to Brugmann (33, II, p. 400), the demonstrative *to* is one of the very archaic Indo-European forms; characteristically, it is paralleled in early infantile expressions such as *da* and *ta.* See Stern (242, pp. 366 f).

by a symbolic field in which lexical units become interconnected with one another, one is confronted with the important question of the ways in which these autonomous linguistic structures can portray or represent realistic happenings despite their obvious "dissimilarity" to these happenings. In other words, how and in what way can there be a *correspondence* between linguistic formulas and reference?

Bühler maintains, we believe rightly, that language as a dichotomized word-sentence system does not portray events materially or "iconically." Essentially the correspondence is not a material correspondence but a formal one: the correspondence between linguistic representation and reference obtains with regard to *relationship;* its truth is a "relational truth." Bühler illustrates such formal correspondence using the thermometer as a model. A thermometric column does not "portray" fever as such; fever intensities are translated—or encoded—into a metric system of length, so that there is a relational correspondence between intensity of fever and height of the mercury column.[4]

If one applies this notion of "relational" or "formal" correspondence to linguistic representation, one may say that a sentence of the structure "A acts on B" expresses relationships which formally-syntactically correspond to the relationships ingredient in the referential event.

At this point we would maintain that Bühler overemphasizes the formal-logical character of language: the understanding of linguistic messages is not merely a matter of grasping the *formal* relationships between concepts but is also a manner of grasping the *content* carried by verbal forms. One important gap in Bühler's analysis is, it seems to us, that the verbal concepts, the lexicon per se, has no systematic place in his treatment of language.

This omission in an analysis of language becomes increasingly glaring as it becomes recognized that there are "semantic fields" and as the area of "semantic fields" is more and more cultivated by linguists. It seems necessary and feasible, therefore, to supplement Bühler's treatment by extending the field-concept to include the lexicon as well as syntax. It is with respect to such semantic fields that single con-

---

[4] This kind of instrument of representation presupposes that the referent is conceived in such a way that it becomes fit for representation by the device; it may be suggested, for instance, that the intersensory experience of fever as "high" or "low," etc., is the basic connotation that makes the referent fit for depiction by the thermometric scale.

cepts acquire meanings; or, perhaps more precisely stated, the semantic field is one of the determinants of the meanings attributed to elements of the lexicon. This field is "constructed" in terms of such conceptual relations as similarity and dissimilarity, inclusion and exclusion, etc.[5]

In sum, then, we would propose the view that three linguistic fields rather than two enter into language: the *field of pointing*, the *lexical-conceptual field*, and the *symbolic-syntactic field*. Of these three, the last-mentioned contributes the most in Indo-European languages—at least with regard to the formal aspects of reference—to the autonomy of linguistic representation. The *field of pointing*, strongly bound up with concrete space, is of course greatly dependent upon the perceptual-motor context and therefore contributes much less to the autonomy of language. The lexical-conceptual field lies somewhere between the other two fields in terms of contribution to linguistic autonomy.

Let us consider briefly the reasons for this lesser autonomy of the lexical-conceptual field. On one side, verbal concepts ordinarily lack clear-cut univocality and determinateness: they require some context to achieve relatively full determination. On the other side, in Indo-European languages of the present day, there are generally no linguistic indices which clearly relate the various lexical concepts to each other in terms of subordination, similarity, etc.; in other words, the structuring of the semantic field takes place internally rather than through external devices.

Languages differ in the lingual structurization of the semantic fields. There are many languages throughout the world (for example, Melanesian, American-Indian, African Bantu) in which special affixes exist for defining classes of objects in terms of certain common properties (roundness, length, angularity, etc.).[6] Some languages, such as Bantu, have gone so far as to employ classificatory concept-formation as a principle for the construction of the syntactic field. Thus, Bantu has twenty-one prefixes which indicate the classes of concepts and which are used for the syntactic connection of the words of an utterance. In Suaheli, the sentence "the knife has cut the child" is formed by add-

---

[5] The notion of a semantic field—a network of lexical units as typical for a language—has been advanced by such linguists as J. Trier (253), G. Ipsen (113), and others. For a discussion of semantic-field theory, see S. Ullman (258, pp. 155 f). S. Öhman (179), Schweidweiler (218), and Kronasser (142, p. 136).

[6] See Swanton (249, pp. 216, 227); Codrington (47, pp. 146 f); cf. Cassirer (42, I, p. 296).

ing the prefix *ki* of the instrumental class (for knife) and the prefix *m* of the person class (for child) to the verb: *ki-su* (knife) *ki-me-m-katha* (has cut) *m-toto* (child).[7] One may state, then, that in languages of the Bantu type, the lexical-conceptual field and the syntactic field are merged, with the consequence that these languages manifest a higher degree of linguistic autonomy of (predominantly concrete) verbal concepts than do Indo-European languages. Indo-European languages, probably because of forces pushing towards increasing abstractness, have developed in the direction of formal-relational autonomization rather than in the direction of the lingualized autonomy of the lexicon.

Let us at this point pursue somewhat further the problem of correspondence between symbol and reference as it is linked up with linguistic autonomy. We have stated that language establishes its symbolic field by formal-syntactical rules; with symbolic units (words) one uses the symbolic field to build up substructures (sentences) which serve to represent referential reality—in some way "corresponding" to this reality.

It seems to us that for correspondences to occur, a mutual process of *convergence* [8] must take place, a convergence which leads to a fittingness of connotations and vehicular forms of representation. To build such correspondences, languages utilize certain *models*. In Indo-European languages, the model used for connoting states of affairs and articulating them linguistically is the *human action model*.[9] A total event is basically articulated into agent, action, and object; the relationships between these are portrayed in sentences in which the vehicles for the referents are related to each other through a "syntax of action."

The potency of this linguistic model becomes evident when one considers its extension even where such an extension, from a logical point of view, makes no sense. One says not only "X kills a dog" but also "X feels pain," as if the state of feeling would be an action and pain an object acted upon. In Indo-European languages, one is even constrained to formulate attributive propositions and propositions about conceptual relations in terms of that *action model*, using auxiliary

---

[7] Meinhof (165, p. 28).

[8] We have designated this process of vehicle-connotation convergence as "rotation." Though the process of rotation can hardly be demonstrated historically, the process can be unearthed through experimentation (see Part V).

[9] See Wundt (284, p. 60), Finck (66, p. 13), Bühler (37, p. 239).

verb forms and other devices: one says, for instance, "X has a dark skin" or "A equals B."[10]

The potency of the action model as a means for establishing an autonomous language in terms of formal correspondence is thus evident in its pervasive exploitation. A further indication of its importance is the role it plays in the developmental transformations that language undergoes in the *shift from concrete to more abstract reference.*

An area well suited for a discussion of such transformations is the *case system* in Indo-European languages. Since Wundt's treatise on language (284), there has been a considerable controversy about the origin and the history of the case system, particularly with respect to the most basic cases: Nominative and Accusative (or Dative). Whereas Wundt was unable to link up the so-called "abstract" or "grammatical-logical" cases to those which have a concrete localistic function, Bühler offers a reasonable interpretation of the common character of all types of cases by deducing their function from the structure of the action model (Bühler, 37). In other words, the emergence of cases and their differentiation derives, by necessity, from a syntactical schema in which an action word demands the filling in of two "empty," function-specific spaces, one in front (subjective case) and the other at the end (objective case), thus:

$$. . . ? . . . action . . . ?. . . .$$

Bühler, having given us a relatively clear account of the role which syntactic models play in the formation of an autonomous linguistic medium, does not, however, turn to the changes these models have to undergo as language comes into the service of greater abstraction. This important problem can only be discussed briefly here.

First of all, one may start with observations concerning early child behavior. Most students of child behavior have observed strong tendencies in young children to perceive and conceive their expanding universe in terms of certain formula-like schemata or connotative models.

---

[10] Other languages, of course, may use linguistic models of quite different types. F. N. Finck, in particular, has attempted to provide a systematic survey of the main structural types of languages. He points out that there are languages, like the Greenlandic, in which events are formulated in terms of phenomenal appearances rather than in terms of action; such formulations would be best translatable into English in terms of participial constructions—for example, what would be "I kill him" in English would have its parallel in Greenlandic in a form which could be approximately rendered as "my his dying" (66).

Such models, which aid tremendously in the cognitive ordering of the multiplicity of happenings to which the child is exposed, are already observable at a prelinguistic, gestural-motoric level.[11] An excellent example of such an anticipatory action model is one quoted by H. W. Brown (30), referring to the activity of a boy of 1;10 years:

> W has a rubber ball that he throws on the floor and watches while it rebounds. He takes his kitten and throws it on the floor in the same way, and looks quite disappointed that it does not rebound like the ball.

Linguistically more advanced children will often indicate verbally their comprehension of events in terms of concrete human action. Here are two of Brown's observations.

> C (1;10 years) was watching some horses drawing a load up the hill in front of the house one cold, frosty morning. As he noticed the breath coming from their mouths and nostrils, he turned to his father, who uses a cigar occasionally, and said, "Horses 'moke, papa, horses 'moke."
>
> S (3;0 years) was in the kitchen when her mother turned on the hot water; observing the water spurting out in jets, she exclaimed, "O, mamma, the water is choked; see how it coughs!"

These examples, which could be supplemented by innumerable other illustrations from the literature on child behavior, suggest two things: first, they indicate the operation of a genuine cognitive urge to conceive of events in terms of action-models; second, they point up the concrete-analogic character of these early models. As we shall indicate in subsequent chapters, there is, in the course of ontogenesis, a development of symbolic representation of happenings, a development during which these models become freed of their concrete contents and become encoded in *autonomous formulas,* which can be used with increasing independence from concrete perceptual motor contexts.

As to the historical-linguistic development of these action models in Indo-European languages, it may be conjectured that the very early sentences in these languages portrayed *concrete action* involving a tangible agent and object. With the development of technology and civilized life, demanding the articulation of more abstract relations, this action-model is not given up but is rather *transformed* functionally so that it becomes fit for the expression of judgments pertaining to states of affairs quite removed from concrete, practical action. Intimately related to this *functional shift* of the action-model is the functional shift of the case system. One can understand these shifts

---

[11] See the discussion of gestural schemata, Chapter 7.

in terms of the basically "analogical" character of any symbolic system, including language.

Language, by its very nature as an instrument of symbolization, is directed towards the construction of forms which "correspond," that is, are in dynamic analogy, with their referents (see Kaplan, 131, 132). It is in conformity with this basic function of language that during its development it is employed to represent the abstract in analogy with the concrete (12). As has often been noted, most abstract words emerge from a concrete, sensory-motor-affective origin; for instance, they often spring from "manual concepts" (Cushing, 50). It is our belief that what is true of words is also most probably true of syntactically expressed relations.

It is likely that one will acknowledge the analogical application of the action-model for such statements as "I grasp the idea," in which the accusative case appears almost like a concrete object upon which action is performed. But it is probably more difficult to sense an analogical application of the action-model in sentences such as "The book mentions several facts;" in this latter instance, apparently, a purely syntactical construction has supplanted the original concrete action-schema. If there is an analogical application of that schema it has become *remote*.

The question then arises: does one deal here with a completely discontinuous phenomenon, a "supplanting" of concrete linguistic models by abstract models which are unrelated to the concrete schemata? This is what Wundt seemed to imply in his dichotomization of cases into those indicating concrete-localistic relations and those having purely grammatical-logical functions. Or is one able to apply the developmental notion of *transformation*, in which discontinuity and continuity are intertwined?

We maintain, as we have insisted throughout this work, that the latter view is more tenable. We believe that the shifts which take place from concrete action models to syntactic relations of a more abstract sort reflect the operation of the basic development principle pertaining to *form-function relationships*. As one will recall, according to this principle, wherever functional shifts occur during development, the novel function is first executed through old, available forms; sooner or later, of course, there is a pressure towards the development of new forms which are of a more function-specific character, i.e., that will serve the new function better than the older forms.

There is ample evidence from the history of European tongues (as well as in ontogenesis) to support this principle in its application to language (see, for example, Breal, 29). The sentences composed of agent-verb-object refer at early stages not only to simple concrete happenings but also to the expression of more complex, abstract relationships. The linguistic connectives formed in such cases are initially, in themselves, words having concrete reference; that is, particles such as prepositions, conjunctions, and so on appear initially as concrete in content, both etymologically and ontogenetically; even modulation by flexion is considered by many linguists to have been derived from the agglutination of tangible, independent words attached to principal words—the attached elements only gradually being divested of their concrete reference and becoming purely syntagmatic units with increase in abstract formulations. In other words, originally concrete forms are used to represent the more complex content and then are voided of their concrete meaning or else replaced by novel forms that fit the progression towards increased abstractness.

In sum, in order for vehicular forms to serve adequately for the depiction of abstract notions and relationships, they must become abstract grammatical-syntactic indices, independent of concrete reference. We may, therefore, conclude that there is a close relationship between increasing abstractness of reference and increasing autonomization of the linguistic medium. In particular, the transformation of the case system from indicators of concrete relations to indicators of abstract ones—a transformation that aroused many discussions in linguistic circles—is easily comprehensible as part and parcel of the transformation of the action model itself.

In order fully to understand such transformation as a process of analogy formation, i.e., as a process which fundamentally retains some features common to both the primordial (concrete) and the derivative (abstract) relation expressed by linguistic models, we have to turn to our organismic interpretation. Our contention here is that the vehicular formulations of sentences, both simple and complex, are grasped as meaningful when articulated in terms of organismic-dynamic patterns.

Therefore, in simple sentences, for instance, the agent (A), the verb (V), and the object (O) are presumed to be linked to one another in terms of a *vectorial configuration* which has the same dynamic structure whether the reference is concrete or abstract.[12]

---

[12] This assumption of organismic theory, concerning the dynamic-organismic formulation and apprehension of sentences, will receive some further clarification in Chapter 14.

A final word may be added concerning the *limitations of languages,* even of the highest degree of autonomy, with regard to their amenability to the expression of abstract relations. Languages, because of the human capacity for analogical transformations, have been quite capable of serving the highest conceptualizations of scientific thought. They could do this because the linguistic formulations of science always involve reference to "reality" and therefore never completely leave the realm of things. The action-model of Indo-European language is, in other words, meaningfully applicable wherever one is concerned with the expression of a dynamic relationship even remotely analogous to action.

When human cognition reaches a level at which relationships *per se,* freed from reference to reality, are to be presented, language no longer suffices as a medium for these operations. As Dantzig (51) has clearly shown, the development of modern algebra hinged on the formation of a new medium for the expression of thought, a medium entailing the construction of symbols having no reference to human perception and action. Letter notations, such as a and x, are "not a mere formality; the symbol is the very essence of algebra." Even if one expresses an equation through verbal forms, for example, "A equals B," one has not reached the level of completely abstract notation; one is still using the human action-model which carries reference to reality. Only the purely algebraic expression, $A = B$, lifts one out of the field of reference-to-action and into that of purely abstract operations.

These limits on language composed of words and sentences bring home, once again, the essence of linguistic autonomy. Autonomous language is to be characterized in terms of *independence* of vehicular construction and by *correspondence* to the field of reference; it is a system which contains its immanent principles of construction, enabling its users to build forms which represent or "correspond to" happenings in the referential field.

part **II**

Ontogenesis

Introduction

The major concern in Part II is with the emergence and development of the representative function, that is, with the ways in which this function is realized in the course of ontogenesis.

Although infrahuman animals are known to use bodily movements and cries in the expression of affective states, appeals, or warnings, the use of bodily movements and vocal utterances to represent some content is generally acknowledged to occur primarily, if not exclusively, in human beings.[1] In other words, the *representative function* is a peculiarly human function.

This representative function does not, however, manifest itself in a discrete and "pure" fashion in early ontogenesis; rather, the bodily movements and vocal utterances of the infant and young child, when they begin to function representatively, remain affective and conative as well; that is, they not only represent some "object" but also express the child's feelings and desires with respect to it. It is only gradually that special means are developed for realizing the representative function—distinctive tools for *referring to* and *describing* events, objects, etc.; in other words, it is only gradually that a relatively *autonomous medium of representation* develops.

Were one concerned only with the most typical form of representative activity, namely, language at its full-fledged level of operation,

---

[1] See Köhler (136, p. 277)

one could restrict oneself to a discussion of representation through linguistic means, and forego consideration of prelinguistic and nonlinguistic modes of representing. Although the independent inquiry into linguistic representation per se may have great value, it is our belief that a fuller psychological insight into all representation, including linguistic, will be attained only by operating on the assumption that linguistic representation emerges from, and is rooted in, nonlinguistic forms of representation. Accordingly, representational activity shall be considered here in its genetically related manifestations, that is, in terms of the precursory prelinguistic stages leading up to linguistic stages and in terms of the intrinsic transformations which these manifestations undergo in the course of ontogenesis.

In delineating the stages towards the full realization of the representative function, we shall describe certain bodily movements and vocal utterances which are "overdetermined" as to function, that is, which subserve multiple functions. We shall deal with such expressions precisely because they are, at least in part, representative in function—whatever other ends they may subserve. The occurrence of such precursors to full-fledged representation may thus be taken as an exemplification of an important developmental tenet: *a novel emerging function becomes actualized at first through the use of means articulated and structured in the service of genetically earlier ends.*

The following discussion of the emergence and development of representational activity will be divided into relatively separate treatments of three fundamental operations—intimately related to each other—which we regard as constitutive of clear-cut representation. These three closely intertwined operations are: (1) the formation of objects-of-contemplation; (2) the denotation of objects, that is, reference; and (3) the depiction of objects. In our discussion we shall treat the precursors, initial stages, and early developments of these three aspects of representation: this will constitute Part II, Section I. In Section II, we shall examine certain later developments of these operations.

Precursors and Early Stages of Reference and Depiction

chapter *5*

The Formation of Objects-of-Contemplation

It is generally assumed that a differentiation between subject and object is absent in the experience of the new-born infant. This means that the experience of a world of objects, distinct from and standing against the self, must emerge in the course of ontogenesis.

As important as is this genesis of the object for developmental psychology, a full treatment of object formation is beyond the scope of this book: we must limit ourselves to a discussion of object formation only insofar as this process is relevant to symbolic activity.

In delineating the phases of object formation which are relevant to symbolic activity, one important distinction must be made at the outset: *action on or with things* must be distinguished from *contemplation of things*. It is our view that those objects which enter into symbolic activity must be things-of-contemplation, that is, objects that one "regards out there," rather than things upon which one merely acts in the service of immediate biological need-satisfaction.

Although the theoretical distinction between things-of-action and things-of-contemplation can be clearly made, and although empirical evidence for this distinction is easily available at later stages in ontogenesis, the indices reflecting the beginnings of this differentiation in early ontogenesis are not unambiguous. Because of the dearth of specific studies directed towards the emergence of this differentiation in ontogenesis, the evidence pertaining to this question must be gleaned primarily from the data provided by such careful observers of early ontogenesis as M. Shinn (227), the Scupins (219), C. Bühler (35), A. Gesell (76), and J. Piaget (191).

Most of these observers agree that the responses of a very young infant to visual stimuli cannot be considered indicative of a contemplative attitude towards objects—although such responses might bear some superficial similarity to later contemplative behavior. Thus, the visual pursuit movements of a moving stimulus, often observed in very young infants, is most likely a reflex-like "tropistic" response. Again, "staring behavior," which C. Bühler has claimed is typical of the normal 2-month-old, does not seem to reflect an orientation towards objects-out-there; the infant appears to be "gazing through" objects rather than "looking at" them.

There is some visual behavior, characteristic—according to C. Bühler —of the 3-month-old infant, which some may conceivably take as indicating a "true object" in the experience of the child: in following moving stimuli, the child seems to "seek them out" rather than to be "pulled" by them. Bühler herself interprets this activity simply as "active interest in optical stimuli." Although it is always difficult to determine whether the infant is looking at objects or at transient appearances, we are inclined to accept Bühler's interpretation: at least, there are no sufficient grounds for positing a world of "true objects" at this stage.

Somewhat later on, probably between the fourth and fifth month the infant shows some very significant advances in behavior—advances which seem to signal the establishment of a world of "true" objects. Before this time, the infant, in making contact with things, appears to be dominated by a "mouthing" tendency, or evinces grasping and looking unrelated to each other. Now, however, a coordination of grasping and looking—with little or no mouthing—occurs, a change which has been superbly described by M. Shinn, and which in its general features has been observed in large groups of children by C. Bühler and A. Gesell. Shinn, in her *Biography of a Baby* (227), writes:

"Just at the end of the third month the baby had once gazed at her rattle as she held it in her hand; but it was not till the second week of the fourth month that she seemed really to learn that when she felt the familiar touch in her hand, she could see something by looking. Then her eyes began to rest on things while she picked them up; but in a blank and passive way—the eyes looking on like outsiders, while the awkward little hands fumbled just as they would have done in the dark. The baby seemed to have no idea that what she saw was the same thing as what she felt.

"There was about a fortnight of this. Then, on one great day, when three weeks of the month had passed, the baby looked at her mother's hand, held up before her, and made fumbling motions toward it, keeping her eyes on it, till her hand struck it; then took hold of it. She had formed an association between the sight of an object and the groping movement of her hand toward it.

"In this fortnight she (still) grasped better with the mouth than with her hands, and was more disposed to use it."

But then a new advance was made.

"She sprang into this era suddenly, within four days: when the baby had passed ten days of her fifth month, she was still grasping half-mechanically. On the eleventh day, lying on her back, she held her rattle above her and looked at it carefully. Her attention had turned to the things that she grasped. She had come before to the perception of a world of objects, but apparently only now to the realization of it. And thereupon, that very day, I saw that she was no longer using eyes and hands merely as means of getting mouth sensations; she was holding objects, looking at them, and pulling them about, for some moments, before they went to her mouth. But soon the supremacy passed from mouth over to the hands, and from this week the habit of grasping with the mouth declined and disappeared. In a few hours, the baby was reaching for everything near her."

This shift in emphasis from the incorporation of a thing into one's body to a holding and beholding of something out there, so aptly described by M. Shinn, seems to us to be a clear indication of the operation of a contemplative attitude—an attitude establishing the relative independence of objects. With the emergence of this attitude, a fundamental intentionality has come into being: the child is no longer solely in a world of things-of-action and of changing appearances; he has entered the world of true objects.

There are further advances in contemplative behavior as the child develops: a higher level is reached when the child begins to regard objects visually, in relative freedom from such sensory-motor activity as reaching or grasping. Such advances have been studied experimentally by Hetzer and Wiehemeyer (105, pp. 113, 275) in 9- to 16-month-old children. These authors presented cards containing a variety of nonrealistic, differently colored forms (see Fig. 5-1). As is indicated in Table 5-1, a developmental shift occurs—measured in percentage of total time of response—from a predominance of handling and touching the cards and figures to a predominance of visual contemplation.

It seems to us that the Hetzer-Wiehemeyer study points up an in-

FIGURE 5-1. Nonrealistic patterns used in Hetzer-Wiehemeyer study.

verse relationship between contemplation of objects and pragmatic-sensory-motor activity with objects: contemplation, in its pure form, seems to emerge as sensory-motor activity of a pragmatic character (for example, grasping) declines. As the grasping activity becomes subordinated to visual regard or contemplation, it is possible that sensory-motor activity undergoes a partial *shift of function:* freed from involvement in the satisfaction of peremptory demands, sensory-motor activity can now accompany visual regard in the form of a deictic gesture (pointing).

Such deixis or reference—invariably involving another individual—reflects the importance of sharing and interpersonal commerce in the formation of true objects and in the subsequent activity of symbol-formation. We shall discuss here, rather cursorily, certain aspects of sharing and interpersonal commerce in the formation of objects.

In the preceding theoretical chapters, we characterized the human Umwelt as uniquely a world of 'true objects,' that is, of things not merely acted upon but contemplated—through knowing. We also stated, in the preceding chapters, that since the human world, strange

Table 5-1

Responses to the Hetzer-Wiehemeyer cards in terms of average percent of time

Age (months)	Predominantly Touch	Predominantly Regard
9–12	80%	20%
12–15	40%	60%
15–18	0%	100%

at first becomes attainable through rather complicated operations of cognition, the mental life of the human infant is one of helplessness, of insecurity, and of confusion. In this earliest period, as far as security does obtain for the infant, this security is achieved by virtue of an intimate contact—to the point of near-identity—with the mothering one.

During the many months of the infant's struggle towards the acquisition of a world of objects, the mother-child bond is always maintained and loosens only slowly. This bond seems to surround the child with the necessary atmosphere within which objects can be formed in relative detachment from need or anxiety: the objects which the child confronts from this vantage point participate, as it were, in the atmosphere of the mother and hence become secure-familiar things, which can be viewed without evoking fright or fear (cf. Spitz, 240, pp. 60 f).

We may assume that, for the normally developing child, the *sharing* of objects is not simply a secondary condition helpful to the learning about objects or symbols but is rather of vital significance in the child's establishment of a life-space, in which he may move with security and confidence. From this point of view, the relatively slight differentiation between mother-child and object must not be considered in negative terms, that is, simply as a "lack of articulation," but rather in terms of providing that necessary primordial basis in which relationships are rooted and from which self, objects, and others emerge and become differentiated from each other without losing their mutual ties.

There is little direct information about the stages, in the normally developing child, of this emergence of objects and symbols from an interpersonal matrix. During recent years, however, a good deal of indirect information has been gained from various studies pertaining to the psychopathology of object formation. These studies deal with two deviant groups: one group consists of children who, because of unfavorable social conditions, have never been able to build up objects in the normal way; the second group comprises individuals—mainly quite disturbed schizophrenics—who have regressed from a once-familiar world into a pathological life space, in which people and objects in the normal sense do not exist.

With regard to the first group, Spitz and others (237; 239) have found that infants and children, cared for in foundling homes, without the necessary intimate human contact, show symptoms of "marasmus" and "anaclitic depression." Spitz's inquiries suggest that the lack of a constant mothering one results in a retardation and even in a complete inhibition of object formation. Such a lack of 'mothering' also seems to influence adversely many subsequent activities resting on object formation, specifically symbol formation: thus children of four years who have been deprived of a maternal atmosphere seem to show almost no speech behavior.

The inquiries with the schizophrenic individuals—especially insofar as they have dealt with the phenomena of object-loss and subsequent regaining of a world of objects—provide us with perhaps the best available insight into the genesis of object formation which we possess today.

It is not our task, nor are we equipped, to analyze the psychodynamics underlying schizophrenic regression. It suffices for us to know that, because of impairments in early mother-child interchanges (in combination with other factors), the worlds of certain individuals lack that stability of organization found in normally developed individuals: these worlds, therefore, break down rather easily under external or internal stresses and there follows a dissolution, often painfully profound, of the self-other-objects articulation.

The reports of the reeducation of certain deeply regressed individuals, undertaken by such therapists as Marguerite Sechehaye (223), Silvano Arieti (7), Harold Searles (221), and others, start with the patient desperately engulfed in a labile universe where there is neither a true self, nor true people, nor true objects. Especially valuable information about such a universe comes from the vivid descriptions which patients themselves, such as Mlle. Sechehaye's patient Renée, give of their experiences (224).

In her autobiographical report written after her recovery, Renée tells how, at the onset of her illness, the things surrounding her lost their solidity and substance, appearing like stage-accessories made of cardboard, with people transformed into lifeless statues or mechanical puppets as part of the pasteboard scenery.

"I look at her (a friend) praying to feel the life in her through the enveloping unreality. But she seems more a statue than ever, a mannikin, moved by a mechanism, talking like an automaton. . . . With heart despairingly empty I reach home. There I find a pasteboard house, sisters and brothers robots . . ." (224, p. 18).

Of special interest to us, in view of our thesis that organismic activity enters into the formation, maintenance, and stabilization of a world of objects and symbols, are instances in which the normal tie between self and objects or self and symbolic forms breaks down; one then witnesses the upsurge of nameless demonic things. Renée provides a fascinating illustration of this kind of occurrence.

"When, for example, I looked at a chair or a jug, I thought not of their use or function—a jug not as something to be used for holding water or milk, a chair not as something to sit in—but as having lost their names, their functions and meanings; they became 'things' and began to take on life, to exist. . . . The stone jar . . . was there facing me, defying me with its presence, with its existence. . . . My eyes met a chair, then a table; they were alive, too, asserting their presence. I attempted to escape their hold by calling out their names. I said 'chair, jug, table, it is a chair.' But the word echoed hollowly, deprived of all meaning; it had left the object, was divorced from it, so much so that on one hand it was a living, mocking thing, on the other, a name, robbed of sense, an envelope emptied of content" (224, pp. 34 f).

In the case of Renée, as in the cases of many other schizophrenics whose histories have been reported in the literature, a fundamental factor entering into the pathological formation seems to have been some disturbance in the early mother-child relationship. The same factor seems to enter into child autism and so-called child psychosis. Whatever the exact nature of this disturbance, it seems to preclude that calm atmosphere of interpersonal sharing which we believe to be necessary for object formation and subsequent symbol formation.[1]

Let us now turn to the recapturing of a world of true objects. It seems to us that in practically all cases in which there is a regaining

---

[1] E. Rodrigué (202, p. 7) remarks: "The most immediate consequence to be drawn from Melanie Klein's work with psychotic children is the realization that symbolism plays a fundamental role in ego-development; and that symbol formation miscarries when . . . the infant's relationship with the mother is seriously disturbed."

of a lost reality through successful therapy, the steps in such a return conform to a general developmental principle: the redevelopment of the life-space must start anew, that is, at a point where there is relatively little differentiation in that global triad, self-object-other; progressively the life-space becomes articulated in terms of an increasing distancing of each of these components from the others.

During the normal, ontogenetic process of "weaning," the individual goes through various stages critical for the formation of referential objects and symbols. Perhaps the most important early stage in the reconstruction of a world of true objects and symbols occurs with the formation of what we shall, after D. W. Winnicott (283), term "transitional objects." [2] For us, this phrase refers to early objects which are not yet articulated as self-contained entities, but which to some extent overlap with the self and with the mothering one. It is likely that food, offered by the mother to the child in either liquid or solid form, constitutes the first transitional object. A little later on, such things as a Teddy-bear, a comforter, or a particular pillow, may serve as a transitional object. Through these security-engendering objects, the child gradually begins to conquer and know a world which belongs to the self, and yet is not fused with the self, a world of familiar, independent objects. Perhaps nowhere is the significant role of such transitional objects as clearly manifested as in individuals who have regressed to an objectless world and are beginning to emerge from this chaotic universe into a world of true objects.

Let us return to Sechehaye's patient Renée, who in her autobiographical report describes the revolutionary impact which the acquisition of the first transitional objects had on her apprehension of the environment. The transitional objects in question were apples, "Mama's apples," which she identified with the breasts of the mother-analyst and with the nourishing "milk" food. Leaning her head against "Mama's" breast and "drinking" pieces of apples which the therapist put into her mouth, the whole world underwent for her an astonishing transfiguration:

"I realized that my perception of things had completely changed. Instead of infinite space, unreal, where everything was cut off, naked and isolated, I saw Reality, marvelous Reality, for the first time. The people whom I encountered were no longer automatons, phantoms revolving around, gesticulating without meaning; they were men and women with their own individual

---

[2] The meaning we give to this phrase is, however, not quite identical with that given to it by Winnicott, although there is considerable similarity in significance.

characteristics, their own individuality. It was the same with things. They were useful things, having sense. Here was an automobile to take me to the hospital, cushions I could rest on. With the astonishment that one views a miracle, I devoured with my eyes everything that happened. 'This is it, this is it,' I kept repeating, 'this is it—Reality' " (223, p. 80).

The new world of Renée's clearly was a "world at home," linked to "Mama" by this significant object, the apple.

At this stage of redevelopment, however, the structure of this newly gained reality was still rather fragile; it broke down whenever there was some occasional disturbance in the "Mama"-patient linkage, which reflected itself immediately in the loss of meaning of apples as a transitional object. The stabilization of reality through further increase in object-mother-self distancing correlated rather closely with the changes in the nature of the transitional object: after the raw apple pieces, she successively accepted apple sauce, unpeeled apples, and finally many different forms of solid food. But with each new step, the new object had to be accompanied by a piece of raw apple offered by the analyst-mother, just as during the weaning period the breast is still given occasionally to the infant.

One should not think that the therapeutic process of recapturing reality which Renée underwent is unique to her particular case. Various therapists have reported instances of a very similar nature. E. Rodrigué, for instance, described the therapeutic construction of reality in a severely autistic, "objectless" 3-year-old boy. There, as in Renée's case, reality was introduced through linkage with a significant transitional "mama"-object, namely, *water* in a basin, into which the boy dipped his arms, splashing water round the room and sucking it in (202, pp. 9 f).

The studies we have just cited, and others like it, contribute not only to an understanding of object-formation but also to an understanding of the earliest stages of symbolization. In the foregoing chapter, we maintained that the symbol-referent relationship becomes articulated in a situation in which four basic moments became increasingly differentiated from each other. These four basic moments were self, other, symbol, and object. From a developmental point of view, there is an early stage at which the distinction or difference between symbol and referential object has not yet been clearly established: in other words, there are phenomena which are neither objects per se nor symbols per se but partake of both.

In terms of the development of symbols, the so-called "transitional objects" again seem to be of critical significance. In this regard, it is noteworthy that among the therapists who have utilized such objects in their patients' experiences to guide their patients towards 'reality,' some speak of "transitional objects" and others talk of (real) symbols. In fact, it is likely that these "objects" are transitional forms—prior to differentiation—of both true objects and true symbols. From the point of view of the development of symbolization, therefore, we may designate them as *protosymbols* (in contrast with representational symbols, in which there is a duality between vehicle and referent). For example, Renée's apples clearly have some object characteristics—they are "mama-objects"—otherwise they could not possibly serve as links to the world of true objects. However, the apples possessed characteristics not found in pragmatic objects: they carry connotations of the maternal breast. In certain respects, therefore, Renée's apples, and similar 'objects,' are like true symbols; they are incarnations of certain profound meanings which present themselves in the objects; yet they are not true symbols, insofar as there is no duality between vehicle and referent.

Just as one moves through the transitional objects to true objects, that is, objects that are familiar, comprehensible, and stable, so too does one move—in ontogenesis as well as in the redevelopment of reality—from protosymbols to true symbols, symbols confounded neither with the objects they represent nor with the "mother"—or others—with whom one shares the objects.

chapter 6

Precursors and Early Stages of Denotative Reference

The earliest concrete and clear-cut expressions of reference to objects are, on the one hand, the characteristic bodily gesture of *pointing* and, on the other, vocal utterances such as "da" or "ta." It is our contention that these formations emerge together from a total organismic matrix and then gradually differentiate: in other words, the motoric activity and vocalizations culminating in (denotative) reference are assumed to be, initially, aspects of action patterns by means of which the child interacts pragmatically with his surrounding milieus.

Eventually, a point is reached where the infant organism "refers" to, or better, is directed toward, distant objects with his entire body: he strains towards objects and at the same time emits "call-sounds," which are part and parcel of the bodily directedness. It is from this global unity of sound and bodily movement that the development of the specific modalities (media) of motor and of vocal reference occurs. Though these two modalities are intertwined at the outset and remain more or less interrelated at much more advanced stages, their development will be considered separately.

Development of Motoric Reference

The act of pointing—that clear-cut expression of reference on the motoric level—is the culmination of a series of pre-deictic and globally deictic patterns of behavior, whose features we shall briefly survey here in their ontogenetic sequence. Only if one compares pointing per se with its precursors and preliminary stages does one get a clear understanding of its continuity with pre-referential activities, as well as its distinctiveness, and emergent character.

It has often been contended that pointing derives from grasping and is, in fact, an abbreviated grasp.[1] This contention seems to be based on the material similarity of the two behaviors rather than on any functional analysis of them. The simple fact that no infrahuman animal is known to point, although many are capable of grasping, should at least raise some doubt about this assumption of an inner relationship between grasping and pointing. Functionally considered, grasping is a behavior which subserves *incorporation,* taking in; in contrast, the essential characteristic of pointing is that it is DIRECTED OUTWARD, it is an acknowledgment of an object located at a distance from the self. Thus, while grasping is tied up with pragmatic things-of-action, pointing is linked to a world of contemplated objects.

Although grasping per se does not appear to be a preliminary stage of, or even a precursor to, the referential act of pointing, there seems to be some element of reference in the bodily acts of *reaching.* Unlike prehensive grasping, the material activity of reaching may be exploited within the act of reference. The amenability of reaching to subsequent referential use seems to be based on the fact that the dominant vectorial character of reaching is outward. Reaching, moreover, is a sensory-motor acknowledgment of something distant from the body. Whether reaching is quasi-referential or not depends on the context of the action: reaching-for-touching is genetically related to reference; reaching-for-grabbing is not.

The act of *touching*—the next activity to be considered—is, even more than reaching, potentially open for concrete expression of reference. One has to be aware, however, that not all touching has this relation to reference. There are at least three kinds of touching behavior. In early infancy, touching is a necessary condition for prehension, and even later on may be in the service of voluntary grasping. This type of "touching-for-grasp" is hardly relevant to reference. There is a second kind of touching that appears at a later stage, touching in the service of exploration of the world of objects; this kind of touching has been mentioned in relation to the contemplative attitude

---

[1] Thus, Wundt (284, p. 137) declares: "Genetically considered, pointing is nothing but an abbreviated grasp movement."

and will be reconsidered later in relation to depiction. Finally, there is a kind of touching which is referential in the true sense; it typically arises in an interpersonal context and indicates for oneself and for others a "something" articulated at a distance from the self and the other.

The suggestion that referential behavior emerges through sharing of contemplated objects in an interpersonal context may recall our previous remarks on the intimate connection between visual regard and deictic behavior. There is a close analogy between "reaching-for-touching" and "turning-for-looking" in an interpersonal context of sharing. The motor activity of turning towards objects, when exploited in the service of reference, is only a short step away fom full-fledged pointing. Such a relationship between turning to and pointing has been clearly observed by the Sterns (242).

For example, they report such a sequence in the behavior of their daughter, Hilde, in response to the question, "Where is tick-tock?" The girl, at 10 months, *turned towards* the clock and listened; later she *turned towards* a clock, even when no auditory stimulus could be heard; finally, at 14 months, she *pointed to* the clock. Again, they note that their son, Gunther, up to 11½ months, *turned towards* some of the objects named by his parents; at 12½ months, he *pointed to* them, *saying "da."* (242, p. 85).

In sum, then, all these preliminaries to motor reference, occurring within reaching-for, touching, and turning-to activities, culminate in *pointing*. Pointing, in its most characteristic manifestation, is the use of one outstretched finger to denote an object in space. In this characteristic form it uniquely reflects the function of reference: it is, in other words, the specialized motoric means for the expression of reference. This specialized, characteristic manifestation is, however, itself an end-form in a sequence of gestural patterns, some of which are clearly linked to the pre-stages to reference discussed above. The observations of Miss Shinn and the Scupins may serve as typical illustrations of this sequence.

Miss Shinn remarks on the acquisition of pointing in her niece, during the ninth to tenth month, as follows: "First the baby began to use her forefinger tip for specially close investigations; at the same time she had a habit of stretching out her hand towards any object that interested her—by association, no doubt, with touching and seizing movements. Combining these two habits, she began to hold her forefinger separate from the other (outstretched) fingers when she thus threw out her hand towards an interesting object; then, in the second week of the month, she directed this finger alone towards what interested her; and by the third week, the gesture of pointing was fairly in use." (Shinn, 227, p. 220)

The Scupins [2] first observed pointing behavior in their son Bubi during the twelfth month: "If asked for an object, the child does not only look at it (as he has done previously) but now extends his arm and hand, saying 'da!' The fingers are spread apart, but the index finger is not stretched particularly. This *gesture of pointing is completely separate from the gesture of desiring an object:* in this latter case the child stretches both arms forward and bends the upper part of the body toward the object."

The thirteenth-month entries read: "Yesterday (he) acquired the name for clock (tick-tock): *degda-dagda,* looking at the clock. At the ringing of the bell he pointed with the finger at the clock, saying 'da-dig-da!' The *pointing with the index finger is entirely newly learned;* he does it with left as well as with the right hand." "A week later, wanting some sugar he took his mother's hand and pulled her toward the sugar bowl. When the mother did not respond he *pointed* with the finger at the bowl and said impatiently: *'da, da!'* "

As these observations illustrate, the development of the characteristic gestural features of pointing follows, in general, the genetic principle of increase in articulation of form out of global bodily patterns, that is, gross bodily movements involving the arms in toto, become refined to a form in which arm and hand, ending in the outstretched forefinger, assume the very configuration of a "pointer."

These observations on the development of pointing also serve to exemplify another important developmental principle, which pertains to the interrelation of form and function in human organizing activity: an organism, initially realizing a novel function through operations which subserve other, more primitive ends, eventually "creates" or "shapes" a more specialized, function-specific means for the execution of the novel end. Thus, as we have seen, the function of reference is initially realized at the level of sensory-motor activity in a syncretic manner, that is, within such behaviors as reaching-for, touching, etc.; eventually, however, it comes, so to speak, to "create" its own instrumentality, specifically "designed" for it.

The close relationship that exists between pointing and vocal utterance is borne out by many observations, analogous to those just presented. These observations show that pointing, in contradistinction

---

[2] Scupin (219, I, p. 48).

to its pre-stages, appears quite frequently in association with demonstrative vocalization. This relationship between pointing and vocal reference will perhaps become clearer in the following discussion.

Development of Vocal Reference

Corresponding in the vocal-articulatory medium to indexical pointing in the motor-gestural medium are the demonstratives of full-fledged speech, for example, "this" or "that." Like pointing, these are final forms, the culmination of a genetic sequence of vocal expressions, some of which have been mentioned incidentally in the discussion of motoric reference. In the following, we shall briefly survey major precursors and pre-stages of vocal reference.

The earliest vocal manifestations are the cries of the infant, typically ingredient in affective states. Such cries, little differentiated originally and solely symptomatic of the general state, soon become differentiated in intensity and quality and begin to subserve appeal functions. Since these early appeal sounds cannot be considered part of a context of contemplated objects, they do not in our view bear a genetic relationship to vocal reference.

Following the early expressions of differentiated internal states, but still prior to the first precursors of vocal reference, one can distinguish a stage of babbling or lallation. This stage, although not directly related to the development of vocal reference, bears on this development insofar as more or less playful practicing of vocal articulation occurs during such lallation.

The first sounds uttered in the context of object-directedness are manifested as ingredients of the straining movements of the child towards objects in the environment which are beyond his immediate reach. Such sounds may be designated as *"call-sounds."* In a systematic study of the vocal behavior of twelve infants, H. Tischler (252, p. 247) concluded that there is a shift in the quality of vocal utterance as the child goes from the stage of babbling to the stage of call-sounds. Whereas babbling sounds are typically lax and spread over a wide range of qualities, call-sounds are short, scarcely modulated sequences, formed within a very small range of qualities. It is characteristic that the first call-sound patterns consist of the repetition of almost the same sound over days and weeks for a particular situation. Tischler, examining the children in various experimental situations, determined that these specific call-sound patterns typically emerge in the context of goal-directed activities; he found distinctive call-sounds of the type mentioned above in the 10–12-month-old child. By 17 months, the call-sounds changed into modulated sound-patterns approaching the intonational patterns of adult speech.

Observations of call-sound patterns have also been made by M. M. Lewis (152, p. 151) and the Scupins (219, p. 41). Lewis observed the emergence of call-sounds in his child, *K*, at about the 11-month period. Lewis noted that the call-sounds were related in quality to the affective expressions of an earlier age but that they were intoned in a distinctive way. Thus, K first used the sound 'a-a' in the context of being delighted at something (0;9,16); about a month later (0;10,28), he used this sound-pattern, now intoned excitedly, in the context of an unsuccessful attempt to reach a fallen toy. The Scupins reported that their 10-month-old son uttered the call-sound pattern 'ha-ha-ha,' while straining himself toward any "interesting" object.

Following the stage of call-sounds, vocal utterances again undergo a change of function from *calling-for* to *denoting*—a shift which appears to be analogous to the change from *reaching-for* to *pointing*. This shift should not be taken to imply that denotative utterances are genetically derivable from call-sounds (or that pointing is genetically derivable from reaching-for); we have, indeed, maintained (Chapter 2) the nonderivability of speech from vocalizations in the service of pragmatic activity. Nevertheless, one must realize that call-sounds, as far as they entail a directiveness towards an object occupying a more or less distant point in space, provide a fertile ground for the emergence of denotative utterances. In other words, although denotative utterance—a cognitive reference to something "out there"—is not derivative from any other activity, the directive character of call sounds renders them easily amenable to exploitation by the newly emerging denotative "attitude": the call-sounds then undergo a *shift in function* and begin to subserve denotation. Following this inner transformation of the function of call-sounds, that is, their use in the service of denotation, there occurs the formation of vocal forms that are specific for the denotative function, for example, *da*. These early denotative utterances then progressively approximate the demonstrative utterances of adult speech, for example, *that, this*.

Many investigators (for example, Wundt, Stern), noting the frequent occurrence of dentals in deictic sound patterns, have argued that dentals function deictively because of their outwardly directed character (Stern, 242, pp. 366 ff). Some support for this view comes from certain observations which show the emergence of the "da" pattern from utterances expressing a desire for objects. Thus Gutzmann (92,

p. 25) reports that his 8-month-old child called out "da," "dja-dja," "hedai" in a high-pitched, drawn-out tone at the same time as he made reaching gestures towards a desired object. At 11 months, the child used "da-da" in a clearly deictic way, now connected with pointing. The more comprehensive recent investigations, such as those by Tischler (252, p. 259) and Bühler (37, p. 219), generally confirm the conclusions of older writers about the frequent occurrence of dental sounds in well-articulated deictic patterns. Bühler, in assessing the detailed recordings of the vocalizations of his own three children, observed: "It is surprising how consistently Brugmann's (Indo-European) 'to'—deixis is actually taken over by dental sounds in all three children."

Summary

In attempting to summarize the early genesis of denotative reference, one must note first that a good deal more observational and experimental evidence will be needed before one can present a complete and detailed account of this development. One can, however, with reasonable assurance, enumerate at least certain major features and steps in the formation of symbolic reference.

(a) There are two main media through which reference is expressed: the motor-gestural and the vocal-articulatory.

(b) Within the motor-gestural medium, referential behavior emerges within pragmatic situations, syncretically bound to such acts as 'reaching-to-touch,' 'turning-to-look.' Somewhat analogously, within the vocal medium the referential function emerges through utterances that express strain toward an object: call-sounds.

(c) These two developmental sequences culminate in the formation of patterns which, in their particular structure, specifically and precisely express the function of denotation: pointing and demonstrative vocal forms. One needs to add that these patterns gain their significance as denotative symbols insofar as they refer to objects-of-contemplation which are shared—by the child and the other—in an interpersonal context.

chapter 7
Precursors and Early Stages of Motor-Gestural Depiction

As noted in the introduction to Part II, symbolic representation involves not only object-formation and reference but also depictive activities, that is, the formation of patterns which serve to *represent* an object and yet are distinct from the object itself. Such patterns may be formed in a variety of media. Some of these emerge early in ontogenesis and are very close to bodily action, e.g., gestures; others, such as conventional language, occur later in ontogenesis and are seemingly quite removed from bodily action—we say "seemingly" because we believe that depictive activity generally involves some patterning of bodily activity.

In this and the following chapter we shall be concerned chiefly with the precursors and early stages of depiction. Here, we deal with the development of depiction in the motor-gestural medium; in the next chapter, we consider the early genesis of depiction in the vocal medium.

Our discussion of motor-gestural depiction will be presented under three general headings: we shall first consider the importance of stable nondepictive sensory-motor patterns as a basis for gestural depiction; we shall then discuss the development of depiction as a process of "distancing," that is, the increasing differentiation between gestural-motor depiction and the contents depicted; finally, we shall treat the problem of the increasing autonomy of the gestural medium.

Importance of Stable Sensory-Motor Patterns for Gestural Depiction

The earliest movements of the child, whether as outward symptoms of global affective states (rage, joy, etc.) or in direct response to external stimulation, may be considered expressive but not depictive: depiction comes into play only when the expression and the presented content are to some extent differentiated—on two different dimensions, as it were. In the early movements of the child, there is an affective-sensory-motor unity: expressive movement does not "refer" to or represent the affective content but rather includes this content in the reactive pattern. Again, bodily movements directly involved in pragmatic commerce with objects are response patterns, not depictive in themselves.

Nevertheless, it is important to consider the early nondepictive activity here, because only after the establishment of a repertoire of well-structured and relatively stable sensory-motor patterns can the child advance towards the exploitation or restructuring of such patterns in the service of gestural depiction.

The establishment of such a repertoire characteristically follows a series of ontogenetic changes which are, in general, consonant with the orthogenetic principle of increasing differentiation and hierarchic integration. Thus, as has been pointed out by K. M. Bridges (cf. Werner, 274, p. 87), there is a rapid differentiation of expressions of affective states during the first few months of life. Similarly, Bühler's summary of observations of 69 infants reveals that, within the first year, the differentiation and establishment of the expressive patterns of so-called "primary" emotions takes place rapidly during the first 3 to 4 months, very slowly during the next 4 months, and shows no further progress during the remaining months.[1] Furthermore, with regard to sensory-motor responses to environmental stimulation, the first reactions are characteristically global, involving parts of the body which are not directly relevant to the stimulation; gradually, finer and more discrete movements emerge, with the more remote movements becoming subordinated.

For instance, the sucking pattern first involves a relatively generalized motor activity of the body, with its center around the mouth. Subsequently, there is a decrease in general bodily movements and an increase in the articulation of the specific mouth movements: the bodily

---

[1] C. Bühler (36, pp. 170–185).

movements are differentiated from each other and subordinated with respect to the focal goal-directed activity. The same sequence is found in many other processes, for example, prehension and locomotion. Through this development the child acquires a number of response patterns, differentiated as to elements and integrated into units that become progressively stabilized as stylized, recurrent, habitual sensory-motor forms.[2]

There is one fundamental characteristic of such patterns that must be stressed here because of its extreme significance in the later exploitation of these patterns in the service of depiction: we refer to the *dynamic-vectorial* nature of these patterns. By this we mean that the sensory-motor patterns possess qualities which defy a merely physical analysis of the movements of specific bodily parts: they have such qualities as direction, force, balance, rhythm, and enclosingness.

That such qualities pervade sensory-motor patterns is clearly suggested by certain observations of Piaget, Guillaume, and others. These writers provide illustrations of the ways in which children early form patterns of response which are of a relatively general character, that is, they are enacted alternately by various organs of the body rather than being bound to specific organs, such as the hand or the mouth. For example, two of Piaget's children, between the ages of 9 to 11 months, imitated the opening and closing of the experimenter's eyes by alternately opening and closing the hands, the mouth, or the eyes (Piaget, 191, p. 40). It seems that the children were sensitive to the dynamic properties of "opening" and "closing" and expressed these properties through different parts of the body capable of carrying these dynamic features. Similarly, Kaplan's son, D, at 13 months, laughingly rocked his head from side to side in response not only to his father's head movements but also arm movements, trunk movements, etc.; also he seemed to "accept" equally his father's movements of head or arms as a satisfactory response to his own "soliciting" head movements. Another instance illustrating this phenomenon is that of a 9-month-old girl, reported by Piaget, who imitated the experimenter's extrusion of the tongue by consistently raising her forefinger. Here again the vectorial quality of protrusion brings into relief the common dynamic quality, elongation of the motor patterns, formed by the two organs.[3]

---

[2] Gesell (77, p. 341), Halverson (94, 95).

[3] The fact that the same vectorial-dynamic features can be realized through different organs seems clearly to be the primordial basis for "displacements" from one organ to another; see Erikson (58).

Such performances as these seem to have considerable relevance to later symbol formation. They reflect the fact that there is an early experience of dynamic similarities obtaining between entities—here body parts—that are materially different. Thus, such different body parts as the upper and lower lips or jaws, upper and lower eyelids, fingers and palm, left and right hand or arm, may, by virtue of their being members of a pair moving in opposite directions, be employed vicariously in realizing a dynamic quality of 'opening and closing.'

It is our thesis that the precursors of depiction and eventually the true depictions emerge from such dynamic sensory-motor formations. It is to the emergence and development of true motor-gestural depictions that we now turn. As we have noted, our discussion of this genesis will be first in terms of the principle of increasing *differentiation*, that is *increasing distancing* between symbol and referent; we shall then treat gestural depiction in terms of the principle of *increasing autonomy*, that is, the building of a system of symbolic vehicles, possessing its own distinctive features and rules of organization.

Distancing: Increasing Differentiation of Gestural-Motor Depiction from Contents Depicted

Before the child reaches a stage at which he clearly uses bodily movements to depict events, he already executes bodily patterns of movement that seem to be mimetic-depictive, but are, in fact, only reactive or co-active; that is, the infant does not represent an event but responds to it by changes in bodily posture or limb movement. Thus, for instance, the young infant may respond to the mother or father rocking back and forth by rocking movements of his own, or he may react to rhythmic sound patterns by moving his body in a corresponding rhythmical pattern. Such a response pattern does not truly imitate the model event depictively but is only a motor resonance of it or, at the best, co-active with it; it is the kind of pattern manifested by adults when they 'unconsciously' tap their feet to music.

A change in the nature of these patterns occurs in the course of ontogenesis when the child begins to use them in the imitation of a model. Such imitative depiction involves some degree of decoupling of the two segments—perceived event and immediate expressive reaction to it—that comprise the original 'circular reactions.' From this initial differentiation, the further developments can be characterized in terms of an increase of *distance* between the motor-gestural expression and that which the expression depicts. This distancing is manifested both in regard to the degree of similarity between the material of the depictive element and of the depicted content and in regard to the temporal-spatial relations between the depictive and the depicted moments.

In Part I, we advanced the view that a symbolic relation between an expression and a referent emerges genetically on the basis of a close material similarity between the two moments: this material similarity, we contended, decreases at later stages. Since the similarity of a bodily movement and an event which that movement somehow 'mimics' is usually considered in terms of a concept of *imitation,* we may consider the distancing between depictive element and depicted content in terms of this concept.

As far as true imitation presupposes an experienced duality between the model and the motor-reaction pattern, the early reflexoid movements of the infant—such as eye movements that trace the path of visual stimuli—would clearly fall outside of the domain of imitation. Such clear-cut exclusion, however, is not possible for so-called *"co-active movements,"* which are often difficult, if not impossible, to distinguish empirically from true imitations. This close affinity between co-active movements and true imitative movements suggests, therefore, that co-active 'imitation' might be considered a transitory form toward true depictive gestures.

Studies by Guillaume, Stern, Piaget, and others suggest that such co-active movements emerge during the second half of the first year: infants begin to show "empathic" movements with regard to certain visual presentations and not to others; thus they show swaying movements in response to the swaying of some person or persons in their milieu but not in response to the swaying of objects. For example, Werner's nephew, E. S., at 8 months, did not sway to the rhythm of moving objects such as the pendulum of a big clock and the swinging of a pencil with the experimenter hidden behind the screen; he did, however, immediately start to sway when the experimenter started a left-right swaying movement directly in front of him. If more systematic investigations would confirm these observations with regard to a period of "selective movements," that is, expressive movements evoked by certain presented contents and not others, such differential expressions might well be taken as one index of a shift of function from a level of "reflexoid" tracking to one of co-active imitation.

During this transitory stage, one can already observe the beginning of a trend toward an increase in material dissimilarity between imitative pattern and model. Thus, the child imitates not only the actions of *persons* like himself *but also movements of things or involving things*. At 10 months, Piaget's girl, J. P., reacted to the swinging of a brush by waving her hand; at 14 months seeing a swaying lamp that hung from the ceiling, she at once swayed her body, saying "bim-bam." Piaget's other daughter, also at about 14 months, imitated the movement of a bicycle which her father pushed forwards and backwards by swaying her body in analogous fashion. Although there may be some doubt that the movements of a child at 10 months were truly imitative in character, the gestures of the children at 14 months were, according to Piaget, undoubtedly mimetic (Piaget, 191).

Another advance in gestural depiction comes when the child uses bodily movements to imitate *nonkinetic properties of things*, such as form, size, etc., or when he imitates movements of things which are quite distinct from movements of people. Such kinds of gestures emerge, according to Guillaume, at about the end of the second year, and become more numerous during the third year (87, p. 18). For instance, Guillaume's 3-year-old daughter, speaking of a big orange, inflated her cheeks to represent the fat and round form of the fruit. At the same period, she imitated the flickering of the electric bulb by fluttering her eyelids and expressed the agitation of the water stirred up by a passing steamboat by trembling her hands. Werner's nephew, E. S. (at 2;9), imitated the typical oscillating movements of boats chained to the river shore by raising his shoulders in alternation.

The emergence—after a period of close imitation of action—of gestures "descriptive" of properties of objects or events is thus consonant with the view that there is an ontogenetic increase of distance between depictive expression and presented content. Descriptive movements differentiate themselves from those utilized in practical action; more and more, the child—in addition to the use of realistic patterns— utilizes patterns such as oscillation of shoulder-raising, trembling of hands, and inflating of cheeks, which are distinct from the forms of motion frequently employed by him in such utilitarian acts as grasping, climbing, and digestive mouth movements. The formation of descriptive gestures of this sort seems to suggest that the child has begun to translate realistic events into a medium with its own expressive features: the imitative expressions have developed into truly *pictorial* or *iconic* representations. Thus, with apparent spontaneity, the child, by means of sensory-motor patterns, creates what have been termed "natural symbols."

Although we have here centered on the exploitation of *imitative movement* in depiction, one should not overlook the importance of *re-*

active and pragmatic movements in depictive activity: we allude to the formation of gestures which derive, not from the imitation of movements or external properties of objects, but from the child's own manner of handling things or dealing with his milieu. As an illustration, one may cite Perez' observations (188, p. 251) on the emergence of a gesture of negation in one child: at 11 months, the child showed his aversion or dislike for certain things by pushing them away; at 13 months, this pushing away gesture had become a gesture of negation, consisting of a waving of the hand back and forth; later on this movement was integrated with speech, so to speak, as a gestural device for negating or qualifying some utterance; for example, the child would look attentively at someone resembling his father or mother, say 'papa' or 'mama,' yet accompany the utterance with the hand movement of 'negation.' In the cases cited by Perez, and in the writings of others (see below), one can clearly see the transformations of pragmatic or reactive movements into depictive forms; one might say that in these cases primary action has undergone a *shift of function* in the service of gestural symbolization.

Depiction takes place not only through the exploitation of bodily movements, but may indeed occur through "extensions" of bodily activity, for example, in *drawings*. As Wallon and others have noted, the earliest forms of drawings are primitive scribblings caused by arm movements projected on a surface.[4] The later drawings of children still have this close tie to bodily activity, but now the tie is to movements which are depictive of objects. Thus, as studies by Muchow, Volkelt, and Werner have shown, when children between the ages of 2 and 4 are requested to copy two- or three-dimensional forms, their drawings appear to be translations of bodily-gestural depictions of objects rather than representations of solely visual properties of objects. For example, one of Muchow's 3-year-olds, after having been presented with several straight-line figures and then asked to copy a circle, inflated his cheeks and then drew an inordinately big, puffed-out circle. Another child, before copying a narrow triangle presented to him, stretched out his tongue and then made rapid forward movements with his stretched-out forefinger; following this, he drew angular strokes so sharply that he tore the paper with the pencil. It was as if the presented triangle were grasped in terms of bodily movement—penetration, etc.—and then drawn in terms of bodily depiction. Again, some children depicted such a property as 'sharpness of edge' by pressing the pencil into the paper, or by making cutting strokes, or by boring movements; the roundness of objects—apparently mediated by bod-

---

[4] See H. Wallon and L. Lurcat (264).

ily experience of such roundness—was represented by soft strokes.[5] It seems that for the young child, in the transition from scribblings to graphic representations of visual content, there is a stage where the line drawings are basically translations of gestural imitations descriptive of presented contents.[6]

Having discussed the distancing in terms of material similarity of depictive element and depicted content, we may now turn briefly to distancing in terms of time and location.

In early forms of imitation—reactive and co-active—the imitative action occurs at the same time, and in the same locale, as the presented content. Later on, imitation occurs at some temporal remove from the presentation of content, that is, one witnesses so-called *deferred* or *delayed imitation*. Theoretically, such a delay in imitation is an extremely important step. It seems to us that its manifestation presupposes the liberation of gestural depiction from concretely presented content; in other words, for the gestural depiction to take place in the absence of concrete content implies that it must be activated and regulated by some kind of *internal model* or *'schema.'* [7]

The increasing distance of gestural depiction from presented content, and also the increasing subordination of overt gestural representation to an internal schema, is attested by the child's tendency to *correct* a deferred imitation, even where the model is no longer present. Piaget observed one of the first instances of correction in his daughter at the age of 16 months: the child, in her attempt to imitate the experimenter who had touched both of her cheeks in alternation, first patted the two corners of her mouth, then laid her forefinger on her

---

[5] M. Muchow (171, p. 45).

[6] Children not specifically trained in drawing probably begin to use such dimensions as size, brightness, form, and direction of a line medium in a more or less consistent manner as expressive properties around the age of 6 or 7. We may refer here to V. Lowenfeld's experiments (156). Lowenfeld has shown how size may be used to describe such abstract properties as social distance, inner state of a person (big head may mean 'headache'), and importance of value of an object or person; how darkness may be used to depict fearful nature of a person or heavy weight of an object. When linear dimensions are employed in this manner, the child is well on the way to using the medium as a self-contained domain for the representation of all events and all aspects of events.

[7] This notion of 'schema' has a long history, dating back to formulations by Kant (126, p. 181). In an early publication, Werner (267) pointed up the developmental significance of sensory-motor and internalized imitative patterns and schemata for the genesis of concepts—a viewpoint more recently expounded particularly by Piaget (191). See also R. d'Allonnes (3).

right cheek, and finally succeeded in touching her cheeks alternately.

When correction occurs at some temporal distance from the presented content and is found in depictive behavior initiated by the child in a content completely different from the original one, one can plausibly assume that the gesture has now become a *representational vehicle,* one of a medium of bodily movements which can be freely used to represent objects even in their absence. It is clear that the increasing distance in time and the increasing differentiation of *context of execution* from *context of original presentation,* coupled with the increasing differentiation of the qualities of the imitation from the qualities of the presented content, already implies that the gestures have entered into a more or less autonomous medium of their own. This trend towards increasing autonomy of a gestural medium will be more specifically discussed in the next section.

Tendencies Towards Increasing Autonomy of a Gestural Medium

A fully autonomous medium of representation is one that is clearly differentiated from the events represented by it: the vehicles which constitute such a medium are distinct in form and context of execution from the contents such vehicles serve to depict. Now, as has been suggested, bodily gestures rarely, if ever, attain a level of full autonomy. Although they could potentially reach such a level,[8] they typically do not comprise a full-fledged system of significant signs.

Several factors militate against the formation of a fully autonomous medium of gestural representation. First, commerce with objects preempts bodily movements, so that the organism is not always free to use gestures to represent events, since the material means are used in pragmatic activity. Again, gestures can typically provide only a gross determination of the referents and their relationships; for the gestures to succeed in communication, the addressor and addressee must usually be co-present in a situation. Perhaps the most important factor working against the full-fledged development of an autonomous gestural medium is the development of the medium of speech: the linguistic medium is "free" from direct involvement in pragmatic action and can be formed to depict and describe contents with much greater precision than can gestures. We shall return to this last consideration later on.

---

[8] The existence of fragmentary gesture-languages in nonliterate societies points to this possibility.

Nevertheless, there are indications that the gestural medium does become more and more autonomous during the course of ontogenesis. Since some of these indications are related to increasing differentiation, our discussion here will overlap to some extent with the discussion in the preceding section.

In ontogenesis, before depictive gestures clearly emerge, there are reflexoid and co-active forms of imitation—materially and spatio-temporally close to the presented contents; there are also pragmatic actions, which subserve the mastery of the world of sensory-motor objects and sensory-motor spatiotemporal relationships. As has been noted, the early imitative patterns and pragmatic actions, when impressed in the service of representation, gradually undergo a metamorphosis: imitative patterns become more and more distanced qualitatively and temporal-spatially from the presented content; and the initially pragmatic patterns are changed to gestures that are less and less like naturalistic reactions to stimulation.

In the previous section we have focused mainly on the *imitative* patterns. Here we shall initially emphasize the exploitation of *pragmatic forms* of behavior in the service of representation. Such a tendency towards exploitation is indicated by the *shift from anticipatory behavior to representative gestures of pragmatic origin.*

Anticipatory behavior, as exhibited in preparatory motor patterns, is a part of a total pragmatic action and can, of course, be observed in many infrahuman beings, for example, in the dog who opens his mouth or even makes biting movements when food is shown to him. A representative gesture of pragmatic origin may bear a close similarity in form to such an anticipatory pattern; on the other hand, it differs in function from the latter insofar as it is not a part of, but refers to and depicts, a pragmatic activity.

The close genetic relationship between anticipatory and depictive forms is attested by the fact that there are periods in which it is empirically difficult to determine whether one is viewing a representative gesture or a preparatory motor pattern. M. Muchow and H. Werner have observed numerous instances of such borderline activity in children from 10–15 months of age. To illustrate: one 13-month-old child, approaching a staircase, lifted his legs in a climbing fashion fully three feet before he reached the first step; two months later, looking for a sand spoon, the same child made shoveling movements with his right arm, holding his hand in a scooping position (173). In the first instance it is difficult to determine whether the activity is anticipatory or representative, but in the second instance it is more likely a depictive gesture. Even in this latter case, of course, one cannot completely determine whether the depictive gesture is actually controlled by an internal guide (*dispositional schema*), differentiated from its specific manifestation. At later ages the child may use such shoveling movements to communicate to others that he wishes a shovel and pail, even when he is completely outside of a shoveling context. Such *decontextualization* of the gestural movements is one of the indices of autonomy.

It is important to note that the transition from anticipatory behavior to representative gesture is often marked by a change in the form of the activity: movements which derive from pragmatic actions but which have become depictive gestures are in subtle ways distinct in pattern of execution from anticipatory responses. A good example of this is the difference observable between *anticipatory movements* in cutting with scissors and *representative gestures* of cutting with scissors. In the first instance, the individual sets thumb and forefinger in a way to fit into the handles of the scissors. When, however, one exploits the pragmatic action for representation, there is a change in the selection of fingers and in the manner in which they are held. The movements do not correspond with those of actual cutting; instead, they express the dynamic activity of "scissors-cutting" by imitating the movements of the instrument.

The increasing autonomy of a gestural medium during ontogenesis can probably be most clearly observed in the domain of *child-play,* especially as the play activity becomes patently make-believe. Make-believe play, that is, an essential *attitude of playfulness,* entails an intention towards representation of something external to the play activity. The older the child becomes, the more this intention comes to the fore, in other words, the more the sphere of playful representation becomes an autonomous domain separated from the sphere of 'serious action.'

As the child enters the sphere of make-believe play and distinguishes this sphere from that of serious action, there is a growing trend toward realism; the play content becomes less 'subjective,' 'fantastic,' 'idiosyncratic,' and more directed towards the depiction of events and objects of everyday life. The child, having distinguished his play activity from the sphere of "reality," increasingly shapes his make-believe play for the representation of this sphere of "reality."

Interrelated with the development of an orientation toward an autonomous sphere of play is the increasing autonomy of the *vehicular medium.* In case of role-taking, with which we are concerned here, one may observe the development in the way in which the child uses his own body and objects—to represent persons or events. As the Scupins, Piaget, Muchow, and others have shown, the ability of the growing child to imitate persons and events increases in complexity and precision. E. S., for instance, previously able to represent only rather vaguely, and mostly with the aid of verbal remarks, began at about 2;8 to represent gesturally in a more complex manner. He imitated a coal-man carrying a sack of coal, by walking stiffly from side to side with a towel slung around one shoulder; he thus formed a recognizable gestural picture of the coal-man, using body and towel as vehicles for representation. In other words, the child constructed a *novel gestural schema*, selecting for the characterization certain postural 'diacritica' not contained in his ordinary gait, such as swaying from side to side and stiffness of limbs. And again, by taking the towel in the role of a sack of coal, he selected certain shape and dynamic properties of an object for inclusion into the gestural representation.

In regard to vehicular mediation, then, symbolic play stands between imitative acts and the symbolic forms (such as 'arbitrary' linguistic signs) that differ entirely from naturalistic events and objects. Gestures and play objects, used as symbolic vehicles, do not differ in their material character from any realistic gesture and object used in social intercourse, but as the child develops the gestures are increasingly treated as *constructions* separated from the child's "natural" or habitual forms of behavior.

At the beginning stages of symbolic play, where play sphere and reality sphere are little differentiated, we may assume that from the child's viewpoint he *is* what he represents; there is little awareness of the body as being a *medium* of representation. At first, completely immersed, egocentrically, in play activity, he is not prompted toward communication and does not select properties of his body or specific postures in order to convey something to others. Later on, however, in the course of separating his habitual way of behaving from that of playful representation, the child often develops considerable skill in constructing characteristic gestural representations quite removed from his ordinary daily conduct.

An indication of this trend toward an autonomous medium of playful representation is a growing emphasis upon the formation of gestural action through the use of objects constructively detached from their naturalistic handling. The child selects objects of everyday life and transforms them, imaginatively, so that they become fit to serve playful representations. In other terms, a growing autonomy of the medium implies a "denaturalization" of the symbolic vehicles. The increasing separation of properties of the vehicle from those of the referent pertains to bodily gestures as well as to the naturalistic objects used for representation. For instance, Piaget's daughter (1;3), in representing sleep by appropriate postures, successively employed various objects in place of a pillow, for example, a cloth whose fringed edges vaguely recalled those of her pillows: "she seized it, held a fold of it in her right hand, sucked the thumb and lay down on her side, laughing hard." The next day, she treated the collar of her mother's coat, and still later, the tail of a rubber donkey, in the same way— as a substitute for a pillow.[9] The creativity of Piaget's daughters in constructing vectorial-physiognomically apprehended relationships with objects having no realistic similarity to the depicted events increased considerably during the second half of the second year. Thus, at 1;8, one child put two shells on top of each other, remarking delightedly, "sitting on a pot." Two months later, the same child put a shell on the edge of a big box, and made it slide down, saying, "cat on wall."[10]

It is to be conceded that in these and similar cases of imaginary transformation of objects the child is 'aided' by his tendency to perceive things in terms of physiognomic properties, rather than in terms of geometric-technical properties. One may therefore question whether in some of these instances the discrepancy between the vehicular symbol and the symbolized is, for the child, as great as it appears to the adult. Yet there are certain indications of the operation of a make-believe attitude, in contradistinction to a primary physiognomic identification of symbol and symbolized, which come from the behavior and remarks of children, e.g., the fact that they may *playfully* change the referent depicted ("it's a cup—now it's a hat—now it's a boat," etc.). An unpublished study by Martha Muchow, conducted at the Hamburg Laboratory, indicates that there is a noticeable increase in make-believe behaviors observable in children between the ages of 2 and 4½.[11]

The same trend toward decreasing realism in the vehicles is clearly evidenced with regard to the bodily characteristics involved in representation. Some examples taken from Piaget's reports may serve to

---

[9] Piaget (191, p. 75).
[10] Piaget (191, pp. 122, 124).
[11] Referred to in Muchow (172, pp. 40 f).

illustrate this: at 2;2 one of his daughters let some gravel trickle through her fingers and said, "It's raining;" at 2;4, holding a piece of sugar between her fingers, she said, "Oh, I can't open the door." The other daughter, at 2;1, moved her finger along the table and said, "Finger walking . . . horse trotting." [12] In all these cases, body parts are activated in a quite extraordinary manner for the representation of realistic situations and actions. Again, a child may, for depicting events or objects, reduce these acts to abbreviated outlines. Thus, a child (1;8) who at previous occasions pretended to sleep by lying down, at a later date—in referring to her doll lying under a blanket—laughingly pretended to show sleep, simply by closing her eyes but standing erect.[13]

The exploitation of postural modifications for representing rather complex shape properties of objects appears to increase considerably during the third and fourth years. As Muchow and Werner have observed, children during this period showed great ingenuity in the forming of descriptive gestures in make-believe situations: one child represented a house by standing erect with the arms slightly raised sidewise to indicate the roof; similarly, by bending down he tried to represent a mountain. Another child represented a chimney and, by raising one arm perpendicularly, depicted smoke. Similar observations have been reported by Stern, Scupins, and Piaget on their own children. We already mentioned Guillaume's conclusions—which he derived from his extensive study on imitation—that gestures descriptive of objects typically develop after 2 years of age.

The formation of gestures severed from pragmatic action and employed in a purely representative function culminates in *"empty gestures,"* gestures performed without the use of concrete objects. The developmental trend toward "abstract" postural schemata per se out of more realistic situations is well illustrated in the following observations by Piaget. His daughter (1;7) playfully imitated drinking from a glass of water, later on pretended to drink out of an empty glass, and finally performed the action without a glass, while making smacking noises.[14] According to Guillaume, "empty gestures" appear late in

---

[12] Piaget (191, pp. 124, 125).

[13] Piaget (191, p. 122).

[14] We are reminded here of some of Head's and Goldstein's brain-injured patients who, suffering an impairment of the function of representation (Head's 'asymbolia'), were unable, on request, to demonstrate how to drink under conditions of no glass or empty glass. (See 83; 98).

the ontogenetic development of imitative behavior (see Guillaume, 87, p. 135). Frances Markey also has demonstrated the relative increase of "empty gestures" in her study of 2- to 5-year-old children (see Werner, 274, p. 80).

In sum, the creation of "nonhabitual" gestures, executed in "empty space" without the support of realistic objects, reflects a considerable development in representative activity. Such behavior indicates some mastery in the handling of one's own body for the formation of vehicles of representation.

Even at its best, however, depiction through gestures remains at a relatively primitive level when compared with the tremendous development of the representative function realized through, and carried by, the vocal articulatory medium. In the next chapter we turn to the precursors and early stages of depiction in that medium.

chapter 8

Precursors and Early Stages of Vocal Depiction

Before we undertake our discussion of the ontogenesis of depiction via the medium of vocal forms, we wish to remind the reader that the presentation here is guided by the concept of *development* and does not constitute a résumé of behaviors ordered *chronologically*. At this time, when empirical data are still quite sparse and fragmentary, it would be presumptuous to claim more than the fact that available observations appear, on the whole, to justify our thesis that vocal representation undergoes changes in accordance with the orthogenetic principle of increasing differentiation and hierarchic integration. One might add further that since speech development can rarely, if ever, be examined under conditions completely optimal for that development, the "ideal" ontogenesis of speech will always, to some degree, have to be "reconstructed."

We shall initiate our treatment of vocal depiction in a manner analogous to our discussion of motor-gestural depiction, that is, in terms of the concept of *distancing*. We shall discuss distancing first with respect to increasing qualitative dissimilarity between vehicle and referent and then, briefly, with respect to the spatiotemporal interval between vehicle and referent. Following this discussion we shall examine, at some length, that process of *differentiation* and *specification* whereby a vocal form, first global and nonspecific, becomes increasingly function-specific and is eventually used to refer to a delimited and circumscribed content in the same manner as are the vocal forms used by socialized normal adults.

Throughout this chapter we shall concern ourselves with the function of designation per se, as distinguished from the function of communicating messages or judgments. In Chapter 9, we shall undertake a brief theoretical discussion of the relations between vocal expression and referent in the course of ontogenesis. In Chapters 10–12, we shall turn to the early tendencies towards the establishment of an autonomous medium of speech, that is, a system of vocal expressions, with distinctive features and rules, by means of which one conveys to others statements and judgments about events.

Our suggestion that, in entering the domain of vocal depiction, the primary focus of the child is on designation should not be interpreted to mean that we believe that the child is initially directed towards some sort of self-contained activity of connecting the right vocal patterns with the right objects. For us, the child's orientation towards naming reflects an intensely social motive of sharing experiences about objects with others. By learning the names of objects, the child, on one hand, continues to build a common universe of contemplated things and events, begun—on the sensory-motor level—at a much earlier age. On the other hand, however, the child, in using names, enters an entirely novel stage, as far as his and the other's experiences are now shared or shareable through the quasi-objective, externalized medium of audible symbolic vehicles.

Distancing: Increasing Dissimilarity between Vocal Utterance and Depicted Event

Although representation, in our view, is an emergent activity that cannot be reduced to or derived from any other operation, one may still inquire about forms of behavior that precede representation and that set the stage and provide the "material" for representational activity to come into play. In dealing here with representation through vocal utterances, we shall again study precursors and ontogenetic changes—here with regard to vocal depiction—in terms of a sequence of stages governed by the principle of "distancing," that is, in terms of an increasing differentiation between the properties of the vocal utterance (variations in sound quality, pitch, intensity, etc.) and the properties of the presented events which they depict. On the basis of genetic theory and empirical observations, three steps of the sequence may be distinguished: (1) naturalistic-onomatopoetic depiction, (2) physiognomic depiction, and (3) conventional representation.

Naturalistic-Onomatopoetic Depiction

The widespread tendency of young children to imitate all kinds of noises—noises of objects as well as of persons (including those the children make themselves)—provides basic material from which vocal depictive forms may be constructed. According to Stern (242, p. 374), young children typically find great pleasure in imitating a great variety of distinctive noises which reach their ears—those from animals, from squeaking doors, from the rattling of toys, the splashing of water, coughing, sneezing, gargling, or kissing.

Before the child reaches the age at which he is able to exploit these imitative patterns for representation, that is, as *designators,* he may use them for the production of signals indicating a need. For instance, a self-imitative vocal signal was uttered by Pavlovitch's 5-month-old son, who indicated his desire for a pacifier by a clicking or smacking sound (186, p. 28).

Theoretically, signals of this sort have to be distinguished from imitative vocal gestures used in the service of designation. The following vocal utterances seem to be in the service of depiction, though empirically, of course, it will often be difficult, if not impossible, to determine when such signals have started to undergo the *shift of function* from imitation per se to depictive imitation. There is no such ambiguity in somewhat older children where denotative gestures (pointing, turning toward, etc.) accompanying these vocal patterns are clear indications of the intent of the child to exploit these primordial signals depictively.

In the list given by Leopold of the earliest, relatively well-established "nonstandard words" of his daughter, one will easily recognize their imitative (and self-imitative) nature (150, p. 140):

> *dididi* (scolding, comfort)—9 months
> *nenene* (disapproval)—10 months
> *mjamjam* (food, tastes good)—12 months
> *kx* (tastes bad)—19–22 months
> *bu* (thunder)—23 months

Stern's children provide a good many illustrations for these kinds of designatory vocal imitations: G. Stern, at 1;10 years, pointed to a picture of cherries and said, *psi.* This sound-pattern, originally the lingualized form of sneezing, was later used by the boy to designate flowers, leaves, and all kinds of trees. At the same age, G. Stern also designated a horse carriage by *ö-ö-ö* pronounced rhythmically, with effort, apparently signifying the strain of the horses involved in the pulling of the car. Hilde Stern, at 1;5 years, called a dish *ssi*. This sound-pattern, originally identical in function to her brother's *psi* (sneezing reaction), was used by the girl to designate the dish, after the flower design with which it was ornamented. She also designated a match stick with *f-f-f,* a sound-pattern that imitates the blowing noise made when putting out the light of a match. She subsequently extended this vocal pattern to include candle, lamp, and other objects of light.

The following report [1] illustrates rather well the exploitation of imitative vocal patterns for designating desired objects: "A. (1;10) wants her mother to put into the water a whistle that lies on the rim of the bathtub. She grabs the mother's hand, puts it into the water and looking at the whistle, out of her reach, calls out: *f-f-f.*"

In assessing the so-called onomatopoetic patterns in their role within the development of representation, one must realize their characteristically *linguistic* nature: however slight the "distance"—the material dissimilarity between the uttered patterns and the depicted event—may seem, onomatopoetic forms never duplicate such events but rather construct them, as it were, by means of speech sounds previously practiced by the child for a long time. Whether the onomatopoetic expressions are offered to the child by the adult or formed spontaneously by him,[2] these patterns always involve a *translation* of the perceived noise into a given linguistic medium. When, for instance, Stern's child uses such simple expressions as *r-r-r* to "name" a coffee grinder, or *s-s-s* to indicate by this hissing a flower syringe, he utilizes phonemes available to him within the German linguistic medium. This is, of course, one of the main reasons, as Wundt and others have pointed out, that so-called imitations by infants of animal sounds differ in different languages; thus the baby word for 'dog' in German is 'wau-wau'; in French, 'oua-oua'; in Dutch, 'waf-waf.' 'Miau-miau' is the name for cat in German, but 'nyanya' is used in Japanese, etc. (242, p. 383).

The nature of onomatopoetic expressions as products of translations into a speech system can probably be best understood when one con-

---

[1] Communication by our colleague, S. Wapner.

[2] In our opinion the problem of free "inventions" has been unduly stressed in literature. In regard to the genesis of symbol formation the question whether the child produces patterns by himself or with the aid of the adult is of far less importance than the question as to the character of these early patterns.

siders the manner in which adults "read" verbal patterns into animal cries and other natural noises. This point is well illustrated by the following observations of Chamberlain (43, pp. 116 f). While in the region of Kootenay, British Columbia, he heard some owls hooting, *tu-whit-tu-whit-tu-whu*. When he asked his Kootenay companion what the owls were saying, the Indian unhesitatingly replied that the owl was saying two things: (*a*) *k'setikenetl patlke;* (*b*) *katskakitl patlke.* "By and by, the writer without being conscious of any particular effort on his part, ceased to hear the tu-whit-tu-whit-tu-whu, so familiar to him, and the sounds that reached his ears were: *k'setikenetl patlke, katskakitl patlke,* these phrases unknown to him, and he being ignorant of their real signification. Moreover, by a very slight effort, he was able to interchange these sounds, and to hear at will the common English or the Kootenay Indian rendering of the owl's cry." Chamberlain quotes one further fascinating observation by an educated Mohawk Indian, bearing on the role of the linguistic system in determining the sounds-heard-for-imitation. Concerning the sounds of the whippoorwill bird, he stated: "When I listen with my Indian ears it seems to me utterly impossible to form any other word from an imitation of its notes than *kwa-kor-yeuh*, but when I put on my English ears I hear the bird quite distinctly saying *whip-poor-will*."

It is by their very virtue as linguistic patterns built by definite speech sounds and not by indefinite babblings that onomatopoetic forms can be further shaped into more complex products, assimilated to the rhythmic structure of the surrounding language, and stabilized into units that are handled like other words in the child's speech. Utterances such as the following, typically heard from children 1;6–2 years of age, are reported by various observers: *shüdde-shüdde* = ball (vocal imitation of the sound of rhythmic bouncing); [3] *ling-dong-mang* = church bells; [4] *didi-lip-didi-lip* = key (originally used for jiggling noise); [5] *nōt-nōt* = walking (imitation of shuffling); [6] *bugge-bugge* = reading; [7] *degatte-degatte* = reading.[8]

The steps by which such patterns, derived from primordial sound material, become lingually and morphemically stabilized in the service of depiction have occasionally been well observed. For example,

---

[3] Meumann (166, pp. 11, 28).

[4] Preyer (194, p. 291).

[5] Pavlovitch (186, p. 15).

[6] Stern (242, pp. 378 f).

[7] Gutzmann (92, p. 29).

[8] Lindner, cited in Stern (242, p. 379)

M. V. O'Shea noted his child uttering some sort of combination of sounds resembling *ndobin;* this pattern was uttered while the child was eating. With the aid of the adults who responded to this sound-pattern by repeating it, the child soon came to use it, quite purposefully, for some particular kind of food (see Stern, 242, p. 380).

A. Gregoire (86) has also provided some illuminating examples. His son, Charles, at 0;8, imitated the sound of church bells with *apu-apu;* at 12 months, he used this pattern to signify the pigeons to which he also pointed. Again, Edmond G., at 0;9½, used *m-m-m* to express impatience and desire at the sight of his bottle; at 14 months, the *m* sound became clearly established and became ingredient in the pattern *menom,* indicating the child's desire to have food. As has been often suggested,[9] such *m*-sounds related to need within a food situation, may grow rather smoothly into the still more formalized and conventionalized name for mother, *ma-ma.*

That depiction of events through speech sounds is a process of "translation" will be clearer the greater the material dissimilarity between the events and their vocal representation. This becomes increasingly evident when one turns from onomatopoetic depiction to physiognomic depiction in the vocal medium.

Physiognomic Depiction

One must distinguish, from those onomatopoetic expressions which imitate sonic properties of objects, articulated vocal patterns which depict *other* than sonic properties of events. For instance, a *visual* property such as size may be depicted linguistically by translating variation of length into variation of sound duration: a long vowel would then indicate a large object; a short vowel, a small object. Again, the vowels *i* versus *u* may indicate 'high' versus 'low,' or 'far' versus 'close,' etc. It is obvious that the depiction of such nonsonic properties by means of vocalizations entails a higher degree of material differentiation between the depictive vehicles and the depicted content than obtains in the case of onomatopoetic expressions.

Such relationships between sounds and nonsonic properties of events have been studied by a number of authors, usually under the concept of "sound symbolism." We shall discuss some of these studies in a subsequent chapter (see pp. 218 f). Here we would like to state briefly the organismic view that the translations of nonsonic properties into sound-patterns are based on sim-

---

[9] Cf. Stern (242, pp. 356 f).

ilarities deriving from the primordial unity of the senses; we maintain that qualities such as "long" or "short," "hard" or "soft," etc., are organismic rather than merely sensory phenomena. This organismic, "sensory-tonic" view enables us to understand why the same terms are often used to characterize events presumably experienced through different, and ostensibly discrete, sense modalities—a *harsh color*, a *sweet sound*, etc.

Many observations have been reported in the literature pertaining to the formation—in children between 1 and 2 years of age—of articulatory vocal patterns for the designation of nonsonic properties of events. In several instances, the vocal utterances served to express *size* differences. For example, Neugebauer's child showed a remarkable ability to express size differences through *intonational variation:* he uttered the name for "stone" (= *teinn*) with a high, thin, short intonation when pointing to pebbles but with a low, long intonation when looking at rocks. At the same time, this distinction was also manifested in his *mouth posture:* lips pressed tightly together in a thin line versus mouth open wide and rounded (with wide-open eyes). Similar observations were made with regard to the child's designations of other objects varying in size, for example, trees, flowers (174, p. 299). An analogous observation was made by Stern on his 2-year-old son: the child called a big tree *ha-psi*, uttered with a deep, long intonation; a small flower, on the other hand, was designated with the same vocal form, but with the second syllable, *psi*, accentuated in a high, peeping voice (242, p. 184). Gabelentz reported similar instances concerning his grandchild, who employed *vowel variation:* a doll-chair was called *likill;* an ordinary chair, *lakell;* an easy chair, *lukull.* Father's name, *papa*, was transformed into *pupu* when he stood in front of the child clothed in a big fur coat (242, p. 185).

Another group of observations suggests even more strongly the involvement of the "posture" of the articulating organs in the formation of physiognomic depictions: for instance, a 1½-year-old boy whom the speech pathologist, Kussmaul (144, p. 49), observed almost daily, designated all round, rolling objects such as balls, coins, rings, etc., by *golloh*. As Kussmaul notes, this pattern involving the "rolling" of the tongue not only seems to imitate the noise of the rolling objects but also their movements. Kussmaul quotes an analogous observation by the linguist Steinthal concerning his 1½-year-old daughter: her name for "barrel" was *lululu* which Steinthal interpreted as an imitative pattern. Again, the 1½-year-old Greif Sander called an old straw hat with which he used to play (and later on, any straw hat) *gugl-gugl*. The observer interpreted this vocal pattern as very expressively portraying the round object as it rhythmically bounces down the staircase from step to step.[10]

As stated, the appearance of physiognomic vocal patterns in early childhood has a particular bearing on the problem of genesis of names, insofar as it points up the nature of onomatopoetic and physiognomic words as "translations" rather than duplications. (See 184.) The import of these "translations" for the formation of speech symbols will be further examined in the following sections dealing with the trend toward conventional vocal representation.

Conventional Representation

As outlined in the introductory chapter, it is our view that linguistic symbols, whether "natural" or conventional, are basically representational, that is, depictive—in a wider sense—of a referent. The difference between onomatopoetic or physiognomic forms, on one hand, and conventional or "arbitrary" forms, on the other, is not therefore in the basic nature of the symbolic relationship: rather, it pertains to the "distance" between vehicle and referent.

As the child advances from his "idiomorphic" speech, his "baby language," to conventional speech, one would not expect that this marked increase in distance between vehicle and referent would occur abruptly; rather, one would assume that a series of transitional steps would intervene between the use of onomatopoetic or physiognomic depictions and conventional depictions. Some of the most frequently reported transitional phenomena will be described briefly here.

The transitional steps towards conventional depiction, that is, the steps towards increasing distance between vehicle and referent, occur, so to speak, in two directions: in the distancing of referent from vehicle and in the distancing of vehicle from referent. The first movement involves primarily a decrease in the concreteness of the referent designated by an onomatopoetic or physiognomic vehicle; the second movement involves a "denaturalization" of the vehicular form.

Thus, when a child utilizes a vocal expression, either onomatopoetic or physiognomic, to designate *qualitatively diverse situations* rather than one specific event, a specific referent becomes less closely linked to the vocal utterance used. Again, when the child begins in some way to take over, in whole or part, the conventional designation for events

---

[10] Citations from Stern (242, p. 379).

and objects, this also increases the distance—in this case, by way of *denaturalization* of the vocal symbol.

The first kind of distancing, the widening of the range of referents designated by a given vehicle, is well illustrated by the example pertaining to the extension of *gugl-gugl* from its original reference to a particular straw hat to its subsequent use for any straw hat. Another illustration comes from Stumpf. His son, at 1;10, initially used the onomatopoetic form *tap* for the opening of a bottle; he later extended this pattern to designate the bottle itself, then to designate scissors and pliers (apparently on the basis of a similarity in snapping movement and sound). Similarly, Gutzmann's son first used *bugge-bugge* to imitate the reading of adults, then to indicate the actual reading event; later this vocal pattern became the name for newspapers, books, and letters. Tögel's son first imitated the noise of a locomotive by *hjhj*, and then used this pattern to designate "train"; later on he also called a flock of geese (marching on the street) by that name. Jespersen gives the example of a 1;9-year-old girl who called a match *pooh* (blowing noise in putting out the lighted match), later extending this name to include cigars and pipes. The same author cites another case of a child who used *fff* (again imitation of blowing noise of putting out the match) as a name for smoke, steam, later on for funnel, chimney, and finally for anything standing upright against the sky, as for instance, a flagstaff (119, p. 183). A number of instructive illustrations showing the referent extension of onomatopoetic sound patterns are also reported by Gregoire. For instance, Edmond G., 22 months old, imitated the hammering of a nail by uttering *pigne* (p-i-ñ) which soon became the name for 'nail,' then also for 'key' and for a 'metallic pencil.' (86, I, pp. 241 f).

With regard to the second kind of distancing, namely, via change in the vehicle, it seems to us that, important as it may be to study the increase in conventional vocabulary, a deeper insight into the ontogenesis of linguistic representation is gained from the study of types of *transitional forms,* intermediate between onomatopoetic-physiognomic expressions and conventional designators. Four such types of transitional forms may be mentioned.

The *first* group of transition phenomena reflects a noticeable tendency to retain the onomatopoetic expressions but to assimilate them into the conventional language code. This evidence of the child's urge to conform to codified speech even when clinging to infantile "word radicals" has been commented on by a number of students of child language, for example, Stern, Meumann, and Gregoire. Thus, Charles

Gregoire formed the verb *bumer* (= to fall) from the original interjection *bum* (boom) used for imitating the noise of things dropped. He also developed the verb *bimer* from *bim* originally employed to indicate tapping on the wash bowl (86, I, p. 185). Neugebauer's son (1;8) built a verb *wiehen* (= to slide) from *wieh* (sliding down an incline) (174, p. 305). E. S. (2;0) derived the verb *bimmen* (to ring the bell) from *bim* (bell). He also built a verb from his "adjective" *aij* (soft)—*das aij-aijt-ssön* (That softs-nice!). Hilde Stern, after having previously formed the term *atze* for indicating the tearing apart of material such as paper or cloth, used it later (2;6) like any other verb, *Hab geatzt mund* [have torn off (bread with my) mouth]. The 2-year-old G. Stern constructed the verb *reuren* (from *reureu* = imitation of the noise of grinding meat) as his expression for "to grind." (242, p. 375).

The *second* group of the transitional speech forms concerns the use of composite forms, one element of which is infantile-idiomatic, the other conventional. These are examples: Ament's nephew (1;6), from the infantile name for "hammering," *poch,* formed the word *pochmacher* (= pochmaker), meaning "workman" (5, pp. 73 f). Bubi Scupin, from the emotional expression *fui* (= phoui) built the word *fui-ordnung* (= dis-order) (220, II, p. 242). Stumpf's son composed *hapman* (= eating man, eater) from *hap* (= eat) (242, p. 387). A composite form which appeared relatively late in Hilde Stern's vocabulary was the name for piano: *tinkeli kommode* (= tinkeli chest) derived from the the onomatopoetic form *tinkeli* (= piano playing) (242, p. 387).

Stern has drawn our attention to a *third* group of transitional speech forms. The child builds a combinatory name composed of the idiomatic plus the conventional word: *wau wau-dog; bah-sheep; muh muh-cow; pee pee-bird; ada-go; tatei-sleep; shu shu-train;* etc. Later, the child begins increasingly to omit the first part, thus finally employing solely the conventional name. Meumann, Ament, Gheorgov, and others have also observed this development in regard to animal as well as object names: *didde didde-clock, mamma-milk, tate tate-scissors* (E. S., 2 years), etc. (242, p. 243).

The tendency of children to use "baby" and traditional speech patterns in combination seems to be related to a *fourth* group of transitional phenomena, mentioned by several investigators: this pertains to the peculiar fact that some children when asked to repeat a conventional word will respond with their own corresponding idiomatic word form. "The trend toward natural symbolics," says Stern, "is sometimes so dominant that even when urged to repeat a conventional word which has been understood for many months these childen will react with their infantile idiomatic expression." [11]

To illustrate, when Gunther was asked to say "bottle," he responded *huhu;* when asked to say "ring," he responded *dintz;* when asked to say "shoe," he responded *buph;* when asked to say "spoon," he answered, *ta;* when asked to say "chicken" he responded *peep-peep.* Stumpf's son behaved in a similar manner: when asked to say "gun," "snow," and "milk," he responded with *pu-pu-pa,* *kjob,* and *prullich* respectively. P. F. (personal communication) showed a somewhat related peculiarity: he used certain baby words such as *puff-puff,* *mimmi,* *dig-deg,* when talking to his mother, but employed the adult German words, equivalent to train, milk, and clock, when talking to others.[12]

We may, at this point, refer briefly to certain features in abnormal speech behavior which seem to be related to the last-mentioned group of transitional phenomena. Some of these facts come from studies in remedial reading. Children with reading disability sometimes misread a word, apparently difficult for them, by substituting a simple synonym. An example is that of a 10 year old child who read "farmer" for "peasant," "rug" for "carpet;" he repeated this performance over and over again without being aware of this error and without being able to correct it without considerable help. Thus, he appeared to behave analogously to the way the above-mentioned young children "repeated" adult word patterns by uttering child-like synonyms. Paralleling these instances of "paralexia" are certain responses given by paraphasics when requested to repeat single words.[13]

Before turning to other manifestations of distancing, we shall elaborate briefly on *the role of "natural symbols" in the development of vocal representation.* If one accepts the thesis advanced in this book, that symbols are not simply substitute signs, pointers, labels, or coins, but rather represent or connote the referent, symbolization must always, and basically, include an element of depiction—however dissimilar the "picture" and the referred object may appear to be.

For those who hold our view, it would be incomprehensible that a child could enter human speech, that is, begin to understand the symbol

---

[11] Stern (242, pp. 242, 93).

[12] In regard to these so to speak "bilingual," features of a transition from baby language to adult language, one is reminded of certain parallels found in children raised in a truly bilingual environment. Cf. Leopold (150, III, pp. 174 ff).

[13] Cf. Goldstein (83, pp. 244, 280).

function of speech, in any way other than through "natural symbols"—forms which most tellingly impress upon the child the inner relationship of name and thing. Label theorists, however, whose basic notions are essentially those of a contiguity-learning theory, may point to certain empirical phenomena which apparently are quite at variance with the developmental viewpoint presented here: Is it not a fact that the child acquires names of things very early through a repetition of the conventional speech patterns of adults? We shall try to answer this argument as follows.

(1) Though it is true that the child early understands and employs some conventional forms, this does not prove that the child apprehends and uses these patterns in the adult manner or sense. It is quite possible—even probable, as we shall point out in several sections of this work—that such patterns may for the child have a physiognomic character: because of the tremendous malleability of auditory-motor forms, because of their embeddedness in organismic activity, and because of the predominance of intonational elements, these seemingly conventional patterns may be conceived by the child as "natural symbols" rather than as conventional signs. Therefore, the occurrence of conventional word-forms in early childhood cannot be taken as proof of the label theorist's thesis.

(2) If one peruses the lists of the earliest stable and meaningful vocal patterns given in the diaries of such careful observers as Ament, Stern, Scupin, Gregoire, and Leopold, one is impressed by the prevalence of "natural" (deictic, onomatopoetic, and physiognomic) forms. This character of baby language, consonant with developmental theory, seems to us to be inexplicable by label theorists.

(3) Finally, there is a body of facts—small, but of greatest significance for our understanding of the manner in which the child passes over the threshold into human speech—that strongly supports our viewpoint concerning the representational nature of speech symbols. This body of facts comes primarily from reports on the learning of language by deaf and blind children. For example, there is a well-known episode, related by Helen Keller and her teacher, Miss Sullivan, which has not often been recognized in its full significance. Here are some of the pertinent remarks by Helen Keller (134, p. 315).

"One day, while I was playing with my new doll, Miss Sullivan put my big rag doll into my lap also, spelled "d-o-l-l" and tried to make me understand that "d-o-l-l" applied to both. Earlier in the day we had had a tussle over the words "m-u-g" and "w-a-t-e-r." Miss Sullivan had tried to impress it upon me that "m-u-g" is *mug* and that "w-a-t-e-r" is *water,* but I persisted in confounding the two. In despair she had dropped the subject for the time, only to renew it at the first opportunity. I became impatient of her repeated attempts, and seizing the new doll, I dashed it upon the floor. I was keenly delighted when I felt the fragments of the broken doll at my feet. Neither sorrow nor regret followed my passionate outburst. I had not loved the doll. In the still, dark world in which I lived there was no strong sentiment or tenderness. . . . We walked down the path to the well-house, attracted by the fragrance of the honeysuckle with which it was covered. Someone was drawing water and my teacher placed my hand under the spout. As the cool stream gushed over one hand she spelled into the other the word water, first slowly, then rapidly. I stood still, my whole attention fixed upon the motions of her fingers. Suddenly I felt a misty consciousness as of something forgotten—a thrill of returning thought; and somehow the mystery of language was revealed to me. I knew then that "w-a-t-e-r" meant the wonderful cool something that was flowing over my hand. That living word awakened my soul, gave it light, hope, joy, set it free! There were barriers still, it is true, but barriers that could in time be swept away. . . . I left the well-house eager to learn. Everything had a name, and each name gave birth to a new thought. As we returned to the house every object which I touched seemed to quiver with life. That was because I saw everything with the strange, new sight that had come to me. On entering the door I remembered the doll I had broken. I felt my way to the hearth and picked up the pieces. I tried vainly to put them together. Then my eyes filled with tears; for I realized what I had done, and for the first time I felt repentance and sorrow."

The unique value of Helen Keller's retrospective statements lies in the unmistakable proof that names are symbols that connote, represent, or depict, and as such are *toto coelo* set apart from signs which label things or direct behavior. There is evidence that the child has learned through endless repetitions, and however incompletely, to connect the handling of objects with the tactual patterns; this should have been sufficient, according to a label theory, for these patterns to function as names. Miss Keller's account attests to the superficiality of the notion that it is a contiguous connection which binds the symbol and the referent; her beautiful description documents the very *shift of function* from signal to symbol which, in the normally growing child, can rarely be directly observed but must be inferred from his behavior.

One might probe further and ask the question: what may have been the critical elements in the events at the well which brought about the sudden understanding of the symbolic function? We doubt that a conclusive answer can ever be given. We may, however, from the point of view of developmental theory, at least offer some conjecture as to the potent factors inherent in that memorable event. In consonance with our theory one would have to argue that a child cannot cross the threshold of language in any way other than by "natural symbols." In the "mug" situation, there was an entirely external connection between a static object and certain tactual signs. In the "water" situation, the object was in itself an *event:* the flowing of cool water over the hand. And as Miss Sullivan "poured" the tactual signs over one of Helen's hands, and the cool liquid over the other, there perhaps occurred two tactual experiences that may have been internally linked in the child's mind —a linkage based on common dynamic features: "water" comes to mean the "cool something flowing over the hand."

Through the attention which is at present given to the education of deaf-blind children, further information of great significance for the problem of early development of symbolization is now available. Educators of the deaf-blind have found a most successful teaching method, which is now widely in use. This method consists of the following steps.[14] The child places his hands on the lips and throat of the teacher and thus observes the formation of sounds through vibrations and touch. The variations of sound are understood by linking them with bodily postures; thus the teacher makes the child raise his hand when he perceives a high tone and lower his hand with a low tone. After this training, the learning of words begins. The first words learned are action words such as "jump" and "bow." Thus, the teacher placing the child's hand on her face, says emphatically "jump"; then placing the child's hands on her hips, proceeds to jump. This performance is repeated several times, then it is the child's turn to jump. Once the connection between mouth patterns and body posture and motion has been established with a very few of these action words, the most important step has been taken: the child has crossed the threshold of human speech. Clearly, this grasp of the representative function of names occurs in exactly the way that organismic theory of symbol formation would predict: the process involves bodily postures and motor action patterns whose dynamic features are somehow "repeated" by the postural and articulatory action-patterns of the mouth organs. Thus, the deaf-blind older child arrives at the understanding of the representative function of speech through the "natural symbols" of mouth gestures, that is, through patterns that are quite analogous to the onomatopoetic and physiognomic forms by which a younger normal child enters speech.

---

[14] Inis B. Hall (93, p. 244); Berthold Lowenfeld (155, p. 7); Gabriel Farrell (62, p. 85).

Distancing: Increasing Spatiotemporal Interval between Vocal Depiction and Depicted Content

This aspect of distancing is of utmost importance in speech development. Since practically all students of child language have commented upon it and have presented pertinent observations with regard to it, we may limit our discussion here to a few remarks.

A distancing between vehicle and referent with respect to space and time reflects the increasing use of the linguistic medium as a means for transcending the immediately given, and hence as a means of extending the human universe into the realms of the nonpresent, that is, into the spatially remote and into the temporally past and future.

Modest beginnings of this development occur at quite early stages of child speech. One illustration taken from M. M. Lewis' observations on his child, K, may suffice to exemplify such early occurrence. Lewis' observations pertain to the response of the child to "ballie" (Where's the ballie?). Lewis distinguishes three stages in the sequence: at 0;9,14, the child touched the ball on hearing the phrase, "Where is the ballie?"; at 0;10,29, the word "ballie" evoked looking at the ball without touching; finally at 1;1,5, the child, lying in the corner of his playroom, on hearing the phrase turned around and crawled toward the ball at the other end of the room. This behavior, according to Lewis, shows "that the phrase causes the child to refer to an absent ball; the behavior that was previously aroused by the presence of the ball is now aroused by the hearing of certain sounds" (152, p. 150).

Lewis' set of observations is one of the many reported in the literature, all indicating the early beginnings of a genetic trend towards relative separation of vocal names from the immediate, concrete happenings or events to which the names refer. One must, however, keep in mind that the full actualization of this trend does not occur for some time: for a long period, the language of the young child remains tied down to the immediate, the concrete—to that which is close in space and time. This closeness of vehicle to concrete referent is reflected in the lack of designators for that which is not given immediately, that is, in the lack of abstract spatial and temporal terms. The gradual comprehension and use of names for location and temporality, for here and there, past and future, reflects the child's growing capacity to increase the distance between vocal utterance (depiction) and depicted event and thus to make language an instrument for articulating and communicating about rather abstract and remote contents.

Differentiation and Specification (Decontextualization) of the Vehicle-Referent Relationship: The Formation of Specific Names

In contradistinction to the circumscribed referents to which adult vocables refer, the early names typically designate global, rather undifferentiated events. From an initial point at which there are only a few name-vocables, there is a gradual increase in the number of distinct vocables used for reference to events; this increase in vocabulary attests to the tendency of the growing child to differentiate among and to specify events in his environment, so that the referents of his vocables progressively approximate the referents of adult names.[15] Students of child behavior and language have provided illuminating examples of this process of differentiation and specification at early levels.

In studying this aspect of naming, one must be aware of the distinction between vocables as designators and vocables as parts of speech. Our present concern is with vocables in their purely designatory function, as names, though it should be clear that only under special circumstances does the child center on the naming function per se when he utters a vocable: such special circumstances obtain when there is an eagerness to *learn names* of things and persons, so that they may be used subsequently in communication through speech. In this respect the child's eagerness to know and practice names stems from the same need for practicing activities which is exhibited earlier in the endless imitation of noises, repetition of meaningless sound-patterns, etc.

Our first illustration of the process of differentiation and specification comes from Ament's discussion of the progressive delimitation of the sphere of reference of his little niece's vocable, *mammam*. M. M. Lewis has presented a schematic summary of Ament's discussion, a summary we reproduce in Figure 8-1. Here one can see how the original sphere of the vocable is progressively delimited as specific vocables come into play for more circumscribed classes of events; finally, the near-interjectional vocable *mammam* disappears, with the types of events to which it originally referred now designated by distinct, separate vocables.

Another illustration of this process of differentiation and specifica-

---

[15] It might be worthwhile to note here that some students of child speech, misinterpreting the over-inclusive, vague, global character of early names as indicating "general" reference, have made the statement that general concepts emerge before specific concepts, a view quite in opposition to modern developmental notions. For further discussion of this problem see Chapter 10 and Chapter 13.

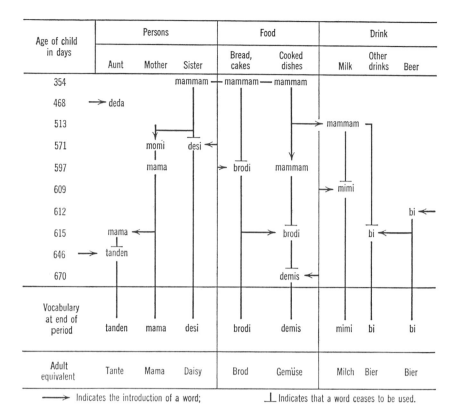

FIGURE 8-1. Development of meaning of *mammam* and its substitutes (Ament's niece). (After Lewis, 152, p. 214.)

tion is provided by Leopold. This example, like the preceding one, again pertains to the domain or sphere of food-eating. Originally, for Hildegard Leopold, *m* referred to a very large sphere of events related to food-getting and food-eating activity. Progressively, the semantic sphere of this interjection-like vocable was restricted as new vocables were added to the vocabulary—new vocables applying to more delimited referents within the larger sphere. Part of this development is reconstructed in the following diagram (Figure 8-2).[16]

Still another illustration is provided by M. M. Lewis, in his tracing

---

[16] After Leopold (150, III, p. 150; I, pp. 67, 83, 84).

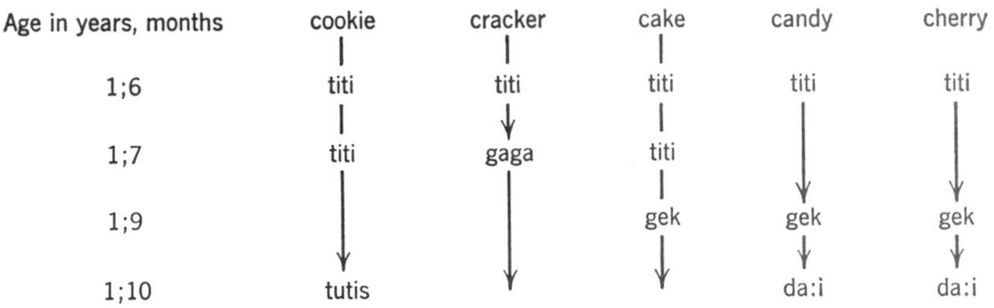

Age in years, months	cookie	cracker	cake	candy	cherry
1;6	titi	titi	titi	titi	titi
1;7	titi	gaga	titi		
1;9			gek	gek	gek
1;10	tutis			da:i	da:i

At the end, each of these spheres of sweets or desserts is designated by a special vocable of more or less restricted reference.

FIGURE 8-2. Vocables used to refer to desserts, sweets (compiled from Leopold's report on his daughter).

of the process of linguistic differentiation in his child, this time within the sphere of references to animals (Figure 8-3) (Lewis, 152, p. 216).

In all of these cases, one sees clearly how a sphere of events becomes progressively articulated and specified through the emergence of specific terms for denoting specific types of events within originally global spheres.

It should be emphasized that such early differentiation and specification in naming does not entail that each of the vocally depicted referents is now distinctly circumscribed in the adult manner—as agent per se, action per se, etc. For a long period of time, the referents of early vocables remain relatively global in character, that is, total situations in which agent, action, and object are intimately fused. A good illustration of this fusion is provided by Ament (5, p. 91). Ament's niece, Louise, at 2;1,3, had begun to refer to the originally undifferentiated sphere of "milk" by two distinct names: one, *mimi*, referred to *milk as drunk out of a bottle*, and the other, *te*, referred to *milk as drunk out of a cup*. It is clear from this that *milk* was not a circumscribed thing but rather entered into total situations which included agent's action as undifferentiated components. Another example from the same observer illustrates the lack of distinction between thing and condition of its appearance in a named event: Louise ordinarily called her cousin, Karl, *darl;* when, however, he had black hands, she called him *manden*, which was her name for "he-who-carries-coal."

There are many indications that the fusion of thing and its context-of-action persists for a considerable period. One indication is in terms

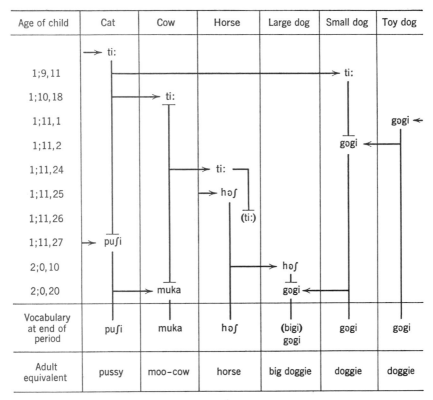

Age of child	Cat	Cow	Horse	Large dog	Small dog	Toy dog
	→ ti:					
1;9,11					→ ti:	
1;10,18		→ ti:				
1;11,1						gogi ←
1;11,2					gogi ←	
1;11,24			→ ti:			
1;11,25			→ hoʃ			
1;11,26				(ti:)		
1;11,27	→ puʃi					
2;0,10				→ hoʃ		
2;0,20		→ muka		gogi ←		
Vocabulary at end of period	puʃi	muka	hoʃ	(bigi) gogi	gogi	gogi
Adult equivalent	pussy	moo–cow	horse	big doggie	doggie	doggie

⟶ Indicates the introduction of a word; ⊥ Indicates that a word ceases to be used.

FIGURE 8-3. Vocables used to refer to animals (Lewis, 152, p. 216).

of the range of referents to which a child applies a particular vocable; the fact that a vocable applies to referents in which thing and context-of-action are fused can best be observed when the range of objects denoted by a name differs greatly from adult classification. In such instances, one frequently finds that the feature common to the phenomena named by the same vocable includes the manner in which the child *handles* these diverse things.

For example, Hilde Stern at 11 months used the vocable (*doll*) in referring not only to her doll but also to a small toy rabbit and a toy cat, and, as a matter of fact, to a great many more toy objects, with the definite exclusion of a little bell which she called *didelideli*. This range of referents designated by the same vocable can best be understood in terms of the way the child affectionately handled these various objects. Hilde's use of the name *pin* is another illustration. This vocable was used in reference not only to a *pin* but also to *breadcrumb, fly, caterpillar,* all in contexts of being picked up from the floor. The implicit concept defining such a "class" may be described as "something small to be picked up gingerly with the fingers." Still another example concerns the vocable *door* applied by Hilde to such diverse things as the *food tray of her high-chair, cork,* and *door.* This vocable clearly referred to "obstacle standing in her way of getting out of, or at, something." Again, the vocable *nose* was used to refer not only to *nose* but also to *handkerchief* and the *point of a shoe.* The common link was that all of these were "pullables" for the child.

These illustrations suggest that the early names do not depict stable, circumscribed things but rather refer to global events in which things and the agent's (the speaker's) action upon things are intimately fused.

In our discussion thus far of the early use of vocalization in the service of naming, we have relied exclusively on the reports of careful observers: these reports, however anecdotal and sporadic they may be, have provided sufficient basis for highlighting the manifestation of developmental principles in the ontogenesis of vocal depiction.

In contrast to the richness of diary observations, on which the foregoing discussion has been based, experimental inquiries dealing with this problem are extremely scarce. One of the very few experimental investigations—and at present probably the most important one—is that by A. R. Luria and his co-workers (159) on a pair of twins who were retarded in their speech. This study presents valuable documentation pertaining to the characteristics of early designators and to the changes which occur in designation during ontogenesis.

The subjects of Luria's study were two 5-year-old identical twin boys who, without any signs of congenital mental deficiency, showed a gross retardation in their speech behavior. The main factor leading to language retardation appears to have been their closely knit companionship, ostensibly so gratifying as to forestall any pressure towards communication with the surrounding world.

Luria's experiment involved separating the twins from one another and placing them in normal situations of communication with other children. Furthermore, one of the twins was given special training in speech. Following the experimentally induced breakdown of the socially isolated state, there occurred a relatively rapid development from speech forms characteristic of very early levels to speech forms of a genetically more advanced level.

At this point, we shall report only certain of Luria's findings pertinent to the ontogenesis of naming. Table 8-1 summarizes the overall nature of the names employed by the twins at the beginning of the experimental "socialization;" the findings, pertaining to the degree to which the names were "contextualized" or "decontextualized," are based on a representative time sample.

As is clearly indicated in Table 8-1, vocal utterances ("names") which acquired their meaning only from an immediately given, concrete context comprised somewhere between ⅝ and ¾ of the twins' speech performances. The *relative lack of spatiotemporal distance between the vehicle and referent* is clearly suggested by Luria's conclusions: "As a rule, our twins' speech acquired meaning only in a concrete-active situation. Outside this situation, a word either did not possess any kind of permanent meaning, or only indicated what they were talking about without disclosing sufficiently clearly in what sense it was being used" (159, p. 40).

The relative lack of spatiotemporal distance between vehicle and referent, that is, the embeddedness of the names in contexts-of-action, was also reflected in various play activities. It was manifested with special clarity in an experimental situation originally designed by Vygotsky. The children were given a number of everyday objects which were to be endowed with a make-believe meaning for purposes of play; thus, a penholder acquired the meaning of "papa;" a pencil, "mama;" a wooden ring, "the house;" a box, "the tramcar;" an ashtray, "the workplace," etc.

The imaginative apprehension of the objects and their new "names"

Table 8-1

Contextualized versus context-free use of words *
(Percent frequency of use)

	Twin A	Twin B
1. Names with meanings determined by concrete context		
(a) Proper names of the twins	23%	21%
(b) Other context-determined names	47%	44%
Total	70%	65%
2. Intermediate group: names of objects with more or less diffuse or unstable meaning	27%	33%
3. Words with stable conventional meaning	3%	2%

* Condensed from Luria's and Yudovich's Table III.

was easily achieved by the twins as long as this transformation took place through *manipulation* of the objects in concrete situations; when establishing the make-believe meaning of the objects through action and gesture, the children could play out the project, "papa traveled to his work in a tramcar." In contrast, a make-believe name could never be grasped and applied by the children through speech *divorced from concrete action.* Thus, a metal spoon with which the experimenter made chopping movements was recognized as "axe" and a knife with which one pretended to sweep the floor was called "brush" by the children, but the twins were unable to attach such imaginary meanings when merely *told* "this (a pen) is a knife" (159, pp. 84 f).

From our theoretical standpoint the behavior of the twins in these situations reflects the fact that the original fusion of names and concrete actions has not undergone sufficient differentiation, to a point where the name evokes an *internal dispositional schema,*[17] which can in turn instigate a novel articulation or transformation of a perceived entity.

Prior to the dissolution of social isolation, the twins also tended to use *names which were quite diffuse and equivocal in their reference,* that is, *they lacked articulateness and specificity of meaning.* This characteristic again parallels that found in the speech of much younger, normally reared children. Thus, quite analogous to the names used by young children, the referents of the twins' namings were fusions of things and contexts-of-action: for example, *amá* (from *slomal* = I broke) signified "I broke," but also was used to refer to *a painful spot, a tear,* etc.; again, *pipis* (*pit-pit* = to drink) signified *to drink, water, a cup,* and *a teapot.*[18]

Once the twins were separated and placed into situations where

---

[17] The process of internalization is discussed in later chapters.

[18] Prior to the Luria-Yudovich study, several writers had mentioned cases of twins, reared in relative linguistic isolation, who developed their own speech forms, of little communicative value to others. Jespersen, in particular, was able to observe—rather unsystematically—such a pair of twins; these 5-year-old identical twins, who had been neglected by their mother, were left almost completely to themselves. From the examples which Jespersen gives (119, p. 186), one can infer that the twins' speech showed characteristics quite similar to those observed by Luria and Yudovich. For instance, the referents of names, even proper names, were fusions of things or persons with context-of-action. Thus, Jespersen was called *py-ma, py* being their name for "smoking," "pipe," "cigar;" he got the name from the chocolate cigars which he frequently gave to them. Again "to break something" was designated *dop* (= piece); *lhal* meant "getting wet" as well as 'water;' etc.

normal social intercourse obtained, the changes that took place were as rapid as they were striking. We shall deal with various aspects of this acceleration in speech development in greater detail in later chapters. At this point we shall limit ourselves to a presentation of some of the findings pertaining to the comprehensibility of the speech of the twins, *outside of contexts-of-action*, at various periods following their entry into social communication. It should be noted that these findings are not restricted to naming per se or to simple designation; nevertheless, they highlight a phenomenon which pertains to names per se, the increase in spatiotemporal distance between vehicle and referent in the course of development.

From Table 8-2 it will be seen that the development towards decontextualization of vocal symbols progressed tremendously even during the twins' three months of separation. The table also indicates that special coaching (of twin A as against twin B) had little influence: the potent factor in the change from relatively contextualized to relatively context-free vocal symbolization seems clearly to have been the placement of the twins in a natural social habitat where each was compelled to develop and articulate his speech in order to achieve open commerce with others.

We may conclude this chapter with a note on some striking parallels from psychopathology, which may serve further to illuminate the formation of highly contextualized symbolic vehicles under conditions of extreme concretization. Of particular pertinence here is the study by Hanfmann, Rickers-Ovsiankina, and Goldstein (96) on the celebrated Case Lanuti, a patient who, as a consequence of a brain trauma, displayed a striking concretization of symbolic functioning among his many other symptoms of "primitivized" behavior.

The authors emphasize, first, that the patient's use of spoken lan-

Table 8-2

Comprehensible speech outside of context-of-action
Time sample in terms of speech units (sentences) *

	Before separation	3 months after	10 months after
Twin A	17%	89%	100%
Twin B	22%	81%	100%

* After Luria and Yudovich (159, p. 65).

guage in many everyday situations was not impaired; his ability to respond correctly both with action and word in such situations enabled him to get along well with others. In the setting of simple manual work, done with others, the patient's verbal behavior was so adequate that his supervisor judged him as capable of normal linguistic responses in general. The highly contextualized basis of the patient's behavior became clear, however, in his inability to utilize verbal symbols, even where they normally referred to concrete objects or events, when the symbols were not embedded in actual, concrete situations: "Lanuti is unable to understand any statement that does not refer to the situation at hand, unable to understand even a simple story as such. . . . His understanding and use of language is fully as much dependent on the situation as is his recognition of objects: without the situational support, words and objects alike are for him merely shifting patterns of sounds or colors. Thus the use of language as a means of operating at will with non-present or even nonexisting things is closed to the patient."

chapter 9

From Onomatopoetic to Conventional Naming: A Brief Theoretical Discussion of Vehicle-Referent Relationships

In the two preceding chapters, we discussed the ontogenesis of naming in two media of representation, the motor-gestural and the vocal-articulatory. An attempt was made to show that there is, ontogenetically, an increasing differentiation between the *external form* of the symbol (the vehicle) and the *contents* represented by that vehicle. As we noted, one of the chief manifestations of this increasing differentiation is the ever-widening distance in substance and quality between vehicle and referent.

If one assumes—as we do—that the linkage between a vehicle and its referent always entails some degree of similarity between the *inner forms* (*symbol* and *significate*) of these two moments, one must try to explicate the nature of this similarity relationship and also show how this inner analogy might be maintained despite the greatly increased distance between external forms of symbol and referent.

In the theoretical section of this book we advanced the thesis that depictive expressions are related to depicted contents by virtue of twin form-building processes, one directed toward the establishment of a referent, the other directed toward the articulation of a symbolic vehicle (sound-pattern) (see Chapter 2). It is through such *two-pronged schematization* of symbol and significate that vehicle and referent are linked to each other.

Though the schematizing activity builds and articulates the symbol and the referent as *inner forms,* it must necessarily also take into account—and interact with—the external forms and properties of both the vehicle and the referent. That means that there is a mutual interaction between schematizing activity and external forms: just as the schematizing activity articulates the external "Gestalt" of object and vehicular pattern, so do object and vehicle, in their external forms, influence the process of schematization. This *reciprocal relationship* has an important bearing on the problem of ontogenetic changes in the formation of concepts and their symbolic expression. Because vehicle and referent are both rooted in a similar underlying schematization process, any developmental modification in the referent would entail some structural change in the symbolic vehicle designating it; conversely, any change in the symbol would entail some modification in the significate (the internal organization of the referent).

In order fully to understand the nature of the developmental changes in vehicle-referent relationships, two further notions must be introduced: these are *plurisignificance of a vehicle,* that is, the use of one vocable to designate several referents ("homonymy"), and *multiformity of referential expression,* that is, the use of several vocables to designate "one" referent ("synonymy").[1] In the following we shall utilize the notions of vehicle-referent reciprocal interaction, plurisignificance of a vehicle, and multiformity of referential expression to describe what we believe occurs in the structurization of symbols when there is a change in referential connotations ("significates") and in the articulation of referents when there is a change in symbolic expression.

Turning first to the issue of *change in significate,* we maintain that the *schematizing activity* leading to this change must have been correspondingly modified, affecting not only the inner structure of the referent but also the inner structure of the verbal form. Let us, for example, consider those typical cases where the (developmental) change is one of an expansion of the range of referents—where there is an increase in the variety of events or objects designated by a common name. For instance, in the example from Gregoire, the child-like (onomatopoetic) utterance *pigne* for "nail" might be conceived as partaking in a schematizing activity which structures (among other things) the ways in which a nail is handled in the activity of hammer-

---

[1] These aspects of the process of representation are discussed in more general terms in Chapter 20, especially with regard to the studies by Cirillo (46) and Bodansky (27).

ing. The subsequent extension of the name *pigne* to such referents as "key" and "pencil" must then, we conjecture, have entailed some modification of the formative schema and hence also of the structure of the symbolic utterance that partook in the total organismic act. For example, there might have been a modification of the schematizing activity to include "fingering of a long, thin object" or the "piercing movement of an elongated object," into the initial postural-kinaesthetic organization involved in "hammering."

Again, let us take the instance quoted by Jespersen, in which a child extended the reference of *f-f-f* from "smoke" to "funnel," "chimney," "flagstaff," etc. As in the case of *pigne,* one may assume that the extension of reference entailed a modification of the schematizing process and hence the total symbol of which the vocable was the external form. For example, one might assume that a dynamic schema involving a bodily set to "blow" was reorganized so that features of "ascendingness" or "straightness" were given greater emphasis.

If one considers the considerable malleability of these child-like utterances—compared with the relatively stable adult forms—one may expect that *changes in referents* might sometimes entail not only changes in the inner form of the verbal symbol but also alterations in the external form (vehicle). Consider the example just mentioned. Assuming a shift from the dominance of the significate "blowing" to an emphasis on the significate "ascendingness," one would expect a related change in the internal organization of the total symbol in which the *f-f-f* pattern uttered by the child is embedded. Moreover, especially at such a genetically early stage, where the inner and external aspects of a total symbol are very intimately bound to each other, the internal change might quite possibly be overtly reflected in the way the name is uttered by the child.

To the present time, there have been no empirical or experimental studies of infant speech which could provide evidence that these conjectured modifications in symbol formation and vehicular patterning do, in fact, take place as a consequence of changes in reference. However, several experiments—discussed in detail in a later chapter (20)— have demonstrated such effects of referential change on symbol formation in the representations by adults in nonverbal media. In these studies, subjects were asked to represent referents by means of expressive line patterns. The spontaneous reports of the subjects indicated clearly that changes in the connotational structure of a referent (the significate) went hand in hand with a reorganization of a materially invariant and seemingly constant linear pattern ("vehicular rotation"). Such findings, although indirect and hence only suggestive, serve nevertheless to lend credence to our thesis.

Another line of indirect evidence comes from earlier experiments in which subjects were asked to apprehend word-forms belonging to German (their native language) while adopting a physiognomic attitude (see Werner, 269). Of particular pertinence were the reports of the subjects with regard to homonymous vocables: *Tor* (door) and *Tor* (fool) or *faul* (decayed) and *faul* (lazy). The statements of the subjects concerning their self-observations clearly indicated that basic differences in inner-dynamic organization and in the outer structure of the vocables occurred when these vocables, having an (objectively) identical external form, were taken to refer to quite different meanings (see Chapter 14).

From such empirical evidence of fundamental differences in the apprehension of two homonymic vocables—at least under conditions of physiognomic apprehension of word-forms—one may perhaps better understand a frequently noted peculiarity of child speech, the *plurisignificance* of many child-like utterances. Gregoire, Bloch, Leopold, Kaper, and other students of child language all agree that there is an early period during which the child utters a great many identical sound patterns for quite different referents without showing any signs of being confused by this state of affairs.

Thus, Leopold (150, p. 5) remarks on the speech of his 1-year-old daughter: "Homophony did not bother the child at all; '*mai mai*' was not an exclamation, but meant 'my money.'" Bloch (22, p. 705) states about the speech of his 2-year-old children: "It is remarkable that these homonyms create no confusion in the mind of the child." Gregoire (86, II, p. 275) makes the same remarks about the speech of his 2-year-old boys.[2]

In the light of the evidence coming from the studies on linear "naming" and on physiognomization of vocables, it seems quite reasonable to interpret the child's lack of confusion in the use of homonymous patterns as due to actual differences in the schematizing processes underlying the superficially identical verbal forms: just as *Tor* (door) and *Tor* (fool), though identical in their external form, are distinguished by adults through underlying processes of schematization, so, we maintain, must the child show an analogous organismic differentiation between homonymic vocables.

The fact that very young children are usually unaware of the hom-

---

[2] See also Kaper (128, pp. 29 ff).

onymity of names appears to be because of an undifferentiatedness (relative "lack of distance") between the inner and external forms of the symbol. Only when the vehicle as an auditory form has become sufficiently differentiated from the inner processes of symbol formation can the child become aware of the homonymity. According to Kaper (128, p. 30), children generally become aware of the possibility of confusion in the use of some homonymous vocable at about the beginning of the fourth year; as a consequence of this awareness, there gradually emerge manifestations of a *tendency towards a deliberate differentiation in external forms of the original homonyms.*

This tendency appeared rather early in Leopold's daughter: for example, at 1;11, she used *meow* as an imitation of the cat's voice; in a phonetically quite different form it became the generic term for "cat." At 1;3, *baba,* voiced, meant "Papa;" the same form, whispered, meant "byebye." At the same time, *dada,* voiced, meant "Carolyn," whereas the same name, whispered, meant "Thank you" (Leopold, 150, III, p. 152). Similarly, Kaper's son, at 3;1, observing the homonymic character of his names for a pear and his Teddy-bear (*beertje,* in Dutch) pointed to the two objects, saying: "Dit is beertje, dat is bèèrtje;" he thus attempted to distinguish between the two names by modification of the sound *e* (128, pp. 29, 31). Still another example of differentiation in vocal forms comes from Gregoire (86, II, p. 347). His son, Charles, during the second half of the third year, dropped the prefix, *ré,* in *régardez,* retained *ré* in *répander,* and pronounced *prender* (= prendre) with an *r,* ordinarily omitted in the *pr* pattern. To this, Gregoire makes the following comment: "That the child kept the prefix *ré* in one case, and the *r* in the other cannot be interpreted as occurring by chance, without a motive: the two words have escaped the confusion which would have inevitably arisen with homonyms such as **pander, *pender.*" Finally, we may mention M. Durand, who, in an article devoted to the issue of the child's tendency to differentiate homonyms by vocal means, gives an instance of a 3-year-old boy who reduplicated his own monosyllabic name to *žaža,* and thus avoided confusion with *ža* (chat = cat), his word for cat (cited by Kaper, 128, p. 33).

Since most of the examples presented above involve alteration of *phonemic form* as the means for distinguishing among homonyms, one might assume that this is the only way in which the child begins to distinguish homonyms externally, as two separate vocables. That this is not true is quite evident to those who are cognizant of the richness in intonational expressiveness characterizing child speech— in contrast with the relatively colorless, monotonous speech of adults (a striking difference rarely, if ever, discussed in the literature). Children often exploit such dynamic qualities as melodic-rhythmic modulations, variations in voice timbre, increase or decrease in pitch, stress, duration, etc., sequential shifts from sharp to soft, explosiveness, abruptness—all qualities that serve tremendously to enrich the repertoire of expressive means available for the vocal depiction of objects and events.

It seems to us that cooperation of two factors is necessary if the tendency towards the differentiation of an originally homonymous vocable is to be actualized: one factor pertains to the differences in schematizing activity where different referents (significates) are involved, the other factor to the malleability or pliability of the vocal patterns. Due to the operation of the genetic principle pertaining to *the development of specific means for specific ends,* there is a push towards the elimination of homonyms: referents, once they are differentiated by the organism, require specific vehicles: especially in situations involving increased distance between symbolizer and addressee, there is a demand for the elimination of ambiguity. But in ontogenesis, as in the evolution of languages, the shaping of new means (novel vocables) is preceded first by the attempt to use "old" forms for new functions, that is, to use aspects of the old forms which are sufficiently pliable to allow for vocal differentiation.

Having discussed the effects of changes in referents on the organization of symbolic vehicles, we may now focus on the complementary phenomenon: the effect of *changes in symbolic vehicles* on the structurization of referents. One problem is particularly pertinent here: how to account for the maintenance of a linkage between vehicle and referent as the child progresses to the use of conventional word-forms. There, clearly, the distance between vehicle and referent has become so great that one can no longer see any material similarity between the two.

Let us take the characteristic instance where the child moves from the infantile (onomatopoetic) name *boom* for "hammer" to the name *hammer* by a series of transitional steps. As already discussed, the child may for a while employ a combinatory name composed of the infantile plus the conventional word, "boom-hammer," omitting the first part later on; according to authorities on child speech, such as Stern and Meumann, the advance from baby words to conventional names through such transitory forms is quite common. The frequent occurrences of such behavior may perhaps be best understood by assuming that this combinatory naming permits the child gradually to shift the schematizing act underlying the idiomatic expression to the conventional expression.

The question that remains is how to account for such transfer of a schematizing activity from one vehicle to another when the two are so disparate in external form. This problem can be solved, we believe, by invoking the notion of a physiognomic mode of apprehension and by maintaining that a schematizing activity, once established with regard to one vehicle, possesses a sufficient degree of *malleability and pliability* to be linked to another vehicle. To be sure, conventional names are externally rather rigidly structured and possess a stable and constant form; however, in the speaking and listening person, they come alive, participating in that (internal) schematizing process through which the word-forms of the code become transformed into living speech.

Thus, when a child utters *boom* for "hammer," the auditory-kinaesthetic event is onomatopoetically portrayed in the phonemic form. When, however, the child shifts to the name *hammer,* he no longer has at his disposal the phonemes so closely linked with the features of the referent. It is our contention that, under these circumstances, he now molds the schematizing activity so that the new vocal material becomes dynamically-physiognomically organized to fit the event represented. Though this physiognomized form, in comparison with the onomatopoetic pattern, is clearly at a greater distance from the referent, it still *portrays* aspects of the referent (significates) not materially, but through the way in which it is apprehended internally by the user.

Indirect evidence suggesting that two entirely different vehicles (here the infantile and the traditional words) may partake of the same symbolic process—may form *equivalent* (synonymous) symbols by virtue of the same dynamic organization—comes from a previously mentioned study on lapse of meaning in bilinguals (cf. pp. 31 f). The study—by Jakobovits and Lambert—was concerned with the transfer effect of lapse of meaning, induced experimentally in a word of one language (*house*) on the equivalent word in the second language (*maison*). It was found that such a transfer of lapse of meaning clearly occurred in those bilinguals in whom the two languages were intimately linked as interdependent systems but did not occur in those bilinguals in whom the two languages existed as internally separate, independent systems. These findings allow us to conclude that, in the case of transfer, two semantically equivalent but externally different verbal forms possess the same connotational dynamics by virtue of their participation in an internal schematizing process common to both.

Obviously, the physiognomizing of conventional names, as postulated here, can hardly ever be observed directly in childhood. As mentioned before, however, indirect evidence is available from experiments with adults which concern the individual ways by which people shape a given vocable into a physiognomic pattern (see Chapter 14). In regard to the word "hammer," for instance, one subject had this to say: "I hear it as two equally sharp syllables which mean for me repetitiveness of hammering—its precision is given to me particularly by the incisive, short 'ha' that comes to rest on the drawn-out humming of m-m."

One may add that the differences between infantile onomatopoetic expressions and physiognomic words of conventional language widen still more when the child begins to take cognizance of the categorial nature of vocables, for example, their grammatical status, syntactic function, etc. As the study just mentioned shows, however, these formal characteristics can also be apprehended physiognomically. For instance, vocables such as *hammer* carried the physiognomy of a noun for a number of the German subjects. The ending, *er*, was then not only grammatically conceived, but was often physiognomized as "masculine" compared with the "soft," "feminine" ending, *e*, etc. (see Werner, 269, pp. 183 ff; also, Chapter 14).

Finally, it should be clear from this discussion that the "maintenance" of a (denoted) referent despite a change in name does not imply that the significate of the referent (its inner connotational structure) remains unmodified. On the contrary, the shift from onomatopoetic to conventional names is quite likely accompanied by changes in schematizing activity with concurrent changes in significates: the denoted referent may remain the same, but the connoted referent is typically modified.

We shall return again to the issues discussed in this chapter when we consider the nature of vehicle-referent relationships in nonverbal representation (see Chapter 20).

Development towards an Autonomous Linguistic Medium for Representation of States of Affairs

chapter *10*

From Early One-Unit Expressions to Early Sentences

In the preceding chapters, we have focused mainly on the designative or *naming* aspects of early representation. We have there attempted to show how "names"—both motor-gestural and vocal—become increasingly differentiated or distanced from the pragmatically organized events which they come to denote and to connote. In this and the following two chapters, we shall deal in an analogous fashion with verbal expressions subserving the *communication of messages* concerning states of affairs. We shall again seek to show how—in the course of ontogenesis—expressions that carry messages become increasingly differentiated and articulated, so that distinct aspects of an expression come specifically to represent distinct aspects of a complex state of affairs, such as the intent of the speaker, the different components of the situation, and so on.

There is no doubt that the increasing differentiation and articulation of expressions for states of affairs goes hand in hand with the increasing preeminence of the verbal-linguistic medium of representation: more and more the various aspects of situations become articulated and represented through verbal symbols. We therefore center, in this chapter, on the process by which the expressions employed by the growing child for the conveying of messages become increasingly lingual in nature: we explore the steps by which verbal symbols progressively take over functions initially carried by other—either nonsymbolic or symbolic nonverbal—means.

In this process towards the *autonomy of the linguistic medium*, we will observe the manifestation of three general developmental principles. In the progressive articulation of speech units ("vocables") out of a matrix of bodily movements and vocal-intonational patterns, with the gradual subordination of intonation and gesture to speech symbols, we shall see the manifestation of the orthogenetic principle of *"increasing differentiation and hierarchic integration."* In the use of intonation and gesture for novel functions and in the changing significance of individual vocables, as more and more speech units come into play in an utterance, we shall witness the manifestation of the genetic principle of *"shift of function."* And, in the temporary return to more primitive means of representation, such as intonation and gesture, when realizing more complex acts of mentation—a return to means already superseded in simpler acts—we shall see a manifestation of the genetic principle of *"spirality."*

For our developmental analysis of the stages in the establishment of an autonomous medium of linguistic representation, it is important to make a distinction between two major aspects of a message. One concerns the *attitudinal mode.* Various main attitudes are expressed through vocal forms: one is the attitude toward making social contact (it appears in expressions of greeting, of saying good-bye, of communicating one's affection); other attitudes are those of *wish* or *command,* of *declaration,* of *questioning,* etc. The second aspect of a message is *reference;* that is, reference to a state of affairs articulated in terms of its components, e.g., self, other, object of discourse. In the light of this distinction, we shall examine the genetic trend towards *increasing differentiation*—the progressive distinction between the *expression of attitudes of the addressor* on the one hand and *reference* on the other; furthermore, the progressive distinction and articulation of the *components of a situation or context,* such as self, other, object of discourse. The complementary trend towards *increasing integration* will be examined as it reflects itself in the progressive linguistic articulation of relationships among the components.

Our analysis of the early stages of speech will be preceded by a brief consideration of the nonlinguistic precursors of vocally articulated expressions. We shall then deal with the ontogenesis of linguistic expressions as they reflect the unfolding of articulated speech

—in external form and in content—from the earliest undifferentiated one-unit utterances to utterances comprising two, three, and more vocables. Whereas the study of such development in terms of increasing differentiation of form and content applies to all stages, it is, of course, only with utterances including more than one vocable that the development in terms of increasing integration—the forming of lingualized relational structures—can be observed.

Vocalizations Preceding Speech

Whereas, at pre-linguistic stages, the infant does not typically articulate and represent any of the three major components of a situation (self-other-object), it does appear that *attitudinal modes,* such as *demand, desire for contact, questioning,* and *quasi-declaration or assertion* do gain some expression.

The principal means used to express these attitudes at this stage is a combination of intonation and gesture. To a great extent, the intonational means are acquired and executed through the imitation of the patterns of adult speech; eventually, intonation is used spontaneously. Mary Shirley observed in the twenty-five infants she studied that such pre-linguistic expressions of attitudes typically occurred between 10 and 11 months. During that period, the infants "jabbered in 'sentences,' combining several incomprehensible 'words,' and uttering them with assertive, interrogative and exclamatory inflections. . . . Such conversational jargon was carried over into and mixed with early comprehensible speech." (228, II, p. 51)

Because of both the general lack of differentiation characterizing infantile behavior and the specific lack of articulation and control of the intonational-gestural means of representation, it is unlikely that there is an exclusive expression of any one of the principal attitudes at this pre-linguistic stage. It is more probable that the various attitudes are at this point more or less syncretically fused, with perhaps one or another of them dominant in any particular expression.

These attitudes—here considered at the stage just prior to symbolic reference—are probably foreshadowed in certain very early behaviors of the infant. Thus, the contact attitude is to some extent manifested in the smiling and early babbling activity of the child in his relations with significant adults; the demand attitude is to a degree presaged in the reaching behavior connected with call-sounds of the infant; and the attitude of quasi-declaration is adumbrated in the contemplative inspection of things and certain forms of pre-symbolic interaction of the child with the surrounding milieu, for example, placing things next to each other and throwing things.

Before the first expression of reference, therefore, there is at least some articulation of attitudes: this aspect of vocal expression remains important throughout all later development of speech. Eventually, however, the child begins to use vocal patterns not only to communicate or express attitudes but also to refer *denotatively* or *depictively* to a total situation or to one of its components. When this occurs, the child has advanced to the earliest level of articulated speech, that of the *one-vocable utterance*.

Level of One-Vocable Utterances: The "Monoreme"

Among the global expressions of the child, which consist of bodily movements and vocalizations, there emerge certain ones which, in some way, *refer* to a situation rather than being solely interjectional, that is, expressive of addressor-attitudes towards it. Such patterns, insofar as they include a discriminable, vocally articulated element ("vocable"), have usually been designated "one-word sentences." This term, however, does not seem appropriate in view of the fact that these utterances are actually neither words nor sentences: they are indeed prior to the correlative emergence of both word and sentence forms. For this reason, we shall designate these early one-unit referential patterns as "monoremes." [1]

Though theoretically monoremes are clearly distinguishable from pre-monoremic utterances by their referential nature, it is difficult, and often even impossible, to determine empirically whether a particular early vocal form is a monoreme or not. One of the main reasons underlying this difficulty is that the stable vocal elements of the earliest monoremes are often quite close in sound form to interjections, that is, they are like interjections (call-sounds, etc.) in articulation and have no relation to later, conventional, standard forms of vocal utterance.

Furthermore, addressor attitudes and reference to the context or situation are syncretically fused within a global intonational-gestural pattern. This "double fusion," that is, of attitude and reference and

---

[1] The term "monoreme" is used approximately in the sense given it by A. Gregoire (86, II, p. 178). Bean (15) mentions that A. F. Chamberlain was the first one to use this term to refer to functionally sentential utterances, consisting of one vocally articulated unit.

of vocalization and gesture, renders it difficult to determine whether, within the total pattern, the vocal form really carries reference, and hence whether the expression is monoremic. Only when it becomes relatively clear that the interjection-like vocable does function referentially can it be said that the infant has reached the monoremic level.

The distinction between expression of attitude and representation of reference is typically more marked in the declarative orientation than in either the contact or demand-wish attitudes. This is true, in part, because the attitudes of contact or wish do not, per se, require an actual reference to something, while the declarative attitude can only be said to be truly governing an expression when some indication of reference is present. In developmental terms, representation of reference is least clearly differentiated from expression of attitude in the contact attitude; such differentiation is intermediate in the wish-demand attitude, where the referent is fused on one side with the addressor's needs and on the other with the demanded or wished-for action on the part of the addressee; and it is greatest in the declarative attitude, where the object of discourse is relatively distinct from addressor needs and addressee action.

From this perspective, the very early ontogenetic changes from babbling to call-sounds to deictic and depictive "naming" may plausibly be taken as implying, on a primary level, the successive emergence of the vocal expression of *contact,* of *demand* attitudes, and finally of *declarative* orientation.

Because it is in the declarative orientation that the aspect of reference is most clearly distinct and differentiated from the aspect of attitudinal expression, one can more easily determine whether a child has reached the monoremic level when the declarative attitude is dominant than when either the contact or wish attitudes govern expressions. A lucid illustration of this point comes from Leopold's discussion of the first "word" of his daughter, Hildegard.

Leopold (150, pp. 21, 81) writes that the first "word" used by his child was a nonstandard utterance 'a! (short a with a glottal stop); this vocable derived from an emotionally laden, high-pitched interjection (in our terms, probably a "call-sound"). At 8 months, this vocable, embedded in a "questioning" intonation, appeared to be an element of a pattern expressing a syncresis of attitudes, with the declarative attitude dominant over the demand-wish attitude; the dominance of the declarative attitude was more or less clearly indicated by the presence of a deictic (pointing) gesture. At this point, one could probably not determine clearly whether the interjection-like vocable was itself a means of deictic reference. Increasingly, with age, '*a*! became more and more clearly deictic and more and more tied to a declarative attitude: thus, whereas at 9 months '*a* was used in a syncresis of demand and declarative reference to a toy which had fallen, indicating both "Look at the toy" and "I want it back," at 12 months it was used in a context clearly devoid of wish or demand, namely, calling attention to music being played in another room. Paraphrasing Leopold's comments, we may say that, although there may not yet be a clear-cut indication of a monoreme in the declarative attitude, such expressions are at least forerunners, "because they show the progressive diminution of wish and even of emotion" and also because they are apparently more or less referential.

Following this early use of nonstandard interjection-like expressions, a further development in the formation of monoremes occurs when the child adopts vocal patterns resembling adult demonstrative forms, for example, *da* or *ta*, as vehicles of reference. An analogous development occurs when the child utilizes such onomatopoetic forms as *wau-wau* and *tictoc*.

The question may arise whether, generally speaking, the earliest patterns are functionally deictic, depictive, or both; on the basis of the present evidence, no clear-cut empirical answer can be given. Theoretically, however—since representation of an object through depicting devices is a more advanced operation than indication of an object—we might expect that functionally deictic vocal patterns would, in general, precede vocal patterns functionally depictive of referents. At any rate, it is characteristic, for deictic as well as depictive monoremes, that attitudes continue to be expressed by means of intonation and gesture.

Thus, the intimate linkage of monoremic expressions with gestures of pointing may be exemplified by the following observation of Leopold (150, III, p. 159). He reports that the first pointing gesture recorded in Hildegard's diary came at 0;10, in connection with the only three "real words" used at that time: she would point at a picture with her hand, saying *peti* (pretty) or *de* (there). *De* was always accompanied by pointing with the right hand, and *peti*, as well as *bi* (picture), were also frequently linked with gestures.

In considering the monoremic stage within the ontogenesis of speech, one is struck by the length of time during which this period persists. According to Stern (242, p. 180) children remain at this level for about 6 months, and sometimes for even as long as a year. The long duration of this monoremic stage becomes understandable if one takes cognizance of the fact that a notable development occurs within this stage. First, there is a substantial increase in the *variety* of vocal forms utilized by the child in articulating various moments of the speech situation. Second, there is a considerable development as to the *nature* of the monoremes: the child begins with monoremes which, through variation of intonation, indicate that there is some degree of differentiation among attitudes but which do not yet indicate a differentiation between important elements of the situation, such as direction towards addressee and object of discourse. Eventually, the child produces monoremes in which such aspects of the situation as orientation toward an addressee and reference to an object of discourse are differentiated respectively by intonation and gesture, on one hand, and by the form of the vocable, on the other.

Furthermore, it is particularly during the later months of the monoremic stage that the child's vocal expressions seem, at least implicitly, to indicate a differentiation among various components of the situation referred to. Though, to be sure, monoremes characteristically refer to total happenings and never to precisely delimited components such as action per se or thing per se, the beginnings of such an implicit "categorization" of events through vocal expression seem to form, closely tied up with the attitude governing the expression. Thing-dominant monoremes appear, occurring most often in a quasi-declarative attitude, while activity-dominant monoremes begin to occur, most often in a request-demand attitude. This relationship is suggested in Leopold's discussion of the utterances of his 1;4-year-old daughter. Leopold found that where the dominant attitude was one of wish, there were "three interjections, no 'nouns,' five activities" represented; when the attitude governing expressions was predominantly declarative ("without wish"), there were "two interjections, ten 'nouns,' and three activities" (150, III, p. 8).

As we have noted, however, such references to things and to activities can only be expressed implicitly on the monoremic level. In order for such references to become explicit, a relationship between *two* elements has to be articulated; this, of course, can occur only when the child has entered the two-vocable stage.

Level of Two-Vocable Utterances

Words Versus Sentence

Since the ontogenetic progression in speech is from a stage of one vocable to a stage of two and more vocables, a considerable controversy has arisen concerning the genetic priority of, and the developmental relationship between, *words* and *sentences*. In earlier times, some students maintained that sentences were built up by the joining together of isolated words; more recently, the argument has been advanced that sentences come first (so-called one-word sentences) followed by the formation of words.

It seems to us that much of this controversy hinges on certain misconceptions about both the nature of the early one-unit vocables and the relation between word and sentence. The early vocables, both structurally and referentially, are neither words nor sentences. Such vocables, considered (abstractly) in their designatory function, are "names": considered in their function of carrying messages, they are "monoremes."

A name becomes a word only insofar as it fulfills a grammatical and syntactic function in an utterance, a function beyond its role as designator of something. Correspondingly, sentences are formed only when speech units become articulated into words. Hence the issue of the priority of words versus sentences turns out to be no issue at all: words and sentences are necessarily correlative in their unfolding. That is, hand in hand with the articulation of an utterance as a *sentence,* the vocables constituting the utterance become *words*.

Because there is a shift from names to words and monoremes to sentences during the two-vocable stage, this stage represents a great advance over the period of the single vocable. In terms of the formation of symbols, these shifts entail a progressive change in the nature of reference as well as in the vocal forms that depict that reference.

Although we strongly maintain the co-emergence of words and sentences, it is not feasible here to deal with the formation of both of these moments simultaneously. We shall, therefore, discuss the formation of words and sentences separately, dealing initially with the transformation of names into words and then with the transformation of monoremes into sentences.

The Beginnings of the Transformation of Early "Names" into "Words"

As we have stated, one must distinguish between the purely designatory function of vocables and the syntagmatic function of vocables. Vocables qua designators are used by the individual to refer the hearer to an event presented perceptually. Vocables qua syntagmas are used by the speaker to indicate to the hearer how he, the speaker, conceives of relations among referents.

During the monoremic stage, the vocables that are uttered by the child for the purpose of designation are to be regarded as "names" rather than "words" for the following reasons. These vocables have a global rather than circumscribed reference; there are no specific forms tied to specific classes of events; there is nothing in the form or referential character of these vocables that would indicate their fitness or use in a syntagmatic role—which alone would justify terming them "words." It is only at the two-vocable level that one observes the beginnings of a transformation, at least in the referential, if not the formal, nature of the vocables, that warrants talking about "words."

The process of transforming primitive designatory vocables into words is a gradual one, which persists for quite a long time in ontogenesis: this is because a vocable becomes more and more a word as its role in a sentential utterance is delimited and defined with regard to the roles of other vocables participating in complex expressions. Accordingly, the formation of words entails a change in reference as well as in formal structure: on the one side, there must be a differentiation, specification, and categorization of reference; on the other side there must be a correlative external shaping of the vocal material toward the expression and articulation of this differentiation in reference.

In contrast to the monoremic utterances, two-vocable expressions permit certain early manifestations of three principal kinds of differentiation: one kind of differentiation pertains to attitude (demand, declaration, etc.); a second kind pertains to the distinction between attitude and referents; and the third pertains to the distinction among referents as components of the context. In the following we shall dwell only briefly on the differentiation of the first two kinds, involving attitudinal expressions; our main concern will be in regard to differentiated linguistic representation of referents.

Intonation, the primordial means for the expression of attitudes, is of course operative on the two-vocable as it is on the one-vocable level. In contradistinction, however, to monoremic utterances, which can at best carry only one attitude at a time—and which, furthermore, typically entail a fusion of attitude and referent—at the two-vocable level, there is the possibility of various kinds of differentiations involving attitude. For instance, with two vocables there is the possibility of intonational patterning, that is, different patterns of intonation with each of the two vocables; thus, one vocable may intonationally express contact predominantly (calling attention) while the other vocable may intonationally express a demand for action or object.

Intonation, however, is not the only means on the two-vocable level for the expression of attitudes: the vocables themselves may be used to designate, rather than to intone, attitudes. This points to a difference in the way in which vocables are utilized for the differentiation of attitudes at different levels. As mentioned before, on the monoremic level the observer can sometimes infer the attitude governing the utterance from the kind of vocable used, for example, interjections often indicate demand attitudes, noun-like forms indicate declarative attitudes, etc.; in general, however, it is much less through vocables than through context and intonation that generic attitudes are expressed on the monoremic level. With two vocables, the child has the possibility not only of articulating an attitude by vocal patterns but also of differentiating vocally between attitude and referent.

Thus, at the monoremic level, a vocable referring to "milk" may be uttered in a context in which either the demand attitude or the declarative attitude is predominant; here, intonation, gesture, and context provide the main clues for determining which attitude governs the utterance. On the two-unit level, however, if "milk" is combined on one hand with "please" and on the other hand with a vocable equivalent to "look," the difference between a predominantly imperative utterance and a predominantly declarative-informational utterance is, to a considerable extent, carried linguistically.

Thus far, we have restricted our discussion on the differentiation of attitudinal expression to a rather general analysis. Because of the intimate linkage of attitude and reference, some further discussion on the articulation of attitudes will be included in the following analysis of the linguistic differentiation of referents.

As mentioned before, the period of two-vocable utterance ushers in the possibility of linguistic representation of different aspects of a situation: the child may now refer in one two-vocable utterance to an addressee and to an object, an addressee and an activity, an activity and an object, an object and an attribute, etc.; he may also linguistically express an attitude towards the situation (e.g., demand) with one vocable and refer to some aspect of the situation with the other. Although two-unit utterances allow such possibilities of differentiation between referents or between attitude and reference, one finds that such possibilities are, in general, realized only at later stages of two-vocable utterances.

As one will recall, the increasing differentiation of reference via vocables has already been discussed once before, namely in the section on the development of representation through the vocal medium (see Chapter 8, pp. 114 ff). There, differentiation of reference was discussed mainly in terms of the child's need to depict a variety of referents. In the present analysis, the basic concern is with differentiation that comes about when the child begins to represent a single, complex happening by multiple reference: in other words, differentiation is discussed here in terms of the growing need of the child to articulate referents *as related to each other* within given contexts.

The general nature of this tendency towards differentiation of referents within a unitary situation will perhaps best be understood if one reconsiders the nature of primordial names, viz., their globality or lack of circumscribed reference on one hand, and their vagueness, indefiniteness, and lack of specific reference on the other. The process of differentiation we shall consider here, therefore, pertains to two closely related phenomena: one, the increasing *delimitation of referents;* and two, the increasing *specificity of referents.*

Turning first to the aspect of *delimitation*—which can only be distinguished theoretically from the process of *specification*—one will recall that many of the early vocables are evoked by total happenings and are expressive not only of reference to an event external to the child, but also reflect the child's attitudes, states, reactions, etc. They are, in effect, *predicates of the situation.* Such expressions as *mm* or *mammam,* for an eating-situation or *boom* for closing or falling situations are illustrations of such undifferentiated vocables.

When the child advances beyond the monoremic stage and begins to refer to the situation, by adding another vocable which emphasizes an aspect originally embedded in the monoremic expression, the original monoremic vocable almost inevitably becomes restricted in its reference. Of course, there is *mutual* restriction when two primordial vocables, which are overlapping in reference, are joined together: in such cases, the bringing together of the two vocables may serve to *polarize* features of reference that are distinctive to each.

To illustrate, in one of Gregoire's children *bum* first referred, in an undifferentiated manner, to situations in which there were loud, abrupt sounds as pervasive features. Later this vocable served to refer to situations of door-closing or door-being-closed; in such situations, it could be used alternately with *popot* (porte, door). At the two-vocable level, *bum* was joined to *popot* in the form *bum-popot.* In this joining with *popot, bum* became more sharply removed from the door aspect of the situation and more delimited in its reference to the banging sound. These distinctive referents—as will be discussed—subsequently become fixed and stabilized when each of the two vocables is combined with other forms, for example, *bum-sonnette* or *ouvrez-porte*. (86, II, p. 191)

In sum, one of the most common conditions for the delimitation of global reference of primordial vocables is the emergence of terms that take over the designation of some aspect of that global reference. This process is clearly exemplified in certain utterances of Leopold's daughter, Hildegard, from the age of 1 year to 1 year, 10 months (150, I, p. 97). At 1;0, Hildegard used the interjection *m* to designate global happenings in the sphere of eating activity. At 1;8 *m* was joined to *Frau* (*Frau-m*) to signify a woman (in a picture) engaged in eating. *m* also became connected with food names such as one designating "cake," etc. At 1;10, "eat" became part of the child's vocabulary and was joined to various vocables. For a time then, *m* continued to be used for a delimited aspect of the total eating situation, that is, good taste of food, while "eat" was used to refer to the activity of eating. This increasing delimitation of the reference of the vocable *m* is represented diagrammatically in Table 10-1.

We may now turn to the second aspect of differentiation of reference at the two-vocable level, *specification*. As we have already pointed out, delimitation and specification are so closely intertwined that they can only be theoretically separated. Therefore, the examples of delimitation mentioned can just as well be taken as illustrations of specification, that is, of the ontogenetic change from vocables having a vague, over-inclusive referent to vocables having a definite, more clearly specified referent. In one important respect, however, the ontogenetic trend toward specificity of reference warrants some further discussion, namely in regard to the particular significance of

Table 10-1
Delimitation of reference of m in Leopold's daughter, Hildegard

(Compiled from Leopold's data)

Utterances	Referent of *m*
1;0 *m* used monoremically	eating—tasting good—food
1;8 *Wau* (*Frau*)—*m*	eating—food
1;9 *gek* (*cake*)—*m*	eating—tasting good
gaga (*cracker*)—*m*	
1;10 *it* (eat).....	
m..........	tasting good

this trend for the formation of "words" as designators of "categorized" experience and thus for the formation of sentences articulated through such words.

There is probably no language which does not, in some way, categorize experience through certain formal means. In an Indo-European language, such as English, the general difference between a noun as a "thing word," a verb as an "action word," etc., is clearly expressed grammatically and syntactically. Long before the child masters the linguistic distinctions of such categories in his expressions of complex reference, he advances through a series of steps that only gradually culminate in the formation of nouns, verbs, etc.

Following the monoremic level, at which only total events are designated, the child progresses, at the two-vocable level, through various stages towards a relatively clear distinction between *reference to thing* and *reference to dynamic state of thing*.

This direction towards categorization—related to operations of generalization, etc.—may seem, superficially, to be antagonistic to the child's tendency towards delimitation and specification of reference. It has, indeed, often been asserted that the child, in his speech development, shows two "opposing" tendencies: on one hand, he *limits* the range of application of his vocables; on the other hand, he *extends* the range of application of his vocables. A closer analysis, however, reveals that these two tendencies are not in opposition to each other but are, rather, correlative aspects of the general developmental trend towards increasing differentiation of reference.

This bi-directional tendency becomes particularly manifest in the differentiation of *things* versus *actions*. Thus, when the child, through two vocables, begins to articulate and specify two spheres within a global field of reference—one sphere pertaining to object the other to dynamic state (movement, action)—such specification carries with it an underlying, implicit notion of two classes of phenomena: things versus actions.

The progression towards this categorization, of such great importance in setting the stage for the linguistic articulation of noun-verb relationships, may be illustrated by some of Leopold's observations.[2] These observations pertain to the articulation of reference to a situation involving vehicles-in-motion which the child enjoys watching or being within. At 1;0, Hildegard, used *sh* as the event-designator for all such situations. At 1;5, *auto* emerged, more or less representing the object-in-motion. At 1;7, such terms as *bai-bai, choo-choo, hai-*

---

[2] Leopold (150, I, p. 121; III, p. 150).

hai came in to accentuate motion, such as moving or riding. These forms were still very close to designators of total events and yet were used to refer to situations where the focus was now primarily on the thing, now primarily on the action or movement. For instance, Hildegard at one time referred to the car-in-motion as *choo-choo-train* and yet, a little later, juxtaposed *auto* with *choo-choo,* where *choo-choo* involved much more emphasis on the movement as distinct from the vehicle (thing).

From this point on, between 1;8 and 1;10, the infantile names for riding and moving (*hai-hai* and *choo-choo*) came more and more to refer specifically to action, correlative with the increasing definiteness of thing-reference carried by the joint vocable (e.g., *auto*). An important factor, contributing to and reinforcing the establishment of a relative independence of action versus thing, is the *combination* of the name for action with names for other objects and the *combination* of the name for the object with names for other actions. Thus, at 1;10, Hildegard combined *hai* with vocables other than *train* and *auto,* saying for example, *hai-baba-nik* (I want to ride on papa's neck). Leopold remarks that from then on *hai* functioned definitely as a verb (150, I, p. 85).

In concluding our discussion on the designatory function of vocables at the two-vocable stage, we may briefly summarize the principal advances made during this period of speech development: in general, situations become articulated vocally in terms of multiple reference made possible through joint designators. In particular, the global reference of monoremic vocables is superseded by combined designations which, in relation to each other, are subjected to delimitation and specification; at the same time, however, the child becomes directed toward the articulation of situations in terms of basic general features, which lead to a change in function of the vocables from mere designators of distinctive concrete events to designators that implicitly include categorial distinctions such as *thing* versus *action.*

To be sure, this development from vocables as concrete "names" to vocables as "words" carrying full categorial significance is only begun at the two-vocable level; it cannot be fully realized and consummated before true grammatical and syntactical formants and notions become available as concomitants of sentential structuring. The emergence of such "categorial names" (as one may call them) at the two-vocable level might well be considered as a preparatory stage, necessary for the full-fledged articulation of experience via "words" as constituents of sentences.

The Beginnings of Sentence-Formation: Integration of Referents

As remarked in the introduction to this section, the gradual transformation of vocables from their merely *designatory* function as "names" to their specific and *categorial* function as "words" is correlative with the integrative trend toward the structuring of sentences. Only if vocables have become fit to serve syntagmatically, that is, only if "words" are available, can one fully articulate and construct sentences. Until now, we have dealt with the developmental trend from names to words in terms of *differentiation;* here, our concern is with the correlative trend, namely, with the development from monoremic expressions to sentences in terms of *integration.* In a discussion on sentential integration one should distinguish between two aspects: "referential" integration, which pertains to the relations between referents, and "vehicular" integration, which pertains to the external (vocal) expressions of such relationships. For convenience, these two aspects will be treated separately.

Turning first to the problem of *referential integration* at the two-vocable level we may start out by quoting the conclusions which the Sterns (242, p. 199) have drawn from a survey of the earliest two-vocable utterances recorded in various diaries, including their own: "In the earliest periods forms prevail, in which one member of a two-vocable utterance is either a vocative (e.g., *Mama*) or a deictic interjection (for example, *da*) whereas the other member represents the essential center of reference (the object of discourse)."

At this early stage, then, there are frequently two vocables, one deictic-vocative, the second depictive. The vocative is predominantly oriented toward the addressee but still implies some orientation toward the object; the depictive vocable, though more oriented towards the object, still includes the addressee to some extent. At this point, therefore, neither of the vocables seems to be clearly employed for exclusive reference to one as against the other of two components of the situation. At a somewhat later period, one of the vocables becomes more clearly a reference to one part of the situation, the addressee, and the second comes to refer to the other part, the object of discourse. This changing character of early two-vocable reference is well illustrated in those two diaries, which contain probably the most continuous and detailed observations of infant language behavior relevant to this stage, viz., the observations of the Scupins on their son, Bubi, and the observations of the Sterns on their daughter, Hilde. (See Table 10-2, *A* and *B*.)

Table 10-2
Earliest two-vocable and three-vocable utterances

A. Bubi Scupin

Age (months)	Utterance	Meaning	Comment
12	da-bu	'da' Bubi	Holding a piece of cloth in front of his face and then removing it.
13	da-digda	'da' clock	Pointing to clock.
13½	da-ball	'da' ball	During ball play.
14	da-tickta	'da' watch	Points to watch, utters da-tickta, and then puts finger on ear.
14;4	aff-u	auf! zu! (open! close!)	During opening and closing of cupboard door.
15	da-ssss	'da' fly	
	da-paap		'da' parrot.
	da-ba		'da' lamp (ba represents blowing noise).
15⅓	ba-ssss	gone! fly	
15⅓	da-mam-bah	'da' biscuit gone!	3-word sentence
17⅓	papa-auf-nini	papa open (the door so that I can) snuggle up in blanket	3-word sentence
17⅓	da-mon-ba	'da' moon lit up (ba = blowing noise)	
17½	putü-titi	chick twitters	
17⅔	hoach! titi!	hear! twitters	At hearing a rooster in the yard.
17⅔ (an hour later)	papaap titi!	bird twitters	After being brought to the window, without hearing the rooster; talking from *memory*.
18;0	hoach! rrrr	hear! rrrr	Said at hearing the alarm clock.
18;0	bah, papaap	gone bird	Surprised at not seeing the bird, while standing in the zoo, looking at bare cage.
19⅓	mann dach bah	(The) man (on the) roof (is) gone	Refers regrettably to the departure of the roofer he saw working before.
19¾	wau wau nini	dog lies-on-blanket	'nini' previously only used in regard to himself.
	wau wau beiss	dog bites	Looking at dog.
	au beiss	I am hurt! bitten!	Playfully uttered.
	mils eiss	milk (is) hot	(H)eiss used also in regard to stove.
20	tatta kugl lugl	Martha reads	

B. Hilde Stern

Age (months)	Utterance	Meaning	Comment
17½	da-is brrbrr	there-is horse	Pointing at picture.
	da-is wauwau	there-is dog	Pointing at picture.
	dada-papa	there-is papa	Pointing at bust.
19	alle-alle milk	gone-gone milk	"gone" also gesturally expressed by stretching both arms outward, palms up.
	alle papa	gone papa	
21	papa stuhl	papa (sit on) chair!	
	mama hute	mama (put on) hat!	
	pickel pickel hol	napkin bring!	
	anzieh ahm	put (sleeve back) (on) arm	(Sleeve was rolled up)
	kind kalt	baby (is) cold	
	muh is put	cow (is) 'caputt'	Points at torn picture.

Glancing over these diary observations, one is impressed by certain subtle, yet characteristic, shifts which are apparent when one compares the two-vocable utterances of a later age with those which occur at an earlier period. Whereas in the early utterances the referents of the two vocables are not greatly differentiated, in the later utterances there is less overlap in reference, that is, different components of the situation are more or less explicitly represented by each of the vocables.

For instance, in *da-digda,* both *da* (there) and *digda* (clock) refer to the total situation of the sounding clock; in *putü-titi,* however, the first unit refers predominantly to the bird and the second to the sound the bird makes. Thus the two elements of the first utterance refer to the same presented event and, therefore, with regard to reference, the total expression is actually not very far removed from a monoreme. On the other hand, the two elements of the second two-unit utterance emphasize relatively different features of the presented event. Examples of this sort suggest that what appears on the surface to be a unitary stage in the development of linguistic representation may actually turn out to comprise a number of distinct steps in the ontogenesis of speech.

Let us briefly consider the possibility of such a series of steps. If one takes, as one extreme of the two-vocable stage, those utterances in which there is one deictic and one depictive form, each referring to the same global event, and at the other extreme, those utterances in which each vocable represents distinct and nonoverlapping referents, then one may at least theoretically assume that there are, inserted between these two extremes, a number of intermediate two-vocable utterances varying in the degree of distinct reference of each of the two forms.

In such utterances as *da-digda* and *dais-brrbrr,* in which both the deictic and the depictive vocable appear to be directed towards the same, relatively undifferentiated happening, there is, of course, the least degree of differentiation with respect to reference: these two-vocable forms, so close to monoremic expression, we shall designate as *"duoremes."* In such duoremic forms, *integration* is very concretely assured through the referential *overlap* of the two vocables.

In such an expression as *putü-titi,* used by Bubi Scupin at 17½ months, there is some degree of differentiation of reference, but the component vocables still seem to be holophrastic in character and there still seems to be some overlap of reference. Within the global referent *putü* does seem to refer predominantly—but not exclusively —to the chicken that makes the noise: chicken (twitters), and *titi* seems to refer predominantly—but again not exclusively—to the noise made by the chicken: (chicken) twitters. In other words, each vocable seems to refer to the same global event, but each has a different focus. In instances of this kind, the two aspects of the global event are linked to each other by way of the overlapping holophrastic reference of each.

Similar examples of such intermediate forms of two-vocable utterance—forms in which there is an overlapping in reference—may be found in Gregoire's comprehensive study of the speech development of his two sons. For instance, consider these two utterances of Charles Gregoire, at about 2 years: *bum, popot* (boom, porte = door), *gigi-pum* (lit = bed, boom). The first utterance was made in the context of a door closing, and the second was made in the situation of the child falling out of bed. In the first utterance, *popot* seemed to have a relatively more circumscribed reference than *bum*—*popot* referring more or less to "door," while *bum* expressed the total happening of "something banging shut;" it would be erroneous to take the child as asserting something like "the door closes;" the reference was more like "door–lots of noise–banging." In the second utterance, again, one cannot legitimately formulate the reference as "bed—I fell out of it;" rather, the reference would be more like "out of bed–plump!" We are confident that the interpretation of overlapping reference in such two-vocable utterances is not an arbitrary one imposed by us upon the material; Gregoire, himself, comments on the "pleonastic," that is, semantically overlapping, character of the two units in such utterances. (Gregoire, 86, I, p. 184; II, p. 191)

A still more marked degree of differentiation of the referents at the two-vocable level occurs when the child brings together, into one utterance, vocables referring to phenomena which are not intrinsically, that is, characteristically, overlapping with each other. Into this class of utterances fall expressions which typically appear with greater frequency during the later months in the diary samples cited from B. Scupin and H. Stern, for example, *wau-wau beiss, mils eiss, kind-kalt*. These expressions closely resemble true simple sentences composed of intrinsically independent units.

These hypothesized steps of increasing differentiation of reference on the two-vocable level may be presented diagrammatically as follows (Fig. 10-1).

This diagrammatic presentation may also serve to indicate significant shifts in the modes of *integration* of the referents—integration that must be assumed to occur on the two-vocable level, since the process of differentiation tends to sunder the referents. Of course,

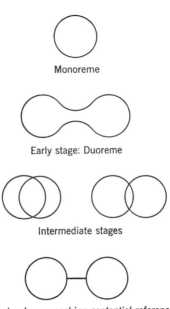

Monoreme

Early stage: Duoreme

Intermediate stages

Stage closely approaching sentential reference

**FIGURE 10-1. Diagrammatic sketch of increasing differentiation of refer-
ents on the two-vocable level.**

as long as there is a considerable overlap in the reference of two
holophrastic vocables, the referents are linked together by virtue of
their participation in, or equivalence to, one global and concretely
given situation. With further advance, however, that is, as the holophrastic terms become delimited and specific in their reference, the
nature of the integration must shift correlatively. The two referents
can no longer be linked through their "equivalence" or their mutual
overlapping; they must, therefore, be linked through some *intrinsic
relationship,* e.g., one referent is thing-like and the other is a movement of the thing or something that happens to the thing. One will
note how a shift in the *content* designated by the two vocables is correlative with a shift in the *nature of the integration:* that is, how a
shift from global overlapping referents to circumscribed referents,
from contextual names to "primordial words," entails a shift towards
sentential relationships.

We may designate vocables that have a circumscribed referent and
a quasi-categorial status "primordial words," because they have a
syntagmatic function and yet lack those morphological features which

express the specific relationships they would have to each other within a full-fledged sentence. For example, Hildegard Leopold, at 1;10, used the monoreme *dash* (dress) in situations having something to do with clothes being put on her. A little later on, *dash* more specifically connoted "dress me," without any explicit reference to the person; at 1;11, the little girl said *dash-me,* the reference to herself now becoming explicit. At this point, the reference of *dash* to dressing became more or less severed from reference to herself, and this "primordial word" was now open to combination with other noun-like forms (e.g., *doll*) within a primordial sentence (150, I, p. 70).

Another impressive illustration showing the correlative interdependence of primordial word- and sentence-formation comes from P. Guillaume (88). Guillaume's 2-year-old child at one point was able to understand the request *brosse-mama!* (brush-mama) and *brosse-papa!* (brush-father), but not *brosse-chapeau!* (brush-hat). Guillaume attributes the child's inability to understand the latter combination to the fact that *chapeau* was still used by the child as a monoreme, expressing "putting on a hat;" hence, it could not simply refer to an object which, among other things, can be brushed; only later on, when *chapeau* acquired a *noun*-like character would it as a primordial word be capable of entering into a sentence structure of the type *brosse-chapeau.*

Up to this point, we have discussed integration at the two-vocable level in terms of the referents. Our analysis of the development of sentence formation cannot, of course, stop here: the question immediately arises as to how the linkage between the two vocables becomes externalized and communicated: what marks a two-vocable utterance as a primordial sentence?

This question bears directly upon the issue of the *establishment of an autonomous medium;* it also leads us once again to the notion of the increasing distance between symbol and referent, reflected in the genetic shifts in the nature of *the vehicular means of expressing integration.*

The problem of integration naturally does not arise with monoremic utterances: in such utterances, there is a primordial unity in outward expression as there is in reference. As one will recall, this unity is not ruptured, even where some differentiation of reference occurs: the intonational features of the monoreme may be expressive of the attitude of the speaker or be directed towards the addressee, and the articulated vocal features may represent the object or event.

At the two-vocable level, however, and with increasing differentiation between referents, some means must be exploited to relate or integrate the vocables so that they constitute a unified expression; only in this way is it possible to depict relationships between referents within a representational medium such as speech.

Probably the most important early means for achieving such integration of vocables is *intonation*. As stated, intonation, on the pre-referential and the monoremic levels, is symptomatic of affective and conative states of the child vis-à-vis events in the environment; this feature of intonation remains dominant during the early stages of two-vocable utterance. Progressively, however, intonation undergoes a *shift from a designatory to a syntagmatic function;* that is, more and more, intonation subserves the integration of vocables in the formation of primordial types of sentences.

In examining the transition from intonation as expressive of affective-conative states to intonation functioning primarily as a distinct means for the integration of vocables in sentence-like forms, it is possible to distinguish several developmental stages.

Werner Leopold is probably the only major student of child language who has specifically pointed out the importance of intonation in the ontogenesis of speech, and his writings present some evidence that the development from early (paratactic) structures to later (hypotactic) structures initially takes place via the medium of intonation. There seems to be a characteristic progression in accent from *"level stress,"* that is, a pattern of the same intonation in both vocables, to *"uneven stress,"* expressed through differences in intensity, pitch, and/or duration; with "level stress," there is typically a brief pause between the two vocables, and with "uneven stress," the pause tends to disappear. Such developmental changes in stress or accent patterning is indicated diagrammatically in Fig. 10-2.

It may be pointed out that the progression from a pattern of even stress to one of uneven stress conforms to the orthogenetic principle of increasing differentiation and hierarchic integration: generally, in ontogenesis, one finds a shift from a primitive synthesis of homogeneous elements to a higher synthesis of heterogeneous elements. Genetic changes, analogous to the one discussed here with respect to intonational patterning, are found in the patterning of melodies, motor rhythms, and many other activities. (See Werner, 274, p. 124.)

In this context, one should especially emphasize the fact—frequently overlooked—that the side-by-side placement of "monotonous" elements does not reflect a lack of synthesis but is actually a very early manifestation of attempts at synthesis. A primordial bond between the elements is established

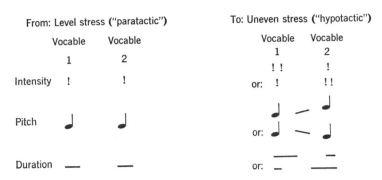

FIGURE 10-2. Developmental changes in intonational patterning of two-vocable utterances (schematic presentation).

through a similarity of some of the properties of the elements such as sameness or similarity of accent. One should also stress the fact that the *brief pause* typically inserted between the two elements is not merely an empty gap but an intrinsic part of the whole rhythmic pattern.

In turning now to some illustrations of these trends in *intonational integration,* one should be cognizant of the fact that there are certain general differences in intonational patterning, depending upon the *attitude* governing the utterance, that is, whether the utterance expresses wish or demand or is of a declarative-assertive nature, etc. Accordingly, we shall present illustrations of intonational patterning for utterances under, first, the demand-wish attitude and, second, under a declarative orientation. These illustrations come from Werner Leopold's acute observations of his daughter Hildegard.

As to Hildegard's two-vocable expressions of *wish* or *demand,* most of them, up to about the age of 1;8, seemed to be "paratactic," that is, each vocable carried the typical inflection of demand without any difference in the intonation between both. Schematically, the most typical form was ! ! . To illustrate, at 1;8, Leopold's child used such expressions as *Come on! Papa!* and *open! door!,* in which both vocables apparently were given the same kind of stress. With regard to an expression at 1;9, *Bau! Haus!* (Build! House!), Leopold remarks (150, III, p. 24) that there was still a level stress, indicating a juxtaposition of two (overlapping) monoremes, that is, a paratactic construction, rather than the integration of the two vocables within a single imperative sentence structure. Expressions of this sort preceded and finally led to integrated imperative sentence structures around 1;11

e.g., *Ring bell!*, *Spiel* (= play) *Haus!*, *Spiel Piano!*, all announcing the child's desire or intention; thus, at this age, as Leopold (150, III, p. 25) states: "the combination of verb and object into one (hypotactic) stress-group was achieved." A particularly clear manifestation of the attainment of intonational integration in imperative expressions was Hildegard's utterance *Dress me!*, in which the *me* was given a very strong, main stress while *dress* was given a secondary stress; this utterance occurred also at about 1;11 (150, III, p. 23).

Compared with imperative utterances, the development towards intonational integration of *'declarative-assertive'* utterances seems to be of a somewhat more complex character. This is partly due to the fact that early expressions involving a 'declarative' attitude are never pure, "sober" declaration but are syncretic fusions of affective states and assertions: there is joyous declaration, surprised assertion, doubtful declaration, etc. Even at the two-vocable level, therefore, intonation in so-called declarative utterances still functions, initially, more in the service of emotional expression than as a means for integrating the two elements. At this initial stage of the two-vocable level, intonation has no syntactic function, whether the two vocables carry the same or different intonations.

In the process towards intonational integration a number of intermediate steps occur, in which intonation appears partly to be exploited as an integrational device, but in which it is still to a marked degree affective-conative in character. For example, in an utterance like *Mama-sh!* (Mama-sleep!), formed by Hildegard at 1;6 the intonational patterning seemed to be of a *question-answer* character, which may be schematically translated into: Mama (sleeping)?–(Mama) sleeping!. It will be noted that each of the vocables (differing in intonation) appears to be, to a great extent, monoremic and overlapping in reference—the first unit emphasizing primarily the agent, the second emphasizing the action (150, III, p. 28).

When intonational integration in a true, formal, sense occurs, it is first manifested through a *"level-stress"* pattern, that is, the same intonation for both vocables. As already indicated, however, the level stress here must be distinguished from any prior emotional pattern of stress, since intonation is no longer functioning primarily as a carrier of affect and wish. An example of such level stress in a "declarative" statement is Hildegard's utterance, at 1;8: *Dada wascht* (= Carolyn-washing) (150, III, p. 28).

At a still later stage, a "hypotactical" form of intonational integration is achieved, through an *uneven stress* on the two vocables: the vocables represent distinct and relatively circumscribed referents, and the pattern of intonation clearly resembles declarative statements of adults. For example, Hildegard Leopold, at 1;11, in pointing to the door, exclaimed: *this zu* (= this, the door, is shut), with the first vocable enunciated with high pitch, the second with low pitch (150, III, p. 29).

At higher levels, beyond the two-vocable stage, intonation is still retained and further developed as an important means of integration. At the same time, however, entirely novel means of integration emerge: that is, morphological and other structural means come into play which indicate the syntactic role of each vocable within a complex structure. Through such means the various vocables become differentiated from each other as to their function in the total expression; reciprocally, they become integrated with each other in such a way that the manner in which the speaker conceives a complex relationship is externalized and communicable in a relatively unambiguous way to the hearer. Since the role of each vocable in a sentence utterance is defined in terms of every other vocable, the specific morphological modifications in any vocable will be dependent on how the other vocables are morphologically handled. This distinctness and yet interdependence of the morphological modifications of all the vocables clearly determines in a direct way the level of integration of the sentence structure.

Thus the vocable becomes more a word the more it partakes in a specific (syntactic) structure designed for complex referential expression. Correlatively, the complex referential expression becomes more and more a sentence as its constituent vocables are modulated to reflect their distinct (grammatical-categorial) roles in the total structure.

Some Remarks on Developmental Antecedents of the Morphological Modification of Vocables

At this point, it seems appropriate to add a few paragraphs on some of the steps that lead to the child's understanding and use of morphological features as a means of sentential articulation and integration.

On purely a priori grounds, one would expect that such steps would occur in a certain sequence: the child would first come to understand that sound-patterns are modifiable, that is, that they can be varied without losing their basic identity. Secondly, he would grasp that such external modifications can serve to express qualifications of the referent. Thirdly, he would apprehend that modifications are systematic, that is, that certain kinds of modifications occur, given certain characteristics ("grammatical categories") and relational positions ("syntactic features") of the referents. In other words, one would expect first a nonreferential play with the forms of vocables (ludic handling), then a modification of vocables to express certain characteristics of the referent (referential qualification), and finally a modification of vocables in the service of sentential integration (syntactic handling).

With regard to the *ludic modification* of vocable forms, practically every student of child language has mentioned this phenomenon. Gregoire, for instance, remarks that the play with words became a favorite pastime of his children around the age of two years; for example, *compote* was jokingly changed to *compette, grain* to *giyiyigain,* and so on (Gregoire, 86, II, pp. 65 f). The Sterns, interestingly enough, point out that around the end of the second year, when their daughter's flexionless epoch of speech reached its end, playful modification of words became very frequent (242, p. 31).

As to the second kind of pre-syntagmatic modification, which pertains to the *qualification of referents,* there are some indications reported in the literature which suggest that long before the child grasps the role of form-changes as grammatical devices, he grasps the fact that forms of vocables may be modified to express some qualification of, or affective reaction to, an event. Thus, as is well known, modifications related to affect occur as reduplication of the vocables, changes in intonation (stress), etc.

Repetition of a vocable has often been observed as a means of emphasis in requesting an object. Thus Bloch notes that his daughter Francoise, at 2;0, when she first wished to be picked up by her father, said *we* (viens); when she was not immediately picked up, she cried *we-we-we.* Another time, in the same situation, she used *ba* (bras). When this did not have an immediate effect, she said *ba-ba!* In these instances, it is clear that reduplication of the vocable was a means of intensification or insistence: "In the ordinary usage of Francoise," Bloch remarks (22, p. 699), "monosyllables such as *balle, sac, sucre,* etc., are the most often reduplicated; she uses them also in monosyllabic form, but when she wishes to have one of these objects, it is most often the disyllabic form which appears, the other marking calm assertion."

Changes in quantity or quality of sounds are another form of modification employed to express affective variations with regard to the referent. Gregoire (86, II, p. 255), for instance, notes that his son, Charles, from the beginning of his third year, deliberately modified the names of persons to indicate affection. Thus at 2;7, he changed *papa* to *papal* and *papap*, the ending having an affective value. At 2;9, he used an internal vowel change, *poupa*, the change reflecting something like "dear little." *Pou* subsequently became a "caressing prefix" for calling other persons, for example, *pou-fere* (petit-frère = dear little brother). Modifications of this sort came rather close to some of the modifying means employed systematically in conventional language.

As to precursors of *systematic modification,* various investigators have reported on certain peculiarities in the young child's handling of verbal material which seem to relate to early systematization tendencies. We refer here to the trend, noted by Stern, Gregoire, Bloch, and others, that children may prefix a common sound or sound complex to words, or may add a common suffix to words, etc. Thus Bloch notes that his daughter, Jacqueline, at 1;11, after using some vocables with a final 't' sound, began to say *papat* instead of *papa, tatat* instead of *caca, patet* instead of *parterre, feut* instead of *f(l)eur;* at 2;0, on the model of the terminal ending of *soupe,* she added the final explosive, *p,* to many vocables, such as *lop* (l'autre), *kokop* (coco-egg), *bap* (boite), etc.; at 2;1, using the initial sound of "ici" as a model, she began to say *isha* (sac), *ishe* (chaise), *isou* (sou), *iba* (bras), etc. Similarly, Bloch's other daughter, Francoise, at 2;0 prefixed an *a* sound to so many vocables that her brother, Raymond, remarked one day that "Francoise puts *a* everywhere" (22, p. 699). Similarly, around 2;4, Gunther Stern started most words with an 'h' ('ch'), substituting it for the conventional initial sounds: for example, *heuer* (for 'Feuer'), *chein* (for 'fein'), *heck* (for 'Schreck'), etc. (242, p. 95).

These peculiarities of speech behavior of the young child are of considerable significance, for they presage a stage of speech development during which the child begins to grasp the functions of morphological features. When one now looks for sure indications that this stage has been reached, one finds them in the creative though unorthodox handling of speech-forms rather than in the occasionally correct use of word-forms. From the mere fact, for instance, that a child in a particular circumstance takes over several expressions of the adult language involving morphological variation, such as "Father eats," "we eat," etc., one cannot infer with certainty that the child has really grasped the function of the morphological features in utterance; the behavior may simply be an instance of imitative learning. Thus, as the Sterns rightly observe (242, p. 37), when Hilde used the vocable *bennt* (brennt = burns) at an early age, she was not using a verb in the third person singular, present tense; it was only coincidental that the child's utterance was identical with that particular grammatical form.

There is, however, a universal and quite striking phenomenon in child speech which seems to indicate clearly that the child has begun to grasp the functional significance of morphological features, namely, the employment of "analogical" formations. Students of child language have extensively discussed—what parents have always observed —the child's tendency to use constructions such as *finded* rather than *found, gooder* rather than *better, gegebt* rather than *gegeben, dormer* rather than *dormir*, etc.[3] Again, as was the case with Stern's 1;11-year-old daughter, a child may extend to verbs certain formal elements, conventionally used with nouns; thus Hilde applied the diminutive ending, *-le* to all kinds of adjectives and verbs for indicating "littleness" —often affectionately. For example, side by side with *appele* (apple), *bildele* (picture), etc., Hilde said *bittele* (please!) *bautele* (build), *atzele* (tear apart), etc. (242, p. 31).

The increasing capacity of the child to handle morphological variations as a means of expressing qualifications in referents and relations among referents becomes particularly evident in those instances in which the child exploits linguistic features, not specifically offered by the speech of the adult. An impressive instance of this sort is manifested in Charles Gregoire's use of *bodome* and *badame*, at 2;0 to refer to "father" and "mother" respectively. Interestingly enough, Charles inadvertently pointed to the physiognomic basis of this vowel variation in referring to the voice of his father as that of a 'beggar,' and of his mother as that of a 'fairy.' (86, II, p. 253).

Thus one finds, paradoxically enough, that it is the emergence of these "incorrect" morphological variations which—as the child's own creations—give us some degree of certainty that the child has begun to acquire a "feeling for grammar." One may refer here to statements by K. Bühler, P. Guillaume, J. Sully, and others (all cited approvingly by Leopold) which emphasize the great significance of "incorrect" analogical formations. For example, Sully writes (248, p. 178): "This . . . not only has the quality of originality, but shows the germ of a truly grammatical feeling for the general types of the norms of language." In this context, one may better understand the findings of A. Collin—cited by H. Delacroix (53, p. 313)—that retarded children are sometimes closer in their speech forms to adults than are normal,

---

[3] Leopold (150, IV, p. 41); Stern (242, p. 140); Gregoire (86, II, p. 356).

intelligent children: the retarded children imitate and do not make "errors" deriving from analogy formations.[4]

In conclusion, it may be pointed out that another, later-occurring, manifestation of the child's increasing sensitivity to morphological characteristics of a language is the *self-correction* of errors in the handling of speech forms. This tendency shows up in the correction of idiosyncratic modifiers, 'false analogies,' etc., with subsequent adoption of the conventional ways of inflecting a vocable, carrying a certain function in a sentence. One illustration of this tendency comes from Jespersen (119, p. 131) who mentions a child, at 2;9, who—alone in his bed—remarked that one must say *small* (*små*) *hands* and not *little* (*lille*) *hands* (Danish *lille* is not used with a plural noun). von Gabelenz offers a beautiful example of a child correcting himself in three steps: *"Papa, hast du mir was 'mitgebringt'-'gebrangen'-'gebracht'?"* (cited after Delacroix, 53, p. 313).

Having, in the present chapter, traced certain general aspects in the development towards words and sentences, we turn in the next chapter to a closer examination of the formation of a specific class of sentences, namely, predicative utterances.

---

[4] With regard to analogy-formations, see Stern (242, p. 140); Guillaume (87, p. 220); Leopold (150, III, p. 79)

chapter 11

Early Stages in the Development
of Predicative Sentences

One of the basic cognitive capacities of human beings is that of making and understanding judgments, that is, utterances that assert (or deny) something about something else. The realization of this capacity is intimately bound up with symbolization and especially with linguistic representation: so much so, in fact, that some have maintained that there cannot be judgments in the absence of speech while others have contended that vocalizations only become speech when such vocal utterances are in the service of the expression of judgments.[1]

It is our view that there are forms of judgment—or at least, of proto-judgment—which are not expressed explicitly in speech or in other overt vehicles of representation: such forms are implicit in the goal-directed behavior of everyday life and are frequently designated as practical judgments. Our concern here, however, is with judgments as explicitly represented through symbolic—chiefly linguistic—means. Where acts of judgment are reflected in symbolic activity, they are manifested in "statements" or "predications;" it is therefore with statements or predicative utterances, in the form of simple sentences, that we deal in this chapter.

In examining acts of judgment ontogenetically, one must distinguish

---

[1] One may recall here the contention of Hughlings Jackson to the effect that "The unit of speech is the proposition." See H. Head (98, I, p. 41).

between the general capacity to make any kind of judgment and specific capacities to make particular kinds of judgments. Predicative utterances are not all of one piece, and particular kinds of predications emerge at different points in ontogenesis and show a distinctive development, setting them off from other kinds of predications. Here we shall trace three principal types of predicative expressions occurring in early childhood. We shall designate these three types of judgment, in terms of the nature of the predications involved, as *judgments of identification, judgments of agent's action,* and *judgments of attribution.* Although there may be occasional difficulty in determining the type of judgment involved in a given early utterance, it seems quite feasible, on the whole, to describe and illustrate the main lines of development of each of these types on the basis of observations made by astute students of child behavior.

Judgments of Identification (Identifying Predications)

These are ontogenetically the earliest kinds of judgments. Basically they involve the identification of an apprehended event as a such and such. In explicit verbal manifestation, these judgments take the form "this (pointing) is a B" or "A is a B." The earliest forms of identifying predications occur in situations in which the child "names" a presented content. The tremendous interest and delight of the child in the names of events and things have been noted by almost all students of infant behavior.

The interest of the child in names and his general efforts to know the names of things are not, it seems to us, primarily in the service of biological need-satisfaction or tension-reduction. Naming, we would maintain, is essentially an intellectual activity more directed towards knowing about the world than towards acting upon the world. This view is supported by the fact that naming and the quest for names occur most typically in contexts where the child is clearly "satisfied," that is, in contexts where there is no tension with regard to unfulfilled biological drives or other imperative needs. The child, under the press of needs or desires, cries out or utters call-sounds: names are searched for when such pressures are not operative.

Humboldt (111, LXXXI, LXXXV) in his analysis of the primordial motives for the emergence of language arrives at conclusions closely related to those presented here. It is one of the most fallacious notions one may hold about language, says Humboldt, to attribute the origin of speech to pragmatic need or mutual help. Inarticulate sounds would have been sufficient to satisfy such needs; speech emerges through the need or intent to give thought a representation by sound.

Clear evidence for the cognitive rather than pragmatic motive in primordial naming can be derived from the examination of the first words uttered by infants as reported in various diaries. If one examines the comprehensive list of such expressions as compiled by the Sterns (242, p. 172), one is struck by the fact that there is little indication of vocables involving reference to bodily biological needs; the early expressions consist overwhelmingly of denotative interjections expressing bewilderment, delight, surprise, etc., of names of persons, and of (mainly onomatopoetic) names of animals and objects.

The intellectual activity underlying naming—here considered as the earliest form of identifying predication—is the fundamental cognitive activity that makes possible all later types of judgment. Through such identifying predications, the first inroads are made towards the isolation and articulation of aspects of events, which leads eventually to the formation of sentences in which some features of a total event are predicated of some other features, both sets of features and the relations between them having become articulated for knowledge via naming. Without such isolation and articulation, the child cannot form judgments. As the philosopher Bosanquet (28, I, pp. 8 ff) has put it: "To give a name is for civilized thought the first step in knowledge."

Identifying predications are evident in the earliest monoremic utterances of the child, for example, *tick-tock, wau-wau, fff*, especially when these are accompanied by deictic gestures, such as turning towards the presented content or pointing to it. At the two-vocable level, one finds that the deixis is represented by demonstrative vocal forms, for example, *da* or *ta*. Characteristically, at early stages of two-vocable utterance, declarative utterances predominate over quasi-imperative utterances; this fact again supports the view that "cognitive needs" are the prime movers in the genesis of speech. Thus, it does not appear accidental to us that in both of the diaries cited in the previous chapter most of the early two-vocable utterances belong to the class of identifying predications, for example, *da bu, da digda, da ball* (B. Scupin), *da-is brrbrr, da-is wauwau, da-da papa* (H. Stern).

Gradually, in early childhood, conventional forms replace the infantile demonstratives and names. For English-speaking children, the identifying predication in concrete situations takes the form "that is a ———." Subsequently, at stages beyond those considered in this chapter, identifying predications subserve class inclusion and exclusion: one asserts that "A is a B" or "A is not a B."

It is important to recognize throughout, with regard to identifying predications, that one is not merely engaged in attaching labels to already determinate states of affairs. Through identifying predications, one so-to-speak creates for knowledge a recognizable arrangement of things, qualities, and relations: one makes so-to-speak contours and lines of contact within densely packed experience and establishes the objects of one's thought and the relations obtaining between one's cognitive objects.

Judgments of Agent's Action (Predications of Action)

In contradistinction to identifying predications, which become differentiated rather early from other kinds of predications, judgments of agent's action as well as judgments of attribution become only gradually differentiated from each other and articulated in specific and distinctive forms. For both kinds of judgment there are a number of steps prior to full realization. First, the child must come to distinguish between thing and some state of thing within a global, concrete happening—a distinction requisite for all forms of predication beyond that of identification.

This basic distinction, however, does not in itself insure a differentiation between predications of action (by an agent) and predications of attribution (of a quality to a thing). "States," themselves, must be differentiated in terms of "doing" and "belonging to." This differentiation emerges only gradually; consequently, one would expect that many early statements cannot be assigned to one class or the other of predications. For instance, such an expression as Hilde Stern's *kind-kalt!* (child-cold), which from an adult point of view might be considered an attributive predication, was uttered while Hilde saw a picture of a child with its arms clasped around its body, and might actually have referred to an action (for example, "the child shudders") as if it were a quality. Only when the child begins explicitly to employ the conventional means offered by the adult language does the distinction between predications of attributes and predications of action become clearly manifest.

Let us turn now to a brief discussion of the genesis of predications of action, that is, those types of judgments in which either an action by an agent or a state of a person (or thing) is asserted. One must here consider three interdependent moments which—though organically related to, and mutually dependent upon, each other—will, for convenience, be discussed separately. These three moments are: (1) the establishment of vocables which more or less clearly represent an agent, (2) the establishment of vocables which more or less clearly represent and refer to activity or state, and (3) the establishment of a relationship of predication between these two kinds of vocables.

(1) With regard to the formation of vocables that refer to an *agent* (person, thing), a truly stable and precise representation of a circumscribed agent most probably occurs only in a context of opposition to action reference within a single sentential utterance. Such precise agent reference is therefore interlocked with the establishment of a relationship of predication between two vocables. Nevertheless, careful observers such as the Sterns and M. M. Lewis have pointed up certain anticipations of thing-reference even with *pre-sentential utterances* of early childhood.

An early step occurs in those very familiar situations where the child responds to a word or sentence uttered by an adult in a questioning intonation by pointing to or turning toward an object. Subsequently, the child utters that word himself, using it to refer to the particular 'object,' as a thing-in-action or a thing-in-a-state. Progressively the vocable comes to refer more and more to the thing aspect, with the action (or state) aspect receding into the background.

Such an ontogenetic sequence may be illustrated by the Sterns' report of their daughter's understanding and use of the vocable *didda* (tick-tock): at 0;10, Hilde, hearing *tik-tak* pronounced by one of her parents, responded by turning towards the clock standing on the mantlepiece; at 10½ months, she uttered *didda* on seeing the clock and hearing it tick—a fusion of thing and state; shortly afterward, she uttered *didda* with respect to a grandfather clock, even while the clock was not ticking; then her father's pocket watch was so designated. After 1;0 she used *didda* to refer to pictures of clocks in books (242, p. 18).

This genetic sequence points up the presence of a trend, even at the pre-sentential level, towards the differentiation of the thing aspect from specific activities and states. The observations of the Sterns, as well as analogous observations made by others, seem to us to establish the existence of preparatory stages leading to the formation of linguistic symbols for agent representation as distinct from action representation. One may maintain that the emergence of the agent referent within a context-of-action or context-of-state is itself preparatory to the later specific articulation of a referent as an "agent" within a linguistically expressed predication of action (e.g., "this-ticking-thing" may thus lead easily to: "this thing (is) ticking").

(2) A second prerequisite for the formation of predications of action is the establishment of vocables that refer primarily to *activity* or *state*. Here again one may discern several steps preparatory to the use of vocables as action- or state-designators in full-fledged linguistic predications. One important step, noted by practically all students of child language, is the early pre-sentential use of vocables, referring holophrastically to sudden change, rapid motion, and the like: these are references that seem particularly to stress "action-event" rather than "thing."

Once again we may illustrate from the Sterns' observations: Hilde, at 0;11, used *bu* or *buä* to refer to the falling of thrown objects or to her own being thrown to and fro in a carriage; at 11½ months, the vocable was used to designate situations in which something suddenly appeared (242, p. 20). Similarly, Deville's daughter, at about 1;0, used *bam* to refer to a situation in which there was a falling object making considerable noise; at 1;1½, she used *pa* to designate events in which some object suddenly disappeared (55).

Other situations conducive to the formation of action-designators are those in which the child's own activity plays a dominant role. Often such vocables are tied up with the play or eating activities of the child and are frequently used in the course of initiating or completing such activities. For example, Hilde Stern, at about 17½ months, used *alle* (all gone) while emptying her bottle of milk or finishing her meals (242, p. 24). Deville's daughter, at about 1;4, used *toutou* in playing "hide and seek;" previously, at about 1;2½, she used *tout* (approximately: 'all gone') while emptying a pitcher (55).

Perhaps the most promising situations for the formation of vocables emphasizing actions or dynamic states are those involving a request for action by others. These early vocables of demand—all holophrastic monoremes—may take the external form of a 'noun,' 'verb,' 'adverb,' etc., but they always serve one principal end, the communication of the child's desire that something be done or that some action be stopped, etc. Vocables uttered in request intonation such as *Mama!, Papa!, mit!* (in the sense of 'come with me!'), *up! down! auf!* ('take me in your arms'), *à terre!* ('put me down'), etc., all contain such a demand. Because these vocables are employed to refer to action and its effects, they may later fulfill the role of a predicate in declarative utterances of two vocables: for example, Leopold's child used *away* at 1;8 as a request to move things away from her; shortly afterward, she was overheard saying *away* after she had put away her toy—the total expression being predicative in import, approximately equivalent to *the toy, I—put away* (Leopold, 150, III, pp. 22–27).

(3) We now turn to the third moment operative in the formation of predications of action, the establishment of the *relationship of "predication"* between thing and action (or dynamic state). As repeatedly noted before, the full-fledged expression of a predicative relationship between thing and action requires linguistic means (morphological features, particles, sequence, etc.) which serve both to differentiate subject and predicate, and to relate these two to each other. Here again, we first direct our analysis toward speech behavior at a level which can be considered preparatory to the full-fledged linguistic expression of predication.

Since the predication of action involves a connection between two terms, a thing (person) and an action, one might logically expect that the formation of predications of action require, at a minimum, two-vocable utterances. Even a cursory perusal of observations reported in the literature indicates that this is not true. The beginnings of predications of action are found in situations in which one member of the relation is not linguistically articulated; rather, it is present only as a perceptual object or implied in gestural activity. Leopold's observation, just cited, on the predicative use of the vocable *away* illustrates this point rather well: only one member of the predicative statement (*away*) was linguistically expressed; the other member (*toy*) was nonlinguistically given in the pragmatic-perceptual context.

O. Bloch (22), especially, has demonstrated rather convincingly that some of these partially lingualized predications are typically formed in situations in which the adult, through his questions, leads a child to predicate an (anticipated) action. These are some of his observations on his daughter: Jacqueline, at 1;10, when asked by her father—as he began to take off his shoes—"Qu'est-ce que je vais faire?" answered: *yeye* (soulier = *shoe*). At 1;11, when asked a similar question by her father as he prepared to wash himself, she responded: *wowo* (sapon = soap). In these instances, again, part of the predicative statement is given in the pragmatic-perceptual context (father as agent, preparing for a particular action), and the lingualized part is uttered in monoremic fashion. One might conceivably translate those statements in terms of two-vocable utterances by means of two monoremes with overlapping reference; for example, *"father* (taking off shoes)–(he, takes-off-) *shoes."*

When such lingualized utterances, involving an overlapping relationship of agent-designator and action-designator, actually do occur, there is a further advance towards fully articulated predications of action.[2] Several observations by Leopold provide instructive illustrations of such an intermediate step. Interestingly enough, Leopold's observations are linked to Bloch's in that they, too, pertain to a question-answer situation: the significant difference here is that both question and answer were uttered by the child. As Leopold (150, III, p. 28) relates, during the transition from one- to two-vocables, Hildegard, at 1;6, used such expressions as *Mama? sh!, Dada? by-by!*, etc. That is, the child first expressed a question about a person's activity or whereabouts, and then answered this question in the intonation of a declarative statement. The two-vocable utterances just cited might be translated: "What is mama doing? She is sleeping." "Where is Carolyn? She has gone out."

Utterances such as these indicate that the child has reached a level where he understands the relationship between a person (thing) and its action. Once this level is reached, the child is prepared to take over devices in the language which, on the one hand, serve categorially to distinguish thing and action, and, on the other hand, serve syntactically to integrate thing and action in predicative sentences.

Judgments of Attribution (Predications of Attributes)

A fully articulated judgment of attribution involves the cognition of two relationships between object and quality: a relationship of *inherence* and a relationship of *adherence*. The meaningful utterance of a sentence such as "this paper is white" requires, first of all, that one perceive a quality, "whiteness," inherent in an object, "paper." Inherence, however, does not suffice to establish a relationship of attribution. In order for this relationship to be established one must be able to decontextualize the quality and then to apprehend the newly detached quality as "belonging" or "adhering" to the object.

The process of *decontextualization*, the detachment of a quality from an object in which it inheres, is of course a manifestation of the orthogenetic principle, and hence it requires only a brief discussion here. In accord with this principle, one would expect to find that the vocables stipulating a "quality" of an object would, in early precur-

---

[2] One will here recall our previous discussion (Chapter 10) concerning the significance of overlapping reference in the ontogenetic change from the monoreme to the two-vocable stage.

sors of predication of attributes, be monoremes, that is, would refer to such a characteristic attribution as not yet detached from the total event, and would often include the child's personal, affective reactions. A typical illustration of such monoremic utterances comes from Leopold (150, I, p. 121): he observed that Hildegard, at 1;4, used *pooh* to express disgust when finding the bed wetted by herself or when imagining a doll wetting the bed. Gradually this quasi-attributive reference became de-emotionalized and decontextualized: after 1;11, *pooh* was used to predicate the attribute 'dirty' of various objects; thus, she used *all pooh* to render, without emotion, the fact that the three little kittens of the Mother Goose verse were 'all dirty.'

The Sterns, too, in their discussion of the development of attributive adjectives, point to the origin of such forms in contextualized affective expressions (242, p. 35): for instance, *ä!* was Hilde's negatively toned expression for referring to black-colored objects; similarly, *heiss!* (hot!) was first uttered by Hilde not as a descriptive statement of the property of an object, for example, a stove, but as an expression of an experience in which perceptual elements and affective-motor reactions were indissolubly fused.

Expressions indicating *"belongingness"* are some of the very early utterances that are directly related to predications of attributes. Manifestations of this relationship can be found in situations in which a child expresses a desire or a claim of possession. Many of the child's early monoremes (typically complemented by gesture) entail such a desire or claim. For example, Hildegard Leopold (150, I, p. 99), at 1;6, used *mai* (mine!) repeatedly, pressing an object to herself with an emphatic asseveration of possession. At 1;7 *mai* was used as part of a paratactic construction, *mai! dadi!* (my! stocking!). At 1;9, in *this (dress) my!*, the *my* had lost much of its emphatic character and had come much closer to being an expression of belongingness.

Once expressions of belongingness have become less emotional, the child can see things belonging to others. Expressions reflecting this awareness are often comprised of a deictic gesture and a vocable. For example, Bloch (22) reports that his daughter, Francoise, at 2;1, pointed to the pants of her brother, and remarked *memo* (Raymond), i.e., (these are) Raymond's; the next day she pointed to her sister's napkin, and said *ninin* (Jacqueline), i.e., (this is) Jacqueline's. Several days later, she carried her mother's boots into the room, and showing them to her father, remarked *mama*, another day, handing her father the paper, she said *papa*. Of course, the child will eventually go beyond gesture and use demonstratives such as *this, ça,* etc., to denote the object. Usually at the same time that such expressions occur, one may also find the flourishing of forms such as *Ida house, mama shoe,* etc., where a thing detached from context is brought into a relationship of belongingness to a person via the use of two vocables.

The development of the tendencies to decontextualize properties and to relate one thing to another thing (or person) in terms of belongingness finally culminates in statements in which a relatively detached property is brought into a relationship of *adherence* to an object, for example, *paper white.* In such two-vocable expressions, the statements are still pre-sentential in nature, insofar as there is still no clear-cut linguistic expression of a subject-predicate relationship. In this respect, these utterances are analogous to the two-vocable forms which come before true action predication, that is, those in which there is as yet no inflection of the verb-like form, e.g., *Mama sh, Frau m, auto ride,* etc. Just as, in children of Indo-European linguistic cultures, true predications of action and, correlatively, true verbs come into existence with the adoption and systematic use of morphological devices, so too do true predications of attributes and, correlatively, true predicate adjectives come into being with the adoption of syntactic means such as copula forms.

In summing up our discussion of the early development of the various forms of judgment (or predication), we may note that, despite differences in detail, they all follow the same general sequence. We may also add that, though the development of request or imperative utterances has not been considered here, the available evidence suggests that these forms also follow the general sequence obtaining for the forms of predication. This general sequence, to recapitulate briefly, is comprised of four main steps. (1) The earliest pre-predicative (and pre-imperative) utterances are, both referentially and linguistically, of an undifferentiated character, that is, they are monoremic. (2) Next come two-vocable utterances which are initially a junction of monoremes, in which each denotes the same event, while connoting somewhat different aspects of it (pleonastic reference); the structure of the utterance here is typically paratactic—a loose joining of relatively separate vocables. (3) At a later stage of two-vocable utterances, the units become relatively distinct in reference and are eventually linked together in an intonational hypotaxis (uneven stress)—indicating that one referent is in some way dependent upon the other. (4) Finally, specific morphological means, such as form-words, come into play to establish integration of the vocables entirely within the linguistic medium per se; at this point "sentences" are fully established and, correlatively, so are "words."

This shift from speech utterances whose full meaning unfolds only in reference to the concretely given immediate context to utterances in which the meaning of the vocables is actualized predominantly by means inherent in the speech medium itself reflects what we have called the developmental trend towards *the increasing autonomy of a medium of representation.*

chapter *12*

Early Stages in the Linguistic Expression of Relations Between Thoughts

In the previous chapter, an attempt was made to trace the steps leading up to simple predicative statements, for example, A is B, A does B. In this chapter, we focus on the steps leading towards the linguistic expression of *relations between thoughts*—relations expressed in full-fledged English through connectives within *compound sentences*. As we shall see, the progression towards the linguistically articulated expression of relationships between sentences is formally parallel to the progression towards simple subject-predicate sentences: more specifically, in the attempts of the child to articulate relationships between thoughts, he progresses, in a sequence of steps—from parataxis through intonational hypotaxis to linguistic (morphemically indicated) hypotaxis—thus going through the same series of steps that culminates in the linguistically autonomous expression of simple judgments of predication. This formal parallelism—the initial return to more primitive means in the attempt to attain more complex ends—is another instance of the operation of *the genetic principle of spirality*.

From the developmental point of view, one would expect no clear-cut differentiation, at the outset, between those forms eventuating in simple sentences and those culminating in compound sentences: in other words, early two-vocable forms, comprised of monoremes in juxtaposition, are not expected to be segregated into those which are precursors of simple statements and those which foreshadow sentences in relationship to each other. Empirically, this genetic expectation is borne out: without knowing the context, one cannot distinguish a two-vocable utterance presaging a simple sentence and one adumbrating a compound statement. For example, among the two-vocable utterances of Hilde Stern, at 1;9, it would be impossible to determine, without information supplied through gesture and action, that *mama-hute* was a statement to the effect that "mama should put on the hat," while *mama-hilde* was a statement to the effect that "mama should hide; Hilde will search for her." (Stern, 242, p. 43)

Nevertheless, in examining the development of the linguistic expression of thoughts in relation to each other, we must make the assumption that the chains of monoremes eventuating in compound sentences involve in their utterance certain *vectors* which polarize the two monoremes as separate thoughts or judgments and yet at the same time link them together. In this respect the juxtaposed monoremes culminating in compound sentences would be different from those culminating in simple sentences. In other words, we assume that a distinction between, and a relating of, two thoughts is experienced organismically, in a *dynamic* way, and that gradually these covert and inchoate vectors reach full articulation through a process of externalization in linguistic vehicles.

Before discussing the progression from paratactic to hypotactic organization in the *linguistic expression* of relations between two events, it is important to recognize that events themselves may be apprehended in different relations to each other. For instance two events may be experienced simply as co-occurrent, or in sequence; on the other hand, they may be apprehended in terms of a causal or conditional relationship, that is, one event may be dependent upon or subordinated to the other. Whereas a paratactic linguistic formulation would more or less correspond to the first kind of experienced relationship and thus be a relatively adequate expression of it, only a hypotactic linguistic formulation would be fully adequate to the second kind of experienced relationship. With these considerations in mind, therefore, we may expect the linguistic expression of relationships to take place in three steps. First, there is the use of paratactic patterns that correspond closely to the apprehended relationships of events, that is, of events standing in juxtaposition or sequence to each other. Second, there is the continued use of paratactic patterns, employed—inadequately—for the expression of relationships of dependency, that is, causality, conditionality, etc. Finally, there is the emergence of hypotactic patterns which do, more or less, correspond to the perceived relationships of dependency, subordination and the like. With the full-fledged use of linguistic hypotaxis, these various relations may become actualized in an autonomous linguistic medium.

Paratactic Patterns Corresponding to Relationships Between Events

Beginning our discussion with paratactic patterns of the first kind, that is, those representing nonsubordinative relationships between events, we may distinguish four types of such relationships: *coordination, sequence, simultaneity,* and *antithesis* As mentioned, we assume that these different relationships between events are initially experienced in terms of organismic states (inner gestures); only later on is there an externalization of these inner vectorial states in linguistic expressions, for example, through the use of coordinating conjunctions ("and"), indicators of sequence ("then"), conjunctions of simultaneity ("while"), and conjunctions of antithesis ("but"). In this section, we treat only the expressions of these relationships in *paratactic patterns*, reserving until later a discussion of the emergence of conjunctions.

Coordination

Paratactic utterances reflecting a relationship of coordination between two experiences are expressed quite early. Such patterning of utterances, for example, *this (is) chair; this (is) table,* corresponds closely to the actual manner in which two events of equal value are experienced—as two discernible happenings in spatiotemporal contiguity. Such paratactic utterances often suffice to express coordination in situations somewhat removed from contexts-of-occurrence.

Sequence

An experience of a sequential relationship between events is also expressed quite early through paratactic patterns; such patterns are utilized for the expression of sequence for a considerable period of time before linguistic means (e.g., "first . . . then") are brought into play. The expression of sequential relationships through parataxis appears to take place, generally, during the second year; the juxtaposition of two or three vocables, uttered within certain contexts, suffices to express a temporal ordering. To illustrate: *papa-auf-nini* ["papa, open (the door), (I want to) snuggle-up-in-blanket"]; *miede-stuli-setzen* ["(I am) tired, (in the) chair (I want to) sit"]; *my hu?-hanzu?*

["(I go to) my room, (get a) handkerchief"]; *Mary Alice home-eat*
["Mary Alice (takes me) home, (I want to) eat"]; *Bottle piek-wehweh*
["Glass pricks (you), (and it) hurts"].[1] As one will note, all of these
utterances, in which monoremic vocables are arranged in a sequential
order, concretely mirror the sequence of the experiences or thoughts
represented.

Simultaneity

Utterances in a paratactic arrangement are also employed by the
child to express *simultaneity,* a more advanced type of temporal relationship than *sequence.* The *apprehension* of simultaneity may be
regarded as more advanced because it entails either the differentiation
of a unitary experience into two events or the bringing together in
time of two *sequentially experienced* happenings (looking at A, then
at B); the *expression* of simultaneity may be considered more advanced because language as a succession of utterances cannot directly
mirror simultaneity in the order of the vocables. To illustrate, the
utterance *papa brrbrr-fasche put* ["papa horse-bottle kaputt"] was
made by Hilde Stern at 2;6; the intended meaning, according to the
Sterns was: "While papa was near the horse, the bottle broke." It is
clear that there was nothing in the utterance per se which warranted
the interpretation that the child was relating two events in terms of
simultaneity; it was rather the emergence of the utterance within a
concretely given context that made it easy for the observers—and
makes it easy for parents generally—to interpret a paratactic formation as alluding to simultaneity. The mastery of speech has to progress quite a bit more before a child can convey simultaneity of events
when he and the addressee are removed from the concrete context,
that is, before the expression of simultaneity is expressed linguistically
and can be understood from the utterance itself as a message in an
autonomous linguistic medium.

Antithesis [2]

The relationships of contrast, discordance, opposition, etc., between
conceptualized experiences are again expressed initially through para-

---

[1] The first utterance comes from Bubi Scupin at 1;5, the second from Hilde
Stern at 1;9, and the last three utterances from Hildegard Leopold at 1;11.

[2] It is recognized that "antithesis" is much closer to the subordinative relations
than are coordination, sequence, and simultaneity.

tactic patterns which do not, in themselves, serve for the full articulation of such relationships. Full articulation comes only through the use of linguistic form-words ("but," "rather") which come into play later on. As Stern has observed, expressions of antithesis through parataxes typically emerge in situations where the child rejects one object or state of affairs while voicing a preference or demand for another, that is, where negation and affirmation are affectively rather than logically related. Thus, at 1;8–½, Hilde Stern reacted to her mother's attempt to put her to bed with *nei nei-fasche!* ["no no (good night yet)–(first I must have my) bottle"]. Two months later, at 1;10, the negation had become somewhat more explicit, but the expression was still a paratactic one: *stuhl, nei, nei-schossel!* ["chair, no, (I don't want to sit on that)–(rather, I want to sit on your) lap"]. And even at 2;5, the same child expressed antithesis through paratactic formations: *Sáuba nich taschentuch, bába taschentuch* ["clean not (is this) handkerchief, dirty (is this) handkerchief"].

These illustrations should make clear how, at early levels of linguistic expression, a variety of different kinds of relationships may be realized with relative adequacy through an externally paratactic structure. Despite this common mode of external organization, however, it is our contention that the different kinds of relationships must be grounded in different organismic experiences, different dynamic-vectorial patterns. Eventually, these different dynamic patterns push towards articulation in increasingly distinctive linguistic forms.

Paratactic Patterns for Expression of Relationships of Dependency

Up to this point, we have considered the use of paratactic patterns for the representation of those kinds of relations between events which, in themselves, reflect a more or less "paratactic" apprehension, that is, relationships of coordination, sequence, etc. Because of this correspondence, linguistic parataxis is a relatively adequate means for the expression of such relationships. Sooner or later, however, the child advances towards a grasp of causal, conditional, and other kinds of *dependency relationships* between two events. How does he first express such novel relations? What are the steps by which he advances toward the fully articulated linguistic expression of such relationships involving the subordination of one event to another?

Briefly stated, the child initially *persists in the use of a paratactic mode of expression* as the means for carrying dependency relationships. Probably because the concrete contexts in which such paratactic formations occur suffice to suggest relationships not embodied in the paratactic pattern itself, the child can continue to cling to these more primitive means as long as his utterances are intimately bound up with situations shared by his addressees. Only when the child becomes ready to utilize speech at some distance from those immediate, perceptual-gestural contexts in which he, the addressee and the concrete events (or objects) are immersed—only when, in other words, the child is directed towards the expression of relations which are not "given" through the context—must he forge or adopt new instruments in order adequately to realize the externalization of those relations. There is thus in the child's progress towards the linguistic expression of dependency relationships an exemplification of the developmental principle that *available means are exploited for new ends until function-specific instrumentalities are forged for the novel functions.*

In line with this principle, one would expect what does indeed occur: paratactic patterning is "over-extended"—used for the expression of dependency relationships—side by side with the early steps towards the formation of hypotactic expressions; eventually fully articulated linguistic hypotaxis ensues.

Precursors to Full Linguistic Hypotaxis in Expression of Dependency Relations

Let us now consider some of the precursors to linguistic hypotaxis. From a developmental point of view, one would expect that linguistic hypotaxis would not emerge full-blown but would be preceded by a number of stages in which true hypotaxis is merely foreshadowed. Such precursors should be found in forms that are closely linked to organismic-gestural activity, that is, "vocal gestures" or "rhythmic-melodic-intonational patterns." And, indeed, this is what one finds: in the development towards the full linguistic expression of dependency or subordinative relationships between events, intonational-rhythmic-melodic patterns once again seem to play a role analogous to the one that such patterns fill in the earlier expression of relations between the elements of simple sentences.

As many observers have noted, long before rhythmic-melodic patterns subserve the function of expressing dependency relationships either within sentences or between sentences, such patterns are often "practiced" in a nonreferential way, that is, in a babbling manner.

In a previous chapter, we cited Shirley's observations concerning the emergence of such nonreferential yet "conversation-like" patterns often during the last quarter of the first year.

When the child becomes ready to grasp and to undertake the expression of hypotactical relations, he may draw on this reservoir of "conversation-like" rhythmic-melodic patterns, embedding the principal vocables in them, yet leaving out those rather "abstract" connectives by which adults conventionally symbolize these dependency relationships. Typically, then, what occurs is a melodic-rhythmic configuration into which essential vocables are inserted; intermingled with these vocables are sounds that serve to complete the intonational "tune." Among the observations of those who have reported on this development, the ones by the Sterns (242), E. Norman (176), and M. M. Nice (175) are particularly relevant.

The Sterns, on the basis of their many observations, conclude: "The first hypotactical (dependency) forms are often not recognized because particles are only implied or are indicated by filling sounds (expletives) such as 'a,' 'mm.' For the attentive observer, hypotactic forms are recognizable on the basis of intonation, modulation, and word-position" (242, p. 208). One may add that "pauses" are also an essential part of intonational patterns and often fill the place into which vocables expressing dependency-connections are later placed.

To elaborate: in filling out a melodic-intonational pattern, where no vocables have yet been developed for denoting specific relationships, the child may first use expletives, which function in a relatively undifferentiated way, that is, they may be used instead of the prefixes of participial forms, in place of connectives, etc. Gradually —and still prior to the adoption of conventional forms—there may be a differentiation of the "fill-ins," so that one type of expletive occurs in the connective position, and another kind functions as prefixes in participial constructions, etc. Still further differentiation may subsequently occur, culminating in the actual adoption of conventional forms.

To illustrate, Gunther Stern (242, pp. 102 ff) first used *e* as an expletive to fill in various parts of melodic-rhythmic structures, that is, *e* was used in place of a prefix in a participle, in place of a connective, in place of an auxiliary verb, etc. Take, for example, Gunther's statement: *"e else zu-e-nöpft hat* (will ich) *wieder sand spielen"* ["when Else buttoned (my dress), (I will) again (in) sand play"]; here, *e* was used in the first instance as an analogue to *wenn* (when), and in the second (e-nöpft) as an analogue to the participial prefix *ge*. Subsequently, a differentiation occurred: more and more frequently *ge* replaced *e* as a prefix in verb forms, and *e* was limited to function as a substitute for connectives.

A further differentiation between expressions for the connective and the prefixing functions took place during the fourth year when *e* was replaced by *mm;* this appears to have served phonetically to mark off the connective more sharply from the prefix. Thus, at 3;3, *mm* was used to express "so that," "because," and "which:" *will de tasse holen, mm wasser trinken kann* ["(I) want to get the cup *so that* (I) can drink water"] ; *mmm keine tasse da is* [because no cup is there]— said in answer to his father's question, "Why don't you drink from a glass?"; *das is ein pilz, mmm in walde is* [that is a mushroom which is in the woods] (Stern, 242, p. 112). It appears that such quasi-vocables as *mmm* could be employed to express a diversity of relationships because the different overall melodic patterns served in themselves to indicate the specific relationship intended.

E. Norman (176) reports a somewhat similar case of a child who reached a point in her language development where she used two or three 'real' vocables with 'nonsense syllables' interpolated between them. In so doing, she managed, via the rhythm of the total utterance, to convey the relations between thoughts. Again, M. M. Nice (175) gives an account of a 2-year-old girl, who employed a number of meaningless syllables to fill in a melodic-rhythmic structure and was able, through vocables embedded in this structure, to convey particular relationships. For example, she used *Mama her her Mama* embedded in a rhythmic structure to convey "Mama (called) Grandma Mama."

Such expressions of *dependency relations* through rhythmic-melodic patterns may be diagrammatized as in Fig. 12-1.

It was briefly noted that a child, in order to maintain a melodic-rhythmic pattern, may use a *pause* rather than an *expletive* in place of a conventional connective. This seems to occur more frequently in utterances where certain linguistic devices, for example, inversion of word-order, already serve to some extent to carry dependency relations. For instance, Hilde Stern, at 2;5, expressed the idea of "that which" or "what" through a construction in which (correct or incorrect) inversion of principal verb and auxiliary, plus a pause (= what) between two phrases, carried the relationship: *papa siehmal–(pause) –hilde macht hat,* i.e., ["Papa see–(what)–Hilde made has"]. Again, at about the same period, she stated, *is nich da schieben–(pause)–kann*

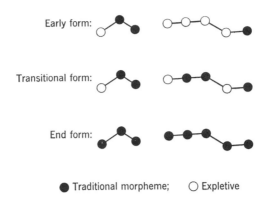

Early form:

Transitional form:

End form:

● Traditional morpheme;　○ Expletive

FIGURE 12-1.　Paradigmatic model of development of hypotactical sentence structure through rhythmic-melodic patterning.

nich mahle mahle ["is not there (something) to push–(therefore)–cannot stir (the pap)"]. Another example comes from Gunther Stern at 2;6: *mutter hagen–ebaut hat egunter*, i.e., [" (I want to) mother tell–what–built has gunther"]. Again, at 2;7, he remarked, *fettig bin–Else haushingen* ["(When I'm) finished (with my eating)—Else (may) take away (my dish)"]. In all these instances, the total melodic pattern had to carry the dependency relationship, since it was expressed neither in the inverted order of grammatically correct German nor through specific connectives.

At a somewhat more advanced level of speech—at a point where the function of word-order was already realized—Hilde Stern uttered sentences such as the following: *freust du—mama wagen ekauft hat* ["are you happy (that) mama a carriage has bought?"]; *mein simmer is so kalt—fenster aufemacht is* ["my room is so cold (because) window open is"]. The Sterns remark (242, p. 69), with respect to such utterances: "Word order and intonation leave no doubt . . . that actual hypotactic sentences are intended." [3]

In sum, then, we feel justified in maintaining that rhythmic-melodic patterns, in which only central vocables are embedded, probably play a much more significant role in the development of expressions of relationship than has generally been recognized. Patterns of this sort are close to internal gestures in that they have vectorial character-

---

[3] In the two examples, the word-order of the dependent clause was—correctly—reversed.

istics, which serve to depict certain dynamically apprehended relationships between events. It seems to us that only by positing such dynamic-vectorial properties of rhythmic-melodic patterns can one understand how a child can manage to express dependency relationships between events without utilizing specific form words: the intonational patterns express the dependency relationships *physiognomically*. These rhythmic patterns—vectorially-physiognomically differentiated —eventually guide the child towards the adoption of certain linguistic devices, for example, in German, the prefix *ge-*, indicative of participial forms, or inversion of word-order. With the adoption of such devices the child may, for some period of time, manage to suggest dependency relationships and yet concurrently show a peculiar absence of the linguistic particles, etc., which more completely and explicitly articulate the specific kind of dependence.

The Emergence of Linguistic Connectives and Their Role in the Expression of Dependency Relations

Having examined the more primordial means used for the expression of relationships between events, we may now consider the emergence and development of specifically linguistic means for the representation of such relationships. As is well known, such morphemic devices as "form-words" or particles serve as principal devices in Indo-European languages for the expression of both coordinative and subordinative relationships. Their value for thought and communication lies in the fact that they manifestly serve to *polarize* two events (or thoughts), while *uniting* the polarized moments in an integrated utterance. Whereas in complex utterances lacking the full explication of relationships via form-words the component parts of an utterance are knit together only through the concrete context in which they are embedded or through intonational patterning, here the conceptualized events become more clearly segregated and self-contained and yet are shown as clearly linked to each other in specific ways.

As the child (of Western linguistic communities) begins to free his expressions of relationship between thoughts from their initial embeddedness in concrete contexts, there are several characteristic steps he takes until he finally reaches that level where he employs specific vehicles adequate to the expression of specific abstract-logical relations. In other words, the child does not suddenly—and all at once —arrive at the full-fledged linguistic expression of all the relationships. There is rather an order in the emergence of linguistic connectives, the expressions for the more advanced relationships occurring much later than expressions adequate to the more primordial (spatiotemporal) linkages. Thus, the first connectives between sentences that emerge in ontogenesis are conjunctions that subserve the general function of "binding" two events either in space or time, that is, usually "and" and "then." For example, the first two conjunctions of Hilde Stern's, uttered during her third year, were: *leich ba gähn und sand (s)pieln*, i.e., "soon go out *and* play in sand," and *äst anzie, dann ba gähn*, i.e., "first dressing, then going out (for a walk)" (Stern, 242, p. 58). It is noteworthy that Hilde, as well as Gunther Stern, during their third year, narrated primitive tales composed of chains of simple sentences—sentences which were generally connected by *un(d)* and *dann* (Stern, 242, pp. 61, 108).[4]

When the child takes the first steps towards the linguistic expression of dependency relationships, once again the principle pertaining to the use of old, available means for the realization of novel ends comes into play. For a long period of time, dependency relationships are carried by the explicit use of coordinate clauses linked by coordinating conjunctions. This is made possible by a strong tendency on the part of the child to transform intrinsically subordinative relationships (e.g., conditionality, causality) into more concrete relations of a merely spatiotemporal character.

Eventually, however, there is a significant leap forward—sometimes within the span of a few weeks (see Leopold, 150, IV, p. 19)—as the child grasps the function of, and utilizes, novel linguistic devices, namely, subordinative conjunctions such as *if, when, because*, etc. True to the principle of conservation of old means for new ends, however, even at a point where the child can use connectives of various kinds, he will still often draw on coordinative connectives for the expression of subordinative relations. Thus, as Piaget and others have shown, the child will often use an *'and'* referring to concrete sequence instead of a *'because'* of causal relationship (see Werner, 274, p. 319). In other words, a form is used which is midway in function between a designator of spatial relation and a designator of logical relation. A similar phenomenon is found with respect to the German conjunction, "da" (concretely, "there;" logically, "since"). The Sterns (242, p. 111) give a number of instances, from their son Gunther, where 'da' was used in this syncretic way. For example, Gunther, at

---

[4] The first conjunction noted for Hildegard Leopold (at 2;3) was also 'and.'

3;1, justifying his calling an alley a 'woods,' remarked: *da doch bäume sind–is doch wald*, ["there indeed (= since) trees are—is indeed woods"].

A brief note may be added concerning the development of explicit causal constructions, such as "while," "because," "when," etc. A typical sequence is as follows: (*a*) "The toy is broken–it doesn't move;" (*b*) "It doesn't move because it's broken;" and (*c*) "Because it is broken, it doesn't move." The first type of utterance is close to the perceptual event; what *is* first is *expressed* first. The second type of utterance shows, in the reversal, a move toward a concrete apprehension of causal relations; an effect is observed and the cause is looked for. The third type of utterance puts the causal ground first; despite the superficial similarity to sequence (*a*), the relationship is not a temporal but a logical one. Compared with (*b*) it is even one step further removed from concrete description; the child now looks at particular events in terms of their grounds. This progression is part of the general movement in development towards viewing the world in terms of abstract, logical relationships.

One may also cite here an interesting finding by F. and G. Heider in their study of deaf-mutes (160, I, p. 97); this finding bears directly on the issue of sequence in the expression of dependency relationships. The Heiders state that deaf-mutes, when compared with normal, hearing children in the recital of stories, used relatively few of the constructions in which the subordinate clause precedes the main clause. In particular, with regard to temporal clauses, the deaf child used relatively more of those constructions, where subordinate clauses follow the main ones, that is, form (*b*) rather than (*c*).

A very informative account of the development of linguistic expressions of subordinative relations between thoughts in pre-school children is contained in a comprehensive study by A. Huth (112). Huth's analysis is based on a sample of narrations and conversations of children from 4½ to 6 years of age; it clearly points to the relatively high frequency in the exploitation of paratactic structures by the younger in comparison with the older children for the expression of dependency relations. The study contains some excellent illustrations of the way in which paratactic forms are used by these children to indicate dependency, for example, causal relations: one 4-year-old girl, in talking about a picnic, related in the following way the idea that the girls could not sit down because the benches were too wet: *Wir sind nicht daraufgesessen, die Bänke waren so nass* ["we did not sit down–the benches were so wet"]. Huth notes that the two seemingly "independent" sentences were run together without a pause, as they otherwise would have to be if they were truly independent of each other. He feels justified in interpreting the relation between the two sentences as one implying causality.

Again, the protocols give evidence of the frequent use of the "and" particle for expressing causal relationships; for example, a 5-year-old boy, telling about an autumn fair at which an organ grinder played a hurdy-gurdy, stated: "There turns all the time the man, *and* inside plays the music." It is clear that the "and" here was not intended to mark a simple relationship of sequence, but was used rather to convey the fact that the music-playing was in some way dependent on the turning; of course, the precise character of the dependence, whether finalistic, causal, or conditional, was left undetermined.

These instances are exemplars of sentence structures which superficially indicate a mere conjunction of two principal sentences and yet intrinsically involve vectorial characteristics of the dependency of one thought upon another.[5] Huth has appropriately designated such constructions as "masked dependent clauses." Such phenomena are transitional between the simple coordination of thoughts and the subordination of one thought to another: they reflect the fact that conjunctions such as "and" must syncretically carry both types of relationship, coordinative and subordinative.

The observed ontogenetic changes in Huth's study with respect to explicit expression of logical and causal (dependency) relationships (112, p. 178) may be summarized as follows (Table 12-1).

We shall conclude this chapter by emphasizing that the ontogenetic changes in the structure of lingualized expressions pertaining to logical relations between thoughts clearly illustrate the phenomenon of *increasing autonomy of the medium of representation:* whereas the structures of the earlier utterances, depictive of the order of pragmatic-perceptual happenings, are closely tied to, and interwoven with, concrete contexts, later utterances are increasingly freed from contextual embeddedness: this decontextualization of speech goes hand in hand with a stress on conceptual-logical rather than pragmatic-perceptual relationships among experiences (thoughts).

In the formation of logico-conceptual dependency relationships between thoughts, development seems to proceed along two lines: on one hand, the child initially utilizes existing *paratactic constructions* for the expression of these new, higher level, relationships; on the

---

[5] See the similar examples given by Piaget in his investigations of children's descriptions of causal events (189, p. 117); "I turn the faucet and the water runs out" for: The water runs out because I turn the faucet.

Table 12-1

Forms of subordinate clauses at various pre-school ages
Obtained from a sample of spontaneous narrations (after Huth)

	Age in years			
	$4\frac{1}{2}$	5	$5\frac{1}{2}$	6
"Masked" subordinate clauses	74.3%	29.6%	33.3%	8.0%
Subordinate clauses: "incorrect"	2.6%	7.5%	—	2.4%
Subordinate clauses: "correct"	23.1%	62.9%	66.7%	89.6%
(a) dialectically correct	—	37.0%	—	12.8%
(b) grammatically correct	23.1%	25.9%	66.7%	76.8%

other hand, he takes over certain *rhythmic-intonational* patterns from adult usage, patterns which lead eventually to *hypotactic constructions.* We assume that there is a constant interaction of these two ways of expressing dependency relationships. Primordially, the *paratactic constructions* express dependency relationships indirectly, through the nature of the *contents referred* to and the embeddedness of such utterances in action-gestural contexts; the *rhythmic-melodic, quasi-hypotactic constructions* are primordial ways of expressing dependency relationships through vocal patterning per se. As special linguistic forms (primitive connectives) are inserted within the rhythmic-melodic (quasi-hypotactic) utterances, and as dependency relations between thoughts via *reference to content* merge with the early expressions of hypotaxis by *vocal patterning,* the child is on the way toward the use of adult (linguistically autonomous) forms of expression of abstract-logical relations between thoughts.

chapter 13

Later Developments Toward Autonomy of the Linguistic Medium

The progress towards the autonomy of linguistic mediation—involving an increasing *distance* and independence of language from the domain of concrete, perceptual-motor experiences—reflects itself in several ways: increasing reference to phenomena remote from concrete perception, formation of names to refer to class concepts rather than to individual concepts, formation of designators of abstract rather than context-bound relations, etc.

Perhaps the clearest indication of the increasing autonomy of linguistic mediation in speech activity is the use of purely linguistic operations for constructing referents and relations among referents. Such operations are reflected in the constructions of names (and hence conceptual referents) out of names, e.g., formation of *composites* and *derivatives;* in the interpretation of names in terms of other names, e.g., in *definitions;* in the establishment of certain relationships among names (concepts), e.g., *relations of analogy;* in the *formation of verbal concepts through linguistic contexts;* and so on. In this chapter, we shall touch briefly on developmental aspects of some of these activities.

Formation of Composites and Derivatives

One of the general methods by which verbal concepts are formed within language is that of *composition,* the joining of two names to form a new unitary name. Another basic method is that of *derivation*, the adding of form-elements to a name in order to derive new names (and concepts).

Composition

After the child has acquired a sufficient number of names—generally, after the second year—and indeed, after he has formed sentences and words, he begins to give some indication that he understands that linguistic means can be used to form new words; he now denotes specific referents by forging new names from those already available to him in his repertoire. Perhaps in analogy to adult composite forms known to him, he brings together two names to form specific verbal concepts (specific referents). Characteristically, in the formation of such composites, the part of the new name that specifies the concept is joined to the general term, which it specifies. The sequence is usually in accord with the peculiar genius of the language of the community into which the child is growing: thus, in German and English-speaking children, the composite names are formed with the specifying component preceding the principal name, and in French-speaking children the specifying component predominantly follows the principal name.

In their classic work, the Sterns devote nine pages to the formation of composites, mainly in German-speaking children.[1] We may here cite some of the composite-formations of the Sterns' own children. For example, Hilde Stern, between the ages of 3 and 5, constructed composites such as the following: *hosennackedei* (pants-nakedy)—referring to her brother, who was running around without pants; *bauernschnecke* (peasant-snail)—referring to a snail found among peasant children; *geschenkvater* (gift-father)—referring to her father on the eve of her birthday. Gunther Stern, at 3;2, formed the composite *raupenbank* (caterpillar-bench), to refer to a bench on which he had recently seen a crawling caterpillar; at 3;5, he formed the composite *geburtstagbaum* (birthday-tree), to refer to a Christmas tree which had been present in the house at the time of his sister's birthday.[2]

Many of these early composites are of a momentary character; they are used in a specific context and then disappear. Some, how-

---

[1] Stern (242, Ch. XXII).
[2] For further lists, see Chamberlain (43).

ever, persist and are used in recurrent situations. For example, Hilde Stern formed the composites *wachhemdchen* (wake-shirt, in contrast with night-shirt) and *singewagen* (sing-car, a trolley car making screeching noises); these and other composites were of a more enduring character.

It must be stressed that such composites are for the most part, strongly *context-bound*. In this regard they clearly resemble very early names. That is, like early names, the spontaneous composites apply to referents in very specific, concrete contexts; without the support of such contexts the utterances would be more or less void of meaning. Thus, once again, we have a manifestation of the *principle of spirality:* when the child embarks on the novel operation of forming referents through composition, he again takes recourse to a mode of handling language which he had already passed on the level of sentence usage.

Derivation

At a level where a child, in building sentences, clearly distinguishes between nouns as thing-words and verbs as action-words, he may nevertheless, for the construction of new names through derivation, take recourse to the primordial interpenetration of thing and action. Children's records between 2 and 7 years of age contain numerous instances of such spontaneous creations, which give evidence of the tendency to name action as qualified by the nature of the object involved and to name an object in terms of its action.

Following are illustrations of action words created by Stern's children that are derivatives of nouns:

2;6   *schlachten* (from "schlacht" = battle) = to play soldiers
2;6   *die Raupe raupt* = the caterpillar caterpillars
3;6   *bezähnen* (from "zähne" = teeth) = to show one's teeth
3;8   *du klavierst* (from "klavier" = piano) = you play the piano
3;9   *metern* = to measure with a meterstick
3;11 *aufperlen* = threading pearls
3;11 *dieben* (from "dieb" = thief) = to steal

These are illustrations of French-speaking children, taken from Gregoire (86, II, pp. 69 f, 77 f):

4;6   *rater* (from "rateau") = to rake
5;5   *assiette entartée* = napkin soiled by eating tarts

6;0   *je vais m'ensoldater* = I will arm myself for playing soldier
      (soldat)
6;0   *je vais m'empropir* = I am going to make myself proper
7;0   *pain ennoeuffer* = bread dunked into egg (oeuf)
7;3   *enconfituré* = cake with confiture
7;3   *ensiruter* = immerse into syrup

The reciprocal phenomenon, that is, the taking over of "action-names" for the formation of "thing-concepts," is illustrated in the following examples from the Sterns:

3;5   *eine schliesse* ("a closer") = a doorhandle
3;5   *eine drehe* ("a turner") = a windowlatch
5;11 *eine rauche* ("a smoke") = a cigar
5;11 *der wurster* ("the sausager") = the butcher

Bean (15) gives illustrations from an American child. His son (5;0) called a towel a *wipe-it-dry*. Particularly interesting are the word formations of Stumpf's son (246), who employed, up to 3½ years, his own idiomorphic language. He formed names such as *wausch-kap* ("Meat-tearing up") = a knife; *pip-sh-sh* ("point-scratch") = a pencil.

One will note that in derivation, as in the case of composition, the *principle of spirality* again is evidenced. When the child embarks on the operation of forming new referents through derivation, he again starts at that primitive point where the segregation of thing referents as against action referent—already clearly attained at the level of his sentence usage—is partially dissolved.[3]

Defining of Verbal Concepts

Up to this point, our discussion has centered on linguistic operations executed in concrete situations. As the child advances towards cognitive tasks of a higher order, involving new operations, the *principle of spirality* is again manifested. Thus, when the child undertakes the operations involved in defining a verbal concept, given in isolation—

---

[3] It is, of course, in the "spirit" of Indo-European languages that there is at all times the powerful tendency to form new words by composition and derivation. Characteristically, in technologically and linguistically advanced cultures, such activities spontaneously emerge from a primordial sphere of linguistic functioning where speech is less bound by convention, for example, in colloquial talk, in the slang of special groups, in advertising, etc. See Werner (271, p. 202); Sperber (235).

and later on, in forming relations between verbal concepts—his linguistic activity at each of these higher levels of functioning is again, at the outset, global, diffuse, and concretely contextualized. In other words, as the child seeks to realize these new demands, he again begins in a relatively primitive manner: for example, he dissolves distinctions such as that between thing-name and action-name, which were long since established in genetically earlier activities.

The answers given in the task of defining verbal concepts—"What is a bottle?" or "What is a flower?"—show clearly that many of the definitions of thing-concepts (noun-like names) given by young children are in terms of concretely contextualized action. For example, in Pohlmann's study (193) of the meanings of words in school children, the following definitions were given by children between the ages of 5 and 6 for "bottle": *There's lemonade in it; Where you put water; When a little boy drinks milk out of it; Where you pour something out of.* It is clear from definitions such as these that the young child's verbal concepts are rooted in specific, concrete, action-contexts, and that their meaning cannot be formulated in symbols remote from such contexts.

The definitions of such younger children may be contrasted with typical definitions for "bottle" given by older children in Pohlmann's study: *that's a hollow, round glass vessel into which one pours drinks* (child of 12;0); *a container into which all kinds of liquids go* (child of 13;0). Here one sees a movement away from the defining of words in terms of action-contexts towards definition in terms of relatively context-free, general thing-names.

In this connection one may mention a comprehensive study by Barnes (14), dealing with the definitions of children from 6 to 15 years of age. His findings present an impressive picture of the ontogenetic decline of definitions formulated in terms of concrete action from 82 percent at the 6-year level to 33 percent at the 15-year level. It is worthy of note that, according to these findings, even in children of 10 years of age, more than 50 percent of the definitions of thing-names are still in terms of concrete acton.

Relating Verbal Concepts: Analogical Relations

There are many studies concerned with the child's growing ability to form relationships between verbal concepts; among these, investigations on the formation of analogical relations are particularly well suited for an ontogenetic analysis. Here again, with linguistic operations applied to a cognitive task of a higher order, developmental changes are in accord with the *principle of spirality:* the child of school age evidences in his everyday sentence usage the fact that he rather clearly distinguishes between thing-names (nouns), action-names (verbs), property-names (adjectives), etc.—but when he is faced with a task in which the names have to be used in relative isolation to express relationships between concepts, the categorial distinctions may break down.   Thus, in a situation requiring the naming of concept d, which stands in the same relationship to concept c as b stands to a, the younger the child the more frequently will he construe the isolated conceptual names in a holophrastic, almost monoremic manner, that is, as referring to a global context.

In a comprehensive study on the formation of such analogical relationships, M. Muchow (171, p. 53) has provided evidence that even children of 8 to 10 years of age frequently give solutions based on an holophrastic conception of names.   To illustrate, an 8;3-year-old boy completed the analogy, *train : engineer,* as *carriage : ?* with the response *horse;* he justified his response in the following way: "as for the train, the engineer is in front of it, and looks around and his job is to watch where the train goes, and as to the carriage, there is the horse in front and he also looks where he is going." Another child, of about the same age, completed the relationship *apple : peel* as *rabbit : ?* by giving the word *brown.* "The apple has a peel around it; the rabbit is so brown (gesturing) all around it." Here a property name, designating a color, is used by the child holophrastically to signify the "brown fur around the rabbit." Still another child of the same age, completed the relationship *carpenter : wood—smith : ?,* with *smiths.* She accompanied this verb by a movement of hammering intensely and commented on her solution by remarking: "so strongly!" The child, according to Muchow, formed this relationship on the basis of the fusion of the object 'wood' with the action of the carpenter: in other words, the carpenter (*woods*) *wood* and the smith *smiths* (*iron*).

The kinds of "errors" noted by Muchow seem to derive principally from the fact that the child transforms a task requiring a logical relationship between relatively self-contained verbal concepts into one in which the names (concepts) are no longer categorially defined but signify referents of a more global, contextual character.[4]

---

[4] At present there is in progress at Clark University a comprehensive developmental study by Arlene A. Roberts dealing with the processes involved in the forming of analogies. Subjects range from 5-15 years.

Generalizing Verbal Concepts Through Verbal Contexts

At a certain point in development, words come to acquire meanings relatively independent of specific, concrete contexts of application, that is, words become lexicalized. This process of establishing a stable, relatively general meaning for words, a meaning which transcends specific significances of a word in different contexts, is a long and difficult one. A child who already uses a word fluently and adequately in a variety of linguistic utterances may meet with considerable difficulties when asked to take the word out of the contexts and to give it a general meaning which will apply in all contexts. The developmental process eventuating in the relative autonomy of lexical units was studied by H. Werner and E. Kaplan (275) in children from $8\frac{1}{2}$ to $13\frac{1}{2}$ years of age, by means of a specially designed "Word-Context Test." This test consisted of twelve series of six sentence-contexts each, with an artificial "word" placed in each of the six sentences of a series. The task was to arrive at the meaning for the artificial word which would fit all six sentences of a series. Of these series, only those involved in our discussions are reproduced here.

Series I. Corplum (adequate translation—stick, or piece of wood)

1. A corplum may be used for support.
2. Corplums may be used to close off an open place.
3. A corplum may be long or short, thick or thin, strong or weak.
4. A wet corplum does not burn.
5. You can make a corplum smooth with sandpaper.
6. The painter used a corplum to mix his paints.

Series II. Hudray (grow, increase, expand, etc.)

1. If you eat well and sleep well you will hudray.
2. Mrs. Smith wanted to hudray her family.
3. Jane had to hudray the cloth so that the dress would fit Mary.
4. You hudray what you know by reading and studying.
5. To hudray the number of children in the class there must be enough chairs.
6. You must have enough space in the bookcase to hudray your library.

Series III. Contavish (hole)

1. You can't fill anything with a contavish.
2. The more you take out of a contavish the larger it gets.
3. Before the house is finished the walls must have contavishes.
4. You can't feel or touch a contavish.
5. A bottle has only one contavish.
6. John fell into a contavish in the road.

Series V. Ashder (obstacle, obstruction)

1. A lazy man stops working when there is an ashder.
2. An ashder keeps you from doing what you want to do.
3. Mr. Brown said to Mr. Smith, "I don't think we should start with this work because there are ashders."
4. The way is clear if there are no ashders.
5. Before finishing the task he had to get rid of a few ashders.
6. Jane had to turn back because there was an ashder in the path.

Series VIII. Prignatus (deceive)

1. Boys sometimes prignatus their parents.
2. Mary did not know that Jane used to prignatus.
3. Mother said, "Jimmy you should never prignatus your own mother."
4. If you prignatus someone you will not get away with it often.
5. A good man who tells the truth will never prignatus you.
6. If John prignatus somebody he makes sure they don't find out.

Series IX. Bordick (fault)

1. People with bordicks are often unhappy.
2. A person who has many bordicks is not well liked.
3. The plan to build a house was a bordick because it cost too much.
4. People talk about the bordicks of others and don't like to talk about their own.
5. A person has many bordicks because he doesn't listen to wise men.
6. If you are smart and work hard your work will not have a bordick.

Series X.   Lidber (gather)

1. All the children will lidber at Mary's party.
2. The police did not allow the people to lidber on the street.
3. The people lidbered about the speaker when he finished his talk.
4. People lidber quickly when there is an accident.
5. The more flowers you lidber the more you will have.
6. Jimmy lidbered stamps from all countries.

From the wide variety of semantic and syntactic processes analyzed in the original study, we shall select for discussion here only processes that are directly related to the child's attempt to form a general lexicalized concept.

The task of construing an artificial word as a general, categorially circumscribed, concept which fits semantically and syntactically in a number of different sentence-contexts requires that such a vehicle be self-contained, circumscribed, and relatively invariant in its meaning (reference); this can only be attained where the child can grasp the fact that a word may carry an autonomous meaning, independent of particular contexts in which it may appear.

The results of the "Word-Context Test" showed clearly that, for younger subjects, the artificial pattern or vehicle was not endowed with a self-contained meaning which could be inserted within a context and yet which could remain semantically independent of that context. There was, in other words, no *lexical concept* for the younger children. The meaning of the word tended to be some global connotative sphere which the entire linguistic context evoked in the child.[5] The following examples may serve to illustrate the relative *lack of differentiation between words and sentence-contexts* in the young child seeking to attain a general concept. One may note with respect to some of these examples that such a word-sentence undifferentiatedness may be manifested in the very first context with which the child copes. It is more characteristic, however, for the child to fit a circumscribed meaning into the first sentence-context, but to regress to *contextualized* meanings when obliged to arrive at a "general" meaning adequate to two or more sentences of a series.

For instance, a 10-year-old child endowed *hudray* (Series II) with a global-contextual meaning in one sentence-context and then retained

---

[5] In other words, when the vocable was isolated from the context, it reverted to the status of a *name,* that is, a status prior to the differentiation of word and sentence.

that meaning for all the other sentence contexts, despite the fact that that meaning could not be inserted in the other contexts without radically altering the structure of the sentences: the meaning assigned by the child to *hudray* "fit" all the contexts only insofar as the word was fused with the contexts, and the contexts were globally and diffusely apprehended. Thus, for the first sentence, "If you eat well and sleep well you will *hudray*," the child substituted *feel good* for the artificial word. For the second sentence, "Mrs. Smith wanted to *hudray* her family," the child retained *feel good* as his solution by rearranging the sentence, i.e., "Mrs. Smith wanted her family to *feel good*." For the third sentence-context, there was again a radical rearrangement of the sentence, and *feel good* was again found to fit: "Jane had to *hudray* the cloth so that the dress would fit Mary," the child stated, "Jane makes the dress good to fit Mary so that Mary *feels good*." Similarly, for the fourth context, "You *hudray* what you know by reading and studying"; the child stated: "Well after reading and studying, you *feel good;* at least you learn something and know something." Again, for the fifth context, "To *hudray* the number of children in the class there must be enough chairs," the child asserted: "When there are enough chairs for the children in the class, they *feel good*." Finally, for the last sentence-context, "You must have enough space in the bookcase to *hudray* your library," the child stated, "If you have enough space in the bookcase to put in some books, you *feel good*."

One should note that, in these cases of word-sentence undifferentiatedness, there is little "respect" for the structure of the sentence-context. It is as if the sentence-context were a take-off point rather than a stable structure. The child so to speak goes directly to the complex referent and then elaborates upon this referent, without considering the necessity for retaining the sentence-context as it is given. This lack of differentiation between the structure of the sentence and the ideas aroused by the various vehicles comprising the sentence attests to the fact that the linguistic medium, at this stage, has not yet reached a stable autonomous status.[6]

At a somewhat more advanced level than the sort of word-sentence fusion we have discussed thus far are instances in which the meaning assigned to the artificial word appears to be partly independent of and

---

[6] It seems to us that some of the interpretations made by others, e.g., R. Brown, in Bruner, et al. (31, pp. 297 ff) of the findings obtained via the "Word-Context Test" have emphasized rather peripheral aspects of the study and have overlooked central aspects pertaining to the acquisition of word-meanings and the formation of verbal concepts.

partly fused with the sentence-context. In these cases, parts of a verbal context, surrounding the artificial word, creep into the meaning assigned to that word-form and then remain incorporated in it as it is applied to other sentence-contexts. One may designate this process as one of *word-sentence overlap*, or as involving a *contextual gradient*. One illustration may suffice to show this process in operation.

A 10-year-old child, for the sixth sentence of the *lidber* series, inserted *collect* for *lidber:* "Jimmy *collected* stamps from all countries." Ostensibly *lidber* just meant *collect*. When, however, the child went back to the previous sentences of the series, it became clear that part of the sixth sentence-context, "stamps," was involved in the meaning assigned to *lidber*. Thus, for the second sentence, the child remarked, "The police did not allow the people to *collect stamps* on the street;" he continued, "It wouldn't be tidy to collect stamps on the street on a windy day—they would all be flying around."

When one looks at the various examples, coming from subjects as old as 11 years of age, one is struck by the paradox that such a lack of differentiation between a word and its linguistic context can occur at a period when words are ordinarily *used* in sentences with complete regard for semantic and grammatical considerations.

This discrepancy indicates, as we have briefly suggested, that the operations involved in the apprehension of words as bearers of circumscribed, context-independent, general concepts are quite different from the operations involved in the utterance of sentences in everyday discourse.

It is again noteworthy that, when the child goes to a new, higher level of functioning, he starts out in a syncretic, relatively undifferentiated manner, formally analogous to his behavior at earlier levels of linguistic activity. This again is a manifestation of the *principle of spirality*.

In the progression towards the formation of context-independent, general word-meanings, several stages can be discerned, which are more advanced than those just discussed but where true lexical concepts have not yet been attained. In one such stage, which we may designate as that of *word-embeddedness*, the child has little or no difficulty in assigning a meaning to the artificial word in each sentence-context; in fact, he often construes the artificial word in a way eminently suited to each individual context. Nevertheless, the child cannot form an overall solution precisely because the meanings suited to the various sentence-contexts are *context-specific*. The child either cannot change a meaning once it has been inserted in a certain sentence-context, or he cannot subsume context-specific meanings under a more general concept. Yet the task demands of him somehow to reconcile the adequacy of fit in *specific* contexts with a *general, unitary* word-meaning. One of the intermediary ways in which children attempt to realize these superficially incompatible ends is by assigning to the artificial word a meaning comprised of an *aggregation* of the context-specific meanings: two or more context-specific meanings are intertwined, linked to each other now in a quasi-causal way, now in a finalistic way, etc.

To illustrate, one child (at 9;1) gave *paint* as the meaning for *contavish* in the third sentence-context of that series: "Before the house is finished the walls must have *paint*." For the fourth context, the child inserted *air* for *contavish:* "You can't feel or touch *air*." When asked what *contavish* meant, the child said, *paint and air*. He fitted this meaning into the third sentence-context as follows: "The walls must have *air* before the house is finished so that the *paint* will dry."

A 10-year-old child, in dealing with the same series, inserted *cardboard* for *contavish* in the first sentence of that series: "You can't fill anything with a *cardboard*." For the second sentence-context, the child inserted the word-meaning *room* for *contavish:* "The more you take out of a *room* the larger it gets." At this point, the overall meaning of *contavish* for the child was *cardboard and room*. This meaning was fitted into the second sentence-context as follows: "The more *cardboard* you take out of a *room*, the larger the *room* gets."

In these and similar instances, the attempt to meet the demands both of *specificity to context* and *generality of reference* leads to the formation of meanings for the artificial word, which neither attain the requisite generality, nor actually fit—in a semantically and syntactically adequate way—into the specific contexts as these are presented to the child.

In a stage more advanced towards lexical conceptualization, the demands for generality of reference and context-specificity come closer to being reconciled, although they are still not fully harmonized. At this stage, the child characteristically gives an overall meaning to the artificial word and a series of specific meanings for the individual contexts; he then globally connects the specific meanings to the overall meaning in a vague, subsumption-like relationship. Thus the overall meaning is not itself inserted or insertable in place of the artificial word in the various sentence-contexts; it "enters" into the various contexts only by way of the context-specific solutions. This process of "indirect" insertion of a general meaning into specific contexts via particular meanings may, after William Stern (241, Chapter 27) be designated as *pluralization*. There are two main characteristics of a "plural concept": it subsumes, in a vague way, the word-meanings specific to individual contexts, and yet it is either too over-inclusive or too vague to fit the individual sentences.

To illustrate: one child gave the following context-specific meanings for *prignatus:* (1) *hit back*—"Boys sometimes *hit back* (at) their parents;" (2) *lie*—"Mary did not know that Jane used to *lie;*" (3) *holler at*—"Mother said, 'Jimmy, you should never *holler at* your own mother,'" etc. Asked for the overall or general meaning of *prignatus,* the child replied, *"not respect your elders."*

Another child, 10 years old, gave *dripple glass* as the meaning for *contavish* in the first sentence of that series: "You can't fill anything with a *dripple glass."* He gave *jack-in-the-box* as the meaning for *contavish* in the second sentence: "The more you take out of a *jack-in-the-box* the larger it gets."* Asked for the overall meaning of *contavish,* the child said, *"plaything."* Though there is actual subsumption of various specific meanings under one term, that term in itself is too vague for an adequate semantic fit into each context.

Closely related to pluralization, but entailing a greater advance towards the lexical concept is a process which we may designate *transposition.* Here, too, there is a struggle to reconcile the conflict between the two opposing tendencies—one towards the formation of an overall, general meaning, the other towards the retention of context-specific meanings. In contradistinction to *pluralization,* however, in using *transposition* the child seems clearly to recognize the demand for a syntactically adequate fitting of the general concept in each specific sentence-context. This demand is here met by expanding the meaning of one context-specific solution—equating all the other context-specific meanings with that one solution. This "equating" is done by means of such expressions of assimilation as "like-a," "sort-of," "kind-of," etc. Through this operation, the child achieves a general meaning which is, for him, both semantically and syntactically adequate.

To illustrate: a child (11;8) employed *bar* in sentence 2 of the first series: "A *bar* may be used to close off an open place." Coming back to sentence 1, he says: "a *leg of table* may be used for support; *bar* fits—a *leg of table* is a sort-a *bar."*

Another child (9;3) offered *teacher* as the meaning for *ashder* in the second sentence of that series: "A *teacher* keeps you from doing what you want to do." In the first context, he had inserted *boss* for *ashder:* "A lazy man stops working when there is a *boss."* In attempting to show the generality of his meaning for the second sentence-context, the child remarked: *"Teacher* fits sentence one, because let's say the 'boss' tells you to do something else—he bosses you around—well, the owner of the store is sort of like a teacher, right? The owner in the store bosses the people around—so *'teacher'* fits here and there."

The next and final step, of course, is the actual formation of *general lexical concepts.* Here, the artificial word, the potential vehicle, is construed so that it is both general—transcending any of the particular contexts—and yet sufficiently specific to be applicable in each of the particular contexts. To illustrate: for *prignatus,* one child gave *lie to* as its meaning in the first sentence: "Boys sometimes *lie to* their parents;" for the second sentence, the solution was *cheat:* "Mary did not know that Jane used to *cheat;" deceive* was the solution for the fourth sentence: "You may *deceive* someone but you will not get away with it often." *Deceive* was then used to subsume both *lie to* and *cheat;* it was a word-meaning that could be fitted into all the sentence-contexts without entailing either vague reference or syntactic distortion.

Before summarizing the various stages just discussed, we may first look more closely at the characteristics of the fully developed lexical concept. The criteria for a lexicalized concept are: (1) that it is symbolized as a word, that is, as a vocable having a syntactic-grammatical as well as referential function; (2) that it is isolable from specific linguistic contexts; and (3) that it is capable via the word-form of being placed in a variety of linguistic contexts (sentences) as a unit in the building up of complex references. In other words, a lexical concept in its development grows out of sentence structures, becomes independent of particular sentences, and then can be used in building up new sentences. The difficulties of arriving at lexical concepts are caused by the necessity of considering—and harmonizing—in *one* act the demands, on one hand, for generality of reference, isolability from contexts, and on the other hand, for amenability to particular interpretations within particular sentence-contexts without loss of generic identity.

As we have implied, one must—to arrive at a fuller understanding of the processes involved in the development of lexical concepts—take into account not only the handling of the word but also the *structuring of the sentence.* As will be recalled, we have maintained that the structuring of the word and the structuring of the sentence are correlative phenomena: from this, it would follow that the degree of stability of word structure is intimately linked with the degree of stability of the sentence structure.

In deriving a general meaning for a vocable occurring in various sentence contexts (as in the "Word-Context" test), there is, therefore, not only the problem of contouring the word within the larger context of a sentence but also the problem of "setting off" each sentence-context from the other contexts in which the vocable appears. In order to achieve a lexical concept, therefore, one of the basic prerequisites is that of keeping the reference of one context distinct from the reference of each of the other contexts.

As we have seen, one of the earliest attempts of the experimental subjects to arrive at an overall concept involved a *fusion of word-meaning and sentence-meaning:* the word, so to speak, was taken as a condensed sentence. Characteristically, at the same time, the various sentence-contexts were more or less fused or intermingled with each other.

At the next step, that of the *contextual gradient* or *word-sentence overlap,* there is still a considerable lack of differentiation, but this fusion is somewhat diminished. There is, to some degree, an independence of word-meaning from sentence-context; the child can give a meaning to a vocable occupying a certain syntactic position, but this meaning is only in part separate from the context. Such meanings, which are fully or partly fused with the meanings of one context, can be applied in other contexts because the two (or more) contexts are themselves not very sharply distinguished from each other.

When the child reaches the next stage, that of *context-specific meanings* and the attainment of generality through *aggregation* of concepts, he has to some degree achieved the understanding that a vocable in a particular sentence-context has a discrete, specific meaning. His mode of attaining *generality,* however, indicates that the vocable (artificial word) has not yet been grasped as having a stable unitary decontextualized meaning; at the same time, the sentence structure is still so labile as to permit the easy incorporation of alien elements.

With the stage of *pluralization,* the child not only achieves context-specificity, that is, specific, circumscribed meanings for each context, but he is able to keep the sentence-contexts distinct from each other and to maintain the vocable as a lexical unit. However, he still lacks the articulation of word-sentence relationships to the extent that he can *simultaneously* grasp the word as a self-contained (lexical) unit and as an element of a sentence.

With the use of the operation of *transposition,* that is, the inordinate extension of a context-specific solution, the child achieves some "generality" and context-specificity; he is now only one step removed from the formation of true *lexical concepts.* The sentence-contexts are relatively well structured and distinct from each other, but the overall meaning of the circumscribed vocable is not yet of a truly general character. Only when the general meaning assigned to a vocable transcends and subordinates meanings given in the specific contexts has the child attained true lexical concepts (see Figure 13-1).

In sum, in the light of the results from the "Word-Context" test, the interdependence of word-formation and sentence structurization is clearly reflected in the high correlation between increasing *lexicalization* of the vocable and increasingly *stable structuring* of the *sentence-contexts*. The findings provide evidence for a lability and diffuseness in the structuring of sentences accompanying the earlier attempts at generality of meaning: the contexts are fused with each other, additions are made to the contexts, parts are omitted, etc. As the overall word-meaning becomes increasingly lexicalized, distortions and changes in the structure of the sentences disappear. It is significant that during

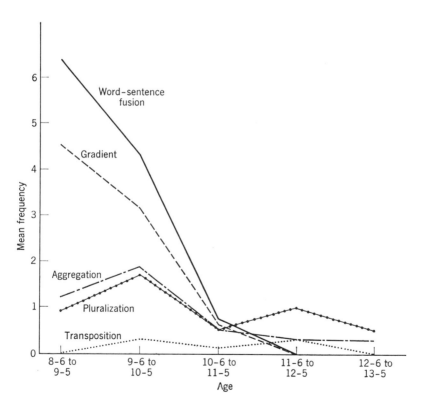

FIGURE 13-1. Word-context test performance: Frequency of processes lacking lexicalization.

the age period (10;6–11;5) in which the word is given a more or less self-contained, context-independent meaning, the more marked distortions of the sentences drop out almost completely; and at the (later) age period (12;6–13;5) in which the artificial word has been assigned a general meaning (has become completely lexicalized), even the minor alterations of the sentence structures tend to disappear.[7]

---

[7] Cf. (275, pp. 85 ff).

part III

The Primordial Handling of the Linguistic Medium in Special States

Introduction

In Part II, we concerned ourselves mainly with the ontogenesis of representation in the vocal-linguistic medium; there we digressed only slightly with regard to pathological or specialized deviations from the normal ontogenetic sequence. In this Part, we examine the handling of the verbal medium in some special states and under special orientations of the symbolizer; that is, we discuss the handling of speech-forms in three primordial ways: (a) where a special physiognomic attitude is taken towards words (and sentences); (b) where vocal-verbal forms enter into dreams; and (c) where schizophrenics utilize language in a regressed manner.

chapter 14

The Physiognomic Apprehension of Language Forms

In our theoretical exposition on the development of symbolization, we emphasized the genetic primordiality of "natural symbols," that is, vehicles formed in intonational, gestural, and other media, which manifestly express or depict dynamic aspects of the meanings they represent. Symbol formation, we maintained, originates during a stage in which the pattern forged into a symbolic vehicle and the material shaped into an object of reference are so closely linked that the relation obtaining between them is one of tangible, perceptible similarity.

We also pointed out that in the handling and shaping of the vocal medium, onomatopoetic forms reflect this primordial relationship of external similarity. Following this stage of onomatopoetic forms, there occurs a progressive "distancing" between the external form of the vehicle and the referent represented by that vehicle. Eventually, the manifest iconic relationship between symbolic pattern and referent becomes so remote that many students of language have argued that an inner bond between vehicle and referent disappears altogether, to be replaced by a relationship of contiguity or external association.

It is an essential tenet of our organismic-developmental theory of symbolization that the basic relationship between any speech-form and the referent it represents cannot be one of mere contiguity or association. We have maintained that the contiguity thesis has a superficial plausibility only if one views vehicle and object as end-forms or products, that is, only if one overlooks the organismic activity essential both to the formation of objects and to the formation of symbolic vehicles. From our theoretical standpoint, all symbolic relationships involve a structuring of vehicle *and* referent, so that for the symbolizing individual an inner relationship (one of analogy or similarity) obtains between the two moments.

One is, of course, cognizant of an immediate obstacle which seems to arise when one attempts to apply this theoretical viewpoint to the relationship between conventional word-forms and the objects to which they refer. Though most people will perhaps admit a depictive relationship between vehicle and referent for such onomatopoetic forms as *boom* and *sizzle,* they will be far less inclined to concede, or even acknowledge the possibility, that such an inner relationship may obtain between words like *gay, true, move,* etc., and their referents.

It seems to us that both the acceptance of a similarity relationship in the case of onomatopoetic forms, and the questioning of such a relationship in the case of conventional forms, typically rests on a "naive realism" in which objects and the relations (e.g., similarity) between objects are presumed to exist in pure 'objectivity,' independent of any activity on the part of subjects. For many, the onomatopoetic form is simply a copy of an event or happening, objectively existing in a fixed form in the nature of things. Since an 'objective' similarity cannot be seen between conventional forms and their referents, any connection is here assumed to be external and arbitrary.

We have already noted that onomatopoeia is not a simple mirroring of an independently given "reality." The onomatopoetic relationship involves the *establishment* of a bond of similarity between an object formed in the medium of perception and a vehicle shaped in the medium of sound or vocalization. There is an unwitting "translation" from perception into a phonemic medium, or better, a concurrent shaping of material in two media, perception and vocal articulation.[1] There is no more an independently given similarity between onomatopoetic forms and their referents than there is between conventional forms and the objects to which they refer. In both cases, there is an *establishment* of "similarity."

It is our contention that, underlying the handling and active use of conventional linguistic forms as symbols of an individual's referents, there is organismic activity which involves the putting into play of primordial operations. These operations are often overlooked in

---

[1] See Chamberlain (43); also Grammont (85), Hornbostel (110).

our day-to-day use of symbols, because—as with other primordial operations in normal activity—they are subordinated to, and integrated within, higher levels of functioning. Nevertheless, they can be brought to the fore—again as with other primordial operations—under special experimental conditions.

It is in this light that the discussion of an early study by Werner (269) on the physiognomization of linguistic forms may be of particular relevance. It is here implied that the spontaneously established physiognomic forms are midway between onomatopoetic forms, which seem to mirror their referents, and conventional forms which are externally, though not internally, remote from their referents. Where one observes what occurs when a physiognomic attitude is induced with regard to conventional forms having a relatively stable phonemic organization, one may gain a greater insight into the persistence of organismic activity in symbolization through conventional forms.

In the following presentation of Werner's study, we shall deal first with the *major characteristics of physiognomized words,* then with the *nature of the physiognomizing process,* and finally with certain findings pertaining to the *physiognomization of grammatical categories.*

Major Characteristics of Physiognomized Words

Following from the thesis that symbolic development entails an increase in distance between vehicles and referents, one would expect a "denaturalization" of symbolic vehicles. Applied to language, this means that there would be an ontogenetic decline in the physiognomization of verbal forms. This process of "denaturalization" does not imply, however, that the verbal symbols at advanced levels are entirely 'objective' phenomena, divorced from the formative activity of the symbolizer or the listening individual. We submit that even the most conventionalized units of speech—words and sentences—are still part and parcel of an articulatory process, bodily postural activity, which, through its dynamic features, links those conventionalized units to their referents.

The typical ontogenetic shift from strongly physiognomized vocal forms to the conventional forms of everyday speech does not, in other words, mean a loss of dynamic structurization: rather, it involves a decline in intensity, a decrease in fullness and, perhaps most important, a change in the degree to which the dynamic processes of formation and articulation are realized outwardly in the visual and phonic-auditory patterns that are shared by addressor and addressee. Indeed, we maintain that were such dynamic processes to be eliminated or impaired—such processes involving postural-affective-dynamic schematization—the conventional forms would undergo "loss of meaning." [2] Furthermore, we contend that only on the assumption of the presence of such tendencies toward organismic structurization can one understand the relative ease with which individuals can adopt instructions to physiognomize conventional forms, that is, to bring to the surface their articulatory activity.

It is important to recognize that the ontogenetic shift from physiognomic patterns to conventional forms comprises a range of stages, which differ in the degree to which the dynamic structuring activity is realized or externalized in the vehicular patterns.

It may be remarked further that, in living speech, these various stages may appear side by side or in quick alternation, depending upon the nature of the communication situation, the character of the addressee, the momentary and pervasive orientations of the symbolizer, the universe of discourse, etc. Thus, conventional forms are much more likely to be selected and shaped in terms of greater externalization of dynamic features in poetic discourse or in advertising than in discourse aimed at the communication of sober information about impersonal states of affairs.

In the experiments by Werner to be reported here, the subjects were required to alter their everyday manner of dealing with (perceiving and comprehending) words, so that these linguistic forms tangibly—visibly and/or auditorily—portrayed their meanings. After having carried out this task for a particular word, the subjects were requested to report their introspections concerning the characteristics of the physiognomized forms. Twenty subjects were employed in the study. Though there were considerable individual differences with regard to the ease with which a subject took to the task, everyone succeeded to some extent in the task of physiognomization of the verbal forms. The verbal material—mainly words, but also some sentences—was printed on cards. The reports of the subjects were taken down verbatim.

The analysis of the protocols unearthed a number of characteristics of physiognomized language. We may briefly discuss and illustrate the three most significant ones, namely: (1) the quasi-substantial, thing-like character; (2) the pictorial-dynamic character; and (3) the organismic character, i.e., the embeddedness in, and emergence from, postural-affective-motor states. All these characteristics reflect the genetically primordial nature of such physiognomized language, that

---

[2] See the discussion of "lapse of meaning," pp. 29 ff.

is, a *decrease in distance* between the symbolizer (agent) and symbolic vehicle, on the one hand, and the symbolic vehicle and referent, on the other.

The Quasi-substantial, Thing-like Character of Physiognomized Words

In contrast with the way in which linguistic forms are apprehended in everyday commerce, physiognomized words were quite frequently characterized by the subjects as possessing a kind of substantial, thing-like nature: they were experienced as possessing properties which were "out there" in space, confronting the observer with a peculiar objectivity of their own. This substance-like character was particularly apparent with regard to visually apprehended forms but was also experienced when the word-forms were apprehended auditorily. A few typical reports may suffice as illustrations. (Werner, 269, pp. 35, 55)

Holz (wood): "Something crude, raw, uncouth. One gets stuck at its splinters if one moves over the word with one's eyes. This quality seems to be (visually and articulatory-auditorily) centered particularly in the *o* and the *z*."

Wolle (wool): "The word has the material properties of what it signifies. It looks to me like the soft, somewhat dull, woolen hair at the bottom of fur. Softness lies particularly in the *w* and the *o* while the articulatory quality of *ll* has something dull, fibrous, stringy, which for me is characteristic of wool. One looks and moves tactually over some dull, unsmooth surface; the hollow *o* and *e* are like very dull spots in an altogether lustreless woolly fur."

Such substantiality and tangibility pertained not only to nouns, but also to forms generally subsumed under other parts of speech, such as adjectives.

braunrot (brownred): "Glancing over it, it's like touching the disagreeable sandy quality of rusty iron."

faul (decayed): "One dips into the word without finding resistance, like into rotten fruit."

kalt (cold): " 'kalt' is structured from the sound *a*. This *a* goes through my spine like a cold wave; from here the word visibly and auditorily acquires some rigidity and stiffness. At the same time the word has something of a 'don't-touch-me' quality; it is something which one must not take into one's hand—something one might approach gingerly, with a flat hand, but which, before contact is actually made, would make one shrink away from it."

In a few instances, the physiognomically perceived words reached such a high degree of realism that there occurred what one might call a "coherence" of the physiognomic pattern with perceptual reality. A good example of the coherence of the physiognomized visual pattern with actual space is the following.

The German homonym, "Tor," has two meanings: 'door' and 'fool.' One subject reported that he got one or the other of these two meanings best by manipulating the card in space: "In order to get 'Tor' (fool), I have to stand the card upright but somewhat inclined backwards, that is, with its upper edge farther back. As soon as I straighten the card so that it stands perpendicularly, the word meaning changes to 'Tor' (door)."

Another subject, quite analogously, stated that when the card was lying directly in front of him, 'Tor' had the meaning of 'door;' it was most easily grasped as 'fool,' when the card was placed somewhat to the left. (Werner, 269, p. 39)

The Pictorial-Dynamic Character of Physiognomized Words

As has already been suggested, physiognomically shaped or apprehended patterns differ in at least one major respect from patterns regarded in a conventional, everyday, pragmatic-technical way. In conventionally apprehended forms—and here we are concerned with forms used symbolically—the symbolizer is typically unaware of any manifestation in the material pattern of the meaning (referent) which that pattern represents; in contradistinction, in physiognomic apprehension, *dynamic-expressive features* of the pattern are vividly experienced as directly exhibiting or depicting what it means.

In principle, the physiognomic shaping of linguistic material is no different from the physiognomic structurization of any other kind of material. In actuality, however, there is one important difference: in the physiognomic apprehension of *nonconventional forms*, whether vocal or otherwise, one is free to select any expressive features in the material and to structure the material in any way so as to embody or adequately exhibit a meaning. In the physiognomization of conventional linguistic forms, however, the individual is restricted in his handling of the material pattern. He must preserve the linguistically given form, that is, he is obliged to carry out any shaping or modulating of the pattern (whether written or heard), without encroaching upon its basic linguistic structure.

We have already illustrated the concrete pictorial dynamics inherent in physiognomically perceived words in the examples given. To these instances, a few more may be added which are particularly valuable in exemplifying the concrete dynamics of words apprehended in this way.

One subject remarked that *Seife* (soap) "has for me the character of something viscous, smeary, gelatinous, something spreading without definite form and consistency. It is particularly in the broadly spreading *ei* and the gelatine-like flowing sound, *f*, where these characteristics are centered."

For *fromm* (pious, devout), the following remarks were made: "Have it before me, first as a printed word—know its meaning, but inaccessible to me as expressive of its meaning—there is a certain lack of closure, quite unsatisfactory—have the feeling the word lacks something most important. . . . But now I'm aware of my (bodily) attitude; it's quite ineffective. . . . By taking a different attitude (a posture of humility) the word suddenly gets a 'religious' face: now it appears very closed, resting in itself, rounded, drawn into itself at its end. It appears humble—the *f*, the *mm* rounded, bent downwards, but—in its being closed within itself, inwardly secure. . . ."

The apprehension of physiognomized words in terms of their peculiar dynamics becomes particularly clear in the responses to synonyms. Such terms, which may well be used interchangeably in everyday pragmatic discourse, differ quite significantly when apprehended physiognomically. The following reports concerning the manner in which subjects handled the synonyms *ruhig* (quiet, calm) and *still* (still) may serve as illustrations:

One subject, for *ruhig*, remarked: "has inner movement, very regular, like quiet up-and-down motion of waves;" for *still*, he stated: "that is something stiff, almost lifeless." Another subject, for *ruhig*, stated: "has in it a calming down, a becoming rather than a being quiet;" *still* was "completely encapsulated, sharply separated and closed up against the outside." For a third subject, *ruhig* "is not at all motionless, there is movement like that of slowly, regularly advancing ocean waves;" "*still*, so to speak, holds its breath like tightened muscles; nothing moves. It can be compared with a tensely bent spring."

The Organismic Character of Physiognomized Words

This characteristic of physiognomized words—their intimate linkage to, or fusion with, organismic bodily activity—is, clearly, most crucially related to our developmental theory of symbol formation; it is, of course, a reflection of the primordial *lack of distance* between the organismic activity (postural-affective) involved in the bodily schematization of meaning and the meaningful symbol itself. The following is typical of the reports of subjects to the word *hart* (hard).

"At the sight of the word I immediately experience a definite 'steel-like' structuring of my body with the center in the back and the neck, particularly strong around the uppermost vertebrae. This structure coalesces fully with the visual structure of the word. Now, the organization dissolves and with it the pictorial expression is lost for a while. I gain it back, however, rather quickly by emphasizing the vertical structure of the *h* and the *t*: but now what previously was all in me, is now partly before me: a visual pattern structured in stern and stiff vertical strokes. The word now has an external existence, out there, rigid, angular, unbendable."

Another illustration of the genetic relationship between bodily schematization and verbal structure can be found in the report of a subject concerning his response to *rot* (red).

"I attempt to grasp the color word *rot* (red) as an expressive pattern, but it remains a mere sign whose meaning I know. Certainly it's no 'red word.' But suddenly I feel how the word so to speak 'glides' into my body; and at this moment, there is in me a round fullness, difficult to describe, expanding within my body, shaping my inner mouth into a spherical cavity. And suddenly I become aware that the word on the paper gets its 'right' expression; it is sensed as a rather darkish red with the central sound *o* possessing that spherical hollowness which my mouth felt first."

A final example of the articulation of word-forms within organismic activity is the following experience of a subject while responding to *feucht* (moist):

"At the start, experience of cold-moist, impression of something diffuse, a strongly dynamic motion of 'sucking-in,' from a surface toward a middle; this dynamic is in the word and in the body: I feel myself organized with a strong tension formed at the surface of my body, a tension drawn inward, sucked inward toward my body center. This dynamic organization pertains to the meaning structure of the word and the body structure which are thus fused in perfect unity: there are not two entities corresponding with each other, but there is sameness, identity. But after a while the whole thing collapses—and it takes some time before the word gets a 'face' again. But now there is twoness where there was one-ness before: now I look at the word as if it were an object—it possesses now some substantial consistency, is now almost a moist substance (cloth, soil, or the like)—but mind you—there is still the suction-like dynamics in my body with its direction from the periphery toward a middle—but this is clearly set apart from the perceived word—both distinct entities though still united."

The problem of the articulation of expressive word-forms within organismic structures is obviously closely related to the more general question concerning the nature of this physiognomizing process; the following discussion in dealing with that problem will therefore refer again to some of the observations already presented.

Nature of the Physiognomizing Process

Having described the main characteristics of physiognomized verbal forms, we may now turn to a consideration of the physiognomic process itself. Here we shall attempt to set forth some of the principal features of the process involved in molding words, that is, forms already possessing a definite phonemic structure, into expressive, physiognomic, forms. In so doing, we shall refer to a number of other studies, which have particular relevance to the understanding of the physiognomizing process.

As we have already mentioned, physiognomization of words differs from physiognomization of nonconventional vocal patterns (or patterns in other media) in that there is a restriction imposed upon the symbolizer. The freedom in shaping the pattern (potential vehicle) to fit the meaning and the referent to fit the vehicular properties is limited, because the relations of the phonemic configurations to their referents (meanings) are, to a great extent, already pre-established in the conventionalized language, and have to be adhered to.[3]

In order to physiognomize the word *soft*, for example, so that it clearly embodies its meaning, one must retain that configuration and operate within that configuration. It may be that one would, given completely free choice, choose other material, or configurate the vocal medium in another way, for the representation of the meaning of *soft*, but once given the conventional code one must operate within it or suffer the probability that the neologism created through the free handling of the vocal medium will be of limited value in communication of reference. Paradoxically, it is precisely the restriction with regard to the malleability of the material which, as we shall see, brings into relief some of the typical features of the physiognomic process.

That one is able to physiognomize already established and relatively stable visual or auditory configurations appears to us to derive from certain characteristics of symbol formation in general. We shall first elaborate on the most important of these characteristics, *the articulation of the physiognomized word within an organismic-bodily matrix.* We shall then discuss *plurisignificance of the vehicular (visual or phonic) material*, the multiplicity of dynamic properties relative to the geometric-technical, conventional singularity of the word-form; *the polysemantic character of the referent*, the multiplicity of connotations relative to the singularity of the referent qua denotatum; and finally, *the bilateral handling of the vehicle and referent*, the selection of ve-

---

[3] Cf. A. MacLeish (160).

hicular properties in terms of the referent, and referential connotations in terms of the vehicle.

Articulation of the Physiognomized Word within an Organismic-Bodily Matrix

In the preceding section, we cited a number of protocols illustrating the genetic significance of bodily organismic structurization in the shaping of physiognomic forms. In such cases, typical of many in the study, the printed word seemed to serve as a signal for a primary psychophysical organization in which the postural set and the verbal form were experienced as a unity. From this fusion, a differentiation took place, leading to a state in which the postural organization and the physiognomized word-form still corresponded to each other, but in which the word-form had *distanced* itself from the organismic matrix and stood as an objective entity, vis-à-vis the observer.

One need only read the observations of the various subjects on the processes leading up to the physiognomization of words like *hard, red, moist,* etc. (see pp. 211 ff), to appreciate the importance that postural sets, inner strivings, and internal gestures have for the establishment of an organismic matrix from which the word as an external form eventually emerges. Interestingly enough, some of the protocols seem to indicate that, in a number of instances, the genetic change from a unitary experience, in which body-posture and word are fused, to a differentiated two-ness, where body-posture and word-form are distinguished, may be abrupt rather than gradual and continuous. In such instances, there seems to be a quick shift from the earlier stage of undifferentiatedness to the later stage of duality between posture and word-form; during this transitional period, the structurization established during the earlier stage ostensibly dissolves.

One gains a particularly clear insight into the nature of this genetic process from certain instances where a subject, in response to a word, first builds up a "wrong" bodily organization: that is, in groping for the "right" bodily attitude, he adopts an inadequate postural set with the consequence that the physiognomization of the word-form does not emerge. This "incorrectness" or inadequacy of bodily organization is well illustrated in the protocol previously cited, dealing with a subject's response to *fromm* (pious). It will be recalled that there the word initially remained expressionless, because of an inadequate postural attitude; only after a change to a more appropriate posture (inner gesture of bowing and humility) did a "religious" physiognomy emerge in *fromm*.

These reports bear a close relation to experimental findings on the "microgenesis" of word-formation, conducted by one of us (Werner, 272) some years ago. The study utilized tachistoscopic presentations ($\frac{1}{50}$ second) of single words, two-word combinations, three-word combinations, and phrases. After each single exposure, the subject had to report everything in his experience pertaining to the presented material. Each stimulus was repeated until the subject was certain of the meaning of the word. This method thus permitted one to study the sequential stages (microgenesis) in articulation of verbal symbols. The words were in German, the mother tongue of the ten subjects.

As one knows from the numerous studies pertaining to tachistoscopic reading, individuals differ greatly in attitude and behavior. In this study, there were subjects at one extreme, who seemed to rely almost entirely on the visually given: they either reported only when the word appeared to them in full visual clarity or they constructed the visual word-pattern from fragments seen during the successive trials. On the other hand, however, there were subjects whose reports consistently reflected a *microgenetic* unfolding of meaningful patterns: the stimuli aroused 'feelings of word-meanings,' inner experiences of the semantic sphere of the linguistic forms, etc., that were apparently prior to any specific articulation of the words. Among the ten subjects of the study, there were two on each of the extremes; the other six oscillated more or less between the extremes.

Where the pattern of responses indicated a microgenetic sequence, one found, for the early stages of the sequence, that there was a prevalence of bodily experiences, which anticipated, in their dynamic features, the meaning sphere of the word before the word per se was fully formed as a visible entity. The following samples may serve as illustrations. The first report is that of a subject who succeeded in reading the tachistoscopically presented words, *Sanfter Wind* (gentle wind), at the fifth presentation.

(1) "—? Wind." What stood before "wind" feels like an adjective specifying nature of wind; feels like "warm" or something similar.

(2) "—ter Wind." Know now that the word is "heavier" than "warm" . . . somehow more abstract.

(3) "—cher Wind." Now it looks more like an adjectve of direction.

(4) "—ter Wind." Now again somewhat more concrete; it faces me and looks somewhat like "weicher Wind" (soft wind), but "ter" is in my way.

(5) Now very clearly: "Sanfter Wind." Not at all surprised. I actually had this before in the characteristic feel of the word and the looks of it.

This report illustrates one remarkable feature of early organismic organization of verbal forms, the apprehension of a *general sphere of meaning* before a more specific determination (recognition) of the word-meaning: thus, the subject first remarked, "feels like warm," and only later recognized *sanfter*.

The following report by the same subject is somewhat similar. Here two verbs, *Ächzen Schwirren* (groan whir), were presented; the pair was recognized on the fourth presentation.

(1) Two long forms equal in height. The last seemed to have something vibrating, something almost like "schwirren," "wirbeln," or the like.

(2) "ächzen" (?). The left word rather guessed than actually seen; its first part impressed me as something depressing, distressing, torturing. Second word not grasped.

(3) "ächzen." The first word almost certain, still same feeling as before (see 2). The second indefinite; nothing vibratory experienced.

(4) "ächzen schwirren." Both words very unclear. The impressions are about the same as in 1 and 2, however, not as precise.

The following are responses of another subject to *Blanke Waffe*, a word combination equivalent to "naked weapon" or "naked sword." For understanding the reactions of this subject, it should be noted that the German, *blank*, also refers to "polished," "smooth." The phrase was recognized on the third presentation.

(1) "—Waffe." Unclear about the first word.

(2) "—nk-Waffe." Read "nk"; before it something from which one slips off, also, impression of something shining; from this, I would guess "blanke."

(3) "Blanke Waffe." Yes, it's correct!

The Plurisignificance of the Vehicular Material

It will be recalled that this characteristic refers to the fact that a pattern which is stable, invariant, and more or less unchanging from a geometric-technical point of view may arouse a multiplicity of dynamic features when viewed physiognomically. This plurisignificance may allow a person, faced with the task of creating or perceiving a meaningful symbol out of visually or phonetically structured material, to select those qualities from the whole range of potential dynamic properties that are pertinent to the representation of a referent. It is precisely because of this plurality of expressive features in a constant phonemic form that an individual is able to shape a given word-form into a physiognomic structure.

For example, subjects in the study on the physiognomics of words (269) were able to seize the quality of "penetratingness" in the *i* in order to express the pointedness in *spitz*. Again, they could grasp the quality of "thinness" in the *i* to express the narrowness in *Ritze* (split), *Schlitz* (slit); or they could grasp the quality of "shrillness" to express the sharpness of motion in *Riss* (a rip), etc. Similarly, *u*, for many subjects, had the property of "depth" adequate to express that quality in *Ruhe* (calmness); or the property of "dull opaqueness" fitting for *stumpf* (blunt). Again, *o* could be perceived now as having the property of "roundness," now the property of "hollowness;" thus for a number of observers, *o* was round in *Gold*, hollow in *Tor* (door).

The handling of diphthongs and umlauts—vowel forms of greater complexity—afforded a particularly clear insight into the plurisignificance of vehicular material. In *grau*, the diphthong, *au*, was perceived by several subjects as embodying a mixture of light and dark; in *faul* (decayed), it was grasped by some subjects as a movement expressing a process of "becoming muddy;" and in *faul* (lazy), the same motion from *a* to *u* expressed an "undisciplined tottering."

The umlaut in German, as the term indicates, is a modification of a pure vowel: *a–ä, o–ö, u–ü*. Most subjects in their utilization of these forms for depiction exploited one of two general characteristics of the umlaut, considered in relation to the primary vowel: increased articulatory tension and/or decreased purity or clearness. These characteristics were exploited specifically with regard to the total physiognomy of a particular word. Thus, in *Mühe* (effort, exertion), *ü* was taken to embody "strain;" in *wüten* (to rage), *ü* was taken to exhibit "exploding energy." For many subjects the expressive difference between *u* and *ü* in *Lust* (delight) versus *Lüste* (unclean, depraved pleasure) was much the same: *u* in *Lust* was expressive of "honest depth," *u* in *Lüste* was depictive of "impurity," "being off-color."

One can observe such plurisignificance with regard to expressive qualities in languages which utilize vocal forms for the depiction of things and events much more than do the Indo-European tongues. For instance, as Westermann (278) has shown, for West African languages, *high pitch* versus *low pitch* may, depending upon the word, be used to signify whole spectra of opposite referential qualities. Thus low pitch versus high pitch may express: something big, broad, massive versus something small, narrow, fine; something awkward, slow versus something agile, swift; something blunt versus something pointed; something dull, stupid versus something sharp, alert;

something swollen, bloated, sick versus something smooth, healthy; something colorless, tasteless versus something colorful, spicy; something frail, weak versus something strong, intense; something hoarse, loose, versus something shrill, dense, etc. Consonantal properties similarly have a wide range of expressiveness: *b* signifies something soft or decayed, rotten, for example, *bayā* (soft), *àbòbŏ* (snail), *botō* (soaked); *kp* signifies something hard, or strong, or stiff, for example, *kpam* (forceful), *kpaladzā* (stiff); *f* signifies something thin or brittle, for example, *flā* (thin), *flofloflo* (loose, brittle).

The fact of plurisignificance of vehicular material has a fundamental relevance to the much-discussed problem of "sound symbolism." Various studies have demonstrated that vowels, in particular, are correlated with certain meanings. Peculiarly enough these findings, and the conclusions drawn from them, have tended to obscure rather than to promote an understanding of what occurs in "matching sound-patterns to meanings."

Sapir (208) was one of the first to demonstrate that vowels possess a "volume" quality which may be utilized for the representation of referents varying in size. When subjects were presented with such patterns as *mal* and *mil* and were asked which of the two forms symbolized the larger object, the observers showed a very high consensus in judging the former pattern to be representative of the larger object. Experiments aimed at correlating vowel quality with brightness differences were equally successful. These findings led to the expectation that languages such as English might make extensive use of this type of sound symbolism in the formation of its vocabulary. However, experimental attempts to find such significant links between, for example, volume qualities of vowels and English words connoting different sizes of referents have not been successful. In our view, positive findings could hardly have been expected. Any expectation of finding such a universal relationship in a living language, especially an Indo-European one, derives, we believe, from two erroneous assumptions.

The first assumption that has obscured the relationship between sound-pattern and meaning is to the effect that synaesthetic links play a dominant role in the phonemic patterning of any contemporary language. This assumption is certainly at odds with the contention of most linguists, who maintain that onomatopoeia, based in part on synaesthesia, is of only minor importance in the lexicon of a contemporary language: the dominant principles underlying word-formation, and changes in the external forms of words, are of a quite different order, typically overriding any onomatopoetic tendencies.

The second erroneous assumption may be termed the "fallacy of constant elements," that is, the fallacy which presumes that there are fixed "bricks" from which verbal forms are built for the conveying of meanings. This elementaristic assumption enters into the interpretation of a certain vowel (or consonant) as entailing a fixed and constant signification such as largeness or brightness. As we have indicated, single sounds are plurisignificant, that is, they possess a wide range of dynamic properties. Furthermore, single sounds rarely determine the *symbolic pregnance* of a word: whether a sound has this or that expressive value, or any expressive value at all in a word, depends upon the dynamic structurization of the word as a whole.

Sometimes these pervasive dynamics of the word as a whole are of a homogeneous simplicity, completely overriding the characteristic forms of the single elements. For example, in Werner's study one subject, for *gelb* (yellow), remarked: "I see and hear it as an acute, sharply rising, form, very pointed—I am somewhat puzzled when I compare this very clear impression with the actual shape of the letters and sounds that at close inspection, seem round, broad, soft, and thick."

More often, however, there is a heterogeneous complexity, i.e., the various parts of the word contributing different features to the total physiognomy. Take, for example, one subject's observations on his physiognomic impression of the word *schwarz* (black): "Immediately had the impression that the word begins with something towering, rising and shadow casting; the *schw* seems to me to be something over which one has to move forcibly to come to the main part of the word—something which in its forbidding gesture toward the perceiver and the gloom cast over the rest of the word, gives the whole thing an almost sinister appearance."

Because these erroneous assumptions have furnished the theoretical ground and justification for most of the studies on "sound symbolism" —and have thus oriented attention towards the presence (or absence) of manifest onomatopoesis in languages or towards the constancy (as manifested through consensuality) [4] of the expressive values of vowels and consonants—the basic issues in the problem of the expressive representation of meanings through sound-patterns have either been overlooked or obscured.

To return to our discussion of the *plurisignificance of vehicular material*, it seems to us worthwhile to outline, at this point, certain parts of a rather comprehensive study recently carried out under our direction by T. Iritani (114). Although Iritani's major focus was on the influence of naming upon the articulation of the perceptual field, certain portions of his inquiry pertain directly to the issue of plurisignificance.

---

[4] The issue of consensus is given special consideration in Chapter 20.

In his first experiment, which is of less direct import, Iritani presented 35 nonlinguistic sound-patterns to each of 30 subjects. The task of each subject was to listen to a pattern, repeat it to himself, and then write down whatever was conjured up by the sound-pattern. The *initial point* to be made here is that each of these artificial sounds—although lacking any conventional 'attachment' to a referent—evoked some referent (conception) in the great majority of the 30 subjects; in other words, once these artificial sounds were taken as names, they tended to evoke referents, even though there had been no prior stipulation or direct associative connection. The *second point* concerns the range of referents evoked by the given artificial sound-pattern. Were the referents which were evoked by a particular sound-pattern all of one sort, or was there a wide variety of referents evoked by a particular sound-pattern? This question is important, because if a sound-pattern contains some fixed expressive value, independently of the subject who apprehends and signifies the sound, one would expect considerable consensus as to the referents evoked by a given sound-pattern. Does such consensus actually obtain under a condition of spontaneous evocation? It is clear that the answer to this question, on the basis of Iritani's inquiry, was 'No!' In general, each of the sound-patterns evoked different referents in the different subjects. For example, the pattern, *Voag,* in one subject evoked "bear;" in another subject, "tent;" in a third, "stormy sky;" in a fourth, "basketball;" in a fifth, "go away!" etc. In the absence of a constraining *universe of discourse* or *stipulation of a dimension,* it seems, at least superficially, that a given sound-pattern will evoke a great variety of different referents in different subjects.

Despite this superficial diversity of referents evoked by a given sound-pattern, Iritani surmised that there might be an underlying expressive factor operating, which might produce more unity or consensus than appeared on the surface. For example, he suspected that for a sound-pattern like *Wauk,* although the range of referents might be quite wide, any referents evoked by that sound-pattern would be of a relatively larger size than, let us say, objects evoked by the sound-pattern *Twie.* These underlying expressive qualities would be masked by the elaboration of them into a complex, multi-qualified referent. With this consideration in mind, Iritani analyzed the referents given to each of the nonlinguistic sounds in terms of six dimensions, each comprising two polar values. In his analysis, he examined only those evoked referents where there was either an explicit (for example, a *small* twig) or implicit reference to one of the two values of a given dimension (as an example of implicit reference, one may mention that he took the reference to 'ping pong ball' as implying 'roundness' in contrast to 'angularity'). The six dimensions used in Iritani's analysis were: size (large versus small), shape (round versus angular), brightness (bright versus dark), texture (smooth versus rough), movement (moving versus static) and affective-hedonic (pleasant versus unpleasant). His findings suggested that certain patterns 'sub-evoked' the same expressive property in many members of his sample—an expressive property masked by the subsequent elaboration of the experience into a complex referent. For example, *Wauk* tended to evoke referents which had 'largeness' ingredient in them; *Dutu* to evoke referents which had 'smallness' ingredient in them; *Srik* to evoke referents which had 'angularity' ingredient in them, and so on. In a spontaneous situation, then, that is, in the absence of restrictions, such expressive properties of sounds may be presumed to interact with other expressive features culminating in an object (referent) where the specific features are submerged or masked.

The part of Iritani's inquiry of most direct relevance to the issue of multivalence of vehicular material was his second experiment. Here, he was directed towards the determination of meanings evoked by given sound-patterns when the "universe of discourse" was *restricted*, that is, when the subject was told that the sound-pattern represented some value of a specific dimension and was asked to choose between one of two extreme values. Using a group of 30 subjects, Iritani presented each of them with each of 35 sound-patterns and asked them to evaluate each of the sounds with respect to each of the six dimensions employed in his analysis in the aforementioned experiment.

The first question here pertains to the degree to which each of the 35 sound-patterns evoked one or the other (e.g., large or small) of the polar values on each of the dimensions, irrespective of which of the extreme values is consensually chosen. For example, was there a consensus among the 30 subjects with respect to *Wauk* as referring to the dimension of size, irrespective of whether this particular pattern was taken consensually to express large or small?

In Table 14-1, we have presented the findings with regard to each of the sound-patterns for each of the dimensions. It will be noted that, for each of the dimensions with the exception of texture, more than 40 percent of the sound-patterns evoked a consensus, that is, an overwhelming agreement among the subjects as to the extreme value expressed or depicted by the sound-pattern. It will also be observed that all but four of the sound-patterns evoked consensual choice with regard to at least one dimension.

Of central importance in the present context is the striking fact that many of the sound-patterns evoked consensual choices along more than one dimension. In other words, in terms of a criterion of consensuality, many of the patterns were *multidimensionally expressive;* or, to put it another way, the sound-patterns qua symbolic vehicles were clearly *plurisignificant.*

In order to show the extent of this multidimensional expressiveness

Sound patterns ("Names") †	Dimensions					
	Size	Shape	Bright-ness	Tex-ture	Mo-tion	Affect-Mood
Wauk	**				*	*
Dlaa	**	**		*		
Fuep	*	*	**		**	
Riru						
Dutu	**		*		**	**
Nosa	*	**	*	**		*
Kiri	**		**		**	**
Psie	*					
Ruma	**	*		*		
Zeca	*	*	**		**	*
Salo	**	**	**		*	**
Piru	*	**	*	**		*
Ftoa	**					
Nics	**	*	*			
Jipi	**		**		**	**
Doem	**	**				*
Grup		**	**	**		*
Pfai	**		**		**	
Srik	**	*		**		
Pocq				*		
Buru	**	**	*			
Stai						
Voag	**	*	**		**	*
Taki	**	*	**		**	**
Twie	**		**		**	**
Huoh	**	**	**		**	**
Smok						**
Nboi			*		*	**
Gumu						
Kimu	*	*		*		
Jeed						
Mzri					*	
Barm	**	**	**	*	**	**
Kuut	*		*			*
Paru	**	*		**		

* Indicates significance at .05 level of confidence.
** Indicates significance at .01 level of confidence.

† For the phonetic transcription of the sound-patterns used, see Iritani's Ph.D. thesis (1962).

Table 14-2
Multidimensional expressiveness: number of sound-patterns eliciting consensus along several dimensions

Number of dimensions along which consensus obtained for a given sound-pattern		Number and kind of sound-patterns
Six	1	Barm
Five	7	Zeca, Nosa, Salo, Piru, Voag, Taki, Huoh
Four	6	Dutu, Kiri, Jipi, Grup, Twie, Fuep
Three	12	Wauk, Dlaa, Ruma, Nics, Doem, Pfai, Srik, Buru, Nboi, Kimu, Kuut, Paru
One	5	Psie, Ftoa, Pocq, Smok, Mzri
None	4	Riru, Stai, Gumu, Jeed
	35	

or plurisignificance of the vehicular material, we have in Table 14-2 organized Iritani's findings to point up the number of sound-patterns consensually expressive of meanings along six, five, four, etc., of the dimensions.

It will be observed that multidimensional expressiveness character- ized 26 of the 35 sound-patterns. In other words, almost three-quarters of the sound-patterns used in Iritani's study evoked a statistically significant agreement among 30 subjects as to their expressive value, along *more than one dimension;* in fact, these 26 sound-patterns evoked consensual choice along *three or more dimensions.* Thus, for most of the patterns, where they were taken to have a certain expressive value (e.g., large) in one universe of discourse (size), they were also taken to have a certain expressive value (e.g., dark) in another universe of discourse (brightness), and yet a third expressive value (e.g., rough) in still a third restricted context (texture).

Thus far, we have not considered which particular values within a specific dimension were chosen by the subjects for a given sound-pat- tern. Thus, although it has been noted that 26 of the 35 sound- patterns evoked a consensus with respect to size, that is, to either large *or* small size, we have not yet spelled out which of these extreme values was evoked by a particular sound. We shall, therefore, now summarize the specific expressive values of each of the sound-patterns, under the condition of forced choice and within restricted "universes of discourse." The pertinent findings are presented in Table 14-3.

Table 14-3
Expressive values of the sound-patterns
(restricted-choice condition)*

Sound patterns	Expressive values †
Wauk	large, moving, sad
Dlaa	round, smooth, small
Fuep	angular, bright, moving, small
Dutu	small, bright, moving, happy
Nosa	large, round, smooth, dark, sad
Kiri	small, bright, moving, happy
Psie	small
Ruma	large, round, smooth
Zeca	small, angular, bright, moving, happy
Salo	large, round, dark, static, sad
Piru	small, round, bright, smooth, happy
Ftoa	large
Nics	small, angular, bright
Jipi	small, bright, moving, happy
Doem	large, round, sad
Grup	angular, dark, rough, sad
Pfai	large, bright, moving
Srik	small, angular, rough
Pocq	rough
Buru	large, round, dark
Voag	large, round, dark, static, sad
Taki	small, angular, bright, moving, happy
Twie	small, bright, moving, happy
Huoh	large, round, dark, static, sad
Smok	sad
Nboi	dark, static, sad
Kimu	large, round, smooth
Mzri	moving, angular
Barm	large, round, dark, smooth, static, sad
Kuut	bright, happy
Paru	small, round, smooth

* After Iritani (114).

† A given sound-pattern is taken to have an expressive value along a dimension when the number of subjects choosing that value significantly exceeds chance distribution.

Table 14-4
Expressive synonymity of sound-patterns

Synonymic sounds	Expressive values
Zeca, Taki	small, angular, bright, moving, happy
Salo, Voag, Huho	large, round, dark, static, sad
Dutu, Kiri, Jipi, Twie	small, bright, moving, happy
Ruma, Kimi	large, round, smooth

A closer inspection of this table yields some very important information. It will be noted that certain sound-patterns, quite different from a material or geometric-technical standpoint, functioned in the experimental situation as *expressive synonyms:* that is, each of these patterns expressed exactly the same values for those various dimensions where they elicited consensual choice. In certain cases, such synonymity ranged *over five of the six* dimensions utilized.

This phenomenon indicates that *patterns which are quite different from a geometric-technical point of view may, through physiognomization, be apprehended as quite similar to each other* (see Table 14-4). It thus points to the fact that not only may one symbolic sound-pattern be plurisignificant, that is, have a multiplicity of expressive properties, but that different sound-patterns may, when physiognomized, possess similar dynamic-expressive features, that is, may be expressive synonyms.[5]

It may be noted that in Table 14-4, we have presented only relatively "perfect synonyms," that is, only sound-patterns which were identical in their expressive values. There were, of course, many cases of partial synonymity; for example, *Ruma* and *Kimu* overlapped with *Salo, Voag,* and *Huoh* in that all five of these sound-patterns consensually connoted *large* and *round;* they diverged in other respects, however.

One final note: just as there were cases of relatively 'perfect synonymity,' so were there instances of relatively 'perfect antonymity.' Limiting ourselves only to those instances where several dimensions were involved, that is, where the sound-pattern was plurisignificant, we note that *Zeca* and *Taki* were, within Iritani's set-up, the exact opposites of *Salo, Voag,* and *Huoh:* whereas the latter patterns each

---

[5] These issues are discussed again and in greater detail with regard to non-verbal representation in Chapter 20.

connoted large, round, dark, static, and sad (unpleasant), the former sound-patterns were each taken to express small, angular, bright, moving, and happy (pleasant).

The findings of Iritani's study, in connection with the detailed qualitative analyses in Werner's inquiry, clearly indicate that the *plurisignificance of the vehicular material* is an essential factor in the transformation of "objectively" given phonemic patterns into symbolic vehicles for the physiognomic depiction of meanings.

The Polysemantic Character of the Referent

On the basis of our discussion thus far, one might conclude that the physiognomization of words consists simply in the selection of dynamic features of sound-patterns for fitting pre-established and pre-determined connotations of the referent. Such a conclusion would be erroneous and would involve a gross oversimplification both of the process of physiognomization of word-forms and of the processes involved in vehicle-referent relationships. Another equally important factor is the polysemantic character of a referent, that is, the multiplicity of connotations comprising any concept. Since we shall go into this factor in great detail in Part V (see pp. 343 ff), we shall only briefly touch upon it here, citing but one illustration from Werner's study on the physiognomics of word-forms.

For many of the subjects in Werner's study, the word *keck* (roughly *fresh* or *pert*) had basically the same *general* dynamic form, the *k* returning, so to speak, to itself. This dynamic form, however, depicted different connotations for different people. Thus, for one observer, it depicted a "gay elasticity, a swinging from one to the other end;" for another subject, it expressed "in the jumping motion, a carefree, almost reckless mood;" for a third observer, the word had "something comical in it . . . it's like a fresh guy—starts out with a dash, but in the end it's not much farther than in the beginning."

Such reports as these point to the final characteristic of the process of physiognomization, the bilateral handling of the vehicle and referent, or their mutual interaction.

The Bilateral Handling of the Vehicle and Referent

Here again, we shall be brief, since this factor will also come up for a detailed discussion and analysis later on (Part V). It suffices to mention, at this point, that the achievement of a *relationship of fittingness* between a physiognomized word-form and the meaning of the vocable typically requires an interaction between the selection of vehicular properties and the selection of connotations of the referent. To be sure, the bilateral handling of vehicle and referent—the mutual adjustment of these two moments, or their *"reciprocal rotation"* with respect to each other—is difficult to demonstrate directly, especially with regard to conventional language. However, since the subject is obliged to start out with a given referent and a given phonic pattern, without any "objective" (onomatopoetic) linkage between them, it seems reasonable to assume that an activity of mutual fittingness is involved in the physiognomic realization of referential meaning in vehicular patterns.[6]

Before concluding this section on the *nature of the physiognomizing process*, one must consider certain questions which may be raised with regard to the observations on the physiognomization of words or vocables, that is, the tangible embodiment of dynamic features in the visible or audible pattern.

Might it not be, one may ask, that these ostensible experiences of dynamics seen or heard in the patterns are actually no more than fanciful, intellectualized elaborations of imaginative minds? Can one really demonstrate the actuality of such experiences in perception? Closely related to these questions is the following: how can one reconcile the existence of words as stable visual or phonemic patterns and their simultaneous existence as dynamic-expressive entities? If physiognomization were actually realized in the patterns would not the phonemic structure necessarily dissolve and disappear, giving way entirely to the perception of a word physiognomy? These are, indeed, interrelated questions. Though we cannot, at this point, provide a complete and definitive answer, we can at least suggest the lines along which a satisfactory solution may be reached.

One method for gaining insight into the problem of the relation between phonemic and physiognomic forms was, indeed, spontaneously suggested by the subjects of Werner's study: they used drawings to communicate the nature of their perceptual experiences in a tangible,

---

[6] The studies on nonvocal representation, e.g., linear representation, discussed later (Chapter 20), in showing the reciprocal influence of connotations on vehicular organization and vehicular patterning on the connotational organization of a referent, strongly support this presumption.

intersubjective way. In Figure 14-1 are presented two drawings by one of the subjects—drawings intended to indicate the nature of his physiognomic impression with regard to the color words *grün* (green) and *rot* (red) (Werner, 269, p. 143).

The subject commented on the drawings as follows: "'green' is gay, frisky; a moving upward. At the same time there is something brisk and cool in the word which is expressed in the rather slim triangles of the crystalline forms; the elongated jagged rays radiate greenness all over it. Quite different with 'red.' It stands out as something warm and red against a cold background. Immensely energetic, closed and yet intensely in motion—everything is infinite inner motion, like a swiftly rotating ball."

These drawings and the subject's remarks provide us with considerable insight into the present problem. They clearly suggest that it is possible to demonstrate tangibly the perceptual reality of physiognomic dynamic properties; in particular, they point rather impressively to the fact that specific dynamics perceived in a word-form may modulate the shape of each element of the word so that these dynamics become actually embodied in all parts of the whole.

In this connection, one may mention a preliminary study carried out some years ago by M. Muchow and H. Werner. Seven- to 10-year-old children were asked by the experimenter to write down certain words of emotional content so that "I can see what they are from the way you have written them down." For many of the older children this task seemed to be quite a natural one. In Figure 14-2 we present the physiognomized written forms of two 9-year-old girls. Note, in

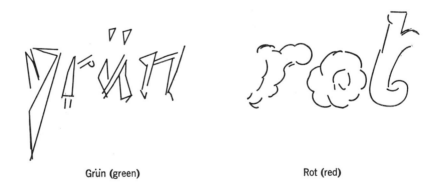

Grün (green)   Rot (red)

FIGURE 14-1. Drawings by a subject to indicate his physiognomic experience of two color words.

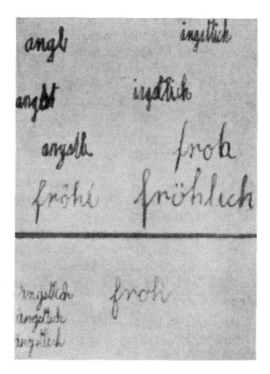

FIGURE 14-2. Physiognomic word forms written by two nine-year-old girls.

these forms, the cramped, narrow representation of *ängstlich* (scared) in comparison with the rounded, swinging, broadly written character of *froh* and *fröhlich* (glad).

The fact that subjects are able to write words in such a manner as to exhibit their meaning through dynamic features gives us some understanding of how words can retain their visible or phonemic constancy and still be physiognomically apprehended. In the case of written (and seen) forms, each letter, and the entire word, may be maintained in its basic structure, and yet at the same time certain features, which do not interfere with the constancy of the letter or word-pattern, may be exploited to carry the meaning physiognomically.[7]

If one extends this thesis to the physiognomization of speech patterns, one may state it as follows: linguistic forms—whether names,

_____
[7] Cf. the study by Honkavaara on recognition of physiognomically written words (109, pp. 69 f).

words, or sentences—are idealized constructs which, in living speech, become actualized in vocal-auditory-postural-kinaesthetic configurations. As has often been noted (for example, by K. Bühler, 37), such idealized constructs retain their constancy and identity despite the actual variability which obtains with regard to the use of any form in living speech—variability due to individual differences in pronunciation, accentuation, intonational modification, etc. There is, in fact, considerable experimental evidence indicating that phonemic patterns remain perceptually constant despite considerable phonetic distortion.[8]

Paradoxically, it is this virtual stability of a phonemic pattern actualized in articulated utterances of considerable variability which is perhaps the main factor permitting the wedding of phonic and physiognomic properties. Were it not for this virtual constancy of phonemic patterns, the molding of phonic material for the exhibition of physiognomic properties would lead to phonemic distortion and would thus work against the formation of a stable system of interpersonal entities for social communication.[9]

Many years ago—long before advertisements in magazines and on television had begun to make use of the physiognomization of word-forms—a German artist, Hans Reimann, published a sensitive and amusing book (200), in which the letters of the alphabet were drawn to carry physiognomic-dynamic properties. For instance, he drew the letter *t* as expressing two different moods (See Fig. 14-3). The first *t* might perhaps fit into an expressive script presentation of such words as "wit" or "witty"; the second into a word like "tipsy." In any case, such drawings again exemplify the fact that one may maintain a stable literal (or phonemic) configuration and yet express variable dynamic features.

Perhaps the most familiar manifestation of the wedding of phonemic and physiognomic properties occurs in the much-discussed intonational variation of words (or sentences) to express variation in affect or attitude. Such expression of affect and attitude through intonation is,

---

[8] One need only recall how quickly one can become adapted to the idiomatic speech of others, even to the 'distorted' speech of foreigners; such stability or constancy is, of course, also found in handwriting, which remains legible despite a wide range of individual variation.

[9] Regrettably, in his criticism of physiognomics of speech, K. Bühler thoroughly misconceived Werner's position in regard to the role of physiognomics in language. Werner did not consider physiognomics to be involved in the construction of language as an "ergon" (la langue) as Bühler seems to impute, but in the—individually produced—language as "energeia" (la parole).

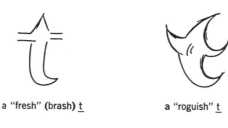

a "fresh" (brash) <u>t</u>   a "roguish" <u>t</u>

FIGURE 14-3. A "fresh" (brash) *t*. A "roguish" *t*.

however, only one—and probably not the most important—manifestation of the molding of phonemically invariant verbal forms for the expression of meanings.

It is crucial to recognize in this connection that verbal units, such as names or words, are not purely sensory phenomena: that is, they are neither isolated visual nor isolated auditory events. The dynamics that constitute the physiognomy of a word are carried not only in the modulated properties of sounds but in visual, auditory, tactual, and kinaesthetic qualities which accompany the utterance or understanding of a vocable. In other words, meaningful vocables are components of total organismic activities (inner sensory-motor gestures), and the physiognomic aspects need not be, and typically are not, carried solely by the visual or auditory components of such total organismic activity.

In sum, then, physiognomization of conventional speech forms typically emerges through an integration of phonemic and expressive-dynamic features, in which the latter are subordinated to the former. The expressive features are realized through total organismic activity whereby the linguistic material is molded to permit the actualization of the dynamic features. The physiognomization of linguistic forms makes use of *the plurisignificance of vehicular properties, the polysemantic character of a referent* (multiple connotations), and *the bilateral handling of vehicle and referent* (reciprocal rotation).

In these respects, as we shall see in Part V, the physiognomization of conventional linguistic forms is no different from the physiognomization involved in the exploitation of nonverbal media for the "natural" representation of meanings. Nevertheless, the physiognomization of conventional words does differ from physiognomic activity with respect to such nonverbal media as expressive line patterns. Whereas expressive lines do not enter into a system of signs whose distinctness and stability must be maintained, speech forms do partake of such a system. In the physiognomization of conventional word-forms, one

Physiognomic Apprehension of Language Forms   **231**

docs not have the freedom to create new forms; one cannot—without the danger of excommunication from the linguistic community—go beyond the limit set by the requirement that the phonemic structures of words be maintained.

The Physiognomization of Grammatical Categories

The physiognomization of language would be of rather limited importance if it were restricted to single names, that is, isolated vehicles referring to isolated events, objects, or concepts. In order to demonstrate the considerable significance of physiognomization of language, therefore, one would have to show that such activity also pertains to grammatical-syntactical aspects of speech. Since Werner's monograph has dealt with these aspects only in a rather preliminary way, we shall be able here merely to point up the feasibility of a comprehensive study of the processes involved in the physiognomizing of grammatical categories: we shall do this by selecting a few examples from Werner's monograph pertaining to the ways in which subjects did physiognomize forms belonging to different grammatical categories.

First of all, it must be recognized that for the Indo-European languages, with which we are chiefly concerned here, the distinction between nouns, verbs, and adjectives is a basic one. The protocols of the subjects in Werner's study showed that all of them were able to physiognomize vocables belonging to these three categories in terms of characteristic dynamic properties. There were, however, at least two essential differences between the linguistic and the physiognomic modes of categorization: one concerns the degree of differentiation among the three categories in terms of their general constitutive properties; the other concerns the degree of differentiation among the categories in terms of the discreteness of their existence or the extent of their overlap.

The protocols of the subjects clearly indicated that the physiognomically apprehended categorialized forms were *less differentiated* from each other compared with the degree of categorial distinctiveness of words at the nonphysiognomic level (269, pp. 120 ff). One reason for this lessening of categorial distinctiveness seems to be the basic dynamic character of all physiognomized forms: *linguistically*, it is the verb in contrast with the noun that typically represents activity; *physiognomically*, nouns and adjectives, as well as verbs, tend to be imbued with dynamic properties.

A second peculiarity of physiognomized categorial forms distinguish-

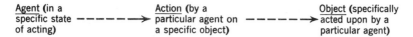

| Agent (in a specific state of acting) | ------> | Action (by a particular agent on a specific object) | ------> | Object (specifically acted upon by a particular agent) |

FIGURE 14-4. Diagrammatic representation of the physiognomic structuring of a simple sentence.

ing them from nonphysiognomic forms is this: physiognomized "nouns," "verbs," or "adjectives" do not represent more or less *circumscribed* aspects of a total event, but—in their concreteness—typically include aspects which would be carried linguistically by other categorial forms. Thus a noun-form, when physiognomically apprehended, usually entails not solely a thing- or object-reference, but an activity-reference as well; similarly, a verb-form, physiognomized, is specifically modulated in terms of the object or agent involved.

This overlap of the categories in physiognomic apprehension is closely tied up with the way in which a sentence is grasped physiognomically: *linguistically* seen, a sentence consists of discrete vocables related to each other through morphological indices and abstract order arrangements, but the unity of a sentence is achieved *physiognomically* through a successively changing accentuation within a global event, that is, with syncretic rather than discrete categorial forms constituting the sentential integration. The physiognomic structurization of a simple sentence may be diagrammatized as shown in Figure 14-4:[10]

A few examples may suffice to show, first, that subjects can and do physiognomize distinctive categorial characteristics of nouns, adjectives, and verbs, and second, that at the same time the dynamic nature of all expressive manifestations makes for the lessening of categorial distinctiveness, the relative lack of differentiation among the vehicles with thing-reference, the vehicles with activity-reference, and the vehicles with attribute-reference.

One method that was found useful for studying these two phenomena consists in the presentation of homonyms that represent now a verbal form, now a substantive. Following are some typical responses given by two subjects to the homonymic pair, *Wand* (wall) and *wand* (past tense of *wind*— to twist):

One of the subjects, for *Wand,* remarked "something straight, built in a vertically straight upward direction, opaque, a barrier between me and you;" for *wand,* he stated, "dynamic movement like that of an injured worm— movement upward." The other subject, for *Wand,* remarked "stiff, verti-

---

[10] See Chapter 22.

cally downward, standing opposite me, cutting short any attempt at movement toward it; smooth surface, impenetrable by touch or look;" for *wand*, he said, "strong inner dynamics, a slow moving in waves from left to right."

Schlangen (snakes) and *schlangen* (plural past of *schlingen*, to sling) comprised another homonymous pair used in the study. Typical responses here were: "*schlangen*—a winding movement from left to right and back; at the same time the motion as a whole is perceived as advancing;" for *Schlangen*, "there is a similar winding motion, but here with a center, a fixed point around which the motion occurs; in comparison with the verb, *Schlangen* is closer, bigger, more solid—substantial, bound to a definite location in space."

Another feature of linguistic codification is the expression in grammatically categorialized forms of such aspects of the experience or conceptualization of events as number (e.g., singularity versus plurality of objects), case (e.g., the relation of subject to object of action), temporality, etc. We shall here refer to certain parts of Werner's inquiry dealing with the manner in which subjects physiognomically apprehended temporal aspects of events, linguistically encoded in tense indicators.

By presenting word-forms differing in tense indicators, Werner was able to determine how his subjects differentiated, for example, present activity from past activity through the physiognomization of the linguistic vehicles expressing such temporal distinctions as *laufe* versus *lief* (run versus ran), and so on. Characteristically, it seems, the subjects selected certain connotational properties of pastness versus presentness and realized these through dynamic features of the different linguistic vehicles. In Table 14-5, we have presented in a schematic way differences along perceptual dimensions, which served to distinguish present and past of actions.[11] Following are some actual illustrations.

For the pair, *laufe* (run) versus *lief* (ran), one subject remarked for the verb in the present tense, "character of ongoing without ending—I perceive the duration of the two syllable structure, the two-bar rhythm indicates for me repetitiveness, the vowel sound of the second syllable, lack of closure;" with regard to *lief*—"in contrast (it) is thinner and more closed; the monosyllabic structure ending on the harsh *f* brings out very impressively the dynamically sharp contour of the word."

For *bleibe* (stay) versus *blieb* (stayed), it was stated, " 'bleibe' is closer

---

[11] As will be shown subsequently, the concrete means used for representing temporality in physiognomized linguistic forms are practically identical with the means used for depiction of time-of-action in a medium of expressive lines (see Chapter 23).

Table 14-5

Schematic presentation of characteristic ways of handling dynamic features in different perceptual dimensions for distinguishing present and past of action

Perceptual dimensions	Present	Past
Space	close	far
	right	left
	front	back
	surface	deep
	figural	background
Size-magnitude	big	small
	long	short
	thick	thin
	wide	narrow
Overall and internal shape	complex	simple
	sharpened	leveled
	open	closed
	repetitive	single
	without termini	with termini
	infinite	finite
Intensity	strong	weak
	vital	faded
Kinesis (motion)	quick	slow
	forceful	lacking force
Substantiality	dense (packed)	ethereal
Personalization	personal	impersonal

than 'blieb;' the latter is farther in the background, less distinct in visual and auditory color; also decreasing in size, almost fading into the distance, like something seen in depth perspective."

These illustrations indicate, in consonance with what one finds with regard to physiognomization of words in general, that temporality is realized in sound-patterns through the mutual fitting of connotations of time with qualities perceived and selected in the speech material. The following illustrations may further exemplify the manner in which individuals mold the concrete phonemic material to express temporality in the word-form.

For *ich breche* (I break) versus *ich brach* (I broke), one subject remarked: " 'breche'—sharp, vital, active—the fricative *ch* sounds like breaking; in 'brach,' the *ch* is more of an aspirated sound indicating the breathing out, the exhaling away, of the activity—*ach* sounds like a far away echoing; again, the double syllable of 'breche' gives the impression of something doubly jagged—the whole word splintered, broken up—'brach' more unitary, melodic, closed."

Of particular interest here is the way in which the *ablaut*, a typical linguistic index of the preterit of so-called "strong verbs," is handled to express this pastness physiognomically. Many subjects sought to exploit the fact that the ablaut is a modulation of the primary vowel, that is, they used the ablaut to depict the modification or the modulation of the action in going from a present status to a past status.

For example, one subject, for distinguishing *schiebe* (push) from *schob* (pushed), remarked: " 'schiebe'—*ie* (is) immediate, very near, vital-concrete; *o* in 'schob'—far away, a sound that implies getting dull and hollow, fading out like a sound moving away in a long tunnel."

In order to understand fully this handling of the ablaut for the expression of temporality and the variation in the handling of the ablaut among different symbolizers, one must recall—in addition to the fact that the ablaut is a modified form of a primary sound—that central factor in physiognomization, *the plurisignificance of the vehicular material*. These considerations may help us to resolve the paradox of the "same" sound—now conceived as primary sound, now as ablaut—being used to express opposing temporal connotations. For example, for one subject, the sound *ie* was seen as expressive of the present tense *biege* (I bend) vis à vis the past tense, *bog* (I bent); yet this same subject used the sound *ie* to express the pastness of *lief* (I ran) vis à vis *laufe* (I run). These phenomena became clear from the subject's protocol: in the first case, he grasped *ie* as being more intense than *o*; in the second case, he grasped *ie* as being thinner, more polished, more uniformly leveled than *au*.

One may add a final note on the physiognomic expression of temporality: this note concerns the distinction between "weak verbs" and "strong verbs." The majority of the subjects distinguished physiognomically between pastness linguistically reflected in the ablaut from pastness linguistically realized through dental suffigation. Whereas the past represented by ablaut was frequently characterized—in relation to the present—as simpler, more finite, more closed, these traits rarely ever appeared with regard to the past represented by suffigation; this latter linguistic representation of pastness was typically characterized as repetitive—incomplete [12] without definite closure, etc. For example, one subject, for *segne* (I bless) versus *segnete* (I blessed), remarked, "the past is actually not a complete past—though in the main the action is ended, it still swings out in the *ete* a few times."

Thus, although the two forms for constructing the past tense are fully equivalent from a linguistic point of view, they clearly differ in general physiognomic features. These physiognomic differences may call to mind one of the distinctions which has been preserved in Romance languages—but not in Germanic ones—that between a simple or 'definite' past and an 'imperfect.'

The fact that the differences in dynamic connotations of the past are here realized through differences in the forms of the two linguistic means for encoding "pastness" points up, once again, the nature of the physiognomizing process as one involving a *bilateral handling of vehicle and referent,* that is, a mutual fitting of vehicular and connotative features.

In concluding this chapter, we may briefly elaborate our views concerning the pertinence of such studies as have been described to an understanding of everyday linguistic representation. We have, in our discussion of the physiognomization of words and "parts of speech," emphasized the tangible embodiment of the meanings in the visible (written) or auditory (phonic) configurations, that is, a tangible embodiment to a perceiver when oriented towards the linguistic form almost as if it were an object confronting him. It will surely be conceded that such a tangible embodiment occurs, and is indeed quite often employed today, in advertising, both visual and oral-auditory; it will also be acknowledged that experiences of word-forms as exhibitors of their meanings often occur in the creation and in the reading of poetry.[13] Such tangible embodiment seems, however, far from manifest to the man in the street or to most of us in our everyday use of language in the service of representation. Hence arises the question of the relevance of physiognomization of language and phenomena of "sound symbolism" to the everyday handling of speech.

Perhaps the best way to begin to answer this question is to recall some of the remarks made in Part I pertaining to the genetic relationships between the inner and external forms of a symbol. There we

---

[12] Somewhat analogous to a "progressive present" put into the past.

[13] See the poem, "Take Sky," by David McCord, in *The New York Times* Book Review Section, June 11, 1961.

maintained that there is, in the course of development, a progressive differentiation or *distancing* between the inner form of the symbol (the connotational dynamics) and the external form (the phonic or written vehicle). At primordial levels the inner form is fused with the external form and is hence visibly and auditorily carried by the vehicle. With the progression towards the use of conventional forms, the inner form of the symbol (the connotational dynamics) becomes more and more *covert* in character—carried by "inner gestures," "imagery," "postural-affective sets," "feelings," etc.

This embodiment of dynamics of meaning in a covert manner, often on the periphery of awareness, is the subject of one of William James' most pregnant passages (118, p. 245): "There is not a conjunction or preposition, and hardly an adverbial phrase, syntactic form or inflection of voice in human speech, that does not express some shading or other of the relation which we at some moments actually feel to exist between the larger objects of our thought. If we speak objectively, it is the real relations that appear revealed; if we speak subjectively, it is the stream of consciousness that matches each of them by an *inward coloring of its own*. . . . We ought to say a feeling of *and,* a feeling of *if,* a feeling of *but,* and a feeling of *by* quite as readily as we say a feeling of blue or a feeling of cold. Yet we do not; so inveterate has our habit become of recognizing the existence of the substantive parts alone, that language almost refuses to lend itself to any other use."

A somewhat related observation, also pertaining to grammatical connectives, has been made by the German psychologist, W. Betz, in his book on "The Psychology of Thought" (18). Thus, Betz notes: "If I slowly pronounce to myself the particles *frankly, anyhow, but* . . . without putting them into specific sentences, then I observe that I take, with each of these words, a different intellectual attitude or set; these differences are so great that it is impossible for me to keep the same attitudinal set with the word *frankly* that I formed with *but* and *anyhow*. If, on the other hand, I articulate for myself particles like *in spite of, but, however,* then I also observe a difference in attitude, but these differences are much smaller than those noted before. I may even exchange these words for one another without basically changing my set (postural attitude). At these attempts at exchange I notice something else, however: namely, that with *but* and *in spite of,* I form not a single unchangeable set for each of them, but that I vary the attitude within a certain range until I have found that attitude which permits the exchange of these words. All this gives us assurance that the 'understanding' of particles consists in much more than a mere recognition of the word as a percept . . . that we are truly dealing here with experiences of meaning" (18, p. 71).

One may also note, in connection with the covert experiences of the meanings of categorialized forms, an early study by Eleanor H. Raymond (196) on "the psychological experiences connected with different parts of speech." Whereas the observations of James and Betz are those of highly sophisticated individuals, Miss Raymond's study deals with the observations of a relatively naive undergraduate student. A study at Clark University (Langer, 147) has dealt with both covert and externalized representations of different parts of speech in ways which extend the work of Werner and Raymond.

The increasing importance of a covert representation of connotational dynamics—the widening distance between inner and external form of a symbol—obviously does not entail a rupture between inner and external form. The two moments remain connected, for without such connection the linguistic forms would lapse in meaning and finally degenerate into mere noises or marks. It is this residual connection of the external with the inner form, despite the increasing distance between these two facets of a symbol, that permits one to realize visually those connotational dynamics which, in adults, are typically realized covertly, that is, in inner gestures, feelings, etc.

Our answer, then, to the question of the relevance of studies on physiognomization to an understanding of symbol formation in everyday life is that such studies serve to bring to the fore (to make tangible) tendencies which are typically carried in a covert manner in various domains of that total organismic matrix from which any symbolic vehicle emerges and in which it remains embedded. These tendencies, which are covertly realized through inner gestures, postural-affective sets, etc., in everyday speech, can be "translated" into visual or auditory properties when such "translation" is required, because connotative dynamics (meanings) transcend particular psychophysical modalities, and may therefore be manifested equivalently in materially different forms of organismic activity.

chapter 15

Handling of Linguistic Forms in Dreams

Although the predominant medium for the objectification of experiences in dream states is a pictorial-realistic one (percept- and image-like), verbal utterances or phonic-like forms do occur, with varying frequency, in the dreams of many persons. For various reasons—for example, their greater refractoriness to recall in a waking state—such linguistic-like forms have rarely been discussed in the psychological literature; even less often has "speech in dreams" been subjected to a comprehensive description, analysis, and classification. Freud (70), it is true, did deal to some extent with "dream speech"; his major focus, however, was on the psychodynamic factors and unconscious motives presumably underlying distortions and aberrations. Perhaps the only one to provide a considerable body of examples of "dream speech"—examples accumulated over a period of 20 years—was E. Kraepelin; it is, therefore, on the protocols presented in his monograph (138) that we chiefly, although not exclusively, rely in discussing the ways in which words and sentences are handled in dreams. In our brief discussion, we shall consider "speech in dreams" in terms of our diagram of the four generic components of symbol-situations (Chapter 3).

Relation between Addressor (Dreamer) and Addressee

There would appear to be little question that the "distance" between addressor and addressee in a dream state is far less than that which obtains in everyday waking communication. In fact, it has often been taken for granted that in the dream state there is an identity between the dreamer and the person to whom he "communicates" his dream; some, indeed, have raised the question whether communication, in a strict sense, is operative in dreams at all. Even if one does not completely accept the view that addressor and addressee are identical in dream states (cf. Ferenczi, 64; Kanzer, 127)—even if one acknowledges that there are various levels of dreaming at which some degree of polarization obtains between the dreamer and his communicatee—one can scarcely deny that the addressee, in dream representation, is much closer (in terms of shared feelings, attitudes, interests, and, above all, prior knowledge of the object of reference) to the symbolizer than he is in almost any waking state.

This closeness of addressor to addressee renders "communication" in the dream state analogous to communication under conditions of *inner speech* (see Part IV). Indeed, "dream speech" seems to be quite close to an extreme condition of inner speech, where the boundary between self as addressor and self as addressee is scarcely established. The extreme fusion of addressor and addressee results in the symbolizer not being confronted with those demands for highly articulate representation—involving the selection of communal forms—that occurs when there is a considerable distance between addressor and other. One is not constrained to use those lexical forms and syntactic patterns that comprise an *autonomous medium of representation*—forms and patterns that are enjoined upon a symbolizer communicating to another who does not share his feelings, his interests, and his prior awareness of that to which reference is being made. Some indication of this closeness of addressor and addressee is reflected in Kraepelin's observation that he often did not recognize the nonsensicality of his dream utterances until he could examine them in a more alert state, as a somewhat detached observer.

Relation between Addressor (Dreamer) and Vehicle

Correlative, therefore, with the "shrinkage" of distance between addressor and addressee, there is a dwindling of distance between the addressor and his vehicle of representation. His vehicles are either personal, idiomatic ones arranged with relative disregard for the "rules" of communal syntax or they are conventional forms endowed with more than, or other than, conventional semantic values.

In order to highlight this closeness of the symbolizer to his vehicles in dream states, we may first essay a somewhat speculative description of the major steps involved in the microgenetic process of transforming felt meanings into appropriate linguistic expression for communication to others.[1]

We assume that this process is essentially an orderly, sequential one. It begins with a phase in which meanings are felt or suffered rather than cognitively apprehended. The earliest representations are presumed to be of an affective-sensory-motor nature, representations which serve perhaps to establish global outlines of the experience but which do not establish circumscribed connotations or lead to an articulation and inner organization of the total experience. Gradually, the diffuse and interpenetrating sentiments and meanings gain some degree of embodiment in personal, idiomatic, and contextualized gestures or images—these mobile, plastic forms participating in, and rising out of, the total experience, and comprising but isolated islands within the experience. Increasingly, as the experience is shaped more and more for communication to others, there is a progressive differentiation and articulation of connotations (for example, a differentiation of subjective and objective spheres), increasing individuation of connotations, and a progressive channelizing of meanings towards communally adequate verbal forms. At the same time, there is a progressive differentiation of representation from bodily experience and also a progressive differentiation among the various media of representation. Lingualization becomes increasingly detached from imagery and gesture and becomes dominant over these more personal and covert media. Communication about the experience is more and more directed towards, and facilitated by, the communal lexicon and syntax.

One might consider this entire microgenetic process as one entailing recurrent operations of selection, modification, rejection, correction, channelization, transformation, etc., until a matching is attained and a compromise effected between the felt meanings and texture of the experience and the verbal-syntactic forms of the communal code.

In contrast to this eventuation in highly articulated and syntactically organized ("autonomous") expression of reference, when such reference is intended for others, dream representation—even where the

---

[1] Some support for this speculative description of major steps in the microgenesis of symbolic reference comes from creative artists and poets who have reflected upon the genesis and gradual formation of a work; support also comes from a totally different quarter, viz., from students of aphasia (see, for example, A. Ombredane, 180, Chapter XVIII). See also (48; 213; 216).

vehicles are verbal or linguistic-like in external form—is presumed to emerge from a phase in the process where the articulation and integration of meanings are, to varying degrees, below the level attained in normal communication to "generalized others." One may say that "dream speech" occurs at levels of *subcodification;* connotations are still diffuse and interwoven; subjective and objective domains are not sharply distinguished; logical connections are not articulated; vehicles are immersed in affective-sensory-motor states and are typically personal, idiomatic, concrete, and relatively labile in character. Linguistic-like forms, when they appear in dreams, are not articulated in terms of the "objective" linguistic code but are personalized, either in form (e.g., neologisms) or in meaning (displacements, homophonic extensions, etc.). Furthermore, such forms are often shaped and related to each other as if they were things, fusing with each other and following patterns of organization quite removed from those reflected in the formation and integration of words enjoined by the communal lexicon and syntax.

Among the consequences of this formation of dream vehicles at levels of subcodification is *a lesser differentiation of the verbal medium from other, typically more personal, media of representation, especially those of gesture and imagery.* Moreover, there is a very close tie between bodily states and representation in any form. One finds that bodily states and postural-gestural representation very easily glide over into verbal expressions which "stick close" to the bodily patterning; conversely, verbal conceptions are easily transmuted into postural forms and into bodily states. Again, verbal conceptions are easily transformed into concrete images, and images are quickly "translated" into verbal expressions. In other words, the various media which are relatively segregated from each other on the level of communication to others are, in the dream, interwoven with each other and with ongoing bodily states.

Psychoanalysts have often pointed to the "translation" of bodily experiences and postural representations into verbal forms and have also highlighted the transformation of verbal conceptions into bodily states ("organ language"); for example, a verbal insult may literally be experienced as a slap in the face, with consequent pain. Kraepelin provides several illustrations of this close relationship between the verbal medium and other media of representation. For instance, in one dream the idea "she does not like to do it" was apparently experienced in terms of bodily postures and imagery and emerged verbally as "she puts her feet leftward" (#249).[2] In another dream, a bodily state (an urge to urinate) eventually emerged in verbal form as "the frontally built waterhouse" (#234). It will be noted that in both of these cases the literal reference is quite removed from the intended reference: the words, understood by the dreamer, would have little communication value for another, who was not privy to the reference.

The interpenetration—often close to fusion—between verbal forms and concrete imagery has also been emphasized by psychoanalysts. Facilitating this linkage of imagery and verbal formulations are two factors: the originally concrete reference of many relatively "abstract" words and the "regressive" nature of dreams, their tendency to concretize or literalize abstract conceptions. As Freud has remarked, "the fact that language has at its disposal a great number of words that were originally used in a pictorial and concrete sense . . . has made it easy for the dream to represent its thoughts." The concretization of the abstract and the transformation of words into imagery is exemplified in one dream mentioned by Freud in which the idea of "superfluous" appeared as "inundation"—overflowing, as a terrible storm, water dripping from walls, damp beds, etc. (Freud, 70, p. 398). For another dreamer, the idea of "being manipulated by someone else" was transformed into a literal "having his hand shook by that person." In another instance mentioned by Freud, the dreamer "translated" the abstract notion of "editing a review dealing with the Far East" into a visual image of one climbing a mountain from which an extensive view is obtained" (Freud, 70).

Kraepelin provides a number of examples in which experiences were apparently articulated in terms of concrete pictures which were then "read off" in verbal formulations: these formulations almost have the character of metaphorical creations. For example, the idea of "a lack of thorough knowledge and industry" was verbally expressed in the dream as "he does not possess a solid mental seat-of-pants" (#250); the idea of "let yourself go" was formulated verbally as "take off the mental shirt collar" (#251); the conception of "body and spirit meeting in man" was verbally subcodified as "the mushrooms and the angels find each other" (#238); "he writes differently from what one would expect" came out as "the straight director—a crooked writer" (#242); the thought of "all these insignificant collections . . ." emerged in

---

[2] The translations of Kraepelin's examples, even when there are no neologisms or syntactic distortions, can never be more than approximate. The numbers following the dream items are those used by Kraepelin in notating his examples.

verbal formulation as "Think—all these wild-apple galleries" (#244). It is clear that the reference of these expressions would only be understood by someone who was already privy to the intended referent. It is also clear that the vehicles are rather personal, idiomatic ones.

Another consequence of the closeness of the vehicles to the symbolizer is the *corralling of diffuse, vaguely formed, and organismically embedded meanings into one or a few verbal units*. In such cases, the verbal vehicles are *holophrastic* rather than circumscribed or delimited in their reference; in this respect they are like the genetically early names discussed in Chapter 8. Entailed in this reference of the verbal utterances to relatively diffuse and atmospheric connotational spheres, all interwoven with each other, is the consequence that the vehicles are necessarily of an implicit, elliptical, condensed, and allusive character. Single words or phrases often hit their intended reference (i.e., what would be the fully articulated and explicated referent) *at a tangent* that is, they are *parasemantic*. Again, the verbal vehicles often have reference to a number of meanings—meanings which would be sharply distinguished on waking levels, meanings which would each have their more specific verbal expressions—that is, the vehicles are *polysemantic*. Finally, the verbal utterances are often arranged without regard to logical and/or syntactic considerations, that is, there is *dystaxia*. These various manifestations of subcodification may, and often do, occur together in one dream utterance.

The *parasemantic* character of many dream vehicles can be observed in most of the examples cited in this chapter: the literal meanings of words uttered in the dream are only remotely related to the intended meanings. In *parasemy*, the connotations, instead of becoming increasingly individuated before they are formulated linguistically, are often channelized into word-forms whose communal significance bears only a relatively remote "family resemblance" to the intended verbal concepts. Kraepelin's example of the word "plantar" used to refer to the notion of "friendship" via an implicit analogy between the sole of the foot and the palm of the hand is a nice illustration of such paraphasia-like displacement: "friendship" is concretized into a component of friendship (handshake), but instead of "handshake" emerging, or some word pertaining to it, there emerges a word alluding to the sole of the foot.

Such *"derailments"* are manifested in many other dream items mentioned by Kraepelin. For example, the evaluation of an epileptic maid who is "not particularly skillful as a worker but who is at least painstakingly conscientious in whatever she does" is articulated in dream speech as "not clean, enjoys unhampered freedom but cleans the horses well" (#272); the idea of someone lacking control is linked to incontinence, and hence diarrhea and uncleanliness, and comes out as "not clean, enjoys unhampered freedom"; the idea of painstaking conscientiousness in menial activity is concretized into an activity usually far removed from the duties of a maid, "cleaning horses." Thus the intended evaluation of the maid, when verbally articulated prematurely, comes out in a statement whose literal reference is quite distant from the intended reference.

In another instance, the idea that "one should drink the tea and not let it get cold" was verbalized in dream speech as "one wishes this ass should be eaten and not dream away" (#268); one can almost see here how the global idea of taking something into the mouth is derailed from drinking to eating, and how neglecting to drink tea while it is hot, presumably because one is preoccupied with something else, gets expressed in words related to "asinine" and "dreaming."

An especially good illustration of parasemy is the following. "It would have broken the girl's heart if her boy friend had left her" was transformed into "the maid would fall (= break) into rods and sticks (= pieces)—it would be said that the fellow had gone up (= gone off)" (#175). In still another dream, the verbal expression "Mr. N was awarded the prize (for an article on dentistry) though he was not working at the notary office" (#247) was uttered to allude to the fact that Mr. N did not belong to the professionally recognized (and thus certified) group of research men: "notary office" alluded tangentially to "authorized dental office."

The *polysemantic,* essentially condensed, character of verbal vehicles in the dream—their simultaneous multiple reference to what, at later levels, are distinct connotational spheres—is evident in many of the examples already cited. Such polysemy is manifested in a number of ways, varying from the use of neologisms [3] to the use of conventional word-forms which are invested with more than their normal, circumscribed significance.

With regard to neologistic utterances, Isolde Kurz, in her book *Traumland* (143, p. 14), reports that in one of her dreams, the word-form "sök" seemed to her to express a long series of aesthetic-philosophical ideas. It may be noted that the neologisms which occur in dream speech are often produced through a contamination in which pieces of word-forms intrude into conventional forms, or in which

---

[3] An extensive discussion of neologisms is given by Bobon (24).

pieces of several words become glued together so that all resemblance to a conventional form disappears.[4]

Let us consider a few more examples of such polysemy via neologisms. In one dream, the word "peticularity" was uttered; it condensed in one form reference to "petty," "meticulous," and "regularity." Kraepelin mentions the occurrence of the neologism "Eistubulat" (#136)—an idiomatic expression to allude to "Russian Secretariat with unrestricted rights over finances;" the "Eis" part (German, "ice") alluded to Russia, that is, icy place; the "-at" part alluded to public office, as in Konsulat. In another dream, "pseudointabloid" (#143), condensing "pseudo" and "tablette," was used to refer to a "phony drug against alcoholism."

In another dream cited by Kraepelin, the expression "she sang commando-red" was uttered (#186); this phrase elliptically carried the idea "she sang loudly (commando) at dawn (red, alluding to reddish clouds or the rising sun)"; the neologism, "commando-red," nicely illustrates the use of a condensed composite form to allude to a total atmospheric context of a particular morning scene.

Occasionally, *homophonic* or clang relationships between verbal vehicles contribute to polysemy, the verbal form including in its reference the content designated by its homophone. For example, the word "senile" was heard by a dreamer, enunciated almost like "snail"; there was also a clang connection experienced to "sail" as well as a smoothness of gliding character of the sound, s-n-l. Altogether, the thought expressed by the verbal form was approximately, "Old age is not so bad; slow but quite smooth sailing in old age." Another dreamer experienced the word "crate" in his dream; this was homophonically linked to "create"; the single word condensed reference to a felt connection between creativity and death (crate = box).

Polysemy is also manifested in certain seemingly conventional words or phrases, carrying more than one meaning: the two spheres of meaning are condensed in one external form. For instance, in one dream, the phrase "the so-called guardparade" was uttered (#117); this phrase reflected the channelization into verbal form of "the drinking bout of a boisterous South American buccaneer troop"; the verbal expression,

---

[4] In this respect such contaminations stand in sharp contrast to the manner in which a number of meanings are conjoined or linked to each other on the level of linguistic codification: in these latter cases, the external forms of words maintain their integrity; where composites are formed, the constituents keep their external form, with sequence and stress defining relationships of subordination (e.g., motherland, housemother).

alluding to the marching back and forth of soldiers in a changing of the guard, also pertains—through what would normally be a far-fetched analogy—to the moving to and fro of a filled bottle from one corner of the mouth to the other. It will be noted that the dream verbalization alludes grossly to a context of warfare and to a context of drinking at the same time.

In another dream, the utterance was "Just give him a tube to describe the time from half past eight to nine" (#266). This utterance referred to "Give him a microscope to study the posterior horn of the spinal cord, the substantia gelatinosa." "Tube" refers to microscope as well as to spinal cord. "Describe the time from half past eight to nine" implies first that the student should take time for that observation; in addition, however, that period before nine, ordinarily not reserved for specifically defined work, bears a (remote) analogy to the little differentiated structure of the substantia gelatinosa. As one will observe this example demonstrates particularly well the very intimate relationship often obtaining between *polysemy* and *parasemy*.

In still another instance, two comprehensive ideas were condensed in the single utterance, "ladle"; the meaning of that word was "I hope there will always be a high level of social togetherness for me; always plenty and richness." The word concretely referred to a big spoon made of silver which, in its weightiness and preciousness, pertained to good table manners in lavish social gatherings; the hollowness and great capacity of the ladle indicated expansiveness and connoted plenty of food.

Polysemy is finally manifested in the use of conventional verbal forms which may be used in everyday speech with different meanings in different contexts; such words often enter into double-entendre and pun-like expressions. Such compression of two meanings in one word is exemplified in the following. In one instance, the utterance was "Now I can be free of this blame" (#185); "free" here referred both to "free from guilt" and "freedom to marry." In another case, the utterance was "The soldiers are in the field; now will be forked" (#27); "forked" here pertained both to the "forking of hay" and the "forking (bayonetting) of people."

The final manifestation of premature articulation that we shall consider here pertains to *dystaxia*, or violations of the rules of communal syntax, in dream speech. One often finds agrammatism in construction, lack of codified means such as word order, conjunctions or flexions for the articulation of relationships, perverted or aberrant handling of grammatical categories, etc.[5] One also finds a somewhat para-doxical combination of ellipsis and redundancy—omission of reference to some of the contents and the representation of other contents several times.

Often, several of these dystactic features are combined in one dream utterance. Take, for example, the utterance "Understands no distin-guish" (#188) which the dreamer felt expressed fully the idea "no-body understands me when I speak Italian with a friend in Madrid"; actually the dream phrase redundantly expressed "understands not a word" and "cannot distinguish." Here we note the condensation of a complex thought in three vocables, a merging of the negative particle with both "verbs," the presence of ellipsis (much of the con-tent does not gain linguistic representation) and the presence of re-dundancy (the same idea is expressed in both "verbs"). Or consider the utterance, "In 'Bullrich' I stand as I last possessed my dear mother" (#189); this utterance alludes to a battle song "I shall hold out amid the roaring of cannons as I was taught by my teachers, the French." 'Bullrich' is used neologistically to connote "combat" via "bullern" (to roar) and "Pulver" (gunpowder); "last possessed my dear mother" condenses "as I was previously taught by my teachers (= mother) and whose lesson I will retain."

Among the dystactic formations in dream language, those pertain-ing to *grammatical-categorial aberrations* are of particular interest to developmental theory: for example, fusion of categorial functions in one word, shift in such categorial functions, contrary to codified usage, etc. Such aberrations are relatively frequent occurrences in dream speech. One finds the use of a verb form where there should be a noun or adjective and vice versa, a change in the syntactic posi-tion of grammatical subject and grammatical object, a displacement of attributes pertaining to the noun from nouns to verbs and vice versa. For example, in one of the dreams mentioned (#268), the idea normally carried by an adjective ("asinine") is expressed through a noun ("ass"); again, the asinine person who should drink the tea becomes the ass that should be eaten. In another dream, "scoopy ironcasting" (#167) was uttered instead of "iron scoop"—an exchange of nominal and adjectival functions. In still another instance, "the

---

[5] In his book, *Das träumende Ich*, A. Hoche reports that only 20.7 percent of the dream utterances which he lists consisted of grammatically well-articulated sentences (quoted from F. Kainz, 125, p. 416). Kraepelin's list contains about 30 percent of such grammatically correct sentences.

handling of voluntary coals" (#203) was uttered for "the voluntary providing of coals." These are but a few of the illustrations of dystaxia in dream speech that can be taken from Kraepelin's material.

Relation between Addressor and Referent

We shall just briefly touch upon the "shrinkage" of distance between the dreamer and referent. Many psychoanalysts have maintained that the referents of dreams are ultimately bodily states or "wishes" of the dreamer: every expression is taken to allude to these states or wishes, with varying degrees of directness. Even if one does not concede the general validity of this thesis, it seems clear that the referents of the dream utterances are of a much more personal nature than are the referents of much of everyday speech. In the dream utterances one expresses one's attitudes, feelings, etc., towards whatever "objective" content one may be referring to. In terms of the relation between addressor and referent, therefore, one may speak of a decreased distance in dream speech.

Relation between Vehicle and Referent

We have, of course, touched upon the relations between vehicle and referent throughout the previous sections. Here we consider certain other features, not previously discussed. As we have remarked elsewhere (see Chapter 3), one of the consequences of a lack of distance between vehicle and referent is that *the vehicle is treated as if it were a thing;* it is endowed with thing-like properties and relations. As Freud has pointed out (70, p. 330), "words are often treated as things in dreams." In dream speech, as in early child speech and in schizophrenic speech, one finds frequent occurrences of *word-realism,* that hallmark of a close interpenetration of vehicle and referent. The handling of words and even syllables and letters as if they were things is well exemplified in a number of Kraepelin's items. For example, in one dream, the utterance "The Gingobi cannot pre-pick the G" (#255) was voiced to express the idea that "the giaour (Turkish, infidel) cannot seize his advantage" (kann seinen Vorteil nicht wahrnehmen). "Vorteil" (advantage), literally meaning forepart, is in the dream utterance equated with the G of Gingobi, i.e., its first letter or forepart. Kraepelin also notes that the strange neologism ("Gingobi") suggests the strangeness or alien character of a giaour or infidel. In another dream, the utterance "13 words of an oracle speech" (#256) alluded to a landscape (apparently like a stage setting) in which 13 wings were ranged one behind the other. Here again, the material arrangement of the 13 words served to reflect or mirror the referent.

Another manifestation or a lack of distance between vehicle and referent, closely related to word-realism, is *the treatment of a given sound-pattern as if it somehow carried its meaning glued to it;* even when that sound-pattern occurs as part of another word, it is invested with its "fixed" significance. We have noted already how this characteristic often leads to a polysemy of a verbal vehicle. For instance, the word "liability" (spelled "lie-ability") is used in a dream to refer to a man the dreamer distrusts. The idea of "auto-erotism" is expressed in a dream by a kiss in an auto; "auto" is endowed with a fixed meaning even where it appears as part of a word having nothing to do with automobile. A French patient of Freud's pictured him in one of his dreams as an elephant. This represented his thought that Freud was deceiving him (vous me trompez); trompez was linked to elephant through "trompe" (trunk) (Freud, 70, p. 401).

Still another manifestation of a reduced distance between vehicle and referent is *the use of physiognomic properties of sound-patterns to convey reference.* Kraepelin provides a number of examples. For instance, the word-form "Knietschengiebel" (#272) occurred in one dream, representing a "hackney driver's seat"; "giebel" (gable) alluded to a high vantage point; the word physiognomically imitated the characteristic slang talk of Berlin cab drivers; it gives the phonic impression of the high "squeaky" (allusion to "quietschen") seat. In another dream, "Graschendassel" (#73) was uttered, a neologism used as a nickname for a cleaning woman; this expression alluded by its sound to the crude, uninhibited manners of an ungroomed person; there was also a connection to "quasseln," "quatschen" (twaddle), and "Drache" (quarrelsome woman). In a third instance, "stintzig" (#214) was uttered as referring to "dainty"; again the physiognomic features of the sound-pattern reminded the dreamer of "zierlich" (delicate).

Concluding Remarks

In this chapter, we have touched very briefly upon the fascinating, but still little explored, area of "speech in dreams." In concluding this discussion, we may again emphasize the significance of such dream speech for an organismic-developmental theory of symbol formation.

We contend that symbol formation is realized at various developmental levels, each defined in terms of the degree of differentiation or "distance" obtaining among the four components of symbol-situations —addressor, addressee, vehicle, and referent. To a certain extent, then, the developmental level of symbolic functioning will be determined by the material nature of the medium in which the vehicles are formed, that is, their closeness to bodily activity, their amenability to externalization, etc. As the instances of "speech in dreams" indicate, however, the level of symbol formation does not depend unilaterally upon the material nature of the medium of representation. A medium such as speech, typically employed at an advanced level of articulation and integration, may be used at developmentally lower levels of functioning; under such circumstances, the characteristics of symbolization and the relations of the symbolic vehicle to addressor and to referent bear a close similarity to the characteristics and relations one finds in the use of "naturally" more primitive media, such as gestures and imagery.

chapter **16**

Primitivized Handling of the Linguistic Medium in Pathological (Schizophrenic) States [1]

Although reservations have been voiced about the justification for applying a single term "schizophrenic" to individuals differing markedly in their manifest symptoms, there is general agreement that the overwhelming majority of persons thus diagnosed are alike insofar as they have undergone a striking transformation in the organization of their worlds. Practically all those who have studied "schizophrenics" concur with Bleuler's view (21) that such patients live in fundamentally *autistic* universes.

In terms of our developmental analysis of symbol-situations (see

---

[1] It must be stressed that we are here concerned with schizophrenia only as a means for gaining some insight into genetically early levels of symbolization. We are quite aware that the behavior of schizophrenics varies from acts that are practically normal to those that are totally idiosyncratic and "bizarre;" such a range obtains also for linguistic utterances. Our focus here—as was true in our examination of speech in ontogenesis and speech in dream states—is on certain deviant handlings of linguistic material in schizophrenia that seem to us to reflect the operation of genetically early modes of symbol formation. Even in this regard, we touch on only a few of these genetically early processes. A more comprehensive treatment is beyond the scope of this work. Readers interested in an examination of the entire range of schizophrenic language behavior should consult the writings of Jean Bobon (23; 24; 25), who has perhaps done the most extensive work in this area.

Chapter 3), schizophrenic autism corresponds to *an extreme shrinkage in distance,* a radical dedifferentiation, among the four basic components of such situations—addressor, addressee, referential object, and symbolic vehicle. The distinction between self and nonself (other persons and things), the differentiation between a world of independent objects and one's attitudes and expectations concerning such objects, the distinction between the meanings one feels and seeks to convey and the semantic values of conventional words, the polarity between symbolic vehicles and objects—distinctions all gradually attained during the course of ontogenesis—appear to break down, to varying degrees, in schizophrenic states.

Our primary focus in this chapter is on the relations of symbolic vehicles, principally linguistic and near-linguistic forms, to the person (addressor) who uses them and to the referents they seem to represent or express. However, the interdependence among all four basic components of symbol-situations renders it necessary to consider, at least briefly, the transformations in addressor-addressee and addressor-referent relationships in schizophrenia. Let us turn first to these latter relationships.

Addressor-Addressee Relationship in Schizophrenia: Shrinkage of Distance

Since the addressor-addressee relationship is a special instance of the general relationship between self and other persons, one would expect that an alteration in that general relationship would reflect itself in the special case. Numerous investigators [2] have stressed the extreme dedifferentiation between the self and others in schizophrenic patients. Many impressive illustrations have been given of the breakdown, or perpetual threat of a breakdown, in the boundaries separating the self from other persons: one may feel oneself transformed, or threatened with transformation into another; often, even the bodily boundaries between self and others dissolve.

This general undifferentiatedness between self and others—reminiscent of the condition obtaining in early infancy and in dream states —is manifested in those special circumstances in which the patient is an addressor communicating to others. For the schizophrenic, even

---

[2] For example, Arieti (7; 9), Bleuler (21), Federn (63), E. Jacobson (115), Searles (221; 222), Storch (243), and Sullivan (247).

those persons who are objectively remote and unrelated to patient's life tend to be transformed into familiar, intimate, need-relevant persons—"internalized objects"—who are privy to the patient's experiences, needs, and fears. No matter whom the patient is addressing, the auditor is construed as someone psychologically relevant to, and involved in, the patient's preoccupations. As Kreitler (141) has observed, the auditor to whom the patient addresses his remarks—whether such an auditor is actually present or imagined as in apparent monologues—is always someone involved, for good or ill, in the patient's fantasies. This collapse in interpersonal distance in schizophrenia results in modes of handling language strikingly analogous to the ways employed by normals in more or less extreme conditions of inner speech (see Chapters 17 and 18), and in dream states (see Chapter 15).

Addressor-Referent Relationships in Schizophrenia: Shrinkage of Distance and the Autistic Transformation of the World of Objects

Just as the schizophrenic unwittingly infuses his wishes and fears into other persons, confounding his notion of himself with his conceptions of others, so too does he tend to endow the objects of his environment with qualities reflecting his own impulses, desires, and sentiments of catastrophe. The inert, stable, impersonal things of the normal world may take on, in schizophrenia, awesome physiognomic-dynamic features. Filled with the patient's anxieties and fears, the everyday things often become demonic, terrifying entities, occupying a twilight zone between the domain of persons and the domain in which things are ordinarily located. In extreme cases, the shrinkage of distance may lead to an experience of the self dissolving into objects, fusing with objects, constructed out of objects, invaded by objects, etc.

Hand in hand with this shrinkage of distance between self and things, the everyday objects lose their contour, their inert, stay-put character, their constancy and stability. Things are no longer just there in the world, segregated from each other and endowed with their conventional, communal, pragmatic-functional properties; they are woven together into strange entities, having direct pertinence to the patient's momentary rages, fears, and fantasies. As Arieti (10, p. 3) has remarked: "The patient who is becoming psychotic no longer experiences certain aspects of the external world as his fellow human beings do, but in private, bizarre ways, difficult to understand and even more difficult to share."[3] Often, as in the case of Mme. Seche-haye's patient, Renee (223, pp. 35 f), the things confront the patient as if they were alive—wilful "persons" rather than inert objects.

The shrinkage of distance between self and things frequently leads the schizophrenic to take as a real, material connection between things, a connection which the patient has merely entertained in imagination or thought. What is connected in experience is taken as connected in the objective world: the patients manifest what Freud has character-ized as "omnipotence of thoughts." To illustrate, Freeman (69, p. 931) mentions a paranoid schizophrenic patient who felt that his stubbing out of a cigarette had caused a man's death because after reading about the man's death in a newspaper he had put out a cigarette he had been smoking.[4]

This tendency to endow objects and states of affairs with a profound meaning, to read deep significance into the prosaic objects of everyday life, leads to ordinary things taking on what we may designate as a *protosymbolic* status: the distinction between referential objects and symbolic vehicles tends to dissolve so that both kinds of "entities" occupy the same intermediate domain.[5] A number of illustrations may be taken from Storch. One patient remarked, concerning some "red bricks," that these bricks "are my transformed thoughts on love, nothing but red love" (244, p. 340). Another patient took the black color of doors as signifying "dying" (243, p. 85). A third patient saw in the twisted legs of a table the meaning that "the whole world is twisted" (245, p. 802).

In sum, through the extreme shrinkage in distance between the self and the surrounding world, the objects and states of affairs in the

---

[3] This transformation of the world in schizophrenia is often overlooked. As Searles (222, p. 6) notes, there is a tendency on the part of less experienced therapists to assume that patients experience situations in the same way as do normals (e.g., the therapist himself) but merely communicate these experiences in a highly distorted way. "It seems usually to require any therapist some years of work in this field (of schizophrenia) to dare to see how remarkably distorted is the subjective experience of the patient itself."

[4] As Cameron (40) has demonstrated in experimental studies, schizophrenics "cannot keep the environment out" of a circumscribed situation: presumably working with a delimited group of objects in an object-sorting experiment, schizophrenics tended to incorporate into the experimental situation any hap-penings which captured their attention, linking such happenings to their han-dling and arranging of the experimental objects.

[5] See below with respect to the shrinkage of distance between symbolic vehicles and referents.

schizophrenic's environment become completely unstable in their inner form (their connotational structure) and often undergo alteration in their external form (their appearance). Those features of things stand out and those meanings become dominant which pertain to the momentary needs, desires, and fears of the patient; the world of things becomes egocentric and idiosyncratic.

These alterations in the inner and external forms of referents, deriving from the extreme collapse of distance between the self and nonself, have an important bearing on the ways in which schizophrenics handle conventional symbolic vehicles and construct new forms; they will, therefore, come in for consideration again in the following sections.

Addressor-Vehicle Relationships in Schizophrenia: Shrinkage of Distance and the Radical Alteration in Attitude towards Linguistic Forms

In dealing with the schizophrenic's handling of language, it does not suffice to determine merely that the patient's utterances deviate in certain external characteristics from the utterances of normals. One must at least consider the possibility that the basic attitude of the patient towards language differs from that of the normal adult. One cannot conclude from the fact that the schizophrenic may exploit conventional linguistic forms in his utterances that he actually uses or regards language in the same way as does the normal. Indeed, it is our contention—following from our theoretical viewpoint—that the extreme change in orientation towards the world that occurs in schizophrenic states must entail a fundamental transformation in the patient's attitude towards language.

Thus, the regression to an autistic world—a world in which the boundaries between the subjective and objective are washed away—entails a merging and interpenetration of different domains of experience: the perceived, the dreamed, the remembered, the wished, the imagined, the thought, etc.—realms more or less distinguished in the experience of the normal adult—tend to occupy a single, in-between domain. We have already mentioned the radical transformation of perceived objects and states of affairs into "protosymbols," entities and events having a profound significance for the schizophrenic, far transcending their ordinary pragmatic-functional meaning. Correspondingly, symbolic vehicles, which function in normal thought as the "transparent" carriers of ideal meanings, tend to lose this status and to become material, actual, concrete-objective entities;[6] in this transformation, of course, they do not become like prosaic, ordinary objects but like the physiognomic-dynamic entities of the schizophrenic's object world.

In sum, autistic regression leads to a collapse of distance between vehicles and referents (objects). Both kinds of entities lose their distinctive "substance" and tend to become of one "stuff"—a stuff that is more or less imagery-like in character. With regard to the handling of linguistic forms in schizophrenia this means that such forms are often treated as if they were "things" and molded or deformed as if they were fluid images.

Autistic Realism and the Thing-like Handling of Linguistic Forms

Because of collapse of distance between self and not-self, the patient believes himself able to regulate and control the "external world" as if it would be an aspect of himself. He feels himself, through his "subjective productions"—words, images, gestures—able to create things, to abolish them, to control them. He also experiences such productions as if they were things having an influence or efficacy upon himself. One of Schilder's patients, for instance, acted as if the substance of her thoughts and words could act in the world in exactly the same way as do physical objects and physical forces. She believed that she could destroy objects by thoughts and words, an act she neologically referred to as "shooting down" or "bumping off" (*bumbse ab*) (Schilder, 215, p. 64). Bobon (23, p. 56) refers to a patient who believed that he could disinfect parts of his body or insure these parts against infection through the recitation of verbal formulae; for this patient, various regions of his body were at the same time letters of the French alphabet (23, p. 65).

The undifferentiatedness between the substance of words and the substance of things also underlies the way in which the schizophrenic manipulates, prunes, reshapes, and alters linguistic forms. Just as two objects may be grouped together in terms of a similarity in their visible properties, for example, shape and size, so may two word-forms be endowed with the same significance—irrespective of their communal meaning—on the basis of a similarity of visible, external features. Again, just as a bad or rotten part of an object may be excised or cut off, so too may a word be truncated, its evil parts being left unsaid.

---

[6] See Arieti's discussion of "the process of active concretization" in psychosis (10, pp. 5 ff).

For example, one of Schilder's patients (215, p. 66) repudiated democracy because the word "Demokratie" contained a number of sounds identical or similar to "demütigen" (to debase); the meaning of *democracy* was equated with the meaning of *"to debase"* on the basis of the external similarity of sound-patterns designating these notions. Bobon's patient (23, pp. 57 f) truncated a number of words because their complete (conventional) form contained parts which carried a bad meaning. Thus he used *tection* instead of *protection, seption maculée* instead of *conception immaculée, m* instead of *homme,* and *amme* instead of *femme.* Interestingly enough, such truncation of the initial parts of words was not used with regard to *enfant* because of the invariable innocence of children.

In many ways closely related to, and often indistinguishable from, the shrinkage of distance between symbolic vehicles and referents (things) in the behavior of schizophrenic patients is an underlying collapse in distance between the inner and external forms of symbolic vehicles. The intention to say something no longer determines the choice of words, but the word-forms seem to carry meaning in their very substance. Just as parts of objects have a relatively stable meaning even when torn out of the larger object context, so too may parts of words, for example, sounds, letters, syllables, be given a relatively fixed significance when isolated from the word or when occurring in different words. The patient seems to look within the external structure of the word for clues to its meaning.

This mode of handling verbal patterns has been discussed with respect to ontogenesis in a monograph by H. Werner and E. Kaplan (275, p. 61). Under the concept of "homophonic word realism," these authors have pointed to the fact that young children will often take a nonsense (artificial) word-form and endow it with a certain meaning simply because this artificial form resembles in its syllabic structure or in its component parts some word which the children know, such as *corplum* interpreted as *corporal.* It is clear that the same phenomenon occurs in schizophrenia.[7] Many of the translations of Tuczek's patient from the communal lexicon into her idiosyncratic vocabulary were apparently based on this kind of homophonic realism; for example, *Meer* (ocean) = *die See* (sea); therefore *diese* (these), homophonically close to *die See,* was translated as *Meer* (254, p. 291). Another illustration may be taken from the protocol of a patient studied by

---

[7] A discussion of such occurrences with respect to schizophrenic performance on the Word-Context Test is presented on p. 278.

M. Lorenz (154, p. 604). Attempting to give the meaning of *content-ment,* the patient remarked: "Well uh, contentment, well the word contentment, having a book perhaps, perhaps your having a subject, perhaps you have a chapter of reading, but when you come to the word "men" you wonder if you should be content with men in your life, and then you get the letter t and you wonder if you should be content having tea by yourself or be content with having it with a group or so forth." One can see here how the meaning is garnered by the patient from pieces of fragments of the word given a meaning in and of themselves.[8]

A somewhat similar handling of language was manifested by Tuczek's patient (254, p. 299). This schizophrenic translated the conventional words by fractionating them into pieces and then equating these pieces homophonically to pieces of her neoformation. For example, *Schwester* (sister) was translated into *den-holz* (wood): *Schw-* was elaborated into *Schweden,* and then the second syllable (*den*) was pulled out; *-ster* was translated into *Holz* (wood) because one speaks of "a ster (a measure) of wood." Similarly, *Trachthund* was given as the translation of *Zwieback: Zwie-* was elaborated into *Zwietracht* (= disunity), and again the second syllable (*Tracht*) was taken; *-back* gave rise to *Hund* (dog) in that the patient elaborated a sentence "The dog (Hund) bit into her cheek (Backe)"; since Back(e) and Hund were elements of the same thought, they were equated with each other.

The Undifferentiatedness of Media of Expression in Schizophrenic States

In the course of ontogenesis, gradual distinctions are forged between symbolic vehicles and referents: representation is distinguished from the presented object or state of affairs. Concurrently, various media of representation are distinguished from each other and take over different functions. Thus language becomes the medium *par excellence* for the communication of precise, objective reference, and inner experiences tend to be embodied in internal feelings and strivings, imaginal forms, etc.

One of the important consequences and manifestations of the autistic

---

[8] Although Lorenz does not offer an explication of the patient's remarks, it seems plausible that the concern with "book" and "chapter of reading" derives from the shift in stress from *content'* to *con'tents.*

regression in schizophrenia is the dissolution—often to the most extreme degree—of all these ontogenetically established distinctions and polarities. As we have noted in the preceding section, the differentiation between linguistic forms and things tends to dissolve, with linguistic forms being deployed as if they were things. As we shall emphasize in this section, so too is there a collapse with respect to the various media of expression: the sharp distinction between an autonomous, interpersonal medium of language, necessary for communication to others, and personal idiosyncratic media of imagery and gesture used in "communicating to one's self" breaks down. In a sense, all the experiences of a schizophrenic tend to occupy a single domain—a 'twilight zone'—where words are equivalent to things, where concrete actions have ulterior, 'profound' meanings, where abstract word meanings glide over easily into imagery, and so on.

Thus, as Schilder and others have shown, a schizophrenic's actions or gestures cannot be taken at their "face value" but are often enactments of delusional ideas. For example, a patient of Spiegel's (236, p. 937) kept throwing things out of her bureau drawers: this concrete action had the esoteric meaning of "putting her house in order." Another patient ate his own excrement, thus "freeing his fellow man from sin." A patient of Storch's made circular movements with his body, thus keeping the 'wheel of the world' in motion (Storch, 243, p. 52). A patient of Segal's (225, p. 269) brought her a canvas stool and was very embarrassed; he behaved as if he had brought her an actual fecal stool.[9]

Likewise, the drawings and paintings of schizophrenics, even where they resemble those made by normals, cannot be taken at their purely realistic-depictive value but often function as if they were gestures or quasi-linguistic expressions which could magically control the world.

As a consequence of the interpenetration of all the media, linguistic forms *lose their autonomy:* schizophrenics tend to express their ideas through an amalgamation of forms from different media rather than limiting themselves mainly to the linguistic code. For example, Gerson's patient, in greeting her doctor in the morning, accompanied her verbal salutation with hand and arm movements which transformed the linguistic utterance into a magical wish: the everyday verbal greet-

---

[9] Though one must deny the status of true "representations" to these "magical" actions, there is at least one feature pertinent to symbolization in them, the creation of a depictive form; the depictive form is, however, given "real" status and hence *is* rather than *refers* or *means* or *represents.*

ing now meant something like 'you who have the power should release me from the hospital.'

The linguistic forms may amalgamate with particular "objects" in the patient's environment, the total complex (words and object) carrying the patient's meaning. Again in Gerson's patient, the vocable *tuck* generally referred to a situation of loving; uttered in connection with a 'red carnation' in the patient's environment, it signified a "wish to kiss someone" (Gerson, 75, p. 166).

In order to understand such amalgamations of linguistic forms and objects, one must keep in mind not only that both kinds of entities occupy the same domain but also that the patient's world of objects is at any time open to transformation into a universe of protosymbols. We have already mentioned such transformations of the object-world; here, we call attention to the interpenetration of such protosymbols with linguistic utterances. The way Tuczek's patient "codified" the number zero in her personal language highlights this interpenetration: zero (0) seen as a testicle was verbally represented as *nenn früh le le* (call-early mornings-urinate). The verbal utterance itself referred to the situation of "mother (the patient) *calling* to her boy *in the morning* to ask if he has *urinated* before going to school."

The closeness of schizophrenic linguistic utterances to other media is perhaps most strikingly seen in the concrete-pictorial, image-like way into which abstract notions are transformed. Just as a patient may see a profound significance in the "twisted legs of a table," so may an abstract thought be realized either through a transformation of the perceptual world or through language which refers more directly to concrete situations.

The realization of linguistically abstract thoughts in altered perception is exemplified in Bleuler's patient (21, p. 351) who saw a nurse who entered his room as standing on her head; the patient interpreted his vision as revealing the fact that the nurse has become a religious "convert." In other words, the abstract-verbal notion of "conversion" was concretely materialized as a turning upside-down of the body.

The translation of abstract thoughts into concrete-pictorial language reflects the closeness of schizophrenic speech to the handling of linguistic forms in dreams. In the previous chapter we cited dream phrases such as "take off the mental shirt collar" for "letting oneself go" as examples of such concretizations. Quite parallel to this is the expression of one of Gerson's female patients: *This is too one-eyed for me,* which was a verbal-pictorial transformation of the relatively abstract thought: "I cannot quite fully comprehend ('overlook') this whole situation" (75, p. 174).

In sum, the patient's handling of language as a concrete realistic substance fused with imagery, action, objects, etc., and often treated as interchangeable with them, reflects the decreased distance between the addressor and his symbolic vehicles in schizophrenia.

The Shrinkage of Distance between Vehicles and Referents: Its Role in the Meanings and Forms of Schizophrenic Utterances

Certain aspects of the vehicle-referent relationship in schizophrenia have already been discussed in previous sections of this chapter. In considering the shrinkage of distance between the self and others, the self and the world of objects, and the self and vehicular forms in schizophrenic autism, we necessarily touched upon the dissolution of the boundaries between words and things in psychotic states.

In examining further the ways in which schizophrenics handle linguistic material with respect to reference, we shall be primarily concerned with the *nature of the connotations* revealed in schizophrenic utterances and with the ways in which linguistic material is arranged and organized in the expression of these meanings. These two abstractly distinguishable aspects of verbalization are of course actually intertwined; therefore, although an attempt will be made to stress each aspect separately, an inevitable overlapping is to be expected.

In our exposition of the meanings and forms of schizophrenic utterance, we limit ourselves to two general issues: first we consider the problem of *"naming"* in schizophrenia, that is, the meanings carried by "names" and the forms that "names" take; then we examine *"sentence-like"* utterances, i.e., linguistic formations apparently serving to express some assertion. In treating this latter issue, we focus mainly on the word-sentence relation, that is, the degree to which the units entering into sentence-like expressions are lexically and syntactically circumscribed.

Connotations and Vehicular Forms in Schizophrenic *"Naming"* (Designation)

Insight into the kinds of connotations carried by schizophrenic "names" comes from two sources: from seemingly conventional word-forms used in strange, idiosyncratic ways, and from the construction of new forms ("neomorphisms"). Much has been written about the tendency of schizophrenics to invest the communal forms of language with personal meanings; little need be said about such phenomena here. Rather we shall focus mainly on neomorphic utterances. Such novel formations—though not too frequently occurring [10]—are of great significance because they highlight most clearly the extreme collapse of distance between meanings and vehicular embodiment in the schizophrenic's attempt to give verbal expression to his experiences.

As indicated, the connotations carried by the names the schizophrenic employs reflect the patient's immersion in a world that has lost its solidity and stability, a world in which the boundaries between self and not-self are constantly fluctuating, a universe in which things and persons undergo rapid and unexpected metamorphoses: the objects of this world are analogous to those which occupy us in fantasies and dreams rather than those which exist in our normal adult perceptions. In referring to the objects and events of this world, the schizophrenic finds much of the communal lexicon—stable forms with stable transpersonal meanings—inadequate. The meanings that he is prompted to express—fluid, diffuse, rooted deep in his personal existence—have no autonomous forms available to them. The patient, therefore, either pours his diffuse experiences into conventional vehicles or, in more extreme cases, re-forms and re-shapes the linguistic material until a new form emerges which carries his felt meanings.

In other words, the process through which our experiences are progressively articulated into sharply contoured meanings, susceptible to expression via stable and autonomous word-forms in stable syntactic patterns, does not run its full "microgenetic" course in typically schizophrenic speech. It is prematurely brought to a stop and externalized: a pattern of organization is revealed in speech which is, to varying degrees, more diffuse and less integrated than the pattern exhibited in normal codification.[11] Thus, what is expressed, what is

---

[10] The relatively infrequent occurrence of neomorphic utterances in schizophrenia should not lead one to underestimate their extreme theoretical significance. Some of the theoretically most important phenomena in psychology occur rarely under natural conditions and may indeed come into existence only under very special experimental conditions. For example, the relatively rarely occurring optical illusions bring to light processes operative in all percept-formation; again, as Freud has shown, slips of the tongue, though rare, highlight processes that are always operative; finally, many of the not frequently occurring "errors" of children in the process of acquiring the adult language provide greater insight into the process of language-acquisition than do the far more frequently occurring "correct" responses.

[11] See Chapter 15; see also the article by Arieti on "microgeny of thought" (11).

represented and referred to in words, is not a domain of stable things, specific actions, circumscribed attributes and relations, etc., but states of affairs that are fusions of affective-impulsive-sensory-motor-perceptual impressions. Analogous to the forms emerging in dream speech,[12] the "words" of the schizophrenic designate referents that are *"spheric"* [13] in nature: their inner forms lack the contour and stability that make possible the formation of true lexical units and syntactic relations.

Such spheric connotational structures, constituting the meanings of the linguistic vehicles schizophrenics employ in "naming" (and hence the inner forms of schizophrenic referents), are characterized by a number of features, each one of which tends to complement and promote the others: (a) the spheres are suffused with highly personal themes and hence are egocentric-idiosyncratic; (b) they lack contour and hence tend to "leak into" other spheres and to assimilate other spheres to themselves; they thus may undergo sudden alterations, expansions, mergings, transformations, etc.; (c) they are global-holophrastic, cutting across, between, and around the meanings expressible via the communal lexicon; and (d) they are affective-conative-imperative, containing the fears, wishes, commands, etc., of the speaker.

It seems to us that vocables having such spheric connotational structures may be properly regarded as *monoremes*. It will be recalled that in our treatment of ontogenesis of language, we introduced the term "monoreme" to designate single vocables that were neither words nor sentences nor any part of speech; they were prior to any syntactic differentiation. The just-mentioned features of the connotations carried by single-vocable utterances of schizophrenics are remarkably similar, *formally*, to the kinds of connotations carried by infantile monoremes. To be sure, since schizophrenic vocables differ both in content and in comprehensiveness from those formed in early childhood, one should emphasize that they are monoremes of a special kind. Following are some illustrations of such "schizophrenic monoremes," provided by one of Gerson's patients (75); these monoremic utterances highlight one or more of the various features of spheric connotational structures mentioned above.

---

[12] Despite the many analogies between schizophrenic speech and "speech" in dreams, one must not overlook essential differences: although schizophrenic handling of language is image-like, an intent to communicate is still operative, however autistically the addressee may be conceived.

[13] See Rapaport's (195, p. 518) characterization of "sphere" as a "realm of sensuous, emotional and drive experiences."

For example, the patient referred to the fact that she was "waiting for the highest (heavenly) moment when my son comes close to me (visits me in the hospital on school holidays)" by the utterance *to stand in schu* (from *Schule*, school); the form *schu* connoted a total situation including her wishes, expectations, religious preoccupations, etc. Again, the patient used a monoreme, *tuck* (from *Turteltaube* —turtle-dove) to refer to herself as a loving person, as one immersed in a situation of affection and love, and—through the fact that Noah had released two turtle-doves from the "box" (Ark)—to diffuse religious notions (75, p. 166). The monoreme *schum* (probably derived from the slang term *schumrig*—cozy) was used to express the comprehensive wish and thought to take her boy in her arms and embrace him, and also to have him close to her (75, p. 162). Finally, the monoreme *mirwihipe* (derived from *Mürbeteig*—pastry-dough, and *pe*—papa) was used by the patient to express the global idea that "I, who am of a higher order (i.e., one who eats cake), expect my release from you (doctor = papa)"; the expectation of release was embodied in the bringing together in a condensation the holophrastic notion of pastry dough (= I of a higher order) and papa (75, p. 167).

One should emphasize a phenomenon apparent in the last illustration: the holophrastic character of the conventional word-forms into which Gerson's patient, and other patients as well, often "translate" neomorphic utterances. "Pastry-dough," for example, carried an aura of "one who was an elevated person, of a higher order, one who is in a position to eat cake." Another example of this phenomenon is the following: Gerson's patient used *schirpflich* to mean "a solid 'serious' person or character." The patient's further comments indicated the global-holophrastic meaning of 'serious'—its embeddedness in religious-biblical preoccupations: "The cricket chirps (*schirpt*). It sets the tune. It chirps because it belongs to the beasts, animals and worms. It is like the preacher who sets the tune, intones the liturgy. Beasts, animals, worms are created by God—which is very 'serious.'" Thus 'serious,' itself, refers to religious content, to God as creator, to a preacher, as an elevated person who leads in liturgical prayer (75, p. 160).

One may also illustrate this global-diffuse structure of connotations from Tuczek's patient (254), who formed a language of her own by constructing a special vocabulary. This patient often translated conventional words into her own "terms." It is interesting to observe that the seemingly conventional circumscribed "words" of her lexicon did not have the delimited meaning they possessed in ordinary language. This may be seen from these two examples: *spider*, and later *tearable* (from *web*), was the patient's designation of "cellar;" she translated *evening* into *le passed* (the day has passed).

These global-situational connotations of seemingly conventional words were frequently comprehensible only when one had a knowledge of the patient's personal experience and personal "life theme." For example, *thistle* was translated as *le stone* and vice versa; the patient clarified these "translations" by noting that when she went with her mother into the fields they used to rest at noon on a big stone standing close to a beautiful red thistle (254, p. 293). Another example: the patient translated *doctor* by *le Komlarah;* the basis for this "translation" became clear from the patient's recall that once, when one of her relatives lay very sick in the village, a doctor could not be found; suddenly she saw a doctor coming around the corner and said to him, 'Komm mal ra' (dialect for 'come down here') (254, p. 293).[14]

Because the schizophrenic tends to give verbal embodiment to vaguely articulated and organismically embedded experiences and thoughts, the linguistic utterances that are emitted are often *obliquely* or *tangentially* related to the "appropriate" word, that is, the vocable that would have been used had the microgenetic process of formulation and externalization run its full course. At the level at which schizophrenic thought is arrested, parts have not been clearly differentiated from wholes, similarities are experienced as identities, and all relations may lead to the fusion or identification of the related elements.[15] The consequence of the "premature" channelization of such global-affective thoughts into words is that the utterances, from a normal point of view, are *parasemantic:* there occurs, in Cameron's terms (39), a "metonymic distortion." Thus a patient does not say *body* where that term would be appropriate but rather utters the related term *flesh* (Cameron, 39, p. 20). Again, Gerson's patient used *fluent dialect* for *rapid speech*, talked of ideas being *worked up to her* rather than *communicated to her*, spoke of *culture life* rather than *country life* (75,

---

[14] We may direct the reader to Goldman's study, discussed in Chapter 21, where similar processes may be observed. For example, one of his schizophrenic patients, asked to represent "Evil," drew a skirt; asked how a skirt represented evil, the patient remarked, "When I was young, they took my Indian skirt away from me."

[15] See in this connection Levy-Bruhl's (151) concept of "participation," Cassirer's concept of "concrescence" in mythical thought (42, II, Chapter 2) and Arieti's formulation of "Von Domarus' principle" (7, Chapter X).

pp. 161, 173). Tuczek's patient used the expression *Erdnuss* (*earth-nut*) for *potato* (254, p. 290). Many other examples of such parasemy could be given, all reflecting the tendency of schizophrenics to externalize their thoughts in language at a point where the thoughts are still spheric, fluid, and more or less undifferentiated among themselves and with respect to things.

The same spheric, fluid character of thought—the interpenetration of connotations, the material identification of referents that would normally be related only ideally—leads to *polysemy of reference* or/and *plurisignificance* of linguistic utterances. The same external form may connote now an amalgam of feelings and ideas, now one or another of the constituents of the amalgam.[16] Illustrations of such plurisignificance are legion. A few examples may suffice here:

Gerson's patient (75, p. 161) used the vocable *sü* (from *Sünde = sin*) to express not only the idea or feeling of sin but also concerns about prayer, a preacher, and herself. *Sü* actually pertained to a holophrastic complex and could be used whenever this complex or any part of it preoccupied the patient. Again, this patient used the vocable *dü* (from *dünn = thin*) to express concerns about *thinness, working hard,* etc.; underlying this polysemy of reference was a holophrastic situation binding together the notions of thinness and working hard: "Thin comes from overeating; animals eat so much that, as people say, they (have to) become thin. People work hard driving the animals around till they get thin." A patient of Piro's (192, p. 130) used *postilla* not only in the usual sense (= *note, marginal note*) but for *calumny* as well; underlying this plurisignificance was the patient's attitude that "people always add something evil. . . ." Another patient, performing on the Rorschach, used *cintura* (= *belt*) both for *belt* and for *tie:* underlying this plurisignificant use was the patient's conception of a tie as a "belt worn around the neck" (Piro, 192, p. 147).

Just as the premature embodiment of thoughts in linguistic forms underlies the *plurisignificance* of verbal utterances, that is, the one-many relationship between a certain vocable and its referents, so too does the premature *polysemantic* formulation of reference lead to a heightened manifestation of *multiformity* in expression: there is a tendency to use a variety of terms to refer to what would normally be taken as a relatively constant content. Because the schizophrenic

---

[16] This does not mean that the schizophrenic will distinguish multiple meanings of a conventional term where such meanings are part of the linguistic code.

tends to give verbal expression to unstable referents, referents that are constantly fusing with each other and hence altering with regard to the characteristics they present to the patient (polysemy of reference), he is prompted to use expressions that capture whatever momentary features of the object are dominant for him at the time; thus the same general (polysemantic) sphere may now be expressed through one term, now through quite another. For example, one of Freeman's patients (69, p. 931) referred to nurses as either *capes*, *hems*, *ruffs*, or *waterproofs*.

The simultaneous operation of both of these tendencies—plurisignificance or "spheric homonymity," on one hand, and multiformity or "spheric synonymity," on the other—leads to a considerable instability of the patient's lexicon. Vocables may at one moment be unrelated to each other and at the next moment share a common sphere of reference—a sharing sufficient to lead to their identification with each other. For example, in Gerson's patient, the vocables *sü* and *dü* originally pertained to two different spheres. Later on, because of the interpenetration of spheres, they were used interchangebly: one has to *pray* when *working hard* so that Christianity can expand, hence the domains of praying and working hard interfuse and *sü* and *dü* become "synonymous." At the same time, however, each may still retain its other connotations and hence have little connection with each other.

Let us now turn from the connotations to a brief consideration of the *vehicular structure* of schizophrenic names. Although, in the main, pathological (schizophrenic) thought is embodied in conventional linguistic forms (these forms, to be sure, functioning holophrastically and idiosyncratically) there are certain instances in which the underlying collapse of distance between experienced content and representational form (referent and vehicle) is more *directly* revealed in the vehicular structure. These are in particular, of course, the cases of *neomorphic utterances*. Reflected in such utterances are the diffuseness and interpenetration of connotational spheres, the lack of differentiation between thing and action, part and whole, substance and attribute, etc. Furthermore, the neoformations—in the mode of their composition—directly correspond to the flowing, interweaving, condensed organization of inner experience.

Thus, in neomorphic utterances (for example, *dü*, *schum*, *tuck*), there is an absence of any external indicators which would reveal such utterances as possessing a nominal, verbal, adjectival, etc., status; although often "cut-outs" or "cut-offs" from conventional linguistic forms,[17] they lack the features that would convey determinate and circumscribed aspects of happenings. In their relatively *amorphous* structure, they mirror the lack of determinateness and circumscription of the experiences they express. In some instances, indeed, full words are cut down to mere letters, quasi-interjections, which may function now to denote a person, now an action, now a quality, etc.: for example, *ü* (from *übermütig* = vivacious) used to indicate now the total quality of a person, now—noun-like—to express "a (powerful) oath" (75, p. 164).

The direct correspondence of the peculiar organization of inner experience in the neomorphic linguistic expression is perhaps most clearly revealed in the manner of *molding* the linguistic material. Just as images flow together and become compacted through conglomeration, or agglutinated through intimate association, so too are many neomorphic utterances built up by the *conglomeration, agglutination, incorporation,* or *condensation* of material deriving from conventional language or from previous neomorphic utterances.[18] Following are illustrations.

Schunk is a contamination of *schun* (= slaving) and *K* (first letter of "Kaiserreich," empire). This schizophrenic monoreme combines two ideas: "I am slaving hard" and (associated with the Russian empire) "liberation from czarism." The meaning conveyed then approximates "slaving hard to be released" (75, p. 164).

Uf is an agglutination of *u* (condensed from *usch* = *unschuldig*, innocent) and *f* (= father). It contains two notions: Innocent (I am kept here)—father (responsible for this, and for my eventual release).

A striking feature of many neomorphic utterances, built up from different words, is the redundant or pleonastic expression of the same sphere of meaning by different parts of the utterance. Just as the interpenetration of connotational spheres leads to a charging of each of the interpenetrated spheres with a common atmosphere, so too, different fragments of a neomorphic utterance may overlap in their meaning. For example, in the neomorphic expression *mirwihe*, of

---

[17] However deviant schizophrenic expressions may be from language proper, they are in the main morphemically related to ordinary speech, that is, they are not entirely glossolalic; this fact suggests, as noted, that some intention towards communication to others is still operative in pathological speech.

[18] So-called "contaminations" in imagery are best known to us from Freud's analysis of condensed dream images; Kraepelin has pointed to condensation as one of the characteristic methods of composition of dream language, for example, *voisit* = voilà and termites (= expression of surprise about the many termites crawling all over the place).

Gerson's patient, *mir* conveyed the idea of the patient (from German "mir" = me, hence, I), and so too did *wihe*, which was a deformation of the patient's name (75, p. 167). Similarly, in *süf, sü* in one context meant the "highest one, the preacher, father" while *f* also conveyed "father."

Primitive Modes of Formulating Statements in Schizophrenia: The Relative Lack of Differentiation between Words and Sentences

Up to now, we have been mainly concerned with the function of designation ("naming") in schizophrenia and with modes of realizing this function that clearly reveal primordial levels of operation. We now consider briefly the function of "making statements" or relating thoughts to each other—a function normally realized through sentences. Here again, our emphasis is on primitive ways in which this function occurs in schizophrenic speech.

We have already mentioned several times that schizophrenic thought is characterized by an interpenetration of connotational spheres, by globality and lability, by a dedifferentiation of activities that are more or less distinguished in normal adult functioning. One of the consequences of the regression into autism in schizophrenia is that the activities of designating (denominating) objects and making statements about them reflected in a distinction between names and sentences, tend to merge or fuse with each other: the utterance of isolated vocables is no indication that a patient is making a delimited designatory reference to a circumscribed thing, action, or event; such vocables, even when they are conventional words, often have a quasi-declarative, quasi-optative, or quasi-imperative function, or reflect some fusion of these various "attitudes."

Many of the neomorphic utterances discussed in the previous section —the schizophrenic "monoremes"—already illustrated the lack of differentiation between words and sentences—between naming and making statements—in pathology. One additional example is the following: Gerson's patient (75, p. 166) used the vocable *exis* to designate an *x*, which, itself, referred to *crossing, embracing;* however, in one of its plurisignificant meanings, *exis* was also equivalent to the statement that "two shans (= neoformation for important persons) embrace each other."

The lack of articulation between the meaning of the word and the meaning of the sentence in pathological verbal thought is, in a certain sense, the principal factor underlying the global-holophrastic, tangential, implicatory, and multifocal (Arieti) meanings of single vocables. To give one further illustration here: [19] Tuczek's patient translated the word *white* into her idiosyncratic lexicon as *le sent*,[20] because "God has *sent* the *snow* (which is *white*)" (254, p. 292): since *sent* was part of the global thought involving the *snow which is white*, it could be equated with the whole thought or with any part of the sentence meaning.

The fact that single vocables (whether conventional or neomorphic) can carry, for the patient, an elaborate and comprehensive thought does not mean, of course, that the expression of diffuse thoughts of a patient is limited to such single vocables (*monoremes*). Patients whose linguistic utterances clearly deviate from those of normals may also express their thoughts through *composites* and through *asyntactic, agglutinative conglomerations;* these latter types of utterance reflect a less severe dissolution of syntactic structurization than does the monoremic kind of expression.

An illustration of the expression of sentence-meanings through composites (juxtaposition of monoremes) is the following: Gerson's patient used *isch-ki* (from *ich-schwöre Kind*—I swear-child) to convey the idea that "children ought to (and do) tell the truth." . . . Other illustrations are: *mür-auf* (from *misericordia*, an utterance pertaining to a religious practice, and *auf*, here signifying "go there!") was used to convey the meaning that "one ought to go more often to Church!"; *mirwihe-pe*, derived from the juxtaposition of a neomorphic utterance signifying "I, hoping for release" and *pe*, referring to "papa," was a means of emphasizing "I expect my release from papa (doctor)" (Gerson, 75).

Quite frequently the composites uttered by schizophrenics have the character of "duoremes" (see Chapter 10): the two components of the utterance are pleonastic, that is, overlapping in their reference. In other words, each component expresses a global connotational sphere from a somewhat different angle, emphasizing a somewhat different aspect, but still referring to the whole sphere. Such pleonastic constructions are particularly apparent in the *asyntactic agglutinative conglomerations*, which comprise the main bulk of distinctively neomorphic speech in schizophrenia.

---

[19] A number of other illustrations will be given in the course of the discussion of Baker's study (13) at the end of this chapter.

[20] Tuczek's patient had a predilection for using the French article "le" in her translations.

Such conglomerations are often combinations of neoformations with syntactically and grammatically distorted words or phrases. They exhibit all of the characteristics which we have discussed under the concept of "dystaxia" in the preceding chapter on speech in dreams: the utterances are fragmentary, disordered and lacking in grammatical and syntactic devices for indicating the categorial and conceptual status of the units. One example, from Gerson's patient, may suffice to illustrate the nature of these conglomerations. Every morning she greeted her psychiatrist with the following utterance which was always accompanied by a gesture of invocation: *Papa sang schan ang schock schunk wie wir hier stehen* (75). Without going into a detailed analysis, this "sentence" was, in its first part, a chain of neomorphic monoremes and, in its second part, a conventional phrase. The entire utterance reflected a *pars pro toto* as well as *totum pro parte* organization. Each of the monoremes was closely, pleonastically, interwoven with the others in its reference, most of the units carrying the total sphere as well as more delimited meanings. Thus each part as well as the whole utterance embodied the patient's wish to be released from the hospital by the psychiatrist (doctor, papa).

Up to now, we have considered pathologically primitivized expressions of simple statements or thoughts as these have occurred in clinical settings. Before turning to an experimental analysis of the relations between word and sentence in pathological thought, we may touch briefly on some other clinical findings pertaining to the verbal expression of so-called *"logical relations" between thoughts.*

Generally speaking, the expression of such "logical relations" by patients reflects, once again, the underlying diffuseness, interpenetration, and concretization characterizing most of the thinking of regressed schizophrenics. Thus, thoughts pertaining to causal relations, conditional relations, in-order-to relations, etc., may be carried linguistically by monoremes, composites, or agglutinative conglomerations—those forms of utterance that have been seen to characterize primitivized expressions of simple thoughts. In other words, logical relations, in many instances, are not realized through the special forms, arrangements, and syntactic devices of the linguistic code, but are fused with the expression of contents.[21] We may again illustrate from utterances by Gerson's patient.

For example, *dü*—a *monoreme* used by this patient—was sometimes

---

[21] See Chapters 12 and 24 respectively for parallels in ontogenesis and in nonverbal representation to primitive expressions of relations between thoughts.

employed to convey not only its multiple global meanings, *thin* and *working hard*, but also a *cause-effect relation* between these holophrastic notions. When thus used, *dü*—explicated in normal, communicable language—was a statement to the effect that "the animal, having over-eaten, has become thin because it was worked out (driven around) a great deal" (75, p. 161). The use of a *composite* to express a causal relation was exemplified in the patient, writing *Flottengut* (= *fleet-riches*) below a drawing of houses, trees, and animals enclosed by a fence; explication and interpretation revealed that there was an underlying causal connection between fleet and riches—"Because of the (German) fleet, riches are created." The use of *agglutinative conglomerations* expressing logical relations is revealed in the following: the patient drew a sequence of single pictures—a man jumping over a dust- or garbage-heap, a pail (to put the garbage in), a house (representing property and wealth), a symbol of the world—and designated the ensemble *rein Müljartem draufschläge* (= pure-billion hitting at it). *Müljartem* was a corruption of milliard (billion) but was also related through the initial syllable to *Müll* (*dust, garbage*); it thus expressed in condensed form the notions of wealth and dirt—misery dished out to the patient. The approximate meaning of the conglomerate, normally explicated, was: "In order to overcome (cleanse, purify oneself from) dirt (misery), billions have to be spent (75, p. 172).[22]

All these instances show the lack of differentiation between circumscribed word-meanings and comprehensive sentence-meanings. Vocables—whether they are neomorphic or seemingly conventional, whether they are uttered singly or occur as part of larger expressions —often convey a number of thoughts, thoughts that are normally distinguished and normally rendered in discrete phrases or sentences. Furthermore, such vocables often express in a condensed, syncretic manner not only multiple contents but also relations between contents. Let us consider one additional instance: Gerson's patient uttered the phrase, *Die Milch ist mir nicht zugekniet worden* (= *the milk was not kneeled to me*). This rather bizarre utterance made sense once it was realized that *zugekniet* (*kneeled to*) holophrastically expressed the idea of "praying for something (on one's knees) and getting it"

---

[22] See Cameron's study (39) on causal reasoning in schizophrenia. Using one of Piaget's tests, requiring the completion of a causal clause ("because . . ."), Cameron's findings led him to the conclusion that the articulate causal reasoning of normals is replaced in schizophrenia by "asyndetic" thinking, manifested in the form of conglomerations.

or "if one prays for something, one should get it, i.e., it should come to one." The meaning of the utterance, then, was: "Although I prayed for milk, I did not get it" (75, p. 173).

Such schizophrenic utterances may remind one of parallel kinds of expressions occurring in dreams. For example, Kraepelin reports the following dream utterance: *Der Fischer hat sich wattmüde erhalten* (= the fisherman kept himself shallows-tired): the meaning of this utterance, when fully explicated, was approximately, "Because the fisherman was tired, he could only manage to wade through shallows (not through deep water)." Another illustration: *mainly due to weak and arrogant digestion;* this condensed utterance, when expanded, conveyed the thought that "a weak and arrogant government will not be loved even if it feeds its people well" (138, p. 34). One sees from these instances, as from the above-mentioned schizophrenic utterances, the relative dissolution of syntactic-relational organization; the seeming "words" (*kneeled to, shallow-tired*) actually function as holophrastic quasi-sentential "names."

Thus far, we have discussed and illustrated primitive modes of handling linguistic forms ("words" and "sentences") as these modes are sometimes manifested in cases of relatively advanced schizophrenia. We conclude this chapter with a brief consideration of some findings from an experimental-comparative inquiry into the ways in which "words" occurring in sentences are endowed with meaning by schizophrenics who have been matched for age, intelligence test scores, and level of education with normal individuals. This inquiry, carried out by R. W. Baker (13), involved the use of an abbreviated form of the Word-Context test.[23]

One will recall that the essential task for a subject with respect to any one series of the Word-Context test is to give an "adequate" or "suitable" meaning to an unknown (artificial) word, embedded in six different sentence-contexts. The sentences are exposed progressively and cumulatively, that is, the first, the first and second, and so on. As each additional context is exposed, the subject is required to endow the artificial word with a meaning, to indicate how that meaning fits the context, and also to show how that meaning fits each of the previous contexts. Ideally, the subject is directed towards the formulation of a word-meaning that will be semantically and syntactically fitting, i.e., that will be semantically and grammatically insertable into each of the sentence-contexts without alteration or transformation of the structures of the sentence-contexts.

---

[23] Six, rather than the original twelve, series of sentences were employed, including the *corplum, hudray, contavish, and bordick* series described in Chapter 13.

Confronted with the task of giving meaning to an artificial word in sentence-contexts, schizophrenics—to a far greater degree than the matched group of normals—tended to give to the artificial word meanings *equivalent* to the (diffusely apprehended) referents of the sentence-contexts in which the word occurred. That is to say, rather than endowing the "word" with a meaning that was semantically and syntactically insertable in the sentence-frames, schizophrenics tended to *equate* the meaning of the word with either the whole or part of the sentence-contexts. Following are several illustrations of such extreme lack of differentiation between word and sentence.

Presented with the last sentence of the *hudray* series—"You must have enough space in the bookcase to *hudray* your library"—one patient stated: ". . . 'hudray' means a bookcase that's sizeable to the amount of books to be had." As can be seen, the meaning attributed to the artificial word was not circumscribed so as to fit organically into the sentence as a distinct element or part; rather the meaning of *hudray* was equated to a globally apprehended meaning of the context.

Another patient, with regard to the third sentence of the *bordick* series—"The plan to build the house was a *bordick* because it cost too much"—remarked: "I can say what a 'bordick' would be; a house is a shelter—it's a plan to be sheltered." One can perhaps best grasp the character of word-sentence undifferentiatedness by trying to fit the word-meaning advanced by the patient into the sentence-context, thus: "The plan to build the house was a *plan to be sheltered* because it cost too much."

It should be emphasized that a subject is asked to show how the meaning he gives to the word fits each of the sentence-contexts. One may then wonder why the patient does not reject or change his "solution" (the word-meaning) once he becomes aware of the lack of "insertability" of the meaning into the sentence-frame. The answer to this question, it seems to us, is that subjects who manifest word-sentence undifferentiatedness do not apprehend the sentence-contexts as stable structures, as autonomous linguistic patterns: they "disregard" the sentence-frames and go directly to the underlying referents, that is, the ideas the sentence-contexts evoke. As long as the meaning assigned to the artificial word shares the same "atmosphere" as the meaning evoked by a context, there is a "fittingness": the subject feels no need to fit the word-meaning into each of the contexts in a syntactically as well as semantically adequate fashion.

The meaning assigned to an artificial word is not always taken over entirely from the sentence-context(s). At a somewhat more advanced level than the kinds of word-sentence fusions illustrated, there were instances in which the meaning assigned to a "word" was *partly fused* with the sentence-context but also *partly independent* of the context. In our discussion of ontogenesis, we designated this kind of word-sentence relation *overlap* or *contextual gradient.* In such instances, parts of a sentence-context surrounding an artificial word creep into the meaning assigned to that word-form and then remain incorporated into the meaning of the word in other contexts. The following examples from Baker's patients may serve to clarify this process.

One patient, for the sixth sentence of the *contavish* series—"John fell into a *contavish* in the road"—gave the seemingly circumscribed meaning "hole" for *contavish,* i.e., he substituted "hole" for *contavish* in the sentence.[24] His subsequent comments, however, indicated that *contavish,* considered in relative abstraction from the context (in response to the question, "What does "contavish" mean, then?") meant not merely "hole," but "hole in the road, etc." Thus, the subject spontaneously remarked: "in the sixth one (sentence-context) it would be a physical condition in the roadway he was traversing caused by tempo condition, a year date, in respect to John whatever year date he had gone to—he fell into a hole in the road." Asked at this point for the meaning of *contavish,* the subject replied: "it would mean a *hole in the road caused by a tempo condition, a year date.*"

The infusion of the sentence-context into the word meaning may become manifest when the subject is asked for the meaning of the unknown word per se (as in the previous example), or it may reveal itself when the subject tries to show the fittingness of an assigned meaning in a new context. For instance, a patient, for the sixth sentence of the *corplum* series—"The painter used a *corplum* to mix his paints"—inserted or substituted "stick of wood" for *corplum.* In conformity with the task requirement for a general meaning, the patient attempted to fit this meaning in the previous (fifth) sentence —"You can make a *corplum* smooth with sandpaper." He first asserted that "stick of wood" did fit in the fifth sentence and then went on to state how it fit: "Because you use sandpaper, it says, and you make it smooth, it says in the fifth sentence, and the words 'smooth' and 'sandpaper' indicate that it's a *stick of wood to stir paints.*" In

---

[24] The difference in the meaning given the unknown word in the process of substitution in the context versus the characterization of the word-meaning per se highlights the difference in the two operations: one may fit a circumscribed meaning in a given context, e.g., "hole," and yet when asked for the meaning of the word, to some degree abstracted from the context, one may assign a much more holophrastic meaning, e.g., "hole in the road."

the final meaning assigned to *corplum,* the subject had incorporated a portion of the sixth sentence context, "to stir (mix) his paints."

Insofar as a subject concerns himself with the sentence-contexts and does not merely assign a meaning to the word irrespective of context, complete and partial equating of word-meaning with sentence-meaning are the most primitive forms of signifying a word. Such processes of word-meaning formation are polar extremes to *lexical autonomy*—the formation of a verbal concept that remains relatively invariant in diverse sentence-contexts. In a statistical analysis (median test) of the differences in incidence of these primitive processes, it was found that a considerably larger number of the patients showed an incidence above the common median: thus, with regard to *complete equating* of word- to sentence-meaning, twelve of fifteen schizophrenics but only two of fifteen normals showed an incidence above the common median—a difference significant at the .01 level; with regard to *partial equating* or *contextual gradient,* thirteen schizophrenics but only one normal showed an incidence above the common median—once again significant at the .01 level.

In the preceding paragraph, we intimated that subjects sometimes seemed to disregard the sentence-context in arriving at a meaning for the artificial word. Actually, such signification, without regard for sentence-contexts, occurred only among schizophrenics. To illustrate: one patient, for the first sentence of the *corplum* series—"A *corplum* may be used for support"—gave as his meaning for the "word"—"an ancient Chinese pressure machine; there's a square box and they push a rod in the square box, and it pumps air out the other end." In such cases the meaning attributed to the unknown word seems to derive either from associations evoked by the word-form or by expressive properties apprehended in the sound pattern; the sentence-context plays little if any role in determining the meaning assigned to the unknown word. As an illustration of such neological signification based on the expressive features of the artificial word, we may mention the following: a patient, again for the first sentence, *corplum* series—A *corplum* may be used for support—remarked, "You know what the word corplum means? It's a pile-driver work—the sound of a pile-driver at work—did you ever hear a pile-driver? (The subject then repeated *corplum* several times rhythmically, pronouncing it 'corplume')—Corplum is the same thing, a fanfare." It is noteworthy that patients when asked, on such occasions, how the assigned meaning fit the sentence-context, typically replied either that they did not know or that "it doesn't."

We may now sum up the findings of Baker's study with respect to processes of signification in schizophrenics and normal adults. First, schizophrenics seem more disposed than normals to assign a meaning to a word-form on the basis of associations evoked by the word-form or on the basis of expressive features apprehended in the word-form. In this respect, schizophrenics signify word-forms in ways more typical of younger children than of older ones (see H. Werner and E. Kaplan, 275). Second, schizophrenics tend, more than normals, to equate the meaning of an unknown word, either in whole or part, with the linguistic context (or referent of that context) in which the word appears. In this respect, again, schizophrenic word-handling is much closer to that of the younger children on the original Word-Context Test (see pp. 192 ff).

part IV

Linguistic Characterization of Objects in Inner versus External Speech

Introduction

In Part I, we emphasized the importance of "sharing" both in the formation of objects-of-contemplation and in the process of symbolic representation of referents. It is our view that in the symbolic formulation of one's experience, one takes into account one or more audiences to whom these experiences are represented via symbolic vehicles. Such audiences may range from the symbolizer himself to any person capable of sharing the medium of representation and communication with the symbolizer.

Underlying our concern with the audiences of symbolic representation is the belief that the structure of symbolic representation is intimately tied up with the audience to whom a communication is directed. Where the audience is envisaged as "distant," removed from the symbolizer and the event which the symbolizer confronts, it becomes necessary to formulate the message via vehicles that are impersonal, objective, and disentangled from the symbolizer's idiosyncratic experiences. Where the audience is one's self or an alter ego, the nature and organization of the vehicles of representation would be expected to be of quite a different, contrasting, order.

In the chapters included in this Part, we shall be concerned primarily with two kinds of audiences: one constituted by the symbolizer himself and the other constituted by some person clearly apart from the symbolizer (hence, someone ostensibly exemplifying the "generalized other"). Where the explicit or implicit orientation of the individual is towards communication to himself, we shall designate the situation as one of "self-directed symbolization" or as one of "inner speech"; symbolic activity intended for others shall be designated as "other-directed symbolization" or as "external speech."

In Chapter 17, we shall focus primarily on the nature of linguistic representation in normals under the two conditions of self-directed and other-directed symbolization. In Chapter 18, our emphasis will be comparative: we shall concern ourselves with linguistic representation under the two conditions of communication not only in normal adults but in schizophrenics as well. Finally, in Chapter 19, we shall consider inner versus external speech ontogenetically, attempting to show how these two orientations in representation differentiate out from a primordial matrix in which the distinction between inner and external speech does not obtain.

chapter 17

Inner versus External Speech in Normal Adults

In this chapter we concern ourselves with the ways in which normal adults handle the linguistic medium for conveying experienced events to themselves as contrasted with their manner of handling this medium when the audience is some other (nonfamiliar) person. The primary basis for our discussion is an experiment performed by Edith Kaplan (133).

In this experiment, ten male and ten female college students served as subjects. Each subject was requested to describe different kinds of stimulus material under different conditions of communication, that is, for different kinds of audiences. The descriptions were written. The stimulus material to be linguistically characterized comprised two exemplars each of (1) a visually articulated configuration, (2) a visually diffuse configuration, and (3) a relatively unfamiliar odor. Exemplars of the visual stimulus material are reproduced in Fig. 17-1; the olfactory stimuli were two chemical compounds, resorcinal dimethyl ether and phenylacetic acid. The different audiences for whom the stimulus material was described were (1) the symbolizer himself, and (2) some person unknown to the symbolizer: these different audiences permitted a comparison between "inner speech" and "external speech."[1]

---

[1] Technically, of course, the study did not deal with speech but with written representation. The phrases "inner speech" and "external speech" are used, however, in the sense of self-directed and other-directed symbolic communication irrespective of the mode of representation. For early treatment of the problem, see (57).

Visual diffuse stimulus

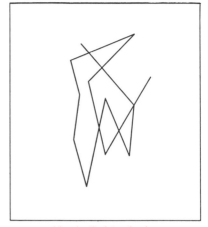

Visual articulate stimulus

FIGURE 17-1. Two patterns used in E. Kaplan's experiment.

The procedure in the study was as follows: in an intial phase, each subject was told that he would be confronted successively with six different stimuli: four visual designs and two odors. As each of these stimuli was presented to him, he was to write down any reactions, feelings, and thoughts that came to mind—taking as much time as he wished to record these responses. This phase of the study was designed to acquaint the subject with the stimulus material; it was also aimed at obtaining a sort of base-level reaction to the stimulus material prior to actual communication to the self or to another.

After a subject had completed writing his reactions to the six stimulus-objects, he was again presented with each of the stimuli and asked to write a description for himself: this description was to be such as to enable him to identify the particular stimulus-object at some future time. It was stressed that this description be no longer than one sentence.

In the next phase of the study, the condition of other-directed communication was introduced. In order to make the subject aware of communication as entailing messages to be fully understood by others, the experimental situation was "rigged" by design so that the subject experienced first failure and then success in his attempts to communicate. This design involved the aid of an experimental accomplice who played the role of the communicatee. The subject was introduced to the experimental accomplice, and given the following instructions:

"You are to tell Mr. ――― as much about the figure (or odor) as you feel is necessary for him to identify it correctly from among the four figures (or odors) in front of him."

In the presence of the subject, the experimenter then gave the following instructions to the accomplice:

"If you can identify the figure (or odor) with certainty on the basis of what has been told to you, then point out the figure (or bottle containing the olfactory stimulus). If, however, there is any doubt at all, then do not guess but rather, say that you need more information."

Prior to the experimental situation, the accomplice had been told to fail to identify the figure (or odor) twice, and to succeed on the third trial.

When the subject had completed this phase of the experiment (when he had characterized all of the six stimuli for the accomplice), he was made aware of the actual role of his communicatee.[2] He then engaged in the last phase of the study: in this phase, the subject was requested to write a description of each stimulus which would serve to enable any other person to identify the stimulus; here again, it was stressed that the description be no longer than one sentence.

In presenting the findings of this study, we shall deal only with the one-sentence descriptions, that is, the one for the self and the one for "any other person," since it is upon these descriptions that E. Kaplan focused in her analysis. The discussion of the differences in linguistic representation under the two conditions of communication and with regard to the different kinds of stimulus material will be primarily concerned with three aspects of the written descriptions: explicitness of expression, communicability of expression, and linguistic organization of the expression.

Explicitness of Expression: Number of Words Comprising a Sentence

One issue in the comparison of symbolization for the self and symbolization for another is the "fullness" or explicitness of that part of the communication which is public or overt: to what extent is the nature of the referent made explicit in communication for oneself as against communication for others?

A gross indication of "fullness" or explicitness is the number of words one uses in forming his descriptive sentences. An examination of the sentences employed by subjects in characterizing the various

---

[2] It was believed that unless the subject were informed as to the role of the accomplice, he might tend to base his final written description of the stimulus material on the information and mode of formulation used in his third trial with the accomplice, i.e., in the trial that ostensibly succeeded in enabling the "other" correctly to identify the stimulus material.

Table 17-1

Mean number of words in sentences characterizing stimuli under conditions of inner versus external speech

	Visually articulated	Visually diffuse	Olfactory material
Inner speech	13.35	19.70	11.35
External speech	52.20	55.00	24.50

stimuli under the two conditions of communication revealed clearly what one might plausibly expect: a relatively fewer number of words in sentences intended for the self than in sentences intended for an "other." For each of the three types of stimulus material, the number of words used in characterizing the material for one's self was significantly less than the number used in characterizing the material for another person. The relevant findings are presented in Table 17-1.

In general, then, linguistic representation in inner speech is more *laconic* than in external speech.[3] One may next inquire whether there was the same degree of laconicism of inner relative to external speech for the various kinds of stimulus material. An examination of Table 17-1 suggests that such was not the case. The difference in the number of words per sentence under external and inner speech conditions (number in external speech minus number in inner speech) was most marked for the visually articulated stimuli (ratio, approximately 4:1), less marked for the visually diffuse stimuli (ratio, approximately 3:1), and least marked for the olfactory stimuli (ratio, approximately 2:1). In other words, a shift from inner to external speech evoked an increase in verbal output that was proportionately greater for the visual stimulus material than for the olfactory material.[4]

In sum, then, irrespective of the kind of stimulus object described, representation for another person was relatively more explicit than was representation for oneself. This overall difference between inner

---

[3] The reader should be reminded that all conclusions drawn are with reference to linguistic representation in the service of giving information about objects.

[4] Analysis of variance, using difference scores, indicated that the differences in degree of discrepancy between external and inner speech when each of the visual stimulus-types was compared with the olfactory material were statistically significant; however, the discrepancy between external and inner speech for visually articulated stimuli did not differ significantly from the discrepancy obtained for visually diffuse stimuli.

and external speech was, however, clearly affected by the kind of stimulus-material considered for description: external speech differed most markedly from inner speech with regard to explicitness when the material was visual in nature; when the material to be described was olfactory, representation for another was closer—in terms of explicitness—to representation for the self.

Communicability of Expression: Kinds of Referents Characterized in Descriptions of Stimuli under Conditions of Inner and External Speech

The issue here concerns the communicability of the linguistic messages when one is representing for oneself as compared with one's representation for another person: the question then is, to what extent are the referents (e.g., objects or properties of objects) implicated in the linguistic characterizations of the stimuli communicable? Is there any difference in the kinds of referents referred to under the two conditions?

One may distinguish two generic classes of referents, viz., those that are of a more "communal" nature and those that are more personal and "idiomatic" in character. "Communal" referents are those which are established through the use of terms referring to conventional and transpersonal properties of perceptual objects, such as location, geometrical shape, size, quantity; "idiomatic" referents are those which are rooted in similes or analogies, described in evaluative terms, characterized physiognomically, assimilated to personal experiences, etc. It is clear that this distinction is only a relative one. As illustrations of *communal referents* with regard to the visual stimuli, one may cite the following: "a thick arc, which seems separated from the rest," "a continuous, broken line," "a series of joined, straight lines;" an example with regard to olfactory stimuli is "acid-like smell which is sour." The following are illustrations of *idiomatic referents:* for visual stimuli, "looks like a native in his ceremonial enjoyment," "looks like a talking penguin," "an interesting design," "looks like a bird's head;" for olfactory stimuli, "a pleasant smell," "a sweetish odor, reminding me of a toothache medicine."

With regard to the two conditions of communication, two questions were asked pertaining to the communicability of reference. What is the distribution of communal and idiomatic referents in inner speech as compared with external speech? To what extent does the nature of the stimulus material (visually articulated, visually diffuse, olfactory) affect the distribution of communal as compared with idiomatic referents under the different conditions of communication? The relevant data are presented in Fig. 17-2 (*a* and *b*).

Examining first that part of Fig. 17-2 dealing with the incidence of communal referents, one will note that there were more communal referents in external speech than in inner speech with regard to each of the stimulus materials. In absolute terms, this difference in incidence of communal referents under the two conditions was greater for the visual stimuli than for the olfactory material; however, the relative or proportional increase in communal referents under external-speech conditions as compared with inner speech was not significantly greater for any one kind of stimulus material than for the others.

Turning now to that part of Fig. 17-2 dealing with the incidence of idiomatic referents, one obtains quite a different picture. In contrast to the incidence of communal referents under the two conditions, the frequency of idiomatic referents for visual stimuli was approximately the same for inner as for external speech. For olfactory stimuli, how-

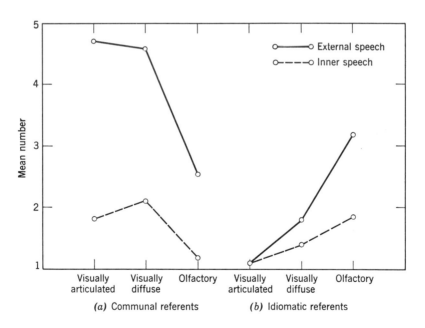

FIGURE 17-2. Communicability of expression: mean incidence of (*a*) communal and (*b*) idiomatic referents, in inner versus external speech.

ever, there was a (significant) increase in idiomatic referents under external speech, somewhat comparable to the increase of communal referents under that condition of communication.

The findings presented in Fig. 17-2 (a and b) may be formulated in another way, to answer a question about the relationship between the incidence of communal and idiomatic referents for each of the two conditions of communication. Under inner-speech conditions (broken lines of both sections of Fig. 17-2), there were no significant differences between the incidence of communal and the incidence of idiomatic referents; this was true in general and for each of the stimulus types. Under external-speech conditions (solid lines of both sections of Fig. 17-2), on the other hand, there were significant differences between the incidence of communal and idiomatic referents: these differences, however, pertained only to the visual stimuli; for the olfactory material, there was no significant difference.

In other words, the difference score, communal minus idiomatic referents, clearly distinguished external from inner speech with regard to the visual stimuli but not with regard to olfactory stimulus material. Using this score as an index of the communicability of expression, one may say, therefore, that there is a greater communicability of expression in external over inner speech for visual stimuli than for olfactory stimulus material.

Linguistic Organization of Expression: Syntactic Forms and Contents of Qualifying Descriptions

In describing stimulus material for oneself and for others, one may organize the linguistic characterization in different ways. In examining the ways in which the descriptions were linguistically organized, E. Kaplan focused on the relations of *qualifiers to nouns;* this was essentially a *formal* analysis pertaining to the *position* of the qualifier in relation to the principal noun. A second analysis pertained to the *kinds of content* referred to by qualifiers.

Formal Analysis

In organizing his description of a stimulus, for the purpose of communication, a subject may focus first on the qualifiers and then on the noun qualified or he may first stipulate the noun and then append the qualifiers. In the first instance, the qualifiers have a primacy and almost dominate the thing qualified; in the second, the thing is first linguistically articulated and circumscribed and only afterward qualified. It seems to us that this difference in the relation of qualifier to noun is not only a matter of grammar but is also psychologically significant: there is, for instance, a difference between describing a visual configuration as "a headless, armless, unfinished *statue*," and describing the same configuration as "a *statue* that is headless, armless, and unfinished." The first description involves a *global conception* in which reference to the statue is implied by each qualifier before it is made explicit at the end of the phrase; in contrast, in the second description the statue from the beginning is named as a *discrete* object, with its properties articulated one by one afterwards.

Where the qualifier precedes the noun qualified, one may designate the process as *modification;* where, on the other hand, the qualifier follows the noun qualified, the process may be designated as one of *specification.* In certain descriptions, of course, both processes may occur; for example, "a thick *arc*, which seems separated from the rest," "a very dark *drawing*, with white patches."

Before turning to a discussion of the distribution of these two kinds of qualifiers under the different conditions of communication and for the three types of stimuli, we may note that both modification and specification imply some degree of differentiation and articulation of a referent. From a developmental point of view, therefore, one would expect both processes to occur more frequently under conditions of external speech than under inner speech. This expectation is fully confirmed by the analysis of the data: as one will note in Table 17-2,

Table 17-2
Mean frequency of modifications and specifications in inner and external speech

	Stimulus material					
	Visually articulated		Visually diffuse		Olfactory	
	Inner	External	Inner	External	Inner	External
Modification	2.25	5.40 *	3.05	5.45 *	1.90	2.85 *
Specification	1.00	8.55 *	2.60	9.25 *	.70	2.70 *

* Difference between inner and external speech significant at .01.

the mean frequencies of both modification and specification increase from inner to external speech for all three kinds of stimulus material. These results serve to support and clarify the previous conclusion —based on the gross difference in number of words used in inner and external speech—that external speech is characteristically more *explicit* than inner speech.

We may now turn to the absolute incidence of modification and specification for the different types of stimuli under the two conditions of communication. Let us consider *modifications* in *inner speech* first. As may be seen from Table 17-2, under conditions of inner speech, more modifications were used in the characterization of visual stimuli than in the characterization of olfactory stimuli; the differences here, however, were not significant. With regard to the incidence of *modifications* in *external speech*, one finds that both types of visual material elicited significantly more instances of modification than did the olfactory stimuli.

A further inquiry pertains to the extent of the increase in the number of modifications in going from inner to external speech. Table 17-2 indicates a large increase for the visually articulated material compared with a relatively small increase for the olfactory stimuli. The extent of the increase for both types of visual material (number in external speech minus number in inner speech) was significantly greater than was the extent of increase for the olfactory material.

Examining now the absolute incidence of *specification* under the two conditions of communication, one will note that the findings closely parallel those obtaining for modification. Under inner-speech conditions, the greatest incidence of specification occurred for visually diffuse stimuli and the least incidence for olfactory stimuli. In going from inner speech to representation for others, the mean number of specifications increased significantly for all types of stimuli. It will be noted, however, that the increase (difference between inner and external speech) was much more marked for the visual stimuli than for the olfactory material; this difference in extent of increase between the visual material (both articulated and diffuse) and the olfactory material was statistically significant.

In sum, then, representation for others seems to be characterized by a greater incidence of both modification and specification than is representation for the self. This greater use of both kinds of qualifications in external speech seems to be more marked for visual stimulus material than for olfactory material.

We may turn now from the analysis of the *absolute* incidence of modification and specification to the incidence of these two kinds of qualifications *relative to each other.* Would one, on theoretical grounds, expect differences in the relative distributions of these two kinds of qualifications in inner as compared with external speech? In our earlier remarks pertaining to modification and specification, we suggested that in the context of describing an object for communicative purposes of identification, description through modification involves a rather global conception in which reference to the thing is carried perceptually during mention of the qualifiers and is only later formulated. Description through specification, on the other hand, implies an initial accentuation of a rather circumscribed thing—a representation of the thing in the medium of language—before there is further qualification. This distinction between modification and specification would suggest that specification in the service of identification involves a greater use of an autonomous linguistic medium than does modification. These considerations would lead one to expect that modifications would predominate over specifications in representation for oneself and that the reverse would obtain in representation for others. The data bearing on this issue are given in Table 17-2.

In general, the findings were in striking accord with the expectations: under the conditions of inner speech, modifications exceeded specifications for all three types of stimulus material; under the conditions of external speech, specifications exceeded modifications for the two types of visual material. True, the expected predominance of specification over modification did not occur for the olfactory material; nevertheless, it will be noted that in the shift from inner to external speech for the olfactory material, modifications increased relatively slightly (from a mean incidence of 1.90 to an incidence of 2.85) and specifications increased relatively sharply (from .70 to 2.70); thus, whereas modification exceeded specification at about 2.7 to 1 in inner speech, the incidence of specification and modification in external speech was about equal.

In sum, then, one may conclude that there is a tendency for the predominant mode of qualification to be modification in inner speech and—at least for visual stimuli—specification in external speech.

Content Analysis

Thus far, we have considered the *position* of the qualifiers without raising the issue of differences in kind of modifications and specifications. In this section, we consider such different kinds of qualifiers, breaking down generic categories of qualifications into distinct types.

Since descriptions involving modifications were—quite understandably—much less explicit, and therefore yielded less information, than those involving specifications, we shall, in the following, restrict the discussion solely to E. Kaplan's analysis of specifications.

In this analysis, seven types of specifications could be clearly distinguished; these, in turn, could be ordered in terms of degree of objectification. This ordering was as follows: *spatial specification,* in which the qualifier is a term or phrase stipulating the location of the object referred to by the noun, e.g., "there is a loop, in the lower left hand corner" (for a visually articulated stimulus), "a prominent figure, at the left hand side" (for a visually articulated stimulus); *figural specification,* in which the qualifier presents the shape or essential property of the thing specified, e.g., "a series of joined, straight lines, forming one closed diamond" (for a visually articulated stimulus), "acid-like smell, which is sour" (for an olfactory stimulus); *specification by simile,* in which the qualifier relates the stimulus material to something radically different in kind, e.g., "light ink drawing, with goblin-like figure" (for a visually diffuse stimulus), "a sweetish odor, reminding me of toothache medicine" (for an olfactory stimulus); *specification by contextual inclusion,* in which the qualifier serves to locate the thing qualified within a larger context, for example, "a formless abstraction, like modern art" (for a visually articulated stimulus), "a dark, forbidding cavern, like those in New Mexico" (for a visually diffuse stimulus), "a leaf-like design, for a modern fabric print" (for a visually articulated stimulus), "a compound used in a lab" (for an olfactory stimulus); *specification by contrariety,* in which the qualifier refers to characteristics which are in opposition to those initially stipulated of the thing qualified, for example, "a sweet odor, with a trace of saltiness" (for an olfactory stimulus); *atmospheric specification,* in which the qualifier establishes a certain atmosphere or ritual-affective context for the thing qualified, for example, "a native in his ceremonial enjoyment" (for a visually diffuse stimulus), "a musty odor, reminding someone of something old and unused" (for an olfactory stimulus); *aesthetic-evaluative specification,* in which the qualifier is used to characterize the thing qualified in terms of affective reactions, for example, "a sharp odor, leaving a mildly pleasant effect" (for an olfactory stimulus), "the smell of pine tree pitch, yet not too disagreeable" (for an olfactory stimulus).

The question now arises concerning the incidence of these various types of specification in inner and external speech and with respect to

Table 17-3

Proportions of types of specification characterizing visually articulated and olfactory stimuli in inner versus external speech

Degree of objecti-fication		Visual		Olfactory	
		External	Inner	External	Inner
High	Figural	59	50	19	8
		91%	64%	19%	8%
	Spatial	32	14	—	—
Medium	Simile	9	12	47	32
		9%	29%	52%	40%
	Contextual	—	17	5	8
Low	Contrariety	—	7	9	30
	Atmospheric	— 0%	— 7%	9 29%	22 52%
	Evaluative	—	—	11	—
	Total	100%	100%	100%	100%

the different kinds of stimulus material. Data pertinent to this question are presented in Table 17-3.[5]

An examination of the distributions of the various types of specification under conditions of external speech, showed that for both visually articulated and visually diffuse stimulus material, the overwhelmingly preponderant types of specification were highest in degree of objectification, namely, figural and spatial specification. Specification by simile, a type of qualification of lesser objectivity, also occurred for both kinds of visual stimulus material, though rather infrequently. Atmospheric specification, relatively low on the scale of "objectification," occurred very rarely for visually diffuse stimuli, not at all for visually articulated material. None of the other "less objective" types of specification appeared in the characterizations of visual material under the conditions of external speech.

The distribution of the types of specification for olfactory stimuli under conditions of external speech present quite a different picture:

---

[5] Since there was little difference between the two kinds of visual stimuli in regard to distribution of specification types, we present only the data for visually articulated stimuli. Whatever difference there was in this regard between the two kinds of visual stimuli is indicated in the text.

of the two types highest in degree of objectification, spatial specification is of course absent and figural specification occurred with comparatively low frequency. The most prevalent type of specification was specification by simile, a type lower on the scale of "objectification" than either spatial or figural specification. The remaining three types of specification which must be considered to be lowest on the scale of "objectification" and which, practically, never occurred under external speech conditions with visual stimuli were utilized to some extent with the olfactory stimulus material.

Turning now to inner speech, one notes in general that types of specification highest in the scale of objectification occurred with comparatively lesser frequency, with the lowest types of specification showing a comparative increase. The shifts in the distribution of the various types of specification, however, did not depend simply on the condition of communication but also on the kind of stimulus material characterized.

Let us first consider the visual material. Here, there was a clear decline (relative to external speech) in the incidence of the two types of specification, highest in degree of objectification; nevertheless, even in inner speech, figural and spatial specification comprised together the greatest number of specifications occurring for visual material. Correlative with the decline in those types of specification that are highest in objectification, various lower types of specification increased.

With regard to olfactory stimuli, specifications highest in degree of objectification occurred with lesser frequency in inner than in external speech. At the same time, types of specification lowest in degree of objectification showed a relatively greater incidence in inner than in external speech with the exception of evaluative specification which occurred only in external speech. Furthermore, among the specifications of medium range of objectivity, simile characterizations of odors —in contrast to visual stimuli—decreased in inner speech.

In sum, then, the findings presented in this section lead to the conclusion that inner speech differs characteristically from external speech in the kinds of specifications used for describing objects for identification: that is, in going from speech for oneself to speech for others, those types of specification implying the higher degrees of objectification will tend to increase while those implying lower degrees of objectification will tend to decline and even perhaps to disappear. The occurrence of the various types of specification, furthermore, seem to be dependent not only on the condition of communication but also on the nature of the stimulus material to be described. Thus the findings suggest that visual stimulus material tends, even in inner speech, to evoke types of specification relatively high on the scale of "objectification;" olfactory material, on the other hand, evokes the use of "lower" types of specification even in representation for others, although the incidence of the lowest types does, in general, increase in inner speech.

Concluding Remarks

In concluding this chapter, we shall attempt to formulate the findings from E. Kaplan's study in terms of the concept of *distance* (Chapter 3). One of the basic principles of organismic-developmental theory pertains to increasing differentiation or "distancing" between the self and the world of objects—this world comprising both things and persons. In terms of this principle, we have contended that representation for oneself ('inner speech') involves a lesser degree of distance between self and others than does representation for others. Also, with regard to the things of the world, olfactory "objects" must be regarded, in general, as much more closely bound to the experiencer than are visual things; phenomenologically, visual "objects" are characteristically experienced as standing opposed to the individual and have a much more "out there" character than do odors.[6]

If there is validity in our contention that cognitive organization is achieved principally through symbolic mediation, the kinds of vehicles employed to characterize presented contents should reflect the developmental level of cognitive operations. Thus, with regard to the particular issue of the *types of specifications* used in communication, one would expect that variations in the distance between self and audience and between self and stimulus material should reflect themselves in variations in the degree of objectification of the symbolically formulated referents. The experimental findings are clearly in agreement with these expectations. Table 17-4 may serve to clarify some of these pertinent findings.

A glance at this table shows, first of all, that there was a remarkable equivalence—with respect to the frequency distribution of the different types of specifications—for changes in "distance" due to conditions

---

[6] Many studies, particularly those by Henning, have shown that the olfactory sense is not only "lower" phylogenetically but has many characteristics—such as the inseparability of subjective impression and objective qualities, the absence of true "configurations" articulated in space and time, etc.—which make it an experientially "primitive" sense. Cf. Werner (274, p. 40); Henning (101).

Table 17-4

Shifts in incidence of different types of specification under different conditions of communication and for different types of stimulus material (after E. Kaplan)

| | Types of Specification in terms of Degree of Objectification | | | | | | |
| | Highest | | Intermediate | | Lowest | | |
Increased distance in terms of:	Spatial	Figural	Simile	Contextual	Contrariety	Atmospheric	Evaluation
(1) Change from Inner to External Speech							
with Olfactory Stim.	*	+	+	−	−	−	+
with Visually Diffuse Stim.	+	=	=	−	*	−	*
with Visually Articulated Stim.	+	+	−	−	−	*	*
(2) Change in Stimulus Material from Olfactory to Visual							
with Inner Speech							
(Olf. to Vis. Diffuse)	+	+	−	=	−	=	*
(Olf. to Vis. Articulated)	+	+	−	+	−	−	*
with External Speech							
(Olf. to Vis. Diffuse)	+	+	−	−	−	=	−
(Olf. to Vis. Articulated)	+	+	−	−	−	−	−

+ indicates an increase; − indicates a decrease; = indicates that the incidence remains approximately the same; * indicates that a comparison could not be made because there was no incidence under either condition of communication or there was no incidence for the two types of stimulus material being considered.

of communication and changes in "distance" due to nature of stimulus material. In general, with a shift towards external speech and with a shift towards visual stimulus material, specifications reflecting higher degrees of objectification increase in incidence and specifications reflecting lower degrees of objectification decrease in incidence. A closer inspection of the table 17-4 reveals three instances of an apparent reversal of this general trend: specification by simile increases for olfactory material in going from inner to external speech; specification by contextual inclusion increases under inner-speech conditions in going from olfactory stimulus material to visually articulated stimuli; and finally, aesthetic-evaluative specification increases for olfactory stimulus material in the shift from inner to external speech.

With regard to the initial two deviations from the general trend, it may be noted, first of all, that the types of specifications are intermediate in degree of objectification. Again, it may be observed that the increase in specification by simile in the case of the olfactory material conformed to the general trend insofar as it occurred at the expense of types of specification lower in the scale of objectification rather than at the expense of figural specification. A somewhat analogous point may be made about the greater incidence of specification by contextual inclusion for visually articulated stimuli compared with olfactory stimuli under conditions of inner speech. The relatively greater number of such intermediate-level specifications in the characterization of visually articulated material is accompanied by a relative paucity of the low-level specifications by contrariety and atmospheric specifications as well as of specifications by simile, whereas the relatively small number of specifications by contextual inclusion for olfactory material is accompanied by a rather large number of low-level specifications, namely, contrariety and atmospheric specifications.

The only finding obviously in opposition to the general trend is the increase of aesthetic-evaluative specifications in external over inner speech with olfactory stimuli. The increase in such specifications goes hand in hand with a decline in types of specification which, though relatively low, are higher in the scale of objectification than are evaluative-aesthetic specifiers, namely, atmospheric specification, specification by contrariety, specification by contextual inclusion. Apparently, some individuals act as if reference to the malodorous or sweet-smelling character of an olfactory stimulus serves better to identify that stimulus for another than does reference to a context or evocation of an atmosphere.

In any case, these minor deviations notwithstanding, the general picture is clear. With a shift from inner to external speech and with a shift from olfactory material to visual material, that is, with *increasing distance* from other persons and from things, one uses those vehicles which will serve to specify referents in a more communal, conventional manner and tends to play down those vehicles which serve to specify referents in a more idiomatic, idiosyncratic, personal way.

chapter 18

Inner and External Speech in Schizophrenics as Compared with Normals

In E. Kaplan's study, the focus was on changes in the linguistic descriptions of stimulus material under conditions of variation in addressee and in stimuli; the addressors were all normal subjects.

The study to be discussed now was carried out by H. Slepian (231) at Clark University. Its aim was to supplement E. Kaplan's work and to extend its scope; in particular, to gain some information on the interaction of mental status of the symbolizer, conditions of communication, and nature of the stimulus material.

The stimulus material to be represented for self and others in Slepian's investigation was similar to that employed by E. Kaplan. It comprised *three* exemplars for each of three types of stimuli, visually articulated, visually diffuse, and olfactory. The olfactory stimuli, selected for non-noxiousness as well as unfamiliarity, were oil of cumin extra, cyclamal cyclo-acetal, and oil of vetivert.

Rather than the two generic conditions of inner and external speech, five conditions of communication were utilized in Slepian's study, the initial two subsumable under inner speech and the latter three under external speech. The five conditions were as follows: (1) *immediate reaction,* a condition in which the subject gives whatever reactions come to mind upon presentation of the stimulus-object; (2) *communication to the self* or *inner speech proper,* one in which the individual directs his communication to and for himself; (3) *initial communica-*

tion to a hypothetical or absent other person, a condition in which the communicator is asked to formulate his characterization of stimulus material to enable any other individual to identify such material without any actual addressee being present; (4) *communication to a real other person,* a condition in which the addressee is visibly present to the addressor; and (5) *final communication to a hypothetical or absent other.*

A few remarks should be added about the fourth and fifth conditions. The fourth condition, communication to a real other person, was designed to determine how far descriptions were affected after the addressor's awareness that he had been unsuccessful in conveying information sufficient to permit identification of the stimulus. Therefore, as in E. Kaplan's study, a "rigged" situation was introduced: an experimental accomplice was brought in, and the subject was asked to write a description which would enable that person to identify the stimulus with certainty from among four stimulus objects, known by each subject to be in front of his addressee. In the presence of each subject, and for his benefit, the accomplice was told to respond only when he was certain of his choice; otherwise he was to inform the addressor that the information was not sufficient. By pre-arrangement, the accomplice was to report twice to the subject that he was unable to identify the stimulus with certainty; thus each subject was obliged to write a total of three responses (*a, b, c* under condition 4) in his effort to describe the stimulus adequately to his addressee (the accomplice).

By introducing the fifth condition—final (second) communication to a hypothetical (absent) other—one was able to determine the effect of actual communication to a real other or communication to hypothetical others: one simply had to compare descriptions in the third condition with those for the fifth condition. (In order to eradicate any false notions a subject might have formed during the "rigged," fourth, situation as to the efficacy or inefficacy of his formulations of the message, each subject was acquainted, prior to the fifth condition, with the pre-arranged character of the fourth situation.)

The analyses were carried out on the one-sentence descriptions of the exemplars of the three types of stimuli under the five conditions of communication. These descriptions were provided by thirty-six subjects, all female, equally divided into a normal group and a schizophrenic group.

In general—although not with respect to specific details—Slepian's analyses were of the same nature as those undertaken by E. Kaplan: he thus dealt with (1) explicitness of expression, (2) communicability of expression, and (3) linguistic organization of expression. We may now consider the findings with regard to each of these aspects.

Explicitness of Expression: Normals versus Schizophrenics

Here, the protocols were examined to determine the degree to which the written messages of the two groups, under the different conditions of communication and for the different types of stimulus material, were explicit or laconic in character. The analysis centered mainly on three questions: (1) To what extent did the descriptions by the normals and schizophrenics differ in explicitness for the same type of stimulus material and under the same conditions of communication? (2) To what extent did differences in conditions of communication lead to differences in the explicitness of descriptions by the schizophrenic subjects as compared with the normals? (3) To what extent did the nature of the stimulus material (whether visual or olfactory) influence the explicitness of descriptive representations in the patient group as compared with the normals?

For the analysis of the data in terms of the dimension of "explicitness," the notion of "structural unit" was introduced. A structural unit was defined as "a part of a linguistic expression containing not more than one primary noun." A structural unit might, therefore, be composed of single words but might also consist of phrases serving to qualify the primary noun.

A "primary noun" was distinguished from a "secondary" or attributive noun, that is, a noun that enters into a phrase qualifying a primary noun. A "primary noun" was taken to indicate an initial categorization of the stimulus as some particular sort of thing. "Secondary nouns" were regarded as serving some further determination of an already established object.

The notion of "structural unit" was employed in the analysis instead of the concept of "word"—as used in E. Kaplan's study—in order to circumvent problems introduced by echolalic and perseverative responses, occurring often with schizophrenics, for example, responses in which the same word is repeated several times, or where there is a flood of speech without coherence, connection, etc. The concept of "structural unit" may be clarified by the following illustrations:

(a) "Percy's ghost—abstract vase." This description was considered as consisting of two structural units: the primary nouns are "ghost" and "vase;"

(b) "A rock with moss on it." This description was considered as one structural unit: the primary noun is "rock;" "moss" appears here as an attributive noun, a constituent of the phrase which qualifies and more fully determines "rock."

Let us now turn to the main findings pertaining to explicitness of messages of schizophrenic and normal subjects as measured in terms of *number of structural units per response.*

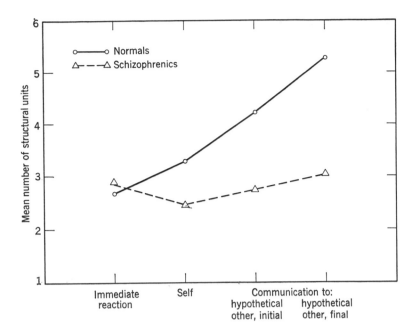

FIGURE 18-1. **Mean number of structural units per response for both groups under various conditions of communication.**

Explicitness and Conditions of Communication

The messages of schizophrenics were found to be less differentiated in explicitness with respect to *various conditions of communication* than were the messages of normal individuals. Schizophrenics tended to show little variation in the mean number of structural units per response, whether they were communicating to themselves or whether they addressed themselves to another (hypothetical) person. In contrast, in the normal group there was a step-wise increment in the number of structural units per response in going from the condition of immediate reaction to the condition of final communication to a hypothetical other: though they tended to be relatively laconic in conditions of immediate reaction, they were quite explicit under conditions of communicating to a hypothetical (absent) other.[1] (See Fig. 18-1.)

---

[1] As indicated in the next footnote, this difference between the two groups also held in regard to communication with a real other.

The messages of schizophrenics appeared also to be less differentiated in explicitness of descriptions for *various types of stimulus objects*, that is, schizophrenics were almost as laconic in their characterization of visual stimuli as they were in their characterization of olfactory stimuli. Normals, in contrast, manifested a strikingly higher degree of explicitness for visual than for olfactory stimuli. In other words, schizophrenics showed a much greater homogeneity in their explicitness for the different kinds of stimuli; normals and schizophrenics were much closer to each other in degree of explicitness for olfactory material than they were for either type of visual material. Normal individuals and schizophrenics tended to be comparatively similar in laconicity under inner-speech conditions and also for olfactory stimuli, but they tended to differ greatly from each other under external-speech conditions and for visual stimuli. (See Fig. 18-2.)

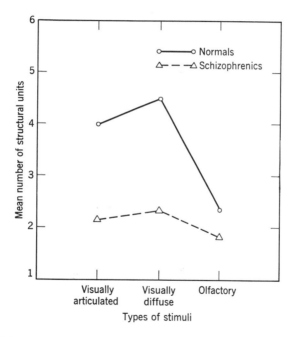

FIGURE 18-2. Mean number of structural units per response for both groups to types of stimulus material.

As will be recalled, between the initial and final communications to a hypothetical other where there was inserted a triune set of communications to an actual person (who, unknown to the subject, was an accomplice of the experimenter), schizophrenics and normals differed strikingly in regard to the effect of this interposition. In normals, communication with a real other strongly affected (increased) the explicitness of subsequent communication with an imagined person; in schizophrenics, the explicitness after the interposition of the condition of communication to a real person was almost the same as the explicitness before the interposition.[2] (See Fig. 18-1.)

Communicability of Expression: Normals versus Schizophrenics

The concern here is with the extent to which the different groups of subjects represented *communal* as contrasted with *idiomatic* referents in formulating their descriptive messages to self and other. It will be recalled that communal referents entail the use of terms referring to geometrical, quantitative, or physical characteristics of stimulus-objects, and idiomatic referents are established through terms referring to physiognomic, affective, or evaluative properties.[3]

In his study, Slepian distinguished among three types of referents, direct-descriptive, allusive descriptive, and evaluative, with the latter two types regarded as more idiomatic in character than the first-mentioned type. In our discussion of Slepian's study we have taken his direct-descriptive referents as equivalent to communal and his other two types as subsumable under idiomatic referents.

Turning now to the findings, we shall first discuss the analysis of the relative frequency of types of referents occurring under the various conditions of communication, irrespective of the mental status of the symbolizer.

Considering first only the responses to the visual material, one sees (Table 18-1) that the fewest communal referents occurred under the condition of immediate reaction and that the greatest number of such

---

[2] In a further analysis, Slepian showed that communication to a real person (condition 4) versus a hypothetical other (condition 3) did not appreciably alter explicitness in schizophrenics. In contrast, with normals, explicitness increased sharply when they were first faced with a real rather than an imagined person and, characteristically, this increase was maintained from conditions 4 to 5.

[3] For illustrations, see the previous chapter.

Table 18-1

Relative frequency of communal referents characterizing the three types of stimuli under different conditions of communication

Stimuli	Conditions of communication:				
	Immediate reaction	Self	Hypothetical other, initial	Real other	Hypothetical other, final
Visually articulated	3%	45%	64%	85%	74%
Visually diffuse	12%	48%	65%	80%	76%
Olfactory	8%	25%	20%	21%	25%

referents was manifested under the condition of communication to a real other. One will also note that there was a shift towards more communal referents in the final communication to a hypothetical other (as compared with the initial communication). Finally, although the relative incidence of communal referents was far greater in communication to the self than in immediate reaction, there was still a considerable difference in incidence between communication to the self and any of the various conditions of external speech.

Let us now examine the influence of type of stimulus (olfactory versus visual) on the kinds of referents employed. One may recall the findings in E. Kaplan's study which suggested that olfactory material, irrespective of condition of communication, lends itself to idiomatic characterization more than does visual material. Slepian's inquiry yielded similar findings: once again, communal referents dominated the characterizations of both the visually articulated and the visually diffuse stimuli; in contrast, the olfactory stimulus material was characterized predominantly in terms of idiomatic referents. One will further note, leaving aside the condition of immediate reaction, that there was much greater homogeneity among the various conditions of communication for the olfactory material than for either of the visual stimulus materials. In other words, in terms of Slepian's index of communicability of expression, there was a lesser tendency to differentiate between *inner* and *external* speech with regard to the olfactory material than with regard to the visual material. In brief, then, olfactory stimulus material had an effect with regard to the communicability of expression (defined in terms of communal versus idiomatic referents) analogous to the condition of schizophrenia and a situation of communication to the self: in all these cases, the symbolizer tended to employ idiomatic rather than communal referents.

Let us next compare the overall communicability of expression among the schizophrenic subjects as compared with the normals. Irrespective of conditions of communication and variations in stimulus type, the descriptions by normal subjects employed more communal referents than idiomatic referents (66.4 percent to 33.6 percent); in contrast, the descriptions by the schizophrenic subjects involved more idiomatic referents than communal referents (55.8 percent to 44.2 percent).

Let us now examine the incidence of communal referents produced by each of the two groups under each of the five conditions of communication. One will note from Fig. 18-3 that for each of these con-

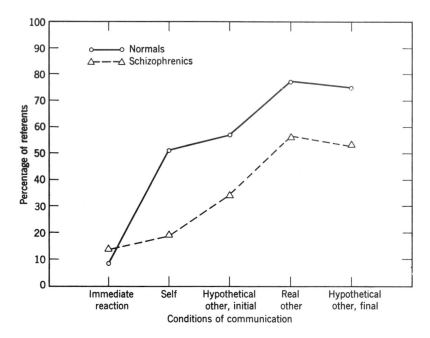

FIGURE 18-3. Percentage of communal referents under various conditions of communication: normals versus schizophrenics.*

* The proportion of idiomatic referents may, of course, be obtained by subtracting above-mentioned percentages from 100%.

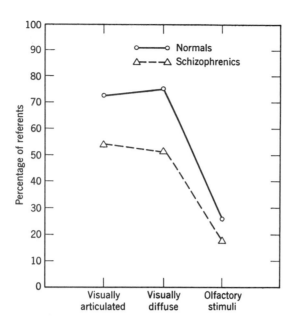

FIGURE 18-4. Percentage of communal referents in characterizations of the three types of stimulus materials: normals versus schizophrenics.

ditions, with the exception of that of immediate response, the normal subjects exceeded the schizophrenics in the relative incidence of communal referents. The difference between the two groups is particularly striking with regard to the condition of communication to the self (inner speech proper). Under this condition, the normal subjects employed communal modes of reference in more than half of their characterization; in contrast, less than one-fifth of the characterization by the schizophrenics employed these modes of reference. In other words, even under the condition of communication to the self, the normal subjects to a considerable extent employed the same modes of reference that they utilized in communicating to real or hypothetical others: *their inner speech was relatively socialized.* With schizophrenics, on the other hand, communication to the self differed little from immediate personal reaction.

Finally, we may consider the differences between normals and schizophrenics with regard to communicability of expressions referring to the different types of stimulus material (Fig. 18-4). In general, the normals used proportionately more communal referent characterizations

Inner versus External Speech in Schizophrenia **309**

for all types of stimulus material than did the schizophrenics. It is important to note, however, that this disparity between normals and schizophrenics was much greater for the visual stimuli than for the olfactory material. In other words, the normals and schizophrenics were much closer to each other in their modes of referent-formation for the more "primitive" olfactory material than for the two types of visual stimuli. Thus, once again, we arrive at the conclusion that the introduction of olfactory material affects the communicability of expression in ways analogous to a condition of schizophrenia and to an orientation towards communication for the self.

Linguistic Organization of Expression:
Normals versus Schizophrenics

It will be recalled that in E. Kaplan's investigation, linguistic organization of the descriptive messages was assessed in terms of the relation of qualifiers to primary nouns: a distinction was made between *modifications*, which preceded primary nouns, and *specifications*, which followed such nouns. The same distinction was adopted by Slepian for his analysis of linguistic organization. Thus, in such responses as "a scribbled design," "a dark tuft," or "an unpleasant odor," the qualifier was considered a modification; in responses such as "lines going every way," "a rock with moss on it," "odor used in paints," the phrases "going every way," "with moss on it," and "used in paints" were considered specifications.

We may remind the reader that we assume that any explicit determination by qualifiers (whether modifications or specifications) includes a process of differentiation and articulation of experience and implies a greater externalization and lingualization of experience than does a primary noun standing alone. Thus, in identifying or characterizing something presented to us, we make our experience of this presented material more overt and social by describing it as "a black car" or as "a car that is black" than by simply stating that it is "a car."

From the developmental standpoint, one would therefore expect that both modes of qualification indicating a higher degree of articulation would occur more frequently under conditions more conducive to comparatively higher levels of symbolic articulation. As one will remember, the findings of E. Kaplan were in full agreement with these expectations. It may be mentioned, in this connection, that Slepian's findings pertaining to the number of "structural units" per response were, in general, fully consonant with the notion of a greater degree of linguistic articulation as a function of external speech, developmentally higher mental status, and less "primitive" sense material.

Turning from this gross determination of linguistic articulation to more refined distinctions, we may follow Slepian in his examination of the incidence of specifications per structural unit and also of the incidence of specifications relative to modifications. The rationale for such analyses is implied in our developmental interpretations of modification and specification: as one will recall, it is our assumption that specification in the service of communication presents a higher level of articulate speech than does modification.

On these grounds, it was expected that specifications per structural unit as well as the incidence of specifications relative to modifications would be more frequent: (a) under conditions of "external speech" compared with conditions of "inner speech," (b) for "visual stimuli" as compared with "olfactory material," and (c) in normal subjects as compared with schizophrenics. In the following, the findings with regard to specifications per se will be presented first; [4] then we will refer to the results pertaining to the incidence of specifications relative to modifications.

Inquiring now about the overall effects of the conditions of communication on the incidence of specifications, the results appear to be fully consonant with the expectations; that is, after pooling subjects and types of stimuli, the amount of specification was found to be significantly greater under conditions of external speech than under conditions of inner speech.

The next analysis was again concerned with the differences in specification under the various conditions of communication, but here, however, in interaction with types of stimuli. From Table 18-2, which summarizes the findings, one notes first that there was an increase in the amount of specification for each type of stimulus material as the subject went from conditions of inner speech to those of external speech. Second, the disparity in the amount of specification for external versus inner speech was more marked for the visually articulated and visually diffuse stimuli than for the olfactory material. The amount of specification for olfactory material, even under the two conditions of external speech, scarcely reached the amount of specification for the

---

[4] In order to control for differences in explicitness for the various groups, and under the different conditions of communication (see above), differences in specification were measured by *mean number of specifications per structural unit,* rather than by number of specifications in an absolute sense.

Table 18-2

Mean number of specifications per structural unit under different conditions of communication and for the three types of stimuli

	Immediate reaction	Self	Hypothetical other, initial	Hypothetical other, final
Visually articulated	.14	.42	.74	1.15
Visually diffuse	.22	.53	.82	1.01
Olfactory	.07	.27	.42	.45

visual stimuli under the conditions of communication to the self. Third, in comparing the final with the initial communication to hypothetical others, one finds an increase in specification occurring with both types of visual stimuli; no such increase was found for the olfactory material. Ostensibly, the interpolated experience of speaking to a real other conduced to an increase in number of specifications for stimuli amenable to "objective" characterizations, such as the visual forms, but not for the less objectifiable, olfactory stimuli.

We may turn to the differences, with regard to specification, between schizophrenics and normals. First, irrespective of conditions of communication and types of stimulus material, the normals used significantly more specifications per structural unit than did the schizophrenics (.83 versus .21).

If one now compares the groups with regard to conditions of communication (Fig. 18-5), one finds, in general, an increase for both groups as one progresses from the condition of immediate reaction to the condition of final communication to a hypothetical other; the extent of increase from one condition to the next was, however, much more striking for the normals than for the schizophrenics. It will be noted further that the normal subjects, even under the condition of communication to the self, used significantly more specifications than did the schizophrenics under the two conditions of communication to a hypothetical other.

Finally, one may compare the two groups with regard to the differential effects on amount of specification evoked by the different types of stimuli. Fig. 18-6 shows that, for both groups, visual stimuli elicited more specifications than did olfactory material. However, the disparity was once again more marked for the normals than for the schizo-

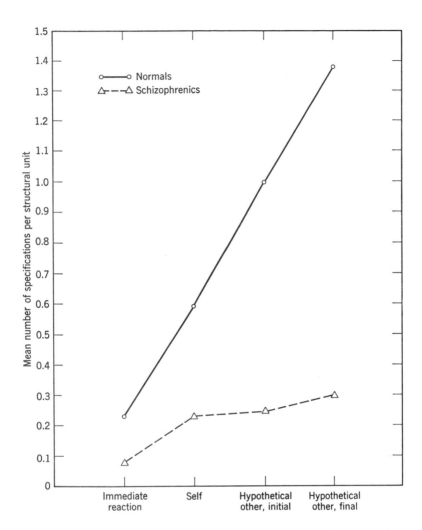

FIGURE 18-5. Mean number of specifications per structural unit for the two groups of subjects under the various conditions of communication.

phrenics: in other words, the schizophrenics—in terms of specifications —showed considerably less differentiation among the descriptions for the three types of stimulus material than did the normals.

In summarizing the various findings on the mean number of specifications per structural unit, we are once again led to the conclusion that there is a *functional equivalence* among the variables of mental

Inner versus External Speech in Schizophrenia   **313**

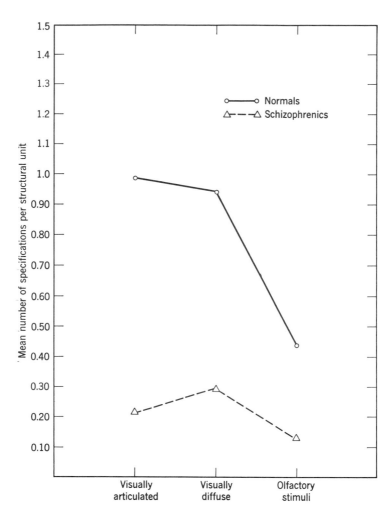

FIGURE 18-6. **Mean number of specifications per structural unit for schizophrenics and normals with regard to the three types of stimulus material.**

status, condition of communication, and type of stimulus material. Normality of symbolizer, representation for others, and visual material to be described all conduce towards the evocation of relatively greater incidence of specifications; conversely, schizophrenic status, representation for the self, and olfactory material to be described each conduces to a lesser amount of specification.

In concluding our presentation of Slepian's work, we may briefly refer to his discussion of the incidence of specifications relative to modifications. In assessing the incidence of these two types of qualifiers relative to each other, Slepian introduced a measure which we shall designate as the *index of disparity;* this index is defined by the following ratio:

$$\frac{\text{Number of specifications} - \text{Number of modifications}}{\text{Number of specifications} + \text{Number of modifications}} \times 100$$

Consequently, where the number of specifications exceeded the number of modifications, the index of disparity bore a plus sign, and where the reverse obtained, the index bore a minus sign.

Based on the previously stated assumption that specification in the service of communication presents a higher degree of articulate speech than modification, the expectations with respect to this *index of disparity* were as follows: (a) normal subjects compared with schizophrenics would show more specifications relative to modifications; (b) in normals, there would be a tendency towards more specifications relative to modifications under external-speech conditions than under inner-speech conditions; this tendency would be lessened in schizophrenics; and (c) there would be a normal tendency towards more specifications relative to modifications for visual stimulus material than

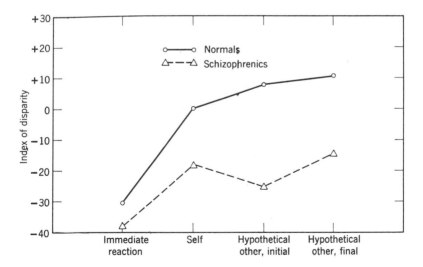

FIGURE 18-7. **Index of disparity for schizophrenics and normals under various conditions of communication.**

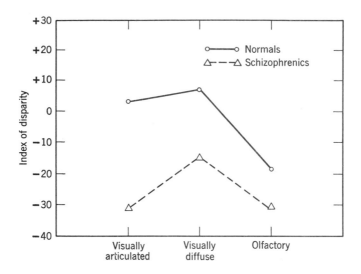

FIGURE 18-8. Indices of disparity for schizophrenics and normals with regard to the three kinds of stimuli.

for olfactory material; again, this tendency would be less apparent in schizophrenics.

The findings, summarized in Figs. 18-7 and 18-8, fully bear out these expectations. Without going into a more detailed discussion, we may simply point out that the analysis employing the *index of disparity* yielded results entirely consonant with those obtained through the use of a measure based on mean number of specifications per structural unit. That is, with more advanced mental status (normal over schizophrenic), under more interpersonal (rather than intrapersonal) conditions of communication, and for stimuli appealing to a more advanced sensory modality (vision over olfaction), specification—as a more articulate mode of qualifying a primary noun—tends to increase relative to modification.

chapter 19

On the Ontogenesis of Symbolic Representation under Different Conditions of Communication: The Differentiation of External and Inner Speech

It has long been recognized that the distinction between communication for others (external speech) and communication for oneself (inner speech), relatively sharply maintained in normal adults, is more or less lacking in young children. One of the earliest accounts of this lack of differentiation between inner and external speech in young children was in terms of the concept of "egocentrism." "Egocentric speech," particularly as characterized by J. Piaget (190), is speech manifested by a child in the earliest phases of the process of socialization. Piaget argued that as socialized speech becomes increasingly prevalent, egocentric speech declines.

One of the major criticisms of the concept of "egocentrism," and of its application to early child speech, came from L. Vygotsky and his collaborators. They concluded, both on theoretical grounds and in terms of their experimentation, that egocentric speech—rather than declining and disappearing in the course of socialization—undergoes genetic transformations, which culminate in the formation of "inner speech" (261, p. 132).

From our theoretical point of view, a primordial stage of speech must be postulated, a stage at which there is a relative lack of differentiation between communication for the self and communication for others. From this relatively undifferentiated stage, speech develops in two interdependent and correlative directions: one towards communication for oneself, inner speech; the other, towards communication for others, external speech. Thus, we see the development of communicative speech as polar: *internalization,* on one hand, and *externalization,* on the other. From the work of Piaget, Vygotsky, A. Luria, and their co-workers, it seems that marked increases in differentiation or polarization occur initially between two and three years of age, and then again between six and seven years of age (see Vygotsky, 261, pp. 134 f).

This, of course, does not mean that the polarization between inner and external speech reaches its terminal form or maximum degree at seven years of age. Since inner and external speech subserve distinctive functions—inner speech serving thought, external speech serving social communication—it seems apparent that, with transformations and elaborations of these functions in the maturing individual, there will be corresponding transformations in, and increasing polarization of, inner and external speech. The studies described in the previous chapters have, in fact, shown that communication to others is, *in normal adults,* rather sharply distinguished from communication to self both formally and semantically. This sharp polarization between inner and external speech does not seem to obtain for *"pathologically primitivized" adults* (schizophrenics).

In the following discussion of the differentiation of external and inner speech in the course of ontogenesis, we shall first comment briefly on developments in externalization of speech and then turn to the problem of internalization of verbal behavior.

On Externalization of Speech in Ontogenesis

In the young child, the lack of differentiation of other-directed communication from inner speech is manifested with regard to linguistic-formal as well as to semantic characteristics: the younger the child, the more fragmentary, linguistically unarticulated, condensed, laconic, holophrastic, and idiomatic is the verbalized communication. These are characteristics of the young child's speech that we have already discussed, in general, in Part II ("ontogenesis of symbol-formation").

In the present context we may again draw on certain findings of Luria and Yudovich (159) pertaining to the development of speech in their twin subjects. As one will recall, the 5-year-old twins, at the beginning of the observations, showed all the characteristics of undifferentiated communicative speech. After they were separated and placed in a normal social environment, external, other-directed speech became sharply differentiated from self-directed speech; this polarization took place very rapidly over a period of 10 months.

The efficacy of situations fostering "normal" social interchanges can be seen in the increase in those formal and functional qualities characteristic of mature communicative speech. Although Luria and Yudovich did not trace the changes in each of the various features of external speech, such changes are implied in their findings; thus, one may recall the impressive evidence (see Table 8-2, p. 121) bearing on the rapid development of the twins' speech with regard to comprehensibility outside of context-of-action; after only 3 months of separation, comprehensibility increased from 17 percent to 89 percent in twin A and from 22 percent to 81 percent in twin B; after ten months of separation, comprehensibility was perfect (100 percent) for both twins. (159, p. 65)

In close correlation with the increase in comprehensibility of external speech outside of action-context, the syntactic articulation rapidly changed from predominantly amorphous sentential forms, with an abundance of monoremic and duoremic expressions, to grammatically and functionally differentiated sentence structures. (See Table 19-1.)

The speech of the twins observed by Jespersen (cf. p. 120) showed great similarity to the speech of Luria's twins with regard to amorphous sentence structure; there was also analogous progress toward grammaticalization of

Table 19-1

**Development of grammatical structurization
of external speech in a pair of twins
(condensed after Luria and Yudovich)**

	Before separation		After 3 months' separation		After 10 months' separation	
	A	B	A	B	A	B
Number of sentences in time sample	69	69	102	32	45	58
Amorphous utterances	82.6%	78.2%	11.4%	18.8%	0%	0%
Differentiated structures	17.4%	21.8%	88.6%	81.2%	100%	100%

speech after the children were brought into social contact with others. These are two examples quoted by Jespersen of the twins' amorphous speech; they consist of flexionless expressions put in sequences totally different from that of Danish: *Bap ep dop* (literally: Mandse horse piece) = Mandse (proper name) has broken the hobby horse; *hos ia bov lhalh* (literally: trousers Maria brother water) = brother's trousers are wet, Maria.

Since they were placed into a children's home, their language, as Jespersen puts it, became to a great extent 'humanized' in comparison with what it was before; even during the short time Jespersen observed the children closely, he noticed the development of flexion, such as the proper use of the genitive case. (119, p. 186)

As we see it, the principal factor underlying the remarkable change in sentence organization was the increase in "distance" between the addressor and addressee. The significance of the experiment by Luria and Yudovich lies in the experimental induction of a relationship ("distance") between the child and the other—a relationship that "naturally" ensues between the child and his addressees under typical conditions of famliy life. One is reminded here of the penetrating observations by Vygotsky (261, pp. 139 ff) concerning the effects of interpersonal intimacy in adults on the style of communicative speech: Vygotsky points out that intimacy allows a style of speech approximating the form of communication for oneself, that is, inner speech.

In connection with the Luria-Yudovich experiment, one must be careful to avoid the conclusion that distance between addressor and addressee can be defined simply in terms of experimenter's manipulations or through external arrangements. The addressor's awareness of distance between himself and the addressee must also be considered, and such awareness is, in itself, a function of ontogenetic development. Some time ago, an experiment was initiated at Clark University aimed at a determination of variations in style and content of communicative speech as a function of variations in addressees: the subjects varied in age from 6 to 12 years, the age differences being taken to reflect differences in the awareness of distance between self and addressee. Each child was required to tell a brief story to someone who was identified as speaking English and to someone identified as a "foreigner," unable to speak English very well; the same story was to be told to each of these "addressees" (both of whom were experimental accomplices). The study itself was not carried beyond the preliminary stage, but the indications of the pilot findings were that a younger child only slightly, if at all, took into account the variations in the addressee, whereas an older child tended to be more articulate in vocal intensity and vocal intonation and more careful in the selection of words and articulation of sentences when addressing himself to the "foreigner" than when communicating to someone from his own linguistic community.[1]

On Internalization of Speech in Ontogenesis

Let us now turn to the correlative development in communicative speech, that of the internalization of speech in ontogenesis. In his critical evaluation of Piaget's work, Vygotsky pointed out that Piaget, having viewed all speech in terms of a tendency towards progressive socialization of the child, neglected to consider the significance of a development towards "inner speech," speech directed towards oneself and subserving thought. Piaget was charged by Vygotsky with having considered egocentric speech in purely negative terms, that is, as a persistence of autistic features and as a failure to attain full socialization: with an increase in socialized speech, egocentric speech progressively disappears. Vygotsky challenged this thesis and maintained that egocentric speech, rather than disappearing in the course of ontogenesis, becomes transformed into inner speech.

However correct we believe Vygotsky to be in his insistence that there is a correlative development of both external and inner speech in ontogenesis, we think that his acceptance of "egocentric speech" as the starting point of this polarization is not warranted. First, it seems to us that Vygotsky misconstrued Piaget's concept of "egocentrism" as descriptive of an asocial attitude; he thus attempted to disprove Piaget's contention of a negative relationship between egocentric and socialized speech through various experiments in which the opportunity for social intercourse was lessened, for example, through the placement of a normal child with a group of deaf youngsters. Under such conditions, where, according to Vygotsky's interpretation of Piaget's views, egocentric speech should have increased, there was rather a marked decrease of egocentric speech. If one recognizes, however, that Piaget's term "egocentric" does not refer to asocial behavior but pertains rather to an early stage of socialization, one would expect exactly the findings obtained by Vygotsky: with a decrease in opportunities for socialized behavior, there would be a decrease in the kind of socialized speech that is characteristic for the young child, egocentric "socialized" speech.

---

[1] In this connection, we may add that John Flavell (67) is conducting a comprehensive program of research which should eventually throw considerable light on this entire area.

These considerations lead us, then, to maintain that the starting point for the correlative and polar development of inner and external speech is not egocentric speech but rather a mode of representation which is undifferentiated with respect to self or other. From this undifferentiated matrix, inner and external speech *co-emerge*, initially with few, if any, characteristics distinguishing them and then becoming further and further polarized as the individual matures and his contexts of communication become diversified and enlarged. From our point of view, therefore, we would expect that early forms of speech for others would be much closer to early forms of speech for oneself and that the later forms of each would be markedly distinct and contrasting in their characteristic features. This, then, is the reason we would give for the appearance in the young child's inner speech of those features found in egocentric speech (as an early phase of speech for others): they are both close to the original undifferentiated matrix.

Until now, we have considered inner speech mainly from the standpoint of communication to others and have therefore characterized it in essentially privative terms, for example, lacking explicitness, lacking communal reference, lacking syntactic formulation, etc. At this point, however, we should like to change our vantage point, and consider the features of inner speech in positive terms, that is, with regard to the functions which inner speech subserves.

One can hardly argue with Vygotsky concerning the central role of inner speech in the *embodiment and articulation of thoughts* and in the *planning for action*. Fully developed inner speech offers a mode of representation which is far better suited for such functions than is speech for others. In the main, there are three characteristics which may be considered as positive features of inner speech in the carrying out of the specific functions of thinking and planning (see Vygotsky, 261, pp. 146 ff). These are: (1) *silence*, representation occurs without audible articulation; (2) *condensation*, a plurality of meanings becomes embodied in one or a few forms and syntactic rules are "disregarded"; and (3) *sense domination*, lexical values of words are subordinated to ideas aroused by words and to the interactions and multiform relations sustained by these ideas.[2] We may discuss each of these features briefly.

---

[2] With regard to the third characteristic of inner speech, the dominion of sense over lexical meaning, one may refer to the valuable paper by L. A. Reid (199), especially sections 1 and 2, dealing with "word and idea symbolization" and "associative and affective symbolization."

Silence is perhaps the most obvious feature of full-fledged inner speech. Young children do a good deal of their thinking "out loud," and only gradually learn to think without reliance on verbalization and external phonetic form (see Stern, 241). This progressive distancing of inner speech from external phonetic form transmutes inner speech into a more phantom-like, abstract medium, well suited to the execution of the abstract operations of thought.

Condensation, entailing a high degree of ellipsis, syntactic incompleteness, the confluence of diverse meanings in one or a few forms, etc., is, of course, a deficiency when the end is one of social communication to a "generalized other." For thought, however, ellipsis, the embodiment of multiple meanings in one form, dystaxia, and incompleteness of syntactical formulation may actually be virtues rather than defects. Such characteristics eliminate unnecessary redundancy and facilitate rapidity of thinking; they also serve to bring together diverse trains of thought, promoting that connection of disparate ideas which is at the basis of productive thinking. The condensation and extreme laconicity characteristic of fully formed inner speech is much more typical of adult inner speech (thought) than of the inner speech of children: paradoxically, because of its intermediate status between fully vocalized and fully internalized speech, the inner speech of children is actually more explicit and more redundant in structure and content than is the inner speech of the more mature person.

Finally, there is the *domination of "signification" by "sense"* (or "denotation" by "connotation") in inner speech. According to F. Paulhan (193, p. 289),[3] "the sense of a word, in its largest acceptation . . . is the totality of psychological facts that this word awakens in a mind, and that this mind does not reject, but welcomes and organizes. These facts are above all tendencies, tendencies to think, to perceive, to act, abstract tendencies, habits, but also images, ideas, present emotions. Their ensemble comprises a mental attitude, a more or less condensed synthesis, or several syntheses more or less united to each other . . . of elements systematized around a word." It is this "sense" of a word, as contrasted with its lexicalized meaning, that Vygotsky takes to be a characteristic feature of inner speech. It is this "sense" which makes it possible to build novel connections, to discover hidden qualities of things and phenomena, to function creatively in one's thinking.

"Sense" as Paulhan formulates it, and as Vygotsky adopts it, seems

---

[3] Paulhan's contrast is between "sens" and "signification," which we have rendered a distinction between "sense" and "lexicalized meaning."

quite close to our notion of a particular organismic state, an "organismic matrix" (see Chapter 2) from which the articulation toward circumscribed meanings issues. In this respect, inner speech as the medium of "sense" rather than external speech would be in intimate, *direct*, commerce with those processes that enter into the organization of the perceptual world and the articulation of the sphere of action. It is this characteristic of inner speech, that is, the domination of sense over strict, circumscribed meaning, that enables one to understand how language can be a formative instrumentality in the shaping of the world of objects and in the guiding of behavior.

Perhaps nowhere else has the ontogenetic relationship between *internalization* of speech and the *planned* performance of tasks within the perceptual-motor environment been more clearly and succinctly demonstrated than in various experiments conducted by A. Luria (himself a student of Vygotsky's) and his collaborators. For instance, in the Luria-Yudovich experiments with twins (159, Chapters VI and VII) it was found that a very striking change occurred in the twins' planning behavior following the period of separation that instigated their rapid development towards normal speech. Prior to separation, there was an absence in both twins of the planning and directing of behavior by means of their own speech; activities such as block building or drawing, which ordinarily require some planning, were carried out aimlessly, and the children seemed to be at the mercy of all kinds of distractions. Within a few months, however, these children became quite able to formulate their plans verbally and to carry them out according to set aims; they began to build and draw constructively, in accordance with stated goals; they could, over a considerable period of time, remember and think about some work that they had left unfinished, and could return to such work with a compelling sense of duty.

This radical change in constructive activity may be briefly illustrated. Before separation, when the children were asked to build something with small blocks—an easy task for a normal 5-year-old—they were unable to do more than to place cubes side by side or to lay out the single cubes along the outlines of circular or rectangular boards, accidentally left on their table. Similarly, drawing was limited to simple scribblings, which were hardly given any representational meaning. In all these attempts, spontaneous verbalization related to play activity was practically absent. Within three months after separation, self-directed speech entered into the scene; appearing in the intermediate form of monologue, audible speech clearly guided the planning and execution of work. For example, in one situation the two children were placed at a table with a screen between them and were requested not to talk to each other; in this situation, they were asked to make something from plasticine. One of the twins (A), who talked continuously about what he was doing, said to himself "Now one more little leg." . . . "Now a leg, I've finished the table"; the other twin (B), more or less silent throughout, also finished making a table. Twin A's plasticine table was more differentiated than Twin B's (e.g., four legs as against two). Taking another piece of plasticine, Twin A remarked: "What else? A carrot," and then proceeded to model a small carrot, etc. (Luria and Yudovich, 159, p. 97). Analogous changes took place with regard to drawings; instead of the previous scribbles, there appeared "goal-directed, differentiated objective drawing" (159, p. 18).

Another series of ontogenetic studies carried out by Luria (158) dealt particularly with the development of the directive function of speech, and here again the central genetic issue was that of internalization of speech. The experimental situations were rather simple: they involved multiple choice tasks, to be solved under varying conditions, for example, immediate versus delayed response, guidance of reaction by visual signals versus verbal instruction. One group of children, 1;4 to 1;6 years of age, were presented with two inverted, nontransparent containers, a cup and a tumbler. After having placed a coin under the cup, without the child seeing the act, the experimenter told the child: "The coin is under the cup—find the coin!" Whereas in a previous experiment, all children had reached for the correct container after they had *seen* the coin placed under it, the mere verbal instruction, in the absense of observation of the placement, turned out, at least at first, to be insufficient for correct performance: a considerable number of these very young children lost track of the task and began to grasp both of the containers before them. Only reinforcement of the command through repetition ("The coin is under the cup—find the coin!") produced correct reactions. (Apparently the verbal command here served primarily as an auditory conditioning signal rather than as a meaningful request.) If the verbal instruction was now changed from "cup" to "tumbler" ("Now the coin is under the tumbler—find the coin!"), very few of the children in this group acted accordingly; they continued to look under the *cup*. In contrast, children in a 1;8 to 2;0 year group solved the task successfully. If, however, the carrying out of the changed instructions was delayed even by a mere ten seconds, even many of the older children did not succeed but perseverated in their previous response. It seems reasonable to assume that one factor underlying the children's failure to carry out the task under the conditions of delay was a deficiency in the internalization of the verbal command necessary for the retention of the instructions during the period of delay and/or a deficiency in integrating the verbal command with the preparatory motor set.

The importance of internalized speech for the execution of sensory-motor tasks can be clearly inferred from another experiment performed by Luria. Children two to three years of age were asked to press a ball every time a red light flashed but not to press it when a blue light went on. Though the children understood perfectly well what the experimenter told them, most of them failed to perform correctly: the excitation aroused by both signals was so strong that after a few times the blue light also elicited motor responses. When, however, the red and blue flashes were accompanied by the experimenter's verbal command, "Press" and "Don't press" respectively, the correct responses became well established. Next, the children were asked to give themselves these verbal commands. Under these conditions, the children of this age group were unable to execute the task: they either ceased to react motorically at all or pressed the ball at the appearance of the light, irrespective of color *and* command. Only older children (about four years of age) were successful, that is, were able to integrate their own verbal commands with their motor responses. Shortly after such integration has been accomplished, self-directed *audible* speech becomes dispensable; according to Luria (158). "As soon as the directive role passes to the semantic aspect of speech (rather than to the external, signal qualities) . . . external speech becomes superfluous. The directive role is taken over by the inner connections which lie behind the word and they now begin to display their selective effect in directing the motor responses of the child."

On the Interaction of Internal with External Speech

Involved in the ontogenesis of "inner speech" is one factor in its development which must be brought more sharply into focus, even if briefly: we refer to the interaction between speech for oneself and speech for others. We have maintained that in ontogenesis there is a progressive polarization of "inner" and "external" speech; we must now insist on the continuous interrelation between these two modes of communication. This interconnection permits us to understand a paradoxical phenomenon, observable in the various ontogenetic studies and particularly in the twin experiment by Luria and Yudovich: the social setting into which the children were placed not only promoted the formation of speech for others but also affected inner speech. It appears that when a child learns to articulate speech in order to communicate to others he also learns to communicate to himself. One arrives here at a most important issue, the organization of inner speech (thought, etc.) in an individual as a member of a social group. Because of his social nature, a person's *inner life* must be fundamentally linked to *socially organized activity* and to communal ways of thinking. In order to function well in an individual who is in healthy contact with his environment, self-directed speech must hold a course between complete freedom and complete conformity.[4] This double aspect of self-directed speech—giving expression to freely moving thought and yet constrained within the bounds of social forms and rules—may well serve to bring into clearer perspective some of our own experimental findings, presented in the previous chapter.

As one will recall, in Slepian's study on communication in normals versus schizophrenics, two conditions of "inner speech" were introduced. One was the condition of "immediate response" to the stimulus material, that is, a reaction to the stimuli as they came into the subject's awareness; the other was the condition of "communication to the self, or inner speech proper," in which inner speech subserved the communication to oneself of one's own reflections and thoughts about the presented material. The results showed a striking difference in the nature of the self-directed communications of normals as compared with the schizophrenic subjects. This difference is most clearly manifested if one compares changes in explicitness, communality of referents, and number and kind of qualifications as a subject moved from immediate reactions to self-directed speech: whereas in normal subjects there was a marked increase in each of these characteristics, there was no increase, or at most a slight one, for the schizophrenics.

In our discussion of Slepian's findings we remarked, ". . . even under the condition of communication to the self, the normal subjects to a considerable extent employed the same modes of reference that they utilized in communicating to real or hypothetical others: their inner speech was relatively socialized. With schizophrenics, on the other hand, communication to the self differed little from immediate personal reaction" (p. 309). Later on (Chapter 21) we shall be led

---

[4] Only if one keeps in mind this "social" aspect of inner speech can one understand the important preparatory role which inner speech has for external articulation and communication of thought—a role which some authors, notably K. Goldstein (83), conceive as the essence of inner speech.

to draw related conclusions from the findings of a study that was quite different in nature, a study dealing with "linear naming" in schizophrenics as compared with normals.

Concluding Remarks on Inner versus External Speech

We may briefly summarize both the analysis of the differentiation of inner and external speech in ontogenesis and the conclusions that we have drawn from the experiments by E. Kaplan and H. Slepian (Chapters 17 and 18). This synopsis will be in terms of the basic components of symbol situations (described in Chapter 3) and of the relationship of "distance" assumed to increase among these components in the course of development.

At ontogenetically earlier levels of functioning where there is little distance between addressor and addressee, the distinction between inner and external speech is relatively slight: speech for the self and speech for the other are little differentiated from one another. In the older child and in the normal adult, with more diversified addressees, varying in distance for the speaker, the differentiation between speech for the self and speech for others becomes progressively more marked.

The increasing polarization between inner and external speech seems to be more manifest when the object of reference is itself more distant from the addressor: thus, visual stimuli, which have a relatively more "objective," "out-there" character, promote a greater differentiation between inner and external speech than do olfactory stimuli. Although we know of no experimental evidence that this is the case in ontogenesis, we would venture to predict that a greater differentiation between inner and external speech for visual stimuli as compared with olfactory stimuli would be more apparent in older children than in younger ones.

The following two diagrams summarize the functional dependence of developmental level of speech upon the developmental level of the three variables (communicator, audience, stimulus-object) introduced in the studies.

In the first diagram are indicated principal conditions (conceptualizable in terms of self-nonself distance) that affect the communicative level of speech. The second diagram pertains to the polarity between inner and external speech as manifested in the contrasting features characterizing the two speech types.

Table 19-2

Communicative conditions in regard to external versus inner speech

Relation of external to inner speech	Communication conditions		
	Status of communicator		Objectivity status of stimulus
	Maturity status	Mental status	
External: Inner speech close ↓ External: Inner speech contrasting	Child ↓ Adult	Schizophrenic ↓ Normal	Less objective (lower sense modality, e.g., olfactory) ↓ More objective (higher sense modality, e.g., visual-articulate stimulus)

Contrasting features of inner and external speech

	Inner speech	External speech
Articulation of referents	Laconicity, condensation (multiple meaning, "hints")	Explicitness in articulation of referents
Communicability of referents	Idiomatic referents	Communal referents
Vehicular signification	Domination by (dynamically fluctuating) sense of words	Domination by (stable) lexical meanings of words
Vehicular organization	Incompleteness (ellipsis), redundancy, dystaxia, agglutinative or holophrastic organization ("monoremic" speech form, etc.)	Syntactic organization

To reiterate: Shifts in the level of articulate speech are equivalently effected through changes in condition of communication, in status of communicator, and in type of stimulus-object. These changes in the characteristics of speech empirically found in the studies may, in turn, all be conceptualized developmentally in terms of the distance between self and nonself. Laconicity versus explicitness, idiomatic versus communal speech forms, organization in terms of relative dominance of modifiers over specifiers, sense domination over syntactic structures built by lexical units—all these can be considered as indicating the relative closeness of the symbol to the ongoing processes (organismic states) of the speaker.

part V

Experimental Studies on Symbolization in Nonphonic Media

Introduction

Thus far, we have been concerned primarily with the representation of referents by means of symbolic vehicles formed in verbal (phonic) media. Our major focus in Part V is, in contradistinction, on the representation of contents through nonverbal, nonphonic mediation. Since the question may arise concerning the relevance of nonverbal representation to the understanding of linguistic representation, it may be worthwhile—before we sketch the kinds of problems encompased in this Part—to comment, at least in a cursory way, on the value of studies employing nonphonic media.

Although often noted in passing, the fact that no entity is, in and of itself, a symbol is rarely appreciated in its full importance. Once one recognizes this fact in its full significance, however, one realizes that theoretically the locus of symbolization lies in the *intentional act* of a human being and not in the material which is utilized qua vehicle. In other words, if one assumes a human act of symbolizing, one can in principle explore the problem of symbol formation using any material whatsoever. To be sure, certain kinds of material are of limited value for such an exploration, while other kinds permit a closer examination of the formative processes entering into the construction of a symbol.

Our utilization of nonverbal, nonvocal media rests on the assumption that these media do indeed permit such a closer examination.

Our argument here rests on four considerations.[1] First, our lifelong, habitual, and intimate use of the vocal-sound medium in the development of speech symbols may tend to obscure our vision of the handling of that medium in symbolic activity. This problem is especially likely to exist in the case of sound-patterns that have already been structured into symbols, i.e., that have become invested with significance. In contrast, the use of nonphonic media, which have not been previously exploited in the service of representation, provides a better view of how the intention to symbolize operates to transform material entities into symbolic vehicles. One may, it seems to us, plausibly maintain that certain findings pertaining to the ways various nonphonic media are handled in the process of representation can, in principle, be generalized to the ways sound-patterns are handled in the process of being transformed into speech symbols. After all, vocally produced sound-patterns are, from a pragmatic-technical standpoint, no more (and no less) like the events they come to represent than are, for example, line patterns or clay forms.[2]

A second reason for our use of media other than vocal-sound is related to our general thesis that symbolic vehicles play a determining and intrinsic role in cognitive functioning. A priori, it is likely that different material media—despite certain generic similarities—are not equally exploitable for the representation or the expression of the innumerable kinds of experiences we undergo: one does not easily express in words what one can express in music and vice versa. Because of these possible differences in the quality and the range of expressivity of different media, it seems to us important to compare and to contrast symbolization of a given kind of experience in various media; doing so allows us to get both a general picture of symbolic activity and a specific understanding of the advantages and the limitations of particular media.

The third reason for using nonverbal media is that they have generally not been structurized into a system of symbols. Individuals obliged to use them for symbolization must begin—as it were—without the advantages and the constraints of an already formed and organized system of vehicles. Through the use of nonverbal means we are enabled to witness, to a far greater extent than would be true other-

---

[1] See Kaplan (129, 131, p. 59).

[2] The fundamental similarity of processes underlying the formation of speech symbols and the formation of significant forms in other media has been most extensively elaborated by Croce (49). See also Sapir (206, preface).

wise, the beginnings in the formation of symbolic vehicles out of a material medium. These observations, then, provide some grounds for reconstructing the way in which articulated sounds are formed into speech symbols and systems of such symbols.

There is a fourth important reason: nonverbal media, such as those of expressive lines and imagery, because of their relative closeness to the symbolizer, are conducive to representation of referents that is paradigmatic of *genetically early stages of symbolization*. The utilization of such media, therefore, provides another important instrument for inquiring into primordial steps of symbolization in general—steps that eventually culminate in the autonomous symbol-systems of speech.

In the light of these considerations, the studies reported in this Part have been undertaken. Most of the studies discussed here are concerned with analogues in nonverbal representation to phenomena occurring in linguistic representation. Thus, the first two chapters of this Part deal with the problem of "naming," while the subsequent chapters deal with more complex phenomena, such as nonverbal representations of simple statements about events, linear and imaginal representations of temporality, and representations of logical relations between statements.

chapter 20

Nonverbal (Linear) Naming in Normal Adults

THE NATURE OF LINEAR NAMES AND THE PROBLEM OF THEIR CONSENSUALITY

The general problem of "naming" pertains to the transformation of material as yet unexploited for symbolic reference into vehicles which serve to indicate and depict events or parts of events. For the examination of this problem here we shall make use of the findings of several studies, all of which deal with the representation of various referents by means of linear-graphic vehicles.

Since the production and apprehension of line patterns qua names are here viewed in relation to the *genetically early, formative* stages in the establishment of names, it will be advantageous to recall briefly the characteristics of vocal names in early ontogenesis (see Chapters 8 and 9). In our previous discussion, we noted that early names were typically *physiognomic in character,* that the referents of early names were of a *concrete-affective-dynamic nature,* that the early referents were characteristically *multiform* as to expression, that the early vehicles were *plurisignificant,* and that the early names were *contextualized,* that is, lacked communication value outside of their concrete contexts of application. In discussing the various studies involving the use of the linear-graphic medium, only data that bear on these features of early names will be emphasized.

Physiognomic Character of Linear Names

One may cite findings from two representative studies, one by H. Lundholm (157) the other by R. Krauss (140), to demonstrate that line patterns are apprehended physiognomically when they are exploited for symbolic representation ("naming").

Lundholm required 8 subjects to represent graphically the referents of 48 adjectives which he grouped into 13 synonym clusters: one group comprised the adjectives "sad," "melancholy," "mournful," "doleful," and "sorrowful;" another "merry," "cheerful," "gay," "jolly," and "joyous;" still another group the words "hard," "harsh," "cruel," and so on.

The physiognomic character of the linear "names" produced by Lundholm's subjects is clearly indicated in their reports. For example, one subject, who used angular shapes to represent certain referents and curved shapes to represent others, remarked:

"Sharp angles are unpleasant—weakness can never be expressed through angles. The rapid interruption through angles gives the impression of furiosity. Angularity of a line suggests sharpness, impatient, hard-heartedness, a certain unfeeling vigor and strength. Likewise, angularity implies absence of gentleness and grace. . . . There is often very much movement in it, but of a jagged, broken, and hard sort. Curves suggest grace, serenity. . . . The curving of a line gives it more maturity, it gives the poise and refinement of nature." (157, p. 52)

Another of Lundholm's subjects reported: "Sharp angles imply the idea of pain, pricking pain, spitefulness, incongruity, instability, moodiness. Angles even imply sharpness and sudden transition, brusqueness, caustic feeling, quick temper, ugliness. Curves imply gradual transition, the more subtle emotions, prettiness, lack of much strength, smoothness." (157, p. 53).

From such typical introspections, it becomes clear that line patterns, when apprehended symbolically, are constituted by a different order of qualities and properties than when conceived geometrically-physically. In other words, when a subject transports the linear product from a geometric-technical universe into a universe of expressive symbols, the geometric-physical features, angularity, curvilinearity, horizontality, etc., give way to physiognomic-dynamic characteristics such as "vigor," "grace," "dullness," etc.

Similar conclusions are warranted from Krauss' findings. In one of his studies, Krauss requested 45 subjects to produce linear patterns for 18 different referents; the referents included moods (joyousness, sadness), colors (red, blue), natural happenings (dawn), material objects (wood, iron, gold), etc. In reporting on the way their linear productions represented the referents, Krauss' subjects characteristically made little or no mention of the geometric-physical properties of the line patterns but rather focused directly on physiognomic-dynamic characteristics shared by the vehicle and referent alike; as a matter of fact, the reader of the reports is often uncertain whether a subject is referring to the vehicle or the referent.

Thus, one subject, after drawing the line pattern reproduced in Fig. 20-1a for the representation of "gaiety" or "joyousness" (*fröhlich*), remarked: "Leaps and then a bound—it is a leaping, bounding joyousness; that's also the case for the line—leaps and then a bound." Another subject, after drawing the line pattern shown in Fig. 20-1b for the representation of "dark" (*dunkel*), commented: "That I experienced directly. That is always deep. With darkness, one has a feeling of sinking. It goes curving towards the bottom; I would have preferred to have the arc suspended from the paper underneath."

In another experiment—to be discussed in greater detail later—Krauss asked a large group of subjects ($N = 242$) to select from several previously drawn line patterns one which allegedly represented a particular referent; this was done for eight referents: "outburst of rage," "melancholy," "sadness," etc. Irrespective of whether the subjects selected the "correct" drawing, they all viewed the line patterns physiognomically rather than geometric-technically, describing them in such terms as: "Massive, softly inclining, sinking into oblivion;" "going on and on without reaching a climax;" "severe and firmly closed;" "narrow, oppressive, impermeable;" "jumping and dancing;" "helplessly sinking;" etc. (140, pp. 93 f).[1]

The difference between the physiognomic and geometric properties becomes highlighted when one inquires about similarity relations obtaining between physiognomic patterns and those obtaining between geometric-physical patterns. Many productions of Lundholm's and of Krauss' subjects give evidence that (a) geometrically similar forms often are physiognomically quite dissimilar, and (b) physiognomically equivalent patterns are often of quite different geometric form.

For instance, with regard to drawings geometrically similar yet physiognomically different, one of Krauss' subjects produced a pattern for "blue" which physically resembled the line pattern produced by another subject for "stone" (Fig. 20-1c and d). Though both drawings were rather similar from a geometrical-physical standpoint—both

---

[1] See in this connection, a recent study by Tagiuri (250, p. 196).

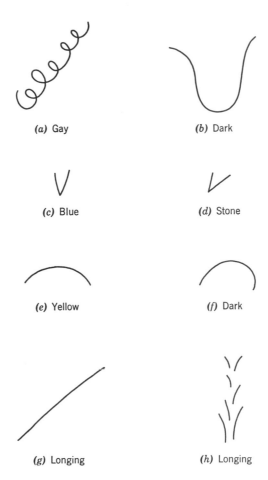

(a) Gay   (b) Dark

(c) Blue   (d) Stone

(e) Yellow   (f) Dark

(g) Longing   (h) Longing

FIGURE 20-1. (*a*) **and** (*b*) **Typical expressive forms.** (*c*) **and** (*d*) **Geometrically similar, physiognomically dissimilar patterns.** (*e*) **and** (*f*) **Geometrically similar, physiognomically dissimilar patterns.** (*g*) **and** (*h*) **Geometrically dissimilar, physiognomically equivalent patterns.** (**After Krauss.**)

angles or v-shapes—they were quite far apart physiognomically: the line pattern for "blue" was taken as an "emanation from inside, outward and downward—more or less as blue light emanates down from above;" the pattern for "stone" was intended primarily as an expression of "pointed, penetrating features."

In another instance, two subjects produced geometrically similar curved forms, one for "yellow" the other for "dark" (Fig. 20-1e and f). There again, the comments of the subjects indicate that these two physically almost identical curves were physiognomically quite different: the first pattern was apprehended as "expanding . . . a radiation outward," the second as a "covering" or "blanketing" . . . "dark being something which covers all things."

Just as geometrically similar patterns may be physiognomically quite different, so, conversely, may physiognomically equivalent patterns be geometrically dissimilar. In Fig. 20-1g and h are reproduced patterns drawn by two of Krauss' subjects for "longing" (sehnsuchtsvoll). Although these patterns were quite different from a geometrical standpoint, they both expressed for the subjects the physiognomic characteristic of "reaching for something far away and out of reach." Thus the first subject remarked of his drawing: "the line is infinitely lengthening, never comes to its goal, and the infinite lies above and beyond." For the second subject, his drawing had a similar meaning: "a striving from somewhere, always bending back, an infinite approximation towards a goal which is never reached."

In sum, then, there can be little doubt that in the transformation of linear-graphic material into "names," physiognomic features are of central significance in the organization of the vehicle.

Concrete-Affective-Dynamic Character of Referents

In our analysis of the ontogenesis of speech, it was noted that the young child employs names to depict referents affective-dynamically, qua things-acted-upon or acting-things. In examining the ways in which normal adults exploit the linear medium for representation of objects and states, one observes, again, how the dynamic-affective features of such objects and states come to the fore.

For instance, one of Krauss' subjects represented "dark" (dunkel) by the pattern shown in Fig. 20-2a, because "in the darkness, I open myself up." Another subject represented "glass" as in Fig. 20-2b, conceiving it as "something cold, flying to pieces, easily breaking." Still another subject symbolized "wood" (Holz) by pattern 20-2c; it represented "the growth of wood tied up with the nervousness aroused in experiencing wood. It is the concentration of the action of wood on me and on itself. I felt it with my fingers—therefore the edge. The openness and growth are in it."

Among the many illustrations which could be cited of the concrete-affective-dynamic character of the referents of linear names, only a

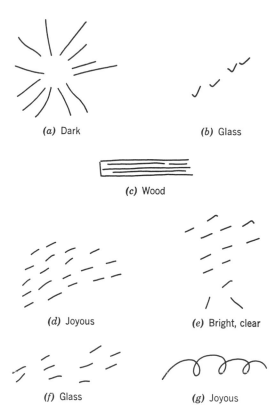

(a) Dark *(b)* Glass

(c) Wood

(d) Joyous *(e)* Bright, clear

(f) Glass *(g)* Joyous

FIGURE 20-2. **(a,b,c) Patterns exemplifying concrete-affective-dynamic character of referent. (d,e,f) One subject's geometrically similar patterns for different referents. (d–g) One subject's dissimilar patterns for same referent. (After Krauss.)**

few more may be given. *"Dusk,* for me, is something unsympathetic to the highest degree." *"Yellow* is agility and bounciness." *"Longing* is reaching in all directions." *"Red* is something prickling and stirring." *"Wood* is something splintery, rugged."

Plurisignificance of Linear Vehicles

The plurisignificance of linear names is clearly manifested in the use of geometrically similar patterns to designate quite different referents. In such instances, as we have already noted, different physiognomic features—deriving from the organismic embeddedness of the pattern qua symbolic vehicle—come to the fore and account for the fittingness of the same (physical) pattern for diverse referents. Plurisignificance of the vehicular material is especially clear-cut where a *single* subject uses the same geometric pattern for different referents. In Fig. 20-2*d, e,* and *f,* approximately the same pattern was used by one subject to represent "joyous," "clear, bright," and "glass."

In the first instance, the pattern represented a "jumping, hopping, relaxed, totally untied, nimble" happening; in the second instance, it depicted a "brightness in the aesthetic sense, nervous, festive, more like candlelight than sunlight;" in the third instance it referred to "something sharp and pointed, piercing." Quite obviously, in the use of geometrically similar patterns to represent such diverse referents, the fittingness must rest on variation in the physiognomic properties of these line patterns.

Polysemy and the Multiform Representation of Referents

In the chapters on the ontogenesis of names (Part II), we noted the frequent use of several names for the "same" object or attribute; we suggested that this phenomenon was due, in part, to the fluid, labile structure of the referents of early childhood—different aspects coming to the fore and "demanding" different names. We also intimated that the relative closeness (lack of distance) between vehicle and referent in genetically early representation prompts the rapid shift in names as the referent is seen in varied ways.

When adults are asked to depict objects and attributes in the lineargraphic medium, one finds such lability of the referents and hence such a multiplicity of names emerging once again.

For instance, one of Krauss' subjects, on two separate occasions, apprehended "joyous" as constituted by different characteristics; he accordingly produced two linear names to represent variations in the meaning of "joyous" (Fig. 20-2*d* and *g*). The first drawing depicted "joyous" as "a little bit of leaping, hopping, relaxed, totally untied, nimble;" the second emphasized the "unsteadily tipsy, blissful" nature of "joyous."

Another illustration is that of a subject's two representations of "wood" drawn by him at different times (Fig. 20-3*a* and *b*). In the first instance, "wood" was conceived as something concretely alive, like a tree, and "tree is a straining, struggling line that shoots and pulls (itself) up into the above;" in the second instance, "wood" represented "something as a log, broken off, dead, rigid."

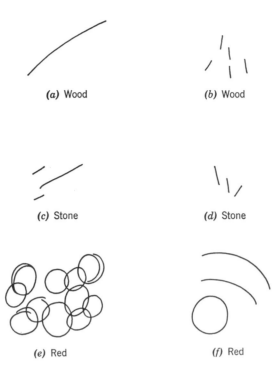

FIGURE 20-3. Subject's two representations for same referent. (After Krauss.)

Still another subject depicted "stone" in two distinct ways (Fig. 20-3c and d): as "a polished surface that one enjoys gliding over with foot or hand;" and as a "fragment from a cliff."

One final example: here a subject, experiencing "red" in two different ways, "named" these different experiences in two distinct linear patterns; as something "vital, energetic" (e), and as something of "enwrapping warmth" (f).

Contextualization of Linear Names

No special illustrations are needed to show that "linear names" presented in isolation, that is, outside of their original context of application, lack communication value. The concrete-affective-dynamic nature and the multiform representability of the referents, together with the plurisignificance of linear vehicles, render it almost impossible for one to know what is referred to by a pattern given in isolation. Thus, if one were confronted with patterns such as those of Fig. 20-2, without any knowledge of the general realm of the referents ("the universe of discourse"), one would surely be unable to determine what the referents were.[2]

Having presented the various primordial characteristics of linear names, we must now face an important question, one that pertains to the status and significance of "natural symbols" in the developmental process of symbolization. "How," it may be asked, "can nonconventional patterns, individually produced, inherently labile and ambiguous, ever be more than idiosyncratic, subjective expressions, incapable of being shared or communicated?" The manner in which one answers this question will reflect the importance that one attaches to the role of "natural symbols" in the genesis of symbolization. Thus, there are those who will concede that linear representations (like the very early vocal names of the young child) are "natural" symbols, depictive of their referents; but they would also maintain that precisely because those symbols have that inherent lability and ambiguity, they (at least indirectly) demonstrate that "natural symbols" are of little or no relevance for the development of language as an eminently conventional and interpersonal phenomenon.

Since we do not accept the view that "natural" symbols are irrelevant to the symbolic process as a social, interpersonal phenomenon, we are obliged to show that "linear naming" of events (as paradigmatic of natural symbols) does not preclude consensus or communication between individuals. Once this is demonstrated, it is important to formulate conditions under which a primordial sharing of linear patterns (or, for that matter, "natural" vocal forms) is possible.

The Consensual Character of Linear Names

Studies concerned with the problem of the consensus in linear naming have dealt with two kinds of evidence: (a) consensus with regard to *productions*, that is, the presence of certain generic similarities in the features of linear patterns produced by a number of individuals for a given referent—features which manifestly distinguish the representations of that particular referent from representations of other

---

[2] One will note the formal resemblance of contextualized linear names to names of the young child, and to symbols used by adults in "inner speech," i.e., in identifying objects for oneself.

referents; and (b) consensus in *comprehension*, that is, the ability of a large group of individuals to recognize the referent of a linear vehicle produced by someone else.

(A) CONSENSUS IN PRODUCTION. Investigations directed toward an examination of generic similarities of line patterns produced by subjects for a given referent indicate a remarkable degree of consensus. Thus, in Lundholm's study, expressive line patterns were examined for various groups of synonyms in terms of "objective" dimensions such as shape (whether angular, curved, or mixed angles and curves), relative size (big, medium, or small angles or curves), and direction (whether horizontal, up, or down). Rather marked consensus among subjects was found as to the values of these dimensions employed for reference to "sadness" in contrast with the values used for reference to "gaiety," etc.

Thus, Lundholm's subjects were in considerable agreement in using predominantly curved-downward line patterns to express ideas of "sadness;" curved, nondownward (horizontal and upward) patterns to represent ideas of "gaiety;" angular-horizontal patterns for ideas of "hardness," etc. That is, transcending the idiosyncratic features of the physiognomic patterns, there were certain externally visible similarities which distinguished each group of representations from the other groups.

Analogous findings are reported by Krauss. The nature of such objective similarities of representation of the same referents and differences between representations of different referents comes clearly to the fore if one compares the drawings of a large number of subjects for two antithetical referents; in Fig. 20-4 are presented reproductions of the patterns produced by some of Krauss' subjects for "raging" and "longing."

Recently, an important study bearing on the problem of linear consensuality has been carried out by Scheerer and Lyons (214). In the major part of their experiment, Scheerer and Lyons had seventy-four college students draw single lines which the subjects felt were adequate representations for a group of word-meanings. The words were chosen on the basis of a preliminary inquiry, as connoting diverse meanings. After the subjects made their drawings, they were asked to assess their own productions in terms of six variables, comprising eighteen possible values. These variables were considered by the experimenters to cover psychologically relevant and measurable properties of line drawings, to take account of salient whole characteristics, etc. The variables

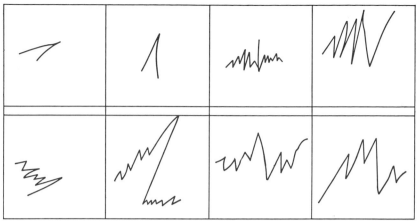

(a) Representations of "raging" (wütend)

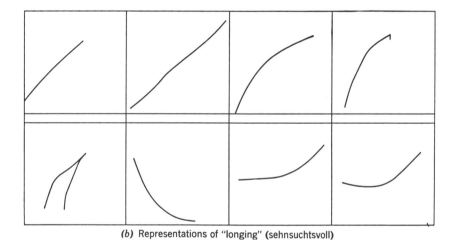

(b) Representations of "longing" (sehnsuchtsvoll)

FIGURE 20-4. Representation of two concepts by various subjects showing generic, externally visible consensus on production. (After Krauss.)

and their values were as follows: design (simple, complex); shape (straight, angular, curved); patterning (regular, irregular, rhythmic-repetitive); dominant direction (up, down, horizontal, alternating up-down, none); pressure (light, medium, heavy); and closure (closed, open).

Scheerer and Lyons' findings indicate a considerable congruity among the productions of subjects about the particular value of a dimension exploited for representing a certain referent and, furthermore, great similarity in the clustering of such values.

(B) CONSENSUS IN COMPREHENSION. The degree of consensus is even more striking when another type of method, that of forced choice, is employed. Thus, in the follow-up study by Krauss, a naive group of subjects were asked to match eight drawings, originally produced by other subjects for certain referents, with these referents. The relatively high percentages of these subjects ($N = 242$) who agreed with the original symbolizer, that is, the percentage selecting the "correct" drawing for each of the referents, can be seen from Table 20-1.

Using a similar method, Scheerer and Lyons (214) presented 109 subjects with three word-designated referents, "gold," "silver," "iron," and three line drawings originally produced to represent them. The subjects were asked to pair the referents of the words with their original linear symbols (Fig. 20-5). A perfect matching was made by 43 percent of the subjects ($P < .01$); 85 percent of the subjects "correctly" matched at least one referent with its corresponding linear name.

These various findings, then, support the view that subjects may, to a great extent, be in agreement with each other in selecting certain nonconventional line patterns rather than others for the representation of certain specified referents. (See also, 182.)

Conditions for Primordial Consensus: The Consensus Paradox

The foregoing evidence shows that "natural" symbolization does not preclude consensus. Despite the malleability of a line pattern when apprehended physiognomically, despite the concrete-affective charac-

Table 20-1
Percentage of subjects selecting "correct" linear pattern for the presented referents *
(after Krauss)

Happi-ness	Melan-choly	Rage	Dawn	Dark-ness	Iron	Gold	Glass
82%	60%	92%	60%	64%	64%	48%	76%

* Chance for each matching was 12.5%.

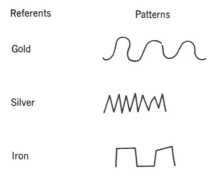

Referents   Patterns

Gold

Silver

Iron

FIGURE 20-5. Patterns and "referents" used in Scheerer-Lyons study.

ter of the referents of linear names, despite the plurisignificance and inherent ambiguity of any linear name considered in isolation, there is ample evidence that some form of agreement or consensus takes place with regard to both the production and the comprehension of linear names.

How is one to understand this paradox of consensuality and communicability despite the presence and operation of forces promoting subjectivity, idiosyncrasy, ambiguity? We suggest that consensus with regard to linear names depends on a number of factors, of which the following seem to be most important.

One of these factors is the *context* within which the referents are located: consensus depends, in part, upon the shared awareness of a particular context or "universe of discourse," within which the linear names are produced and with regard to which they must be comprehended. For instance, in the instance of the matching of three line patterns with "silver," "gold," "iron," the fact that a context of "metals" was shared by the subjects appears to have been an important condition for the relatively high degree of agreement.

A *second* factor underlying consensus pertains to the degree of *differentiation* between the *referents*. It seems that only when referents can be sufficiently distinguished—sharply polarized—within a common context is consensus with regard to the representations of those referents likely to occur. For instance, representations for contrasting moods such as "elation" and "depression" or "anger" and "love" should, in general, invite a higher degree of consensus than representations of "love" versus "sympathy" or of "anger" versus "irritation," etc.

A *third* factor concerns the degree of *differentiation* between the *vehicles* employed in the representation of two or more referents. Specifically, for consensus to occur there must be a sufficiently clear distinction between the properties of the linear patterns exploited for the representation of one referent as against another. For instance, the choice of sharply accentuated, contrasting properties of two linear patterns, such as upward versus downward direction, thick versus thin breadth, long versus short size, straight versus curved shape, is an important factor in the achievement of consensus.

The *fourth* factor, closely related to the third, concerns the degree of *depictive incisiveness* of the vehicles. This factor is directly related to the basic fact that lines are expressive or representative of referents insofar as they are apprehended physiognomically. This physiognomic character of expressive line patterns is at the heart of the paradox with which we are faced in this discussion: on one hand, physiognomic lines, because they are nongeometric, are lacking geometric-physical "objectivity;" on the other hand, physiognomic patterns are "natural" symbols of their referents, and—in the sense that meanings imbued in the lines can be directly "read off"—hence possess a definite "objectivity" of a particular kind.

All this points to a final, all-important factor of inner experience which must obtain so that "depictive objectivity" may be exploited for consensus: that is, the subjects must share not only the "universe of discourse" within which the referents are located but also the physiognomic characteristics of the referents to be represented. Only then can one expect that a sufficiently high degree of congruence between the physiognomic properties of the object to be depicted and the physiognomic properties of the lines be attained. It is precisely the possibility that the "same" event may be construed differently by different individuals that places a potential limit on consensus. For example, in Krauss' study, two subjects selected quite different patterns to represent the state of "joyousness;" the difference in choice of the adequate vehicle—and hence the lack of consensus—was partly due here to the fact that the subject who chose ℳ grasped "joyousness" primarily as a "rhythmic mounting tendency," while the subject who selected ℳ took, as the dominant feature of "joyousness," "a jumping and dancing back and forth." On the other hand, were subjects to apprehend such referents as "joy" and "sadness" in terms of, for example, elation versus depression, their linear names for these states might easily be "read off" consensually from line patterns with congruent features, for example, upward versus downward directionality.

We may now summarize. It seems to us that the study of linear naming, that is, the production and comprehension of linear patterns as symbolic vehicles, provides us with a deeper understanding of the formative processes underlying primordial naming. Despite the obvious differences between early infantile naming and adult naming via line patterns, the striking similarities between ontogenetically early names and linear names in adults serve to reinforce our thesis that an activity of establishing "natural," internal relations between vehicle and referent underlies the primordial formation of names and hence is at the root of symbolic development.

The paradoxical, ambivalent character of "natural symbols"—their idiosyncratic, subjective, and context-bound nature, on the one hand, and their "depictive objectivity," on the other—foreshadows the two-pronged progression in symbolic development, a progression towards vehicles which **serve** both the expression of individual experience and creativity and the realization of interpersonal and communal sharing of referents. It is especially with regard to the genetic increase in the *conventionalization* of symbolic vehicles that the basic fact of consensus with regard to "natural symbols" is of extreme pertinence.

It is our view that, once a consensus is established via "natural symbols," the path is cleared for the introduction of consensus on the basis of conventional relations between names and referents. Such conventionality, of course, is a phenomenon of later stages of onto-genetic development; and when it takes place, there is operative that inner-organismic activity by which the child transforms the "arbitrary" or conventional signs of *la langue* into symbols that serve to depict what they represent. As we shall show in the following sections, even an adult individual confronted with an originally "arbitrary" pattern for the designation of a referent may eventually be able to transform the geometric-technical pattern dynamically so that it serves to represent the referent for him.

PROCESSES UNDERLYING VEHICLE-REFERENT RELATIONSHIPS IN LINEAR NAMING

In most studies pertaining to "sound symbolism" or to the matching of line patterns to word-meanings the central focus has been on the *consensus* obtaining among large numbers of subjects. Rarely was the aim of these inquiries to ascertain the reasons why and how an individual subject was led to make this or that particular choice or matching.

In probing more deeply into the phenomena that were considered in the preceding section, one must separate the analysis of "appropriateness" or "fittingness" from that of "consensus." Having discussed consensus and the conditions for its occurrence, we shall now deal mainly with the issue of "fittingness" between a vehicle and referent. The studies we shall discuss once again involve the use of an expressive line medium; nevertheless, the sorts of findings these studies yield, and the conclusions they suggest, seem to us to have a bearing on the general issue of "fittingness" between vehicle and referent in any medium, including the medium of speech.[3]

Malleability of Vehicular Patterns and the General Nature of Symbolic Rotation

As one will recall, a basic tenet of our theoretical position on symbol formation is that a sense of "fittingness" accrues to the vehicle-referent relationship through the establishment, by the symbolizer, of some inner similarity between the linear "name" and that which is named: the material pattern and content-to-be-represented are shaped by the symbolizer so that an analogy of inner form is attained.

There are at least two general phenomena which seem to run counter to this tenet. One is the *plurisignificance* of a vehicle, that is, the use of one pattern to represent and refer to diverse contents; the other is the *multiformity* in the vehicular expression of a referent directly related to the notion of "arbitrariness" of the vehicle, that is, the possibility of using quite different material patterns to refer to the "same state of affairs." How can there be an inner similarity between a vehicle and a referent when one vehicle can represent many referents or when many vehicles can represent the "same" referent? The studies we shall discuss in this chapter have focused directly on these issues.[4]

A study by Cirillo (46) centered on the general problem of malleability in terms of *plurisignificance* independent of the issue of referential multiformity or "arbitrariness." Twelve subjects were asked to represent, in expressive line patterns, each of the following conceptions: *outburst of rage, state of ecstasy, falling asleep,* and *running.* Each subject, after having produced his linear patterns for these referents,

---

[3] See Chapter 9.

[4] Since these studies were chiefly concerned with delineating the kinds of processes that come into play in the establishment of vehicle-referent relations, the analyses undertaken were primarily qualitative ones.

was then asked to find other referents for which his linear productions were also "adequate" or "fitting" depictions. Characteristically, for every one of the subjects, each of the linear patterns produced for a specific conception was found to be easily exploitable for the "naming" or representation of certain other conceptions.

To illustrate, a subject, after having drawn the four patterns for the four original conceptions, was able to give on request five other conceptions for each pattern. Thus, for Fig. 20-6 he mentioned "crash," "aimless, frightened kind of striving," "weakness," "vulnerability," and "lack of integrity." The central question, now, concerns the subject's apprehension of any one of the patterns as it was employed to symbolize these varied meanings; that is, did the appearance of the pattern itself undergo a change, or did it remain the same throughout?

Let us consider the drawing originally produced by this subject for "outburst of rage." This pattern qua symbol of "an outburst of rage" was seen as consisting of a core, or common center; the lines radiating from this center were without an object, reflecting undirected activity; the jaggedness of the lines expressed the harshness of rage, the center the calmness before the outburst.

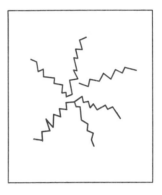

FIGURE 20-6. Line drawing by one subject to represent: outburst of rage.

When taken as a symbol for "an aimless, frightened kind of striving," the subject perceived the lines as: "striving towards something; they're trying to go somewhere; but they're not at all unified. . . . In 'outburst of rage,' they (the lines) all have to start from the core; here, the core isn't necessary—it isn't a core anymore. . . . These (lines) could all be striving lines which just happen to meet at the center in their aimless wandering . . . it could just as well be seen as three lines overlapping."

This example may serve to illustrate the process of *"vehicular rotation."* It shows how a physically invariant pattern is "rotated" in a number of different ways as this pattern is taken to represent different contents: this involves changes in the features selected, changes in emphases, changes in physiognomic qualities that come to the fore with the changes in referents.

Nonverbal (Linear) Naming in Normal Adults **353**

Perhaps the clearest evidence for these different structurings of a physically invariant pattern came from subjects who, by means of drawings, tried to indicate how the pattern was apprehended for different referents. In these new patterns the subjects highlighted and externalized, with "depictive incisiveness," the dynamic qualities they seemed to "read into" their original patterns.

When a pattern (cf. Fig. 20-7) was formed to symbolize "outburst of rage," the subject emphasized "its explosive character and lack of direction." When it was taken as representative of "ideas," it was dynamically restructured so that it appeared to the subject to change sequentially in pressure and at the same time to become more symmetrical around the central point. When it was taken as representative of "enthusiasm," the subject grasped the radial lines as "shorter, darker, not as symmetrical nor as many." When it represented "glee," the subject saw the lines with less pressure, a trifle longer; the spacing between the radial lines was "widened" to express "lesser explosiveness." Finally, when it represented "attention," the original pattern,

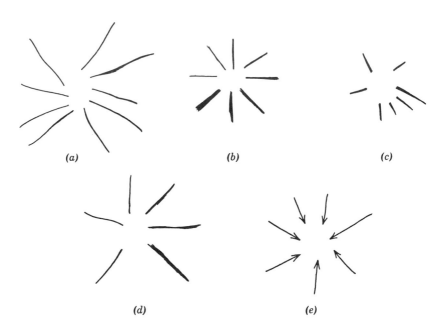

FIGURE 20.7. A subject's original pattern and drawings indicating perceptual restructuring for various new referents: (a) *outburst of rage,* (b) "ideas," (c) "enthusiasm," (d) "glee," (e) "attention."

rather than being seen as radiating outward, was apprehended as directed inward, converging on a point, and possessing greater symmetry.

These illustrations highlight the general process of *rotation* which a physically invariant pattern undergoes when it is exploited in the service of representing different conceptions. They indicate that a subject is able to represent a diversity of phenomena by such a pattern, because the pattern is imaginatively restructured and re-created (through changes in vividness, incorporation of new features, transformations, etc.) so that it possesses, for the individual, those dynamic-physiognomic features requisite for making the pattern a fitting vehicle for the specified referent. It is worthy of note that in Cirillo's study, the original patterns were clearly restructured in practically every instance in which they were taken to represent new conceptions.

Cirillo's findings lead to the further question of the nature and kind of the processes that underlie the establishment of such referent-vehicle relationships in linear representation. Margery Bodansky (27) addressed herself to this problem. She was concerned with three major facets of representational activity: (1) how *linear patterns* were apprehended to form *vehicles;* (2) how *concepts* were handled in the course of being represented in a linear form imposed upon the subject; and (3) how the *relation* of *vehicle to referent* had to be conceived in order to make the pattern function in a representational manner, that is, what were the modes of relating a pattern (vehicle) to a concept (referent)?

We shall discuss the findings in terms of each of these three interrelated aspects.

Ways of Structuring Vehicular Patterns (Vehicular Rotation)

In contradistinction to Cirillo's experiment, Bodansky employed *arbitrary* patterns—patterns which are stipulated by the experimenter as names for conceptions.[5] The patterns to be taken qua symbolic vehicles by the subjects are reproduced in Figure 20-8.

Each of twelve subjects was directed to take first one and then the other of these patterns, now as the representation of *modesty*, now as the representation of *arrogance*. Each pattern was thus "arbitrar-

---

[5] This problem of giving representative meaning to arbitrary patterns—although here raised only within the context of linear mediation—is in itself of signal importance for an understanding of the processes underlying the child's acquisition of the conventional names offered by adults.

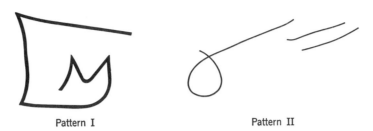

Pattern I   Pattern II

**FIGURE 20-8.   Linear patterns used as "stipulated names" in Bodansky's
study.**

ily" instituted as the "name" for two different—indeed, antagonistic—
conceptions, and each linguistically articulated concept was represented
by two markedly different patterns.

As one can see, the patterns presented to the subjects are, from a
geometric-technical point of view, unfamiliar and meaningless designs;
one is rather square, with sharp points, and rather harsh and dark,
the other is a lighter loop-like figure, with two smooth lines underneath the elongated line to the right.

How were those patterns apprehended when they were taken as
vehicles for the representation of concepts (*modesty, arrogance*)?
Bodansky distinguished four general ways in which the linear patterns
were transformed into representational vehicles.   Though each of these
ways was distinct from the others, a subject nevertheless could—and
often did—use more than one of these modes in the process of forming
the pattern into an adequate vehicle of representation.

The four modes comprised structuring the pattern: (1) as a picture
of a concrete object or event, (2) in terms of configurational-physiognomic qualities, (3) in terms of expressive movement, and (4) in terms
of dynamic relationships between parts.   We may briefly illustrate,
from the subjects' reports, each of these ways of transforming a pattern
into a symbolic vehicle.

Structuring through the Picturing of Concrete Objects or Events

The following protocols (see Fig. 20-9) are typical examples of this
mode of vehicular structuring:

(Pattern I, *modesty*)—"This could look like the picture of a woman . . .
this is both her profile and her breasts at the same time, and she's lying on
her back, and what's happened is she has curled her legs around so that she's
hiding, covering." (Fig. 20-9a)

(Pattern II, *arrogance*)—"This slips much more quickly into a person or individual rather than a concept: an individual who is pretty much empty, yet pushes. This is found in the line drawing . . . in the *empty bag* here. . . ." (Fig. 20-9*b*)

Structuring in Terms of Configurational-Physiognomic Qualities

In the course of taking the pattern as a symbolic vehicle, the subject may organize the pattern in terms of qualities of various kinds. He may perceive the pattern or part of it as "jerky," "soft," "intense," "angry," "supercilious," etc. The manner in which the subjects employed even such seemingly geometric properties as "roundedness" or "pointedness" indicates that these qualities were, as a rule, apprehended expressively or physiognomically. Following are illustrations taken from the protocols of two subjects.

"Well, this (Pattern II) more than that (Pattern I) represents the gentleness of *modesty* that I am talking about. The *gentleness* is in this smooth continuous line (the loop) and the two free-flowing lines which waft rather than jutting out." (Fig. 20-9*c*)

"An arrogant individual (Pattern I). This is given primarily in the *angu-*

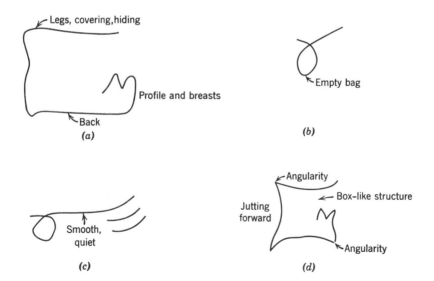

FIGURE 20-9. Perceptual structuring of vehicles for representing concepts. In terms of *concrete objects*: (*a*) Pattern I, *Modesty* ("woman"); (*b*) Pattern II, *Arrogance*: In terms of *configurational qualities*: (*c*) Pattern II, *Modesty*; (*d*) Pattern I, *Arrogance*. (Reconstructed from subject's remarks.)

larity . . . in the *jutting forwardness*. . . . Again, a sort of *bluntness* . . . an indication of a primary lack of capacity." (Fig. 20-9*d*)

Structuring in Terms of Expressive Movement

As geometrical forms, the two patterns are of course stationary and static. As representational vehicles, such patterns become imbued with dynamic qualities; they are often apprehended as endowed with a particular dynamic property, namely, with directional movement, thus exhibiting a line in motion or a line as a directional force. These are illustrations:

(Pattern I, *modesty*)—"It has a lot of movement in it; mainly the turning inward. The reason the turning in represents modesty is that it shuts off the person from view." (Fig. 20-10*a*)

(Pattern II, *modesty*)—"The business at the end (the two lines) is a deprecatory movement like 'No, no'—as if saying, 'The praise that you're giving me really isn't true.' " (Fig. 20-10*b*)

Structuring in Terms of Dynamic Relations between Parts

Any material entity, for example, sounds, line patterns, which has a fair degree of complexity (articulated parts) may be structured as parts in relation to each other. In such structurings, differentiated parts are apprehended as standing in some specifiable relationship to each other. These are some illustrations:

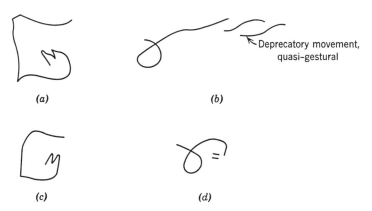

(a)   (b)

Deprecatory movement, quasi-gestural

(c)   (d)

FIGURE 20-10. Perceptual structuring of vehicles for representing concepts. In terms of *directional movement*: (a) Pattern I, *Modesty*; (b) Pattern II, *Modesty*; In terms of *relations between parts*: (c) Pattern I, *Modesty*; (d) Pattern II, *Arrogance*. (Reconstructed from subject's remarks; see text.)

(Pattern I, *modesty*)—"The part with the curving around (points to rounded corner) suggests modesty because it is *under the other thing*—the top part." (Fig. 20-10c)

(Pattern II, *arrogance*)—"Pictorially, this figure, rather than bowing down to the other part as it was before (when Pattern II was taken to represent *modesty*), is *beating them down.* He's lording it over these poor little parallel lines. (Fig. 20-10d)

These, then, were the four generic modes [6] in which the linear patterns were transformed into symbolic vehicles in Bodansky's study. They are the very processes which are exploited in *vehicular rotation,* that is, in the experiential structuring and restructuring that a given pattern undergoes as it is employed to represent different conceptions.

In addressing herself especially to the problem of *vehicular rotation* proper, Bodansky made extensive comparisons of the changes occurring in the structuring of the given patterns as a function of changes in the concepts. Since vehicular rotation has already been well illustrated in Cirillo's findings, we shall abstain from giving further examples from Bodansky's comparisons. We may, however, note that these comparisons did not only yield clear-cut evidence of the often very striking changes that occurred in the structuring of a vehicle when shifting from the representation of one referent to that of a second, antagonistic, referent; they also brought out the fact that these shifts in structure quite frequently entailed also shifts in the generic modes of handling the patterns. The analysis indicated that there was only a single instance when a subject used the same structural mode while changing the representational meaning of a given pattern. In all other instances, the subjects either used completely different modes of structuring a given pattern when shifting from the representation of one concept to that of the other or used different and identical modes in combination.

In sum, then, the overall findings in regard to vehicular structuring allow us to conclude that the subjects, with relative facility, were able to *rotate* the same arbitrary pattern in such a manner that it could represent concepts of great diversity, even of contrast.

---

[6] It may be added that structuring a pattern qua concrete object rarely occurred among Bodansky's subjects. The clearly dominant mode of structuring was in terms of dynamic qualities: this seems to be consonant with the findings presented in the following chapter, showing that under conditions of spontaneous linear expression, normal subjects showed very little inclination toward concrete picturing, in contradistinction to schizophrenics who displayed a strong trend toward pictorial representation.

Handling the Concept: Conceptual Rotation

In order for any ideal concept to be grasped through a medium of representation,[7] it must be articulated (connoted) in such a way as to make it amenable, through the particular means available in that medium, to representation.

The most direct way of demonstrating this process is through experimental situations, such as Bodansky's, in which a subject is requested to represent a concept by two or more different vehicular patterns offered to him. One then inquires whether, and how, the exploitation of different patterns affects the "inner form" of the concept, that is, whether, and how, the connotational structure of the concept changes (is rotated) in order to be amenable to representation by one or the other linear pattern.

Bodansky's analysis of generic as well as particular ways in which the subjects treated the concepts is thus directly related to a crucial problem of vehicle-referent relationships, the issue of *conceptual rotation*. Just as a given pattern undergoes *vehicular rotation* as it is employed to represent different conceptions, so does a concept undergo *conceptual rotation*, that is, changes in connotations, as a function of changes in the vehicles representing it. Assuming that the linear pattern taken as a symbol involved "language" as *energeia* rather than as *ergon*, one would indeed expect that a change in the vehicle for the representation of a concept would entail differences in the way the logical concept is experienced and realized. Before presenting some illustrations showing the particular ways in which connotations are rotated, we may briefly refer to a quite comprehensive analysis by Bodansky in which she attempted to determine the subjects' general modes of handling the concepts for representation. According to this analysis, the following are the most frequently used modes.

(1) *Delimiting.* The range of the concept becomes articulated in terms of one of several subspheres. For instance, *modesty* was apprehended by a subject as "nun-like modesty" when represented by Pattern II and as "schoolgirl modesty" when represented by Pattern I; (2) *Characterizing* in terms of properties. This mode involves the selection of one or several connotational properties of the concept for representation. Such properties are often *central* for defining a concept; for instance, a subject chooses "concealment" as such a property, remarking: "The idea of concealment is central to modesty." Sometimes, however, such connotative properties chosen by the subjects for

---

[7] In regard to the related problem of making abstract, ideal contents amenable to representation in a nonverbal medium, see Freud (70), Silberer (229; 230).

representation strike one as being rather secondary, *peripheral,* or even far-fetched in definitive relevance ("softness" for *modesty,* "impressiveness" for *arrogance,* etc.); (3) *Instancing.* This mode entails the apprehension of a concept in terms of a concrete instance, somehow illustrative of it. For example, *arrogance* was conceived by one subject as ingredient in a situation where one person beats down another.

There can hardly be any doubt that an important factor underlying these various modes of apprehending a concept is the striving of the subjects to make it fit for representation by a given pattern. A subject may particularize, concretize, an abstract notion or may focalize on one or two properties impelled by the material and form of the given vehicle; or he may "force the issue" by overextending the meaning of the concept, by stressing otherwise peripheral qualities, etc. This handling of the concept in terms of general modes is closely related to the particular ways in which the meaning of a concept is apprehended so that it becomes fit for vehicular depiction.

Let us now turn to a few of Bodansky's protocols illustrating *conceptual rotation* in terms of the particular ways of handling the connotational stucture of the concept. In the following are the responses of two subjects: the first two juxtaposed protocols pertain to *modesty* as this concept is realized through the two patterns; the second two protocols show another subject's handling of *arrogance* as mediated by the two patterns.

Modesty Represented by Pattern I

"The idea of concealing one's complexities because here you have this inner business, which is a little more intricate and complex than the outer shell; so you could say that the outer shell is concealing the inner complexity from the outer world. . . .

"I would think it would be modesty with regard to some intellectual or inner attributes of an individual rather than physical attributes. (E: Why?) Just because if this is an organism, what is being kept inside, back, that's what he's modest about."

Modesty Represented by Pattern II

". . . a phrase comes to mind: 'The lady doth protest too much' . . . The business at the end is a deprecatory movement like 'no, no'—as if saying, 'the praise that you're giving me really isn't true.'

". . . But I guess you do have the idea of some sort of barrier (in the long, straight line) . . . before you come to the person; a distance between individual and attributes and the outside world could be looked on as a kind of modesty. A person has isolated himself and this can be related to modesty. . . . The person is trying to shield attributes of his from people, hiding under a bushel."

Arrogance Represented by Pattern I

". . . Arrogance—aggressive superciliousness. It almost swaggers. The pointedness and the blackness—which went against *modesty*—they give the aggressive quality. (E: What about superciliousness?) This part (pointing to the top line) like a 'holier than thou attitude,' supercilious; the extension is almost like a hand gesturing—holding something away (S gestures accordingly). It also has a chompy quality, closing, a vector here (in some way vaguely related to aggression).

"A disdainful turn of the head, made more arrogant by the aggressive qualities involved. It is an active and militant disdain."

Arrogance Represented by Pattern II

"This is a more flighty kind of arrogance. The other was more hostile. And this is the arrogance that is a reaction against something. It is more adolescent. Pattern I is an older person. This is . . . almost a juvenile delinquent. Doesn't have solidity, discombobulated, not sustained. . . .

"Assertiveness, given by the shape —these lines going out. This is more a defiant arrogance and that's adolescent. . . . It has a shooting out quality. The vector goes this way (points), a big thrust and then two little jabs. It's fairly active: the tempo. . . . This is a pushy kind of arrogance, thinner and more wiry. A completely different kind of arrogance."

On the basis of the qualitative analysis of the performances and protocols, Bodansky clearly established the fact that variations in the connotations of a given concept occurred throughout as a function of differences in vehicle of representation. A further numerical survey (Table 20-2) confirmed her conclusions: as the table shows, the great majority of Bodansky's subjects realized the concepts in quite different ways under the two conditions (vehicles) of representation. In only one instance was there a preponderance of similar or identical contents in the two representations.

Table 20-2

Number of subjects giving preponderance of different content versus number giving preponderance of similar or identical content for each of the concepts as represented by the two patterns

Concept	Difference > Likeness	Difference = Likeness	Difference < Likeness
Modesty	9	3	0
Arrogance	10	1	1

In sum, then, the protocols of the subjects led to the conclusion that where the contents did change from one vehicle to the other, the variations in content were intimately connected with the specific structurings of the patterns. Underlying this relationship was, of course, the striving by the subjects to establish, through restructuring of referent and of vehicle, some correspondence between both (*"reciprocal rotation"*).

General Modes of Linking Vehicle and Concept: Kinds of Referring

Whereas the foregoing analyses—though concerned with vehicle-referent relationships throughout—have focused mainly on vehicular structurization on one side, on referent structurization on the other, a further analysis by Bodansky focused on the vehicle-referent relation as such. The problem posed here concerns the general modes of linkage obtaining between concept and vehicle.

The analysis of the subjects' protocols suggests three principal modes by which the vehicle may be taken to refer to the concept, *concrete exemplifying, direct concrete analogizing,* and *analogizing by secondary augmentation.*

In *direct concrete exemplifying,* the vehicle is linked to the concept through the depiction of a particular happening serving to exemplify the concept. It is this embeddedness of the "universal" in the particular that here underlies the use of the vehicle to refer to the concept. One subject's depiction of *arrogance* by Pattern II may serve as an example: ". . . This is a dictator (pointing to the loop and its extension); he's laying down the law. A benevolent despot. He's firm. There's certainty here." That which the vehicle immediately depicts is taken to exemplify *arrogance,* "a good kind of arrogance."

In *concrete analogizing,* vehicle and referent are apprehended as having similar qualities or sharing similar dynamics; for example: "This (Pattern I) is a good representation of *arrogance.* It has all the things that make it so; angularity, brashness—in the angles—the darkness . . . is good here." Here the vehicle clearly exhibits qualities which are also considered to characterize arrogance. The vehicle represents and refers to the concept because it shares certain central qualities of *arrogance* with the concept.

In *analogizing by secondary augmentation,* there is initially established some similarity between vehicle and referent, which is followed by further verbal elaboration. This further elaboration distinguishes *analogizing by secondary augmentation* from *simple analogizing.* Secondary augmentation apparently comes into play when simple, direct analogizing leaves some gap between the vehicle and the concept to which the vehicle refers. The subject ostensibly strives toward filling out the gap in the initially established analogy. The remarks of one subject in regard to *modesty* (Pattern II) illustrate this process: ". . . if you think of modesty as shyness, then it (Pattern II) has a tentative quality which could be represented by those broken lines, headed toward or away from the loop. They (the lines) are tentative in either case, but have different meanings; tentative inward, retreating, retreats into attitude of modesty or shyness; tentative outward, advancing, reaching out attitudes to make contact."

Here the immediate structuring of the pattern qua vehicle is in terms of "tentativity." This expressive feature is not directly connected with *modesty* or with its realization as "shyness." *Secondary augmenting* is necessary to bridge the gap: tentativity is equated with shyness, which in turn is a basic characteristic of modesty.

In sum, then, it is quite clear that of the three general modes of linking vehicle to concept, *concrete analogizing* most directly establishes the relationship of inner similarity between vehicle and referent; here the pattern is structured and the concept realized in such ways that parallel or *isomorphic* relations emerge for both. In other words, *concrete analogizing* brings out "symbolic pregnance" to its highest degree. In the two other modes, the similarity linkage between vehicle and realized concept is less direct and thus less apparent. In *concrete exemplifying*, qualities or relations that link the vehicle to the concept are embedded in the concrete object or situation which the vehicle exhibits as its immediate meaning; only through inquiry does it become clear that it is by virtue of these indwelling, covert features that the concrete object represents and refers to the concept. In *secondary augmentation*, the immediate sense exhibited by the vehicle during the initial phase of analogizing does not suffice to make the vehicle fit the concept fully. The subject therefore elaborates upon or extends, augments, the immediate qualities or relations until an internal linkage is established between vehicle and concept.[8]

---

[8] This process seems to bear a close relationship to *secondary elaboration* operative in the shaping of dream contents—a linguistic elaboration which results in a greater measure of coherence and logical organization than would otherwise obtain.

chapter *21*

Nonverbal (Linear) Naming in Schizophrenia

In the experiments on linear naming discussed in the preceding chapter, normal subjects characteristically seemed to apprehend the lines as expressive or physiognomic vehicles rather than as geometric-technical entities or as pictures of objects. Concomitantly, the subjects seemed to comprehend the conceptions to be represented in terms of dynamic, inner-gestural features—connotations most amenable to overt expression through the physiognomic properties of the linear patterns. Through this *bilateral handling* of pattern and concept—bringing both moments in some way into the same physiognomic-dynamic universe—the normal subjects were able to transform otherwise "meaningless" linear patterns into symbolic vehicles capable of directly exhibiting otherwise abstract, intangible conceptions.

In their ability to segregate the physiognomic qualities of line patterns from geometric-technical properties and from the possible use of lines for pictorial representation, normal subjects are apparently enabled to establish a relatively novel medium (that of *expressive lines*) and to forge and articulate vehicles within this medium for the representation of referents. As we have also noted, normal adults further appear able, *under certain specifiable conditions,* to work this line medium in such a manner as to produce expressive line patterns in a way that permits other normal adults to read off the "embodied" meanings.

In the preceding chapter, we have indicated that there is an inter-dependence between the attainment of consensus concerning the mean-ings exhibited by line patterns and the establishment of a relatively autonomous and distinctive medium of representation. Even the kind of limited and conditional consensus to which we have referred there depends, to a great extent, upon the degree of autonomy given to the medium by the subjects. That is, only insofar as the subjects were able (1) to exploit the line medium expressively, differentiating physiognomic-dynamic properties from other features or usages of lines, (2) to distance the contents to be represented from their own idiosyncratic or momentary involvements with these contents, and (3) to articulate the domain of physiognomic properties in a way that highlighted differential representation of different referents, were the subjects able to achieve the minimum conditions for consensus to ensue.

In terms of our developmental orientation, we were interested in determining whether such relatively *autonomous handling* of an ex-pressive line medium and such *attainments of consensus* as have been found among normal adults is approximated by others who may be assumed to operate, typically, at genetically lower levels of cognitive functioning than do normal adults. One such population is constituted by schizophrenics who, despite their acknowledged heterogeneity, are generally regarded as individuals characteristically functioning at a level of lesser differentiation and hierarchic integration than do nor-mals at comparable ages and of comparable educational status. The study we shall focus on here, therefore, is one that deals with the ways schizophrenic individuals produce linear vehicles to represent contents and interpret linear patterns as representative of referents.

In this investigation, carried out by Alfred Goldman (80; 81), fifteen normal and fifteen schizophrenic females were employed as subjects. The study consisted of two parts. In the first part, the subjects were asked to represent verbally designated conceptions via linear patterns which they were to construct themselves; in the second part, the sub-jects were asked to match already formed line patterns with verbally designated concepts. The part dealing with the self-produced linear representation of concepts will be considered first.[1]

---

[1] Our analysis of the first part of Goldman's study differs from his since our concerns were different. We are obliged to Dr. Goldman for providing us with his original protocols for this reanalysis.

Linear Representation of Concepts:
Normals versus Schizophrenics

In this part of the study, after rapport had been established with a subject and the general nature of the task—representation of concepts by expressive lines—had been concretely demonstrated, the subject was asked to draw a line that would represent the word *angry*: "Draw a line that looks angry; draw an angry line." [2]

The stimulus-words, in the order of their presentation, were as follows: *angry, powerful, excited, laughing, soothing, misery, irritating, healthy, cruel, gentle, evil, sick, hate, kind, crying, love, sad, weak, happy,* and *disgust.*

In the main, the analysis of the performances of the two groups of subjects was based both on the actual drawings made by the subjects and the explanations of these productions brought out during the inquiries that followed each response. There were some cases, however, in which the subjects showed either an inability or unwillingness to produce a line drawing for a particular verbal concept or to interpret a pattern once they had drawn it. We refer to the behavior in such cases as *blocking*.

The psychological reasons underlying *blocking* vary in different instances. One reason for *blocking* may be simply that the individual lacks the ingenuity to forge a particular linear vehicle for a given concept. Again, one may be blocked in the linear representation of a concept because one is sidetracked into the use of another medium; for example, a schizophrenic subject, for the concept *hate*, grasped her pencil and, wielding it like a knife, remarked, "hate is a knife, that's hate;" there was no use of the linear medium before or after the use of the gestural medium. Another factor which may block linear representation is a strong personal reaction to the content to be represented: the subject may wish to have nothing to do with the concept, and hence may refuse to represent it. This latter reason seems to have been operative in one subject's refusal to draw any pattern to represent *disgust*. We may add that, in addition to *blocking of line production*, there occurred also *blocking of interpretation*—an inability or unwillingness on the part of a subject to indicate how the pattern he had drawn served to represent the particular content.

In regard to the linear productions that were formed and interpreted by the subjects, three types could rather clearly be distinguished:

---

[2] If the subject responded by writing a word or if he drew a picture, the instructions were repeated and it was made clear that linear forms were wanted, not words or pictures. If the subject, in three instances, persisted in giving only words as responses she was not included in the sample.

extra-medium productions, pictorial-realistic productions, and *true linear productions.* In the following, various kinds of drawings falling under each of these types will be described and illustrated.

Extra-Medium Productions

Under this heading are included instances where a subject, though drawing certain linear forms, did not use them qua linear expressive patterns per se to represent a concept; instead, such a subject produced a "letter" of the alphabet, belonging to the medium of script rather than to the medium of expressive lines.

To illustrate, a schizophrenic subject drew the letter *i* to represent *excited*. She stated, "it carries the motions of any letter in the word 'excited,'" explaining further, "it's the letter 'i' in 'excited.'" The same subject, for *soothing,* produced the pattern: $\smile\!\!\nearrow$, remarking: "It's part of an Hebraic letter—the first part of the Hebraic letter 'samach.'" Another schizophrenic drew Fig. 21-1a for *laughing,* explaining: "almost like an *E*—more like an *L* in *laughing.*" Hardly any of the responses of the *normal* subjects could even remotely be considered as belonging to the class of *script productions.*

Among extra-medium productions we also included certain line patterns which did not seem to differ, on the surface, from the usual linear-expressive vehicles, but on closer examination, turned out to have no true representational relation to the concept. They were *mood-related productions;* that is, rather than representations of a conception, they appeared to indicate the affective reactions of the subject to his or her own drawing. For example, one schizophrenic subject, after having

(*a*) Laughing   (*b*) Angry   (*c*) Irritating

FIGURE 21-1. (*a*) **Script production by a schizophrenic subject.** (*b*) **and** (*c*) **Mood-related productions by two schizophrenics.**

drawn the pattern of Fig. 21-1b for *angry,* said: "It's scribbled—
you're angry." Another schizophrenic subject, for *irritating,* produced
the pattern of Fig. 21-1c, interpreting it as follows: "I had no power
over it when I drew it, so it's irritating."

We may mention that mood-related productions did not occur at all
with the normal subjects, whereas fifteen such responses were given
by the schizophrenics. Altogether, 12 percent of the total productions
of the schizophrenics were either script-like or mood-related drawings
falling completely outside of a linear medium of representation.

Pictorial-Realistic Productions

We turn now to a group of instances in which the line medium was
used in a more or less indirect manner for the representation of concepts. These comprised drawings in which lines were organized to
depict some concrete object or event which then served as vehicle of
representation. Such *pictorial-realistic productions* were of three
kinds: *depiction of an object, depiction of the motion of an action,* and
depiction of a combination of object and action-motion.

In Fig. 21-2a–e are reproduced drawings by both schizophrenics and
normal subjects, involving *depiction of an object* as a means for the
representation of concepts. The drawing (a) for *powerful* was interpreted by its schizophrenic producer "as a piece of nut in a cake"; on
the basis of this subject's overwhelming concern with food as a source
of strength, one could quite readily infer the relation between the object drawn and the concept to be represented. Drawing (b) is a schizophrenic's representation for *gentle;* her explanation was this: "It's
like hay; hay is gentle; you can lie on it." *Evil* was represented in (c)
again in terms of an object: "It's a skirt—once they took my Indian
skirt away." The two drawings (d) and (e) were those of normal subjects. To the first, a representation of *crying,* the subject remarked,
"sort of like teardrops . . . yeah, they're teardrops." The second pattern, drawn by another normal subject for *laughing,* was interpreted by
her as "a bubble—when you laugh it's like bubbling over with
laughter."

Another means of pictorial-realistic representation of concepts is
through the *depiction of motion typical for an action.* Fig. 21-2f shows
one schizophrenic's drawing for *angry,* produced with the comment:
"If a person's angry, they'll force—like a punch." The same subject
interpreted her drawing for *powerful* (g) as: "someone climbing upwards—doesn't have to be a person, could be a thing." Another schizo-

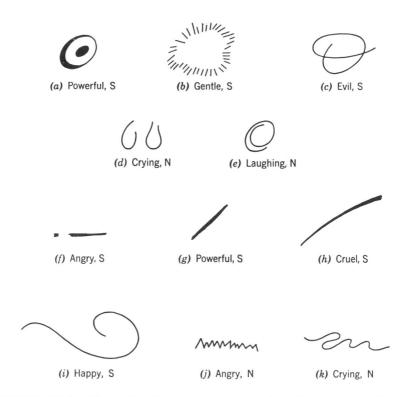

FIGURE 21-2. Pictorial-realistic representations by schizophrenics (S) and normals (N): *a–e* Depiction by way of objects. *f–k* Depiction by way of motion of action.

phrenic drew pattern (*h*) for *cruel*, remarking: "It's a strike—a blow is cruel." Pattern (*i*), a drawing for *happy*, was explained by its schizophrenic producer as: "something like a wave, like a wave to somebody, somebody waving." Patterns (*j*) and (*k*) are representations of two normals for *angry* and for *crying* respectively; they were interpreted as follows: *angry*—"it means that you're up and down; blood rising and falling with anger;" *crying*—"There are sobs, intake of the breath."

Finally, there were pictorial-realistic line drawings (occurring only with schizophrenics) which depicted both an object together with some characteristic motion. One subject, for instance, drew the pattern ₐ( )ₙ for *laughing*, explaining, ". . . here's the mouth and cheek—and when laughing, the little curved line on the cheek."

Table 21-1 presents the frequencies of occurrence of the three types of pictorial-realistic productions for both groups of subjects. The data indicate, quite strikingly, how much more frequently such productions were used by the schizophrenic subjects than by the normals: whereas such pictorial productions amounted to less than 10 percent of all of the drawings made by the normal subjects, they comprised almost 44 percent of the schizophrenic drawings.

Table 21-1
Incidence of pictorial-realistic productions

	Mean per subject		Percent of total responses	
	Normals	Schizo-phrenics	Normals	Schizo-phrenics
Object depiction	1.40	6.87	7.0	34.3
Motion of action	.53	1.33	2.9	6.7
Object in motion	.00	.53	0.0	2.7
Total	1.93	8.73	9.9%	43.7%

True Linear Productions

The linear patterns subsumed under pictorial-realistic productions involve only an *indirect* use of the line medium: that is, the properties or qualities of the line medium are not exploited as symbolic vehicles but function rather to depict objects or action, which in turn are the true vehicles of representation. In the kinds of productions to be discussed now, the line medium is *directly* exploited: the concepts are represented through expressive properties of the linear patterns as such.

With regard to the direct use of the linear medium, one may distinguish among four types of linear properties exploited for representation: *qualities of extensity and intensity*, such as length, width, brightness, lightness or pressure, etc.; *shape or configurational qualities*, such as roundness, angularity, etc.; *directional qualities*, such as upwardness, downwardness, etc.; *physiognomic and synaesthetic qualities*, such as erectness of stance, harshness, softness, etc. Each of these types of properties were utilized sometimes singly, sometimes in combination with one or more of the other kinds of properties.

Figure 21-3 presents drawings by both normal and schizophrenic subjects exemplifying the use of linear properties. Pattern (*a*) was drawn by a schizophrenic subject to represent *gentle;* when asked how the drawing represented the concept, she simply stated: "no pressure" (i.e., light). Another schizophrenic represented *sick* by line (*b*), explaining: "If this line is sick maybe because it is not long enough in length." For comparison with these rather idiosyncratic drawings of schizophrenics, we present in Fig. 21-3*c* a typical, almost self-explanatory representation by a normal subject of *weak:* a thin, downwardly curved line.

Whereas the drawings just discussed emphasize intensity or extensity, other drawings stress more the property of *shape.* For instance, a patient drew Fig. 21-3*d*, his depiction of *hate*, adding this comment: "the curving is wrathful, the roundness of the line." Pattern (*e*) is

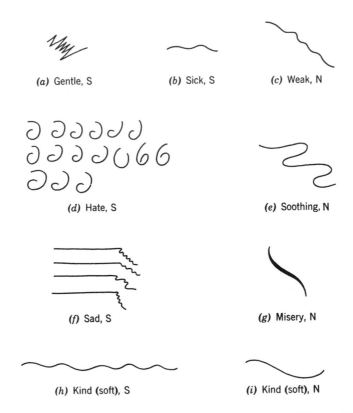

(*a*) Gentle, S   (*b*) Sick, S   (*c*) Weak, N

(*d*) Hate, S   (*e*) Soothing, N

(*f*) Sad, S   (*g*) Misery, N

(*h*) Kind (soft), S   (*i*) Kind (soft), N

FIGURE 21-3.   **Representations by linear properties: (*a*) (*b*) (*c*) Qualities of extensity or intensity; (*d*) (*e*) Configurational or shape qualities; (*f*) (*g*) Directional qualities; (*h*) (*i*) Physiognomic-synaesthetic qualities.**

the representation of a normal subject for *soothing;* she drew it as "slow curves—gentle curves, mostly horizontal positions."

Two patterns emphasizing *directional qualities* are presented in Fig. 21-3*f* and *g*. Pattern (*f*), representing *sad,* was interpreted by the schizophrenic producer as: "going straight along, and then down to show sadness." Pattern (*g*), depicting *misery,* was drawn by a normal subject with this comment: "Let's have that down—it's definitely downward."

In spite of a considerable overlap, we have been able to differentiate qualities of extensity, intensity, shape, and direction from *physiognomic and synaesthetic qualities* insofar as the former essentially pertain to visual properties of lines while the latter are dynamic-affective in nature. Under *physiognomic and synaesthetic qualities* we include the apprehension of line patterns as "drooping," "aggressive," "harsh," "prickly," "cold," etc., that is, where there is some grasp of the line patterns as reflecting human-like states or postures or as exhibiting properties which characteristically belong to sense modalities other than vision.

Two drawings (*h* and *i*), both representations of *kind,* one made by a schizophrenic, the other by a normal subject, may suffice as illustrations. In both cases "softness" was given as the characteristic property of the depictive lines.

We may now turn to the quantitative findings concerning the exploitation of linear properties for representation by the two groups of subjects (Table 21-2). There are quite striking differences between

Table 21-2
Incidence of use of linear qualities in representation

	Mean per subject		Percent total responses	
	Normals	Schizo-phrenics	Normals	Schizo-phrenics
Singly Used Qualities				
Extensive-intensive	.93	.60	4.7	3.0
Configurational	3.60	1.40	18.0	7.0
Directional	3.47	.33	17.3	1.6
Physiognomic-synaesthetic	2.53	2.33	12.7	11.7
Used in Combination	6.47	1.14	32.3	5.7
Totals	17.00	5.80	85.0%	29.0%

Table 21-3
Relative incidence of different ways of dealing with
task of representing concepts via linear patterns

	Extra-medium	Pictorial-realistic	Linear	Other (blocking, etc.)
Normals	0.0%	9.9%	85.3%	4.8%
Schizophrenics	12.0%	43.7%	29.0%	15.3%

these groups: whereas normal subjects exploited linear qualities—either singly or in combination—in 85 percent of their productions, schizophrenics used distinctively linear qualities in only 29 percent of their productions. Moreover, whereas normals employed a combination of linear properties in almost one third of their line drawings, schizophrenics used a combination of properties in only about 6 percent of their productions. In other words, normals tended much more than schizophrenics to use linear qualities for representation and to exploit combinations of different kinds of qualities in symbolizing via linear patterns.

Turning now to Table 21-3, we may summarize the overall differences between the two groups in regard to the handling of the linear medium for representation. It will be recalled that the task posed to the subjects in Goldman's study was to represent verbal concepts in linear patterns *that were not pictorial-realistic in character.* Under this stipulation, the normal subjects, for the most part, abided by the task demands and tended to employ the linear medium as a distinctive one—separate and segregated from a medium of natural objects and events or of private imagery. Schizophrenics, on the other hand, were, in spite of the instructions, far more inclined to use line patterns for the drawing of objects or actions—with these latter entities serving as the direct means of representation. This suggests that schizophrenics have a greater difficulty than normals in establishing a specific, expressive line medium for representation, clearly differentiated from a medium of graphic depiction, of painting, etc. The relatively high percentage of *extra-medium responses* (*script-productions* and *mood-related responses*) attests further to the relative lack of differentiation of a linear medium (limited autonomy) among schizophrenics, compared with normals.

At this point, we may add some further information about the group differences in the use of the three kinds of productions, this time in terms of *number of individuals* in each group. An analysis was undertaken to determine how often and how many of the subjects in each group employed extra-medium, pictorial-realistic, and linear-representation responses: how many of the fifteen normals and how many of the fifteen schizophrenics used extra-medium responses at least once? at least five times? at least ten times? at least fifteen times? How many individuals of each group used pictorial-realistic responses, how many used linear properties: at least once? five times? ten times? fifteen times? (See Table 21-4.)

For this analysis, we identified, on genetic grounds, each of the three kinds of productions with one of three levels of medium-autonomy. One assumption here was that the means of representation specific to the linear medium are linear qualities: thus, autonomy of the linear medium would imply more frequent use of linear qualities for representation. A second assumption was that there is an increase in the autonomous use of a medium with development: the more the vehicle makes use of properties pertaining to the medium, that is, the more distant the properties exploited for representation are from the symbolizer's momentary moods or personal images, the genetically higher the level of representation. From this point of view, extra-medium productions are genetically the most primitive way of using line patterns to represent concepts, pictorial-realistic productions are inter-

Table 21-4

Number of subjects in each group performing at one of three levels of medium-autonomy

	High (linear)		Intermediate (pictorial)		Low (extra-medium)	
	Normals	Schizophrenics	Normals	Schizophrenics	Normals	Schizophrenics
In at least 1 task *	15	13	13	15	0	10
In at least 5 tasks	15	6	1	12	0	5
In at least 10 tasks	14	3	0	4	0	3
In at least 15 tasks	13	1	0	2	0	1

* Total number of tasks (concepts represented) = 20; total number of subjects = 15 in each group.

mediate, and true linear productions are developmentally most advanced.

A glance at the table reveals some striking differences, couched in developmental terms, between the normals and schizophrenics. Thus, thirteen of the fifteen normal subjects operated on the highest (linear quality) level of representation in most (at least three-fourths) of their responses; in contrast, there was only one schizophrenic subject who showed such predominance of the highest level of representation in her responses. On the other hand, the great majority of the schizophrenics (80 percent) utilized pictorial-realistic representation in at least one-fourth of their productions, whereas only one normal subject used this kind of representation so often. As to low-level productions, those which fell outside of the linear medium proper, a majority (two-thirds) of the schizophrenics "represented" concepts at least once in this manner, whereas the normals never employed extra-medium formations.

These differences between the two groups in regard to the *construction* of linear vehicles—differences which we have attempted to conceptualize in developmental terms—may aid us in the understanding of the differential behavior of normals and schizophrenics in the *apprehension* of linear vehicles, that is, in the matching of already formed line patterns with verbally designated concepts. This problem is dealt with in the second part of Goldman's inquiry.

Apprehension of Linear Meanings: Normals versus Schizophrenics

This part of Goldman's study consisted of two experiments, both involving the matching of mood terms with linear patterns. In the first experiment, the subject was required to select one of two antithetical word-meanings as the "best fit" for a given line pattern; in the second experiment, the subject was required to select one of four linear patterns as the "best fit" for a given word-meaning.

In the first experiment, the subjects were shown twenty cards, on each of which appeared one line pattern and two words of opposite meaning, for example, *love-hate, kind-cruel.* Each word-pair appeared twice in the series, on the two occasions with line patterns whose structural characteristics (angularity-circularity, upward-downward direction, darkness-lightness) were in sharp contrast. Thus if a word-pair appeared first with a dark, angular and (or) downward line, the same word-pair appeared later in the series with a light, circular, and (or) upward-directed pattern (see Fig. 21-4a and b). With the presentation of each card, the subject was asked to select one of the two words which was best expressed by the line pattern.

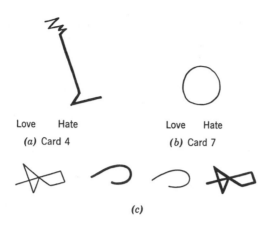

Love   Hate   Love   Hate

(*a*) Card 4   (*b*) Card 7

(*c*)

FIGURE 21-4. Samples of patterns used in Goldman's experiments on matching of words to lines (*a*) (*b*)—Two of the patterns used in Matching Experiment I. (*c*)—A set of four patterns in Matching Experiment II, presented once with GENTLE (Card 3), once with VICIOUS (Card 23).

In the second experiment, the subjects were shown twenty-four cards, each containing one word and four line patterns. Each four-line set appeared twice in the series, each time with one of two words of contrasting significance, for example, *joy-misery*. The four line patterns were not unrelated to each other but were constructed through variation of linear properties of shape, brightness and direction. Thus, on each card two of the line patterns had an angular quality and two a round quality; on ten of the twenty-four cards, one of the angular and one of the round line patterns were drawn in an upward direction, the other angular and round patterns being drawn in a downward direction; on fourteen of the cards, one of the angular and one of the round patterns were drawn heavy-thick, and the other angular and other round pattern were drawn light-thin (see Fig. 21-4*c*). The subjects were asked to select one of the four lines best fitted to the particular word.

Underlying the construction of these cards was the assumption that, at least within our society, certain linear qualities were "naturally" more expressive of certain connotations than of others.[3] Thus it was assumed that circular, light-thin and/or upward-directed line patterns

---

[3] It is of no relevance to this study on group differences whether "natural" refers to supracultural, universal ties between certain linear qualities and connotations, or whether this relationship is culture-bound, that is, "natural" only for members of a particular culture.

are "naturally" more expressive of connotations of "mildness," "goodness," happiness," etc., and that angular, dark-heavy, and/or downward-directed patterns tend to connote "harshness," "evil," "misery," etc.

If one tentatively assumes such linkages between certain connotations and certain expressive properties of lines, then one may inquire about the extent to which members of different groups of subjects agree among themselves (show consensus) in matching certain lines to certain words on the basis of the presumed ties. The relevant findings with regard to this question are presented in Table 21-5a and b.

As one will observe from the table (a), all fifteen normal subjects, in the majority of their matchings in the first experiment, chose a "positive" word-meaning (e.g., *gentle, love, kind*) to go with a circular, light, and/or upward line pattern and a "negative" word-meaning (e.g., *cruel, misery, bitter*) to go with an angular, dark, and/or downward line pattern. The same unanimity did not obtain for the schizophrenic group; still, eleven of the fifteen schizophrenics, in the majority of their matchings, linked "positive" words to circular, light, and upward

Table 21-5a

Number of subjects in each group making majority of word-choices in correspondence with the presumed expressive valences of line patterns

	Normals (N = 15)	Schizophrenics (N = 15)
"Positive" word-"positive" pattern	15	11
"Negative" word-"negative" pattern	15	12

Table 21-5b

Mean frequency of word-choices corresponding to the presumed expressive valences of line patterns

	Normals	Schizophrenics	Diff. (N − S)
"Positive" word-"positive" pattern	9.26	7.00	2.26 *
"Negative" word-"negative" pattern	10.00	7.33	2.67 †

Maximum for each group 10.00; * $p < .05$, † $p < .01$

patterns, and twelve of the fifteen linked "negative" words to angular, dark, and downward patterns. Thus, about 80 percent of the schizophrenic subjects matched word-meanings and line patterns, on the whole, in accordance with the presumed relationship between expressive qualities of lines and connotations of words.

Rather clear differences between the two groups emerged, however, when one examined the *mean frequency* with which these two groups made responses in conformity with the assumed expressive valences of the linear properties (Table 21-5*b*). Compared with the normals, the schizophrenics matched significantly fewer "positive" words with "positive" line patterns and significantly fewer "negative" words with "negative" line patterns. We may add that the word matchings to "negative" line patterns distinguished the two groups with especial clarity, for no normal subject ever matched a "positive" word with a "negative" line, whereas eleven schizophrenics made at least one such matching.

Another issue of considerable importance pertains to the degree to which normals and schizophrenics apprehended linear vehicles as relatively stable and unequivocal in expressive meaning. This issue might be examined in the light of the findings of the *first* of the matching experiments. The ten pairs of word-meanings each appeared twice in the test, once with a round, light, upward pattern and once with an angular, dark, downward pattern. The degree of equivocality could therefore be determined by the number of times (out of a maximum of ten) a given word of a pair was matched with contrasting linear patterns; for example, it would be an instance of equivocality were the word *love*, of the pair *love-hate*, selected as the best fit both for a round, light, upward line and for an angular, dark, downward line.

An analysis indicated that there were significant differences between normals and schizophrenics with respect to average number of equivocal matchings. Out of the ten doublets of matchings, schizophrenic subjects had an average of 3.75 equivocal matchings, and normals had an average of only .73 equivocal matchings. It seems justifiable to conclude that schizophrenics view the expressive meanings of linear properties with much less stability and unequivocality than do normals.

This interpretation is strongly supported by the findings pertaining to the performances of schizophrenics and normals in the *second* of Goldman's matching experiments. It will be recalled that this second experiment differed from the first in two major respects. First, in the second study, one word-meaning was presented with several line patterns, whereas in the initial study, two word-meanings were presented with one line pattern; second, in the study to be considered here, the various properties of lines (circularity-angularity, lightness-darkness, upwardness-downwardness) were more or less independently varied, whereas in the first experiment the line patterns were presented as a complex in which shape, pressure, and direction were not sharply articulated from each other.

This latter deviation of the second from the first study is of special significance here. Where, in the first experiment, the choice of a line pattern for a word-meaning was in terms of a *complex* of linear properties sharply differentiated from another complex of linear properties, in the second study, the matching of word-meanings to line patterns involved a discrimination among linear patterns contrasted along only *one* or *two* dimensions rather than among three properties *en bloc.* In other words, in the first experiment, matching of a "positive" (or "negative") word with a "positive" (or "negative") line pattern could be attained on the basis of relatively *global* apprehension of the linear pattern; in the second experiment, however, the subject had to tease out *single* properties and their variations. Therefore, one could infer, on the basis of the performances of the subjects, the degree to which shape, brightness (pressure) and directional qualities—each taken separately—were perceived as possessing relatively stable and consistent expressive values—sufficiently stable to produce a consensus.

When such an analysis as to the fittingness of distinct and single qualities of lines for specific word-meanings was undertaken, it was found that normal subjects, with few exceptions, matched circular, light, *or* upward-directed line patterns with "positive" word-meanings and angular, dark *or* downward-directed line patterns with "negative" word-meanings. The schizophrenics also, *on the whole,* tended to match the various "positive" linear qualities with the "positive" terms and the "negative" properties with "negative terms;" however, if one considers the linkages of the *separate* linear properties to the word-meanings, one finds that considerably fewer schizophrenic individuals matched on the basis of the assumed linkage than did normal subjects. In particular, the number of matchings of light line–"positive" word and downward line–"negative" word failed to reach statistically significant deviation from chance among the schizophrenic group, but not among the normal subjects (see Table 21-6).

These findings, taken in conjunction with those presented in Table 21-5a and b, suggest the following interpretation. Where the expressive properties of a potential vehicle work to reinforce each other (provide redundancy) in the conveying of certain meanings, the differ-

Table 21-6

Number of subjects in each group matching separate linear properties to corresponding mood-terms

	Round line- "positive" word	Angular line- "negative" word	Light line- "positive" word	Dark line- "negative" word	Upward line- "positive" word	Downward line- "negative" word
Normals	15 ‡	15 ‡	13 †	15 ‡	15 ‡	13 †
Schizophrenics	11 *	12 *	9 n. sig.	12 *	11 *	8 n. sig.

* p < .05; † p < .01; ‡ p < .001

ences between normals and schizophrenics will be less marked than where the redundancy is experimentally eliminated or reduced. Whereas in the latter situation the narrowing down of linear properties expressive of certain meanings only negligibly affected the "appropriate" matchings of normals, in the case of schizophrenics there was an appreciable effect. In other words, schizophrenics seem to be less oriented than are normals towards the exploitation of distinctive and separate linear properties.

These conclusions are in accord with those which may be drawn from the analysis of the self-produced linear forms. As will be recalled, it was found there that schizophrenics were less oriented than normals towards the exploitation of distinctive linear properties for the representation of concepts.

The general lack of orientation of schizophrenics towards distinctively linear properties of a line medium is even more strikingly evidenced by the remarks of the patients concerning the bases for their choices in the matching experiments. As we have already noted in the study on linear naming, schizophrenics tended to use the line medium as a means for the drawing of pictures; similarly, in the matching experiments, where the line patterns confronting the subjects were definitely of a nonpictorial nature, many of the schizophrenics nevertheless tended to construe such patterns as if they were pictures of objects and happenings and then utilized the depicted objects as the vehicles of representation. For instance, the pattern shown in Fig. 21-4a might be taken as "lightning" and then seen as connected to *hate* because "I hate lightning."

This tendency to construe the linear patterns as objects or happenings, coupled with the embeddedness of objects in idiosyncratic-affective contexts, may be among the factors that contributed to the equivocality of the linear meanings. For example, one patient chose an angular pattern for both *good* and *misery*, that is, for a "positive" and for a "negative" term. In both cases she construed the patterns as "lightning"—not, however, as a circumscribed happening, but either as "lightning coming from heaven" or "lightning which is destructive and hence causes misery."

Concluding Remarks: Linear Naming in Schizophrenia and the Issues of Autonomy and Consensus

In concluding this chapter on the formation and apprehension of linear vehicles by schizophrenics, we may consider more closely the two interrelated issues that motivated our concern about schizophrenic linear "naming": the issue of autonomy and the issue of consensus.

In choosing schizophrenics as subjects, we hoped to gain information concerning: (1) the extent to which autonomy of linear vehicles obtains for individuals who are presumably dedifferentiated in their ego-world relationships, and (2) the extent to which such individuals concur with others (normals) as to the "meanings" carried by linear patterns in a limited "universe of discourse."

The results of Goldman's experiments indicate that schizophrenics, both in the production of linear "names" and in the apprehension of the meanings of linear vehicles, treated the line medium in a less autonomous manner than did normal subjects. This relative inability to treat the vehicles of a line medium as autonomous manifested itself in various ways: first, the patients showed a greater difficulty in differentiating the linear medium from other media, particularly from the medium of imaged objects and events; second, the patients were less able than the normals to distance the linear patterns from their personal strivings, momentary reactions, and personal-idiosyncratic life experiences; [4] finally, the patients showed a relative difficulty in

---

[4] One will recall our discussion of "mood-related responses." The same kind of collapse in symbolizer-vehicle "distance" as occurs in such responses was reflected in the matching experiments. For example, a subject would say, "the meaning of this line depends on how I feel—right now it means 'joy'"; or "lines mean different things on different days;" or "it depends from what side you look at it." The general lack of differentiation or reduced distance between schizophrenics and their pictorial or linear productions in cases of spontaneous drawing is illustrated in the case histories presented by J. Bobon, et al. (25), and M. Sechehaye (223).

articulating and organizing separate linear properties such as shape, direction, pressure, etc., an articulation and organization that would have enabled them to establish relatively stable forms in a systematic way, however fragmentary and unclosed such a system might be.

In light of this relative lack of autonomy of the linear medium it is not surprising that consensus—both in terms of the normal standard and with respect to the group of schizophrenics as such—was relatively less marked for the schizophrenic sample than for the normal sample. Goldman's study strongly suggests that a major factor in the relative lack of consensus found for the schizophrenics is the nature of the patients' cognitive organizations. Insofar as one formulates one's experiences so that there is a complete embeddedness in personalized reactions and idiosyncratic contexts, the relatively abstract qualities of an autonomous medium, even if they could be articulated, are of little value. Such abstract properties cannot convey contextualized, personalized feelings and ideas connected with a referent. Furthermore, the tendency towards concreteness and contextualization operates against the formation of vehicular properties that are self-contained, impersonal, objective. Thus, the general lack of differentiation which characterizes the self-object relationships of schizophrenics underlies both the relative lack of autonomy of symbolic media and the relative lack of consensus with regard to the meanings of symbolic vehicles.

chapter 22

The Representation of Simple Statements in a Nonverbal Medium

In going from the problem of the formation of nonverbal names to that of the formation of nonverbal symbols analogous to simple declarative statements, we follow the order in which we presented the ontogenesis of symbolization in the verbal medium (see Part II).

Before entering into the discussion of nonverbal analogues to simple sentences, we may briefly recall some of the issues treated in the chapters on the ontogenesis of verbal expression—issues which have a particular pertinence in the present context.

In Part II, *naming* was treated primarily with respect to the development of the depictive or designatory function. The chapter that followed the discussion of naming dealt with the early expressions prior to sentence-formation and with the emergence of the first sentence-like formations: in that chapter we were concerned with the function of establishing relations between referents, that is, of forming assertions. Thus, with the shift to an analysis of sentence-formation we moved to a new function quite distinct from the designatory function. To highlight this basic shift, we made a distinction between "names," the function of which is solely designatory, and "words," which have a *syntagmatic function*, that is, whose referents are located within a network of syntactic-grammatical categories.

From our analysis of the ontogenesis of sentence formation in the linguistic medium, we concluded that, at the earliest stages of infant speech, there are neither true words nor true sentences. The child's utterances do not have the differentiated structure of true sentences nor do they have that circumscribed reference and specific syntactic-grammatical status (subject or predicate, noun or verb, etc.) characteristic of true words. The earliest precursors of sentences—the *monoremes*—are global, undifferentiated expressions. From such monoremes, there develop linguistically quite articulated expressions, consisting of vocables with relatively delimited reference and specific syntactic functions. We emphasized that this development was a slow one: during a long formative period, the referents and functions of these externally distinct vocables are more or less fused or overlapping; only at relatively advanced stages of speech development do true words appear, correlative with the appearance of true sentences.

As with "names," one of the ways of studying the nature of *assertions* on more primitive levels of representation—other than those appearing in ontogenesis—is to request subjects to symbolize such assertions in a relatively novel, more or less unexploited medium. In one of our studies, the line medium was used as such a novel medium for the representation of assertions—assertions which, on the level of linguistic mediation, were of a subject (pronoun)-predicate (verb-complement) form.

In this investigation, fourteen college students participated as subjects. Each subject was first familiarized, through an illustration, with the fact that experiences can be represented by line patterns. The subject was then asked to transpose the sentences mentioned below into linear symbols, as far as possible utilizing nonrealistic, nonpictorial representations.

There were four series of sentences (assertions) presented for linear symbolization.

Series A: 1. He opens a bottle. 2. He opens a door. 3. He opens his eyes.

Series B: 1. He loves steak. 2. He loves horses. 3. He loves his wife.

Series C: 1. He catches a fly. 2. He catches a lion. 3. He catches a criminal.

Series D: 1. He closes a bottle. 2. He closes a door. 3. He closes his eyes.

After the line patterns were drawn, a series of inquiries was conducted with each subject. The aim of these inquiries was threefold: (1) to determine how each drawing represented the particular content it was drawn to express; (2) to determine the manner in which, and degree to which, linguistically articulated components of the event were represented in the line drawing; (3) to determine whether, and in what ways, properties of the linear medium, for example, size, shape, direction, pressure, repetition of parts, were used for representation of the content.

Turning now to the ways in which the subjects represented simple statements in linear patterns, one is struck by two—related—phenomena: first, despite the fact that each of the linguistic formulations of events consisted of three principal terms symbolizing three distinct components, the majority of the linear symbols consisted of not more than two distinct vehicles; second, although there was discrete and clearly articulated reference to an agent, action, and object in each of the linguistic statements, there was no such discrete articulation of reference on the level of linear representation. The following analysis will be pursued with regard to these two phenomena: first we shall start from the linear patterns and inquire into the manner in which they were organized to represent the assertions; and second, we shall start with the reference and inquire as to how, and to what degree, the linguistically articulated referents were represented in the linear productions.

Organization of Linear Patterns Representing Agent's Action on Object

As we have just noted, most of the linear representations, in contradistinction to the linguistic formulations, consisted of *fewer than three component vehicles*. Indeed, quite a number of linear symbols comprised only a *single, relatively undifferentiated vehicle*, which apparently served to represent the entire content expressed in a sentence. In Fig. 22-1 are illustrations taken from various subjects' drawings.

For example, *He loves steak* was represented by one subject as a stick figure with a distended 'stomach' (*a*), by another subject as a steak (*b*); for *He opens a bottle,* a subject drew a pattern primarily depictive of the action of opening a bottle (*c*); similarly, *He catches a fly* was represented by a subject through the depiction of "quick movement" (*d*); finally, the wavy, spreading-downward pattern (*e*) was a subject's linear expression of *He closes his eyes.*

These kinds of vehicles, in which the total content of a sentence is represented in one relatively undifferentiated form, might be conceived as linear analogues to *monoremes,* the earliest forms in the ontogenesis of sentence-formation. Thus considered, these linear productions provide *direct* insight into the nature of primitive forms of assertion, supplementing that information which can be gained only *in-*

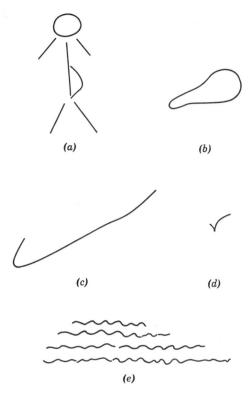

(a)

(b)

(c)

(d)

(e)

FIGURE 22-1. Unitary, undifferentiated symbols, representing: (a, b) *He loves steak*; (c) *He opens a bottle*; (d) *He catches a fly*; (e) *He closes his eyes.*

directly from the examination of infantile speech. Specifically, the adult subjects capable—in contradistinction to the young child—of reflecting on their own productions, gave clear evidence during the inquiries that their "linear monoremes" were intended to be global and situational in reference rather than circumscribed and discrete. For example, the pattern (c) of Fig. 22-1 did not refer to a delimited "action" component of *He opens a bottle* but included in its reference—in a diffuse and syncretic manner, to be sure—the agent who opens the bottle and the bottle top flying off.

Patterns consisting of *two* discernible parts or components were also found quite frequently among the linear productions. Superficially, these distinct components seem to refer to distinct features of the linguistically articulated event; the subjects' reports, however, made it clear that such discernible parts of the two-unit productions were not, in the main, distinct in their reference, but were rather *"pleonastic"* or *overlapping*. Thus, in these two-unit patterns, there were no circumscribed parts referring uniquely to a circumscribed component of the event, that is, no part symbolized agent, action, or object alone.

To illustrate, one subject represented *He catches a lion* by a pattern (Fig. 22-2*a*) consisting of two parts: in the words of the subject, the first part (the small loops) represented "he-in-the-process-of-catching-something," while the second part (the big loop) depicted "both the action-of-catching-a-large-object, and the-object-which-is-caught." Another subject used a two-unit linear pattern—similarly pleonastic —to represent *He opens a door* (Fig. 22-2*b*); one part depicted "opening of a door," and the other referred to "door open." A third illustration of such two-unit pleonastic representations is given in Fig. 22-2*c*. Here, *He catches a criminal* was being represented; the straight horizontal forked line depicted "he-firm-of-purpose-going-ahead-in-a-

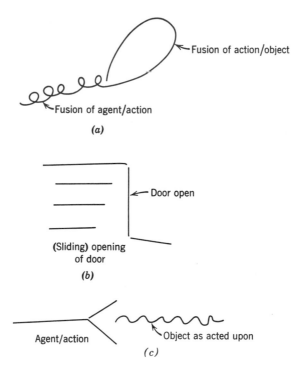

FIGURE 22-2. **Two-unit linear symbols, overlapping in reference:** (*a*) *He catches a lion;* (*b*) *He opens a door;* (*c*) *He catches a criminal.*

straightforward-way-and-blocking-off-escape;" the wavy line depicted "the-criminal-as-crooked-and-devious-being-trapped."

Thus, these two-unit linear symbols, in general, overlapping in reference, appear to be formally analogous to the early two-unit utterances in child speech (see Chapter 10); it will be recalled that much evidence pointed there to the pleonastic, overlapping character of the referents of the early two-unit utterances or *duoremes*.

Though the great majority of the linear productions consisted of one or two units, there were also a number of patterns structured in terms of three relatively distinct units; in practically all these productions, too, the same *pleonastic* and overlapping reference of the symbol-components obtained as was found for the two-unit patterns.

From our analysis of the linear productions intended as representations of sentence-contents, the conclusion may be drawn that, on the level of linear symbolization, distinct components of symbolic patterns do not function as equivalents to true "words" but rather to globally apprehended "names." That is, they do not denote a categorically defined and circumscribed aspect of an event—a thing per se or an action per se but refer to a more or less comprehensive situation.

Representation of Linguistically Separate Components of Events in the Line Medium

Thus far, the relationship between linear vehicle and reference has been examined by starting with the total symbolic pattern and its organization of discernible parts whose meaning (reference) we tried to determine. In a further analysis of vehicle-referent relationship which follows below, we started with the reference rather than with the vehicular pattern; here we sought to determine how and to what extent the discernible components of the linguistically given assertion, namely, agent, action, object, were represented by the linear symbol.

Linear Representation of Agent

In the linguistic assertions—typical of modern Indo-European languages—two general, formal features mark representation of the agent: the agent of action (*he*) is expressed (1) *overtly*, and (2) *independently*. In other words, there is always a vehicle that represents the agent; this vehicle is reserved for the agent alone and refers to none of the other major components of the assertion. To what extent then, we may ask, do these characteristics of *overtness* and *independence* obtain in the representation of the agent in linear productions?

The findings give a clear-cut answer to this question. First, in almost one-half (43 percent) of the linear productions, there was *no overt* representation of the agent altogether, that is, there were no features of the line patterns which served in any way to depict or represent the agent explicitly. Second, *not one* of the subjects, in those remaining linear productions where the agent was depicted at all, showed *true independence* of agent-representation—in the sense that the agent was symbolized in the identical way irrespective of action or object components of the situations.

These findings lead to the conclusion that in the linear productions there is no representation of the agent per se, as a separate and circumscribed component of situations; in other words, the agent is represented in a manner affected by the nature of the action he performs or the object upon which the action is performed.

This relative lack of differentiation of agent from other aspects of a total event was, in the main, manifested in two ways: (*a*) by *fusion,* in which a vehicle serving to represent the agent at the same time syncretically depicted other aspects of the event; or (*b*) by *modulation,* in which a vehicle primarily serving to represent the agent was varied more or less slightly in different contexts to reflect either the action or the object of action.

Turning first to *fusion,* it should be stressed that one is dealing with a truly *syncretic symbol.* To illustrate, one subject, for *He loves his wife,* produced the pattern of Fig. 22-3*a*, where the downward spiralling line represented both the agent and his action in an indissoluble unity.

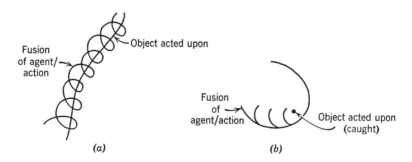

FIGURE 22-3. **Syncretic symbols involving fused representation of agent-action; (*a*) *He loves his wife*; (*b*) *He catches a fly.***

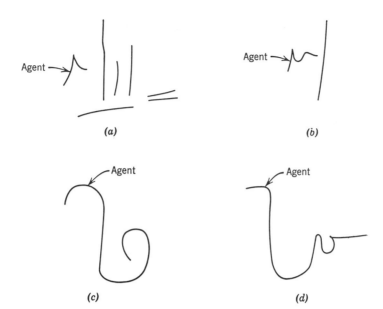

FIGURE 22-4. Modulation of agent-symbol to reflect different action-object contexts: (a) *He closes a bottle;* (b) *He closes a door;* (c) *He opens a bottle;* (d) *He opens a door.*

In another illustration of fusion—a depiction of *He catches a fly* (Fig. 22-3*b*)—the agent and his action were again syncretically represented by one symbol: the hand-like aspect of the pattern represented both the agent who grasps and his grasping.

Agent-representation in terms of *modulation* involves a lesser degree of undifferentiatedness between agent and other parts of the situation than does fusion: here, a particular vehicle is used primarily to represent the agent, but, nevertheless, by some modulation of its basic form, it also reflects some aspect of the action or the object. In such cases, then, there is neither complete fusion with the total symbol nor is there true independence of agent-representation.

Illustrations of modulation of the agent-symbol *he* are given in Fig. 22-4*a* and *b*. For *He closes a bottle*, a subject depicted *he* as "he who bends over sharply because the (strong) activity of closing a bottle is *downward;*" on the other hand, for *He closes a door*, the same subject depicted *he* as a more rounded, wavy-like, horizontal line pattern (*b*) to express that "closing a door is an easy activity—not forceful."

A second subject (Fig. 22-4*c* and *d*) represented *he* in *He opens a* *bottle* by a roundish, upwardly starting line to indicate the roundness of the object (bottle); in his second drawing, for *He opens a door, he* became a straight, horizontal line reflecting the flatness of the object (door).

In sum, then, the findings in regard to agent-representation by linear patterns lead to the following conclusions: (1) frequently, the agent is not represented overtly; (2) where the agent is represented, there is hardly ever an independent representation, but rather one in which the agent is depicted as influenced by his action or/and the object acted upon.

Some quantitative data may be mentioned here pertaining to fusion and modulation in those cases where agent-representation was overt. These data suggest that agent tended to be fused much more frequently with action than object (frequency ratio approximately 8:1); this was not true with respect to modulation. Here, there was a slight inclination to modulate the representation of agent more frequently in regard to the object than in regard to the action (frequency ratio approximately 3:2).

In consonance with the assumption of the line medium as a primitivizing medium, one may then conclude that at earlier levels of representation of agent's action on objects, the symbol for the agent—if it is formed at all—shows all the typical marks of undifferentiatedness. It is, in general, so formed as to reflect various other aspects of the total context in which the agent is embedded; circumscribed representation of agent per se hardly ever occurs.

Linear Representation of Action

As with agent-representation, the characteristics of the representation of action in the linear medium can best be brought to the fore by contrasting them with the features of the representation of action in the linguistic statements; there action was *overtly* symbolized and represented as a relatively *independent* content, that is, it did not include reference to concrete features of either agent [1] or object. Furthermore, action was symbolized as a generalized rather than concrete-specific activity; for example, one of the verbs referred to the general act of "opening" rather than to specific actions such as "bottle-open-

---

[1] Of course, the verb-form in the English statements, in its suffigation, still contains some formal, abstract-general—but never concrete—reference to the agent.

Pushing force

Cork

Open bottle

(a)

Bottle in the "state of being closed'

(b)

He closes a bottle

FIGURE 22-5. Overtness of action-representation in regard to (*a*) a strict criterion, (*b*) a loose criterion.

ing," "door-opening." The question then arises as to what extent overtness, independence, and generality of action were manifested in the linear symbols.

Let us first consider *overtness*. According to a *strict* criterion for overtness requiring the presence of some linear feature expressing action, in 40 percent of the linear symbols action was not at all represented. Even if one adopts a rather loose criterion and attributes overtness of action-representation to productions where the action was at least alluded to by the way in which the object acted upon was represented, there were still a number of the productions (15 percent) without such overt action-representation. The drawings of two subjects for *He closes a bottle* (Fig. 22-5) may serve to clarify the distinction between a *strict* and *loose* criterion of overt action representation.

In regard to *independence* of action-representation, that is, codification by a vehicle reserved entirely for action per se, it can be stated that *not one instance of such independence* occurred in the linear productions: whenever a vehicle was used to represent action, it also referred implicitly or syncretically to the agent or/and object. As a consequence, such interpenetration of other components in the representation of action *precluded* symbolization of *action-in-general:* there was never a representation of "open" per se or "close" per se, but rather of "door-opening," "bottle-closing," etc.

In the main, the relative lack of independence of action-representation was manifested in the linear productions in three ways: (*a*) *fusion,* (*b*) *concrete assimilation,* and (*c*) *modulation.* Each of these types of relatively undifferentiated action-representation is illustrated below.

Fusion of *action* with *agent* has already been discussed and is illustrated by the syncretic symbols of Fig. 22-3. Syncretic fusion of *action*

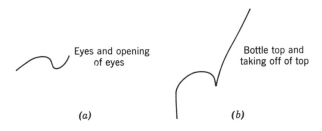

FIGURE 22-6. Syncretic symbol, showing fused representation of action-object: (*a*) *He opens his eyes*; (*b*) *He opens a bottle.*

and *object* are exemplified in Fig. 22-6. In (*a*) is reproduced one subject's drawing for *He opens his eyes;* the syncretic character of the part characterized by the subject as "the hook" is indicated in the subject's remark: "The hook is the opening of the eyes as well as the eyes, all in one." (*b*) is a reproduction of another subject's drawing for *He opens a bottle:* the linear pattern represented both "the top of the bottle" and "the process of the top being taken off."

While fusion involves a relatively extreme degree of globality or undifferentiatedness of the action vehicle, there are other forms of interpenetration that come somewhat closer to independence of action-representation. In *concrete assimilation,* the vehicle functions primarily for the representation of action but is shaped qualitatively to reflect features specific to a particular kind of object acted upon. In other words, the relatively abstract, general, invariant verb forms of the sentences become transformed for linear representation into concrete, object-specific action-symbols.

Assimilation was characteristically manifested through a change in shape of an action-vehicle depending on the concrete situation involved. The drawings of Fig. 22-7, produced by two subjects, exemplify assimilative variations in action-symbols.

In *modulation,* as in assimilation, action is represented by its own distinct vehicle; unlike assimilation, however, the modulation of the action vehicle reflects the influence of the object not through *qualitative* changes, but through *quantitative* variations (size, pressure, etc.) of a basically constant action-symbol.

Since the shape of the vehicle typically carries the basic meaning, the basic "theme," of the symbol, such variations of shape in regard to size, pressure, etc., function as "linear modifiers" (remotely analogous to linguistic modifiers) of the basic theme.

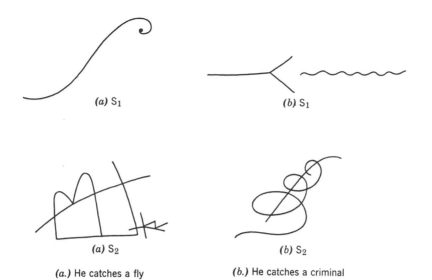

(a.) He catches a fly   *(b.)* He catches a criminal

FIGURE 22-7. Line drawings by two subjects (S_1, S_2) exemplifying concrete *Assimilation* of action-symbol to the particular object and situation involved.

Two illustrations of modulation are given in Fig. 22-8. In both, the action-symbol was varied in size: in (a), this variation reflected for the subject the differential importance of the objects towards which "love" is directed; in (b), the variation referred to the "degree of complexity and effort" entailed in "catching" the different objects.

The various findings with regard to action-representation lead, once again, to the conclusion that the transformation of linguistically encoded assertions into linear encoding conduces to a *dedifferentiation* of representation. In not a single case was there representation of action per se, that is, action independent of other components of the sentence-content.

Nevertheless, from a developmental point of view, one may look at the three kinds of interpenetration as reflecting steps in a genetic sequence, leading from a level of syncretic fusion of action and agent- or object-reference to a level of object-specific action-vehicles and then to a representation of action in which the vehicle is modulated without basic change in order to express variations in size, intensity, complexity, etc., of the object. It is clear that the linear modulation reflects a genetically relatively high level of symbolization: that is,

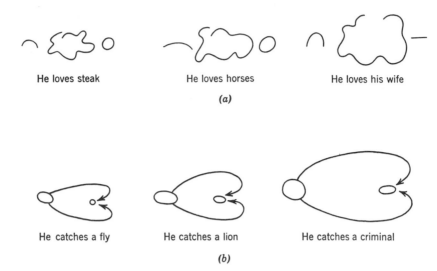

He loves steak   He loves horses   He loves his wife

(a)

He catches a fly   He catches a lion   He catches a criminal

(b)

FIGURE 22-8. *Modulation of action-symbols.*

modulation as a method of action variation comes as close to being analogous to linguistic modification of verbal action by morphemes (adverbs, etc.), as the medium of expressive lines permits.

Linear Representation of Object

In each of the linguistically expressed assertions, the object was *overtly* and, moreover, *independently* represented, that is, there was a symbol which referred to the object per se, irrespective of agent or action. The question again arises as to the extent to which overtness and independence obtained in the linear representations of the object.

Let us first turn to the findings in regard to *overtness*. According to a frequency survey, in about 30 percent of the total number of the linear productions there was *no overt* representation at all of the object. It was also evident from this survey that the nature of action was an important factor determining the presence or absence of overt object representation: overt object-symbolization was far more often lacking with the "love" and "catch" series than with the "open" and "close" series.[2]

---

[2] Overtness was lacking in 48 percent and 37 percent of the representations involving "love" and "catch" respectively, as compared with 19 percent and 14 percent of the representations for the "open" and close" series respectively.

As to exemplifications of linear productions involving the absence of overt object-representation, we may recall those previously presented instances of alteration in the vehicle for action that reflected the objects acted upon, without the objects themselves being depicted explicitly.

As to the degree of *independence* of object symbols in the instances of overt object-representation, the findings are clear-cut: there was *not one instance of completely independent object-representation*. In other words, whenever objects were depicted, they were always represented in such a manner as to indicate or reflect the action, the agent, or both. This relative lack of articulation of circumscribed object-representation was manifested in two main ways: *fusion* and *ingredience*. In *fusion*, the vehicle simultaneously depicts the object and some other content such as action or agent; in *ingredience*, the object is depicted in a certain state so as to indicate the specific action executed upon it.

Since illustrations of fusion have already been presented in our discussions on agent- and action-representation (see Figs. 22-2 and 22-6), we may exemplify here only an instance of representation pertaining to *ingredience* of action in object representation (Fig. 22-9). In the drawing for *He opens a door,* the object (door) is first depicted in the state of being closed and then of being open; this sequence reflects the process of action expressed in the statement, "He opens a door."

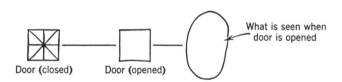

FIGURE 22-9. **Illustration of *Ingredience* of action in object-representation:** *He opens a door.*

Concluding Remarks

The results of our study clearly point up the fact that happenings involving an agent's action on objects are not symbolically articulated in a linear medium in terms of a discrete and independent agent, a discrete, independent, and general action, and a discrete and independent object. In sharp contrast to advanced stages in the linguistic (Indo-European) articulation of events in which—ideally—agent, action, and object referents are conceived in relative independence, in linear mediation these diverse components are represented either in syncretic fusion or in various lesser degrees of interpenetration with each other.

From a developmental point of view, the lack of differentiation and articulation of happenings consequent upon the use of linear mediation suggests that such mediation conduces to a more primitive level of representation. Operation at a more primitive level of symbolization is also indicated by the frequent absence of overt representation of one or more of the major components of happenings, that is, the omission of agent, action, and/or object. Presumably such omission occurs because of the lack of distance between symbolizer and vehicle: much of the representational activity is covert occurring in a medium other than lines, for example, inner gestures, imagery. We shall come back to this point later.

To be sure, the use of a linguistic medium does not preclude representation involving undifferentiatedness of expression. As will be recalled, such lack of differentiation and articulation is characteristic of the linguistic assertions of young children. This leads one to expect that, irrespective of the medium of representation, whenever the conditions (for example, status of the symbolizer, nature of the medium, the context of discourse, etc.) conduce to genetically earlier modes of representation, the categorial distinctions between agent, action, and object will be weakened and even dissolved.[3]

---

[3] This expectation will guide us in our later discussion of some of the characteristics of linguistic representation among nonliterate peoples (cf. Chapter 25).

chapter *23*

The Expression of Time in Nonverbal Media of Representation

The study discussed in the foregoing chapter has shown how a nonverbal medium of representation, that of expressive line patterns, tends to evoke genetically less "advanced" modes of articulating and organizing experience than are attainable through (English) linguistic codification. Those inquiries provided some indication of the ways in which one would be channelized into apprehending agent's action on objects were one limited to a medium of representation close to gesture. In the present chapter we extend our investigation into primordial analogues of linguistically articulated conceptions by examining the ways in which *temporal loci* of action are expressed in nonverbal media of representation.

Space and time constitute the fundamental framework for the establishment of our human world of action and thought. Without this framework, the flux of sensuous experience would remain forever undifferentiated and unarticulated, and we would not be able to experience the universe but as a chaos of formless, fleeting, unrelated happenings. Again, without some sort of *representation* of space and time —however crudely articulated and fragmentary it might be—there would be no cognition of a world of objects, no consciousness of self or others; we would never be able to go beyond animal reaction and action to the human level of *knowledge about* reality. In light of this

399

tremendous importance of space and time for the organization of our human world, it is clear why languages—basic instruments for cognitive construction and organization—possess means, of greater or lesser efficacy, for representing events and objects in spatial and temporal relations to each other.

Despite the importance of both of these aspects of events, it is apparent, at least from the history of Indo-European languages [1] and from the study of ontogenesis with regard to children in Western societies,[2] that the formation of temporal indicators is a much slower, more involved, and "difficult" process than is the articulation of spatial indicators. The main factor underlying this difference in development is, of course, the lesser concreteness of temporal as compared with spatial conceptions. It is this relative abstractness of time that has led us to inquire into the nonverbal representation of temporal, rather than spatial, characteristics of events. By requiring individuals to utilize a rather primitive medium to represent events in time, we hoped to gain some insight into primordial stages of the symbolic expression of time—stages which, at least in formal respects, may be considered as developmental forerunners of the advanced codification of temporal aspects of reality, realizable only through more or less abstract linguistic means.

In regard to such early stages in the representation of temporality, there is, of course, a considerable body of information coming from studies on the ontogenesis of speech. Before entering into the discussion of the experiments on nonverbal representation of temporality, it might be advantageous to outline, briefly, major steps in the verbal expression of time, as these unfold in ontogenesis.

A Brief Excursus into the Ontogenesis of Time Expression

In general, Indo-European languages codify time in two ways: by separate words (adverbs such as *yesterday, later,* etc.) and by verb indicators of aspects and tenses. Underlying this codification is the comprehension of time qua an objective sequential framework, rela-

---

[1] Cf. Chapter 25, on linguistic parallels.

[2] The literature indicates that children's speech is almost completely bare of temporal terms at a period (second year) during which spatial designators are already used in abundance; on the average, it is not before the third year that temporal designators come clearly to the fore (Stern, 242, p. 261; Leopold, 150, III, p. 60).

tively independent of the person speaking or of the particular action taking place. In contrast to these self-contained temporal distinctions, the very early expressions in ontogenesis suggest that time is initially cognized as completely embedded in the child's concrete momentary action, attitudes, or needs with respect to his immediate environment. Leaving aside, for the moment, the formation of adverbial expressions, one may distinguish the following four steps in the ontogenesis of verbal expressions of temporality: [3]

STEP 1. A temporal aspect is implied by monoremic (holophrastic) expressions which may indiscriminately take the external form of a noun, verb, adjective, or simply of an interjection. In any case, temporality is embedded in the total event comprising subjective as well as objective aspects of the situation. Immediate futurity may be implied by expressing a need, such as asking for bread (*pain!*) or for "promener," that is, for going from one place to another (*mené-mené!*).[4] On the other hand, the immediate past may be referred to by thing-words (*huhu* = bottle; i.e., I just drank a bottle of milk) or action words (*sia-butz!* i.e., Look—I just fell down).[5]

STEP 2. With increasing differentiation of thing-words (nouns) and action words (verbs), temporal aspects—although still fused with a particular event and the child's affective attitude—are carried more and more by action-words. The shift from unitary, monoremic expressions, implying *futuric* aspects to words denoting action seems facilitated by the emergence of two-word sentences. "During the third year," comments Stern on the progress of Hilde, "the imperative sentences composed of an infinitive and a substantive increase greatly." Whereas this child had previously made the request *lade!* (chocolate!), she now exclaims *lade essen!* (chocolate eat!). Just as futurity is alluded to by imperative-like action-words expressing a need to be fulfilled, so is *pastness* implied in event-words that connote disappearance, termination of happening, satiation, accomplishment of a performance, and the like. For instance, the 1;9-year-old Hilde called out *fettig!* (finished) after having emptied her bottle; she exclaimed triumphantly

---

[3] A more detailed account of this development would, of course, have to include the preverbal forerunners of temporality such as anticipatory bodily attitudes and gestures, the motoric behavior indicating that an action is "finished," etc.

[4] Both are expressions, one "nominal," the other "verbal," of a 1-year-old French child. Perez (188, p. 249).

[5] Stern (242, p. 89), referring to Gunther's expressions at 1;8.

steh-steh! after having succeeded in climbing up and standing at the top of a chest.[6]

It is noteworthy that almost all vocabularies of children mentioned in the literature have expressions for disappearance (*all gone!*); these expressions, as Miss Shinn has pointed out, are just as much mood terms as terms denoting change of environment. Moreover, the way such terms are used points to another characteristic of early temporal expressions: often enough past and future and even present are merged or fluctuate in the verbal utterances. It depends on the way the child is affectively involved whether the accent is on the "overness" with its implication of the past, the suddenness of change with its implication of the "now," or the desire of reappearance with its implication of the future.

STEP 3. Whereas in the previous stages temporality is *implied* by a particular action word itself, at this stage temporal aspects *as such* begin to be articulated as variable characteristics of an articulated and relatively self-contained action. In other words, the particular action-words now begin to be *modulated,* thus indicating changes in the aspective characteristics of such action. However, although children advance during their third year toward the expression of some such seemingly pure temporal variations of a verb theme, acute observers of child speech, such as Stern and Gregoire, caution us not to interpret this phenomenon as an indication that the child has actually acquired the linguistic notion of "temporal locus" or "tense." For him, these "tense" forms, for a good many months or even years, still seem to refer to characteristic aspects of a *present action* rather than indicate placement of action in a "receptacle of time." Thus, as Gregoire (86, II, p. 129) points out, verbs may be modulated to form imperatives and past participles at a time when true tense expressions of future and the imperfect have not yet appeared. This observation, pertaining to the speech development, not only of French, but also German- and English-speaking children, must be interpreted to mean that these modulated forms still express temporality in terms of the present event. Thus, at this stage, past participles are descriptive words *defining a present state* as a consequence or termination of a preceding (past) action: e.g., *soldat cassé* (soldier broken!); *tombé, papa!* (I fell down, papa!); *aneziet!* (I am dressed up).[7]

---

[6] Stern (242, p. 35).

[7] Gregoire (86, II, p. 129); see also Stern (242, p. 53).

The development toward differentiation of aspects of activity through *verb modulation proper* becomes manifest in such utterances as that of the 2-year-old Hilde Stern (242, p. 47): asking for the milk bottle, she exclaimed *fasche tinken!* (bottle-drink); after having finished the bottle she stated *fasche tunken!* (bottle-drunk).

STEP 4. The final step, covering the longest period of speech development, involves processes aimed at mastery of temporality qua tense. This development is intertwined with and facilitated by the emergence of time words (adverbs). Through such coupling of morphological modification of verbs and adverbs of time, the stage is gradually reached in which tense distinctions are correctly understood and employed, that is, a stage in which the child is able to codify activity at specific positions—past, present, future—on a time line.

In concluding this brief sketch, we may note that the careful study of the ontogenesis of speech provides a remarkable insight into the ways in which the increasing symbolic articulation of experience— into subjective and objective domains, into a world of stable things and actions—goes hand in hand with the increasing articulation of temporality as a relatively independent framework in which events occur, objects change, etc.

The ontogenesis of temporal expressions shows clearly the operation of two important developmental principles. First, it reflects the general *principle of increasing differentiation.* Temporality is initially embedded, or even "buried," in the expression of specific, concrete-affective action. Later, though still bound to action, it begins to be distinguished from the concrete action; this is reflected through modulation of the action-designator (verb). Finally, temporality becomes clearly differentiated from the action themes, insofar as it is now expressed through general linguistic indices which are attached to whole classes of verbs. Second, it reflects the *principle of the exploitation of old means for novel functions.* The child in his initial expressions of temporality employs available action words which imply or allude to time-of-action. Only later does he advance to the understanding and use of specific linguistic devices for codifying temporality.[8]

---

[8] It may be briefly noted that the early development of "adverbs" of time (e.g., *yesterday, tomorrow, now, later,* etc.) closely parallels that of temporality indicators in verbs: many students of child speech have observed their emergence within an ego-involved concrete-action context whereby temporality is *alluded* to through reference to an affectively toned situation including the speaker's

We may now turn to the main theme of this chapter, the representation of temporality in nonverbal media. The two media considered here are those of expressive line patterns and visual imagery. Since both of these media, to different degrees, are assumed to conduce to a "primitivization" of symbolic expression relative to linguistic codification, one would expect parallels between the representation of time in these media and the ontogenetically early linguistic expression of time. It is in this regard that the findings on child speech can be expected to prove a valuable guide in the analysis of linear and imaginal representation of time; conversely, the findings to be presented, in conjunction with ontogenetic studies, should enable one to draw a fuller and more comprehensive picture of the development of temporal representation.

REPRESENTATION OF TIME-OF-ACTION IN A MEDIUM OF EXPRESSIVE LINES

The method employed in this study was quite similar to that used in the inquiry pertaining to agent's action on objects (Chapter 22). In this case, the sentences that subjects had to "translate" into linear vehicles pertained to agent's action in time. Using the pronoun "he" to denote the agent, we constructed sixteen sentences from four verbs and four tense indicators.

He runs	He tries	He yields	He loves
He is running	He is trying	He is yielding	He is loving
He ran	He tried	He yielded	He loved
He will run	He will try	He will yield	He will love

Each subject, after having drawn all sixteen patterns, was presented with a number of questions, analogous to those used in the agent-action-object study. He was asked how each of the line drawings represented the meaning evoked by the sentence; in what way—if at all—agent per se, action per se, and temporal locus per se were represented in the total linear pattern; how—if at all—various components or characteristics of the linear vehicles (shape, page position, pressure, direction, length, etc.) expressed either a part or the

---

attitude. For instance, Decroly and Degand (52) give illustrations of expressions that allude to temporality in expressing *regret* that a pleasant event ceases too quickly, that a disagreeable one lasts too long, or in expressing the *wish* to lengthen, shorten, or postpone an event: e.g., *pas encore dormir* (not yet sleep) = I don't want to go to sleep; *toujours* (always) = I wish this would last long, etc. (2;4–2;8 yrs.).

whole of the sentence-meaning, and so on. Twelve college students served as subjects.

In discussing the findings, we shall deal, in some detail, with the interdependence of *form* and *meaning* in the representation of temporality: we shall show how the *structure* of the linear vehicle and the *connotations* of temporality are closely intertwined. First, however, it is important to stress a very basic characteristic of the linear representation of temporality vis-à-vis linguistic codification, *the relatively global expression of time in the linear medium*.

In our linguistic formulations of events, we characteristically utilize distinct means for referring to agent, to activity, and to time of activity. Each of these means is more or less independent of the other, so that we can—broadly speaking—change one without changing the others. For example, we can change "he" to "she" without altering the means for expressing the activity; again, we can often use the same suffix to indicate past tense, irrespective of the nature of the activity-designator (verb). Linguistically, then, we dissect happenings into conceptual elements which are relatively independent of each other.

Such relative separateness of agent, activity, time-of-action, object-of-action, etc., as one finds in linguistic codification does not obtain in the organization of events, lived through sensory-motorically and apprehended perceptually. When one perceives something happening, one does not see an agent isolated from his action or an activity isolated from the agent acting. On the level of perception, an agent's action is concrete and particularized; one does not see a generalized person engaged in an abstract activity but rather a particular individual, acting in a particular way, with respect to a particular object, and in a particular context. Again, on the level of perceptual apprehension of events, one does not always look on with affective or evaluative indifference; inherent in much of our perception is our feeling about the happenings in which we participate or the states of affairs of which we are spectators.

To be sure, linear representation is at quite a distance from the perceptual apprehension of events; much further away, as we shall see, than is imagery representation. Nevertheless, when compared with the linguistic codification of experience, linear representation still shows its affinity—in certain formal respects—to the organization of events in perception.

Stated in terms of developmental conceptualization, the "translation" of linguistic phrases into a symbolic medium, deriving from organismic-gestural expressivity, leads to a *dedifferentiation* of representation, that is, a reversal of the developmental process of increasing differentiation and articulation. In contradistinction to linguistic codification, events as represented linearly are not expressed in terms of distinct and independent marks for agent, action, time-of-action, etc. Rather, the various (linguistically isolable) components of events are represented in their *interdependence and concrete relatedness to each other.* Thus, the depiction of action affects, and is affected by, the degree and manner in which one expresses his feelings about the action; the depiction of qualifications or specifications of action (carried by independent adverbs in English) interpenetrates, and is determined by, the manner in which one is inclined to characterize the "generic" action; the expressions of activity and of time-of-action mutually interact and determine each other; and so on.

In order to assess the degree of articulation of temporality in linear representation, that is, the degree of distinctness with which temporal connotations are realized relative to the extreme poles of perceptual-affective-motor experience and linguistic codification of such experience, we may first consider briefly the characteristics of an ideal symbolic system, in which action and time-of-action are rather clearly and unambiguously registered. Such a system is characterized, in the main, by the following features: (1) the various events (verb-themes) are distinctly differentiated from one another; (2) each theme is more or less invariantly represented, irrespective of time-of-event, that is, the expression of an action is independent of the indication of temporality; (3) the different temporal loci of an event are represented by distinctly different indicators (past of an action is indicated differently from present or future, etc.); (4) each particular temporal locus is represented in relative invariance, that is, independent of variations in action (e.g., pastness of action A is expressed by the same means as pastness of action B).[9]

Now, an evaluation of the productions of the subjects with reference to these four characteristics of an ideal action-time code showed clearly that linear representation of events-in-time is typically *global and undifferentiated.*

---

[9] It may not be superfluous to note that such an ideal system, though potentially realizable in language, has never been completely realized in any of our languages: languages have not developed solely—or even mainly—in the service of systematic logical organization of experiences. Nevertheless, some languages come closer than others to realizing these requirements.

The analysis of the linear productions revealed:

(1) *Relative lack of differentiation of themes.* The chief means for expressing the distinctive characteristics of an activity in the linear medium is through shape of the pattern; therefore, in assessing distinctness of representation of any one activity with regard to others, the intra-series commonness of shape was compared with intra-series similarity. It was found that the great majority of subjects produced vehicles for one verb-series that could, to varying degrees, be confused with vehicles for one or more of the other series.

(2) *Relative lack of differentiation of theme and time-of-action.* The second characteristic entails that the four vehicles for any given verb-series would show a "family resemblance" with respect to shape, a resemblance indicating that they all pertained to the same theme, irrespective of variation in time. Even on the basis of a loose criterion of "constancy of shape," in only one-half of the sets of vehicles for a verb-series was there visible evidence of theme-constancy, irrespective of time. In the other half of the sets, at least one of the vehicles differed markedly from the others in shape.

(3) *Relative lack of articulation in expression of different time loci of a given event.* Clearly different means for expressing different temporal loci were rarely manifested. The main reason for this lack of articulation was the intimate fusion of theme and temporality already mentioned; it was often not possible to determine the means for expressing time per se; hence, one could not determine in the various expressions for a theme whether temporal loci were distinguished from each other.

(4) *Relative lack of invariance in expressing temporal loci, irrespective of variation in action.* The realization of this—probably the most rigorous—requirement for systematic expression of temporality is, of course, dependent upon the other requirements for ideal systematization. This characteristic, which is at best only approximated in highly developed linguistic codes, did not even come close to realization in the linear productions.

The relative "undifferentiatedness" of linear vehicles for events-in-time does not mean that all of the linear productions manifested the same degree of globality or lack of inner articulation. In fact, the degree of articulation varied depending upon the subject, the verb-theme, the temporal locus of the action, etc. In other words, the linear productions ranged all the way from global-unitary vehicles, in which there were no separate means for the expression of theme and expression of time, to representations in which there was a closer approximation—with regard to articulation of the vehicular form—to the linguistically encoded statements of agent's action-in-time. In the main, the productions occupied a middle region between the two extremes, with only an occasional form at either extreme.

Thus far, we have considered the character of linear representation of action-in-time in terms of the organization of the linear *vehicles*. In light of our discussion of vehicle-referent relationships, especially with regard to the process of *reciprocal rotation* (see Chapter 20), we would also expect a "regression" in the *connotational sphere* of *reference*. Although it can be assumed that every English-speaking adult subject has at his disposal fully articulated concepts of temporality and temporal distinctions, the task of representing action-in-time through the vehicular means of a primordial medium leads to the emergence of connotations that are depictable by such means. In this medium-induced "regression," an adult subject seizes upon more or less earlier temporal notions, still deeply rooted in him and never fully forgotten. It is such exploitation of archaic notions of temporality that warrants relating linear representation of time to linguistic expression in early ontogenesis.[10]

In brief, then, the *expression* of agent's action-in-time in a linear medium was found to be relatively undifferentiated, with the means for expressing time fused with the means for representing other features of a total event, including the symbolizer's affective reaction. Correspondingly, the *reference* to temporality was not sharply separated from the reference to symbolizer's attitude, the reference to agent-characteristics, the reference to concrete action, etc. Although this general characteristic of *undifferentiatedness* marked off the linear representations from linguistic codification, there was a considerable range with respect to the degree of articulation of the linear vehicles and with regard to the abstractness of the temporal connotations expressed by lines. This range renders it feasible to order the subjects' performances, relating them grossly to genetic stages. In discussing these stages, we shall go from the most primitive and indirect ways of connoting temporal locus to connotations that are more closely related to abstract notions of time.

Global-Affective Reference to Temporality

The earliest utterances in ontogenesis having some pertinence to temporality are monoremic expressions that convey a child's wish for something not present, or his unhappiness at the no-longer-presentness

---

[10] The whole process here exemplifies the fundamental principle of *form-function interdependence,* so to speak, in reverse: in order for the linear medium to be used for the representation of temporality, there must be a shift to older "meanings" of time, capable of being realized through the less-differentiated means of the linear medium.

of something he had been enjoying. Such utterances are as a rule affectively intoned—the affective tone implying not-here-now.

In looking for parallels to this earliest stage in the linear productions, one would expect to find them in vehicles that represent one's affective reaction to an event-in-time rather than depicting the event-in-time itself. There was one subject whose representations approached such global-affective reference. For example, in representing *He will love* (Fig. 23-1a), her primary emphasis in the linear vehicle was on her negative reaction to the idea of love in the future: "This just can't be; you either do (love) or you don't . . . you can't forecast. 'He will love' is meaningless to me, so I've used a meaningless line to express it." This affective reaction served to distinguish *He will love* from loving now and loving in the past. It should be noted that there was no representation of either theme ("loving") or temporality ("future") as objective content.

Somewhat more advanced in regard to expression of temporality was the same subject's representation for *He tries* (Fig. 23-1b). Here again there was a strong affective reaction—negative and critical towards the agent of such an action, seen as "some kind of bug sitting there weakly waving its antennae . . . a static figure making weak, pitiable attempts." The affective reaction, thematic content, and

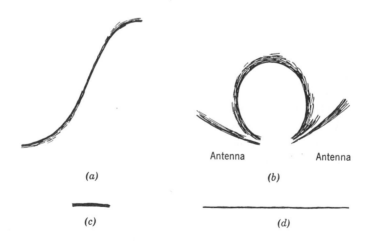

FIGURE 23-1. *a,b* Representations by *global-affective* reference to temporality: (*a*) *He will love* represented by "meaningless" line; (*b*) *He tries* represented by a bug's "pitiable" attempts. (*c,d*) Representation by reference to temporality through *agent-characteristics*: *He ran* expressed (*c*) by certainty; (*d*) by prostration.

temporality (the latter scarcely involved) were fused into a concrete happening. The linear medium was not directly exploited, but was used to picture a global situation. The picture itself primarily revealed the symbolizer's attitude—the thematic content being completely transformed by this attitude.

Reference to Temporality through Agent-Characteristics

Allusion to temporality becomes somewhat less indirect when a linguistically designated agent's-action-in-time is conceived in terms of some *agent-attitude* or *agent-posture,* which holophrastically implies a certain phase (at the beginning, in the midst, at the end) of a temporally extended concrete activity. Such agent-characteristics were typically exhibited in unitary vehicles, in which certain properties (length, pressure, straightness, etc.) served as the means for depicting the attitudes or postures.

For example, one subject grasped *He ran* in terms of the "certainty of the agent about past occurrence of an activity (one can never be so sure about future events)," to express this certainty, she formed a short, sharp, thick line (see Fig. 23-1c), which—through its succinctness, precision, and lack of fuzziness—conveyed the agent-attitude.

Another subject conceived *He ran* in terms of the condition of the agent following the activity, that is, "prostrated;" a more or less 'straight line' (Fig. 23-1d) depicting the posture ("stretched out") of one who, after having run, is now prostrate. The same subject used a similar but somewhat heavier pattern to represent *He is trying;* in this case, the vehicle depicted "tautness"—a posture characteristic of one who "strains" in the act of trying.

Whereas these agent-characteristics were often used rather unsystematically, that is, in only single instances of a verb-series for reference to a particular time, there were a number of cases in which such characteristics were exploited for referring to three, and even all four, of the temporal loci of an activity. Thus agent-characteristics served, to a certain degree, as a *concrete means for systematic reference to temporality.* One subject, for example, depicted all four tense-forms of *Run* in terms of agent-characteristics: "he-graceful-happy" (*He runs*); "he-more-graceful" (*He is running*); "he-awkward" (*He ran*); "he-in-fearful-tension" (*He will run*). Another subject differentiated three of the four temporal loci of *Try* by the following variations in agent-characteristics: "he-pessimistic-strong" (*He tries*); "he-optimistic-stronger" (*He is trying*); "he-pessimistic-weak, exhausted" (*He tried*).

These illustrations may suffice to show that, prior to the emergence of formal indicators of pure tense, it is possible to convey temporal distinctions through agent-characteristics such as posture, attitudes, etc., ingredient in concrete activity. In other words, these findings suggest that temporal reference through agent-characteristics is at least potentially exploitable for those seeking to codify temporal loci of action. Though such agent-characteristics are not typically exploited for temporal reference during the ontogenesis of the Western child,[11] they appear to play a significant role in the languages of some nonliterate peoples (see Chapter 25).

Reference to Temporality through Characteristics of a Phase of Concrete Action

This mode of apprehending agent's-action-in-time is perhaps the principal one under conditions of linear representation. Here, the conception of an action-in-time is grasped in terms of certain features that characterize a particular phase of a specific, concrete, temporally extended event. At this stage, although thematic content and temporal locus are still quite interwoven, both are more clearly articulated than at the previous stage; their fusion is chiefly manifested in the fact that a particular temporal locus is not grasped abstractly, but is conceived in terms of the specific action: *time, in other words, is theme-specific.*

In the main, the linear vehicles for expressing the connotations reflect the interpenetration of theme and temporality: the vehicles are relatively undifferentiated, that is, there are generally no distinct means for representing action on the one hand and temporality on the other. Because of the interpenetration of theme and temporality, a given temporal locus (for example, past) is expressed through different means for different activities; the means often depend upon the shape of the line intended to convey the action. Figure 23-2*a–d* may serve as an illustration: reproduced there are one subject's patterns for *He ran, He tried, He yielded,* and *He loved.* In the first case, past-

---

[11] One of the few reported instances in which variations in agent indicated temporal distinctions is that reported by Stern (242, pp. 20, 83): Hilde, at two years used *ich* (= I) interjectionally for the present and immediate future, e.g., "I get ball;" she employed her own name, Hilde, however, when reporting calmly about the past: *"Hilde-ba"* (= Hilde went for a walk).

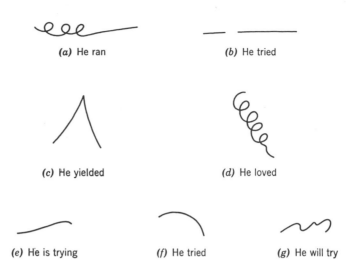

(a) He ran   *(b)* He tried

(c) He yielded   *(d)* He loved

(e) He is trying   *(f)* He tried   *(g)* He will try

FIGURE 23-2. Reference to temporality through characteristics of a phase of concrete action: (*a–d*): *Theme-specific* expressions of temporality (past); (*e–g*): *Time-specific* expression of activity.

ness was revealed in the transition from motion to no motion; somewhat similarly, the second vehicle depicted "something happening—then nothing happening (empty line);" the third pattern suggested pastness of *yield* by symmetrization, depicting "restoration of equilibrium . . . end of conflict;" finally, the pastness of *love* was expressed through "a downward dwindling away."

Now, just as time, at this stage, is theme-specific, so too is a given action (for example, trying) apprehended in terms of particular phases rather than abstractly and invariantly. In other words, *action is time-specific*. To be sure, there is often an *intended differentiation* between theme and temporality; the subject has in mind, for example, a certain shape for depicting the action per se; however, the intimate fusion of theme and temporality leads to different patterns for different tense forms of a given activity. The shape intended for the depiction of action is, so to speak, "deformed," because it also serves to express a particular temporal phase of the action. An illustration is presented in Figure 23-2*e–g*. Here one sees how the interpenetration of theme and temporality led one subject to form markedly different vehicles for the present, past, and future of *try*.

In some of the cases at this stage, one could see beginnings of differentiation between theme and temporality: although the vehicles for different tense-forms of an action (verb) showed considerable variation—reflecting the interpenetration of theme and temporality—the theme itself was dimly visible in each of the patterns. In other words, one sees here the beginnings of the device of *modulating action for the expression of temporality*. Figure 23-3 provides a good illustration. The theme of "yielding" was depicted as a "caving in" (shown in the first pattern, for *He yields*). This "standard" expression of the thematic content appears in modulated form for *He is yielding*, to show a back-and-forth struggle in the process of 'caving in.' The pattern for *He yielded* again expresses a modulation of the thematic content, indicating—by the static symmetry of the pattern—the final status, the irreversible resultant of the process of yielding. The tendency towards articulation of the theme, that is, differentiation of theme from temporality, was only slightly displayed in the representation for *He will yield*. Here the thematic content as well as its expression appear to have been thoroughly infused and altered by the overriding notion of what will happen in the future: "he will give some ground (the caving-in theme is slightly represented at the top), but eventually, he will triumph" (indicated by the upward direction of the linear pattern).

The stage of reference to temporality described in this section has its formal parallel in linguistic ontogenesis to the Western child's ways of referring to time prior to his understanding and use of tense forms (see pp. 400 ff). As we shall see, it is also analogous to the ways in which temporality is encoded in the languages of many non-literate societies (see Chapter 25).

Reference to Temporality through Spatial-Vectorial Relations of Agent's Action to Object or Goal

This stage in the development of reference to temporality is closely akin to the more advanced steps of the previous stage (such as is

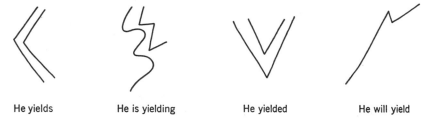

He yields　　　　　He is yielding　　　　　He yielded　　　　　He will yield

FIGURE 23-3. Reference to temporality through *modulation* of a concrete action.

exemplified in Figure 23-3) and yet foreshadows the next stage to be discussed, that of reference to temporality through generic aspects of action (see pp. 415 ff). Here, temporality is still, to some degree, interwoven with thematic content, but in comparison with the typical representations of the previous stage, the expression of thematic content is more clearly articulated and relatively more constant: the ideal theme is more apparent in the vehicles for the different tense-forms of a series. Again, although the means for expressing temporality are still to a great extent dependent upon and influenced by the ideal means for expressing a thematic content, there is at least partially a tendency to express temporal locus by *theme-transcendent devices,* for example, spatial-vectorial relations between agent's-action and goal, etc. In other words, the means for expressing theme and the means for expressing temporality are to some degree differentiated from each other and partly amenable to independent variation. Fig. 23-4 illustrates this mode of representation; it shows the codification by one subject for the progressive present, past, and future tenses of *try, yield,* and *love.*

As can be seen, "ideal" forms for each of the different thematic contents are rather clearly suggested in the representations for each of the tense-forms of a verb series. The ideal forms are not *fully manifested,* however, because temporal connotations still force some modification of the ideal expressions of thematic content per se. In other words, although thematic content is to some degree represented by near-uniform means, there is still considerable interpenetration of temporality and theme.

What is of great significance here is the insight we gain in regard to progress in the representation of temporality per se: it shows that despite the influence of theme on the connotations of temporality, approximately the *same means* can be used to express the same temporal locus for all three activities. For example, the progressive present is here expressed through a *vector of "coming close to" or "making contact with" the object:* thus, the "contact with the object" for *He is trying,* the "partial incorporation of agent by tempting object" for *He is yielding,* and the "interlocking or embracing between agent and object" for *He is loving,* were all realized, in part, through the theme-transcendent device of "close approximation." Again, the "not-yetness of, but intent towards, contact (making the attempt)" for *He will try,* the "not-yetness of giving in, but the attraction by the tempting object" for *He will yield,* and the "not-yetness of, but direction towards, embracing" for *He will love,* were all revealed, in part, through the theme-transcendent device of *vector towards object from a distance.*

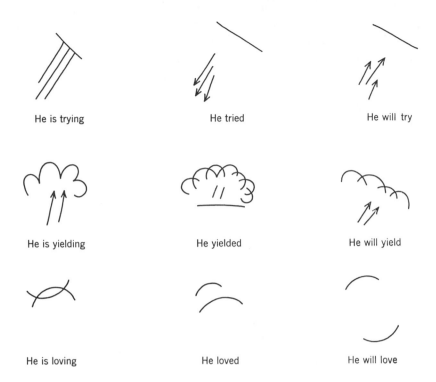

FIGURE 23-4. Reference to temporality through spatial-vectorial relations of agent's action to object or goal.

Even for the representations of activities in the past, there was some degree of theme-transcendence: the "giving up attempts" for *He tried* and the "rejection of the other" for *He loved* were both carried by a *reversal of vector* (from "going towards" to "turning away from"); however, the "complete giving in" for *He yielded* was not carried by such a reversal. Thus, one sees again how the interpenetration of theme and temporality—even when there is a considerable degree of differentiation—works against the complete systematization of temporality in linear representation.

Reference to Temporality through Generic Aspects of Action

A young child, growing up in a community speaking an Indo-European tongue, rarely—and then only for a brief, transitory period—refers to temporality through forms which convey a basic aspect or characteristic of thematic action. Quite early, any tendency in this direction is abruptly checked as the child turns towards the use of those highly developed morphological and syntactic means (i.e., tense indicators) that exist in Indo-European languages for the expression of pure temporal distinctions, irrespective of action.

As is well known, however, there are many languages, particularly those of nonliterate societies, in which means for the expression of true tense distinctions are lacking.[12] This is not to say that these languages lack means for referring to temporality; in fact, they possess very important linguistic devices for temporal reference. These languages, in the main, have available not only morphemes that express specific modulations of a thematic action (modulations that are still more or less theme-bound), but they also possess morphological means for conveying *generic aspects of action,* that is, aspects which transcend a particular theme or even a particular class of activities. Such means affixed to a linguistic form may, for example, indicate that an action is about to begin (*inceptive aspect*) or is coming to an end (*cessative aspect*) and so on. It seems clear that the presence of means for expressing these latter kinds of aspective connotations—means separable from the devices for expressing a specific theme—reflect a greater degree of articulation of temporality (and indicate a more marked differentiation between time-locus and theme) than any of the means thus far considered in our discussion of linear representation. This articulation of means for the expression of temporal locus (and this greater separateness of temporal expression from thematic representation) is, of course, more likely to enter into, and promote, a systematic codification of temporality.

The issue arises whether such generic aspects (for example, inceptive, cessative) were seized upon as a way of conceiving temporality by the subjects representing agent's-action-in-time in the linear medium. This issue really involves two questions, which must to some extent be considered separately. The *first* pertains to whether such generic aspects were conceived at all, irrespective of their mode of realization in the linear medium, or the degree to which they were systematically apprehended.[13] The *second* pertains to whether such generic aspects were not only conceived, but also *distinctively and un-*

---

[12] See Chapter 25.

[13] Here, we relied primarily on the subjects' remarks in explicating their vehicles. Since the subjects possessed linguistically articulated conceptions of time, it was possible for them to *mention* generic aspects—as a sort of secondary elaboration—even where there were no distinctive means for *expressing* the aspects in their linear productions.

ambiguously expressed in the linear medium by means separable from, and transcending, those employed for thematic representation.

The first question must clearly be answered in the affirmative. Whether or not the linear vehicles directly depicted an agent-characteristic (e.g., "he-taut"), a quality or phase of concrete action, or a relation of agent's action to object (e.g., "he-turning-away-from-her"), the subjects often stated that connotations such as "ongoingness," "overness," "nonactuality," etc., were implied or intended.

A further examination of the protocols gave some indication that certain generic aspects were more typically intended where the representations pertained to one temporal locus rather than to another. To determine this relationship more clearly, we tabulated the number of subjects who reported intending certain generic aspects in their representations for one or another of the four temporal loci. This information is presented in Table 23-1.

Table 23-1

Average number of subjects mentioning various generic aspects in the course of explicating linear vehicles for agent's-action-in-time *

Generic aspects	Tense-forms (temporal loci)			
	Simple present	Progr. present	Past	Future
Nonactuality	0.0	0.0	4.5	9.8
Ongoingness	7.5	11.81	.8	1.3
Completedness	.3	0.0	10.25	0.0
Detail-fullness	.3	5.3	1.3	0.0
Anticipative	.8	.3	0.0	9.8
Temporally neutral †	7.0	.3	0.0	.5
Uncertainty	.5	3.0	.5	5.0
Intensity	3.3	3.5	2.0	.3
Quantity (amount)	3.0	3.0	3.0	2.0
Enduringness	3.3	3.8	.8	.3
Cessative	.8	.3	3.3	0.0

* Averages derived from number of subjects mentioning the aspect for each of the four activities (verbs).

† The aspect of temporal neutrality is closely related to the declarative mode, i.e., it expresses activity in general, more or less indifferent to specific temporal locus.

The table suggests that in the main different generic aspects were intended, by a relatively large number of the subjects, for different temporal loci. Thus, activities in the simple present (SP) tended to be conceived chiefly in terms of "temporal neutrality" ("not really in time") or in terms of "ongoingness." Activities in the progressive present (PP) tended to be grasped, even more strongly, as implying "ongoingness" but also as implying "detail." Activities in the past were likely to be apprehended as implying "completedness" and (to a lesser degree) "nonactuality." Finally, activities in the future quite frequently suggested aspects such as "nonactuality," "anticipation," and (to a lesser degree) "uncertainty."

An examination of the table shows that the various generic aspects were not equally effective in distinguishing a particular temporal locus (for example, present) from the others. Thus, although "temporal neutrality" clearly indicated the simple present, "detail" the progressive present, "completedness" the past, and "anticipation" ("incipience") the future, "ongoingness" and "nonactuality" were not as specific with regard to the temporal locus they implied; "ongoingness" could imply either the simple present or progressive present, and "nonactuality" could indicate either the past or the future.[14]

In sum, then, the subjects, conceiving of events in time, were often led to think of generic aspects which to varying degrees served to indicate one temporal locus rather than another.

We may now turn to the second question pertaining to whether such aspects were not only *apprehended* in thought but also clearly *expressed* in linear representation. An examination of the protocols showed that generic aspects were rarely represented by clearly articulated, theme-transcendent means in the linear vehicles. Even where such means were used by a subject, they were mostly confined either to a single verb-series or for only one of the tense-forms.

Two illustrations may show how generic aspects were unambiguously expressed in the linear medium. In Figure 23-5a–d are reproduced one subject's vehicles for *run* in the different temporal loci. One will note that the same means, *shape*, was used throughout to express the thematic content. The principal "dimension" exploited for the repre-

---

[14] One may recall, in this connection, the indiscriminate use of early time words, e.g., *yesterday, tomorrow,* used now for past, now for future (i.e., not-now). "In the mind of the child," writes Gregoire (86, II, p. 129), "that which is not present —and this may refer to the past or the future—possesses a uniform character, *viz.,* that of non-existing at the moment."

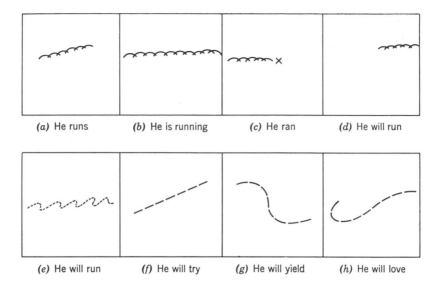

(a) He runs   (b) He is running   (c) He ran   (d) He will run

(e) He will run   (f) He will try   (g) He will yield   (h) He will love

FIGURE 23-5. Reference to temporality through generic aspects of action. (*a–d*) One subject's representations for *Run* in different temporal loci. (*e–h*) One subject's representations for *Future* of different activities.

sentation of temporality was *page-position:* location of a pattern in the center of the page indicated "ongoingness"; location in the center and the absence of visible termini indicated both "ongoingness" and "enduringness"; terminating in the center indicated "completedness"; beginning in the center without termination indicated "uncertainty" and "anticipation of the action."

Figure 23-5*e–h* illustrates the systematic use of a line property for expressing the temporality in all four activities. As can be seen, *dotting* was used for future action in each instance, serving unambiguously to express the connotation of "nonactuality" of the action.

These illustrations are quite instructive. They point up the fact that the linear means (linear "dimensions") most suitable for the expression of generic, theme-independent aspects are those amenable to variation without entailing an alteration in the basic "shape" [15] of the linear pattern. Among the more frequently used "dimensions" susceptible to variation without influencing the shape of a pattern were such linear properties as pressure, size, length, page-position, direction,

---

[15] It is predominantly the "shape" which is utilized for the representation of the action theme.

continuity (full-dotted), and repetitiveness. Furthermore, it was also clear, from the subjects' comments, that such linear properties, physiognamically-dynamically conceived, were easily exploitable for establishing an analogical correspondence between vehicle and referent, between the "inner form" of a linear property and a generic aspect pertaining to temporality. Thus, the *dotting* of Fig. 23-5 as contrasted with *solidity* of the other patterns of a series, was immediately graspable in its visible analogy to "nebulous," "unreal," "nonactual."

Since there were such shape-independent dimensions available for the expression of generic aspects, and since the subjects did vary these dimensions of the linear medium in the formation of different vehicles for a verb-series, why, one may ask, was there not more frequently a clear-cut and systematic *expression* of generic aspects through specific means, separable from those features (shape) used for realizing thematic content?

One principal factor underlying the infrequent use of linear dimensions for representing generic aspects systematically was the *relative globality of apprehension of agent's-action-in-time*—that globality which we noted as the characteristic feature of linear representation: in undertaking the task of representing an action-in-time in the linear medium, the subjects typically tended to grasp such content in terms of unitary, concrete, relatively undifferentiated occurrences. The (isolable) "dimensions" such as pressure, size, etc., rather than functioning as separate elements, entered into the construction of a unitary whole—a single "painting."

In addition to the tendency towards the global apprehension of events-in-time, some other factors working against the expression of generic aspects by stable, invariant and action-transcendent linear means have to be considered. In particular, militating against the unambiguous and systematic expression of generic aspects were certain (previously discussed [16]) fundamental characteristics of *vehicle-formation* and *structurization of referents* in linear representation.

One of the basic features of the expressive line medium is the *plurisignificance of linear properties,* that is, the susceptibility of the same *geometric* property to apprehension as two or more quite different *physiognomic-dynamic* qualities: for example, the "same" short line might be viewed now as expressing "compactness" or "concentration at a point" and now as expressing "abrupt termination." Plurisignificance is, of course, enhanced when a given property occurs not in iso-

---

[16] See Chapter 20.

lation but as a component of different configurations, for example, as in the typical global vehicles produced by the subjects in our study: a given pressure in a pattern of a certain "shape," direction, and size is very likely to be apprehended as exhibiting quite different expressive qualities than the "same" pressure in a pattern of quite different "shape," direction, and size. Furthermore, where it is not clear to which connotational domain a property pertains—e.g., whether it expresses something about the theme or something about temporality—plurisignificance is almost certain to obtain.

The second basic feature to consider is the *pluriconnotative (polysemantic) character of referents,* that is, the apprehension of an abstract referent or concept as comprised of a multiplicity of nuances, each of a more or less concrete, tangible nature. Thus, a generic aspect like "nonactuality" might be conceived in terms of "vagueness," "removed from the focal vision," "nonfulfillment," "incomplete fulfillment," or in terms of one of a host of other meanings, some scarcely formulable. In order to exhibit these different nuances, one is led to *multiform expression,* that is, the use of different linear properties to express the divergent connotations of the abstract notion. Thus the aspect of "nonactuality" grasped in terms of "vagueness" might well receive a different linear expression than that aspect grasped in terms of "nonfulfillment." As one can see, the pluriconnotative character of referents in conjunction with the multiform expression of the variegated connotations also militates against the establishment of stable form-function relationships and systematic codification.

Although plurisignificance, on one hand, and pluriconnotation-multiform expression, on the other, worked *against* the establishment of uniform means for the expression of *abstract* and theme-transcendent aspects, and hence against the sort of sysmatization that one finds in the more advanced languages employing aspects for temporal reference, they worked *towards* the clear-cut *concrete* differentiation of temporal loci of events. Even where two temporal loci suggested the same generic aspect (for example, "ongoingness" for simple and progressive present; "nonactuality" for past and future), the specific, concrete connotations of the generic aspect generally differed for the two loci; to exhibit these different nuances, different means were used (multiform expression). For example, as the protocols indicate, "nonactuality" with respect to past action was often suggested by "shortness" and "abbreviation of form," and "nonactuality" with respect to future action was frequently implied through "lightness of pressure" and "upward movement in space."

Furthermore, the factors of pluriconnotation and multiformity of expression typically led to the expression of a number of aspects for the same time, for example, "completedness" as well as "nonactuality" for the past, "incipience" as well as "nonactuality" for the future. Through the plurisignificance of linear properties and the multiformity of expression of aspects, it was possible to *interweave the particular connotations* in such a way that temporal loci were marked off from each other with great "pregnance" and distinctiveness. In sum, although temporal loci were not differentiated in terms of stable and invariant indices connoting abstract aspects, they were clearly and distinctly marked off from each other through the depiction of a rich variety of features pertaining to particular phases of concrete globally apprehended events.

In sum, then, the global character of the apprehension and expression of events-in-time, coupled with the factors of plurisignificance and pluriconnotation-multiformity operated against the clear-cut, theme-transcendent representation and articulation of generic aspects. The subjects, in spontaneously representing events-in-time, focused mainly on the concrete thematic content and selected those temporal connotations and those linear means that would harmonize with the expression of a particular theme. Yet there was an indication that linear properties, could they be disentangled from "shape" (that is, could they be freed from their role in conveying time as concretely infused in action), were capable of expressing temporal connotations of a generic kind.

This latter fact led us to conceive of an experiment, carried out by M. Bodansky (26), designed to explore the degree to which variations in isolated linear properties (disentangled from "shape" variations) could be exploited to express differences in temporality per se. Using a forced-choice technique, Bodansky presented twenty subjects with pairs of simple line patterns, for example, ——— versus - - - - -; ——— versus ———; ∧∧∧ versus ∧ , and pairs of phrases varying in temporal locus of action, e.g., *he runs* versus *he is running; he tried* versus *he will try*, etc. Fifteen pairs of patterns were individually presented with six tense contrasts (simple present versus progressive present, simple present versus past, simple present versus future, progressive present versus past, progressive present versus future, past versus future) for each of four verbs (*run, try, yield, love*). The study sought to determine whether such an abstract content as temporal locus is "naturally" representable by different characteristics of nonconventional linear patterns. The criterion of such "natural representability" was a significant consensus among the subjects.

One may illustrate the general nature of Bodansky's analysis and the general tenor of her results by examining how her subjects matched the two patterns, ∧∧∧ versus ∧ , with different sentences, varying in temporality. It was found that the progressive present, when paired with the simple present, was closely linked with the replicated pattern. For the pair of phrases *he runs* versus *he is running*, 100 percent of her subjects matched the simple present with the nonreplicated linear vehicle and the progressive present with the replicated pattern; for *he tries* versus *he is trying*, 75 percent of her subjects matched the progressive present with the replicated pattern, while only 25 percent linked the simple present to the replicated pattern; for *he yields* versus *he is yielding*, 95 percent of her subjects matched the progressive present with the replicated patterns, only one subject matching *he yields* with that pattern; finally, for *he loves* versus *he is loving*, 70 percent of the subjects matched the progressive present with the replicated pattern. In other words, in general, where a simple present form of a verb was contrasted with a progressive present form, the great majority of the subjects took the replicated line pattern to be a more fitting representation of the progressive present. When the progressive present was paired with either past or future, similar consensuality in matching of these two patterns was observed. The percentages of agreement in taking the replicated pattern to represent the progressive present rather than the past were: 100 percent for *run*, 95 percent for *try*, 90 percent for *yield*, 85 percent for *love*.

As a second illustration we may consider the subjects' choice of one of the two patterns: → versus ← (right versus left direction), as depictive of the past. Here again, there was high consensus: whether paired with simple present, progressive present, or future, the past was consistently matched to a high degree with direction to the left. Thus, 92 percent of the subjects, on the average, chose left direction for "*he ran*" versus *he runs, he is running,* or *he will run* respectively; 88 percent of the subjects, on the average, matched left direction with "*he tried*" against the present, progressive present and future of *try;* the same agreement in matchings was shown by an average of 80 percent of the subjects for the *yield* series and an average of 85 percent for the *love* series.

A third illustration pertains to the matchings of the subjects with regard to the two patterns ↑ versus ↓ (upward versus downward direction). Considerable agreement obtained in the choice of upward direction as expressive of the future (when paired with simple present, progressive present and past): the average percentages for the four verb-series were 70 percent for *run*, 70 percent for *try*, 80 percent for *yield*, and 75 percent for *love*. There was also considerable agreement in taking downward direction as depictive of the past (when paired with simple present, progressive present, and future); the average percentages were 85 percent for *run*, 82 percent for *try*, 82 percent for *yield*, and 85 percent for *love*.

Bodansky's study thus demonstrates what was only hinted at in our inquiry: that there are potential means available in the *concrete-depictive* expressive line medium for relatively distinct, systematic, and theme-transcendent representation of generic aspects of time. In other words, there is the possibility for systematic codification of temporality and hence for some degree of autonomous representation.

As our inquiry shows, however, in the spontaneous representation of events-in-time in the linear medium, there occur only the barest beginnings of such systematization. In contradistinction to what occurs under the limiting conditions of Bodansky's study (or, for that matter, in the languages of many nonliterate communities, where morphemic indices for generic aspects may attain relative invariance and considerable generality), generic aspects are hardly ever realized through universal and invariant means in spontaneous linear representation; this implies that such aspects are *latent* rather than clearly articulated in the linear medium. We have pointed out that this lack of realization is in great measure due to the global-concrete apprehension and expression of events in time and hence to the subordination of all those properties—potentially available for expression of generic aspects— to the establishment of the "shape" of a linear vehicle, that is, the typical means used for expressing concrete action. Thus, insofar as a subject comes to the medium with a generic aspect in mind, he is led by the pressure of the medium to realize the aspect in a concrete and theme-bound manner (for example, cessation of *love* will differ from cessation of *try*).

In sum, in the medium of expressive lines, where global apprehension, plurisignificance of patterns, and pluriconnotative (polysemantic) grasp of referents are significant factors in the formation of symbolic vehicles, the potentiality for systematic codification of temporality may perhaps come into being in terms of implication and allusion, or may even be partly actualized on certain occasions, but will never come to full fruition.

REPRESENTATION OF TIME-OF-ACTION
IN A MEDIUM OF VISUAL IMAGERY

Having discussed both the potentialities and actualities of symbolic reference to action-in-time in a medium of expressive lines, we may turn to a consideration of ways in which temporal locus of an action is represented and referred to in a medium of (predominantly) visual imagery.

Before dealing with this specific problem, however, it is important to mention why studies of representation in imagery are, in general, so pertinent to a developmental analysis of symbol formation. Such studies, to be sure, would be valuable even if they only provided additional information about ways of expressing thoughts other than through linguistic codification. Their special value for us, however, is with regard to our thesis (see Chapter 3) that the development of symbolization, microgenetically as well as ontogenetically, begins with the building up of vehicles out of the "stuff" that makes up the concrete contents of everyday experience—the recollections of particular, evanescent events that we have lived through.

It seems clear that unless nascent thoughts and conceptions can be apprehended without having any embodiment at all (a thesis we reject), they must gain their early realization—their initial comprehensibility—through concrete perceptual-motor-affective events. In order for concrete events to be used for the *representation* of thoughts, however, such events must be *intended* as having a more general and ideal import than they otherwise possess, that is, they must be viewed as embodying or exhibiting meanings that go beyond their concrete factuality. In other words, out of the reservoir of particular experienced happenings we must put together or *construct*, concrete elements (particular persons, actions, situations) to function as symbolic vehicles. Insofar as we exploit recollections of concrete experiences for this symbolic function, we may be said to be operating in a *medium* of imagery. This medium (possibly in combination with gestural configurations) is perhaps the primordial one in which *intentionality towards representation* of thought is realized.

Adults—especially educated adults—having more advanced means available for the representation of thoughts, tend to exploit imagery rather sparingly in its symbolic function. This fact has led some investigators to overlook or depreciate the role of imagery in the genesis of thought. Yet those who have reported on the process of giving form to new ideas and those who have reported on the struggles to make thoughts clear have generally mentioned the role of imagery in the initial phases of rendering thought explicit (see Ghiselin, 79; Spaier, 233).

To be sure, in communicating information to others about "objective" states of affairs, we are obliged to formulate our thoughts in linguistically coded messages rather than in incommunicable imagery. Yet in the genesis of thought, as we have noted elsewhere (see Chapter 19), there are stages important to investigate where there is little differentiation between subjective and objective and between thought formulated for oneself and thought formulated for others. One can speculate about the concrete, image-formulated thought of young children, in whom this lack of differentiation is manifested most clearly, but children do not have the means for describing such forms to us. If we wish to get some information about the nature of image-formulated reference to "objective" states of affairs, relations of events to each other, etc., we must use another approach.

One way—the way we have chosen—is to have sophisticated adults "translate" linguistically designated states of affairs or objective content into imagery.[17] We maintain that this approach should provide considerable insight into the ways in which this quite primitive medium is shaped and organized in representing thoughts. It should also provide insight into the ways in which abstract thoughts and ideas would be communicated to others if the progress towards the linguistic articulation of thought were arrested at the level of imagery "codification," that is, if we were to express our thoughts in the same way in which we form our image-representations of them.

An objection may be raised to this procedure on the grounds that such individuals characteristically formulate thoughts linguistically and that this fact may influence the reports of their imagery. Doubtless, this is true. However, the likelihood is that any influence will be in the direction of greater articulateness and explicitness than would otherwise obtain. In other words, it would be reasonable to expect that whatever formal characteristics mark off image-representation from linguistic codification, these characteristics would be even more exaggerated if there were not the "secondary elaborations" arising from the fact that subjects have a linguistic medium available to them.

---

[17] The method used by H. Silberer in his pioneering work (229; 230)—hypnagogic and hypnopompic imagery—does not permit a sufficient degree of experimental control over the content to be represented, and hence precludes comparison and ordering of images for the "same" content.

Major characteristics of imagery representation of abstract notions will be more clearly revealed through the findings of a study, carried out at Clark University by R. Erle (59), on the representation of time-of-action in visual imagery.

The procedure was as follows: each subject—there were ten men and ten women—after having been placed in a light, hypnotically induced sleep,[18] was informed that he was to be presented with four groups of four sentences. He was told that each group would contain the same verb, but that the tenses of the verb would vary. He was then told that he would represent the meaning of each sentence as much as possible in visual imagery or pictures while he was in the hypnotic state. He was informed that after he had dreamed imagery forms for all of the sentences, he would be awakened: when awake, he would be presented with each sentence and be able immediately to recall the image produced for that sentence. It was emphasized that he would have no trouble recalling the relevant dream image, and that he would be able to describe the image exactly as he had formed it in the dream state. After a subject had reported his images for the sentences, an extensive inquiry was conducted.

Sixteen sentences were presented to each subject for transformation into imagery:

He runs	He loves	He fights	He thinks
He is running	He is loving	He is fighting	He is thinking
He ran	He loved	He fought	He thought
He will run	He will love	He will fight	He will think

If one keeps the linguistic statements in mind, it is clear that the essential task of each subject was somehow to represent three "conceptions" in the imagery medium: the male agent ("he"), the thematic action ("fighting," etc.), and the temporal locus of the agent's action. The first two of these ideas are more or less amenable to direct exhibition in the imagery medium; temporal locus, on the other hand, does not seem to be directly depictable.

Considering the refractoriness of temporality to direct depiction, one might therefore expect that a subject, oriented towards the imaginal representation of action-in-time, must somehow exploit the

---

[18] Erle used hypnotism primarily because he wished to postpone his inquiries about the image-representations until all the images had been reported. It is an interesting question whether, in terms of the *formal* characteristics with which we are here concerned, hypnotically induced dream imagery would differ from images reported during an alert state. A quick pilot survey did not yield any important differences.

way in which he depicts the agent, the manner in which he exemplifies the action, and the way in which he situates agent's action in a concrete context, in order to refer to temporal locus via imagery.

The Contextualized Character of Representation of Thematic Action in Imagery

Before we turn to the ways in which this reference to temporality was realized, we may note some characteristics of the representation of agent's-action, independent of temporal qualification.[19] In the examination of the images pertaining primarily to agent's-action, one is immediately struck by (*a*) an elaborateness and circumstantiality of the vehicles and (*b*) the extreme, individual-bound variety of expression of a thematic action.

(*a*) In contradistinction to the succinct representation of action in the verb-forms of the linguistic code and to the capturing of salient features of thematic action in the "shape" of linear patterns, *thematic action in imagery was typically embedded in a more or less comprehensive scene;* the details of this scene often obscured the centrality of the action. These are illustrations.

He is running—"a man running down the street in the middle of a city chasing another man, and this other man starts to turn into a store, and the first man who is chasing him is afraid that he is going to lose him, so he runs even faster than before."

He is thinking—"a man on a ship in a storm, looking up at the sky; he seems to be using a sextant to find his location. The water is coming in over the deck. He's wearing a hat, an ivy league cap."

Such profuseness and circumstantiality undoubtedly derive from the *syncretic* character of imagery, that is, the fact that it usually subserves functions other than representation. In "regressing" to the archaic means of imagery for representing relatively circumscribed thoughts, the subjects were often carried away, in part, into fantasies and personal reminiscences of particular happenings.

(*b*) Deriving, in part, from the syncretic character of imagery, but also from the *pluriconnotative* nature of referents, was the extreme

---

[19] To be sure, thematic action per se (that is, in its atemporal notion) was not presented to the subjects for representation. However, most of the subjects took their images for the progressive present of the verbs to represent thematic action as such; hence one may look to the images for that tense-form to gain some notion of how agent's-action per se was expressed in imagery.

individual variability in expression for a single thematic action. Whereas the tendency in linguistic codification is to subordinate the diversity of concrete variants to a generic concept (expressed in a verb-form), the tendency in codification by imagery is to highlight one of the extremely specific and highly personalized meanings. This tendency leads to each individual using a more or less specific personal vehicle to represent a given action. Following are illustrations.

He is running—"A track meet; there is one out in front. I can see the numbers on the uniforms." "A person running down the sidewalk, very fast, as if to get to class, but he's not; he's running away from school up towards the auditorium, as if he's running to catch up to somebody."

He is fighting—"Two boys in front of a fraternity house fighting two other people because they had said something against them or against the fraternity. It's on the sidewalk." "A soldier, clacking with someone, hitting the guns against each other."

We have discussed the images primarily representative of action per se in order to establish a "base line," so to speak, in terms of which one can see more clearly what occurs when action located in time is represented in imagery. As we shall show, the *contextualization* of the vehicle—the intimate dependence upon the attitudes and experiences of the symbolizer—that one finds already in the depiction of action per se becomes even more marked in the representation of temporally qualified action.

The Contextualized Character of Representation of Temporally Qualified Action in Imagery

It was noted that temporal locus is generally refractory to depiction in the image medium. The concrete, particularized happenings that make up the images simply exhibit events as occurrent: they might have taken place in past time, might take place in the future, or might be going on in the present. Just as the utterances of the young child, having tangential reference to temporality, are not marked by formal devices that reflect location of a particular event in past, present, or future, so, too, the images of adults are in general not marked by specific indices pertaining to temporality. In both instances, the vehicles gain relatively unequivocal determination as to temporality only from context. In the case of the child's utterances, the context is what the child has just done and what he is doing at the moment of utterance (for example, *pipi*, after a child has urinated, implies something done;

before urination, something to come). In the case of adult images, the context is comprised of attitudes, states, past experiences, etc., of the symbolizer, not manifested in the image proper but determining how the image is to be taken, what reference the image carries.

The embeddedness of the image-vehicle in the organismic context of the symbolizer, and hence the *lack of autonomy* of the vehicle for carrying temporal reference, is perhaps most apparent in those instances where the same image is employed to represent two different temporal loci of an action. To illustrate, one subject for both *He will think* and *He is thinking* formed the following image: "A fellow at a desk with a book in front of him, leaning forward, one hand on his chin." When intended for "thinking in the future," this image was taken in the context, intended by the symbolizer but not manifest in imagery, of someone studying for a test that was coming up: "He is studying now (to enable him to think on his test in the future)." When intended for "thinking in the present," the image was taken as someone thinking now about the book he is reading. It is clear that an other would have to share the symbolizer's context in order to grasp the temporal reference of the image.

Although the embeddedness of the image-vehicle in a matrix of symbolizer's attitudes, expectancies, personal recollections, etc., is especially apparent in instances where the same "external form" is used in the representation of different temporal loci of a given action, lack of differentiation between symbolizer and vehicle was involved, to varying degrees, in every image: an image did not autonomously carry reference to time-of-action, but required nonimaginal supplementation and explication by the symbolizer for its temporal reference to be made clear to another. Consider the following image, for example. "One kid running away with another kid's toy or ball. There are two small children playing outdoors, and one takes one of the other's toys, and runs away with it. The first kid has a look as if he wanted his ball or his toy back."

An observer, not privy to the intent of the symbolizer, would have difficulty interpreting this image as referring to "fighting-to-come." Yet this image was formed for *He will fight:* the symbolizer felt, although he did not express it in imagery, that the boy whose ball had been taken away would fight to get it back.

Or take the image formed by another subject for *He loved.* "A girl standing in the kitchen of her home, washing dishes. I'm standing in the kitchen there, looking at her; she doesn't see me." For an external observer, the reference to thematic content ("loving" =

domestic happiness) is perhaps vaguely and atmospherically suggested, but the reference to pastness is completely hidden. For the symbolizer, however, the pertinence to the past was quite clear: "She was a girl . . . that I was going pretty steady with two years ago, and it's all over now."

As these typical illustrations make clear, the images represent a specific action-in-time only for the symbolizer and for an addressee who shares the same context of attitudes, experiences, etc., as the symbolizer. This context in which the image is embedded gives it its referential import. Implied in the imagery representations, in other words, are those two closely related hallmarks of genetically primitive representation, *a shrinkage of distance between addressor (symbolizer) and addressee* and *a shrinkage of distance between symbolizer and vehicle.*

Although the symbolizer's attitudes, experiences, etc., were always involved in determining the import of an image vehicle and hence in establishing the reference of the image to thematic-activity-in-time, the degree of determination varied considerably. Sometimes the reference to both thematic content and temporality was carried only to a small extent by the image proper, but mainly by aspects of the total symbol falling predominantly outside of the image vehicle; in other cases, there were some characteristics of the image, which for the symbolizer had clear reference to temporality. This latter fact—the presence of means in the images for the carrying of temporal reference—allows one to determine the variety of ways in which temporality was alluded to in the imagery medium.

Specific Means for Referring to Temporality in Imagery

Before going on to these specific means for referring to temporality, we should mention a typical feature of imagery representation of time-locus—a feature that characterizes imagery representation of time-of-action to an even greater degree than it does linear representation of temporality: that is, means of reference to time are very intimately, often indissolubly, fused with means for referring to action.

Therefore, in most of the instances, the manner in which thematic action was represented completely determined the manner of reference to time. There were also a number of instances, however, in which connotations of action and connotations of time-locus were carried by *different* features of the total image.

If one excludes time reference by nonimaginal feelings and attitudes of the symbolizer, there were six principal means for referring to temporality which could be discerned in the imagery representations. Let us consider briefly these various means, going, in the main, from the more "indirect" or "oblique" devices for referring to temporality to those ways which permitted a more direct reference to time-of-action.

Reference to Temporality through Agent-Characteristics

Here the principal agent ("he") in a total situation was the carrier of temporal connotations. In some instances, agent characteristics referred simultaneously to temporality as well as to thematic action; in other instances, however, thematic action was represented by some component of the image, whereas certain agent characteristics served mainly, if not exclusively, to indicate temporality. Let us consider first some illustrations of the former, *syncretic*, use of the agent component.

In one subject's image of "a big guy holding a beer can in his hand, wearing Bermuda shorts" ("the guy was someone I used to fight with"), the agent was both the carrier of the activity (he-fighter) and the means of referring to temporality (he-who-fought-me-in-the-past). Another symbolizer, for *He fought,* formed an image of "an old man with a broken leg . . . sort of a fat person, gay and talkative, sitting down at home in a comfortable chair." Here, once again, the agent ("old man with a broken leg") carried both thematic activity and temporality; he was "one who had fought in the war." A female subject, for *He will love,* depicted "an old boyfriend of mine . . . ;" this agent was taken by the symbolizer as "someone whose love would continue indefinitely into the future."

It is noteworthy that the great majority of depicted agents that were utilized by subjects to carry activity-in-time reference—like those mentioned—were of a very *personal, idiosyncratic* character. In a number of images, however, the depicted agent carried activity-in-time connotations in a more *communal* manner. For example, one subject, for *He thinks,* depicted "a baseball umpire" as the principal agent; this agent connoted for him "one who is obliged to make decisions all the time" (= thinking). Again, a number of subjects, for *He thinks,* formed an image of "a professor" or "teacher," that is, one typically or generally engaged in thinking.

The use of agent-characteristics primarily for the expression of temporality rather than for the expression of the action-theme can perhaps best be exemplified by contrasting several images from a single set. For example, one subject depicted "a man running to first-base in a baseball game" for *He runs,* and "a trackman running ahead of a number of others in a track meet" for *He is running*. In both cases, the thematic activity was revealed in agent's action; the temporal reference pertained to "different degrees of involvement" in running. The track star, according to the subject, suggested "greater involvement" than the baseball player. Another subject represented the agents of "he runs" and "he is running" by "real" individuals, the agents of "he ran" and "he will run" by "stick figures;" these differences in agents alluded to the temporal aspects of "actuality" and "nonactuality" respectively. In this latter case, the subject hit upon a theme-transcending means potentially useful for distinguishing present from non-present. This means, however, was used only for the *run* series and thus not exploited to its full extent. In the main, where agent components were used to indicate a particular temporal locus, they were typically theme-specific, gaining their particular time value only in terms of their relatedness to a particular action.

Reference to Temporality through Agent-State or Posture

Here, a particular state or posture of the agent, suggestive of a certain phase of an event carries the reference to temporality. Such features may again be employed syncretically, that is, representing a fusion of activity and temporality, or may be more or less reserved for the expression of temporal meanings. These are examples: For *He fought,* a subject produced the image "a kid with head bent and body slumped"; here the posture of the agent holophrastically referred to activity in the past. Another subject for the same statement formed the image of "a soldier lying dead"; here, the nature of the agent ("he-soldier") was the primary means for alluding to thematic activity, while the agent-state ("he-dead") more specifically suggested the overness of the activity.

Once again, one finds the means employed here almost inherently specific to an action: thus, an agent lying dead would have little relevance to the overness of "thinking" or "running;" an agent with head bent and body slumped would have little relevance to the overness of "loving" or "thinking," etc.

We may point here again to the issue of the degree of *privacy versus communality* in representation. For instance, a subject who used the agent-state "he-balding" to suggest "one who had done a lot of thinking in the past" undoubtedly employs a more idiosyncratic means than one who forms an image of "he-lying dead," "he-with-black-eye," "he-bruised and exhausted" to connote "fighting in the past." The agent-states or postures which have a more communal character are, of course, those that typically occur at one of the various phases of a complex, temporally extended action.

Reference to Temporality through Situational Elements

By situational elements, it will be recalled, we mean persons (other than the principal agent), locales of action, etc. Often such elements were used *syncretically*, to refer both to time *and* theme. An illustration of this use is one subject's image for *He will run:* "an empty track . . . grass in the center;" this locale meant, for the symbolizer, "a place where people will run." Situational elements were sometimes used as a means for relatively *discrete* reference to temporality, agent's activity being carried by other components of the total image. For example, one subject formed the image for *He ran* of "a thief running away from a jewelry store, its window broken;" the thematic activity was here carried by the actual running of the agent; the allusion to the past was carried by "the broken window of the jewelry store"— "something that was done." Another subject, for *He is thinking,* saw himself as agent "slumped in a chair in this experimental room:" the agent-posture suggested the thematic activity, while the locale conveyed the notion of "going on now."

Thus, as was the case with agent-characteristics, situational components where they carried or helped to convey temporal reference were theme-specific, never employed for the same tense-form of a different verb-series.

Reference to Temporality through Major Phases of a "Natural" Event

In contradistinction to linguistic codification of the action-themes placed at various temporal loci, there are no means available in imagery by which a conceptualized invariant action can be represented at one time in the past, at another in the present, and at a third in the future. To allude to temporal locus one must, in imagery, always depict an occurrent, actual state of affairs; *one must refer to the past and future under the guise of the "present."* Here is where the major phases of events may be seized upon. By depicting the beginning of an action, one may suggest its futurity; by depicting agent's action or posture at the close of activity, one may imply its pastness; and so on. Invariably, this means of referring to temporal locus is fused with the allusion to specific action.

Several illustrations may serve to clarify this mode of temporal reference. One subject, for *He runs* and *He is running,* visualized "someone running . . ."; the image for *He ran* was "someone walking and panting heavily," signifying the completion of running by depicting how the agent appears at the end of the action. As one can see, both thematic action and temporality were alluded to in the latter representation; the running was not shown but rather implied; and it was implied as "over." Another subject, for *He loves* and *He is loving,* formed the image of "a boy kissing a girl;" this image expressed "loving (kissing) going on now." For *He loved,* the subject visualized "a boy wiping lipstick off his face," signifying the completion of kissing (and overness of loving). Again, there was no depiction of the action, but a global allusion to the overness of the specific action.

A third subject, representing the various tense-forms of *love,* exploited a larger event-unit than "kissing." For *He loves,* he formed the image of "a man and wife in a typical home scene," signifying the enduring, "mental," "always-there" kind of love; for *He will love,* he visualized "Two people getting married at an altar; they're dressed in wedding garments . . . ;" for *He loved,* the image was of "a court scene . . . a divorce case."

To repeat, at this level of reference, as in the previous modes of reference to temporality, there is still *extreme theme-specificity of time.* The images are suitable as means of indicating time-locus only for a specific action: "wiping lipstick off one's face," for example, would not be exploitable for referring to the past of "thinking," "running," or "fighting," and so on.

Reference to Temporality through Spatial Relation of Agent's-Action to the Situational Context

This means is one of the few which, if consistently realized, would permit the representation of thematic action in an invariant manner, simultaneously alluding to various temporal loci. Thus, ideally, it is a step towards the differentiation of action and time. Just as one may represent the passage of time by imagining a constant sun, now rising, now at zenith, now setting, so, too, may one represent temporal locus by envisioning an agent's action with respect to a fixed item of the context: the item, to be sure, would have to be apprehended as segmentable into beginning, middle, and end.

Some notion of the possibilities of this means may be gotten from the following. One subject differentiated *He ran* and *He will run* in terms of the position of the agent with respect to the track: in the former instance, the agent was *"standing* at the *end* of the track;" in the latter, he was *"standing* at the *beginning* of the track." For *He is running,* the agent was visualized as *"running* in the *middle* of the track." Another subject used a road as the constant feature, but otherwise distinguished *He ran* from *He will run* in exactly the same manner; again, for *He is running,* the agent was visualized as "in a running position." By exploiting systematically the means of spatial relation used in these instances, the subjects could have achieved an invariant representation of thematic action, since it was essentially the variation in the relation of agent to contextual object that served to indicate variation of time.

This means, however, was never systematically exploited in the imagery representations of these subjects. Typically, in both cases, the pressure of the medium towards concrete depiction led to the use of another means, for example, agent-posture (*standing*), rather than thematic action (*running*). This push towards concrete realism worked against representation of action as invariant—a basic prerequisite for theme-independent depiction of temporality.

Reference to Temporality through Qualities Inherent in the Medium

Here allusion to temporal locus is carried through such features as size of image, clarity of image, etc. This means ideally permits complete differentiation of theme and temporality and potentially allows theme-transcendent reference to time-locus. It is another indication of the pressure of the medium towards concrete depiction that this means was very rarely used; and furthermore, in those instances where it was employed, it was used fragmentarily, that is, for one tense-form of one or two themes. Thus, two subjects, for a future tense-form of an activity, formed an image that was "less clear" than other images for the verb series: this lesser clarity served to allude to nonactuality. Yet, interestingly enough, in these instances other means were also employed to express temporality, and these means resulted in variation of action-representation.

Summarizing briefly, we have indicated how various components within total images, for example, agent-characteristics, agent-states, relations of agent's activity to situational context, etc., were frequently exploited by symbolizers to refer to temporality as fused with thematic activity. In such cases, the same vehicular component referred to a global unity, *"activity-temporality,"* for example, about-to-begin-running, just-finished-fighting, finished-fighting-some-time-ago, thinking-all-the-time, etc. In certain, less frequent instances, the means for reference to temporal connotation, though always concrete and theme-specific, were to some degree differentiated from the means for primary reference to activity.

In our discussion, we also touched on the issue of communality of expression of the meanings by imagery. We saw that in most of the instances reported, the sense attributed either to total images or to image components—as is the case in inner speech (see Part IV)—was more or less personal and idiosyncratic; nevertheless, there were instances (infrequent, to be sure) where the connotations attributed to the vehicular components were of a relatively more communal nature.

In concluding this chapter, we may briefly comment on the significance of the studies on linear and imaginal representation of temporality from the point of view of an organismic-developmental approach to symbolization. As we have noted previously, there is a wide gap between the organization of concrete, perceptual-motor experience of events unfolding in time and the codification of such events in (the English) language. On the level of concrete experience, events are not dismembered into distinct agents, activities, and locations in time. One apprehends a person-in-concrete-activity-executed-in-a-specific-manner-with-respect-to-particular-persons (or things)-in-particular-contexts; temporality is experienced as concretely ingredient in a person's particular activity or state, in characteristics of the context, etc. In representing such concrete states of affairs for communication to others via the linguistic code, we disentangle and idealize (conceptualize) components of the global events as if they were actually separable from each other and independent of each other. The agent may be designated in an invariant manner irrespective of his momentary attributes, states, postures, or actions; likewise, the activity may be codified in an invariant manner irrespective of its particular manner of execution, the agent who carries it out, its present, past, or anticipated occurrence, etc.; and again, one may express, through special morphemes or auxiliary verbs, an ideal temporal locus, irrespective of the nature of the agent's activity involved.

From our theoretical position, we would maintain that experience is given symbolic form at developmentally different levels of symbolic functioning. At the early levels of symbolic functioning involving a linguistic (verbal) medium, symbolic expression possesses those features that we have highlighted in our discussions of linguistic forms in dreams (Chapter 15), schizophrenia (Chapter 16), and inner speech (Chapters 17 and 18). The studies on imaginal and linear representation take us back still further with regard to genetically early forms of symbolization: their value lies in the general insight they provide with regard to pre-linguistic ways of symbolizing temporal loci of events.

Of the two kinds of media, imaginal and linear, imagery is the one that instigates—in terms of the concept of "distance"—the more profound primitivization of symbol formation. The linear medium—because it provides relatively "abstract" lines rather than concrete pictures (as in imagery)—allows for some small beginnings in the formation of distinctive means for the differential expression of such distinguishable aspects of events as thematic action and temporality; in this respect, the linear medium stands somewhere between the medium of imagery and the linguistic medium. As already stated, it is only at levels of linguistic codification that one observes a progression towards the attainment of full-fledged means for the differential articulation of the various aspects of an event.

chapter 24

The Representation of Relations between Thoughts in Nonverbal Media

In Chapter 12, an attempt was made to trace the major steps in onto-genesis leading up to the distinct linguistic expression of certain relations between conceptualized states of affairs.

We there indicated that, for children growing up in Indo-European linguistic communities, the gradual mastery of so-called "form-words" or conjunctions (e.g., "and," "but," "because," "if") is centrally involved in this progression towards the autonomous expression of relations between thoughts. Such form-words are not necessary for the expression of relations between thoughts as long as the child's utter-ances are embedded in concrete contexts; through the support of such contexts, the child can communicate at least certain relations between thoughts implicitly, even though his linguistic utterances consist sim-ply of a paratactic "naming" of events. As the *context of utterance* becomes more remote from the *context of occurrence*, however, the ex-plicit expression of relations becomes necessary for communication.

When the child begins to express relations linguistically, he typically uses an all-purpose connective, for example, "and;" this form is ini-tially used to express those concrete relations of coordination, co-occur-rence, and sequence which the young child can comprehend. As the child begins to grasp more abstract, logical relations (e.g., causality), he uses the available all-purpose conjunction to express the novel re-

439

lations. Only later does he adopt the conventional form-words for causal, conditional, and other logical relations; even then, it takes some time before the specialized forms are fully coordinated with their particular functions.

The present discussion is once again concerned with the developmental analysis of the process of forming relations between thoughts; here, however, the problem is studied by inquiring into the representations of relations in media which, by their very nature, lead to relatively primordial modes of articulating and organizing experience. Specifically, the issue posed was: "How are relations of coordination, concurrence, sequence, limitation, causal dependence, conditionality, etc.—carried in English by conjunctions such as "and," "but," "because," "if"—expressed in nonverbal media?" To answer this question, two studies were carried out, one dealing with linear the other with imaginal representations of such relations by adult, linguistically sophisticated subjects.

REPRESENTATION OF RELATIONS BETWEEN
THOUGHTS IN AN EXPRESSIVE LINE MEDIUM

In the first study, carried out by S. Speier (234), twelve subjects were asked to represent by expressive lines the content of six sentences:

I am sad if I lose	I lose if I yield
I am sad and I lose	I lose and I yield
I am sad because I lose	I lose because I yield

Each subject, after completion of the line drawings, underwent a comprehensive inquiry.

*General Characteristics of the Linear Expression
of Thought Relations* [1]

In the six linguistic statements, the relations between states of affairs were *overtly* expressed; furthermore, the same relation [2] was expressed

---

[1] Some of the findings reported here are based on additional analyses of the protocols not included in Speier's thesis.

[2] In ordinary language, of course, the form-words are not as univocal in their significance as in these constructed sentences: "and" in one case may subserve the expression of co-occurrence and in another case may express temporal sequence.

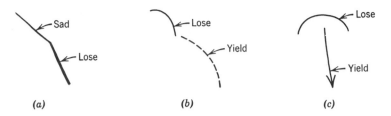

FIGURE 24-1. Illustrations typical of the contextualized, non-explicit representations of relations in the linear medium: (*a*) "I am sad and I lose," (*b*) "I lose because I yield," (*c*) "I lose if I yield."

by the same form-word, irrespective of the contents related; that is, the expression of a relation was *invariant*. Such overtness and invariance of the expressions of relations were *atypical* in linear representation; here, in general, each relation was carried by the organization of the total pattern and was expressed differently depending on the way in which a specific content was depicted. For instance, in Fig. 24-1 are shown the patterns for "I am sad *and* I lose," "I lose *because* I yield," "I lose *if* I yield;" in neither case are there components expressing the particular connection per se.

Thus, in the main, relations between conceptualized events were not expressed through tangible, circumscribed, and specific means; *yet they were realized in the linear medium.* This raises the question: "How, and on what basis, were the relations between thoughts expressed in the nonverbal medium of expressive lines?"

It appears, in light of the subjects' representations and reports, that there is one plausible answer to this question: the sententially formulated relations were organismically grasped and represented in terms of *vectorial-dynamic action patterns,* such inner gestures as "moving toward," "intersecting with," "making contact with," "flowing into," "balancing," "supporting," and so on. Only because the relations between thoughts were formulable in these terms was it possible for the subjects to exploit the linear medium to express the relations. In other words, in the process of articulating and relating experiences to each other, it must be assumed that one organizes thoughts in such vectorial-dynamic patterns. True, such fleeting patterns are only occasionally reflected in consciousness; [3] nevertheless, we would maintain that they are always centrally involved in the "microgenesis"

---

[3] Cf. W. James (118, I., pp. 245 ff), Betz (18, p. 71).

of the expression of thoughts and in the process of understanding statements asserting relations between thoughts. The linear medium, because of its closeness to inner gestural activity, serves only to make these vectorial-dynamic action patterns more manifest.

It seems obvious that unless there were such vectorial-dynamic (organismic) patterns underlying the abstract, logical relations between thoughts, it would be impossible to relate "because" or "if-then" statements to lived experience. One would not have a distinctive inner experience to articulate further and channelize into a causal or conditional statement, nor would one be able even to make the initial inroads into an understanding of such statements made by others. There must, in other words, be some basis in nonlinguistic experience for linking thought to language, no matter how much language may subsequently serve to transform and reorganize thought.

Let us now turn to the particular ways in which the various relations between thoughts were realized in the linear medium.

Expressions of the "And-Connection" in the Linear Medium

As indicated, in every day language the conjunction "and" is a relatively plurisignificant form which, in addition to carrying connotations of "coordination" and "temporal concomitance," may sometimes indicate "temporal sequence" and even "causal influence." "And" is particularly used as a rather "universal" connective in early stages of ontogenesis. Even when other connectives are available, however, "and" may still be used for multiple functions.

The drawings and inquiries clearly reflected the fact that there was an intimate and reciprocal relationship between the patterns formed by the subjects and the ways in which the "and-connection" was construed; it was evident that the "and" as *concomitance* was represented through different modes of expression than was the "and" as *sequence* or the "and" as *causal influence*.

The relation of *concomitance* itself subsumes a number of more specific relations, for example, contiguity of events, temporal overlap, coordination, or equality in status. It was actually these more specific relations which were depicted in the expressive line patterns when subjects grasped "and" as concomitance. The principal linear means employed to express these connotations were *contact, symmetrization, intersection, equalization, balance,* and *divergence from a common point.*

In Fig. 24-2a–d are shown various such representations for "I am sad and I lose": in (a) the vehicle for "lose" was presented touching

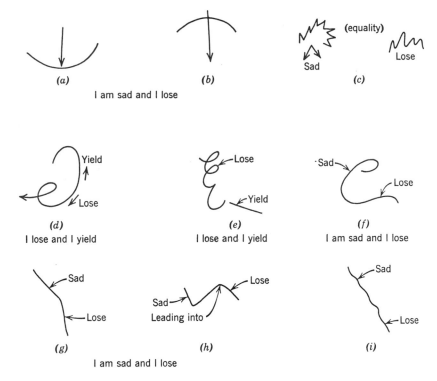

FIGURE 24-2. Representations of the "and" relation. (*a,b,c,d*): "and" expressed as concomitance; (*e,f*): "and" expressed as temporal sequence; (*g,h,i*): "and" expressed as influence.

the vehicle for "sad" at its mid-point; concomitance was thus expressed through *contact* and *symmetrization;* in (*b*) *intersection* and *symmetry* expressed connotations of contiguity, temporal overlapping, and coordination between the two states of affairs; in (*c*) concomitance was realized through *equalization* and *balance* of the vehicles for the two events. Finally, in (*d*) is shown concomitance of two events (lose and yield) expressed by depicting the vehicles for these events *diverging from a common point.*

Next, the apprehension of the "and-connective" as implying a *temporal sequence* was typically realized through *the spatial ordering of the vehicles depicting the conceptualized events,* that is, placing the vehicle for the initially occurring happening to the left of the other vehicle (see Fig. 24-2*e* and *f*). Of course, from a geometric point of view, the deployment of the vehicles in this fashion is a mere juxta-position, which would indicate nothing but spatial contiguity; actu-ally, however, the vehicles were apprehended in dynamic-expressive terms, that is, the one on the left sequentially prior to the one on the right; the arrangement thus clearly depicted a relationship of sequence. We may note that in each of these instances, the subjects intended their vehicles to express the temporal sequence of otherwise *independent* events, that is, "first—then."

A third way of apprehending the "and-connective" was in terms of *influence*. The most typical way in which this mode of apprehension was realized in the linear productions was through the *homogenization of the vehicles representative of the two states of affairs:* the vehicles for the two events were assimilated to each other either in terms of their shapes, directions (vectors), or both. In Figure 24-2g, h, and i are presented several illustrations of such homogenization; it may be noted that, sometimes, as in (h), the expression of "influence" was further indicated by a vehicle depictive of *leading into*, that is, A leads into B.

It will be readily acknowledged that the cognizing of a relationship of "influence" between two states of affairs is further removed from the concrete perception of happenings than is the apprehension of spatiotemporal concomitance or sequence. In this connection, it is quite striking how the character of depiction changes, corresponding to the differences in the degree of abstractness (distance from concrete perception). The depiction of the two previously described kinds of "and" connotations were, to a great extent, of a rather "natural," di-rect form (overlap, contact, balance, symmetry, spatio temporal con-tiguity); in comparison, the expression of "and" as "influence" or "sub-sequence" was somewhat more *metaphorical:* the *similarity of shape* in the vehicles for the two events was not intended to reflect their con-crete-external sameness but served rather as a sign of their *inner* bond. That this shift from the more direct to the more indirect ("distant") forms of depiction goes hand in hand, to a certain extent, with the de-gree of abstractness of the relation will become even clearer in the representations of the causal and conditional relations.

Expressions of the "Because-Connection" in the Linear Medium

In abstract thinking, as articulated and codified in English, the term "because" is typically used to reflect the fact that one state of affairs is taken to occur on account of, by reason of, or due to, another state of affairs. The use of "because" generally indicates that one has reorganized and transformed the concrete perceptual order of events—in which happenings are merely concurrent, overlapping, or sequential—into an order in which the conceptual relations of causal dependence or ground-consequence obtain.

As noted, in the ontogenetically early phases of the articulation of causal relationships, such relationships are often carried by the plurisignificant "and;" the use of this vehicle does not render explicit, but often implies causal relationships in terms of a relation of temporal sequence, etc. It is interesting to observe that, under the pressure of expressing causal relationships in the relatively primitive linear medium, subjects, to varying degrees, *reverted* to such genetically early apprehensions of the causal relation. An examination of the protocols revealed that, in the course of linear representation, the "because-connection" was apprehended as connoting three kinds of relations, *differing in abstractness*. These were: (1) *first* B occurs, *then* A occurs; (2) A's occurrence is *intimately linked* with B's occurrence; and (3) B's occurrence *supports* or *provides the ground* for A's occurrence. In the main—undoubtedly due to the primitivizing effect of the linear medium—"because" was apprehended mainly in terms of temporal sequence and intimate linkage; only rarely was the more advanced and abstract relation of subordination depicted.

Turning first to the linear representations entailing transformation of "because" into *temporal sequence*, the most striking means used here was the *inversion in the order of symbolizing the two events:* whereas the linguistic statement referred to the states of affairs in the order AB, the linear representations presented the states of affairs in the order BA. This kind of organization will recall the ontogenetically early linguistic formulations of relationships between events, in which the child—in his linguistic statements—stays close to the concrete perceptual order of happenings, linking the happenings in terms of pre-causal "and," or "first-then," connections.

Illustrations of this mode of realizing "causality" in the linear medium are reproduced in Fig. 24-3a–d.

Although, in this type of representation, the dominant relation between the two events is one of concrete temporal sequence, it may be pointed out that subjects often used additional means to suggest something more than a mere sequence of happenings. For instance, in drawing (a) ("I am sad because I lose"), the visible effect of bitterness and sadness was delineated in great detail; on the other hand, the causative event (losing) was depicted with much greater intensity

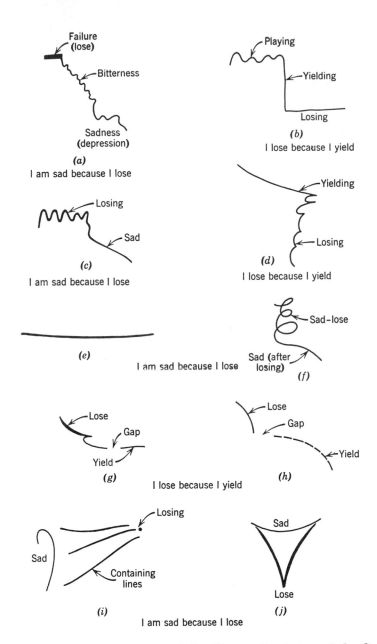

FIGURE 24-3. Representations of the "because" relation: (*a,b,c,d*) "because" expressed as temporal sequence, (*e,f*) "because" expressed as intimate linkage, (*g,h*) "because" expressed as cause separated from present event, (*i,j*) "because" expressed as subordinative dependence.

(pressure). In other words, although the causal relationship was transformed into a concrete temporal sequence, there was at the same time an urge to indicate, *by formal means,* a difference in status between the two events. The first, relative to the second, was exhibited as possessing influence (indicated by greater pressure), but also as less immediate, less actual, more "abstract" (indicated by the relative shapelessness of a single straight line).

Again, in (*b*) ("I lose because I yield"), the representation involved something more than pure spatial ordering: through the *abruptness of angular change,* the drawing indicated a distinction in the status of the two events: one is initiatory; the other "then" follows from the first. Once again, in drawing (*c*) ("I am sad because I lose"), the subject indicated his intention to represent more-than-temporal connotation of "because" by depicting the causative state of affairs with *greater pressure* than the effected event.

Intermediate between those representations of "because" which emphasized temporal sequence and those which reflected an apprehension of the events in terms of some global, intimate linkage were a number of productions in which an attempt was made to indicate more strongly in a sequential patterning the relation of *dependency* between the two events. Whereas the "because" qua sequence was reflected in a *left-right* (inverted) positioning of the event-vehicles, in these latter instances, the relation of a more-than-sequential dependence upon was indicated through a greater emphasis on the *above-below* placement of the event-vehicles rather than on the left-right arrangement. An illustration of this manner of realizing "cause" is given in Fig. 24-3*d* ("I lose because I yield").

This last illustration approaches rather closely a way of symbolizing "cause" (discussed below) which implies an *inner, conceptually apprehended link* rather than an external, sequential connection between two events. Subjects employed various means to indicate such inner linkage.

One was by stressing the *implicatory relationship* between the two events: B implies A. A most extreme method of representing the intimate linkage between the causative and the effected event was to *portray both in indissoluble fusion,* that is, in a global, unitary vehicle. An illustration of this manner of representation is the drawing of Fig. 24-3*e*: a portrayal of the globally apprehended sentence meaning ("I am sad because I lose"), by an undifferentiated vehicle. A less extreme manner of indicating cause in terms of *intimate linkage* is shown in Fig. 24-3*f*. Here, two vehicles were used: one vehicle expressed "lose-sad" in fusion; the second, explicating the effect, expressed "sadness."

In practically every single example presented, the subject inverted the linguistically codified order of the causally related event, thus transforming the abstract connection into a connection more or less close to the concrete sequence of happenings. There were, however, some—less frequent—productions in which the vehicles for the separate events were arranged analogously to the linguistic-abstract sequence, that is, the effected event was portrayed first and then the causative state of affairs. It is quite remarkable how the linear means for expressing an intimate linkage were changed in these instances—*becoming more metaphorical and quasi-abstract*. Let us examine two productions of this type (Fig. 24-3*g* and *h*). In both instances, a gap was introduced between the precedent depiction of the effected event and the subsequent depiction of the causative event, this gap, as inquiry revealed, functioning as a question—why or when? At the same time, these subjects depicted the causative event with *lesser pressure* (*g*) or *dotting* (*h*), trying to indicate that the causal event was more removed from the present in relation to the presently ongoing effect. These examples approach, in some features, the representations of the next group insofar as the attempt was made somehow to indicate the lesser actuality of the cause by specific means, for example, dotting.

The final group of representations—a kind very rarely produced by the subjects—illustrates the closest approach within the linear medium to the expression of "abstract" causal relation. These patterns were intended to convey the notion of *subordinative dependence* implied in "because," through *"spatial metaphors."* These metaphors were equivalent to the notions of cause in terms of "behind of it," "supporting it," "underlying it," "containing (entailing) it," and the like.

Consider, for instance, the drawing for "I am sad because I lose" (Fig. 24-3*i*). The subject intended to convey a three-dimensional effect, with one event "behind," [4] in the past, holding (entailing, containing) the present event (the sadness); the holding or regulating notion is expressed through the lines, emanating from the dot (losing) and contacting the extreme points of the vehicle for sadness.

In the representation of the same sentence (Fig. 24-3*j*), another subject apprehended cause in terms of "underpinning" an effect and supporting it; the effect, dependent on cause for support, was manifested by placing the vehicle for "lose" (downward-converging, heavy

---

[4] Cf. our expression "something is *behind* all this!"

lines) below that of "sad" (curved line on top); and at the same time having it "support" the vehicle for "sad."

Expressions of the "If-Connection" in the Linear Medium

The term "if" is used, in speech and thought, to denote either—more concretely—the temporal proximity of two states of affairs or—more abstractly—the dependence of one event upon another, which may or may not occur. In the first usage, "if" functions more or less as a "first-then" or a "when," alluding to a relation of *sequence* or *co-occurrence;* in the second, "if" refers to a *conditional dependence*, taking one out of the realm of actuality or existence into the realm of the possible, the hypothetical, etc.

As with the expression of "because," the subjects symbolizing in the relatively primitive linear medium—generally reverted to more concrete interpretations of "if." Though less often, drawings also expressed other kinds of relations than simple sequence or co-occurrence. In the main, three kinds of relations—differing in level of abstractness —were realized in the linear representations. These may be indicated approximately as follows: (1) first B occurs, then A occurs; (2) A occurs when(ever) B occurs; and (3) A occurs should B occur.

With regard to the first, and most concrete, connotation of "if," the principal means for expressing it was the *inversion of the linguistic order of presentation of the two happenings;* that is, the subjects interpreted "if" in terms of temporal sequence, in which the conditional event was depicted first and the conditioned event afterwards. For example, one subject represented "I am sad if I lose" (Fig. 24-4a), by three parts: an antecedent state of activity, then failure (losing), then sadness. This subject observed that "if" was not directly realized in his linear symbol; he said, "I intended what 'could' be, but had to draw it as existing." One sees here, quite clearly, how *the linear medium conduces to the transformation of possibility and hypotheticality into actuality.*

The drawings of Fig. 24-4b and c are further examples of subjects' realizing the "if" relation through transformation into a "first-then" sequence.

Distinguished from these instances, in which "if" was apprehended as connoting co-occurrence or sequence of two states of affairs, were other cases where "if" was grasped as implying an *intimate linkage* between two events. One way in which this linkage was realized was

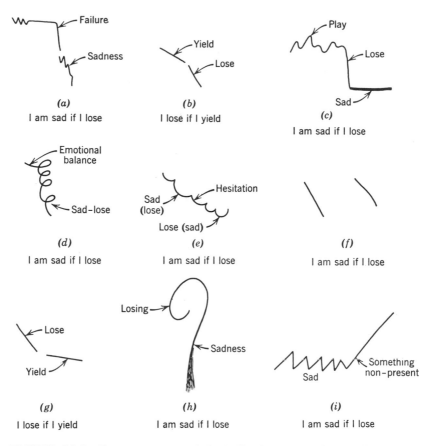

FIGURE 24-4. Representations of the "if" relations: (*a,b,c*) "if" expressed as temporal sequence (when), (*d*) "if" expressed as intimate linkage, (*e,f*) "if" expressed as separateness from present event, (*g,h,i*) "if" expressed as possibility.

through the *fusion of the two events into a syncretic situation* represented by a global, unitary symbol. An example of this manner of realizing "if" is shown in Fig. 24-4*d*, a representation for "I am sad if I lose." The symbol exhibits a state of "sad-losing," following a state of emotional balance (indicated by the short line preceding the downward-spiralling component).

It is interesting to note that the subject who formed this symbol felt that the content would have been much better represented if he would have made a break between the representation of emotional balance and the vehicle for "sad-lose"—a gap that would have ostensibly indicated "what comes next is not yet happening."

A means—quite often used for portraying the intimate linkage of causally related events (p. 447)—was also employed for the realization of "if." This means consisted of the *assimilation or homogenization of the vehicles for the two events,* in terms of such features as shape, direction, etc. As we have noted before, this may be regarded as a rather metaphorical device for indicating the inner connection of the two events. Fig. 24-4*e* and *f* illustrates this mode of "if" representation. In representing "I am sad if I lose," the first subject expressed the idea of "inner linkage" by assimilating "sad" and "lose" to each other; the "ifness" was further indicated here by a rather jerky line interposed between the two event-symbols—a line representing "hesitation." One might thus verbally translate the connotations intended here as: "sad (lose)—hesitation—lose (sad)." The subject went beyond simply symbolizing the inner connection between the two events: he attempted, rather concretely, to indicate the nonactuality of the "losing" by the notion of hesitation pictured by the interceding line. A second subject's linear pattern for the same sentence (Fig. 24-4*f*) showed features formally analogous to those of the first production. Here again, the vehicles for "sad" and "lose" were assimilated to each other in shape and direction. The *gap between the two lines* indicated that, in spite of their relation in terms of assimilated shape and direction, no "real connection" existed between the events. In other words, the subject, although he did not symbolize the hypothetical nature of the "if," at least attempted to concretize the nonreality in the connection between events.

The next illustration reflects a manner of realizing "if" which comes closer to a representation of the abstract notion of "possibility" or "hypotheticality." One subject remarked that the *gap* he used in his representation of "I lose if I yield" (Fig. 24-4*g*) indicated "conditionality." The degree of distance between the two event-symbols was extremely important; it had to be of such an interval that neither "absence of connection" (if too far apart) nor "real connection" (if too close together) were suggested. Here, in contradistinction to those representations which emphasized gaps mainly as indicators of nonactuality, one finds a *spatial-topological relation* ("not too far, not too close") exploited to allude to "possibility of actualization." The drawing of Fig. 24-4*h* shows another manner of representing the abstract conception of "if" in terms of possibility or hypotheticality.

Here, the symbol for "I am sad if I lose" primarily exhibits "sadness;" the "sadness," however, is shown standing, so to speak, in mid-air, without a basis; furthermore, the initial part of the vehicle (which was drawn from bottom to top) is rendered as diffuse and fuzzy, suggestive of "emergence from uncertainty." Finally, in the representation for the same sentence (Fig. 24-4i), another subject so strongly emphasized the abstract aspect of possibility that the conditional event was not even concretely depicted but transformed into a "something to occur in the future," indicated by a line leading "far upwards."

Concluding Remarks on Linear Representation of Thought-Relations

We may conclude this section on linear representation of logical relations with a short summary of the findings presented above. The main aim of this investigation was to uncover primordial ways of representing relatively abstract thought-relations; the technique used to unearth these genetically earlier ways was that of inducing adult subjects to represent statements containing "and," "because," and "if" in a medium—expressive lines—that promotes the representation and articulation of meanings close to the level of concrete-perceptual experience.

The kinds of representations that emerged in linear symbolization showed a number of features bearing a formal parallel to characteristics of linguistic representation in early ontogenesis. For example, in practically all the linear representations, the thought-relation was *implied* in the arrangement of the event-symbols rather than *explicitly* expressed. The study also suggests that certain kinds of inner gestures and bodily organismic patterning mediate the relations between conceptualized events before these relations are explicitly articulated in linguistic forms.

It has been noted in several places that the linearly expressed relations for a particular linguistic connective varied in degree of abstractness. These various degrees seem to have been determined by two factors, one pertaining to the interpretation of the linguistic connective (what it is taken to connote), the other pertaining to the handling of the linear medium.

With regard to the connotations of the linguistic connectives, it was noted that the "and" tended to be taken as connoting conjunction or simple sequence between events—relations which are close to those obtaining on the concrete-perceptual level. "Because," conceived in terms of sequence, is again close to the perceptual apprehension of concrete events; so, too, is "if," when conceived in terms of co-occurrence. On the other hand, when "because" and "if" are apprehended in terms of ground-consequence and conditional-hypothetical dependence, one has grasped connotations which are far removed from the perceptual-concrete.

Second, the degree of abstraction of the represented relation depended upon the ways in which the subjects exploited the properties of the linear medium for the realization of the various relations. There was, on one hand, the general tendency to conform to the promptings towards concreteness engendered by the linear medium, for example, causality realized as simple sequence, conditionality as co-occurrence. On the other hand, there was also the tendency among the normal adult subjects, already in possession of linguistic means for articulating abstract relations, to form their linear vehicles so as to realize, at least indirectly, the abstract connotations of the connectives. Thus, features of the linear medium were endowed with a metaphorical function, for example, the use of pressure differences to indicate differences with regard to actuality versus nonactuality.

Regarded in terms of its more *general implications*, this study—as well as the others we have discussed in previous chapters—provides added insight into the operation of basic organismic-developmental principles.

Consider, for example, *the relation between form and function.* In Chapter 12, on the ontogenesis of thought-relations, we pointed to the tendency of the child to use available forms for the execution of a newly emerging function until forms specifically tailored for that function were forged or adopted by the child. For instance, long before the child uses an adequate *hypotactic* structure, a dependency relationship between events is typically expressed through juxtaposition of sentences, often without any connective. In certain respects, the subjects in Speier's study were faced with a situation somewhat parallel to that of the young child. In attempting to translate notions of dependency ("because," "if") the subjects frequently exploited the concrete-depictive means most readily offered by the linear medium (for example, juxtaposition of event-symbols), thus leaving much of the intended meaning unexpressed in overt forms.

The study also highlights the genetic principle of *increasing distance between symbol and referent.* If one attempts to order the linear productions with regard to the degree of abstractness of the relations represented, one will recognize that hand in hand with increasing abstractness there was an increasing "distance" between the structure of the symbol and the nature of the relations represented. At least three degrees of "distance" between the symbol and the symbolized seem to have been manifested in Speier's study.

At the level of "minimal distance," the vehicles directly pictured that which they represented: coordinate events in time, for instance, were symbolized through the juxtaposition of event-symbols; temporally overlapping events were portrayed through spatial overlap of sub-symbols. At a level of "intermediate distance" the vehicle functioned in a "concrete metaphoric" way in the representation of the referent: concrete properties of lines were exploited to indicate (rather than to directly depict) differences in status between the two connected events; for example, *pressure differences* were used to indicate differences in the degree of actuality of the two events. Finally, there was a third degree of distance, in which the vehicles functioned as "alluding metaphors;" in these cases, configurational-topological features of the linear symbols were exploited to allude to the more abstract thought-relations. For instance, topological characteristics, such as the spatial location "behind" or "up in the air," were used to allude to abstract relations of causal dependence and hypotheticality. This latter kind of symbolization—involving the formation of rather novel specific means from the linear material—seems to come as close as the medium of expressive lines permits to that degree of articulation of thought-relations which is apparently realized fully only through linguistic structures.

REPRESENTATION OF RELATIONS BETWEEN THOUGHTS IN A MEDIUM OF VISUAL IMAGERY

As noted in the preceding chapter, to have individuals represent thoughts in imagery is to have them exploit the perceived, lived-through events of their everyday lives as a medium of symbolization: one thus obliges them to structure concrete events or objects so that, rather than being particular recollections of particular occurrences, they are used as vehicles of representation and carriers of abstract, general reference.

In terms of our thesis (see Chapter 3) that the development of symbolization begins with the formation of symbolic vehicles out of the same "stuff" that comprises the concrete contents of perceptual-motor experience, representation in imagery brings to the fore a level of symbolization that is, genetically, one of the most primitive; therefore, one can expect to gain considerable information as to the ways in which thought-relations are apprehended at a very early stage in the process of conceiving, and giving primordial form to, complex thought-contents.

In the study to be discussed here (see Erle, 60), twelve adult, well-educated subjects were asked to represent, in imagery, first the content of four simple sentences, and afterwards the content of the following six compound statements (formed by joining pairs of simple sentences via the conjunctions "because," "if," and "but").

He paces a great deal because he works hard.
He would pace a great deal if he worked hard.[5]
He paces a great deal but he works hard.
He is intelligent because he is cautious.
He would be intelligent if he were cautious.[5]
He is intelligent but he is cautious.

The simple sentences were presented in order to obtain a gross "base line" from which the investigator could inquire concerning any changes ensuing in the subsequent expressions for the simple statements when these were components of the compound sentences. Since any simple statement was potentially amenable to diverse representations, a change in the representation of a simple statement was taken to reflect the influence of its relation to the other statement only when the subject explicitly indicated that the larger context had played a role in the change or modification of the expression.[6]

Before the modes of expression for the specific conjunctions are discussed, it is important to highlight certain general characteristics of the imagery productions vis-à-vis the linguistic statements that evoked them. In the linguistic statements, clear and distinct reference was made to the different agent-activities or agent-attributes, and the abstract relations between these contents were overtly expressed through relatively circumscribed and discrete forms in syntactically appropriate positions. Furthermore, the same form was used to represent the same relational function, irrespective of the contents related. In contradistinction, in the imagery representations, clear and distinct reference to both contents of a compound utterance was the exception, and the expression of a relation was typically embedded in the particular organization of the total content, rather than through clearly articulated and circumscribed means.

---

[5] These forms were used to emphasize the "if" as a relation of conditionality rather than as one of co-occurrence.

[6] For details as to procedure, see Erle (60).

It is, of course, in the very nature of the imagery medium that a direct realization of linguistically designated content must be carried through the *depiction of a concrete instance:* a statement such as "He works hard" can only be shown directly through a particular situation and can only be alluded to through concrete objects or events. There is, however, no intrinsic reason why the contents have to be condensed in, or omitted from, an image: yet *condensation* or *ellipsis* were typical in the imagery translations of the compound statements. In many instances, the two contents were represented as indissolubly united in one concrete event; in other cases, one—and even both—of the contents was given no direct representation at all.

Involved in the condensation of the contents in the image-vehicles was another characteristic feature of the representations, *indicatory depiction.* An agent's activity or attribute was often alluded to, not through the depiction of action but through some object in the total situation comprising the image, for example, a pipe or a desk for "He is intelligent," machinery, tools, etc., for "He works hard," and so on.

Such depiction through indicators is, of course, intrinsically *implicatory,* that is, it points beyond itself to a more comprehensive state of affairs without actually showing that state of affairs clearly and explicitly. Indicatory depiction and implicatory reference, however, were not limited to the realization of one or the other of the contents of a compound statement; in a number of instances, the content directly imaged did not imply one of the linguistically designated contents but rather some state of affairs which was itself the link to the designated contents. For example, an image of "a traffic light" formed by one subject did not imply either "He is intelligent" or "He is cautious," but rather "He crossed the street safely;" it was this implied content which was itself taken to imply "intelligence and caution."

In sum, then, imagery representations of relations between thoughts typically exhibited certain features, namely, *condensation of contents, ellipsis of content, indicatory depiction,* and *implicatory reference,* which were often exploited as means for realizing a thought-relation.

Let us now consider some of the specific findings. In our exposition here we shall limit ourselves solely to those results pertaining to the "because-" and "if-" connections. Although these thought-relations will be discussed separately, it should be emphasized that the significance of an image symbol for any one of the statements (e.g. "if") depended upon, and was frequently determined (in part) by, his images for other statements (e.g. "because") of a series.

Expressions of the "Because-Connection" in the Imagery Medium

In our discussion of the linear representation of "because-statements," it was noted that there was often a reversion or "regression" to more primordial analogues or forerunners of the abstract conception of "because," for example, temporal sequence or influence, notions more easily realized through the concrete-depictive linear vehicles.

The imagery medium is even less distant from the organismic matrix in which contentual and relational connotations are interwoven; it is not surprising, therefore, that the image representations even more often expressed relations of a "pre-causal" nature.

From the images for the "because-statements" (of the form "A because B") one might infer tendencies to express a number of genetically different connotations of the causal notion—ranging from the primitive apprehension of "because" in terms of *temporal sequence* to the interpretation of "because" in terms of *ground-consequence*. Quite often, to be sure, several connotations were realized in a single image; where this was the case, the different connotations were typically carried by different *material* or *formal* means.[7]

Going from the more primitive to the more advanced ways of construing "because-statements," there was "because" taken as: (1) *temporal sequence,* first B then A; (2) *exemplification,* B illustrates A; (3) *ingredience,* B manifested in A, A containing signs of B; (4) *influence* or *concrete entailment,* B produces, compels, or necessitates A; and (5) *ground,* A as due to B, B as "underlying" A.

The first of these modes may be considered the most primitive because it reduces "because" to a simple temporal relation between two events: it does not go beyond concrete sequence to a notion of a more intimate connection between events.

When a temporal sequence between the events was the dominant connotation [8] realized in an image, the principal means for expressing this connotation was the *formal*—and quite "natural"—one of imaging a

---

[7] By "material" means we mean the particular content of the image; by "formal" means, we refer to the organization of the content, e.g., sequence, condensation, foreground-background relations, etc.

[8] Since all the (well-educated) subjects undoubtedly came to the task with more advanced conceptions of the "because-connection" and presumably attempted to realize one or another of these, *even if only by implication,* it is understandable that none of the images for "because-statements" were taken to express solely a relation of temporal sequence. Nevertheless, it was clear in a number of representations that temporal sequence was one of the guiding connotations in the formation of the image.

sequence of occurrences. That this sequence was intended to express a *temporal* order of happenings was manifested in the fact that the B content was depicted before the A content—a transposition of the sequence of reference (AB) in the linguistic statement.

A subject, for *paces because works,* reported: "I see a person I know; he's working in a grocery store, working very hard; he tries to relax, walks upstairs, then keeps coming down to work again." In her explication of the image, the subject indicated that she had visualized *first* someone working very hard, *then* that someone walking upstairs (= pacing) to relax (sitting on a chair watching TV); then, unable to sit still (implying need to pace), coming downstairs (= pacing) to work again. (From the explication, it could be seen that the image was also exploited to carry a connotation of "because" close to *ingredience,* i.e., "the pacing was that of one who works hard," but this appeared to be a secondary connotation of the image.)

A somewhat more complex image, realizing "because" both as *temporal sequence* and as *exemplification,* comes from another subject, for *intelligent because cautious.*

"An image almost like Siamese twins. One is facing left, tentatively touching a hot radiator, pulling back his finger very quickly (thus exemplifying first caution and then learning), and the part facing to the right is standing with his chest out and his hand in his belt (the posture indicative of one who regards himself as intelligent)." The subject commented: "There is a *sequence* here from the cautious to the intelligent. . . . The caution leads to the reaction 'I'm intelligent.' "

The intent to express a more intimate relation than mere sequence between the two contents was here realized in two ways: through a *material condensation or syncresis*—connotations of both caution and intelligence (= learns from experience) expressed in one part of the image—and through a *formal condensation*—picturing the agent as a unitas duplex. By construing the agent as a unity-in-duality, the subject countered the sequence, expressing the two contents as indissolubly tied together although distinct: "The two parts can't be separated, they have to occur together. They are not two complete men back to back; they are each half a person; they can't exist separately." By materially showing the B content fused with the A, the subject set the stage for construing the left half of the image as exemplifying the A content.

To apprehend "because" as *exemplification* is to go beyond mere temporal sequence in that one grasps an inner bond between the two contents. The chief means for realizing this mode of apprehending "because" was: (*a*) to *condense* the two contents into one event, thus showing an inner tie between the contents, and (*b*) to picture the agent as *embodying* both A and B content while *enacting* the B content. In other words, in exemplification, both contents are depicted in a unitary event but the A content is imaged as more "static" (and hence more indicatory of status or disposition) than the B content; the A content is also partly fused with the B content.

To illustrate, a subject,[9] for *intelligent because cautious,* reported: "a girl with her books; at the same time, she's smiling, she's neat, her mouth is closed, and I see her walking around a puddle." The books, the smile and the neatness served primarily to indicate intelligence; they also served partly to indicate caution, but the chief means of expressing caution was through the girl walking around the puddle. The 'walking around the puddle' (caution) illustrated the intelligence, and in this way the 'because' was expressed. As one will note, the agent in this representation was grasped as an *"intelligent-*cautious individual behaving cautiously."

The next two stages are closely allied: "because" as *ingredience* and as *influence* both reflect the infusion or penetration of the causative state of affairs (B) in the dependent state of affairs (A); the former, however, by emphasizing the A content does not fully show the dependence of A upon B. In "because" as *ingredience,* the characteristic image was one in which *the A content was rather fully depicted, whereas the B content was rendered elliptically, that is, through indicatory depiction.* On the surface, it appears as if the B content is a *part* of A. Only through implicatory reference does it become clear that the B content is taken as determining or compelling the A state of affairs.

One subject, for *paces because works:* "a business man, but a very intelligent one, with a very important job, he has a cigar, pacing. This kind of pacing is a combination of worrying and thinking. 'Because' is shown in that pacing is essential to his thinking (= working hard). The fact that it's a 'worried-pacing' makes it 'forced.'" The subject contrasted her representation of the "because-statement" with the "but-statement" in terms of the amount of compulsion involved in the "pacing."

Another subject, for *intelligent because cautious:* "A person walking away from a race track, leaving fast, with a complacent look on his face." The situation depicted "intelligent behavior," but at the same time the agent's-action in the total context embodied cautiousness.

Where "because" was realized as connoting *influence* or *concrete entailment,* the dependence of the A content upon the B content was shown principally through *the dominant emphasis on the B content in the image.* Here, in direct contrast to *ingredience,* the B content

---

[9] The subject was a girl; the transformation of "he" into "she" reflects the lack of distance between symbolizer and vehicle in imagery representation.

was given rather full depiction whereas the A content was only elliptically depicted. Furthermore, the total image was articulated in such a manner that the dependent activity or attribute (A content) was shown almost as an inevitable or necessary concomitant of the B state of affairs. Following are several examples.

A subject, for *paces because works:* "A guy with a wheelbarrow with a lot of stuff in it, and he's pushing the wheelbarrow and pacing while doing it." Here clearly the "pacing" is shown as dependent upon the "working hard."

Another subject, for *intelligent because cautious:* "A man moving slowly, deliberately in a strange situation." Here the depicted cautious behavior implies intelligence.

We may turn finally to the apprehension of "because" as a relation of *ground-consequence.* To refer to such a relation in the imagery medium, the *foreground-background* relation obtaining in perceptual or imaginal experiences was exploited: for example, a situation or context pertaining to the causative statement was depicted in the background of the image, and a state of affairs pertaining to the dependent statement in the foreground. To illustrate:

One subject, for *paces because works:* "a person pacing up and down in his living room, and in the background there is a desk with a lot of papers on it, and the desk lamp is on. There's a lot of activity implied around the desk (= works hard)." The "pacing" here is literally shown against the background of "hard work."

Another subject, for the same statement: "The desk *shifts* to the background (work *becomes* the ground). . . . I see him walking. There is a waste paper basket near the desk and paper crumpled on the floor." Once again the dependent state of affairs is literally shown against the background of the causative state of affairs.

As one will observe, the foreground-background relation provided, in such instances, a *quasi-metaphorical* way of depicting the relationship of consequent to ground. What was "behind" the pacing literally was also figuratively "behind" the pacing.

In sum, there were at least five genetically distinct meanings given to the "because-connection" in the course of imagery representation of "because-statements." As we have seen, these different connotations were *to some degree* realized through different patterns of organization of the images, for example, sequence, foreground-background relation, etc. It must be stressed, that the image as a symbol is even more fused with the addressor than is the linear vehicle; hence, there is a *lesser autonomy* of imaginal than of linear representation; that is, one can less easily determine the kind of connotation carried by an image simply from an inspection of the external organization of the image as a detached product.

Expressions of the "If-Connection" in a Medium of Visual Imagery

It will be recalled that Erle used a somewhat different format for his "if-statements" than he used for statements including the other connectives. This was done in the hope of counteracting the more concrete connotations of "if" and of orienting subjects towards the idea of *conditional dependence*.

It is true that the statements "He would pace a great deal if he worked hard" and "He would be intelligent if he were cautious" did not lead to connotations of concomitance or temporal sequence; however, they also did not lead to connotations related to conditionality. In the great majority of cases, these statements led the subjects to take one or both of the contents as *nonoccurring;* in other words, the statements as represented in imagery were almost uniformly taken to connote (*a*) "He does not work hard," (*b*) "He is not cautious." It was as if a subject, entertaining a thought such as "He would pace a great deal if he worked hard," were to condense this assertion into "He does not work hard (and does not pace)," and then, unable to realize a negative in the concrete medium of imagery, were to depict an actual situation which implied "He does not work hard." Following are typical illustrations for the two "if-statements."

For *He would pace a great deal if he worked hard:*
(1) "A guy lying in the sun smoking cigarettes trying to make some chick."
(2) "A loafer sitting on a bench rather relaxed."
(3) "A guy, lounging on sort of a chaise lounge, looking up at the ceiling, hands behind his neck, and nesting his head on his hands, feet crossed."
(4) "Man sitting down relaxing, has a cigarette in one hand and a drink in the other."

For *He would be intelligent if he were cautious:*
(1) "Man taking a trip alone, driving very fast and misses an important turn."
(2) "Guy in a car, driving down the street, crashing into somebody else."
(3) "Man sitting in a chair, drink in one hand and cigarette in the other, beginning to fall asleep and the cigarette has dropped to the floor."
(4) "Man crossing the street against the light."

Because of the limited range in kinds of imaginal productions given to the statements used by Erle, sentences more in accord with the original format were introduced: "He paces a great deal if he works hard" and "He is intelligent if he is cautious." Each of these "if-statements" was given to a new group of twelve subjects for "translation" into visual imagery; the subjects were explicitly told that the intended relationship was one of conditionality. The following discussion is based chiefly on the second study.

Although there was a variety of ways in which the "if-connection" in these statements was imaginally construed, one fact was clear: the relatively abstract conception of *conditional dependence* rarely gained even indicatory depiction; and was, in fact, often acknowledged as *not being implied* in the image in any way. In other words, even though the subjects were clearly aware that the sentence referred to a relationship of conditional dependence, the push of the imagery medium toward concrete depiction led most of them to form representations that did not even *imply* conditionality. With this fact in mind, let us turn now to the various meanings of "if" as mediated through imagery. These "meanings" could be ordered developmentally, in terms of the degree to which they realized the dependence of the A upon the B content, and implied—even if globally—the notions of conditionality, presupposition, etc. The following steps could be delineated: [10] (1) *temporal sequence,* first B then A; (2) *concomitance* or *collaterality,* B co-occurs with A, A accompanies B, B 'hangs together' with A; (3) *exemplification,* A is manifested in, or exemplified by, B; (4) *ingredience,* B is implicit in or infused in A; (5) *influence,* B 'contains' or 'prompts' A; (6) *suggestive of conditionality,* B leads toward but is not yet consummated in A, A presupposes B.

To construe an "if-connection" as merely one of *temporal sequence* is to treat the linkage between the contents as solely an external one. Since the subjects—well-educated adults—were aware that the sentence to be translated into imagery referred to a relation of conditionality, it was not to be expected that they would apprehend the connection simply as one of "first B, then A" or "before B, now A." Nevertheless, there was one case in which the "if-connection" was so construed:

"A male, sweat on his brow, an open tie, now pacing in an area." The 'sweat on the brow' and the 'open tie' were taken to indicate work in the past. The

---

[10] These various steps pertain to the meanings of the if-connection and not to the mode of organization, for example, condensation, sequence, of the image per se.

462   SYMBOL FORMATION

image rendered in English was "Having worked hard, he is now pacing." There was no implicatory reference to any linkage between the two contents other than one of temporal sequence. Even the *condensation* of the contents into a unitary occurrence—a *formal* device often used to exhibit intimate linkage —carried no implication for the subject of a more-than-temporal connection.

A more advanced stage in the apprehension of the "if-connection" is the construal of the relation between the contents as one of *concomitance* or *collaterality*. Here there is something more than a temporal tie, even if the inner connection is a loose one and is more closely related to coordination than to dependence. There were two main ways in which "if" as collaterality was expressed: in one, the agent was depicted as exhibiting one content in his appearance and the other in his activity; in the other, both contents were exhibited in the appearance of the agent.

One subject, for *paces if works,* visualized "somebody striding, head straight, determined expression on his face, hands clenched (indicative of one who works hard), taking long steps and moving his arms vigorously.

Another subject, for *intelligent if cautious,* depicted "A very intellectual boy with glasses, studious looking (indicative of intelligence), poring over data, checking numbers on a calculator.

A third subject, for *intelligent if cautious,* visualized "A man who shows both intelligence and caution in his face." Another visualized "A professor, who typifies both intelligence and caution."

In cases such as these, the connection between the contents is palpably more than a temporal one (for example, simultaneity), but it is difficult to characterize the exact nature of the relationship; perhaps the best that can be said is that the A and B contents "hang together."

In "if" as *exemplification,* the relationship between the A and B contents is a more intimate one, and there is some implication of a difference in "weight" attributed to the two contents. The greater weight, however, is on the A rather than on the B content: *the B content exemplifies the A content.* Interestingly enough, all the instances of "if" as exemplification occurred for "He is intelligent if he is cautious." Following are a number of typical examples.

(1) "An individual speaking very slowly and deliberately." The subject observed that the action depicted was that of caution, but that such caution reflected intelligence.

(2) "Someone buying insurance." Here again, the action depicted was that of caution, the sort of caution that an intelligent person shows.

(3) "Someone carrying an umbrella on a cloudy day." Once more, the B

content was depicted and the A content was implied as behind the cautious action.

In these instances, one will observe the marked *condensation*, with the A content given little if any representation. Despite the fact that the B content (that on which the A depends in the sentences) is given the dominant depiction in the images, this content is thought of as emanating from the A content.

We turn next to the "if" as *ingredience*. As was noted in the discussion of the "because-connection," the relations of *ingredience* and *influence* are very closely allied: they differ in the degree to which the subordination of A to B is manifested. In *ingredience*, the A (or dependent) content is directly realized, and the B content (that upon which A depends) is only indicated; the dependence of A upon B is carried only by implication. In *influence*, the B content is given a greater dominance in the image, and the A content is seen as 'contained by' or 'embedded in' the B. In both relations, there is a very intimate tie between the two contents; there is also a vaguely articulated relation of subordination or dependence. There is, however, no implication of conditionality.

In order to realize the "if" as *ingredience*, subjects used indicatory depiction to refer to the B content in images that were primarily depictive of the A content. The B content was alluded to through gestures, postures, or characteristics of the agent or through modulation of the agent's action. These devices for expressing *ingredience* were manifested with especial clarity in a number of images reported for the *paces if works* sentences:

(1) "A person walking in a circle." The subject stated that the 'pacing' was shown in the agent's action, while the 'working hard' was indicated in the *direction* and *repetition* of the pacing. These features implied that the 'walking' was not an action directed towards a goal, but another kind of 'pacing,' a kind prompted by 'working hard.'

(2) "A guy pacing a great deal, walking back and forth intensely." Here the ingredience of the 'working' in the 'pacing' was indicated by the *intensity* of the pacing.

Consider now the following examples, primarily illustrating "if" as *influence*.

(1) "A man in an office, with desk full of papers and books (indicative of a work situation), and he's pacing around in the room." Here the B content was not expressed via agent characteristics or as modulation of agent's action,

but through the *context* in which the action was exhibited as occurring; this sufficed to convey a relation of influence rather than ingredience.

(2) "A library, small room, brown colored books on the walls, desk on one side, papers on top of the desk and some more books (all indicative of a work situation); man pacing on a rug and his hands are on his hips and he's bent over." Here again the principal expression of the B content was through the *context* of action which contained the A content. "If" was also expressed in the same image as a relation of *ingredience:* the *agent's posture,* while pacing, was indicative of working.

In these examples, the A content is exhibited, or very clearly implied, as dependent upon the B content. There is, however, no indication or implication of conditionality.

The "if-connection," as suggesting some connotation even vaguely related to *conditionality,* was rarely realized in the imagery representations. To refer to such a relation required special handling of the medium, for example, making a distinction between reality and irreality within the image, exploiting spatial relations metaphorically, etc.

One subject, for *paces if works,* formed a complex representation comprised of two images. First he visualized "a man standing near a work bench with a lot of tools" (man about to work but not yet working). Then he visualized the man imagining himself "walking back and forth rapidly as he planes boards" (pacing influenced by working). The *dependence* of the pacing upon the working was shown in the second image; the *nonactuality* of the working was exhibited in the first image; the *conditional relation* was implied in the sequence.

Another subject, representing *intelligent if cautious,* alluded to the connection between the two contents, and at the same time the nonfulfillment of the connection in the following image: "Man riding a snail's back up a road (very slow pace indicative of caution); there is a stream of sunlight at the top of the roadway in the distance (illumination equals intelligence)."

These, then, were the principal ways in which "if" was realized in imagery. One will note—in comparing Erle's and the subsequent study—that the meaning given the "if-connection" depended upon the format of the "if-statement": different meanings emerged for "He paces a great deal if he works hard" and "He would pace a great deal if he worked hard." It also appears that the connotation of "if" depended upon the characteristics of the A and B contents: the relation was inseparable from the content. Thus "if" as *exemplification* seemed to occur typically for "He is intelligent if he is cautious," whereas "if" as *ingredience* or *influence* was more characteristic of

"He paces a great deal if he works hard." Attention should also be called to the considerable overlap between connotations of "if" and "because" in imagery-mediated thought: only at the linguistic level do these notions become clearly differentiated.

Finally, the content given fullest representation in an image was that most amenable to *concrete depiction* rather than that which occupied a particular status in (linguistically formulated) thought: thus, for *paces if works,* the more concrete A content ("pacing") was generally given fuller depiction than the less determinate B content, irrespective of whether the connotation was *temporal sequence, ingredience,* or *influence;* for *intelligent if cautious,* on the other hand, the more concrete B content was given the more full-bodied depiction, even where the "if-connection" was grasped as *exemplification,* a connotation which usually emphasizes the A content.

A Note on the Expression of Relations between Thoughts in Dreams

In the studies discussed, we limited ourselves to an examination of only certain of the so-called "logical relations" between thoughts; thus, there was no attempt to deal with the nonverbal representation of such relations as "either-or," "although," "as though," "is like," etc. Furthermore, only two nonverbal media were employed, expressive lines and images. Finally, the subjects in both studies, being awake, were explicitly oriented towards the task of representing specific relations between thoughts.

In the present section, we seek to supplement the experimental findings by considering a special kind of imagery representation of thought-relations, images of the sort that emerge in the dreams of ordinary sleep.[11] Moreover, we deal with a wider range of relations than was done in the experimental inquiries—concerning ourselves not only with the relations previously discussed, but also with a number of others, for example, "A is like B," "A is not B."

Before turning to this discussion of representation of relations in dreams, it is important to highlight some of the differences between the findings derived from experimental studies (such as the one on imagery just described) and those findings that psychoanalysts have arrived at in their interpretations

---

[11] We deal, in this discussion, only with representation in dream *imagery;* the analysis of the syntactical and other linguistic features of actual *speech* in dreams is presented in Chapter 15.

of the dreams of patients. (1) In experimental inquiries, as noted, it is possible explicitly to direct subjects to form images pertaining to specified content; although instruction and orientation do not insure execution, it is reasonable to assume that the images (and linear patterns) produced by the subjects in the studies were directly related to the linguistic utterances that evoked them. Such a direct relationship between the "manifest content" of a dream and specific "latent content" putatively underlying the dream is far more open to question. (2) In experimental inquiries, it is possible to induce subjects to exploit imagery primarily, if not exclusively, in the service of representation; it is problematic that the images of dreams are primarily formed in the service of symbolic representation.[12] (3) In experimental studies it is possible to have a relatively large number of individuals form symbolic vehicles for the same circumscribed content; this fact makes it possible to compare and order the various ways of realizing a specific content. Ordinarily, one does not, and perhaps cannot, prescribe the same "latent content" for a number of dreamers.

Although these factors should make one wary of giving uncritical acceptance to the interpretations of analysts, one may give at least tentative credence to conclusions concerning the representation of logical relations in dreams, as long as there are no better controlled sources of information available, and insofar as there is no evidence which would conflict with these conclusions.

The major source of information concerning the representation of logical relations in dream imagery is Freud's *Interpretation of Dreams*. Almost alone among the psychoanalysts, Freud posed, and sought to answer, the question of how the connections between thoughts, ordinarily articulated by specific linguistic means, are realized in the manifest dream content. "When the whole mass of . . . dream thoughts is brought under the pressure of the dream-work, and its elements are turned about, broken into fragments and jammed together . . . the question arises of what happens to the logical connections which have hitherto formed its framework. What representation do dreams provide for 'if,' 'because,' 'just as,' 'although,' 'either-or,' and all the other conjunctions without which we cannot understand sentences or speeches?" (Freud, 70, p. 312)

Freud's initial answer is that dreams have no inherent means for

---

[12] Since, for us, the typical symbol arises when the symbolizer articulates a vehicle in a medium in order to represent a content of a materially different nature; and since symbolization, in its more characteristic manifestations (e.g., in speech) entails an awareness of duality between vehicle and referent, it will be obvious that our conception of symbol formation differs from that propounded by many psychoanalysts (cf. E. Jones, 121).

representing logical relations between thoughts. The "psychic material" out of which dreams are formed is inherently refractory to the expression of such connections. In this respect, Freud notes, dreams are like painting and sculpture, which are likewise inherently incapable of expressing logical ties.

But then comes a qualification. Just as one may exploit the visual imagery of the wakened state to allude to logical relations, so, too, as Freud puts it, is there "a possible means by which dreams can take account of some of the logical relations between their dream thoughts." This is done "by making an appropriate modification in the method of representation characteristic of dreams." (Freud, 70, p. 313 f) Such modifications do not occur in all dreams. "While some dreams completely disregard the logical sequence of their material, others attempt to give as full an indication of it as possible." (Freud, 70, p. 314)

Let us consider now the means used in dreams to indicate logical relations of different kinds. In discussing these means, we shall, wherever such a procedure is relevant, compare and contrast the means used in dream imagery with those used in imagery representation in the wakened state.

With regard to the primordial, global relation of *connectedness*—carried linguistically by the "and-conjunction"—Freud notes that this tie is expressed in dream imagery through concomitance or simultaneity in time. Two dream-thoughts that are brought into connection with each other are realized concretely in a single situation or event; an analogy may be drawn here to the manner in which a painter may represent poets from different periods in a single picture because they go together conceptually even if they have not historically coexisted.

Although Erle did not include an examination of general connectedness in his final study, he did investigate ways of expressing "and" in visual imagery in an earlier pilot inquiry. He there found a tendency —quite analogous to what Freud reports for dreams—to transform "connectedness" into simultaneity.

Causal relations ("because," "since"), according to Freud's account, are realized in dreams through two essentially similar means. In one, two dreams occur in sequence: the less extensive dream-unit generally, but not invariably, precedes the more extensive dream-part; in any case, the less extensive dream always corresponds to the dependent clause, and the more extensive to the principal clause.[13] In the second

---

[13] Freud notes that one cannot conclude from the manifestation of two dream-units of unequal "size" that the relation expressed is necessarily causal (70, p. 316).

way of expressing causal connection, one image in the dream, whether of person or thing, becomes transformed into another before our eyes. The two means are regarded as essentially similar because in both causal connection is expressed as temporal sequence. (70, pp. 314 ff)

Compared with the means that Freud appears to take as exhaustive for the expression of causal relations in dreams, the representation of "because" in wakeful imagery is much more *multiform*. There are quite definitely means analogous to those mentioned by Freud; there are also, however, means where no temporal sequence is involved, for example, *ingredience, influence*. Because these forms occur in images of single situations or events, they may have been overlooked by students of dream-representation. On the other hand, since ingredience, influence, etc., involve the apprehension of "because" at a more advanced level, closer to the linguistic-conceptual meaning of "because," it may be that they are exploited only in alert states of consciousness and not in the more "regressed" dream state.

We may also recall here Speier's findings concerning the expression of "because" in the linear medium. In many instances, of course, Speier's subjects were able to express connotations of "because" that are refractory to imagery expression. When "because" was grasped in its more primitive signification, however, the linear means for expressing causal relations were analogous to those utilized in dream imagery. Thus there were instances of causal linkage depicted through sequence (indicated by left-right placement in space), with the symbolic vehicle for the main clause being of greater detail and length than the vehicle for the dependent clause. Again, there were instances in which the linear symbolic vehicle for the causative state of affairs merged into the vehicle for the consequent happening—a mode of expression quite analogous to the transformation of one image into another in dreams.

Conditional relations between thoughts are discussed by Freud in a rather cursory manner. He notes in one context (70, p. 335) that "a conditional in the dream thoughts has been represented in the dream by simultaneity: ('if' has become 'when')." In other contexts (70, pp. 429, 438), he indicates that counter-factual conditionals, for example, "If my (dead) father were alive . . . ," "If only I had been the son of a professor," are insusceptible to expression in dreams, unless the hypothetical situation is transformed into an actual one.

Other investigators have uncovered different means for the expression of conditionality in dreams. Thus, Gutheil (91, p. 256) cites an instance in which the "if-relation" was realized in the form of a *sequence* of two events in a dream. The dream (that of a young school teacher) was as follows: "I kissed Mary in the presence of my father—

then I saw my father poisoned." The story behind the dream involved the objection of the father to the son's relations with Mary. He had once said that the son's marriage to Mary would deeply hurt him. The dream, then, expressed the thought: "If I should marry (= kiss) Mary, it would kill my father."

Another, more complicated, dream reported by Gutheil also reveals the use of sequence in the expression of conditionality. The dreamer here was a young man whose father, a rabbi, strongly opposed his son's desire to study law; being a very pious man, the father considered any profession except that of a rabbi as profane and undesirable. Underlying the dream was the young man's conflict as to whether to become a lawyer or a rabbi. This was the dream: "I am standing in front of a synagogue. My father is inside. A lawyer passes by." The dream expresses this thought: "Should I become a rabbi, the chance of having a desired life (as a lawyer) would pass me by." The dream, then, as Gutheil states, transformed the 'propter hoc' relation into a 'post hoc' one, that is, into a sequence (existing 'inside' the synagogue → life outside passes one by).[14]

As one will recall, the images produced for "if-statements" under conditions of wakefulness depicted single events but also events in sequence. We have seen, however, that events in sequence did not necessarily represent "if" grasped as "first-then;" nor did single events necessarily express "if" grasped as "when." A unitary event, depending upon the manner in which the content was exemplified and deployed in the total image, might express "if" as "ingredience," "influence," and even "presupposition," as well as "concomitance." A sequence of images, on the other hand, might be used to express more than temporal sequence; for example, a sequence was used by one subject to show "about to, but not yet working, then pacing while working" (for "He paces a great deal if he works hard").

One may mention further the use in wakeful imagery of such properties as "clarity," "size," etc., and such means as the "image within an image" to express "if-connections"—devices not reported by students of dream symbolization. These devices were typically used to indicate distinctions between actuality and nonactuality. Finally,

---

[14] It may be noted that this dream appears to express some of the atmosphere of "iffiness" by having the agent standing *outside* of the synagogue; in other words, he has 'not yet' entered the temple (= become a rabbi). One will recall similar devices used by some of Erle's subjects to suggest "not yet" of the conditional state of affairs.

one may note the typical way of dealing with counterfactual conditionals in wakeful imagery, namely, transformation of the conditional state of affairs into a contrary (e.g., "if he worked hard" = "he is lazy, is lying down"). Although Freud's comments are ambiguous in this regard, his illustrations suggest that dreams do not transform a counterfactual into a contrary but treat the counterfactual state of affairs as if it were actual (Not $A = A$).

Thus far, we have discussed those relations for which there was available information from experimental studies involving wakeful imagery as well as from clinical observations of dreams. We may now briefly consider a number of relations for which the only source of information on their nonverbal expression are cases cited by students of dream-representation.

Consider the relation of *similarity* or "just as." Conventional language can quite precisely formulate this relation between two contents, for example, one can say "A is like, equals, is similar to, B." Such a precise formulation cannot be attained in the dream. Instead, the dream alludes to the relation of similarity through *identification* or *composition*. Freud notes that the former method is used where persons are concerned, that is, where "Person A is similar to Person B;" the latter method also may be applied to similarity between persons, but is typical for expressing similarity between things (70, p. 320).

In *identification*, one of the two persons who are thought of as similar to each other is represented in dream imagery, whereas the second person is not directly exhibited. Implicatory reference to the second person is manifested in the fact that the depicted agent appears in the dream in all the relations or situations that apply both to him and to the person to whom he is likened. In *composition*, the dream-image contains parts or aspects of the two persons or situations that are likened to each other; thus the image may be of a person whose features come partly from Person A, partly from Person B, or who looks like Person A but behaves like Person B, and so on.

In connection with these means for expressing *similarity*, Freud observes that they are facilitated by the tendency towards condensation or fusion in the dream-work. This tendency, as we have noted, is generally characteristic of imagery in the wakeful state and may occur when the relation between two thoughts is other than that of similarity. Specifically, although identification and composition may subserve the expression of similarity in an image, their operation in imagery may also reflect primitive attempts to express a causal relation, etc.

According to Freud, the *alternativity* relation ("either-or") cannot be expressed in dreams in any way whatsoever. Even where the alternatives in the latent content are mutually exclusive, they are generally all expressed in the manifest dream—juxtaposed or "enumerated," so to speak (70, pp. 316 f). Although there is no available evidence to contradict Freud on this point, contrariety or antithesis was indeed occasionally expressed in *wakeful* imagery, typically for instance, through separate images going in different directions. There is no a priori reason why divergent vectors could not also be a means for expressing alternativity in dream imagery.

Finally we may consider the relationships of *contrariety* and *contradiction,* which are discussed in Freud's treatise as if they comprised a unitary category (70, 318). Although Freud begins his examination of the modes of expressing these relationships by stating succinctly that they are simply disregarded in the manifest dream, his subsequent remarks indicate that there are a number of ways in which contraries and contradictions are realized in dreams. First, because contraries emerge from a common matrix, a contrary may be implied in any aspect of a dream-image that potentially admits of a contrary: for example, something "going up," being a concrete expression of the generic change of direction, may also signify "going down;" something "hot," being a specification of the spheric notion of extreme temperature, may also signify "cold;" and so on (see Kaplan, 130). Second, since the negation of any thought presupposes conceiving of the positive (for example, to assert "He is not running" presupposes that one thinks of the possibility that "He is running"), one may express only the positive state of affairs in the dream proper, the "negation" remaining buried in the organismic setting from which the dream-image springs. Third, and at a somewhat more advanced level with regard to expressing negation, one may realize the idea of negation through some expression of incompleteness; for example, to express "He does not run" one may picture someone trying to run but hampered in his movements.

The representation of ideas of negation in wakeful imagery has not been studied systematically. Preliminary inquiries, however, suggest that methods used in dreams to allude to contrary or contradictory states of affairs are also employed in the imagery of the waking state.

We conclude this chapter on the representation of relations-between-thoughts in nonverbal media with a very brief—and necessarily tentative—comparison between imaginal and linear "codification" of such relations. For this general comparison, we shall overlook differences between wakeful and dream imagery.

Although imagery and linear expression are both relatively primitive vis-à-vis linguistic codification, the two media are not on the same plane of primitivity. In terms of our analysis of the changes in symbol-situations in the course of development (see Chapter 3), imagery representation entails a lesser "distance" between addressor (symbolizer) and addressee, a lesser "distance" between symbolizer and his vehicle, and a lesser differentiation between the medium of expression and the content expressed.

This latter feature is especially important in limiting the degree of autonomy of imagery representation. In order for a medium truly to become established and eventually to become autonomous, its *material* must be susceptible to being distinguished from the "stuff" of concrete, everyday experience. Only in this way is it possible to establish the duality between vehicle and referent that is characteristic of advanced symbolization. Because the medium of lines lends itself to being segregated from everyday experience—because its material is of a different nature—one can, within lines, establish a universe of representation. One can manipulate and modulate the properties of the line medium to a certain degree to express something of a totally different order, such as relations, etc. Because imagery partakes of the same substance as that which it "represents," this manipulation and modulation is scarcely possible: the manipulation of the medium almost inevitably infringes upon the content depicted. Thus, in the linear medium one can carve out means for expressing relations that are to some degree distinct from the means for representing the content related; the imagery medium is typically refractory to any such articulation.

In sum, the differences in the primitivity of the media entail differences in the relative autonomy and communicability of the vehicles formed in the two media. Whereas images are inevitably limited to communication to an alter ego, linear symbols are at least potentially capable of being used as interpersonal carriers of meaning.

chapter 25

On Linguistic Parallels to Nonverbal (Linear) Representation

A major aim of our experimental inquiries into linear (and other forms of nonverbal) representation has been to determine the nature of symbolic organization of experience at levels close to imagery and gesture and to contrast such symbolic organization with that reflected in the codification of experience in a typical Indo-European language, English. Stated in *developmental* terms, we sought to ascertain the changes that occur in representation when a linguistically encoded referent is represented in media conducing to a quite marked shrinkage of distance between vehicle and referent, that is, in media which are structured to form "natural" symbols.

We clearly recognize that all linguistic codes, whatever their structure, differ radically from "natural symbols;" in other words, we are cognizant of the fact that there are probably no linguistic codes whose basic principle of construction is that of onomatopoesis.[1] Despite this distinction between linguistic codification and natural symbolization,

---

[1] It should be clear that we are concerned in this chapter with *codification* as such and not with the *experiences* involved in the *handling* of the code. As we have shown, vehicle-referent distance varies considerably in the personal handling, for example, of English; thus in the adoption of a physiognomic attitude, in the poetic handling of words, in inner speech, etc., vehicle and referent are much closer to each other than in the everyday informational use of language.

however, we still believe that languages may—with respect to their typical features—differ among themselves in terms of the degree of vehicle-referent distance. It seems to us likely that such differences derive chiefly from divergent emphases on the various functions which language, as a fundamental instrumentality of culture, subserves.

In this light, one may plausibly expect that so-called "folk societies" or "nonliterate societies," whose members live to a considerable degree in concrete worlds-of-action, would have a language primarily oriented towards the mirroring of man's relative nearness to his concrete surroundings—that is, a language which, in its lexicon, morphology, and syntax, would place a relatively greater stress on the delineation of events and action in their experienced fullness and concreteness. On the other hand, languages of "advanced societies," whose civilizations are elaborated at relatively greater biosociological distances from natural habitats, would be expected to reflect, in their lexicon, morphology, and syntax, a relatively greater emphasis on the articulation of analytic conceptions and abstract relations.

In the preceding chapters, we have contrasted linear representation with English codification because we wished to bring into sharp relief the characteristic features of representation at levels close to imagery and gesture. It is of equal interest to organismic-developmental theory, however, to compare "natural symbolization" with linguistic codifications that are, in the main, more oriented towards the expression of concrete experience.

In using linguistic materials from nonliterate societies for our comparisons, we do not wish to imply that Indo-European languages, such as English, are devoid of the tendencies that render every language an instrument for concrete representation. It is fully recognized that any living language subserves a variety of functions, ranging from concrete characterization to the articulation of relatively abstract conceptions; it is only the relative emphasis on certain tendencies in the codification of experience that warrants regarding one language as closer to concrete perceptual-motor reality than another. It is also recognized that Indo-European tongues have a long history behind them, and that the numerous languages of this family reflect various stages of this historic evolution—some showing more and some fewer of the archaic features. None of the languages are, of course, completely devoid of features reflecting an orientation towards concrete representation.

With regard to the history of languages, eminent linguists such as Meillet (164) and Jespersen (119)—although acknowledging the operation of a great many nongenetic factors in the formation and changes of linguistic codes—have come to the conclusion that general principles of development are operative in the modifications that languages undergo in their evolution from earlier to more recent forms.[2] Jespersen has, in fact, formulated a comprehensive "law of development" for languages: "The evolution of language shows a progressive tendency from inseparable irregular conglomerations to freely and regularly combinable short elements" (119, p. 429).[3]

Actually, in Jespersen's formulation there are *three* developmental trends implied. One concerns the increase in the differentiation between words (as constant linguistic elements) and the sentence. "The borderline between word and sentence," Jespersen remarks, "was (in the past) not so clearly defined as in more recent times" (119, p. 425). For instance, the Latin *cantavisset* (subjunctive pluperfect of *cantare* —*he had sung*) "is really nothing but a sentence-word"—quite holophrastic, we may add, when compared with the corresponding codification in a language such as modern English, which is far more advanced in the construction of sentences from isolated, separate word units.

Second, and closely interrelated with the first trend, is the tendency towards increasing regularization and systematization in morphology and syntax. If one compares, for instance, the older with the more recent Germanic languages (e.g., (1) Gothic; (2) Anglo-Saxon, Old High German; (3) Middle English, Middle High German; (4) New English, High German), one finds in general a stepwise decrease in the number of classes of verbal conjugations and of nominal declensions and, within each class, a decrease in the variety of flexion forms. The following sample of declension (Table 25-1) may exemplify this trend (Krahe, 139, p. 31).

---

[2] There are, of course, a number of linguists who reject the application of developmental concepts to the analysis of language. Their principal objections seem to be (*a*) that there are many instances of reversal in trend, and (*b*) that more recent codes still retain residues of archaic tendencies and often reflect such tendencies in their contemporary operation. Against these objections, one may assert, first, that a developmental factor is only one of the factors assumed to operate in diachronic linguistic change; second, that the actual evolution of languages—in terms of *overall* direction—seems to be consonant with the developmental principle; and third, that archaic tendencies persist in every actual development, but that such tendencies are generally subordinated to the higher levels of functioning. See Werner and B. Kaplan (276).

[3] See, in this connection, the remarks of A. N. Whitehead (279, pp. 25 f) concerning the relation of mathematics to the development of language.

Table 25-1

Sample of a declension exemplifying trend towards morphologic-syntactic regularization and systematization

(after Krahe)

	Gothic	Anglo-Saxon	Old High German	New English	High German
Singular					
Nominative	sunus	sunu	sunu	son	Sohn
Genitive	sunaus	suna	sunes	sons	Sohnes
Dative	sunau	suna	sune	son	Sohn
Accusative	sunu	sunu	sunu	son	Sohn
Plural					
Nominative	sunjus	suna	suni	sons	Söhne
Genitive	suniwe	suna	suneo	sons	Söhne
Dative	sunum	sunum	sunim	sons	Söhnen
Accusative	sununs	suna	suni	sons	Söhne

The third trend implied by Jespersen's law of linguistic development, closely linked with the first two, is the tendency towards increasing abstractness. This tendency is manifested in many facets of linguistic change: in morphology, syntax, semantics. The rise of isolated constant linguistic elements ("words") out of holophrastic-concrete expressions—elements susceptible to combination with many other units—may itself be viewed as an increase in abstractness. Hand in hand with this process of splitting up small units and combining them in multifarious ways is an increase in "abstract"-formal, morphological-syntactic methods of construction, without which these elements would disintegrate into an orderless mosaic of linguistic pebbles. Take for instance, the English *had* which, as Jespersen notes, subsumes under one short form "everything expressed by the relatively holophrastic Gothic forms *habaidedema, habaida, habaides, habaidedu, habaideduts, habaidedum, habaideduth, habaidedun, habaidedjan, habaidedeis, habaidedi, habaidedeiura, habaidedeits, habaidedeith, habaidedeina*—separate forms employed for two or three persons in three numbers in two distinctive moods" (119, p. 332). But *had* would not function unequivocally were it not combined with other, equally short, abstract forms and were there not available "abstract" syntactic devices such as sentence order, subordinate clauses [4] particles, universal auxiliary verbs, etc., all features of later development.

The developmental increase in abstractness, as reflected in these formal morphological-syntactic features, is paralleled by an increase in connotational abstractness.[5] The evidence for this increase in abstractness is legion. For example, there is the formation of practically all our abstract or semi-abstract words from originally concrete terms through processes of generalization, metaphoric extension and the like. There is the evolution of concepts of pure temporality, independent of the concrete aspects of action. There is the evolution of the concept of space, independent of particular objects or events. There is the progressive building of number systems divorced from the properties of concrete objects. There is the systematization of notions about physical objects and living organisms through superordinate and subordinate concepts; and so on. Thus, as language is used more and more for the codification of happenings in terms of abstract and general subsumptive concepts and categories, and less and less for the relatively direct "painting" of perceptual-motor reality in its concreteness, the linguistic code inevitably loses a great deal of its potency for rich and detailed description.

Linear Representation and Concrete-Depictive Codification of Agent's-Action-on-Objects

Turning now to the main theme of this chapter, we advance the thesis that the closeness of symbol to concrete perceptual-motor reference, characteristic of representation in the linear medium, also plays a role in determining many features of the linguistic codes of folk societies. In the following discussion, we shall seek to clarify this thesis by selecting a number of instances from the languages of various

---

[4] Comparative linguists dealing with Indo-European languages are in general agreement that primitive Indo-European consisted predominantly of independent sentences; the dominant mode of relating sentences was that of paratactic construction. The historical unfolding of hypotactic constructions from coordinate sentences is paralleled by ontogenetic changes in modes of relating sentences (see Brugmann, 33, III, p. 650; and Chapter 12 in this book).

[5] As an impressive illustration of the inner connection between form and function underlying this parallelism, one may cite the statement by H. Sperber (235, p. 109) to the effect that the rationalistic attitude of the Enlightenment brought about—at least in Germany—a tremendous increase in the occurrence of linguistic expressions of causal relations between sentences ("because," etc.).

nonliterate societies. These instances are chosen because they exemplify, rather strikingly, linguistic parallels to some of the basic features of linear representation. In this section, we shall be primarily concerned with linguistic parallels to the linear representation of agent's-action-on-objects (see Chapter 22); in the following, concluding section, we shall deal with linguistic parallels to the linear representation of temporality (see Chapter 23).

In order to forestall irrelevant objections to our viewpoint, we should reiterate that we are not advancing the view either that nonliterate languages are exclusively concrete-depictive in character or that Indo-European languages are exclusively analytic-abstract in character. Our main emphasis here is to show that there are at least parts of *linguistic codes* in which the symbolic representation of experience closely parallels the organization obtained through *linear* mediation.

Furthermore, we do not maintain that the linguistic features discussed here are necessarily the central ones in *all* predominantly concrete-depictive languages. There are undoubtedly other features of concrete linguistic representation which fall outside the scope of this chapter—which is devoted solely to highlighting linguistic parallels to characteristics of representation in the *linear medium*.

As we have indicated, we would expect that linguistic codification in nonliterate societies would reflect—more than would the languages of Western European societies, with their sciences and advanced technologies—the concrete-dynamic-physiognomic richness of perceptual-motor commerce with the world. In selecting our illustrations, therefore, we looked for vehicular expressions of *dynamic features* of referents and for vehicular organization exhibiting the *global-concrete-contextual unity* of perceptual-motor referents. These two features are, of course, closely interrelated; nevertheless, we shall deal with them separately.

Dynamic-Physiognomic Features in Linguistic Codification

We have seen how linear vehicles, when construed as symbols for the representation of referents, are physiognomized so as to possess such dynamic properties as directionality, mounting intensity, extendedness, abruptness, repetitiveness, etc. Such dynamic properties in linguistic symbols are more difficult to point up because, in general, they are not perceptible in such symbols viewed externally, that is, viewed as products detached from their users.

Despite this difficulty, however, the physiognomic character of certain formal means of expression (their depictive relation to the connotations they embody) is sometimes rather clearly apparent. Among the expressive means which serve overtly to depict connotations, one may mention intonation, stress-accent, sound—especially vowel—symbolism, etc. To illustrate, the language of the Kaingang Indians, as Jules Henry describes it, expresses degree and intensity not by grammatical means but by more or less formalized changes in pitch and articulatory force, by modulation of vowels, and by facial expression. For instance, the Kaingang Indian raises his voice to denote some long, drawn-out activity; his voice may then take on what appears to us as a "complaining" nuance. When Henry described a hunting trip to his students at Columbia University in that language, the students were puzzled about what he was saying when he used the "complaining voice;" "it was the usual tone to describe the slow climbing of a hill." Again, Henry notes that the Kaingang cannot state "I struck him very hard" linguistically, except by using remarkable force in saying "strike" and enunciating the vocable with high-pitched, explosive articulation. Henry also observes that the facial expressions used to express degrees of intensity, etc., are just as formalized in many instances as are the formal categories of the language (Henry, 102, p. 252).

A linguistic emphasis on the depictive codification of physiognomically apprehended referents seems to us to be related to a widespread feature of many non-Western tongues, namely, the relatively lesser differentiation among various grammatical categories. In this regard, one may recall that we pointed to such a connection before, in our discussion of the characteristics of linear representation. We there showed that what appears as a sharp distinction between noun and verb in an English sentence does not appear as a sharp distinction in linear representation; the lack of differentiation ensues because the noun-referent and the verb-referent are both apprehended in terms of dynamic features (Chapter 22). We also referred to the lesser differentiation between noun and verb under conditions of the adoption of a physiognomic attitude (Chapter 14). In sum, then, one would expect that languages oriented towards concrete depiction would manifest only a relatively slight differentiation between the noun-category and the verb-category.

An impressive illustration of this point is provided by B. L. Whorf, in his discussion of the codification of an event in the English and the

Nootka languages. The English sentence "The boat is grounded on the beach" is rendered in Nootka [6] by:

tlih	is	ma
I. moving pointwise (boatwise)	II. on the beach	III. third person indicative (= they)

Part I, says Whorf, is not a name for what we should call a "thing," but is more like a vector in physics. The sentence does not contain any unit of meaning akin to our word "boat" or even "canoe." Thus, part I means "moving pointwise," in a way suggested by the following drawing.

Thus, in Whorf's interpretation, the predicative English statement, articulated in nominal-verbal forms, is represented in Nootka in terms of a vectorially characterized occurrence. It is most pertinent to our concern with linguistic parallels to linear representation that Whorf, in order to clarify his interpretation, actually—perhaps inadvertently —takes recourse here to representation via expressive lines, utilizing the properties of "shape" and "direction" (Whorf, 282, pp. 234–236).

The relative lack of differentiation between noun and verb has been pointed to in a number of non-Indo-European languages. For instance, Gatschet, in discussing the nature of the Klamath "verb," comes to the conclusion that it possesses some characteristics shared by the "noun" and some which it shares with the "true verb" of Western languages. As Gatschet characterizes it, "the Klamath verb is not a true verb, but essentially a noun-verb." It is thus presumed to stand closer to an assumed "early period when languages possessed neither nouns nor verbs . . . these distinctions arose gradually" (Gatschet, 73, p. 573). Gatschet maintains that "when the sentence has reached a stage in which the predicative idea in the verb began

---

[6] In rendering the linguistic forms of nonliterate societies we have not been concerned with precise phonetic transcription; such precision is not necessary in the present context.

to distinguish clearly between subject, object, and verb—noun and verb commenced to assume distinctive affixes. . . . Noun and verb, therefore, originated simultaneously, not successively." (73, p. 253).

Similar observations about the closeness of nominal and verbal forms have been made by other students of American-Indian languages, although most of them have not explicitly pointed out the pertinence of predication of action for noun-verb differentiation, and they have not appeared to be as keenly aware as Gatschet of the reciprocity in the emergence of the two grammatical categories.

Gladys Reichard, in her analysis of the noun-verb relationship in Coeur d'Alene, an American Indian language spoken in Idaho, makes these observations: "Relationship between nominal and verbal stem is so close that they are often not distinguishable. . . . I am inclined to interpret nearly every noun as a verb. For instance, *amiyăm* is not only 'woman' but also . . . 'the womaning' " (197, p. 553). One may also note here that so-called pronouns, adverbs, and adjectives are all closely related to the verb, having event significance. To illustrate, the English phrase, "It is tough" is codified in Coeur d'Alene in a way that would be equivalent to an English statement referring to an event; accordingly, the equivalent for *tough* has to be put into one of the various aspective modes, e.g., "it toughs naturally" (197, p. 677).

M. Andrade, in his structural analysis of Quileute, a language spoken by American Indians of the State of Washington, also points to the close relationship between nominal and verbal stems. In this language, most morphemes are used as nouns or verbs, depending upon the proper suffixes. Furthermore, Quileute words which would be classified as adjectives in Indo-European languages are actually identical in their morphology and syntax with verbs (6, p. 179).

B. L. Whorf's discussion of the noun-verb relationship is somewhat close to Gatschet's. Whorf points out that in Western tongues such as English, most of the words are divided into two classes which have different grammatical and logical properties: the class of nouns and the class of verbs. "Our language thus gives us a bipolar division of nature. This division, however, is not inherent in nature; how far events, things, relationships are distinguished depends on the grammatical categories evolved in the particular speaker's language." "In Nootka, all words seem to us to be verbs, but really, there are no classes 1 and 2; we have, as it were, a monistic view of nature that *gives us only one class of words for all kinds of events.* 'A house occurs' or 'it houses' is the way of saying 'house' . . ." (282, p. 215).

In Gatschet's terms, Nootka would represent a type of linguistic codification close to a state in which descriptive painting of an occurrence is maximally stressed, and in which the trend towards a predication entailing noun-verb differentiation is minimal. It is interesting to observe that, whereas many linguists speak about nouns in American Indian languages as having more or less the character of verbs, Gatschet—and apparently Whorf also—see the verb-noun relationship in terms of degree of reciprocal differentiation.

Although we believe that the Gatschet-Whorf interpretation is the more adequate one, the question still remains why one might be induced to interpret as verbs such words as the Nootka expression equivalent to our "house." "These terms," says Whorf, "seem to us to be verbs because they are inflected for durational and temporal nuances, so that the suffixes for 'house-event' make it mean long-lasting house, temporary house, future house, house that used to be, what started out to be a house, and so on" (282, p. 216). Whorf's statement carries the implication that the Nootka expressions, whether equivalent to our nouns or our verbs, refer to "eventing" and thus convey the dynamic nature of their referents. In this respect, Nootka seems to us to represent only an extreme case of many, if not all, American Indian languages. If one tries to press the unit forms of these languages into the categories of Western tongues, the stress on 'eventing,' entailing a lack of differentiation between noun and verb, may make the verb appear as a "noun-verb" (Gatschet) or may make the noun appear as a "verb-noun" (Reichard).[7]

A relative lack of differentiation between noun and verb is overtly manifested in some languages by the attachment of the same affix sometimes to a "verb," sometimes to a "noun." For example, in the Klamath language, the prefix *lxa-* refers to the class of wavy or striped objects when connected with a nominal expression and to undulating motion when attached to a verb-stem. Thus, this prefix, if attached to nominal forms, connotes such things as "articles striped horizontally," "striped vertically," "elongated bag," "animal provided with antlers;" if attached to verbal forms, the connotations are "to undulate," "to billow," etc. Similarly, *shl-* refers to objects of a thin, flexible, sheet-like form, such as cloth, blankets; but it also appears in

---

[7] See Gatschet's statements on Klamath and Reichard's on Coeur d'Alene, quoted previously. Thalbitzer presents the rather extreme view that "the Eskimo verb merely forms a sub-class of nouns" (251, p. 1059).

verbs that refer to "spreading out," "spread over" (Gatschet, 73, pp. 292, 297).

How is one to account for this phenomenon? It seems inconceivable to us that verbal and nominal classes could be treated in such a similar way, unless it is assumed that the properties of objects are perceived as dynamic, kinetic, or physiognomized qualities. It seems most plausible to us that "bridge" in Klamath takes on the prefix *shl-* because this object is apprehended and classified in terms of its dynamic property of "spreading over" (a river, etc.). Again, we may consider a phenomenon from another language, Coeur d'Alene: the previously mentioned fact that, in this language, adjectives are closely related to verbs, and that therefore English "tough" is actually equivalent to something like "state or occurrence of toughening," seems to be most easily comprehensible if one assumes that object properties are here apprehended physiognomic-dynamically.

The noun classification of the Yuchi language (Oklahoma) may serve as another illustration. Yuchi nouns are classified through suffixes into two main groups, animate and inanimate objects. The inanimate objects are further differentiated into (1) upright, vertical objects, (2) horizontally extended objects, and (3) objects of roundish shape (actually of forms not definable in terms of verticality or horizontality). The three classifying suffixes are: *-fa* = vertical, *-ĕ* = horizontal, and *-dji* = round; for example, *yáfa* (tree), *ya'ĕ́* (log), *tídji* (rock). It seems highly significant that these three suffixes are identical with the verbal stems for "to stand," "to lie," and "to sit" respectively (Wagner, 262, p. 321). This kind of classification clearly suggests that the properties of objects on which the categorization is based are dynamic or physiognomic, event-like qualities rather than static ones.

In sum, we may say that however one may characterize the "nominal" or the "verbal" forms in these languages on the basis of grammatical-structural analysis, it seems to us that the relative lack of boundary between the classes can only be accounted for by assuming that nominal referents (objects, subjects) as well as verbal referents (action) both take on some of the basic properties of the concrete-dynamic events of which they are intimate ingredients. In other words, things or persons acting, as well as things or persons acted upon, are represented in these languages in terms of dynamic properties. In this respect they are apprehended just as are movements and actions; that is, they are, in our terms, "physiognomized." In this light, one can perhaps better understand the frequently observed emphasis in nonliterate languages upon the minute and detailed characterization of motion as well as the stress upon the kinetic properties of objects.[8]

Global-Contextual Representation in Linguistic Codification

Intertwined with the tendency towards the apprehension and expression of events in terms of dynamic-physiognomic properties is a tendency towards the representation of events in their unbroken contextual unity. The "spirit" of a language oriented towards the "painting" of reality in tangible concreteness and globality rather than towards the articulation of it in terms of analytic subsumptive notions and abstract relationships has been well formulated by Gatschet. Based on his intimate knowledge of Klamath and related tongues, Gatschet states: "Our (Western-European) intention is to speak with (abstract) precision, that of the Indians to speak graphically; the Indian individualizes while we classify" (73, p. 498). A more recent statement to the same effect comes from Kluckhohn and Leighton in their evaluation of Navaho (135): "Navaho is an excessively literal language, little given to abstractions and to the fluidity of meaning that is so characteristic of English. The inner classification gives a concreteness, a specificity, to all expression. Most things can be expressed in Navaho with great exactness by manipulating the wide choice of stems in accord with the multitudinous alternatives offered by fusing prefixes and other separable elements in an almost unlimited number of ways. Indeed, Navaho is almost overneat, overprecise. There is little 'give' in the language. . . . The general nature of the difference between Navaho thought and English thought —both as manifested in the language and also as forced, by the very nature of the linguistic forms, into such patterns—is that Navaho

---

[8] The history of the Indo-European languages impressively suggests that noun-verb differentiation is an occurrence consonant, in general, with the law of linguistic development. In early Indo-European, nominal as well as verbal "themes" or stems were formed out of roots in *identical* ways; Indo-European nouns were thus forms comparable to the verbal nomina of the later languages (they had the character of "giver," "spender," etc.). Later on, neither verbs nor nouns were derived from the roots, but their construction involved methods entirely distinct from each other (see Meillet, 163, pp. 151, 263). (For ontogenetic parallels to the early derivations of nouns and verbs, see Chapter 13.)

thought is prevailingly so much more specific, so much more concrete." [9]

In linguistic codes such as these, in which there is a strong emphasis on the representation of events in their full, unbroken concreteness, one would again expect a prevalence of certain features more or less analogous to those obtaining in linear representation. Thus, insofar as a language is inclined towards concrete-depictive codification, one would expect a relatively frequent use of *holophrastic symbols,* that is, unitary forms that refer to a complex state of affairs. Secondly, one would expect a reflection in the codification of that close interpenetration of various aspects in a concretely endured and apprehended event; whereas languages oriented towards analysis, abstraction, and generalization are rather removed in their codified statements from the perceptual-motor domain of experience, concrete-depictive languages would be more inclined to exhibit that *interpenetration* of the viewer's attitudes and the events viewed, that fusion of agent and action, that unity of agent's-action-on-specific-object, which obtains in the world of perception and action.

In the following, we shall first illustrate and discuss *holophrastic codification* in languages of nonliterate peoples and then deal with various ways in which the *organic interpenetration* of components of concrete events are exhibited in linguistic codes which are less distant from their referents than are our own.

Let us consider several illustrations of *holophrastic symbolization* on the linguistic level. Gatschet, in his analysis of the Klamath language, observed that this language possessed material or concrete affixes as well as formal-syntactical affixes; these concrete affixes referred to such facets of events as the "shape" of an activity, the distance of the event from the speaker, qualitative dynamics, etc. In codifying an event, speakers of the Klamath language brought these various material affixes into a constellation with a radix and thus "painted" the occurrence. For instance, in *shlelxtchanólatkó,* the prefix *shl-* refers to garments or flexible articles for personal use, *-tchan* indicates an act performed while marching, *lx* indicates a downward direction;

---

[9] Kluckhohn and Leighton (135, pp. 199 f) give this illustration of the concreteness of Navaho speech: "When a Navaho says that he went somewhere, he never fails to specify whether it was afoot, astride, by wagon, auto, train, or airplane. This is done partly by using different verb stems which indicate whether the traveler moved under his own steam or was transported, partly by naming the actual means."

these are combined with relational suffixes, -óla (altogether) and -tko (participial suffix of the passive). All of these, connected with the radical -e, appearing in words connoting 'to lay down,' leads to a unitary expression which would be rendered in English approximately as "dropped and left behind altogether something garment-like while walking" (Gatschet, 73, pp. 280 f).

Another illustration of this holophrastic, graphic mode of symbolizing may be taken from the description of the Chipewyan language by Li Fang-Kuei (153, p. 405). In Chipewyan, verbal statements are formed with indices indicating one of three "aspects" (imperfective, perfective, futuric) and one of five "modes" (neuter, momentary, continuative, customary, and progressive). These indices occur in a symbol in two ways: by affixes and by verb-stem modifications. There appears to be a very close interdependence of these different indices: specific prefixes entail specific modal variations of the verb stem, etc. The meaning of the integral symbol cannot be inferred from stem or prefix taken separately. For example, from the stem signifying "to handle a living being," we have in the neuter mode, "a living being is in position, i.e., to lie" (thi-tĩ = I am lying); in the momentary mode, the symbol signifies "a living being gets into position or acts, i.e., to lie down" (ne-s-téih = I am lying down); in the continuative mode, we get "a living being acts continually, i.e., to dream—to lie around" (na-s-te = I dream); in the customary (transitive) mode, we get "to handle a living being customarily or repeatedly, i.e., to carry it around" (dzéré-s-teih = I am carrying it around); finally, in the progressive (transitive) mode, we get "to keep on handling a living being, i.e., to hold it" (da-ge-s-tel = I am holding it).

In both of these illustrations one sees a unitary symbol formed by bringing into a constellation various morphological elements, each having little significance of its own, but all uniting to produce the integral, semantically more or less determinate symbol. Whorf, in discussing characteristics of Shawnee and Nootka, suggests the analogy of these languages to a chemical compound; in contrast, he considers English as analogous to a mechanical combination: "Shawnee and Nootka suggest a chemical compound; the typical Shawnee or Nootka combinations appear to work with a view not so much to the utility of their immediate references as to the ability of the terms to combine suggestively with each other in manifold ways that elicit novel and useful images." (Whorf, 282, p. 236).

Interpenetration in Linguistic Codification

The exhibition in linguistic codification of the organic interpenetration of aspects of events is closely related to holophrastic symbolization. In interpenetrative representation, the vehicles do not articulate discrete, ideal aspect of events but rather emphasize one feature of a concrete event while at the same time referring overtly or implicitly to other features of that event. Thus, interpenetrative representation is much closer to concrete perceptual-motor reality than is that form of codification which sets off agent from action, action from object, etc. As one will recall, interpenetrative representation characterizes linear symbolization of events (see Chapters 22, 23, and 24). In our view, where such representation occurs it reflects *a decreased distance between person and symbolic vehicle and between vehicle and referent.*

One of the striking findings of our linear mediation studies was that many of the subjects used one or more linear properties in their symbols to express their personal reactions to the events to be represented: they thus included, in their representations of ostensibly "objective" events, their own "subjective" attitudes or relations to the events.

The *"compulsory codification" of the addressor's (or/and addressee's) attitude or relation to an event* occurs in many nonliterate languages. For example, Whorf points out that the Hopi verb differs clearly from the Indo-European verb in that the Hopi verb always indicates by formal means the type of validity the speaker intends his statement about an event to have; the Hopi speaker must express in his utterance whether he is reporting the event, whether the event is expected by him, whether he is referring to an event from memory, etc. (Whorf, 282, p. 217).

An interesting manifestation of the intrusion of addressor or addressee characteristics in the representation of an event is the difference in speech-forms depending upon the sex or social class of the speaker or addressee. Such a difference, found in many languages, may pertain only to a few selected words or to an extended vocabulary but may also apply to the grammatical structure. The origin of these linguistic differences is probably rooted in religious-magical (taboo) notions as well as in social-organizational distinctions (Werner, 268, p. 219). To illustrate, in Old Samoa the common name for food was *ai;* when one addressed a person of higher status, one used the form *tau-sami;* when the addressee was a chief, the term was *taumafa;* for the high chief, it was *taute* (Werner, 268, p. 89).

An excellent illustration of a language that has distinct forms for men and for women is the Yana language, spoken by some Northern California tribes. According to Sapir's analysis (in Mandelbaum, 209, p. 210), the majority of the Yana words have two forms, one used by males in speaking to males, the other used whenever females are the addressors or addressees. With regard to grammatical indices for these two speech-forms, two classes can be distinguished. One class contains "male" forms, ending in a short vowel, and "female" forms, in which the final vowel as well as the preceding consonant are unvoiced: for example, "to eat" is *mô'i* for the male and *mô'ⁱ* for the female; "river" is *dāha* for the male and *daxᵃ* for the female. The second class is characterized by a "male" syllable added to the "female" form: thus, the endings of the causative forms, third person are, for the *usitative* aspect, -*mā* (female), -*mā'a* (male); for the *dubitative* aspect, -*K!ô* (female), -*K!ô'a* (male); and for the *quotative* aspect, -*t'ê* (female) and -*t'ê'a* (male). Thus, "it is said he gives to eat" is expressed through *mot'ê'a* by males and through *môt'ê* by females.

In his study of Nootka, Sapir has presented another illuminating example of the intrusion of phenomena lying outside of the "objective" events themselves in the codification of these events. In this instance, features of the addressee are included in the codification of events in such a way as to affect the representation of other features of an event, for example, mood and person, etc.

Thus, in speaking to a child or about a child, it is usual to add the ordinary diminutive suffix, -*'is,* before terminations which indicate tense, mood, or person in the verb. In talking to persons of unusual size, *aq* is inserted similarly. In speaking to dwarfs or very little people, the diminutive suffix is used and in addition all sibilants are palatalized. The diminutive suffix is also used to people who have lost an eye, or who squint, but in their cases all *s* or *sh* sounds are changed into the corresponding side-sounds (different variants of *l*). Humpbacked people are also addressed with the usual diminutive suffix, but the ordinary *s* or *sh* sounds are here changed to some peculiar 'thickish' *sh* sounds, pronounced with the lower jaw somewhat protruded. In talking of lame persons an *l* is inserted somewhere in the word, and with left-handed people the element *tsh* is inserted after the first syllable of the word. In speaking of greedy people *tshx* is inserted after the first syllable (cited after Jespersen, 120, p. 132).

Another manifestation of *interpenetrative representation,* which one will recall from our studies on linear mediation (see especially Chapter

22), was the frequent *fusion of agent and action* or the representation of the agent in terms of the nature of his action and vice versa. For instance, one of the indications of agent-action interpenetration in the linear productions was the lack of explicit representation of the agent; in our study, this absence of any overt representation of an agent occurred in almost half of the linear productions.

In our search for linguistic analogues to this lack of agent-representation, the following comments by Gladys Reichard (198, pp. 55 f) on the character of the Navaho verb seem to have considerable relevance: "One of the most obvious characteristics of the Navaho stems is the marked division into verbs of state, which I call 'static' (called elsewhere 'neuter'), and verbs of motion and action. *Neither type requires a subject* although both types may have one. The third person, therefore, means 'there is a quality or state of . . .' rather than 'he is . . . ,' 'there is . . . kind of motion' rather than 'he is . . . ing.' The emphasis is on the description inherent in the stem rather than on the person or object to whom the description is attached or directed . . . the third person is remarkable in the fact that no personal subject is apparent. . . ." For instance: *sitt*, which one would translate as 'animate object lies,' actually connotes 'lying on the part of animate objects,' "and for that reason needs no reference to a subject."

Turning from the static verb-stems to the active verb stems, Miss Reichard has this to say: "The understanding of such verbs will be greatly increased if the verb is thought of as essentially emphasizing the kind of motion—'motion of round object takes place progressively,' 'motion of round object starts from a point,' etc. Once this idea is grasped and the general meaning of the stem is ascertained, the forms usually seem reasonable, whereas if one *first personalizes the forms and moves out from the subject* instead of *from impersonal motion,* the forms may make little sense and seem impossible to interpret. . . ." Since all such stems, Reichard argues, imply inherent motion, they do not require an expressed agent or cause: "once the concept of the inherent power of an object to move is understood, it is not difficult to understand why the need for a third person subject, object, or agent is minimized." (Reichard, 198, p. 62)

It is recognized that the Navaho samples do not present a perfect linguistic analogue to agent-action interpenetration expressed in our subjects' drawings, insofar as the Navaho stems do not refer specifically to transitive verb themes. In principle, however, there seems to be considerable similarity as to the general manner in which English phrases concerned with verbal action are "translated" into both media—a similarity which results in minimal agent representation both in the linear drawings of our subjects and in Navaho codification. In both cases, the emphasis is on the concrete depiction of an *event*, rather than on the analytical separation of subject or agent from his action. The Navaho notion of the "inherent power" of an object to act or move in a specific manner seems to imply that a perceived action or motion is the outward manifestation, the overt dynamic characteristic, of the object involved. Since such objects-in-action, which would ordinarily be codified as grammatical subjects, are already implicit in their physiognomic-dynamic forms of motion, it is understandable that a separate codification of an agent per se is omitted.

Another phenomenon that one would expect in codification close to perceptual-motor reality is that *the representation of action might reflect different relations of the agent to that action.* In this connection, Reichard's observations on Coeur d'Alene are quite pertinent. Reichard notes that in Coeur d'Alene, where the emphasis is on the 'coming about of the action,' there are references to different agent-qualities in the expression of different types of completed events; different suffixes are employed, depending on whether the agent controls the event or not; whether the activity requires considerable effort on the part of the agent; whether the event comes to pass with the agent quite passive, etc. To illustrate: *-em* indicates that the action comes to be of its own accord, that is, the agent does not control it; *-p* indicates that the activity was not voluntary on the part of the agent; *-nun* denotes that the agent succeeded after effort, and so on (197, pp. 579, 601).

Some observations by Whorf concerning peculiarities of Hopi grammar seem relevant here. Whorf, in his discussion of the *inceptive* aspect of the Hopi verb, found that *three* different morphological forms, rather than one, are used by that language to translate the English "begins doing." Whorf came to the conclusion that the usage depends on the way in which the agent is related to the action: that is, whether the verb represents an action springing from a subject-initiated impulse (e.g., *running, fleeing*), or an action which comes about through constantly maintained participation of the subject (e.g., *breathing, dying*) or an action into which the subject needs only to be placed in the initial stage to be carried further by a natural tendency (e.g., *'falling,' tipping over*) (282, pp. 103 ff).

Just as one often finds interpenetration of agent- and action-representation in concrete-depictive codification, so would one expect relatively frequent manifestations of *action-object interpenetration* where codification is close to the perceptual-motor referents. It will be recalled that in the study on linear symbolization of agent's-action-on-objects, the degree of interpenetration in the linear productions ranged from practically none (relative independence of verb from variation in object) to almost complete fusion. Such a range may also be found in the American Indian languages, from which we take most of the illustrations about to be cited.

Let us examine, first, some of the characteristics of the Navaho verb-stem, as described by Reichard (198, pp. 55–76). Leaving aside here the basic division of Navaho into verbs of state and verbs of action, one finds that the elemental segment of an event, as signified by the verb stem, is not action per se, but action or motion with respect to a particular object. "If the Navaho emphasis on descriptive motion were thoroughly realized," says Reichard, "the demands by English speakers for words like 'give, take, put, carry, lose, get' would be understood as unreasonable. . . . The interpreter must know what kind of object is to be 'given:' a round, a fabric-like, rope-like, fluffy object, substance in a container, etc.;" that is, different verb stems must be employed, depending upon the nature of the object.

One also finds in Navaho codification that there are variations in the degree of specific concreteness in the ways in which the Navaho stem symbolizes events; this again parallels the findings of the linear-mediation study. Thus, there are stems which refer to action of an object in a more general way, for example, -'al ('round object moves'); but there also exists an "incredible number" of stem forms for symbolizing highly concretized events involving very particular objects, for example, 'motion of objects fastened to a string' (-'ish), 'shattering fragments move' (-ta), 'broad stiff surface sails' (-ki), 'light feather-like object sails' (-zal). In many cases, Navaho stems are even more specific: if one speaks of the 'falling of a long, slender, rigid object,' one must decide whether it is 'club-like' (-l-xal), 'an animate object moving like a stick' (-til), or 'a stick moving so swiftly that it twists' (-kos) (Reichard, 198, p. 65).

In Quileute, action is represented in a similarly contextualized fashion. This language possesses many postpositive morphemes which express action very concretely, including the specific handling of the object; thus, Quileute has a morpheme for the general idea of catching (-qua) but entirely separate stems for such notions as 'to catch an animal or a person who tries to escape' (-'ai); 'to be successful in catching fish in large quantities' (-soq), 'to catch fish for the specific purpose of drying it for future use' (-pats); 'to catch one by surprise at a proper act (*-aqli*), and 'at an improper act' (*bā'*). (M. Andrade, 6, p. 196)

These examples illustrate cases in which *the verb stems themselves are varied,* indicating through these variations the objects involved in the action; such examples reflect a very intimate fusion of action and object. There are other instances where morphemes (affixes) *are attached to a given verb stem* to indicate the nature of the objects involved in the action. To illustrate, the transitive verb of the Klamath language is characterized by Gatschet as one that is controlled and modified by its object rather than by its subject (73, p. 574). Accordingly, there are prefixes attached to a stem to signify the class characteristics of the particular objects involved in the action. For instance, *t* in transitive verbs refers to acts performed with elongated objects, e.g., performed with hands outstretched; *st-* refers to an object placed in a stiff, immovable position, e.g., *stitxa-* to defraud (versus *itxa-* to take away); here, apparently the helplessness or immobility of the victim is, so to speak, "pictured" by the prefix (Gatschet, 73, p. 298).

This kind of expression of object variation, that is, the attachment of prefixes to a relatively intact verb-stem, reflects a rather mild degree of action-object interpenetration, especially when compared with the radical alterations of verb-stem, as a function of object, in the Navaho examples. Such relatively mild interpenetration will perhaps be more strikingly highlighted in the following Klamath expressions: *kshelxa: to lay down*—long object, animate being (e.g., man); *shlelxa:* to lay down—thin, flexible object (e.g., clothes); *kmelxa:* to lay down —object of winding shape (e.g., thread, rope).

In Klamath, the intimate relation between verb and object is indicated with particular clarity in the fact that the expression of plurality versus singularity, as embodied in verb variations, is in terms of objects rather than subjects. There are four grammatical means available in Klamath to indicate the number of objects involved in action, all means of modifying the verb-stem: thus, plurality of the direct object may be expressed through (distributive) reduplication of the verb, e.g., *skútash sha wáldsha* ('they spread a blanket over') and *skútash sha waláldsha* ('they spread a blanket over several objects'). Plurality of objects may also be expressed through changes in the object-classifying prefix, for example, for the symbols for action pertaining to long objects, the prefix shifts from *ksh-* (singular) to *i-* (plural); if round objects are involved, there is a shift from *l-* (singular) to *pe-* (plural); and if one refers to objects to be driven, the prefix for singular is *shu-*; for a few objects, it is *tp-*; and for many objects, it is *n-*. A third way of expressing plurality of objects is through variation in suffix, e.g., *ktuka* ('to strike by hand one object') and *ktuyus* ('. . . several objects'). Finally, one may show the shift from singularity to plurality of the objects by changing the radical syllable in certain verbs, e.g., 'to shoot (one)'—*shlin*, 'to shoot many' —*yúta*; 'to ram one post into the ground'—*téwa*, 'to ram two . . .'— *stálxa*, 'to ram many . . .'—*tetálxa* (Gatschet, 73, pp. 443 ff).

In contradistinction to languages such as Klamath, in which objects are *implied* through verbal affixes, there are other languages in which action and object are both *explicitly* encoded, but in which, nevertheless, the closeness of action and object is exhibited in a sentence by attaching the same classificatory affix to the symbols for both. For instance, in Palaio-Sibiric languages, the identical suffix for the indefinite noun is appended to the transitive verb as well as to the object (Lagercrantz, 145, p. 109). Again, in the Bantu languages of Africa, there is appended to the verb not only the classificatory prefix of the grammatical subject (agent) but also the classificatory prefix of the grammatical object (Meinhof, 165, p. 28).

Having discussed fusions of agent-action and action-object, we may finally treat of instances in which there is *interpenetration of agent-action-object*. Of particular interest here are those cases in which one part of the total action-symbol refers to properties of the agent (subject) and another part refers to properties of the object.

As one will recall, this kind of interpenetration was not infrequent in the linear productions of our subjects (see Chapter 22). We may reproduce again two of the patterns drawn by one of the subjects (Fig. 25-1a and b), the first for "He catches a lion" and the second for "He catches a criminal." The initial part of the first pattern, composed of a series of small loops, repre-

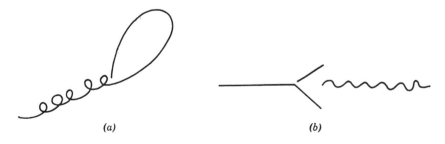

(a)   *(b)*

FIGURE 25-1. Linear representations by one subject for: (a) "He catches a lion." (b) "He catches a criminal."

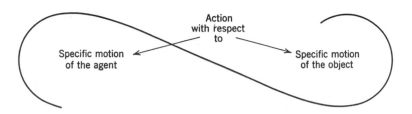

FIGURE 25-2. Scheme of interpenetration of agent-action-object in linear representation and in Chipewyan codification.

sented 'the agent-acting-with-difficulty,' and the latter part, consisting of a big loop, represented 'the-catching-of-a-large (lion-like)-object.' In the second pattern, the left part, consisting of a straight, horizontal, forked line, represented 'the agent's serious, straight-forward, goal-directed performance,' and the right part, a wave-like horizontal line, represented 'the victim's wavering movements in struggling to get away while being caught.'

Certain structural features of the symbols for action occurring in some American Indian languages may, perhaps, be looked upon as linguistic analogues to this "double-barrelled" kind of interpenetration. For example, one may refer here to the description which Li Fang-Kuei gives of the structure of a number of Chipewyan verb themes (153, pp. 405, 418). According to Li, the Chipewyan verb, in general, is a structure consisting of a stem and a number of prefixes. There are verb stems which signify the handling of objects possessing one or another attribute, for example, one stem refers to the handling of a round, solid object, another to the handling of a long, stick-like object, another to the handling of a grain-like object, etc., each object class requiring a distinct stem. On the other hand, the manner of handling, for example, picking up, putting down, carrying around, holding, etc., is itself signified by the prefixes which, with the stems, form the themes. One instance may suffice. "He is picking up a round solid object" is codified as follows: *niyeri'aih* (*ni* = up, *ye* = third person object, *-ri-* = local infix, *'aih* = to handle a round, solid object).

Leaving aside the fact that—in contrast to most linear productions— the third person pronoun is here explicitly (and redundantly) expressed, the diagram in Fig. 25-2 will serve to indicate the general similarity between linear and Chipewyan representation of a verbal theme. The symbol for the verbal theme is shown to be composed of two parts, one concerned with the agent's manner of action, the other with the object's dynamic-kinetic properties.

This kind of "intertwined" codification of agent's action on objects also occurs in Navaho. For instance, in expressing the notion which would be rendered in English as 'to lower an object,' Navaho has to represent the particular shape of the object as well as the agent's specific manner of handling it. Thus the stem *'áál* refers to the handling of a bulky, roundish object, and the prefix *na-* (down) indicates the direction in which the agent moves the object (Kluckhohn and Leighton, 135, pp. 192, 205).

In sum, then, the general parallelism between some aspects of codification in certain languages, more or less directed towards concrete-depictive representation of events, and the linear representation of agent's-action-on-objects appears to be quite striking. In both kinds of mediation, events are represented in such a way as to reflect the interpenetrations of agent and action, action and object, etc., as these are manifested in perceptual-motor experience.

We have also seen that in both media there are varying degrees of *interpenetrative representation*. Thus, we have witnessed instances in which the symbol for action is radically altered with changes in object, and we have also seen instances—in both the linear and linguistic media—where the symbol for action is left more or less intact, relatively slight modulations reflecting variation in the objects acted upon.

Linear Representation and Concrete-Depictive Codification of Temporality

Having thus far considered concrete-depictive codification with regard to agent's-action-on-objects, we may conclude this chapter with a discussion of certain *parallels in concrete-depictive languages to the linear representation of temporality* (see Chapter 23). As one knows, linguistic codification of temporality per se is a relatively late achievement in the history of language; the articulation and systematization of tenses is a highly significant feature of only relatively modern Indo-European grammar. This fact renders an inquiry into the nature of temporal representation in non-Indo-European languages a topic of special interest for an organismic-developmental approach to symbolization. We would expect that, in such languages, there would be striking analogues to the linear representation of temporality; that is, we would assume that insofar as there is an orientation towards concrete depiction, the temporal locus of an event would be represented as ingredient in the event rather than symbolized by a vehicle whose reference is to an "empty" point in an abstract, homogeneous network.

Guided by our inquiry into the linear representation of time, one would look for "primitive" linguistic expressions of temporality either in representations of a total event or in representations of relatively delimited components of events, for example, agent-in-action, action-on-object, attitude-of-observer-towards-agent-in-action, etc. In the latter case, the linguistic indices would be of that kind that linguists have termed "modes" (moods) and "aspects": these usually connote attitudes of the agent and modifications of activity, respectively. However, the close interlocking of the various features of an event often renders it difficult to characterize "primordial" means of expressing temporality in terms of the traditional categories of analysis. This has been pointed out clearly by Reichard, in her analysis of Coeur d'Alene (197, p. 571):

"The primary interest of the language centers on the way in which a state or an action came about. This is not the kind of distinction which we should call mode. It is much more subtle, and besides, the differentiations made would not fit into the classification of 'aspects.' Verbs may be intransitive in meaning and form in which case they express condition (state) or action. The difference between state and action may be expressed by grammatical form. One form will show that the subject has been acted upon and now exists in that 'acted upon' state so that the condition might be removed again; another, that the subject was acted upon so that the condition is within and has become a part of it; and a third, that the condition is within and part of the subject. There is also a differentiation as to how it became acted upon: it acted with or without its own volition; or it came to be acted upon by, or without a natural or human agent; or the action was performed with, or without control. Still another form indicates that a person or object affects in a particular way, or 'has the quality of affecting.' . . . Words denoting action may be modified to show whether the subject is 'in the act of . . . ,' or 'in the position of . . . ,' 'moving in a horseshoe curve,' 'arranging for . . . ,' 'doing artificially,' 'attempting to . . . ,' 'acting playingly,' 'acting seemingly,' 'acting willingly.' "

Recognizing the cogency of Reichard's observations, we shall nevertheless examine linguistic expressions of temporality as if addressor-attitudes, agent-qualities, action features, etc., were relatively distinct from one another. We shall, in the following, first consider how relatively *global, physiognomic-dynamic features* of total events are used to express temporality; then, how *addressor-attitudes* enter into temporal reference; next, how *agent-characteristics* function in temporal indication; and, finally, how *modifications of actions* express temporality.

Global Physiognomic-Dynamic Features and Temporality

In our analysis of the linear transposition of English verb-tense statements, we suggested that such mediation was possible only insofar as the events denoted by the statements were apprehended as possessing dynamic features susceptible to expression through linear physiognomics; some of these dynamic features would then serve as indices of temporality and means of temporal differentiation. In line with our expectation of parallels in linguistic encoding to phenomena obtaining in linear mediation, it is not surprising to find that some non-literate languages possess morphological elements which connote precisely such dynamic-physiognomic features of events—features which often serve to indicate temporality.

An illuminating illustration is provided by B. L. Whorf, in his analysis of the Hopi verb (281, pp. 179 f). Whorf notes that in the Toreva dialect of Hopi there is "a large array of lexemes"—designated by him as "tensors"—"in which denoting of intensities seems to be the leading principle; and tendency, duration, and relative time position seem to be fused with intensity, as with us they are fused with spatial magnitudes." He remarks, "Not only the degree but the kind of intensity is expressed, as to whether it is gentle or rough, punctual or tensive, constant, increasing, decreasing, etc. *Incipient* intensities are the same as tendencies, and are rendered, e.g., 'very quickly, right away, now,' or 'quickly, soon after, soon,' etc.; they may be said to be estimators of *present or future* time. *Punctual* intensities contain a demonstrative sense and so place an event at a point in the *reportive* realm, i.e., the *past*, at more or less remoteness from the speaker, e.g., at *this* event or moment, at *that* event or moment, at *that* remote (long past) event, etc." Thus, "the tensors *pe', pay, pasat*, all may be translated 'now' or 'then,' but *pe'* corresponds to 'this,' *pay* to 'it,' *pasat* to 'that;' *pay* also implies 'this becoming that,' and as predicator means 'become past' or 'depart, quit the scene.' . . . Others have repetitive and long durative meaning like 'again,' 'often,' 'constantly,' 'all day,' 'more and more.' In general the tensors handle notions allied to those of the verb aspects." [10]

Addressor-Attitudes and Temporality

One of the striking findings of our study on the linear representation of temporality was that nine of the twelve subjects used linear properties of their vehicles to express their personal reactions to the events denoted by the verb-tense statements. These reactions of the symbolizer, which often served to set off one tense-form from others, were either in terms of affective responses or of cognitive attitudes (e.g., certainty, expectancy) of the subjects.

Such indications of, and distinctions among, temporal loci through relations of the observer-symbolizer to an event are often found among nonliterate languages. Whorf (282, pp. 144 f) points out that time relations among the Hopi are, in general, not codified in terms of tense (past, present, or future); rather, various facets of the total event, including observer-reactions, can be taken loosely to translate Hopi statements into explicit temporal propositions in English.

Further, expressions of the position of the observer in relation to an event may not only take place through such morphological elements of a spoken language as modal affixes but may also be manifested through other means at the disposal of the speaker—means not constituting part of the linguistic code per se. Manuel Andrade's remarks about the Quileute highlight this fact: "the attitude of the speaker as expressed in his gestures or posture, his emotional attitude, as manifested by emphasis, melody or speed of speech . . . the context . . . all these combined supply temporal reference conveyed by our tense suffixes or auxiliaries." (6, p. 263)

Agent-Characteristics and Temporality

Another phenomenon that was observed in the linear representation of verb-tense statements was that agent qualities served as a means for indicating temporality. This is quite understandable if one con-

---

[10] It is exactly those features denoted by tensors which become visible in linear mediation. The interpretative rendering of 'tensors' by Whorf points up the inadequacy of our present scientific vocabulary for describing dynamic-physiognomic connotations.

siders that an agent's characteristics or qualities actually change during the various phases of a concrete action. Thus, for example, some subjects distinguished "he ran" from "he will run" in terms of such conditions of the agent as "a state of prostration or exhaustion" versus "a state of potential tension."

There are some analogies to this phenomenon in American Indian languages. In contradistinction to a language such as English, in which one generally encodes an agent as separable from the activity in which he participates, in those concrete-depictive languages there are certain ways of indicating time, which can only be understood, it seems to us, if one assumes that agent-qualities bear the reference to temporality. For example, Sapir, in his analysis of Takelma, points to the peculiarity of the verb, in which "tense-modes" (e.g., aorist, potential, future) are distinguishable not in terms of specific tense or mode signs but through specific sets of *pronominal* endings for each "tense-mode." Thus, for example, for the verb-form indicating "to stop" we get for first person future, *hán'sdē,* and for first person potential, *hán'sdē';* for second person future, *hán'sdā* and for second person potential, *hán'sdam;* for third person future, *hán'sdā,* and for the third person potential, *hán's.* In other words, the morphological index for each grammatical person suffixed to the verb-stem was modulated to indicate the particular tense-mode of an action (Sapir, 207, II, pp. 157, 165).

Modifications of Activity as Temporal Indicators

In linear representation, it will be recalled, modifications or qualifications of activity were perhaps the chief means used by the subjects to indicate temporal differences in events. A verb-form was rarely represented with strict constancy from one tense-form to another; rather, variations in temporal loci of the verb-activity were expressed through slight or major shape alterations (the latter analogous to radical change in verb-stem). Though some of the variations in shape were not directly indicative of temporality, others were more or less direct expressions of the temporal locus of the activity. The linear variations expressing temporality, moreover, often referred to relatively *generic* aspects of activities ('ongoingness,' 'completedness,' etc.). Such generic aspects, however, were often given a particularized interpretation binding them to a specific activity, for example, the 'overness' of the Past of 'love' was usually depicted differently than the 'overness' of the Past of 'run.'

In many nonliterate languages, aspects of activity are also a principal means of indicating temporal features of events. In a broad sense, of course, any of the symbolized features of events may be considered modifications of activity and hence "aspects;" this is true because activity is not sharply separated from other components of concrete events. Furthermore, any of these features have potential temporal reference; this is so because an activity unfolds in time, and different features may characterize it at various stages of its unfolding. For example, some of the suffixes mentioned in the following quotation—suffixes which the Klamath Indians join to verb-stems to express various features of activity—may be viewed as implying reference to time-of-event.

"The Klamath Indian employs derivation suffixes to express the following ideas which English can express by separate words only; commencing, continuing, quitting, returning from, doing habitually, frequently or repeatedly, changing into, moving at a long, a short distance, moving in a zigzag or straight direction, going upwards, downwards, circling in air, coming toward or going away from, seen or unseen, moving within or outside of the edge, on or below the water surface, also an infinity of other circumstantial facts, some of which we would not observe at all" (Gatschet, 73, p. 305).

As has just been mentioned, a number of these "aspects" ('commencing,' 'continuing,' 'quitting,' 'doing habitually') are certainly related to temporality, although they do not refer to time in the same way as do our tense indicators; they are not, like tense, coordinated with serial positions along a homogeneous dimension of time. Nevertheless, they do to some extent function indirectly as indicators of temporal locus. For example, the Hopi distinction between *manifested* and *manifesting* aspects of activity serves to set off past or present events from future ones; thus, events as manifested would, depending upon context, be either in the past or present, and events as manifesting would be "located" in the future. The latter would have the status of (*a*) activities coming to be, (*b*) activities expected to occur, (*c*) activities which are realized in the imminent future through an act of thought (Whorf, 282, p. 59).

Another illustration from a nonliterate language which points to temporality through aspective modifications of activity comes from Andrade's analysis of Quileute. In this language, as Andrade points out, reference to an activity as momentaneous suggests the 'overness' of that activity. Such a momentaneous activity "appears to us as a past tense because of the intrinsic nature of a rapid action: due to its short duration, by the time the speaker refers to it, it is generally a recent past event." Thus, *céqwatílas* which means "he-pulling-me-momentaneously" is translatable into English as "he pulled me" (Andrade, 6, p. 263).

As in linear mediation, aspects in nonliterate languages vary in their generality. In these languages, some aspects may be truly generic, that is, a constant means is used for all verbal themes to express an "inceptive aspect," another constant means for a "durative aspect," still others for the "completive aspect," "usitative aspect," etc. However, aspects may often be more theme- or activity-bound, that is, particularized with respect to classes of verbs and sometimes even to individual verb-stems. For example, the inceptive ("inchoative") aspect in the Coos language is differently symbolized (implying particularized nuances) depending on the nature of the activity. Thus the inchoative -*iwe* indicates the commencing of a *uniform* action and is suffixed to verb-stems which express active or transitive ideas; where the verb-stem does not imply a transitive idea, the beginning of the activity is expressed by the suffix -*íye*, which ordinarily indicates a transition from one qualitative state to another. Thus, *gameläniwe* = "he began to swim around" and *gamîlíye* = "he began to swim" (Frachtenberg, 68, p. 339). In this and similar cases where a generic aspect is expressed for different classes of verbs by different morphological means, it is plausible to assume that one is dealing with particularized, more or less theme-specific nuances of the generic aspect.

In conclusion, we may state that such indications of temporal locus through the mode of representing different facets of a concrete unfolding activity are particularly characteristic of languages which have not articulated a relatively clear-cut tense system. Of course, aspects are found to varying degrees in Indo-European languages, for example, English progressive present, but in the main this family of languages, more than any other, has approximated a clear-cut system of tenses. In these languages, tense seems to have evolved from prior states where relatively theme-bound and, later, more generic aspects were the principal means for referring to time. In this connection, the remarks of A. Meillet are particularly pertinent: "The category of *aspect* is more concrete than that of *tense*, and in the course of the history of Indo-European languages, one sees the aspect losing importance and tense gaining it." (164, p. 185)

The unfolding of the category of tense out of the category of aspect is part and parcel of the overall developmental change which the Indo-European languages have undergone, a change to which we have already referred earlier in this chapter, and which Meillet has succinctly expressed in these words: "The advance of civilization is clearly evidenced in the formation of the time category; the trend has been to eliminate the concrete and expressive categories of values and to assign to the abstract categories a role of ever-increasing importance." (164, p. 198)

references

(Numbers in brackets refer to citations in text)

1. Ach, N., 1921. *Über die Begriffsbildung.* Bamberg: Buchner. [34, 35]
2. Agar, W. E., 1944. *A contribution to the theory of the living organism.* Melbourne: Melbourne University Press. [6]
3. d'Allonnes, R., 1934. La schématisation. In Dumas, G. (Ed.), *Nouveau traité de psychologie,* Vol. IV. Paris: Alcan. [91]
4. Allport, G. W., 1955. *Becoming.* New Haven: Yale University Press. [13]
5. Ament, W., 1899. *Die Entwicklung von Sprechen und Denken beim Kinde.* Leipzig: Wunderlich. [108, 114–116]
6. Andrade, M. J., 1933–1938. Quileute. In Boas, F. (Ed.), *Handbook of American Indian languages,* Vol. III. Glückstadt-Hamburg-New York: J. J. Augustin. [482, 492, 493, 499]
7. Arieti, S., 1955. *Interpretation of schizophrenia.* New York: Brunner. [72, 254, 267]
8. Arieti, S. (Ed.), 1959. *American handbook of psychiatry.* New York: Basic Books. 2 vols. (See refs. 9; 236)
9. Arieti, S., 1959. Schizophrenia. *American handbook of psychiatry,* Vol. I, Chap. 23. New York: Basic Books. [254]
10. Arieti, S., 1961. The loss of reality. *Psychoanal. and Psychoanal. Rev.,* **48,** No. 3, 3–24. [255, 256, 258]
11. Arieti, S., 1962. The microgeny of thought and perception. *Arch. gen. Psychiat.,* **6,** 454–468. [264]
12. Asch, S. E., 1955. On the use of metaphor in the description of persons. In Werner, H. (Ed.), *On expressive language.* Worcester, Mass.: Clark University Press. [60]
13. Baker, R., 1953. The acquisition of verbal concepts in schizophrenia: A developmental approach to the study of disturbed language behavior. Unpublished doctor's dissertation, Clark University. [272, 275–279]

14. Barnes, E., 1896–1897. *A study in children's interests.* In: Studies in education. Stanford University. [188]
15. Bean, C. H., 1932. An unusual opportunity to investigate the psychology of language. *J. genet. Psychol.,* **40,** 181–202. [134, 187]
16. Bertalanffy, L. von, 1933. *Modern theories of development.* London: Oxford University Press. [4]
17. Bertalanffy, L. von, 1952. *Problems of life.* New York: Wiley. [4]
18. Betz, W., 1918. *Psychologie des Denkens.* Leipzig: Barth. [238, 441]
19. Blackmur, R. P., 1952. *Language as gesture.* New York: Harcourt, Brace. [37]
20. Blanshard, B., 1939. *The nature of thought.* London: Allen and Unwin. 2 vols. [24]
21. Bleuler, E., 1950. *Dementia praecox or the group of schizophrenias.* New York: International Universities Press. [253, 254, 262]
22. Bloch, O., 1921. Les premiers stades du langage de l'enfant. *J. de Psychol.,* **18,** 693–712. [126, 155, 156, 165–167]
23. Bobon, J., 1947. Les pseudo-glossolalies ludiques et magiques. *J. Belge de Neurol. et de Psychiat.,* **47,** 327–395. [253, 258, 259]
24. Bobon, J., 1952. *Introduction historique à l'étude des néologismes et des glossolalies en psychopathologie.* Paris: Masson and Co. [246, 253]
25. Bobon, J., 1962. *Psychopathologie de l'expression.* Paris: Masson and Co. [253, 382]
26. Bodansky, M., 1956. An experimental and theoretical inquiry into the symbol-meaning relationship. Unpublished master's thesis, Clark University. [422, 423]
27. Bodansky, M., 1961. The representation of abstract concepts through the use of line patterns. Unpublished doctor's dissertation, Clark University. [124, 355–364]
28. Bosanquet, B., 1888. *Logic.* Oxford: Clarendon Press. 2 vols. [161]
29. Bréal, M., 1911. *Essai de semantique.* Paris: Hachette. [61]
30. Brown, H. W., 1893. Some records of the thoughts and reasonings of children. *Pedag. Sem.,* **2,** No. 3, 358–396. [59]
31. Brown, R. W., 1956. Language and categories. In Bruner, J. S., Goodnow, J. J., Austin, G. A. (Eds.), *A study of thinking.* New York: Wiley. [193]
32. Brown, R. W., 1958. *Words and things.* Glencoe, Ill.: Free Press. [viii]
33. Brugmann, K., 1902–1904. *Kurze vergleichende Grammatik der indogermanischen Sprachen.* Strassburg: Trübner. [54, 478]
34. Bruner, J. S., Goodnow, J. J., and Austin, G. A., 1956. *A study of thinking.* New York: Wiley. (See ref. 31)
35. Bühler, C., 1928. *Kindheit und Jugend.* Leipzig: Hirzel. [68]
36. Bühler, C., 1930. *The first year of life.* New York: John Day. [85]
37. Bühler, K., 1934. *Sprachtheorie.* Jena: Fischer. [52–62, 83, 230]
38. Burke, K., 1957. *The philosophy of literary form.* New York: Vintage Books. [37]
39. Cameron, N., 1938. Reasoning, regression and communication in schizophrenics. *Psychol. Monogr.,* **50,** No. 1, 1–34. [267, 274]
40. Cameron, N., 1939. Schizophrenic thinking in a problem-solving situation. *J. ment. Sci.,* **85,** 1012–1037. [256]

41. Carroll, J. B., 1953. *The study of language.* Cambridge: Harvard University Press. [viii]
42. Cassirer, E., 1953–1957. *The philosophy of symbolic forms.* New Haven: Yale University Press. 3 vols. [14, 24, 56, 267]
43. Chamberlain, A. F., 1893. Some points in linguistic psychology. *Amer. J. Psychol.,* **5,** 116–119. [103, 185, 206]
44. Chomsky, N., 1957. *Syntactic structures.* The Hague: Mouton. [viii]
45. Church, J., 1961. *Language and the discovery of reality.* New York: Random House. [viii]
46. Cirillo, L., 1962. A study of the representation of multiple meanings (plurisignificance) in a non-verbal medium. Unpublished master's thesis, Clark University. [124, 352–355]
47. Codrington, R. H., 1885. *The Melanesian languages.* Oxford: Clarendon Press. [56]
48. Conrad, K., 1947. Über den Begriff der Vorgestalt und seine Bedeutung für die Hirnpathologie. *Nervenarzt,* **18,** 289–293.
49. Croce, B., 1953. *Aesthetic.* New York: Noonday Press. [334]
50. Cushing, F. H., 1892. Manual concepts. *Amer. Anthrop.,* **5,** 289–317. [60]
51. Dantzig, T., 1954. *Number, the language of science.* Garden City, N. Y.: Anchor Books, Doubleday. [62]
52. Decroly, O., and Degand, J., 1913. Observations relatives au développement de la notion du temps chez une petite fille de la naissance à 5 ans ½. *Arch. de Psychol.,* **13,** No. 50, 113–161. [404]
53. Delacroix, H., 1924. *Le langage et la pensée.* Paris: Alcan. [157, 158]
54. De Laguna, G. A., 1927. *Speech, its function and development.* New Haven: Yale University Press. [11]
55. Deville, G., 1890. Notes sur le développement du langage. *Rev. Ling. et de Phil. Comp.,* **24,** 330–343. [164]
56. Dowling, R., 1962. Effect of sensorimotor and conceptual activity on perceptual functioning. Unpublished doctor's dissertation, Clark University. [33, 34]
57. Egger, V., 1904. *La parole intérieure.* Paris: Alcan. [285]
58. Erikson, E., 1950. *Childhood and society.* New York: W. W. Norton. [86]
59. Erle, R., 1958. The representation of temporal features of events in hypnotically induced dreams: an exploratory study. Unpublished master's thesis, Clark University. [427–436]
60. Erle, R., 1963. Representation of relations between thoughts in a medium of visual imagery. Unpublished doctor's dissertation, Clark University. [455–466]
61. Ervin, S. M., and Osgood, C. E., 1954. Second language learning and bilingualism. In Osgood, C. E., and Sebeok, T. (Eds.), Psycholinguistics, *J. abnorm. soc. Psychol.,* **49,** *Suppl.,* 139–146. [31]
62. Farrell, G., 1956. *The story of blindness.* Cambridge: Harvard University Press. [112]
63. Federn, P., 1952. *Ego psychology and the psychoses.* New York: Basic Books. [254]
64. Ferenczi, S., 1950. To whom does one relate dreams. In: *Further contributions to the theory and technique of psychoanalysis.* London: Hogarth. [241]

65. Ferenczi, S., 1950. On obscene words. In: *Sex in psychoanalysis.* New York: Basic Books. [37]

66. Finck, F. N., 1923. Die Haupttypen des Sprachbaus. *Aus Natur und Geisteswelt,* No. 268. Leipzig: Teubner. [57, 58]

67. Flavell, J. H. Unpublished papers on ontogenesis of verbal communication. [321]

68. Frachtenberg, L. J., 1922. Coos. In Boas, F. (Ed.), *Handbook of American Indian languages,* Vol. II. Washington: Smithsonian Institution. [502]

69. Freeman, T., 1960. On the psychopathology of schizophrenia. *J. ment. Sci.,* **106,** 925–937. [256, 269]

70. Freud, S., 1955. *The interpretations of dreams.* New York: Basic Books. [240, 244, 250, 251, 360, 467–469, 471, 472]

71. v. Frisch, K., 1950. *Bees, their vision, chemical senses, and language.* Ithaca: Cornell University Press. [17]

72. Galanter, E., and Miller, G., 1960. Some comments on stochastic models and psychological theories. In Arrow, K., et al. (Eds.), *Mathematical methods in the social sciences.* Stanford: Stanford University Press. [4]

73. Gatschet, A. S., 1890. The Klamath Indians of Southwestern Oregon. *Contributions to North American Ethnology,* Vol. 2, No. 1. Washington: Department of the Interior. [481–487, 493, 494, 501]

74. Gelb, A., and Goldstein, K., 1918. Zur Psychologie des optischen Wahrnehmungs-und Erkennungsvorganges. *Z. ges. Neurol. Psychiat.,* **41,** 1–142. [6]

75. Gerson, W., 1928. Schizophrene Sprachneubildung und schizophrenes Denken. *Z. ges. Neurol. Psychiat.,* **113,** 159–176. [262–275]

76. Gesell, A., 1925. *The mental growth of the preschool child.* New York: Macmillan. [68]

77. Gesell, A., 1954. The ontogenesis of behavior. In Carmichael, L. (Ed.), *Manual of child psychology.* New York: Wiley. [8, 86]

78. Gheorgov, I. A., 1908. *Ein Beitrag zur grammatischen Entwicklung der Kindersprache.* Leipzig: Engelmann. [478]

79. Ghiselin, B., 1952. *The creative process.* Berkeley: University of California. [426]

80. Goldman, A. E., 1955. An investigation of symbolic representation in schizophrenia. Unpublished doctor's dissertation, Clark University. [366, 376–383]

81. Goldman, A. E., 1960. Symbolic representation in schizophrenia. *J. Pers.* **28,** 293–316. [366, 376–383]

82. Goldstein, K., 1937. *The organism.* New York: The American Book Company. [4, 6]

83. Goldstein, K., 1948. *Language and language disturbances.* New York: Grune and Stratton. [7, 97, 109, 327]

84. Gombrich, E., 1960. *Art and illusion.* New York: Bollingen. [viii]

85. Grammont, M., 1930. La psychologie et la phonétique: la phonétique impressive. *J. de Psychol.,* **27,** 544–613. [206]

86. Grégoire, A., 1937–1947. *L'apprentissage du langage.* Paris: Droz. 2 vols. [104, 107, 108, 124–127, 135, 141, 142, 148, 155–157, 402, 418]

87. Guillaume, P., 1925. *L'imitation chez l'enfant.* Paris: Alcan. [86, 89, 98, 158]

88. Guillaume, P., 1927. Les débuts de la phrase dans le langage de l'enfant. *J. de Psychol.*, **24**, 1–25. [150]

89. Guillaume, P., 1937. *La psychologie de la forme.* Paris: Flammarion. [4]

90. Guillaume, P., and Meyerson, I., 1930–1934. Recherches sur l'usage de l'instrument chez les singes. *J. de Psychol.*, **31**, 497–554; **33**, 177–236. [10]

91. Gutheil, E., 1951. *The handbook of dream-analysis.* New York: Liveright. [469, 470]

92. Gutzmann, H., 1911. Beobachtungen der ersten sprachlichen und stimmlichen Entwicklung eines Kindes. *Mediz.-pädag. Monatsschr. f. d. ges. Sprachheilk.*, **11**, 1–28. [82, 83, 103, 107]

93. Hall, I. B., 1945. The oral method for deaf-blind children. *Outlook for the Blind*, **39**, 244–245. [112]

94. Halverson, H. M., 1931. An experimental study of prehension in infants. *Genet. Psychol. Monogr.*, **10**, 107–286. [86]

95. Halverson, H. M., 1932. A further study of grasping. *J. gen. Psychol.*, **7**, 34–64. [86]

96. Hanfmann, E., Rickers-Ovsiankina, M., and Goldstein, K., 1944. Case Lanuti: Extreme concretization of behavior due to damage of the brain cortex. *Psychol. Monogr.*, **57**, 1–72. [121]

97. Harris, E., 1959. Teleology and teleological explanation. *J. Philos.*, **56**, 5–25. [6]

98. Head, H., 1926. *Aphasia and kindred disorders of speech.* Cambridge: Cambridge University Press. 2 vols. [97, 159]

99. Hegel, G. F. W., 1949. Vorlesungen über die Philosophie der Geschichte. In *Sämmtliche Werke*, **9**. Leipzig: F. Meiner. [8]

100. Heider, F., and Heider, G., 1940–1941. Studies in the psychology of the deaf. *Psychol. Monogr.*, **52**, 1–152; **53**, 1–155. [181]

101. Henning, H., 1924. *Der Geruch.* Leipzig: Barth. [298]

102. Henry, J., 1936. The linguistic expression of emotion. *Amer. Anthrop.*, **38**, 250–256. [480]

103. v. Herder, J. G., 1827. Über den Ursprung der Sprache. In *Sämmtliche Werke, Philosophy*, **2**. Stuttgart: Cotta. [20]

104. Herrick, C. J., 1956. *The evolution of human nature.* Austin: University of Texas Press. [10]

105. Hetzer, H., Beaumont, H., and Wiehemeyer, E., 1929. Das Schauen und Greifen des Kindes. *Z. Psychol.*, **113**, 239–286. [67]

106. Hofstadter, A., 1941. Subjective teleology. *Philos. and Phenomenol. Res.*, **2**, 88–97. [6]

107. Hofstadter, A., 1941. Objective teleology. *J. Philos.*, **38**, 29–39. [6]

108. Hoijer, H., et al., 1946. Linguistic structures of native America. Viking Fund Publications in Anthropology. New York: Viking Fund. (See refs. 153; 281)

109. Honkavaara, S., 1961. The psychology of expression. *Br. J. Psychol., Monogr. Suppl.*, XXXII. [229]

110. Hornbostel, E. M., 1927. Laut und Sinn. In: *Festschrift Meinhof.* Hamburg. [206]

111. v. Humboldt, W., 1836. *Über die Verschiedenheit des menschlichen Sprachbaus.* Berlin-Bonn: Dümmler. [19–23, 50, 51, 160, 161]

112. Huth, A., 1919. Die Nebensätze in der Kindersprache. *Z. f. Pädag. Psychol.,* **20,** 163–183. [181–183]

113. Ipsen, G., 1932. Der neue Sprachbegriff. *Z. Deutschkunde,* **46,** 1–18. [56]

114. Iritani, T., 1962. A study of the expressive values of non-linguistic sounds and their influence on the articulation of perceived objects. Unpublished doctor's dissertation, Clark University. [219–226]

115. Jacobson, E., 1954. Contribution to the metapsychology of psychotic identifications. *J. Amer. Psychoanal. Assoc.,* **2,** 239–262. [254]

116. Jakobovits, L. A., and Lambert, W. E., 1961. Semantic satiation among bilinguals. *J. exp. Psychol.,* **67,** 567–582. [31, 32, 129]

117. Jakobson, R., 1941. *Kindersprache, Aphasie und allgemeine Lautgesetze.* Upsala: Almquist a. Wiksell. [viii]

118. James, W., 1890. *Principles of psychology.* New York: Holt. 2 vols. [238, 441]

119. Jespersen, O., 1922. *Language, its nature, development, and origin.* New York: Holt. [107, 120, 125, 158, 319, 320, 475–477]

120. Jespersen, O., 1954. *Mankind, nation and individual.* London: Allen and Unwin. [489]

121. Jones, E., 1948. The theory of symbolism. In: *Papers on psychoanalysis.* London: Baillière, Tindall & Cox. [467]

122. Kaden, S. E., Wapner, S., and Werner, H., 1955. Studies in physiognomic perception: II. Effect of directional dynamics of pictured objects and of words on the position of the apparent horizon. *J. Psychol.,* **39,** 61–70. [26–29]

123. Kahler, E., 1960. Nature of the symbol. In May, R. (Ed.), *Symbolism in religion and literature.* New York: G. Braziller. [11]

124. Kaila, E., 1932. Die Reaktionen des Säuglings auf das menschliche Gesicht. *Annales Universitatis Aboensis,* B., **17,** 1–114. [43]

125. Kainz, F., 1943. *Psychologie der Sprache,* Vol. 2. Stuttgart: Enke. [249]

126. Kant, I., 1787. *Kritik der reinen Vernunft,* 2nd ed. Riga: Hartknoch. [91]

127. Kanzer, M., 1955. The communicative function of the dream. *Intern. J. Psychoanal.,* **36,** 260–265. [241]

128. Kaper, W., 1959. *Kindersprachforschung mit Hilfe des Kindes.* Groningen: Wolters. [126, 127]

129. Kaplan, B., 1955. Some psychological methods for the investigation of expressive language. In Werner, H. (Ed.), *On expressive language.* Worcester: Clark University Press. [334]

130. Kaplan, B., 1957. On the phenomena of "opposite speech." *J. abnorm. soc. Psychol.,* **55,** 389–393. [33, 472]

131. Kaplan, B., 1961. An approach to the problem of symbolic representation: non-verbal and verbal. *J. Communic.,* **11,** 52–62. [60, 334]

132. Kaplan, B., 1962. Radical metaphor, aesthetic and the origin of language. *Rev. Existent. Psychol. and Psychiat.,* **2,** 75–84. [60]

133. Kaplan, E., 1952. An experimental study on inner speech as contrasted with external speech. Unpublished master's thesis, Clark University. [285–303]

134. Keller, H., 1903. *The story of my life.* New York: Doubleday, Page. [110, 212]

135. Kluckhohn, C., and Leighton, D., 1948. *The Navaho.* Cambridge: Harvard University Press. [485, 486, 496]

136. Köhler, W., 1927. *The mentality of apes.* New York: Harcourt, Brace. [10, 17, 65]
137. Köhler, W., 1929. *Gestalt psychology.* New York: Liveright. [4]
138. Kraepelin, E., 1906. *Über Sprachstörungen im Traum.* Leipzig: Engelmann. [240–251, 270, 275]
139. Krahe, H., 1957. *Germanische Sprachwissenschaft, II: Formenlehre.* Sammlung Göschen 780. Berlin: DeGruyter. [476, 477]
140. Krauss, R., 1930. Über graphischen Ausdruck. *Z. f. angew. Psychol.,* Suppl. **48**, 1–141. [338–350]
141. Kreitler, H., 1957. Les bases psychologiques du langage des schizophrènes. *Acta Neurol. et Psychiat. Belgica,* **57**, 950–954. [255]
142. Kronasser, H., 1952. *Handbuch der Semasiologie.* Heidelberg: Winter. [56]
143. Kurz, I., 1919. *Traumland.* Stuttgart: Deutsche Verlags-Anstalt. [143]
144. Kussmaul, A., 1885. *Die Störungen der Sprache.* Leipzig: F. C. W. Vogel. [105]
145. Lagercrantz, E., 1950. Primitivismen arktischer Sprachen. *Mem. Soc. Finno-Ougrienne,* **98**, 107–123. [494]
146. Lambert, W. E., and Jakobovits, L. A., 1960. Verbal satiation and changes in the intensity of meaning. *J. exp. Psychol.,* **60**, 376–383. (See ref. 116)
147. Langer, J., 1962. The representation of perceptual phenomena: a comparison of nonverbal (linear) representation with linguistic coding. Unpublished doctor's dissertation, Clark University. [239]
148. Langer, S. K., 1949. *Philosophy in a new key.* New York: Mentor Books. [53]
149. Lashley, K. S., 1951. The problem of serial order in behavior. In Jeffress, L. A. (Ed.), *Cerebral mechanisms in behavior: The Hixon symposium.* New York: Wiley. [23]
150. Leopold, W. F., 1939–1949. *Speech development of a bilingual child.* Evanston: Northwestern University Press. 4 vols. [101, 109, 115, 116, 126, 127, 135–137, 142–144, 150–154, 157, 158, 165–167, 173, 180, 400]
151. Levy-Bruhl, L., 1926. *How natives think.* London: Allen and Unwin. [267]
152. Lewis, M. M., 1936. *Infant speech.* New York: Harcourt, Brace. [82, 113–117, 163]
153. Li Fang Kuei, 1946. Chipewyan. In Hoijer, H., et al. *Linguistic structures of native America.* New York: Viking Fund. [487, 495]
154. Lorenz, M., 1961. Problems posed by schizophrenic language. *Arch. of gen. Psychiat.,* **4**, 603–610. [260]
155. Lowenfeld, B., 1952. If deaf and blind. *California Parent-Teacher,* **28**, 7–8. [112]
156. Lowenfeld, V., 1939. *The nature of creative activity.* London: Kegan Paul. [43, 91]
157. Lundholm, H., 1921. The affective tone of lines. *Psychol. Rev.,* **28**, 43–60. [338, 346]
158. Luria, A. R., 1959. The directive function of speech in development and dissolution. *Word,* **15**, 341–464. [325, 326]
159. Luria, A. R., and Yudovich, F. I., 1959. *Speech and the development of mental processes in the child.* London: Staples Press. [118–121, 318–320, 324–327]
160. MacLeish, A., 1961. *Poetry and experience.* Cambridge: Riverside. [213]

161. Maier, N. R. F., and Schneirla, T., 1935. *Principles of animal psychology*. New York: McGraw-Hill. [10]

162. Mayr, E., 1960. The emergence of evolutionary novelties. In Tax, S. (Ed.), *Evolution after Darwin*, Vol. I. Chicago: University of Chicago Press. [8]

163. Meillet, A., 1909. *Einführung in die vergleichende Grammatik der indogermanischen Sprachen*. Leipzig: Teubner. [485]

164. Meillet, A., 1948. *Linguistique historique et linguistique générale*. Paris: Champion. [475, 502, 503]

165. Meinhof, C., 1906. *Grundzüge einer vergleichenden Grammatik der Bantusprachen*. Berlin: Dietrich Reimer. [57, 494]

166. Meumann, E., 1902. *Die Entstehung der ersten Wortbedeutungen beim Kinde*. Leipzig: Engelmann. [103, 107]

167. Miller, A., 1959. An experimental study of the role of sensory-motor activity in the retention of verbal meaning. Unpublished doctor's dissertation, Clark University. [32–34]

168. Miller, G. A., Pribram, K., and Galanter, E., 1960. *Plans and the structure of behavior*. New York: Holt. [5]

169. Morris, C., 1946. *Signs, language and behavior*. New York: Prentice-Hall. [35]

170. Mowrer, O. H., 1960. *Learning theory and the symbolic processes*. New York: Wiley. [35]

171. Muchow, M., 1926. *Beiträge zur psychologischen Charakteristik des Kindergarten-und Grundschulalters*. Berlin: Herbig. [91, 189]

172. Muchow, M., 1929. *Psychologische Probleme der frühen Erziehung*. Erfurt: Stenger. [96]

173. Muchow, M., and Werner, H., 1930. Unpublished papers on infant behavior. Hamburg: Hamburg Institute. [93]

174. Neugebauer, H., 1915. Aus der Sprachentwicklung meines Sohnes. *Z. angew. Psychol.*, **9**, 298–306. [105, 108]

175. Nice, M. M., 1925. A child who would not talk. *Ped. Sem.*, **32**, 105–142. [177]

176. Norman, E., 1936. Some psychological features of babble in children. *Proc. 2nd Int. Congr. Phon. Sciences*, 155–158. [177]

177. Oakley, K., 1954. Skill as a human possession. In Singer, C., et al. (Eds.), *A history of technology*, Vol. I. Cambridge: Cambridge University Press. [10]

178. Ogden, C. K., and Richards, I. A., 1930. *The meaning of meaning*. New York: Harcourt, Brace. [35, 36]

179. Öhman, S., 1953. Theories of the "linguistic field." *Word*, **9**, 123–134. [56]

180. Ombredane, A., 1951. *L'aphasie et l'élaboration de la pensée explicite*. Paris: P.U.F. [242]

181. Ortega y Gasset, J., 1941. *Toward a philosophy of history*. New York: Norton. [13]

182. Osgood, C. E., 1960. The cross-cultural generality of visual-verbal synesthetic tendencies. *Behav. Science*, **5**, 146–169. [24, 348]

183. Osgood, C. E., Suci, G. J., and Tannenbaum, P. H., 1957. *The measurement of meaning*. Urbana: University of Illinois Press. [24]

184. Paget, R., 1927. The origin of language. *Psyche*, **8**, 35–39. [106]

185. Paulhan, F., 1928. Qu'est-ce que le sens des mots? *J. de Psychol.*, **25**, 289–329. [323]

186. Pavlovitch, M., 1920. *Le langage enfantin.* Paris: Champion. [101, 103]

187. Penfield, W., and Roberts, L., 1959. *Speech and brain mechanisms.* Princeton: Princeton University Press. [viii]

188. Perez, B., 1911. *Les trois premieres années de l'enfant.* Paris: Alcan. [90, 401]

189. Piaget, J., 1930. *The child's conception of physical causality.* New York: Harcourt, Brace. [182]

190. Piaget, J., 1948. *Language and thought of the child.* London: Routledge and Kegan Paul. [317]

191. Piaget, J., 1951. *Play, dreams and imitation in childhood.* New York: Norton. [68, 86, 89, 91, 96, 97]

192. Piro, S., 1958. *Semantica del linguaggio schizofrenico.* Napoli: Acta Neurologica Policlinico. [268]

193. Pohlmann, H., 1912. Beitrag zur Psychologie des Schulkindes. *Pädag. Monogr.* (Meumann), **13.** [188]

194. Preyer, W., 1882. *Die Seele des Kindes.* Leipzig: Grieben. [103]

195. Rapaport, D., 1951. *Organization and pathology of thought.* New York: Columbia University Press. [265] (See refs. 216; 229; 230)

196. Raymond, E., 1907. The psychological experiences connected with the different parts of speech. *Psychol. Rev. Monogr. Suppl.* **8**, No. 1. (Whole No. 32.) [239]

197. Reichard, G. A., 1933–1938. Coeur d'Alene. In Boas, F. (Ed.), *Handbook of American Indian languages,* Vol. III. Glückstadt-Hamburg-New York: J. J. Augustin. [482, 491, 497]

198. Reichard, G. A., 1949. The character of the Navaho verb stem. *Word,* **5**, 55–76. [490, 492]

199. Reid, L. A., 1955. Aesthetic meaning. *Aristot. Soc. Proceedings.* N. S. **14**, 219–250. [322]

200. Reimann, H., 1919. *Literarisches Albdrücken.* Leipzig: E. Matthes. [230, 231]

201. Révész, G., 1958. *The human hand.* London: Routledge and Kegan Paul. [11]

202. Rodrigué, E., 1956. Notes on symbolism. *Intern. J. Psychoanal.,* **37**, 1–12. [73, 75]

203. Russell, B., 1940. *An inquiry into meaning and truth.* New York: Norton. [74]

204. Russell, E. S., 1916. *Form and function.* London: Murray. [5]

205. Russell, E. S., 1945. *The directiveness of organic activities.* Cambridge: Cambridge University Press. [5, 6]

206. Sapir, E., 1921. *Language: an introduction to the study of speech.* New York: Harcourt, Brace. [334]

207. Sapir, E., 1922. Takelma. In Boas, F. (Ed.), *Handbook of American Indian languages,* Vol. II. Washington: Smithsonian Institution. [500]

208. Sapir, E., 1929. A study in phonetic symbolism. *J. exp. Psychol.,* **12**, 225–239. [218]

209. Sapir, E., 1949. *Selected writings.* (Mandelbaum, D. G., Ed.) Berkeley: University of California Press. [489]

210. de Saussure, F., 1959. *Course in general linguistics.* New York: Philosophic Library. [viii]

211. Schachtel, E. G., 1959. *Metamorphosis.* New York: Basic Books. [13]

212. Scheerer, M., 1931. *Die Lehre von der Gestalt.* Berlin: DeGuyter. [4]

213. Scheerer, M., 1959. Spheres of meaning—an analysis of stages from perception to abstract thinking. *J. Indiv. Psychol.,* **15,** 50–61. [242]

214. Scheerer, M., and Lyons, J., 1957. Line drawings and matching responses to words. *J. Pers.,* **25,** 251–273. [346–349]

215. Schilder, P., 1914. Wahn und Erkenntnis. *Monog. Ges. Geb. Neurol. Psychiat.* Berlin: Springer. [258, 259]

216. Schilder, P., 1951. On the development of thoughts. In Rapaport, D. (Ed.), *Organization and pathology of thought.* New York: Columbia University Press. [242]

217. Schiller, C. (Ed.), 1957. *Instinctive behavior.* New York: International Universities Press. (See ref. 257)

218. Schweidweiler, F., 1942. Die Wortfeldtheorie. *Z. f. Deutsch. Altertum,* **79,** 249–265. [56]

219. Scupin, E. and G., 1907. *Bubis erste Kindheit.* Leipzig: Grieben. [68, 79, 80, 82, 173]

220. Scupin, E. and G., 1910. *Bubi im vierten bis sechsten Lebensjahr.* Leipzig: Grieben. [108]

221. Searles, H. F., 1960. *The non-human environment.* New York: International Universities Press. [19, 72, 254]

222. Searles, H. F., 1961. Schizophrenic communication. *Psychoanal. and Psychoanal. Rev.,* **48,** No. 1, 3–50. [254, 256]

223. Sechehaye, M. A., 1951. *Autobiography of a schizophrenic girl.* New York: Grune and Stratton. [72, 73, 256]

224. Sechehaye, M. A., 1951. *Symbolic realization.* New York: International Universities Press. [72, 73, 382]

225. Segal, H., 1950. Some aspects of the analysis of a schizophrenic. *Intern. J. of Psychoanal.,* **31,** 268–278. [261]

226. Severance, E., and Washburn, M. F., 1907. The loss of associative power in words after long fixation. *Amer. J. Psychol.,* **18,** 182–186. [30]

227. Shinn, M. W., 1900. *The biography of a baby.* Boston–New York: Houghton-Mifflin. [68, 69, 79, 80]

228. Shirley, M. M., 1931–1933. *The first two years; a study of twenty-five babies.* Minneapolis: University of Minnesota Press. [133]

229. Silberer, H., 1951. On symbol formation. In Rapaport, D. (Ed.), *Organization and pathology of thought.* New York: Columbia University Press. [360, 426]

230. Silberer, H., 1951. Report on a method of eliciting and observing certain symbolic hallucination-phenomena. In Rapaport, D. (Ed.), *Organization and pathology of thought.* New York: Columbia University Press. [360, 426]

231. Slepian, H., 1959. A developmental study of inner vs. external speech in normals and schizophrenics. Unpublished doctor's dissertation, Clark University. [301–316, 327]

232. Smuts, J. C., 1926. *Holism and evolution.* New York: Macmillan. [4]

233. Spaier, A., 1927. *La pensée concrète.* Paris: Alcan. [426]

234. Speier, S., 1956. The representation and differentiation of grammatical relations in a non-verbal medium: an experimental and theoretical study. Unpublished master's thesis, Clark University. [440–454, 469]

235. Sperber, H., 1923. *Einführung in die Bedeutungslehre.* Bonn: Schroeder. [187, 478]

236. Spiegel, R., 1959. Specific problems of communication in psychiatric conditions. In Arieti, S., *American handbook of psychiatry*, Vol. I, Chap. 46, 909–949. [261]

237. Spitz, R. A., 1945–1946. Hospitalism. In *Psychoanal. Stud. Child.* I, 53–74; II, 113–117. New York: International Universities Press. [72]

238. Spitz, R. A., 1946. The smiling response. *Genet. Psychol. Monogr.*, **34,** 57–125. [43]

239. Spitz, R. A., 1946. Anaclitic depression. In *Psychoanal. Stud. Child.* II, 313–342. [72]

240. Spitz, R. A., 1957. *Die Entstehung der ersten Objektbeziehungen.* Stuttgart: Klett. [71]

241. Stern, W., 1930. *Psychology of early childhood up to the sixth year of age.* New York: Holt. [195, 323]

242. Stern, W. and C., 1928. *Die Kindersprache.* Leipzig: Barth. [54, 79, 82, 101–109, 117, 118, 136, 145, 155, 161–167, 171–178, 180, 185, 400–403, 411]

243. Storch, A., 1922. Das archaisch—primitive Erlebnis und Denken der Schizophrenen, *Monogr. Ges. Geb. Neurol. Psychiat.*, **32,** 1–89. (*Eng. trans. Nerv. Ment. Dis. Monogr.* 1924, **36**) [254, 256, 261]

244. Storch, A., 1923. Bewusstseinsebenen und Wirklichkeitsbereiche in der Schizophrenie. *Z. ges. Neurol. Psychiat.*, **82,** 331–342. [256]

245. Storch, A., 1930. Die Welt der beginnenden Schizophrenie und die archaische Welt. *Z. ges. Neurol. Psychiat.*, **127,** 799–810. [256]

246. Stumpf, C., 1901. Eigenartige sprachliche Entwicklung eines Kindes. *Z. f. Pädag. Psychol.*, **3,** 419–447. [187]

247. Sullivan, H. S., 1962. *Schizophrenia as a human process.* New York: Norton. [254]

248. Sully, J., 1903. *Studies of childhood.* New York: Appleton. [157]

249. Swanton, J. R., 1911. Haida. In Boas, F. (Ed.), *Handbook of American Indian languages,* Vol. I. Washington: Smithsonian Institution. [56]

250. Tagiuri, R., 1960. Movement as a cue in person perception. In David, H. P., and Brengelman, J. C. (Eds.), *Perspectives in personality research.* New York: Springer. [339]

251. Thalbitzer, W., 1911. Eskimo. In Boas, F. (Ed.), *Handbook of American Indian languages,* Vol. I. Washington: Smithsonian Institution. [483]

252. Tischler, H., 1957. Schreien, Lallen und erstes Sprechen in der Entwicklung des Säuglings. *Z. f. Psychol.*, **160,** 209–263. [81, 82]

253. Trier, J., 1931. *Der deutsche Wortschatz im Sinnbezirk des Verstandes.* Heidelberg: Winter. [56]

254. Tuczek, K., 1921. Analyse einer Katatonikersprache. *Z. ges. Neurol. Psychiat.*, **72,** 279–307. [259, 260, 262, 266, 268, 272]

255. Uexküll, J. von, 1921. *Umwelt und Innenwelt der Tiere.* Berlin: Springer. [5]

256. Uexküll, J. von, 1932. Das Duftfeld des Hundes. *Kongr., Deutsch. Ges. f. Psychol.*, **12,** 431–433. [10]

257. Uexküll, J. von, 1957. A stroll through the worlds of animals and men. In Schiller, C. H. (Ed.), *Instinctive behavior*, Part I. New York: International Universities Press. [5, 24]

258. Ullmann, S., 1951. *The principles of semantics*. Glasgow: Jackson, Son. [56]

259. Urban, W. M., 1939. *Language and reality*. New York: Macmillan. [14]

260. Viaud, G., 1956. Taxies et tropismes dans le comportement instinctif. In *L'instinct dans le comportement des animaux et de l'homme*. Paris: Masson and Co. [10]

261. Vygotsky, L. S., 1962. *Thought and speech*. Cambridge: M.I.T. Press and New York: Wiley. [317–323]

262. Wagner, G., 1933–1938. Yuchi. In Boas, F. (Ed.), *Handbook of American Indian languages*, Vol. III. Glückstadt-Hamburg-New York: J. J. Augustin. [484]

263. Wallon, H., 1945. *Les origines de la pensée chez l'enfant*, Vols. I-II. Paris: Presses Universitaires. [viii]

264. Wallon, H., and Lurçat, L., 1957. Graphisme et modèle dans les dessins de l'enfant. *J. de psychol.*, **54**, 257–278. [90]

265. Wapner, S., and Werner, H., 1957. *Perceptual development*. Worcester: Clark University Press. [18]

266. Wegener, P., 1885. *Untersuchungen über die Grundfragen des Sprachlebens*. Halle: M. Niemeyer. [53]

267. Werner, H., 1912. Skizze su einer Begriffstafel auf genetischer Grundlage. *Arch. f. system. Philos.*, **18**, 47–62. [91]

268. Werner, H., 1919. Die Ursprünge der Metapher. *Arb. z. Entw.–Psychol. (Krueger)*, III. Leipzig: Engelmann. [488]

269. Werner, H., 1932. *Grundfragen der Sprachphysiognomik*. Leipzig: Barth. [38, 39, 47, 126, 130, 207–219, 226–228, 232–237]

270. Werner, H., 1940. Musical microscales and micromelodies. *J. Psychol.*, **10**, 149–156. [18]

271. Werner, H., 1954. Change of meaning. *J. genet. Psychol.*, **50**, 181–208. [187]

272. Werner, H., 1956. Microgenesis and aphasia. *J. abnorm. soc. Psychol.*, **52**, 347–353. [18, 215–216]

273. Werner, H., 1957. The concept of development from a comparative and organismic view. In Harris, D. B. (Ed.), *The concept of development*. Minneapolis: University of Minnesota Press. [8]

274. Werner, H., 1957. *Comparative psychology of mental development*. New York: International Universities Press. [8, 85, 98, 151, 180, 298]

275. Werner, H., and Kaplan, E., 1952. The acquisition of word meanings: a developmental study. *Monogr. Soc. Res. Child Develpm.*, **15**, 190–200. [259, 279]

276. Werner, H., and Kaplan, B., 1956. The developmental approach to cognition: its relevance to the psychological interpretation of anthropological and ethnolinguistic data. *Amer. Anthrop.*, **58**, 866–880. [476]

277. Werner, H., and Wapner, S., 1956. Sensory–tonic field theory of perception: Basic concepts and experiments. *Revista di Psicologia*, **50**, 315–337. [18]

278. Westermann, D., 1927. Laut, Ton, und Sinn in Westafrikanischen Sudansprachen. In *Festschrift Meinof*. Hamburg. [217, 218]

279. Whitehead, A. N., 1925. *Science and the modern world.* New York: Macmillan. [4, 476]
280. Whitehead, A. N., 1929. *The function of reason.* Princeton: Princeton University Press. [6]
281. Whorf, B. L., 1946. The Hopi language, Toreva dialect. In Hoijer, H., et al., *Linguistic structures of native America.* New York: Viking Fund. [498, 499]
282. Whorf, B. L., 1956. *Language, thought and reality.* (Selected writings, Carroll, J. B., Ed.). New York: Wiley. [481–483, 487, 488, 491, 499, 501]
283. Winnicott, D. W., 1953. Transitional objects and transitional phenomena. *Intern. J. Psychoanal.,* **34,** Part II, 89–97. [74]
284. Wundt, W., 1912. *Völkerpsychologie; Die Sprache.* Leipzig: Engelmann. [57, 58, 78, 82]

Communication, condition(s) of, 285 ff, 301 ff, 317 ff
external speech, 285 ff, 301 ff, 317 ff
inner speech, 285 ff, 301 ff, 317 ff
with hypothetical other, 302 ff
with real other, 302 ff
see also, Inner speech, External speech
Components of symbol-situations, 40 ff
in dream speech, 240 ff
in schizophrenia, 254 ff
Composites, and principle of spirality, 186
formation of, in early ontogenesis, 184 ff
in schizophrenia, 272
Compound statements, 170 ff
vectorial patterns in expression of, 171 ff
primitive means in expression of, 170 ff
Concept-formation, Ach's experiment on, 34 f
by aggregation, 195
by pluralization, 195 f
by transposition, 196
in schizophrenia, 275 ff
lability of early, 196
lexical, 197
stages of verbal, 192 ff
verbal, in linguistic contexts, 190 ff
Conceptual rotation, 124 f
in linear naming, 360 ff
Concomitance, represented in dream medium, 468
represented in linear medium, 442 ff
Conditionality, 179 ff
represented in dream medium, 469 ff
represented in imagery, 461 ff
represented in linear medium, 449 ff
Conjunctions, coordinating, 179 ff
subordinative, 179 ff
see also, Connectives
Connectives, 179 ff
dream representation of, 466 ff
imaginal representation of, 454 ff
in expression of dependency relationships, 179 ff
linear representation of, 440 ff

Connectives, physiognomic apprehension of, 238
Connotations, 14 f, 50, 226 f, 231
of words in schizophrenia, 263 ff
see also, Inner form, Referents, Significate
Consensus, 219, 221 ff
and depictive incisiveness, 349
and vehicular differentiation, 350
conditions for, 348 ff
in sound-meaning matching experiments, 219, 221 ff
of linear names, 337 ff, 345 ff
of schizophrenic representations, 376 ff
paradox, 348 ff
Conservation of means, principle of, 8, 60, 175
in expression of dependency relationships, 175, 180
Contact attitude, 133, 135
see also, Attitudinal modes in speech
Contemplation, attitude of, 69
objects of, 67 ff
Contextual gradient, 194
in schizophrenia, 277 f
on word-context test, 194, 198
see also, Word-sentence overlap
Contextualization, of children's analogies, 185 f
of definitions in young children, 188
of expression of temporality in language, 485 ff
of expression of time in imagery, 428 ff
of linear names, 337, 344 ff
of word-meanings, 192 ff
see also, Decontextualization
Continuity in development, 7 f
Contradiction (in dreams), 472
Conventional names, development of, 106 ff, 123 ff
Correspondence, establishment of semantic, between vehicle and referent, 21 f, 57, 60
in linear representation, 361 ff
in linguistic representation, 55, 62
see also, Fittingness

Declarative attitude, 132 f
and contemplation of objects, 135
in two-vocable utterances, 153
see also, Attitudinal modes in speech
Decontextualization, 59, 91 f, 166 f
increasing, of word-meanings in ontogenesis, 192 ff
of names, 114 ff
see also, Contextualization
Definitions, 187 f
contextualized nature of, in young children, 188
fusion of thing and action in, 188
Demand attitude, 133, 135
and call-sounds, 133
and predication of action, 164 f
and reaching behavior, 133
in two-vocable utterances, 164
see also, Attitudinal modes in speech
Deixis, 77 ff
and call-sounds, 77, 81 ff
vocal, and pointing, 82 f
see also, Pointing
Denaturalization of symbolic vehicle, 95 ff, 106 ff, 205 f
in play, 95 ff
see also, Distancing, Natural symbols, Onomatopoesis
Denotative reference, 20 f, 77 ff
see also, Call-sounds, Pointing, Reference
Dependency relationships, 170 ff, 439 ff
expression of, by deaf children, 181
in imagery medium, 457 ff
in linear medium, 444 ff
in linguistic medium, 170 ff
masked expression of, 181 f
paratactic expression of, 174 ff
physiognomic expression of, 179
representation of, in dreams, 468 ff
vectorial patterns underlying, 178 f, 182, 444 ff
see also, Causality, Conditionality, Subordination
Depiction, development of motor-gestural, 84 ff
development of vocal, 99 ff
physiognomic, 104 f
via onomatopoesis, 101 ff

Depictive incisiveness, 350, 354
and consensus, 349 f
Derailments in dream speech, 245
Derivatives, in early ontogenesis, 184, 186 f
and principle of spirality, 187
Designatory function, 138 ff, 337 ff
see also, Linear names, Naming
Development, 3, 7 ff
general, of symbolic process, 40 ff
linguistic law of (Jespersen), 476 ff
means-ends relationships in, 128
organism-environment transactions in, 9 ff
principles of, 7 ff, 40 f, 170, 453 f
see also, Differentiaton, Distancing, Form-function relations, Orthogenetic principle, Spirality
Differentiation, 127 f, 131 ff, 162, 383, 473
in gestural-motor depiction, 87 ff
in orthogenetic principle, 7, 403
lack of, 240 ff, 253 ff, 271 ff, 383, 406 ff
of components of symbol situation, 40 ff
of vehicle and referent in early speech, 100 ff, 114 ff
see also, Decontextualization, Distancing, Fusion
Directiveness, assumption of, 5 ff
Discontinuity in development, 7 f
Distancing, 75, 99, 113 f, 238 f, 251 f
addressor-addressee, 41 f, 49 ff, 240 f, 254 f
addressor-referent, 41 f, 44 f, 250, 255 ff
addressor-vehicle, 41 f, 45 f, 241 ff, 257 ff
general problem of, 41 ff
in dreams, 240 ff
in inner speech, 298 ff, 328 ff
in schizophrenia, 254 ff
vehicle-referent, 41 f, 46 ff, 87 ff, 100 ff, 251 f, 263 ff
see also, Decontextualization, Differentiation
Drawing, children's, 90 f
Dreams, addressor-addressee relationship in, 240 f

Dreams, addressor-vehicle relationship in, 241 ff
 expression of logical relations in, 466 ff
 levels of functioning in, 252
 linguistic forms in, 240 ff
 regression in, 244
 vehicle-referent relationship in, 250 f
Duoremes, 147
 in linear representation, 389
 in schizophrenic utterances, 272
 see also, Two-vocable utterances
Dystaxia, 248 ff, 273

Egocentric speech, 317, 321 f
Ellipsis, in dream-speech, 249
 in imaginal expressions, 456
 in linear representations, 452
 see also, Explicitness, Laconicity
Energeia (v. Humboldt), 22, 50, 52, 360
Equivocality, in expression of temporality, 421 f
 in schizophrenic apprehension of linear symbols, 378 ff
Ergon (v. Humboldt), 22, 50, 52, 360
Euphemisms, 37
Expletives in expression of dependency relationships, 176 f
Explicitness, 303 ff
 and types of stimulus material, 305
 in inner versus external speech, 287 ff, 304
 in schizophrenia, 303
 see also, Ellipsis, Laconicity
Expressive antonymity, synonymity, 225 f
Expressiveness, 20 f, 29
 of objects, 20
 in physiognomic apprehension, 210 ff
 in linear representation, 340 ff
 multidimensional, 221 ff
 transcendence of, 20 f
External form, of referents, 41, 44, 46 ff
 of symbols, 45 ff, 238
 of words, 214
 of words in schizophrenia, 268
 shaped to express inner gestures, 239
External speech, in normal adults, 285 ff, 301 ff

External speech, in ontogenesis, 317 ff
 in schizophrenia, 301 ff
 see also, Other-directed symbolization
Externalization of speech, 318 ff
Extra-medium productions in linear representation, 368 f, 374 f

Female language, 489
Field, 53
 lexical, 55 f
 of pointing, 54, 56
 semantic, 55 f
 syntactic-symbolic, 54 ff
Fittingness, and multiformity of expression of referents, 352
 and plurisignificance of vehicle, 352 ff
 in vehicle-referent relationships, 227, 352 ff
 see also, Correspondence, Conceptual rotation, Reciprocal rotation, Symbolic rotation, Vehicular rotation
Formal parallelism (principle of), 170
Form-words, 179 ff
Form-function relations, 7 f, 59 f, 128, 175, 180
 in expression of connectives in linear medium, 453
 in expression of time in ontogenesis, 403
 principle of "conservation of means" in, 8, 60, 66, 128, 175, 180, 403
 see also, Means-ends relationship, Shift of function
Functional shift, *see* Shift of function
Fusion, of action and time, 429 ff
 of action with agent in linear medium, 393 f
 of agent-action symbols in non-Western languages, 491
 of agent and time in imaginal medium, 432 ff
 of object and temporality in imagery medium, 434
 of object and agent in linear medium, 397
 thing-action, 117 f
 see also, Contextualization, Globality, Differentiation, lack of

Intonation, and sentence-integration, 151 ff, 168
and two-vocable utterances, 139 f
hypotactic patterning of, 153 f, 168, 175 ff
in expression of dependency relationships, 175 ff
non-referential use of, 133, 176 f
paratactic patterning of, 152 f
role of, in early sentence formation, 151 f
Intonational hypotaxis, 151
as stage in expression of relations between thoughts, 170, 175 ff
in expression of dependency relationships, 175 ff
on two-vocable level, 151
Invariance (Independence), in expression of components of statements, 389 f, 441
in expression of temporality, 406, 436
Invectives, 37
Inversion of order, in linear expression of causal relation, 445
in linear expression of conditional relation, 449

Jespersen's law of linguistic evolution, 476 ff
Judgments, of agent's action, 162 ff
of attribution, 166 ff
of identification, 160 ff
see also, Predicative sentences

Knowing and symbol formation, 12 ff

Laconicity, in inner speech, 288, 323, 329
see also, Ellipsis, Explicitness
Language, animal, 17
arbitrariness of, 16, 26
conventional, 106 ff, 128 ff
development of, 476 ff
flag, 17
genetic definition of (v. Humboldt), 22
non-literate, 474 ff
physiognomic, 38 f, 205 ff
Lapse of meaning, 29 ff

Lapse of meaning, and bilingualism, 31
experiments on, 31 ff
loss of physiognomy of words in, 30 f, 39, 208
Lexical concepts, breakdown of, in schizophrenia, 275 ff
development of, in ontogenesis, 192 ff
Linear naming, 337 ff, 365 ff
conceptual rotation in, 360 ff
consensus with regard to, 345 ff, 382 f
contextualization in, 344 f
dynamic aspects in, 341 ff
in schizophrenics, 365 ff
multiple representation of referents in, 343 ff
physiognomic aspects of, 338 ff
plurisignificance in, 342 ff
processes underlying, 351 ff
vehicular rotation in, 355 ff
Linear medium, qualities of, 371
Linear representation, consensus in, 345 ff, 382 f
expression of agent's action on objects in, 386 ff
expression of "concomitance" in, 442 ff
expression of "conditionality" in, 449 ff
expression of "causality" in, 444 ff
expression of "time" in, 404 ff
Linguistic hypotaxis, 170, 175 ff
and word-order, 178
in expression of complex thoughts, 170 ff
in expression of dependency relationships, 175 ff
precursors of, 175 ff
Linguistic organization of expression, in inner versus external speech, 291 ff
in schizophrenia, 310 ff
Logical relations, expression of, in dreams, 466 ff
in imagery, 454 ff
in linear representation, 440 ff
in ontogenesis, 439 f
in schizophrenia, 273 ff
vectorial-dynamic aspects in, 441 f
see also, Connectives
Ludic handling of language, 155

Magic, 16, 35 ff
  in schizophrenic handling of words, 258 ff
Make-believe in children, 94 f
Male language, 489
Masked dependent clauses, 181 ff
Means-ends relationship, 6 ff
  in speech development, 128
  see also, Form-function relations
Media of representation, advantages of using non-phonic, 333 ff
  comparison of imaginal and linguistic, 455 f
  comparison of linear and imaginal, 438, 472 f
  comparison of linear and linguistic, 474 ff
  interpenetration of, in dreams, 243 ff
  progressive differentiation of, in microgenesis, 242
  undifferentiatedness of, in schizophrenia, 260 ff
Metaphor, alluding, 454
  concrete, 454
  in imagery, 460
  linear, 448
  spatial, 448
Microgenesis, 18, 22, 441 f
  and progressive differentiation of media of representation, 242
  arrest of, in schizophrenia, 264 f
  in comprehension of word-forms, 215 f
  of the symbolic process, 242 f
"Modifications," in external versus inner speech, 292 ff
  in schizophrenia, 310 ff
Modulation, in words representing action, 402 f
  of linear symbol for action, 393 ff, 413
  of linear symbol for agent, 390 ff
Monoremes, 134 ff
  and addressor attitudes, 134 f, 137
  and pointing (deixis), 136
  development of, 135 ff
  in linear representation, 385
  in schizophrenia, 265 f, 271
  see also, One-unit expression
Morphological modification of vocables, 154 ff

Mother-child relation in formation, 71 ff
Multidimensional expressiveness, 221 ff
  see also, Plurisignificance
Multiformity in expression of referents, in linear representation, 337, 343 ff
  in linear representation of temporality, 421 f
  in ontogenesis, 124
  in schizophrenia, 268 ff

Names, 138 ff
  in schizophrenia, 263 ff, 365 ff
  linear, 337 ff, 365 ff
  motivation of names, 160 f
  transformed into words, 138 ff
  versus words, 384
  see also, Designatory function, Naming
Naming, and process of decontextualization, 114 ff
  and specification, 114 ff
  diffuseness of, 120
  in concrete situations, 43, 120
  in schizophrenia, 263 ff
  see also, Names
Natural symbols, 109 ff, 205, 345
  see also, Onomatopoesis, Sound symbolism
Negation in dreams, 472
Neologisms, in dream-speech, 246 ff
  in schizophrenia, 263 ff, 278
  see also, Neomorphisms
Neomorphisms, in schizophrenia, 263 ff
  see also, Neologisms
Noun-verb relation, in dreams, 249
  in non-Western languages, 480 ff
  in ontogenesis, 143, 168, 186 ff
  in physiognomic apprehension of language, 232 ff

One-unit expressions, 131 ff
  see also, Monoremes
Onomatopoesis, 100 ff, 123 ff, 205 f, 218
Organismic approach, and teleology, 5 ff
  experimental support of, 25 ff
Orthogenetic principle, 7 f, 40
  and autonomy of medium of representation, 132
  and formation of predicative utterances, 166 f

Reality, schizophrenic apprehension of, 72 f, 253 ff
Reciprocal rotation, 24, 227, 408
  in linear naming, 363
  in representation of time, 237
  see also, Bilateral handling of vehicle and referent, Fittingness
Redundancy, in dream-speech, 249
  in neomorphic utterances, 270
  see also, Pleonasm
Reference, act of denotative, 20 f, 77 ff
  delimitation of, 141 ff
  differentiation of, 140 ff
  general development of, 77 ff
  specification of, 142 ff
Referents, communal, in inner and external speech, 289 ff, 306 ff
  concrete-affective-dynamic nature of early, 116 ff, 341 f
  external form of, 44 ff, 257
  idiomatic, in inner and external speech, 289 ff, 306 ff
  inner form of, 44 ff, 257
  multiform expression of, 124 ff, 343 ff
Referential integration, 145 ff
Representation, Ach's experiment on, 34 f
  and duality of vehicle-referent, 16 f
  and symbol, 14 ff
  exemplificatory, 15
Rhythmic-melodic patterns, 175 ff
  see also, Intonation
Role-taking in play, 94 f
Regularization, in language history, 476
  in ontogenesis of speech, 156 ff
Rotation, 57
  in vehicle-referent relationships, 124 ff, 353 ff
  modes of conceptual, in linear representation, 360 ff
  reciprocal, 24, 227, 237, 363, 408
  vehicular, in child speech, 124 ff
  vehicular, in linear representation, 353 ff
  see also, Fittingness

Schema, 91
  gestural, in play, 95

Schema, internal, dispositional, 94, 120
  sensory-motor, 91
Schematization, 17 ff
  and anticipatory set, 19
  and internalization of sensory-motor patterns, 18
  and vehicle-referent correspondence, 17 ff, 123 ff
Semantic field, 55 ff
Self-directed symbolization, 284, 301, 307 ff
  see also, Inner speech
Schizophrenia, addressor-referent relationships in, 255 ff
  addressor-vehicle relationships in, 257 ff
  and expression of logical relations, 273 ff
  and linear representation, 365 ff
  and microgenesis, 264
  and word-context test, 259, 275 ff
  magical handling of language in, 258 ff
  physiognomic-dynamic apprehension of world in, 255 f
  substantialization of word-meanings in, 258
Sentence-formation, 137 ff, 145 ff
  and monoremes, 138
  relation of, to word-formation, 138
Sentence structurization, 192 ff
  and word-formation, 197 ff
  dynamic basis of, 61
  in relation to forming verbal concepts, 192 ff
  in schizophrenia, 276 ff
Sentential integration, 154, 485 ff
Sharing, 42 ff
  in symbolic representation, 283
Shift of function (principle of), 18, 101, 403
  and autonomy of medium of representation, 132
Sign, 9 ff
  versus symbol, 13 f, 36, 111
Signals, 9 f, 53, 101
Significate, 14 f, 26 f, 123
  see also, Connotation, Referent

Time, linear representation of, 404 ff
  ontogenetic steps in verbal representation of, 400 ff
  physiognomic aspects in representation of, 498 f
  systematic expression of aspects of, 422 ff
Transcendence of expressive qualities, 20 f
Transformation, in development of case system, 9 ff, 58, 61
  see also, Rotation
Transitional object, 74
  and symbol formation, 76
Transparency of advanced symbols, 47
Transposition on word-context test, 195 ff
Twin studies, 118 ff, 318 ff
Two-vocable utterances, 137 ff
  and identifying predications, 161
  and word-sentence relation, 137 ff
  see also, Duoremes

Umwelt, 5 ff
Universe of discourse, 220 f, 350
  effect of restriction of, on consensus, 220 f
  in sound symbolism, 220

Vectors, in expression of dependency relationships, 178
  in expression of thought-relations, 441 f
  in non-Western languages, 481
  of sentence, 61 f
  underlying compound statements, 171 ff
Vehicular integration, 150 ff

Vehicular rotation, in linear naming, 353 ff
  see also, Symbolic rotation
Vehicle-referent relationships, 20 ff, 206
  bilateral handling in, 213, 226 ff
  establishment of "similarity" in, 20 ff, 206
  in linear representation, 351 ff
  undifferentiatedness of, in dreams, 250 f
  undifferentiatedness of, in schizophrenia, 263 ff
Vocative, 145

Word-blindness, experimentally induced, 28 f
Word-Context test, 190 ff
  used with children, 192 ff, 259
  used with schizophrenics, 275 ff
Word-embeddedness on word-context test, 194 f
  see also, Contextualization
Word-formation, 137 ff
  microgenesis of, 215 f
  sensory-motor facilitation of, 32 ff
Word-magic, 16, 36 f
  in schizophrenia, 258 ff
Word-realism, 35 ff, 47, 251, 259
  see also, Symbol-realism
Word-sentence overlap on word-context test, 194, 198, 277
Word-sentence relation, 137 ff, 169, 192 ff
  in history of language, 476 ff
  in schizophrenia, 271 ff
  undifferentiatedness of, in young children, 192 ff
Word-sentence undifferentiatedness, in schizophrenia, 265 ff
  on word-context test, 192 ff
Word-tabu, 37